The Information Process

The Information Process

World News Reporting
To the Twentieth Century

Robert W. Desmond

University of Iowa Press ⊔Ψ Iowa City 1978

University of Iowa Press, Iowa City 52242
© 1978 by The University of Iowa. All rights reserved
Printed in the United States of America

Library of Congress Catalog in Publication Data

Desmond, Robert William, 1900–
    The information process.

    Bibliography: p.
    Includes index.
    1. Newspapers—History. 2. News agencies—History
3. Foreign news—History. I. Title.
PN4801.D45   070   77–9491
ISBN O–87745–070–6

To Emily
. . . with love and admiration

Contents

Knowledge will forever govern ignorance, and a people who mean to be their own governors must arm themselves with the power that knowledge gives. A popular government without popular information, or the means of acquiring it, is but a prologue to a farce or a tragedy.

—James Madison

What is all knowledge too but recorded experience, and a product of history.

—Thomas Carlyle

Foreword

Historians pursuing their research have turned regularly to the brittle and yellowing files of newspapers and periodicals, and to the microfilms of such publications.

Whatever is past once was present. Today's newspapers and periodicals, and the tapes of today's radio and television news broadcasts also will interest historians of later days as they reconstruct the life of our times.

Those events of a century past, or of another millennium, were as real and important to persons then alive as are the events of today and yesterday to the present generation. They helped to shape the present.

In the long history of mankind, information always has been the key to knowledge and the basis for action. In the great span of time, it is scarcely a day since newspapers appeared to provide some sort of consistent report upon events. How did our ancestors fare before newspapers existed? What information reached them, and by what means? Why did they need and want information? When did newspapers enter the scene, and who were those persons who made them, and who made it possible for our more immediate forebears to receive an effective service of information?

These are among the questions to be dealt with in the pages following, and it is appropriate to begin the story in the earliest of times. A great part of the story is of the newspaper press. That is an unfinished story, but one ended in these pages in the first years of the present century because by then a logical conclusion is indicated. The Press had reached a point when it was able to bring full and prompt reports of each day's events in most of the world to most of its people.

With full recognition that a newspaper, wherever produced, may properly be expected to inform its readers about events and issues in their own community, these pages will be concerned with its service in a broader sense. An occurrence in any part of the world may have its effect upon any person, wherever he may dwell. Therefore, this will be a wide-ranging view of the public need for information on the national and world scene, and the ways in which that need was met. It will give special attention to the manner in which the newspaper press, once in existence, was able progressively to broaden the horizons of all peoples, giving them opportunity to acquaint themselves with other lands and peoples, with the issues of war and peace, with events of interest and events important to the well-being of nations and of individuals.

In the performance of its function, the press provides a service to the public and at the same time is recording what will become history. Those who made it in the past, and who continue to make it, are the first historians. The history of the press itself is a part of the social history of mankind in his search for information and understanding. As such, it deserves to be recognized—along with its publishers, editors, and reporters—even as governments, statesmen, and military leaders are remembered.

"Beneath the rule of men entirely great, the pen is mightier than the sword." So wrote Lord Lytton a century ago, and Thomas Macaulay observed that "The gallery in which the reporters sit has become a fourth estate of the realm." Yet little has been set down, except in uncoordinated bits and pieces, to make clear the importance of the pen and the reporter in man's advance from primitive existence, or to explain precisely how they contributed. This book is intended to repair that omission in the social history of man, and to establish its relation to political history.

It is usual in any such foreword as this to present a personal note and certain acknowledgments to those who have played a part in making the volume possible. Since what follows is based upon more than a half century of experience and research, a hazard exists that some persons deserving of an obeisance may be overlooked through lapse of memory.

With that reservation and apologia, however, deep appreciation must go, first, to my wife for putting up with my absences and absent-mindedness in periods of research and writing, and for her counsel on matters of content.

Acknowledgments must go to associates in various universities, to certain government officials, and to almost numberless fellow journalists with whom I have worked professionally or socialized in places as widely separated as London and San Francisco, Paris and Tokyo, New York and Rome, Washington and Geneva, Boston and Berlin, New Delhi and Chicago.

A kind of impersonal acknowledgment is due to such rich sources of information as the British Museum Library, the Library of Congress, and the New York Public Library, and to friendly working associations in the International Press Institute in Zurich, Unesco in Paris, the Centre International d'Enseignement Supérieur du Journalisme in Strasbourg, the Instituut voor Perswetenschap in Amsterdam, and the London School of Economics and Political Science. Special dividends also attached to participation in sessions at the Geneva School of International Studies and at the Williamstown Institute of Politics, now both long gone; and to periods of residence in the Middle East.

Benefits bearing upon the backgrounding of these pages also derived from staff work with such newspapers as the *Milwaukee Journal,* the *Miami Herald,* the Paris edition of the *New York Herald,* the *New York Times,* the *Christian Science Monitor* in Boston and London, and work in radio news and magazines.

Grateful mention must be made of the late Dr. Willard G. Bleyer, who stimulated the writer's interest in a journalism of substance as a student at the University of Wisconsin, and to the late Professor E. M. Johnson, who induced him to leave active journalism for a time to join the faculty at the University of Minnesota and there to introduce what may have been the first university course giving specific attention to international journalism. About seven years and two graduate degrees later, and following a return to news work, there emerged a first book dealing broadly with the same subject, *The Press and World Affairs,* happily well received in the United States, Great Britain, and elsewhere.

Further individual mention must go to Dr. Ralph D. Casey of the University of Minnesota, to the late Professor Harold Laski of London, and to Roscoe Drummond, then executive editor of the *Christian Science Monitor,* all of whom encouraged the writer in the production of that first book. Joseph L. Jones and Eugene Lyons, then both of the United Press, gave advice and comment that was more than helpful.

Beyond that, the writer expresses warm appreciation for subsequent support in the later concern for the subject here explored to several educator-journalists, among them the late Professor Kenneth E. Olson of Northwestern University, the late Dr. Chilton R. Bush of Stanford University, the late Dr. Ralph O. Nafziger of the University of Wisconsin, and Dr. Raymond B. Nixon of the University of Minnesota.

It is appropriate, also, to salute hundreds of former students at four universities in the United States and four in other lands who made it pleasantly necessary to seek answers to questions. There was the added satisfaction of seeing some of them go on to solid successes as active journalists and to count them as personal friends.

La Jolla, California   *Robert W. Desmond*

A Search for Understanding 1

Citizens of Rome passing through the city's main public square, the Forum, on a day in 131 B.C., might have observed two framed and hand-lettered bulletins prominently displayed. Pausing to view this unfamiliar thing, the literate among them would have learned that it presented brief items of information about subjects of current importance or interest.

What they saw was the "Acta Diurna," freely translated as "daily events," sponsored by the senatorial government. To historians of the press, it is generally accepted as the first clear prototype of the modern-day newspaper.

For 145 years, from 131 B.C. until A.D. 14, the Acta Diurna was posted regularly, if not daily, in the Forum Romanum. It appeared in two separate parts: single copies, one the "Acta Senatus," reported senate actions and matters of an official nature; the other, the "Acta Publica," reported events of a more general or even popular variety. The content of both was prepared by *actuarii,* surely the world's first professional news writers.

Some Romans read the bulletins, if they could; others heard them read aloud, and still others learned the substance of them by word-of-mouth. Beyond that, however, scribes made copies, sometimes as many as 2,000 of a single posting, for wider distribution. In this way, persons far from Rome itself, including legion members, learned of government actions and decrees, court rulings and legal notices, noteworthy births, marriages and deaths, and a miscellany of events, including the results of gladiatorial combat—a kind of sports news.

The Acta Diurna was exceptional and extraordinary. Never before had the people of any land been provided with current information, even in so limited a fashion. When it vanished, nothing comparable was to appear for a thousand years or more.

This is not to say that the peoples of the earth were wholly uninformed, either before the years of Rome's greatness or after. Yet it taxes the imagination to realize that, with what anthropologists call "true" man inhabiting the globe for perhaps 20,000 years, the flood of information now so generally available represents a development that has taken place, for the most part, only in the last 500 years and, in its most effective form, only since about 1850.

Mankind sought information from the beginning of his existence. It is scarcely an over-simplification to attribute his emergence from the darkness of primitive times into the light of the modern world to those progressive advances by which a variety of information became increasingly available. With information contributing to knowledge, and thus to understanding, man gained a certain mastery of his environment and of his personal life and destiny.

The intent, in these pages, is to trace this progression from its faint beginnings to a time when the world was brought into something approaching a full perspective. It is a story of a triumph of mind and spirit accomplished in large part through the medium of communication.

The Imperative of Communication

The impulse and indeed the need of men and women to exchange information and ideas in the human relationship is amply clear. It is manifested in gesture and sound, facial expression and speech, in music, dance, art, and other forms, including writing and print.

In whatever milieu people have existed through the centuries as individuals or families and groups, they have been concerned with their own safety and well-being, and with the necessities of the day. They have been moved by their instincts, interests, aspirations, and emotions. They have been eternally curious about all things surrounding them, and beyond the horizon.

Anthropologists and archeologists have shed much light upon the early history of mankind, but written history dates only from about 5000 B.C., when the total population of the world is estimated to have been hardly more than five million.

Archeology has demonstrated, however, that life went on, that cities and something like nations existed, that efforts were made to obtain and exchange information, to give passing or permanent expression to ideas, and to preserve in some fashion the memory of men and events. Those particular efforts did not succeed beyond a point and they did not proceed evenly, but it is notable that peoples living in widely-separated areas of the globe frequently arrived independently at comparable means to accomplish that objective.

Communication was primarily oral, for then there was no alternative. But even that permitted transmitting the story of past events from one generation to another in what became legends, and many eventually gained written form. Man's instinctive desire to communicate ideas, impressions, and feelings going beyond the verbal, nevertheless found expression surely no less than 10,000 years ago in pictures and story-paintings on the walls of caves and on cliff-sides in places as widely separated as Spain and India, France and Rhodesia and Mexico. Some survive, in fine colors and style, to tell something of the people and life of those times and places.

Other early clues to events and interests exist in designs and ornamentation on pottery and weapons, in tombs and burial places in ancient Assyria, Syria, Persia, India, Egypt, and China. They exist on the Runic stones of Scandinavia, in the pyramids of Egypt, and in elaborate structures surviving in Iran, Cambodia, Thailand, and Java; in Mayan, Aztec, and Inca remains in Central and South America. The list is long, and archeologists continue to find new examples of past efforts in human expression.

The experience, information, and knowledge mankind had gained through thousands of years brought him to the edge of a new advance from about 5000 B.C. History was not literally written from that time, but forms of communication did begin to permit both a permanent recording of information and its transmission in something other than verbal form.

Precisely how it began is not established, but it seems to have been in the eastern Mediterranean area, and to have arisen out of a particular need by traders for a means to regularize their enterprises. Political and military leaders were not far behind, and both men of religion and scholars followed closely. What seems thus to have begun in the Middle East, in due course was matched, apparently quite independently, in China and in India, and in some fashion in the Western Hemisphere.

It is significant, in the light of later developments, that the needs of traders should have spurred the forms of communication leading to writing and printing, and so to a new world order. As will become obvious, the "business community" was to contribute consistently through the years to important advances in the provision of information to the peoples of the globe, and therefore to the evolution of modern civilization.

Trade, like communication, had its prehistoric beginnings. It is certain that by 5000 B.C. camel caravans were moving about in the Middle East, and small craft were on rivers and at sea. By the first millennium B.C., a "silk route" linked the Middle East to China, where trade also proceeded, and there was a sea route to India.

Merchants, traders, moneylenders, and craftsmen as well came together in a fraternity that was to become world-wide, its members always seeking information required for the proper conduct of their affairs. It became important to them to keep records and accounts, to mark and identify goods for shipment, and to exchange information with buyers, sellers, and suppliers, wherever located.

One early means to meet some such needs was the notching of sticks as an aid to memory. Next, to convey meanings, cords or beads were attached to shipments in various colors, lengths and designs, or with knots added. Signs and symbols were marked on goods or objects, or were carved in stone or bone, on pieces of ivory or carnelian. Signet rings and cylinder seals were used later to form impressions in clay or wax, or to mark documents; in China seals of wood or jade were used.

At some time before 3000 B.C., the Sumerians, living in what now is southern Iraq, devised a cuneiform system to keep records, with signs and symbols impressed in wet clay tablets by using a small bone or a reed stylus. The neighboring Chaldeans added a system of signs for numerals. Professional scribes prepared these records, with the clay tablets baked in the sun, or in a kiln, to give them permanency. Until about 1500 B.C., this system was used throughout much of the Middle East.

In Egypt, even earlier, and in China and India, and also among the Mayans and Aztecs in what is now Mexico, a different form of symbol came into use. Rather than patterns of lines or marks, a system of pictographs or ideographs was introduced. These were recognizable as familiar objects or animals or humans, or parts thereof. Used in combination, they became a kind of pictorial writing, somewhat comparable to a modern-day novelty rebus, to be read phonetically.

Known in Egypt as hieroglyphs ("priest-writing"), these pictographs were variously carved in stone, wood, or plaster, but they also could be painted or drawn upon flat surfaces. The use of hieroglyphs had certain advantages that resulted in their adoption through-

out the eastern Mediterranean area after about 1500 B.C., in preference to the cuneiform system. They continued to be used in Egypt,
at least, until about the sixth century A.D., and the ideograph system
of pictorial writing, although greatly modified, remains in use in
China and Japan to the present time.

The most significant advance toward modern-day writing originated, however, with the Phoenicians, then a trading and sea-going
people occupying much of the eastern edge of the Mediterranean—
the area of present-day Israel, Syria, and Lebanon. Beginning about
1500 B.C., they introduced symbols for sound, although not phonetic
sound; the pronunciation of the sound signified by the symbol had to
be learned. The symbols were relatively few in number and not too
difficult to master. They also were easier to form, carve, or mark
down than the pictographs. They represented what now may be
called "letters." Taken together they formed an "alphabet." In
combination, they formed "words." So used, messages could be
conveyed more briefly and more clearly.

For a thousand years or more, the Phoenicians were notable as
traders and bankers in the Mediterranean world, and they also established settlements in Africa and as far west as Spain. During that long
period, they made their system of writing widely known. The Phoenician alphabet became the basis for others derived from it and adapted
to other languages. Notably, there evolved the Hellenic, Aramean,
and Sabean alphabets, and from them, in turn, came alphabets used
throughout the world today—except for the ideographs in China,
Japan, and related areas.

From the Hellenic came the Greek alphabet, and the Coptic, which
was to replace the hieroglyphic symbols in Egypt; the Cyrillic, as
used in Russia and other eastern European states; and notably the
Latin or Roman, as now used in Europe and most of the western
world. From the Aramean came the Hebrew, Arabic, and certain
other alphabets. From the Sabean came the Bengali, Marathi, Urdu,
and other alphabets of India, and those used in Ethiopia, Indonesia,
and southeast Asia.

Since the earliest placement of pictures and designs upon the walls
of caves, fluids had been used in a variety of colors. Sometimes a kind
of paint, they also were used as an "ink" to produce the pictorial
ideographs in Egypt and China, or to form the "letters" of the
Phoenician alphabet. Derived from the juices of berries, from
lampblack or soot, from indigo, cochineal, sepia, tannin, and alizarin,
substance was given by adding gums and glues to make for even flow,

permanency, and drying qualities. Possibly about 2500 B.C. a process was devised whereby the materials were mixed to form small sticks. A segment of such a stick could be cut off and mixed with water to provide a required amount of ink. In use, it was applied to a flat surface with a pad, or with a reed frayed at the end to make a brush, or with a quill sharpened as a pen.

It was not practical to transmit messages by shipping clay tablets bearing cuneiform markings, or stone tablets with carven hieroglyphics; they were heavy, bulky, and perhaps fragile, and required great space to store as records. With pictorial ideographs in use, and then Phoenician letter-symbols, eliminating the need for incisions in clay or stone, it was possible to mark those ideographs or symbols on a flat surface—if such a surface was available.

In Egypt a particular variety of reed was common along the Nile River. Sometime before 500 B.C. a means was devised to use these reeds to make what became known as papyrus, from which derives the word "paper." On the surface of papyrus, a scribe, using a reed brush or a quill dipped in the ink-fluid, could "write" what he was directed in the form of hieroglyphics. And it was a method to be used by the Phoenicians as well. This was obviously quicker and more convenient than carving, and also solved the twin problems of storage and transport of records and messages. At last, in the history of man, the essentials existed for communication of a broader and more permanent sort.

The process of making papyrus was laborious, however, and was limited to Egypt, since suitable reeds were not commonly available elsewhere. A sheet of papyrus could be used separately, but single sheets were joined to form a scroll. With a stick affixed at each end, and spindle grips extending, the scroll could be rolled in either direction, with a portion of the total visible. This in itself was awkward, but nevertheless marked a great advance.

Scrolls became the repository of a great variety of information, with copies made by scribes, priests, and scholars, often to be sent to Athens, Rome, Constantinople, and other places in the Mediterranean area. Collections of scrolls formed some of the earliest libraries, with that in Alexandria holding one of the greatest number and from the second century B.C. becoming an intellectual center. The ability to read remained an art limited to a small segment of the population, but it was not uncommon for one who could do so to read aloud to assembled groups. Thus the audience grew for information and instruction, and the materials to meet the need were in some degree available.

Vellum or parchment was to become another writing surface, beginning in the second century A.D. Made from the skins of sheep, goats, and calves, it was of superior quality, and available where papyrus was not. By the fourth century A.D., throughout the Middle East, Egypt included, it was used for manuscripts of special importance, as it was in the Greek and Roman worlds.

The skins, prepared and trimmed, were used first in scrolls, but later as pages, written on both sides, and bound as books. This was another advance. Produced in monasteries by monks, or by other artisans, some revealed elegant calligraphy, with color accents and illustrations added. Usually bound in leather, often elaborately tooled and sometimes set with jewels and with gold leaf applied to the page edges, they became ceremonial gift volumes worthy of kings.

Manuscript books continued to appear through the fifteenth and sixteenth centuries, not only in the Mediterranean area but, by then, even more in Europe. Comparable books appeared in India and in China and Japan, where silk scrolls had become another art form. They became treasures—quite literally chained to desks in libraries, even though only specially privileged persons were admitted—preserved in monasteries, temples, and palaces.

In China, meanwhile, a means had been devised to produce something similar to modern-day paper. This was another major advance. Bark from mulberry trees at first, and then vegetable, cotton, and hemp fibres were soaked to form a pulp. Pressed to flatten and mat it, the pulp was permitted to dry, then trimmed, and was available for use as a smooth, white paper. The inventor of the process is believed to have been Ts'ai Lun, a court attendant, and the date was about A.D. 105—the first known name and date in the technical history of communications. Such paper was being used in China and India for several centuries before the process became known in the Middle East, and further centuries elapsed before it reached Europe.

A battle in deepest Turkestan, strangely, brought the knowledge of paper making to the western world. Starting from the deserts of Arabia, Moslems had been carrying the sword of Islam east and west in the century following the death of the Prophet Mohammed in A.D. 632. In A.D. 751 they occupied the area around Samarkand, and were attacked by Chinese, who were extending the domain of their country. On this occasion, the Chinese were defeated. Chinese prisoners taken by the Moslems included some familiar with the paper-making process and conveyed knowledge of the art to their captors. The manufacture of paper began almost immediately in the Middle East, and particularly in Baghdad and Damascus. To produce the paper, workers used flax, which was abundant, and reshredded linen rags.

The Chinese variety of paper was slow in replacing papyrus and parchment, but by the ninth century it was in general use in the Middle East. Papyrus had been entirely supplanted by the twelfth century. Damascus-made paper was being used in Greece by the eleventh century, and the art of paper making had been carried to Sicily and to Spain. Paper manufacture began in Italy and France by the twelfth century, and had spread throughout most of Europe by the thirteenth century. But it did not occur in England until the late fifteenth century, although it was imported before that.

With alphabets simplifying communication in written form, and with supplies of paper available, two great advances had been made toward the presentation and preservation of information and ideas. It was still not easy, however, to disseminate such information. The only means was for scribes to prepare copies of written material. This was done, but even the best of such efforts could make information available only to a few persons.

Again, a start toward a solution was made in China. At approximately the same time as paper began to be used, artisans devised a method for making "rubbings." This involved carving illustrations and ideographs in tablets of stone or wood. A sheet of thin, but strong paper then was spread over the surface, moistened, and—with a stiff brush—worked carefully into the carved, intaglio portions of the block. Time was allowed for the paper to dry. Next, a pad of silk or cotton was dipped in an ink, thick enough to prevent it from running, and wiped or "rubbed" lightly and evenly over the dried surface of the paper. In so doing, only the high spots were inked, leaving the incised areas untouched. After another interval for drying, the paper was peeled off the tablet. The illustration or ideographs appeared on the sheet in white against the dark, inked background.

The "rubbing" could be posted, hung in the style of a picture, or used for sale or delivery. The process took time, but any number of copies could be made. Sheets from two or more tablets could be pasted together to form a larger poster, or a scroll. The Japanese learned this process from the Chinese, sometimes using silk rather than paper to form a scroll, and China in turn borrowed that practice from Japan.

Wooden tablets were easier to carve than stone, and were much used. A preference arose for carving the ideographs or illustrations to stand in high relief, rather than incised in the surface of the tablet. This meant that the ink would be applied directly to the high-standing lines of the illustration or ideographs, with an unmoistened sheet of paper laid over the inked surface itself. Using a block, moved across the paper and tapped with a mallet, the inked impression was transferred to the paper. The result was a more pleasing black-on-white reproduction. Far more copies could be made in a given period of time, since the process eliminated the need to work moistened paper into carved incisions, and eliminated the two intervals required for drying the sheet. What appeared, of course, was no longer a "rubbing," but more properly a block print (a term actually adopted) or xylograph from a wood engraving.

This process was to be used and improved through several hundred years. By the eighth century block prints of considerable size were being produced. Blocks also were being carved in such a fashion that a full printed sheet could be folded perhaps four times to form thirty-two pages of appropriate booksize, printed on both sides. Several sheets, so folded, placed together, stitched and trimmed, became a book, and a great variety were so produced.

Most important, however, in furthering the distribution of information, was a completely new approach to what, by then, might reasonably be called the printing process. Both "rubbings" and block printing required carved tablets. These were time-consuming to prepare, and there always was the hazard of spoilage by a slip of a craftsman's chisel. The tablet so laboriously prepared to convey a message through the medium of ideographs became completely valueless once its original purpose had been served.

Sometime between A.D. 1041 and 1048, an artisan named Pi Shêng found a solution to these problems. Instead of carving a wooden tablet, he used a heavy clay. In this clay he cut single ideographs, each in reverse and in high relief. When a sufficient number had been prepared, they were baked in a kiln. Trimmed as individual and separate ideographs to stand at the same height and fit together, they became what could be called earthenware "type." The single pieces could be assembled to convey a message, spaced out as necessary with chips and strips of bamboo, and all placed and braced in a tray. As with a block print, the surface of the type was inked, paper laid over it and pressed evenly upon it to transfer the inked message and immediately lifted off as a printed sheet of black type on white paper, and then set aside to dry.

The process could be repeated as often as necessary to produce the required number of copies, pausing only to re-ink the type. Illustrations, separately carved in the traditional manner, could be printed with the ideographic text, if desired. Following use, the earthenware type characters could be cleaned, separated, and sorted out, to be reassembled later to convey a new message, and used and reused so long as the type produced a clear image.

So it was that printing from movable type began in China in the eleventh century, and soon in Korea and Japan as well. Experiments followed in making type characters of tin cast in sand molds, but tin did not take ink properly and lost its form under pressure. Characters carved in wood were better, but type cast in bronze, as introduced in Korea in A.D. 1241, was most satisfactory. An improved quality of ink brought still better reproduction.

The advantages of block printing had made rubbings obsolete, except as an artistic exercise, and printing from movable type was equally to supplant block printing in China. Introduced there four centuries before the process appeared in Europe, apparently quite independently developed, it was in regular use through that time in the Far East.[1]

Marco Polo, twice in China for long periods in the thirteenth century, referred often in later writing to the use of paper money in China—it made its first appearance there, and was produced both by blockprinting and from type. Oddly, he said nothing about the printing process itself, then long in use. But he did bring back from China, on his final return in A.D. 1295, some of the carved wooden blocks used there for block printing. Seen in Venice, they almost certainly provided an incentive to European artisans to attempt the process, already in use in Persia and Egypt by that time.

With the Chinese wood blocks thus viewed in Venice at the end of the thirteenth century, the process was used in many parts of Europe during the fourteenth century. Wooden tablets were carved in high relief, both as illustration and as text. Almost without exception, the illustrations were concerned with religious themes, and were termed "image prints." Text matter, originally in single sheets, became known as "block books" when sheets were bound together. This process and practice attained its highest point of development in Italy, Austria, Bavaria, Bohemia, and Holland. Albrecht Dürer and Hans Holbein produced notable wood engravings for use in some true

---

1   The full story of the development in China of rubbings and block printing, of paper making, of printing from movable type, and of an improved quality of ink, the essentials of publishing, is best told by Thomas Francis Carter in *The Invention of Printing In China and Its Spread Westward*(1925), with a revised edition including added material by L. Carrington Goodrich (1955).

illustrated books in the late fourteenth and early fifteenth centuries, and block printing was to continue into the sixteenth century, only yielding then to printing from movable type, at last introduced in Europe.

Credit long has been accorded to Johann (Gensfleisch) Gutenberg, of Mainz and Strasbourg, for the introduction in Europe and, in effect, to the world, of printing from movable type. So far as evidence exists, he was unaware of that form of printing in China.

It appears that Gutenberg had been engaged in block printing in Strasbourg, and there conceived what he believed might be a more efficient method. In 1450 he entered into a partnership agreement with Johann Fust, a wealthy goldsmith in the Rhine River town of Mainz, where Gutenberg had been born about 1400. Fust advanced the money to finance Gutenberg's experiments. The tools acquired and whatever equipment was produced would stand as security for the loan, which was to be increased in 1452.

Pursuing his ideas, Gutenberg proceeded to cast type in individual letters, in reverse and in high relief, even as was being done at the time, unbeknownst to him, in far-off China. Rather than bronze, however, he used lead, mixed with tin and antimony. He devised his own means to space the words and lines, and hold the type together, and produced a suitable ink. To assure even pressure in the transfer of ink from type to paper, he adapted the wine press, familiar in the Rhine country. This was a new concept. It produced excellent results and also introduced "press" and "printing press" as terms of specific meaning.

Gutenberg's experiments continued for four or five years before he was satisfied. He produced some small books from his press. Then, in 1456, he began his first major printing venture, an edition of the Bible.

In 1455, however, Johann Fust brought suit against Gutenberg, seeking repayment of the loans made, which Gutenberg either could not or would not repay at the time. The court decided in Fust's favor, and in 1457 he took over the print shop and all its contents. He and his son-in-law, Peter Schöffer, proceeded with the work already in hand, even made some improvements, and in 1460 the printing of the Bible was completed. Referred to, nevertheless, in years following, as the "Gutenberg Bible," rare surviving copies and pages possess great value today. Gutenberg remained in Mainz, received support enabling him to print other volumes, and died there in 1468.

From that time, printing spread rapidly in Europe and beyond. Among men prominent in its development, Lourens Janzoon Coster, of Haarlem, in Holland, was notable, and is believed by some even to have preceded Gutenberg in bringing the printing process to Europe. William Caxton, an English textile dealer whose business took him to Europe, gained an interest in printing while in Belgium, and became the first printer in England in 1476.

Printers appeared in Milan, Tours, Rome, and Venice, and by 1490 at least one printing press was operating in nearly every city of size in Europe. The first in the Western Hemisphere was in Mexico City in 1539, the second at Lima, Peru, in 1584, with others in Bolivia and Ecuador, and a fifth—the first in the British-American colonies—at Cambridge, in Massachusetts Bay Colony, in 1638.

Despite the earlier appearance of printing from movable type in China, its introduction in Europe in 1456 was the greatest event of the Renaissance period. It made possible the assembling of textual matter in a reasonable time, produced in multiple copies for distribution over an unlimited area, and offered at a moderate price. It made possible the dissemination of information and ideas, and their preservation for all time. It was to advance the quality of civilization at a pace completely beyond any comparable interval during the millennia preceding. It was to revolutionize the world.

That the People May Know 2

Until the printing press appeared in Europe after the mid-fifteenth century there was no means by which information of whatever nature could be provided to more than a limited number of persons at any given place or time. Nor did the printing press change that circumstance overnight. It was still to be nearly three centuries before the average person would have effective opportunity to learn much of what was transpiring in the world beyond his doorstep.

For all that, however, man's interest and curiosity bearing upon the world around him was inbred. His desire to know had been one of the most potent forces in his survival and advancement. He observed, he considered, and he exchanged views. "What's the news?" was a question surely asked early and often, in one form or another. He obtained information as best he could, and used it as he was able. The relevant efforts and means by which he did so during the long centuries prior to 1456, and after that time as well, forms the essence of the story of man's progression from darkness to light.

From the earliest time, in the course of their activities, individuals naturally saw, felt, heard, and experienced certain things. They formed opinions, reached certain conclusions, and acted in accordance with their understanding and beliefs. In their homes with their families, friends, and acquaintances, in the performance of their daily tasks, in shops and market places, they spoke of those things, sharing information and ideas. Some such exchanges could have been called "news," by definition "a report of a recent event; intelligence; information." Some could have been called "gossip," defined as "idle talk or rumor." What men and women did not know at all, or "knew" inaccurately or only in part, could mislead them in thought and deed. All of these elements continue to shape the experience of mankind.

There were occasions, even in those past centuries, when information was available in some random fashion. For example, civil or military officials, men of "religion," or men of ideas sometimes addressed assembled groups. Their remarks were in the nature of "news," and perhaps of historic importance, although not then widely reported or "published."

By the time of the Greco-Roman period, some independent scholars and others were seeking information in a purposeful way, and perhaps writing of what they learned. This may have been little more than an excerise in self-expression, since dissemination of any such writing then was necessarily limited by reason of a general illiteracy, language differences, and the absence of a means to duplicate or distribute what had been written, unless through the slow and laborious efforts of scribes. Some such efforts, nevertheless, were made.

In the view of Sir Richard Jebb (1841-1905), among other classicists, certain of those first writers were performing functions, in their own periods, akin to those performed later by literary men and by journalists of the printed media. They were writing of their own times and people; they were gathering and recording information and setting down their views on a variety of subjects, with or without an audience in prospect.

It is thus suggested that Homer, for example, a Greek epic poet living between the sixth and tenth centuries B.C., was recording in the *Iliad* and *Odyssey* aspects of life, thought, and events in the eastern Mediterranean area.

Herodotus, a Persian by birth but a resident of Greece for most of his life, traveled widely in the Middle East and Mediterranean world between 464 and 447 B.C. He wrote of what he learned and observed, somewhat as a special correspondent might do in a later era, and is known as the "father of history."

Demosthenes, a statesman of Athens, active from about 350 to 322 B.C., is remembered as an orator. But he also prepared addresses for other leaders to deliver, referring to events of that period, and performing somewhat as a public relations officer in the process.

Plato, Pythagoras, Aristotle, Socrates, and Seneca in Athens and Rome, and Confucius in China, all between the sixth and first centuries B.C., dealt with ideas casting light on their times and their contemporaries.

Thucydides, a commander during the long and critical Peleponnesian War of 431 to 404 B.C., wrote eight volumes descriptive of that conflict between Athens and Sparta. Xenophon, an Athenian military leader, also recorded in the *Anabasis* events of the Greek campaign in

Persia about 401 B.C. Both were military historians, but have been likened to latter-day war correspondents.

Julius Caesar might equally be seen as a war correspondent. In his *Commentaries* he reported the wars in which Rome was engaged in Gaul, southern France, and Central Europe in 58 to 51 B.C. This account occupied seven volumes. In three others he described the wide-ranging civil wars of 49 to 45 B.C., during which he established his personal command over Rome and the empire.

Plutarch, a true Athenian who spent years in Rome as well, wrote biographical "profiles" of men prominent in the period of about A.D. 100. Somewhat journalistic in style, his writings still provide an understanding of those leaders.

A parallel has been drawn also between a number of Athenian dramatists and latter-day journalists. Aeschylus, Euripides, and Aristophanes are cited as having exerted an influence on public thought in the fourth century B.C. with their plays, presented in Athens and elsewhere, which reflected events, concepts, and problems of the times—such as might be done later by editorialists on social and moral issues. And a parallel has been drawn with reference to such Romans as Lucilius, a satirist; Cicero, an orator and master of written prose; Virgil, a poet; and Tacitus, an historian—all active in the period from about 160 B.C. to A.D 120.

Paul (or Saul), referred to as the "first great Christian missionary," and others of the apostles, conveyed "news" of another sort to the peoples of the Mediterranean basin during the early years of the first century A.D. Like Jesus himself, the apostles spoke to "multitudes" gathered to listen. Their remarks were noted, it must be assumed, by some early "reporters," ultimately to become part of the New Testament, including Paul's "epistles," as well as the words of Matthew, Mark, Luke, and John. No writings, it seems safe to say, have been read or quoted so consistently through uncounted generations, or have exerted more influence.[1]

Long before the time of the apostles, and before Homer became perhaps the first "writer," men had devised means to communicate, even over long distances. Drumming on hollow logs—the so-called "jungle telegraph"—had been used beyond the memory of man in Africa and in Polynesia. There was the mysterious *kabar angin,* or "news on the wind," a term used to describe the amazing way in

---

1 Pope John XXIII, speaking to news correspondents accompanying President Eisenhower on a formal visit to the Vatican in December 1959, suggested that "If St. Paul were alive now he probably would be a newspaperman. That would give him the means of spreading the doctrines of Christ."

which information seemed to be almost literally carried in the East Indies, even in recent times, with the people dwelling in widely separated areas somehow aware of far-off events.

Runners or "couriers" carried messages in ancient Greece; indeed, Hermes, in Greek mythology, was a messenger of the gods, as was Mercury, in Roman mythology. As in Greece, so later in the Andes of South America, in a pre-Inca period from about A.D. 1100 to 1500, runners or couriers also carried messages. There, in a Chimu civilization centering at Chan Chan, a coastal town 300 miles north of present-day Lima, and once a place of about 250,000 population, the Chimu runners traversed a 5,000-mile network of trails extending into what now are Colombia, Brazil, and Argentina. In leather pouches, they bore messages etched upon the broad surfaces of dried (Lima) beans with tools which are depicted by craftsmen of the time on vases and jugs surviving and on display at Trujillo, near the ruins of Chan Chan.

The Chimu runners, moving in relays, are estimated to have averaged 300 miles a day on their rounds. That would have been faster than the nineteenth-century pony express, which traversed the 2,000 miles of the western United States in 1860-61 between St. Joseph, Missouri, and Sacramento, California, carrying the mail, just before telegraph and railroad lines went into full operation in that part of the country.

The pony express was far from being the first means of the sort to speed information. Horses and horse-drawn vehicles had long been used for that purpose. At least as early as 500 B.C., Cyrus the Great dispatched mounted riders to carry messages through his great empire, extending from Persia to Babylon, Egypt, and Lydia (present-day Turkey). Riders also served Genghis Khan, Mongol leader of about A.D. 1200, then master of China and Central Asia westward to the Caspian Sea and south to India and Pakistan.

It has been contended that smoke signals, used by the Picts in sixth-century Britain, and by American Indians, might be regarded as a kind of communications system. So might torch signals, used in Greece at least as early as 300 B.C., and certainly lanterns, heliographs, flag signals, and semaphore arms used much later to convey messages by a code system. Pigeons had been used to carry messages in Egypt about 300 B.C., in Rome and in Baghdad at least by A.D. 1150, and in Japan and China certainly by the sixteenth century. Carrier pigeons continued to be used extensively in Europe and in the United States as late as the eighteenth and nineteenth centuries, and in Japan in the twentieth century to carry photographic film from the scene of an event to a newspaper office.

Indians in seasonal migrations perhaps a thousand years ago marked signs and symbols, significant to others, on a cliffside near what now is Monticello in southeastern Utah, still visible and known as "Indian Creek Newspaper Rock." Public announcements were made through the centuries by civilian and military officials speaking from some tribune, podium, or balcony, by priests from their pulpits, and by heralds pausing in the market squares of cities, their presence perhaps made known by a trumpeter. There were "town criers" passing through the streets, or "bellmen," who rang handbells to give notice that an announcement was about to be made. In later times, hand-prepared or printed notices or proclamations were posted in public places to convey information, orders, or instructions.[2]

The conveyance or transmission of messages, however important, was only half of the information process. The other half, and the first in point of time, required the gathering of information and its preparation. With the possible exception of that effort represented in the "Acta Diurna" of Rome (131 B.C. to A.D. 14), the first systematic and continuing program for the collection of information probably began in the eighth century A.D. in China.

China was then in one of its most brilliant periods, during the 300-year T'ang dynasty (A.D. 617-906), with Hsüan-tsung as emperor for forty-four years (A.D. 712-756), and with the capital at Ch'ang-an (now Sian).[3] It was a time when the first large, page-size block prints were being produced, with books, poetry, and painting of a high order; civil service and educational systems were advancing, along with a concern, at the court level, for the welfare of the country. The emperor and the imperial court introduced a practice, from about 750, whereby representatives were sent about the realm twice each year to inquire into general conditions and learn of events. Their reports were prepared in a form known as the Spring and Autumn "Annals" for the information of the emperor, at whose pleasure copies went to designated officials.

In addition to the "Annals," a Bureau of Official Reports was

---

2 From these early circumstances, it is understandable that many newspapers should have adopted such names as "Courier," "Mercury," "Herald," "Tribune," and even "Messenger."

3 China's capital was located in various cities through the centuries. It did not become established at Peking until 1409, and even that city had formerly been known as Yenching.

authorized at the same period to issue an official bulletin and a court calendar for more general distribution. Known as the "Tching-pao" (Capital Report, or Great Report), it appeared about once a month at the outset, in hand-written form, but was prepared in multiple copies. Before long it was produced by block printing, and later from movable type.

China was to encounter difficult times after Hsüan-tsung's death in 756, and even more so after about 950. The "Annals" continued, nonetheless, and the "Tching-pao" as well. In about 1361 that monthly bulletin was transformed into a printed weekly, and in 1830 it was to become a daily. Commonly known in its later years as the *Peking Gazette,* always official, it was to continue until the empire ended in 1911. Surely the earliest printed publication in the world, it was and still is by all odds also the publication of longest existence, having appeared in one form or another for nearly 1,200 years.

A third official publication began a long span of existence in China in 950. A kind of newssheet, it was intended for the information and instruction of provincial governors and their staff assistants, but was available also to scholars, a privileged and respected group. Known as the "ti-pao" (palace report), it was issued at intervals, including some information drawn from the "Annals." It, too, continued until 1911. Within that period of 960 years, a number of provincial governors added reports of their own, serving the same general purpose within their administrative districts.

Neither the "ti-pao" nor the "Tching-pao" (*Peking Gazette*) presented any general news. Neither reached members of the larger public. In this, the people of China were themselves in much the same position as the people in most parts of the world in the years prior to 1600 or, more realistically, prior to about 1850.

As mentioned earlier, Marco Polo was in China for two extended periods, first from 1260 to 1269, and again from 1271 to 1295, and was in the Chinese imperial service for seventeen of the twenty-four years of his second expedition. Yet, so far as revealed by his later writing, he was unaware not only of printing from movable type, but of the existence of the palace-sponsored reports.

Even so, he observed well, made copious notes, and after his return to Venice he wrote a long and detailed account of China, or "Cathay," completed in about 1300. He was the Herodotus of his time. For several centuries Marco Polo's account of his travels was to remain as the most informative and authoritative work on the Orient available in the western world. Its value and appeal was such that it was reproduced in hand-written copies for a considerable distribution. It remained so valuable, even after the further passage of two centuries, that *The Travels of Marco Polo* was one of the first books to appear in printed form, in 1559.

The printing press was still relatively new to the world at that period, and information was still a rare commodity. It had always been so. Leaders and peoples alike had to find their own means to gain and transmit information.

In China, as elsewhere, there was an informal exchange of gossip and of information. But it also became common in larger cities for "newshawkers," or storytellers, to appear in market places and perhaps in tea houses. The hawker carried a pole to which was affixed a sheet of bamboo with "headlines" displayed for the benefit of those able to read the ideographs. Beating a gong to attract a group, he presented an oral report of the "news," hoped to receive some coins, and moved on to a new location.

Considering the limited sources of information open to any person, the substance and accuracy the hawkers' reports would have been questionable. The hawkers existed, nevertheless, and had their counterparts in other areas of the world. Storytellers frequented the bazaars of the Middle East. Europe had its bards, minstrels, and strolling musicians. They were entertainers, but they also bore tidings of news and were hospitably received, almost without exception, wherever they might appear, even in inns and palaces.[4]

A version of the oral news-hawker-cum-entertainer were the "balladsingers," a feature of the London scene from the fifteenth to the early seventeenth century. These were small groups whose members moved about the streets, pausing to present news reports of a sort, in sing-song fashion, with listeners expected to toss coins. The "songs" were likely to relate to incidents in the affairs of the town, or of the country, or tales involving royalty or other highly-born or prominent persons. The facts and the names were somewhat dis-

---

4 While such practices were virtually at an end by the late eighteenth century, the tradition survives. The *sadhus,* or "holy men," still travel through India and carry news. There and in some other countries where illiteracy remains common, it is not unusual for a literate member of the community to read aloud from a newspaper to small groups. It may even be said that the role of the newshawker is taken today by the radio news broadcaster. His voice is heard not only in areas of complete literacy, but in parts of the world where literacy is rare, where languages and dialects vary, and where newspapers and periodicals are absent or late in arriving. Television, extending its reach, is adding pictures and even color, with reception in some relatively remote areas.

guised to protect the singers from the possible displeasure of the authorities, yet not so far disguised as to obscure the meaning beyond recognition by listeners.[5]

It has been contended, with some circumstantial evidence in support, that the familiar Mother Goose rhymes, although also held to be of French origin, actually had the British news-ballads as their source. By this interpretation as advanced, among others, by K. E. Thomas in *The Real Personages of Mother Goose* (Boston, 1930), Mary Queen of Scots was referred to in sixteenth-century news-ballads as "Mistress Mary, Quite Contrary," "Little Miss Muffet," and "Little Bo-Peep." Cardinal Wolsey became "Little Boy Blue" and "Old Mother Hubbard." "Georgie Porgy" probably was George I, "Little Tommy Tucker" was a real person, and Henry VIII, Queen Elizabeth I, and others among the personalities of the times were given names recognizable by the auditors. The rhyme beginning, "Baa, Baa Black Sheep, Have You Any Wool?" is said to have related to unrest then current among farm workers in England. The examples may be multiplied and are impressive.[6]

Among the news-hawkers, the élite of the breed were the *nouvellistes* (newsmen) of Paris in the seventeenth and early eighteenth centuries. They also were the last because by that period printed newspapers were appearing, literacy was on the rise, and privately operated newsletters were being circulated in much of Europe.

The *nouvellistes* moved in the parks, gardens, and cafés of Paris, or wherever groups might be attracted to hear them and reward them with small contributions. They were better informed than any of their predecessors, and some were excellent showmen, attracting a faithful following and profiting accordingly. It was usual for them to carry sheets of paper and carbon sticks so they could illustrate their reports, or they used predrawn maps, diagrams, and sketches to be displayed as they recounted the news or read it from notes.

The best of them made it their business seriously to learn the latest news. They were enterprising in developing sources. They found informants in the army, in diplomatic quarters, in positions to know the gossip of society, and even of the royal court. The informants

---

5 The street singer and musician remain figures in the life of London and other British cities even today, and "buskers" entertain outside theaters before performances, but the songs are unrelated to the news. More nearly resembling the ballad-singers are the West Indian Negro calypso ballads concerned with topics in the news, with the singers performing in an informal setting such as the market place.

6 Whether or not the "Mother Goose" disguise for news was, in fact, used by the ballad-singers, devices conceived in a similar spirit to evade official censorships were not uncommon in later years.

could be clerks in government offices, banks, or shops; soldiers or sailors, servants, or tradesmen. Usually of humble status, but so situated or employed as to be able to observe and hear things of some interest, or even of considerable importance, they would be paid for usable items provided, and pleased to receive small sums in return for taking notice and reporting what they knew or suspected. It was in this fashion that the "news tipster" made a beginning in France; he still exists there, as in some other parts of Europe and the world.

Some *nouvellistes* rather specialized in war news—and Louis XIV had a number of wars during his seventy-two-year reign from 1643 to 1725. The time of Louis XV, extending to 1774, saw French involvement in other wars. Both reigns were disastrous for France, but for the *nouvellistes* the scope of the news was wide and sources existed to permit them to deal with general political affairs, crimes, disasters, personalities, art, literature, music, ballet, and even to recount the latest jokes.

The door had been opened a crack in Europe in the matter of public information since block printing had been introduced on the continent after 1400. In addition to image prints and block books, occasional newssheets were produced. Small though they were, they became known as "broadsheets" or as "flysheets," and came from the wooden block untitled, printed on one side only, and presenting one item of news, briefly told.

These were the first news publications ever to be offered for sale to the general public in shops and market squares, at fairs and elsewhere—most commonly in the Germanic states or principalities of central Europe. They were inexpensive but, considering the limited literacy of the times, it is doubtful that many copies were sold. Perhaps for that reason the printer-xylographer went to the effort of carving a block only when he had a dramatic or other potentially popular item to offer.

The broadsheets appeared, therefore, usually only to report a battle, the death or the coronation of a king, the results of a tournament, a burning of witches or heretics, a disaster on land or at sea, a great storm, or a crime. For example, the critical Battle of Agincourt in 1415 was so reported, and a broadsheet in 1493 published a letter from a navigator named Christopher Columbus purporting to have discovered a previously unknown land somewhere across the western ocean. There might also be an account of some strange or miraculous occurrence, a quirk of nature, or occasionally a narrative or instructional song.

Across the world in Japan, something vaguely comparable to the

European broadshect began to appear in the sixteenth century. Known as the "kawara-ban," these were prints produced from tile engravings. The sheets, bearing ideographs and sometimes illustrations, were made primarily for display on shop doors. Each presented a report of a single occurrence, or a form of a song or even a kind of drama. For three centuries the "kawara-ban" continued. The visit to Japan of Commodore Matthew C. Perry and units of the United States fleet in 1853 was the subject of one of the later prints. From the late seventeenth century, however, untitled blockprinted newssheets called "yomiuri," fully comparable to the broadsheets of Europe, were sold by street vendors.

These forms of presenting information still did not account for the *gathering* of information. There was as yet no organized means serving that purpose except insofar as rulers and military leaders used their powers and resources to obtain it for their own interests. The program mentioned as having been instituted by the Chinese Emperor in the eighth century is one illustration. From Rome the Church sent its diplomatic representatives and missionaries to far places and obtained information from them, and also received a stream of visitors bringing news. Rarely was information obtained by church or state shared with the general public.

Among those private persons who most actively wanted or needed general information, traders and bankers once again were the most successful in obtaining it. As for centuries past, their ventures required that they be aware of events and circumstances both at home and abroad.

Traders and shippers in Europe, concentrating their activities in port cities, made the Hanseatic League important from the thirteenth century to the time of the Thirty Years War in the seventeenth century. The League, concerned with the needs of its members and member states, had representatives in at least eight Baltic and North Sea ports, including London.

Traders followed those navigators and explorers who had moved into the Western Hemisphere and parts of Africa and the Pacific in the fifteenth century. Traders and governments together joined to form settlements and then colonies, or to obtain trading rights. European governments—British, French, Spanish, Dutch, and Portuguese—in becoming "colonial powers," wanted information from those areas.

The traders of Holland, England, and France, supported by their governments, brought into being the Dutch East India Company, the East India Company of London, and the French East India Company, all between 1600 and 1664. Portugal, Spain, Denmark, Austria, and Sweden also formed such companies. Together they extended a network of commerce around the world, by no means limited to the East Indies, while also stimulating a flow of information.

Those traders and related banking houses in Europe, growing in numbers and activity after the thirteenth century and extending their interests, understandably wanted and needed information bearing upon their enterprises.

Three family banking houses became particularly successful in obtaining such knowledge. These were the Medicis of Florence, the Fuggers of Augsburg, and the Rothschilds of Frankfurt-am-Main. The Medicis and the Fuggers both gained wealth and power in the fourteenth century. As they passed their greatest period by the early eighteenth century, they were matched and exceeded in resources by the Rothschilds, who were gaining importance through Europe and in England and who remain active.

The Fuggers were the first in arranging to receive reports regularly and in substantial volume from many parts of the world. Their wealth was such that they helped to finance governments and in return received every sort of information from officials, military men, missionaries, ships' captains, traders, and bankers of various countries, as well as others in positions to observe and understand events and situations as they developed at home and abroad.

Much information came to these trading houses through direct personal relationships, but even more came in the form of written communications. Some were lengthy and often included a variety of items, and they were referred to as "newsletters." The letters usually were in German or Italian, but just as possibly in French, Spanish, English, or even Latin, for so long the *lingua franca* throughout much of a European continent living in the reflection of the Holy Roman Empire.

Neither wars nor wartime blockades appear to have stopped letters from arriving. They included reports on the Battle of Agincourt in 1415 and Colombus's first voyage, both of which became the subjects of broadsheets. The Fuggers are known to have received contemporary reports, and sometimes eye-witness accounts of such events as the St. Bartholomew's Eve Massacre of 1572 in Paris, the murder of William of Orange at Delft in 1584, a detailed account of the execution of Mary Queen of Scots in 1587, and the defeat of the Spanish Armada off the English coast in 1588. There were letters from India and Japan, an account of the death of Philip II of Spain in 1598, the execution of

the Earl of Essex in the Tower of London in 1601, accounts of some of
the early voyages of Sir Francis Drake, and a report of the imprisonment of Sir Walter Raleigh in 1604.[7]

As such examples indicate, the Fuggers were receiving reports not
only on matters of a business nature alone, but on general subjects as
well. Recognizing the interest some such reports would have for
others, it became the practice to turn over the general reports to two
Augsburg citizens, first Jeremias Crasser and later Jeremias Schiffle,
to be prepared for a more general distribution in a private commercial
service of newsletters going to subscribers. For that purpose, the
letters were translated, if necessary, edited or perhaps even augmented with further background material, hand-copied by clerks or
scriveners, and distributed.

The Fugger newsletters, presenting a variety of informative items,
were delivered to royalty, public officials, merchants, and other
literate citizens interested and able to afford them. As many as
fourteen different handwriting styles have been identified in surviving
copies. Two different reports appear to have been offered at different
prices. One was known as the "Ordinary" papers at the equivalent of
about two cents a copy for a small folio sheet of four pages. The other
was "Extraordinary," possibly a special or a more extended service
at a higher rate.

So far as is known, the Fugger newsletters, or Fugger-Zeitungen,
were the first of their kind to be made available to a general
readership. They continued for thirty-six years, from 1568 to 1604,
and were possibly printed from movable type during some part of that
time. Distributed chiefly in Bavaria, Austria, and adjacent Germanic
states, the service was imitated in other parts of Europe and in
England. Newsletters were to remain important, the best existing
source of public information until printed newspapers replaced them
in the late eighteenth century.[8]

In England, two notable publishers of newsletters in the sixteenth

---

7 Most of the original newsletters have disappeared, just as all of the copies of the
"Acta Diurna" of Rome have vanished. Among the letters surviving are some directed
to the Medicis in 1536, now preserved in the Magliabecchi Library in Florence. The
most important surviving collection includes many letters written to the Fugger house
during the sixteenth and seventeenth centuries, which are preserved in the Vienna
State Library and in the Leipzig State Library.

8 Actually, newsletters have never ceased to appear. They are not designed for
general news but to provide specialized and sometimes supposedly "confidential"
information, usually relating to business and finance, aspects of government administration, or foreign affairs.

and seventeenth centuries were Sir Thomas Gresham and Henry Muddiman. Gresham, originally a merchant, became fiscal agent both for Henry VIII and Queen Elizabeth I, and also is credited with having established the Royal Exchange in 1568 as a financial center and a center for commercial news in London. He arranged to receive both commercial and general information from parts of Europe, attained success with a newsletter drawing upon that information, and also was to leave his "Gresham's law" as a heritage to economists.

Henry Muddiman was equally successful as a publisher of newsletters at least as early as 1659. He is remembered more particularly as founder-editor of the *Oxford Gazette* in 1665, established at the special behest of Charles II. Moved to the capital in 1666 as the *London Gazette*, it is accepted by historians as the first "true" newspaper. It continues to exist as an official British government publication, appearing twice a week, and is now in its fourth century. Muddiman also continued with the production of other newsletters after 1665.

In Paris, some of the *nouvellistes* converted their oral reports into newsletters, with subscribers in Paris and beyond. Unlike most newsletters, some of these included items of a personal and even scandalous or libelous nature. This resulted in a number of their sponsors being sent to the Bastille. Some French postmasters also produced newsletters, using their positions both to obtain information and to facilitate delivery.[9]

Newsletters also existed during the sixteenth and seventeenth centuries in Italy, Austria, Holland, Denmark, and Norway, and in cities of the North American colonies. Crasser and Schiffle, preparing the Fugger newsletters, referred to themselves as *nouvellanten,* those in England were sometimes called "intelligencers," and the term in Italy was either *gazzettanti* or *corrieri.*[10] While most newsletters began in hand-written form, they were appearing in printed form by the seventeenth century. Most had a secondary circulation or readership by being passed along by the subscriber to a friend or relative. In recognition of that, it was common to leave the fourth page of the folio blank so that the original recipient might use

---

9 The first newspaper in the American colonies, appearing in Boston in 1704, was titled the *News-Letter,* and was established by the postmaster, John Campbell.
10 The "gazzetta" was an Italian coin, and presumably the price of the newsletter. It also became the name and price of early printed newssheets in Italy. But it was to be adapted almost world-wide as a newspaper title, as with the *London Gazette.*

the space to add personal, family, or local "intelligence" for the interest of the later reader.

As printing presses came into use throughout Europe in the late fifteenth century, heads of state and leaders of the church became concerned lest ideas dangerous to established authority be put into the minds of the people through the distribution of printed material. Cardinal Wolsey, as lord chancellor of England under Henry VIII in the early sixteenth century, expressed a sentiment then prevailing both in palace and church. "We must destroy the press," he said, "or the press will destroy us." While it never came to that, restrictions were imposed on printers in England and in most countries, with persistent and recurrent efforts made to control publication and prevent "unauthorized" information and ideas reaching the public.

The civil and clerical leaders rarely objected to the newsletters, however. The letters were few in number, and limited in circulation. Their writers usually worked in close relationship with the leadership, what might now be called the "establishment," both as a matter of personal caution and because it was helpful to them in obtaining information to be incorporated in the letters. Further, the price set for the newsletters was high, in terms of general income; subscribers and recipients were almost all persons of means and position, and members of a literate minority. The ruling group reasoned that persons sufficiently educated, privileged, and prosperous enough to buy and read such newsletters were not likely to harbor ill-will toward the regime under which they were thriving.

For the general public, however, another source of information gained importance in the seventeenth century. These were the cafés and taverns of the European countries, comparable to the tea houses of Asia and the Middle East, and the "coffee houses" that began to appear in England, where the first opened in London in 1652.

Frequented almost exclusively by men, even the humblest might be served in some such place and there hear the latest news and gossip. By the seventeenth and eighteenth centuries it had become the practice in some of the countries of Europe, and later elsewhere, to keep available for customers a file of newsletters and the newssheets and then newspapers, as they began to appear. Those able to read were able to enjoy this pleasant amenity—one that still exists in cafés in some cities of the world.

It was in one such London coffee house that another of the landmark efforts was made, beyond those of the Medicis and Fuggers, to obtain news on a regular basis and to make it generally available.

Edward Lloyd had opened a coffee house in Lombard Street about 1686. Situated not far from the busy Thames River embankment, and between the Tower of London and the city, in the heart of the banking and commercial district, it was a convenient place of rendezvous for ships' officers, traders, merchants, bankers, and brokers. There they could find food and companionship in pleasant surroundings, and enjoy a brief respite.

These patrons of Lloyd's coffee house were men of varied experience and professional occupation. Many were well established, respected, and responsible citizens with an interest in commerce and in the political, social, and economic influences affecting it. Many received information through their own local sources and relationships, and often from far parts of the globe. Usually, they were willing to share information.

It became the custom at Lloyd's to prepare a budget of news—some obtained from patrons—with items to be read aloud to those present at certain hours of the day. A handbell was sounded to indicate that the reading was about to begin, with the reader occupying a kind of pulpit overlooking the main room.[11]

Beyond the reading of news in the coffee house itself, and to give it wider circulation and a more permanent form, Lloyd in 1696 established a weekly paper known as *Lloyd's News*. It appeared for several months, but then was replaced by a printed newsletter, which continued for nearly thirty years. In 1720 the business passed from the Lloyd family control, but the name was retained. In 1726 the newsletter was supplanted once again by a newspaper, now a daily, called *Lloyd's List*.

Concerned primarily with matters of shipping and trade, *Lloyd's List* did not limit its content to such subjects. Nor did it limit itself to presenting information originating in London and the British Isles. On the contrary, by 1788 or earlier it had as many as thirty-two informants, or "correspondents," sending it reports on a fairly regular basis from twenty-eight ports and capitals of the world, with attention given to general news developments as well as to matters of commerce. By that time, daily and weekly newspapers existed in many cities, but *Lloyd's List* may be regarded as having made the first

---

11 Lloyds, Ltd., now long known as a London insurance firm, stemmed from the Lloyd coffee house. So largely patronized by men involved with shipping, marine insurance understandably became the firm's original concern, and remains an important aspect of its service. The tradition of the pulpit and the bell survives in the company's headquarters, with the Lutine bell now sounded preliminary to the announcement of a shipping loss.

substantial effort to report upon the course of world affairs. It is a paper that continues to appear in London as a special commercial daily.

By those later years of the eighteenth century, newspapers had grown from small beginnings in the previous two centuries and were about to enter upon a development whereby they were to become the major source of current information, at last available to the peoples of many countries.

The Newspaper Emerges 3

The great transition that was to bring an awareness and understanding of the world to virtually all peoples began when the process of printing from movable type was introduced in Europe in 1456. The first products of the presses included the "Gutenberg" Bible in 1460, books giving instruction in Latin, almanacs, encyclopaedias of some variety, and volumes intended to be instructive or morally improving. This was only the beginning.

An early product was a variant of the broadsheet, a newssheet printed from type rather than from a carved wooden block. Still a small single sheet, printed on one side only and untitled, the metal-cast type letters were smaller than carving had permitted, and more text could be accommodated on the page. This allowed for the presentation of more detail, or for several short items rather than for one item only. Again, although it required two printing operations, the practice began of presenting news items on both sides of the page, doubling the space available for news. By placing the type suitably in the form, and adding a hand-folding operation, the newssheet later became a folio of four small pages. From such modest beginnings, the newspaper press of the world was to grow.

The monarchs of the time, clerical leaders, and many members of the élite and privileged groups sensed danger to their positions and prerogatives in the new printing process. But it was not possible to turn back the clock. The very existence of useful books and of sheets presenting "tydings of news" stirred public interest, and was to invite the growth of literacy. The rulers of nations responded, however, by using their powers to control the output of the printing press.

The first press in England, brought from Bruges in 1476, was set up in a shop near London's Westminster Abbey. It was under the ownership of William Caxton, then fifty-four, who was highly successful in the textile business and well connected. He had the sponsorship of Edward IV, Richard III, and Henry VII, whose successive reigns spanned his own years, and he also enjoyed the support of nobles and merchants. He posed no threat to the existing establishment, printed only approved books, attempted no news publication, and thus conducted his printing business with full freedom to the time of his death in 1491.

Other printers setting up in London were less favored. In 1530, Henry VII introduced a licensing system that continued until 1695. Licenses were granted only to printers serving the government, the church, or university sponsors. From 1557, a year before Elizabeth I assumed the throne, the printers also were made members of the Stationers Company, established originally in 1357 for court writers and text writers, and later extended to include illustrators and book dealers. For the printers, it meant official control and a weekly search of their premises to determine the work upon which they were engaged, and for whom.

Any unauthorized printing—and there was some—meant a penalty for the printer, if he was identified. The penalties ranged from fines, the pillory, imprisonment, the branding iron, other tortures, or even executions. Such penalties were imposed through the Star Chamber, a closed and inquisitory court existing at the highest level from 1566 to 1641, from which there was no appeal.

Publications were limited almost exclusively to "authorized" books. Until 1621, the printed publication of any sort of news was forbidden. Meanwhile, ballad-singers were active in London and some were arrested in 1540 when certain of the "ballads" found their way into print. Henry VIII was particularly enraged when reports of a battle in Scotland, with which England was at war, appeared in an unauthorized newssheet.

Contrary to the limitation on news publication in England, the early printers in European cities, although under restraints, were able to produce newssheets. One of the first appeared in Spain in 1493. Sponsored by Queen Isabella, it told of Christopher Columbus's discoveries across the Atlantic. It was this account that was reported in a German broadsheet, and doubtless also in the Fugger newsletter. Newssheets, as published in Spain, were known as *relaciónes,* and that term was adapted for use in some other countries.

In Switzerland, where the first presses had been set up at Geneva and Lausanne in 1483, newssheets soon were appearing. In Sweden they were published as *tidende* (tidings). They appeared in Austria, Italy, Belgium, Holland, and elsewhere. Printers in Holland had greater freedom from government restraint than in any other country, and printing flourished accordingly. The newssheets published in Amsterdam were known as *corantos,* again to distinguish them from the earlier broadsheets, and because they presented a variety of news items in each issue. In addition to producing corantos for readers in Holland, they were printed in English for shipment from Amsterdam to London, first in 1603 and then quite regularly from 1619 to 1621. Printings in French were sent to Paris until 1631.

Although "Courant," as a newspaper title, was to evolve from the "corantos" of the seventeenth century,[1] none of the early newssheets bore a title. They did, however, carry general overlines to indicate the countries from which the news items came, or to which they related. An Amsterdam coranto of 1618, published for Dutch readers, bore the overline "Courante uyt Italien, Duytslandt" (news from Italy, Germany). One prepared for London readers bore the overline "Coranto or Newes from Italy, Hungarie, Spaine and France.

It was permissible for printers of the Dutch corantos to include news of Holland itself. Elsewhere in Europe at that time "foreign" reports were permitted in the newssheets, but no local or domestic news items. With such limitations, even the"foreign" item usually was rewritten from a newssheet published in a country at least once removed from that mentioned in the report. Adding the time required for an exchange of corantos in the uncertain postal system of seventeenth-century Europe, and speculating upon the means by which the item had been obtained in the first place, the recency and the accuracy of the news became uncertain.

With the publication of newssheets forbidden in England, the Amsterdam-printed corantos, in English, found a ready sale in London, exclusively, it is believed, through Nathaniel Butter, a bookseller. They were transported and sold in a somewhat secretive manner, however, as at least technically contrary to the licensing regulations affecting printing in England.

It was only in July 1621 that Thomas Archer, a London printer, probably in partnership with Butter, ventured to publish a coranto in London. Promptly brought before the Stationers Company, he was

---

1 The oldest existing newspaper today in the United States is the *Hartford Courant,* established in 1764 as the *Connecticut Courant,* a weekly.

judged guilty of transgressing a specific ban on corantos recently proclaimed by James I, and was sent to prison. There he remained until the following spring.

Another London printer, Nicholas Bourne, this time certainly in association with Butter, produced a second coranto in England in September 1621. In this instance, however, it was "Published by Authority," as stated in an overline, but only to present "foreign" intelligence. The main overline announced it as a "Coranto of Weekly Newes from Italy, Germany, Hungarie, Spaine, and France." Precisely how Bourne gained "authority" to print it is not clear, but it marked the beginning of news publication in London and the British Isles.[2]

There has been some dispute among historians as to when and where the first titled newssheet appeared. It seems to have been either the *Avisa Relation oder Zeitung* of Augsburg, the home of the Fuggers, or the *Relation* of Strasbourg, or the *Aviso* of Wolfenbüttel, just south of Bremen. All three had their beginnings in 1609, and all were published weekly.[3]

The titles began to be used by printers whose newssheets were being published regularly by then, rather than occasionally. Titles also provided reader recognition, since newssheets were multiplying in some places.

The first titled weekly in Paris appeared in 1631. It was very short-lived, and almost immediately was followed by the *Gazette,* soon retitled the *Gazette de France,* and considered the first newspaper in that country. Established by Théophraste Renaudot, physician to Louis XIII, it was closely identified with the court; the king himself and Cardinal Richelieu, secretary of state, were occasional contributors. Presenting foreign reports only, in the manner of the corantos, Renaudot nevertheless had special access through the court to news not available to others. The paper, always official in character, prospered and became a daily in 1772, and only suspended publication in 1819 after 188 years of existence.

Titled papers appeared in Switzerland, Germany, Austria, Swe-

---

2 This was at a time when the Plymouth Colony was just established on the coast of what was to become Massachusetts Bay Colony. Two members of that colony, William Brewster and Edward Winslow, who arrived in the Mayflower in 1620, were former printers in England. It was eighteen years before the first printing press was set up in the colony at Cambridge. Brewster and Winslow remained active at that time, but never as printers.

3 There had been titled publications in Europe before 1609, but they were not concerned with current news; one was in Latin and the other appeared annually.

den, Italy, and Poland—all between 1610 and 1661. The *Frankfurter Oberpostamtzeitung* of 1616, soon retitled the *Postzeitung*, later became the first daily newspaper in the world. It continued until 1866, then merged with the *Frankfurter Zeitung*, which was founded in 1856.

The first titled newspaper in England appeared in October 1621. It was, in fact, the second issue of that first coranto "published by authority" only the month before by Bourne and Butter. Archer, by then several months out of jail, was also associated. It was called *The Courant, or Weekly News*. The third issue, and others to follow, were known more simply as the *Weekly News*.

Government control remained, as it did throughout Europe; indeed, a church censorship was added in Italy, and in some countries news publication still was banned entirely. In England, too, a sharp reverse came in 1632. Charles I had succeeded to the throne in 1625 and instituted an administration so harsh that it put him at odds with Parliament, which he dissolved in 1629.

The youthful press, in its turn, felt the king's power in 1632. At that time the Spanish ambassador in London objected to an item about Spain's royal family, as printed in the *Weekly News*. The king responded by forbidding all news publication in England. For six years following, no printed news publications could appear legally. When the King was persuaded in 1638 to permit Butter and Bourne to revive the *Weekly News*, publication was still limited to foreign reports.

When the so-called "Long" Parliament met in 1640, after a lapse of eleven years, it entered into a bitter contest with the king to assert what it regarded as its rights, and the rights of the people. One result was the abolition of the Star Chamber in 1641, and the contest ended with the beheading of the king in 1649.

The press licensing regulations remained in effect throughout those years, and beyond. But because members of Parliament wanted the people to understand their position in the controversy with the king, and the king and his supporters also wanted their side presented, authorization was at last given after 1640 for the publication of domestic news, in addition to foreign reports. Further, an unprecedented liberalization permitted new publications to appear, with every sort of subject reported and discussed.[4]

Under the Commonwealth, following the execution of Charles I

---

4 Authority was given to refer to Parliamentary proceedings, but not until 1770 was the British press permitted to report such proceedings in detail, including speeches. John Milton, in 1644, published the *Areopagitica*, a classic appeal for press freedom.

and continuing until 1660, Oliver Cromwell, as lord protector with supreme authority, reversed the advances gained by the press in the 1640-49 period. He suppressed all existing news publications, which by then included "news-books" of from eight to forty-eight pages. Instead, he substituted one official publication, the *Mercurius Politicus,* to which a second, *Publick Occurrences,* was added later, both under the same editor. With the restoration of the House of Stuart in 1660, the new king, Charles II, permitted other publications, but with a licenser overseeing the printing presses and their output.

In the years when news publication was effectively halted in England from 1632 to 1638 under Charles I, and from 1649 to 1660 under Cromwell, newsletters became more important than they had been at a time when there were alternative sources of information. Henry Muddiman had conducted one of the most successful of the newsletters during the Cromwell period, and continued to do so after 1660. And he also succeeded to the direction of both the *Mercurius Politicus* and *Publick Occurrences* from 1660-63.

London was visited by the Great Plague in 1665, at its worst between May and December, with nearly 70,000 victims. Charles II and members of the court took refuge in Oxford. There the King missed the news reports available to him in London, but was hesitant even to have papers sent to him lest the plague be brought with them. It was at this time that he called upon Muddiman to produce a paper in Oxford. This was the *Oxford Gazette,* published twice a week as a small single sheet printed on both sides. When the King and his entourage returned to London in December, the paper was continued there, retitled the *London Gazette.* This paper of news, or newspaper, is regarded by press historians as the first true newspaper.

As these events were transpiring in England, the people of the European continent and its infant press had been suffering through the Thirty Years War from 1616 to 1648. Actually a series of wars, having a religious conflict as its cause, it brought eight or more countries into battle, with perhaps ten million lives lost and inestimable damage done. That war was followed immediately by a civil war in France, known as the Fronde, from 1648 to 1652, and by a war between France and Spain from 1653 to 1659. With such deep unrest continuing for forty-three years, the development of the press was delayed and even set back, and the information process was subject to further negative restraints by governments.

Recovery was to take some time in Europe. England had had its difficulties, but had not been involved in the wars on the continent.

It was in a better position to move forward, and the press shared in those advances. Under William III, who succeeded to the throne in 1688, the acts of 1530 and 1557 on the Regulation of Printing and Licensing were permitted to lapse in 1695. As a result, newspapers were able to take political positions editorially. Partly for that reason, they increased in number. The use of advertising notices by commercial enterprises also increased. Such paid notices, occupying greater space in newspapers, both forced an increase in the size of the papers and brought prosperity to some. The first British "provincial" paper published outside of greater London appeared in 1690. It was the weekly *Worcester Post Man,* later retitled *Berrow's Worcester Journal.* The *Edinburgh Gazette* followed in 1699 as a biweekly. Others were to come.

Government restrictions on the press did not end in England when licensing ceased in 1695. Strict laws of treason, libel, and contempt of court continued in effect, as they still do. There was no clear "right" to print news of governmental affairs. The disposition continued at official levels to regard a great deal of information as being none of the public's business, and to favor a curb upon the press.

In 1712, a stamp tax was voted by Parliament to be imposed upon every printed newspaper, with added taxes on advertisements. These taxes were doubled in 1757. Since the taxes were almost necessarily added to the cost of a newspaper, whether purchased in a single copy or by subscription, they had the effect of putting the price of the paper beyond what many readers were able or willing to pay. The measure thereby discouraged the reading of newspapers. This was exactly what the government intended.

The revenue raised from the stamp tax was not the government's first consideration, which was, rather, to forestall public involvement in the business of government. Yet the measures also deprived the people of information. For that reason, the imposts came to be referred to as "taxes on knowledge." There were protests, but the taxes continued virtually unchanged until 1833. At that time they were notably reduced. In 1855 they were almost entirely removed, but did not vanish completely until 1861, nearly 150 years after their beginning.

Restrictions on the press continued in most countries of Europe through the eighteenth and nineteenth centuries and beyond. But newspapers survived; and new ones came into existence, including dailies, and some periodicals appeared as well.

In England, the first daily, the *Daily Courant,* was established in

London in 1702. It survived for some years. *Lloyd's List* became a daily in 1726. Particularly important, however, were five London morning dailies established between 1752 and 1785—all were to figure prominently in the continuing story of press service.

The first to appear was the *Public Advertiser*, published under that title from 1752, but with antecedents going back to 1712. The second was the *Morning Chronicle,* established in 1769. The first was founded by Henry Woodfall and the second by his son, Henry Sampson Woodfall. Together, they helped to open the way for the publication of full parliamentary reports in 1770, and were leaders in general press enterprise.

The *Morning Post and Daily Advertising Pamphlet* was established in 1772. Soon to become simply the *Morning Post,* it gained an important place and continued until 1937. The *Morning Herald,* appearing in 1781, made a special contribution to press development in the nineteenth century. In 1785, John Walter, a coal merchant and insurance underwriter, established the *Daily Universal Register,* retitled *The Times* in 1788. Still published, it has long been one of the great newspapers of the world.

The eighteenth century also brought the establishment of a number of provincial papers that were to become leaders in their communities. These included the *Leeds Mercury* (1717), the *Yorkshire Post,* also of Leeds (1754), and the *Glasgow Herald* (1783). Periodicals added to the publication field at this period included the *Review,* in 1702, bringing fame to Daniel Defoe; the *Tatler,* established in 1709, and the *Spectator,* replacing it in 1711, both identified with Joseph Addison and Richard Steele, whose styles of journalistic writing were to set a pattern for emulation on both sides of the Atlantic. Defoe also was one of a group of "pamphleteers" prominent in the century. Among these writers were Jonathan Swift and William Cobbett. With views on religion, politics, and other subjects, the "pamphleteers" wrote subjectively and often polemically, sometimes with considerable effect.

One of the first papers established on the European continent in the eighteenth century was the *Vedomosti* (Gazette), beginning as a weekly in Moscow in 1703. It was also the first newspaper in Russia. Christian Voss established the *Vossische Zeitung* as a Berlin daily in 1705. The *Hamburgischer Correspondenten,* of that port city, began in 1714 as a weekly; later it became a daily. The *Allgemeine Zeitung* was founded at Tübingen in 1798 and gained importance.

In Switzerland, the *Neue Zürcher Zeitung* appeared in 1780 as a weekly; later it became a daily, and is regarded as one of the important European papers today. The *Gazette de Lausanne* began as a daily in 1798. The *Diario de Barcelona* began in Spain in 1792 and still appears. In Denmark, Ernest Heinrich Berling established the *Kobenhavnske Danske Post Tidender* (Copenhagen Danish Postal News) in 1749 as a weekly. Made a daily in 1831 and retitled the *Berlingske Tidende* (Berling's News), it still appears as the oldest existing newspaper of continuous publication in Europe. In France, the *Mercure de France,* dating perhaps from 1605 as an annual, became a weekly newspaper in 1728 and a daily in 1789, then changed its name to *Le Moniteur.* Another Paris newspaper established in 1789, on the eve of the French Revolution, was a daily, the *Journal des Débats.*

Far to the east in India, the presence of the British East India Company played a part in the establishment of the *Bengal Gazette or Calcutta General Advertiser* in 1780, commonly called "Hickey's Gazette," and the *Indian Gazette or Calcutta Advertiser* later in the same year. Both weeklies, they were perhaps the first newpapers to appear in Asia. The *Madras Courier* appeared in 1785, and the *Bombay Herald* in 1789. The first newspaper in Egypt, or all of Africa, appeared in Cairo in 1789, the *Courier de l'Egypte,* when French forces under Napoleon were campaigning there.

In the Western Hemisphere, the first newssheet was produced in Mexico City in 1541 by printer Juan Pablos. Bearing an overline, "Relación del terremoto de Guatemala," its single report was of a devastating earthquake in Guatemala months before. The second newssheet was published at Lima in 1594 by Antonio Ricardo, reporting the capture of Richard Hawkins, a notorious pirate, off the coast of Peru. These were printed broadsheets.

When the first press in the British North American colonies was set up at Cambridge in 1638, it was under the control of Harvard College, then in its formative period and still without a name until the following year. Other presses were set up in Boston before the end of the century, but not elsewhere in the colonies until after 1700. By 1776 there were printers in all thirteen colonies, although still no more than fifty altogether. For the first century or more after 1638, every press and all the paper, type, ink, and equipment was imported from England. Printers were under the same licensing regulations, with authority to print required from the royal governors appointed by the crown, even after the licensing regulation ended in England in 1695.

In Boston, New York, Philadelphia, and Charleston, the four largest towns, some newsletters were produced for limited distribution. Files of London newspapers, such as they were in the late seventeenth and early eighteenth centuries, were slow in arriving by sea, but were kept by some coffee houses and taverns for their patrons to read.

Two copies of the *London Gazette* are known to have been reprinted in Boston, one of 1684 date, and one of 1696. Increase Mather, Boston church leader, but also licenser of the press, under the governor's authority, sponsored publication of a newssheet in 1689. Bearing an overline, "The Present State of New English Affairs," it reported his effort, on a visit to London in 1688, to obtain a new charter for Massachusetts Bay Colony. Since he was in an official position to grant a license, it was an "authorized" publication, but it carried another line explaining that "This is Published to Prevent False Reports."

The first attempt to print a newssheet in Boston in 1690 was no more successful than that of Thomas Archer's in London in 1621. The effort was made by Benjamin Harris, a former London printer who had been arrested there in 1679 for unauthorized printing and sent to the pillory and to prison. In trouble again in 1686, he then managed to escape to America with his family. Conducting a coffee house and bookshop in Boston, he also was successful as a writer and publisher, "by authority," of almanacs and, particularly, of the *New England Primer,* a spelling book for school use.

In September 1690 Harris produced what some have accepted as the first newspaper in the American colonies, if not in the Western Hemisphere, and by extension the first newspaper outside of Europe and England. Titled *Publick Occurrences, Both Forreign and Domestick,* it was intended to be a monthly, and was a small four-page folio, with the fourth page left blank in the manner of some newsletters.

Four days after it appeared, Thomas Hinckley, the royal governor, with the concurrence of his council, declared that Harris's paper had been published without authority, that it contained "Reflections of a very high nature," "sundry doubtful and uncertain Reports," and was to be "suppressed and called in." The reminder was added that it was strictly forbidden for "any person or persons for the future to set forth any thing in Print without License first obtained."

Unlike Archer in his day, Harris suffered no personal penalty for his effort, and later returned to England. Not for fourteen years was another newspaper attempted in the colonies. Then in 1704 John Campbell, Boston postmaster, produced from the press of Bartholomew Green the first copy of the Boston *News-Letter*, truly "Published by Authority." A weekly of four small pages, it was to continue under Campbell and others for seventy-two years. Never a bright paper, it presented items of local news and news rewritten from papers received from London.[5]

A second weekly, the *Boston Gazette*, was established in 1719 by William Brooker, who succeeded Campbell as postmaster at that time. It continued until 1798, with several publishers. James Franklin, who had been the printer of the *Gazette*, started his own paper in 1721, the *New-England Courant*, which he continued until 1732. It was the most readable of the three Boston papers; partly for that reason, it was in periodic trouble with the authorities. Benjamin Franklin, James's brother, and nine years younger, entered upon his newspaper career with the paper, but left Boston in 1723, when he was seventeen, to continue that career in Philadelphia.

Three other Boston weeklies were started, the *Boston Evening Post* in 1731, the *Post-Boy*, by another postmaster, in 1734, and the *Massachusetts Spy*, by Isaiah Thomas, in 1770.

Meanwhile, William Bradford had become the first printer in Philadelphia in 1685, but moved to New York in 1693 to establish the first shop in that city. His son, Andrew Bradford, returned to Philadelphia later, and in 1719 established the *American Weekly Mercury*, the first newspaper outside of Boston. In New York, William Bradford established the first newspaper in that colony in 1725, the New York *Gazette*. One of his apprentices, John Peter Zenger, a German immigrant, established the *New York Weekly Journal* in 1733. In the following year, Zenger became the defendant in a suit brought by William Cosby, royal governor of New York, holding that he had been libeled. Zenger was cleared in a case establishing precedents in law.

Among other papers important in the colonies in the eighteenth century was the Philadelphia *Pennsylvania Gazette*, acquired by Benjamin Franklin shortly after its establishment in 1726. Franklin made it a useful and informative paper of quality, and also made it

---

5 Seeking to report news from London, and maintain a proper chronology, but having so little space in his paper, Campbell at one time fell thirteen months behind in his news accounts.

profitable. He directed it until 1748, maintained an interest in it to the time of his death in 1790, and the paper itself continued until 1815. Even as he was engaged in public affairs, Franklin also encouraged and helped finance printers who had worked for him to start their own start their own papers, which included the Charleston *South Carolina Gazette* (1731), the New Haven *Connecticut Gazette* (1755), and one of the first in Canada, the *Montreal Gazette Littéraire* (1788).

Important colonial papers also included the *Connecticut Courant,* later to become the *Hartford Courant* (1764), still published, but long a daily; the Annapolis *Maryland Gazette* (1727), the first in Maryland; James Rivington's *New York Gazetteer* (1733); and four Philadelphia weeklies, John Dunlop's *Pennsylvania Packet* (1771), the *Pennsylvania Journal* (1742), Benjamin Towne's *Pennsylvania Evening Post* (1775), and the *Pennsylvania Ledger* (1775).

By 1765 there were twenty-three weekly papers appearing in all the colonies except Delaware and New Jersey. By 1775 the number had grown to thirty-seven. Few as they were, and still relatively small, they were well read and appreciated. Some carried considerable advertising and were profitable. The best of them stimulated interest in current affairs and provided a rather substantial volume of information.

In March of 1765 in London, Parliament voted that a stamp tax, comparable to the "taxes on knowledge" then imposed in England, should also be levied on colonial newspapers, effective November 1. It would mean a tax of a half-penny on a single newspaper sheet, one penny on a four-page folio, and two shillings on each advertisement published in the edition, regardless of size.

Colonial printers and editors, learning of the purposed taxes, considered them improper in every way. They were prepared to refuse to accept the regulations, and made their protests heard in London through Benjamin Franklin, present there as agent for Pennsylvania and Massachusetts colonies. He put the views of the colonial editors before the members of Parliament with such vigor and effect that it repealed the Stamp Act in March 1766. The taxes, meanwhile, were never collected. The issue represented the first serious expression of a colonial grievance, and a first step toward what was to become a war for independence ten years later.

In the press development in the Western Hemisphere, the *Halifax Gazette* was established in 1751 as the first newspaper in Nova Scotia; the *Nova Scotia Gazette* appeared there in 1770. The

Quebec Gazette, published both in French and in English, began publication in 1764 and was the first newspaper inland in Canada.

To the south, the *Gaceta de Mexico* was established in Mexico City in 1722, while the *Gaceta* of Guatemala appeared in 1729. In South America, the first to appear were the *Gaceta de Lima* in Peru in 1744, and in 1785 the *Gaceta* of Bogotá, Colombia, and the *Gaceta de Santafé* of Quito, Ecuador.

In viewing the establishment of these various newspapers in the eighteenth century, it is not that they were necessarily greatly important or long-lived, although some were to become both. What is important is that the century brought the rather sudden presence of newspapers in considerable numbers, and on five continents— Europe, Asia, Africa, and North and South America.

Even with the restrictions and limitations of the times, and the shortcomings of the newspapers themselves, there now was a manifestation of change in the world. The peoples were being offered an imperfect, but still unprecedented service of information. Their ready reception of that service was an incentive to its continuation and improvement.

The Beginnings of News Coverage   4

Information has value only as it reaches those persons for whom it is intended or has meaning, and reaches them in proper time. Even after printed newssheets began to appear, the random and uncertain means through which current information was obtained left most persons poorly advised, virtually to 1800 and beyond.

With corantos and newspapers of title in existence, and newsletters as well, even so major an event as the Thirty Years War in Europe (1616-48) received no consistent or effective press attention—nor did the French civil war and the Franco-Spanish War occupying the years from 1648 to 1659. Indeed, printed newssheets were forbidden altogether in England in 1632-38 and again in 1649-60, and there was as yet no newspaper of any sort in the Western Hemisphere or elsewhere in the world.

Even with the passage of another century, the reporting of news was only moderately advanced. There were more newspapers by then, and somewhat larger ones. But great events still were inadequately reported, including the Seven Years War (1756-63) between France and England, and involving Russia, Prussia, Austria, Sweden, and Saxony. This war extended to North America as the French and Indian War, with the peoples of the British American colonies involved, and France's control in Canada lost to Great Britain.

There were reasons for the inadequate coverage of such events. First, the newspapers continued to operate under restraints imposed by governments; they were not uniformly free to seek information, or to use it if obtained. Second, newspapers did not have the manpower or staff organization to seek information, even locally, much less in far places.[1] Information reached them through office visitors, friends, chance encounters, letters received or made available by their recipients, casual "contributors," and newspapers received from other cities. Third, until the closing years of the eighteenth century, newspapers were published weekly and, although some had grown larger in page size and number of pages, space remained limited.

These circumstances, prevailing late in the century, shaped the coverage of two major events of that time, important then to millions of persons, and important for the world of the future. These were the American Revolution of 1775-83 and the French Revolution of 1789-99.

The American Revolution (1775-83)

The American Revolution was to bring a turning point in the world's history, and also in the evolution of a free press.

The success of the colonists in gaining independence of British rule ended England's control of that vast area of North America occupying the Atlantic seaboard from the Canadian border in the north to the Gulf of Mexico in the south, and westward to the Mississippi River. It resulted not only in the establishment of the United States of America as a new nation, but it helped inspire the French Revolution a few years later, and also inspired the peoples of Latin America of European descent to win their own independence from Spanish and Portuguese rule in the decades following.

Differences between the American colonies and England had mounted since 1765 when the British Stamp Tax had been proposed for application in the colonies, not only with reference to the press, but as a levy upon all documents, official papers, and books. While that proposal had been successfully resisted, other actions and incidents followed that roused emotions among the colonists.

These included the Boston "massacre" in 1770, and the "Tea Act" passed by Parliament in 1773, which was intended to assist the financially ailing East India Company at the expense of a special tax on tea transported to America. Parliament then passed three other acts in 1774, referred to in the colonies as the "Intolerable Acts," or

1 This was particularly so for the young press in North America, where the printer was also the owner, publisher, editor, and advertising director; too occupied to give much time to working as a reporter. he was perhaps more the craftsman than the writer.

the "Coercive Acts," which were followed shortly by the Quebec Act, extending the administrative boundaries of Canadian Quebec southwestward to the Ohio River. These measures, originating in London, brought a growing resentment and resistance on the part of colonial "patriots," at first a minority. James Otis, Samuel Adams, and John Hancock, all of Boston, undertook to establish a unity of voice and purpose, espousing the "rights" of the colonists, by then more than two million in number, but widely scattered through thirteen colonies, and lacking in any means of easy communication among themselves.

Efforts toward the establishment both of unity and of communication were advanced through the formation of an organization, the "Sons of Liberty," the establishment of "Committees of Correspondence" in the various colonies, and later of "Committees of Safety." By September 1774 delegates from all the colonies were prepared to meet in Philadelphia, there to form a Continental Congress. Its object was to restore good relations with the British crown, while also gaining recognition of colonial rights and liberties. A Declaration of Rights and Grievances was drafted and forwarded to London in a petition to King George III.

Meanwhile, a more overt expression of colonial opposition to measures taken in London had occurred in December 1773 in the "Boston Tea Party." Members of the Sons of Liberty there conspired to destroy a cargo of tea, just arrived, as a demonstration against the Tea Act. While some "patriots" even then were advocating colonial independence, this concept was far from general acceptance at the time. Insistence by the crown, however, upon those policies set out in the "Intolerable Acts" and others, and the closure of the port of Boston in June 1774 in a British response to the "Tea Party," stirred great opposition. There were voices of moderation in London, but they did not prevail.

The conflict escalated, clashes occurred at various places in the colonies. At last, in April 1775, British troops marched from Boston toward nearby Lexington and Concord to seize stores of munitions and also with the intent to arrest Adams and Hancock, then visiting there, as dangerous trouble-makers. The British troops were met and challenged at both places by local militia members, the "Minutemen." The skirmishes that ensued and the shots exchanged on that April 19 were inconclusive but critical. After that there was no turning back. The War of the Revolution followed, to become the War for Independence.

The Continental Congress, in its second session in Philadelphia, beginning in May 1775, appointed a Virginia delegate, George Washington, as commander-in-chief of a so far nonexistent colonial army. Experience in military campaigning since 1753, and an officer with British forces during the French and Indian War of 1754-63, he was to take command at Cambridge on July 3 of a Continental Army then counted at 14,500 men.

Much of the colonial opposition to British policies had originated in Boston, and British countermeasures also centered there at the outset. Adams and Hancock had worked from there in rallying the "patriots," organizing both the Sons of Liberty and the Committees of Correspondence. They were early advocates of independence and, for ten months in 1768-69, had produced a "Journal of Occurrences" as a weekly report or special column distributed to all colonial papers. The papers were encouraged to use it to make known what Adams, perhaps the first "propagandist," viewed as inequities in British policy. The *Boston Gazette* became a strongly partisan patriot journal, its content greatly shaped by Adams and Hancock.

There were "loyalist" papers as well. They had many readers among those in the colonies who had no wish to see the differences with England end in a severing of ties. As tensions rose, however, a newspaper that tried to hold to a middle course, in a fair and balanced treatment of events and issues, was likely to suffer reader displeasure.

This was the case, for example, with the *Boston Evening Post.* Perhaps for that reason, it was to report nothing whatever about the Lexington-Concord battle in 1775, and presently suspended publication altogether. To escape the tensions of Boston, Isaiah Thomas had moved his newspaper, the *Massachusetts Spy,* to Worcester, almost forty-five miles west. It happened that Thomas was in Concord on the day of the fateful clash, and an eye-witness to the battle. Yet his account only appeared in his newspaper three weeks later, and somewhat obscurely on the third page.

The best contemporary report of the Lexington-Concord battle is judged to have been published in the weekly Salem *Essex Gazette,* although how it was obtained is not clear. Other papers published versions of the battle rewritten from various "exchanges," but only after delays attaching to the delivery of those newspapers.

General Thomas Gage, royal governor of Massachusetts Bay Colony, and commander of the British troops, wrote his own account of the battle and forwarded it to London as a basis for reports to be published there. An American-written version reached London first, however, by clipper ship out of Salem, and was distributed by Benjamin Franklin in copies for use by London newspapers.

Historians have filled many gaps, and brought background and perspective to the events of the war in the two centuries that have since elapsed. The people of the time, of course, had no source other than the newspapers then existing, and those papers were not able to report the war as effectively or as promptly as would have been possible a century later. Accustomed to no other form of journalism, readers found little objection and indeed were better served than their forebears.

Some colonial papers were quite well supported by advertising and therefore were larger, insofar as newsprint was available.[2] This allowed space for more news. Full publication was given to the activities of local branches of the Sons of Liberty and of the Committees of Safety and Inspection, concerned with the militia and control of shipping, and to information provided through the Committees of Correspondence.

The newspapers also reported the news of town meetings, legislative assemblies, speeches of importance, and resolutions taken. The Continental Congress met during the period of the war, variously, at Philadelphia, Baltimore, Lancaster and York in Pennsylvania, and at Princeton. The sessions were reported by newspapers of those places, with their reports reprinted or summarized in others. Some documents and reports of parliamentary action in London were

---

2 The first paper mill in the colonies was established in 1690 at Germantown, now a part of Philadelphia. By 1768 there were others in Pennsylvania, New Jersey, Massachusetts, Virginia, and New York, and by 1775 about seventy mills were operating, including at least one each in Connecticut and Maryland. The importation of paper from England had been either halted or interrupted between 1767 and 1775, when it ceased entirely. Many of the mills had been established by printers or newspapers to assure their own supplies. The war brought the establishment of new mills, so that about ninety existed by 1783. The quality of the paper was not of the best, rough in texture and of a grey or bluish tint. Made of rags, however, it had substance and permanency. Rags were in short supply during the war years, partly because of demands for paper in making cartridges, for army and official purposes, and for propaganda publications. Every newspaper and every community called upon citizens, as a patriotic duty, to save every scrap of linen and cotton-and-linen material, with prizes offered to those who turned in the greatest quantities, usually to printers acting as agents for the mills. The price paid for the best rags, and the price of paper itself, rose to unprecedented levels.

Printing presses and type, originally imported from England, had been produced in the colonies since the 1760s, so that such requirements were far less a problem than paper supplies during the war years.

obtained, possibly by way of Canada and the West Indies, since a direct exchange of newspapers between the colonies and England was interrupted.

The reports of the war itself also came indirectly: from other colonial newspapers, from letters written by soldiers and shown to the editor-printers, from returning soldiers, and from visitors possessing some special knowledge; by hearsay, and occasionally by official distribution, with lists of army deserters, for example. Papers occasionally advanced their dates of publication to present a particularly important or interesting report.

In the first period of the war, the royal governors remained in colonies where the contest had not been joined, and some undertook to maintain the established restrictions upon the press. This did not continue for long, however, for the governors departed, one by one, on ships bound for England. Lingering efforts by colonial officials themselves, or by the courts, to curb the press also soon ceased. On the contrary, the time was not long in coming when colonial authorities were concerned lest a lack of news reports should reduce public interest and support of the war, and undermine troop morale. General Washington, with that in mind, sponsored the establishment of a new paper, the *New-Jersey Gazette,* during the hard winter of 1777, so that information might be made available to troops encamped nearby. He took special action to obtain newsprint for its use, sending worn-out tenting materials to the mills.

The Declaration of Independence, upon its signature at Philadelphia in July 1776, was promptly published in full text by the *Philadelphia Evening Post* and a number of other papers. It also was everywhere reported, although less promptly and less fully.

The Philadelphia *Pennsylvania Journal,* a strong "patriot" paper, in 1776 and 1777 published two essays by Thomas Paine, "Common Sense," originally a pamphlet, and "Crisis." These were widely reprinted by papers throughout the colonies, with great effect, winning fame for Paine and providing a persuasive rationale in the cause of independence.

Delays in the distribution of newspapers between cities, so important in the provision of news, was a constant problem. Some papers went by coastal vessels, some by overland transport. A lack of proper roads and unfavorable weather conditions had always made difficulties for postriders. And the war added military blockage of some roads and ports. At the very outset of the war, Savannah did not learn of the April 19 battle at Lexington and

Concord until May 31. As late as October 1781 the Battle of Yorktown, the decisive conflict of the war, received only one brief paragraph in the Philadelphia *Freeman's Journal*.

Shortage of newsprint forced some papers to suspend publication. A special problem also confronted newspapers published in cities occupied by British troops. At various periods, these were Boston, New York, Newport, Philadelphia, Norfolk, Wilmington, Charleston, and Savannah. Patriot papers were forced to suspend, or to move if they could, as the *Boston Gazette* was moved promptly after the Lexington-Concord battle to Watertown, across the Charles River estuary. Loyalist papers, if they existed or were started during an occupation, were forced to suspend when the occupation ended.

There were loyalists throughout the colonies. Until the time of the Declaration of Independence in 1776 they were generally tolerated. After that time their position became increasingly difficult. Not all newspapers had been strongly patriot in their editorial expressions; many held to the hope that the differences with England might be settled peaceably. After 1776 that also changed. Most papers then supported the patriot cause and looked toward independence. The few that did not proceeded with caution, but in cities occupied by the British, they could be outspoken. Those clearly loyalist or Tory included, among others, the *Pennsylvania Ledger*, and the *Royal Pennsylvania Gazette*, both of Philadelphia; the *Gazette and Mercury*, the *Royal American Gazette*, and especially *Rivington's New-York Gazetteer*, all of New York.

As the loyalist papers were forced to suspend, where they existed, when British troops withdrew, so those persons of loyalist persuasion either left the country or, if they remained, were subject to special laws until after 1812. Of about 60,000 who departed between 1775 and 1787, some went to England, others to the West Indies or the Bahamas, but most settled in Nova Scotia or Canada. Many had been established and affluent, but lost their property and were recompensed in some degree out of a British government special fund of £6 million (about $29 million).

Of thirty-seven weeklies existing in the colonies when the war began, twenty survived. About thirty-five new weeklies were attempted during the seven years. Some of those survived, so that the net count was thirty-five in 1783, when peace was formally restored by a treaty signed in Paris. Among the newspapers that had disappeared, fifteen had given support to the loyalist side.

The people of England probably were less well informed on the course of the war than those in the colonies. The British newspapers were unaffected, materially, by the war. Aside from some letters from military personnel, their major source of information was the *London Gazette,* the official government paper appearing twice each week. Its reports were reprinted, rewritten, quoted, and commented upon editorially. Those reports were not necessarily reliable, and they were often delayed. These delays in communication across the Atlantic, journalistic or otherwise, were significant, affecting military leadership and decision-making on both sides.

London did not learn of the signing of the Declaration of Independence until forty-four days after that action, with thirty-five hours required merely to move the report by postchaise from the port of Bristol to the capital. Again, the surrender of General Cornwallis at Yorktown in 1781, with French forces under Admiral Rochambeau sharing in the significant colonial victory, was not known in London until forty-nine days later.

In summary, press coverage of the American Revolution, whether in the colonies or in England, was neither organized nor fully effective. However, the main issue was not obscured—the struggle of the colonies to gain independence, and their ultimate success in doing so.

Whatever its shortcomings and its problems, the colonial press did publish a vast amount of information. Perhaps it could have done little better, in the context of the times. It was unquestionably the chief weapon in building the patriot cause and spirit, and readership increased during the war years. Most important, it did provide the public with a better understanding of a major event than ever before in history.

The French Revolution (1789-99)

The French Revolution was less well reported than the American Revolution. The French press was weak and too caught up in the issues to be effective. The press of other continental European countries, none too well established, was literally unable to provide any original coverage. Some slight London press coverage was attempted, but it was seriously handicapped.

Despite this poor press performance, the period of the revolution did set three new "firsts" in reporting. One was the presence in Paris in 1789 of quite probably the first *bona fide* newspaper "foreign correspondent," that is, a staff member of a well-recognized newspaper, writing for that paper from a foreign place. Another was a demonstration of possibly the first special enterprise on the part of a newspaper in reaching out, at some cost and effort, to obtain news reports from another country. The third was probably the first organized service of current news information prepared for distribution to the press. All three of these "firsts," as it happens, were identified with British press development.

France in 1789 was one of the most advanced nations of the world, but beneath the surface of what seemed a well established and orderly society there was discontent. Reform was long overdue, advocated, and discussed for many years by French writers and political spokesmen, including Montesquieu, Voltaire, and Jean Jacques Rousseau, and by members of the press.

At last a serious effort began in June 1789 looking toward proper changes. Louis XVI gave his support to the effort. Disputes soon arose, however, and reached such a pitch as also to arouse public emotions. The king was persuaded to turn out the Royal Guard to assure order. This precaution was misunderstood by some, and an element in the crowds gathered about the National Assembly chose to demonstrate by marching to the gates of the Bastille, the 400-year-old prison-fortress. Long used as a place of confinement for prisoners of the state, the massive stone structure had become a symbol of despotism. The demand of what had become a mob to be admitted to the Bastille was rejected by its commandant. The fortress was stormed by the mob, the seven prisoners held there were freed and the commandant was killed, as were about 100 others. The building was completely demolished later in the year.

This event of July 14, 1789, marked the beginning of the French Revolution. The attack on the Bastille was echoed by other demonstrations in Paris, riots in the provinces, and the departure of some members of the nobility from the country.

The original effort, nevertheless, proceeded in the National Assembly. A Declaration of the Rights of Man, somewhat comparable to the Declaration of Independence, was published in August. A constitution was drafted, and was to be approved by the king in July 1790. Some reforms were in prospect.

In October 1789, however, rumors had gained currency that the king was preparing to use military force to put down what by then was the "revolution." This led to another mob demonstration at the great Palace of Versailles, and seizure of the king and Queen Marie Antoinette. Both were taken from Versailles and installed under guard in the Tuileries Palace in the heart of Paris. The original hopes for reform were overwhelmed by rising passions and the king felt such alarm that in June 1791 he attempted to escape to Prussia. The attempt failed; he was captured, along with the queen and their two children, near the frontier, and all were returned to the Tuileries as virtual prisoners.

These events did not go unnoticed by other monarchs in Europe. After the king's ignominious return to Paris, Frederick William II of Prussia, and Leopold II of Austria, suggested a possible intervention in France. An alliance was formalized early in 1792, in which the island kingdom of Sardinia joined.

In France, the National Assembly, reorganized as the Legislative Assembly, responded to the new alliance by declaring war against Austria in April 1792, and Prussia and Sardinia later. It put three armies in the field against Austria, but they suffered reverses. Fears of a possible successful foreign coalition in support of the king rekindled the revolutionary spirit in Paris. Mobs attacked the Tuileries in June and again in August. The king was unharmed, but his Swiss Guards were massacred on the second occasion.

Throughout this period since 1789 factions were forming among those active in the revolution. Maximilien Robespierre gained leadership in the Jacobin group, which was relatively extreme. Georges Jacques Danton, Jean Paul Marat, and Camille Desmoulins were among the Cordeliers, later to become the Girondists, who were more moderate. The Monarchists recognized the need for reforms but they were conservative. The Marquis de Lafayette, who had played a prominent part in the American revolution, was active in the latter group.

The French press inevitably was drawn into the passionate debates. Such Paris dailies as the *Gazette de France,* the *Journal de Paris,* and the *Journal des Débats* attempted to maintain a balance, but found it difficult to do so. Others, and especially such new papers as were started by active participants, Marat and Desmoulins included, made no pretense of balance. Even more extreme advocacy was reflected in the production of hundreds of pamphlets, known as *libelles,* or "small books." Some resorted to such violent expression and defamation as to bring the word "libel" into the international lexicon.

Violence increased, stemming largely from the Jacobin group. Massacres of suspected dissidents to the revolution occurred in September 1792 in Paris and at least five other cities. Lafayette was forced to flee from France, only to be captured by the Austrians and imprisoned until 1796.

The Legislative Assembly was reorganized as the National Convention, to exercise legislative and executive power for three years. France was declared a Republic on September 21, 1792, with the monarchy abolished. In December Louis XVI was brought to trial before the National Convention, condemned to death, and on January 23, 1793, died on the guillotine in the Place de la Concorde. The queen met the same fate in October.

The execution of the king brought such protests from other countries that France, already technically at war with Austria, Prussia, and Sardinia since 1792, now also declared war February 1, 1793, against Great Britain, Spain, and Holland, and announced the annexation of Belgium.

The king's death brought further violence in France. Marat was assassinated, a Royalist revolt arose in the western Vendée province, and a Reign of Terror continued through much of 1793-94. In this latter, Robespierre was dominant in directing a campaign against suspected counter-revolutionaries. Many were jailed and literally thousands executed, both in Paris and in the provinces. Danton and Desmoulins were among the victims. Such Jacobin excesses brought resistance and reaction. Robespierre himself was arrested and executed in July 1794, and nearly one hundred others were similarly dispatched. The White Terror continued through 1794, with more riots and killings.

By 1795, however, a certain order was restored in France. Some who had fled returned. French forces invaded Holland, but peace was made with Prussia and with Spain. The National Convention seemed at last in a position to consider the original objectives of reform and reorganization. A new constitution for the republic was drafted, and in October 1795 the National Convention dissolved itself in favor of an administrative organization specified in the constitution. This was known as the Directory, with executive powers in the hands of five persons. A bicameral legislative assembly would choose those five.

The Directory, assuming power late in 1795, did not distinguish itself in the four years it was to exist. In an early action, however, it appointed Napoleon Bonaparte, already in the nation's military service, to direct a campaign against the Austrians. This he did with success in 1796-97, while also establishing a French position in Italy and Switzerland, and then in Egypt in 1798-99.

In Paris, during those years, the Directory made a record of ineptitude and corruption. Napoleon was aware of this, not least through his brother Lucien, who was president of the lower house of the new legislative assembly. With a political sense matching his military acumen, he returned unannounced to France in November 1799. Acting in accordance with plans secretly prepared, he proceeded to Paris, used his military prestige and power to overthrow the Directory, and adjourned the legislative body. He took personal direction of the government, with title as First Consul under a new system known as the Consulate, designed by Emmanuel Sieyès, one of the leading advocates of reform prior to 1789. This reorganization in Paris marked the historic end of the French Revolution after ten years and the beginning of the Napoleonic period, which was to continue until June 1815.

Through the years of the revolution, several countries of Europe were engaged in wars unrelated to France. This was true for Sweden and Denmark, Russia, Finland, Poland, Turkey, Austria, and Prussia. At the same time, France itself was in conflict with Austria, Prussia, and Sardinia, with Spain, Holland, and Belgium, seized areas in Switzerland, contested Turkish power in Egypt, and at war with England. In that latter confrontation, British ships under Admiral Horatio Nelson destroyed the French fleet near Alexandria in 1798 in the Battle of the Nile.

It was not possible, in the light of the various belligerent relationships, for the press of European continental countries to provide direct coverage of events in revolutionary France, even had existing newspapers been equipped to do so. The French press itself was so disrupted by the revolution, so restricted and so polemical, as to be basically unreliable—useful chiefly in presenting the texts of official documents or in reflecting changing moods. Almost by default, therefore, the most effective reporting—brief and limited as it was—must be attributed to four London dailies. Yet the French declaration of war on England in 1793 compromised even those efforts.

The London *Morning Chronicle,* published since 1769, was to come under the control in 1789 of James Perry, a Scotsman already possessing a decade of news and magazine experience. Perry was in Paris when the revolution began, and remained through its first year, providing reports for the *Chronicle.* In this he became perhaps the first "foreign correspondent." His reporting, unusual at the time, added distinction to a newspaper already favorably known by reason of the work of its founder, Henry Sampson Woodfall.

There can be little doubt that copies of the *Chronicle* reached the

United States and became the source of information about the revolution, with Perry's reports reprinted or rewritten in New York and elsewhere. Since the papers moved across the Atlantic under sail, the fall of the Bastille on July 14, 1789, for example, was not reported in the United States until two months later.[3]

Robert Cutler Ferguson, a colleague of Perry, was in Paris for the *Morning Chronicle* at various times in 1792 and in 1793, until France declared war on Great Britain. His reports added both to public information and to the reputation of the paper.

The *Sun,* established in London in 1792 to support the policies of William Pitt as prime minister, arranged to receive some reports from a contributor in Paris until 1793.

John Bell, proprietor of the London *Oracle and Public Advertiser,* which he had established in 1789, arranged for reports of British military action in Belgium in the spring of 1794, when France's annexation of that country was an issue. This became an aspect of war correspondence, but relating to the revolution.

Reports from various countries were appearing in *Lloyd's List* at this period. Some such reports bore at least an indirect relation to the revolution, but there is no evidence to indicate any coming from France itself.

In 1785 John Walter had established the *Daily Universal Register* in London, which became the *Times* in 1788. By 1792 the *Times* had engaged resident "agents" in several European capitals, including Paris, to forward newspapers of the countries to the paper's office in London, there to be used in preparing news reports. The agents might also write letters reporting upon events, although they rarely did so. The *Times* was not yet prepared to call such agents "correspondents," nor had that term been used by the *Morning Chronicle* in application to Perry or Ferguson, who wrote anonymously so far as readers were concerned.

---

3 The French Revolution had a profound effect in the United States. The revolution and directly related matters placed personal and official pressures on George Washington, newly in the presidency; on Benjamin Franklin, so soon to die (1790); on Thomas Jefferson and James Monroe, both with ties to France. The relations of the United States to France itself, to Great Britain and Spain were critically involved. The execution of Louis XVI and events following had great public and official impact. The "Genet affair," a controversy over the Jay treaty, the "XYZ affair," and the 1798 Alien and Sedition Acts, with a threat to press freedom, all part of U.S. history and once current news, stemmed from the revolution. So did political differences reflected in the Federalist party (Washington and Adams) versus the Democratic-Republican party (Jefferson). When Washington died in 1799, the last year of the revolution, the key to what had been the Bastille was in his Mount Vernon home.

In appointing agents to regularize and assure a flow of information from European capitals, the *Times* nevertheless was establishing a basis for what was to become the first active "foreign" or world news service.

In a further show of enterprise, the *Times* in 1792 also started its own small boat service, with a light cutter moving back and forth across the Channel between England, France, and Belgium to bring back copies of such newspapers as its new agents forwarded to Calais or Ostend, or as could otherwise be obtained. This was one of the first positive efforts to speed news communication and, along with the appointment of the paper's agents, probably the first purposeful action to obtain prompt news reports from other countries. The effort sponsored by *Lloyd's List,* while also important in pioneering such a service, was less tightly organized than that of the *Times*.

When the *Times* began its special boat service across the Channel, it received an immediate protest from the British General Post Office. The GPO claimed a monopoly on the right to deliver foreign newspapers in the British Isles, along with the mail. It contended that the *Times* was transgressing upon an official government right and responsibility and should desist. There was no law or precedent to support such a contention, however, and the *Times* persisted in its independent effort. The controversy with the GPO continued until 1813 before a settlement was reached.

In 1792, when that controversy began, the GPO had for some time been producing a special service of its own in the provision of foreign reports to London newspapers, government offices, banks, and business firms. The service was prepared from reports originally appearing in newspapers from other countries received by the GPO, with excerpts made, translated where necessary, and distributed twice each week to subscribers. The cost to a newspaper for the service was 100 guineas (about $900) a year. For the press, it was a useful source of foreign news.

Copies of both foreign and domestic newspapers were received in British newspaper offices and used as a source. But the GPO delayed postal delivery of such newspapers a day or more to give its own reports precedence. In any case, the GPO was able to draw upon more newspapers for its service than would be available in any one London or provincial newspaper office, and so could provide a wider range of information. Historically, the British General Post Office thereby was making available to the press the first organized service of world news.

When France declared war on Great Britain February 1, 1793, and also proceeded to annex Belgium, access to continental papers was interrupted. Indeed they became contraband in England and might be seized as such. The GPO thus had a more valid reason for objecting to the cutter service of the *Times*. Nor could that service be totally effective. At some risk, papers could be obtained through French and Belgian fishing ports, and material derived from them possessed a certain interest. For that reason, the service was continued until 1798. A Newspaper Act passed by Parliament in that year then set penalties for the possession of contraband newspapers. This finally halted the cutter service, although some newspapers still were smuggled into Great Britain.

The end of the French Revolution in 1799 and the beginning of the nineteenth century opened a new era in the history of the world and of communication and information. The London press was to lead the way toward the provision of extensive world news reports. The press of the United States was to exemplify a new concept of freedom which grew as the new nation grew. There were to be press advances in other parts of the world, along with advances in science and technology that were to transform society, while bringing to the peoples of many lands an improved service of information. Even so, these advances came slowly.

The Industrial Revolution: Catalyst 5

Four circumstances combined during the period between about 1800 and 1870 to create a situation in which information became available quite suddenly, in an historical sense, to millions of persons throughout the world. Within the possible lifetime of one man, dramatic changes occurred, with the press both recording those changes and contributing to them.

The first circumstance was the beginning in England of the industrial revolution.

The second and related circumstance was an information revolution, wherein the press gained greater freedom, reached out for news in a show of enterprise, and gained in prosperity, professionalism, readership, and influence.

A third circumstance, related to the other two, was a revolution in transportation and communication, which drew the peoples of the world together.

The fourth circumstance, again related, was the evolution of agencies and organizations specifically concerned with gathering and distributing current information in volume, quality, and balance, to be made promptly available through the press to the peoples of many lands, in small towns as well as in great cities and capitals.

Accompanying these events went a growth in general literacy and education, and a lively public awareness of the world.

However indirect it might seem, and however important in itself in changing the face of the world, the industrial revolution was basic to the advancement of the information process. The two go together.

It often has been observed that the invention of the wheel marked a distinct point of advance in mankind's control of his environment. The invention of printing from movable type was equally important.

The industrial revolution was a third, for it harnessed the power of steam to the performance of tasks previously dependent upon the muscles of men and animals, and upon the power of wind and water. It opened the door also to unimagined scientific and technological developments.

Thomas Savery and Thomas Newcomen, later in association with John Cawley (or Calley), in England had devised and improved a steam-operated engine in 1705 to pump water out of coal mines. James Watt, a Scotsman born in 1736, and a maker of mathematical instruments, in repairing one of the early engines in 1764, made improvements, not only for its use in pumping water out of the mines but for lifting the coal to the surface. He also adapted it to supplant hand operation of the flying shuttle, recently invented by John Kay, an Englishman, for use in the weaving of cloth. He adapted the steam engine further to activate a spinning jenny, patented in 1770 by James Hargreaves, and to a spinning jenny roller frame patented by Richard Arkwright and applied later to the cotton gin invented in the United States by Eli Whitney in 1793.

Between 1764 and his death in 1819, Watt manufactured in Birmingham, England, what may still be called in principle the "modern" steam engine. He rated its usefulness in terms of "horsepower," as the terms "watt" and "kilowatt" also derive from his work.

By 1800 England probably was the most advanced country of the world, politically, economically, and culturally. Although the United Kingdom—England, Wales, Scotland, and Ireland—was of limited area, about equal in size to the six New England states, plus New York and New Jersey, British navigators and explorers had given the island nation an empire. At home there were resources of manpower, an agricultural economy, deposits of coal, iron, and tin, and a climate suited to the weaving of wool, linen, and cotton. Articles of commerce were moving from British ports, for an active merchant marine, including ships of the East India Company, had extended British trade around the globe. A royal navy guarded the sea lanes against pirates, privateers, and hostilities by other countries.

This, however, was only a beginning. The steam engine, as adapted to the mechanized weaving of textiles, was to transform the slow handcraft and cottage industries into a giant of production during the nineteenth century. The steam engine also was to make it possible to produce efficiently far greater supplies of coal and iron. Iron ore, for centuries smelted by fires stoked with charcoal, had been processed more effectively since the early eighteenth century in blast furnaces using coal. Then in 1855 Henry Bessemer invented a process for making steel of a superior quality, at a lower cost, and so opened greater prospects for industry. Better equipment and better machines were produced. New machines were devised to do new things, adding useful and merchantable articles for presentation to a world market.

The changes that ensued from the mechanization of tasks formerly performed by hand labor in homes and small workshops had far-reaching results. Few individuals could afford to buy steam engines and machines, or to build blast furnaces. Those who could, or those who joined together to do so, needed banking and financial support. This was to be found only in the larger cities. Logic also dictated the placement of production facilities in locations convenient to supplies of materials, and to ports and highways.

As manufacturing enterprises began to function in such locations, many persons formerly engaged in home industry and workshops turned to the new factories for employment. Families were uprooted, moving from rural areas and villages to the towns and cities in which the factories were situated. Some who had worked in the fields joined in the migration. Others established themselves in the growing towns in retail trade or service occupations. This movement of peoples, continuing over several decades, ended what remained of the feudal system; what had been an agricultural society became an urban society, with stress on industry and commerce.

The products of the factories, as well as coal, were soon moving in great quantities and volume in British ships to other countries. The British Empire became both an assured market and an assured source of raw materials. But commerce with other countries was equally important. The quality of the British-manufactured goods was excellent, and many of the products were unobtainable elsewhere. The volume and costs of production were such as to permit the quotation of attractive prices, additionally possible because deliveries could be made in British ships.

As steam power was used in the factories, so inventive minds put it to other uses. Rail transport, using steam propulsion, began in England in 1825—its first appearance anywhere. After about 1830, ocean-going ships began to move under steam. Earlier, small ships had been steam-powered on rivers, canals, and in coastal waters, but now British enterprise put them to sea. With progressive improvements, increasingly independent of wind and weather, the ships gained in speed, regularity of service, size, and comfort. British-built and manned, they could transport passengers as well as products of the factories to all parts of the world, protected by British naval power and coaling en route at British Empire ports.

So it was, as the nineteenth century advanced, that Great Britain became an industrial and commercial nation, trading with almost all the peoples of the world. Related and peripheral enterprises and services also developed. The profits accruing to British industrialists, businessmen, bankers, and shipping firms were substantial, and the general British economy prospered. Although in some cases seriously disaffected by conditions of life and work in industrial communities, the people nevertheless attained a standard of living and a personal freedom that, on balance, may have been then the best in the world. The conversion from an agricultural to an industrial economy meant that foodstuffs had to be imported in increasing volume, but this was hardly a problem, given the new wealth deriving from empire and world trade.

With international trade centered in Great Britain late in the century, the British pound sterling became a convenient standard of monetary exchange, and a basis for calculations. This made London the main world center for banking, finance, and commodity prices. The British Empire was strong, and the United Kingdom was a "great power." Even the population mushroomed from 10.5 million in 1801, the year of the first census, to 27.5 million in 1851, and 41 million in 1901.

With this beginning in the nineteenth century, the industrial revolution was to continue, giving meaning to a "capitalistic system" under which industry, trade, and commerce might proceed. The system was adopted on the European continent after about 1870 with Germany leading, in the United States after 1900, and later in Japan and elsewhere.

The industrial revolution, as it proceeded in England, became a kind of catalyst in bringing about an "information revolution." The expansion of trade, changes within the country, and closer relations with the empire and with nations of the world, all brought information flowing into London in increasing volume. It was sought and required by the business community, by the government, and by the press. London, in those years, became the greatest world "news center," a distinction it has never lost.

The industrial revolution had an early impact on the press; the basic printing process was altered when the hand-operated press was replaced by the first steam-operated press, which was made by

Frederick Koenig and put to use by the *Times* for its edition of November 29, 1814. It made possible the printing of an edition of the paper, then about 4,000 circulation, in one-third the time previously required. And the process was improved when a new type of steam-operated cylinder press was put to use by the London evening *Courier* in 1824. Invented by David Napier, it permitted still faster production.

The most significant effect of the industrial revolution upon the press was the discovery by those industrialists, bankers, and financiers directly involved that a free and active press was urgently needed if their own enterprises were to continue successfully. Their advocacy and support for such a press was doubly potent because the British government discovered equally that it in turn needed industrial development to maintain a strong national economy and empire.

The new industrialists, along with the business community, became keenly aware early in the century that they needed a sufficient reservoir of human talent to keep the system they had created functioning properly. Such talent was required not only to produce and move goods and raw materials, but also to make necessary decisions, deal with suppliers and customers, keep records, and perform administrative and clerical duties becoming evermore complex. Those qualified to perform such tasks, with proper understanding at every level of responsibility, needed at least a minimum education and needed to be adequately informed about current affairs, both at home and abroad, on a day-by-day basis. This required schooling beyond what had been available, and a press both free to report the news and prepared to do so.

Beyond that, the work, welfare, and prospects of every person and every family in the British Isles were becoming evermore dependent, directly or indirectly, upon the continued successful operation of the system of industry and commerce, and upon its proper conduct domestically and overseas. The total economy was involved, but so were such matters as the maintainence of an orderly society, public health, housing, transport, imports of food and raw materials, and a host of other factors. The government, as well as the business community, was obliged to give attention to these things, and to the world at large, with an awareness of events and pressures bearing upon the entire economic and political structure.

Every individual in the country, whether he realized it or not, had a personal reason to be concerned and informed about the great range of subjects upon which his own well-being depended, and that of his family. Some persons understood this, or sensed it, because they themselves or members of their families were directly involved in the industrial-business complex—some as factory workers and some in offices, some as soldiers or sailors, some as managers or civil servants, some at home and some abroad.

It would have been unrealistic to expect all persons, or even most, to recognize the full import of the industrial revolution as it proceeded, but the horizons of many were extended nonetheless. One result was a recognition of the need for a more effective system of general education, and a more informative press.

Private schools, colleges, and universities had existed in England since the eleventh century, but they were for the children of persons of title and of financial means. An apprentice system had existed since the twelfth century to provide training in the crafts. For most, however, opportunity to receive instruction even in reading, writing, and arithmetic was rare. In 1808, a new effort began to meet what by then was recognized as a need. By 1831 at least 13,000 elementary schools were in operation, originally with church sponsorship. State aid was instituted in 1832, and a Grammar Schools Act was passed by Parliament in 1840. By 1861 about 2.5 million children were attending day schools at no cost. Passage of a Public Schools Act in 1868, and an Elementary Schools Act in 1870, brought truly substantial progress in the provision of free universal elementary education in Great Britain. From these beginnings, a generally literate public appeared, a potential audience for a newspaper and periodical press which also was developing. Public libraries became available through an act of Parliament in 1850, advanced in 1852-53, and aided by formation of a Library Association in 1877.

Press development occurred at somewhat the same rate as education. The government was slow to ease its restraints. The taxes on knowledge were even raised in 1804. Every advertisement was taxed three shillings and sixpence (not less than ninety cents). Beyond that, a tax of threepence-halfpenny (about six and a half cents) was assessed on the price of each copy of a newspaper. The total put the cost beyond the means or pleasure of most persons, and circulations were understandably low.

A Libel Act of 1792, while not without merit, was so used and interpreted as to induce a caution on the part of newspapers that tended to deprive the public of information it might well have had. A Newspaper Act passed in 1798, again possessing some merit, resulted in numerous press prosecutions, with fines and imprisonment for specified offenses, including that relating to possession of contraband newspapers.

The vigor with which the *Times* was conducted drew reprisals from the government, and John Walter, the founder, was arrested in 1789 for a published reference to the Duke of York. He was fined and jailed for a year. He was jailed again in 1790 for an additional four months and heavily fined for further "libels" against the Prince of Wales, the Duke of York, and the Duke of Clarence.

Walter died in 1803, succeeded as proprietor of the *Times* by his son, John Walter II. Under his direction in the next forty-four years, the paper moved steadily into the forefront among London dailies. Its very success and independence of expression irked the government, which sought to trim its growing leadership and influence. This was attempted, in part, by granting secret subsidies to competitive morning dailies willing to accept official guidance as to content and editorial policy. Further, the first important reduction in the taxes on knowledge was made in 1833 in the hope that the lower per copy and subscription prices thus made possible might help other papers at the expense of the *Times*. This maneuver failed completely, for with more to offer and its own price also reduced, the *Times* gained a larger circulation.

Because of this evidence that the taxes on knowledge no longer seemed to be serving effectively to curtail newspaper growth or readership, and perhaps even more because of the recognized need for newspapers in a new industrial society, the government eliminated the taxes almost completely in 1855, and entirely in 1861.

The British newspaper press, responding to the needs of the industrial development, had grown in numbers after the 1833 reduction in taxes, and had grown sharply after the 1855 reduction, both in London and in the rest of the kingdom. General enterprise in news gathering and greater freedom and substance in editorial comment was part of that growth.

The press of the United States, unhampered by any sort of government restriction, and indeed with a constitutional guarantee of freedom and official encouragement, had made great progress in those same years of the nineteenth century.

In many other parts of the world, however, press development lagged until 1870 and later, both by reason of continuing government restrictions and because of limitations in literacy, public education, and economic strength.

The Information Revolution 6

As the year 1800 dawned the time was nearing when a service of current information could be made available to the people by the newspaper press. The "information revolution" was about to begin.

All of the London morning newspapers gave substantial attention to domestic matters, but often with a strong partisan emphasis between the Tories, the party then in power, and the Whigs. Most gave space to foreign news reports as well, but the *Morning Chronicle*, the *Times*, and the *Morning Post* were almost alone in attempting any direct coverage, and then only on the European continent.

Access to news sources on the continent was complicated by a state of war existing between Great Britain and France from 1793 to 1802, from 1803 to 1814, and after a brief interval, from 1814 to the Battle of Waterloo in 1815. With France extending its military power in parts of Europe during those years, coverage was that much more difficult, and sometimes impossible. Further, Great Britain was at war with the United States from 1812 to 1815, but the London press made no attempt to give direct coverage to that conflict.

With French newspapers declared contraband in England, and with the same ban extending to newspapers of other parts of Europe under French control, even the opportunity to obtain or reprint information from such newspapers was rare.[1]

---

1 The *Times* maintained a cross-channel courier system and obtained some newspapers in that fashion, and sometimes by bribing post-office workers in London. Other London newspapers followed the lead of the *Times* in this respect. In the years from 1803 to 1814, when Napoleon was extending French power, John Bell, proprietor of the London *Sun*, for one, is reported to have paid from 10 to 100 guineas (about $50 to $500) for a single copy of a French newspaper, if of recent date and containing a substantial account of a battle action.

Early in 1807, the *Times* ventured once again by direct effort to obtain news from the continent, as it had done briefly in 1792-93. It sent Henry Crabb Robinson, a twenty-four-year-old attorney, to Prussia before Napoleonic power was fully established there. Crabb Robinson, as he was familiarly known, had lived and studied in Berlin from 1800 to 1805 and was well acquainted there. From Hamburg, where the *Hamburgischer Correspondenten* had developed useful sources of information in European areas, and from nearby Altona, and also from Stockholm in 1808, Robinson was able to report on aspects of the wars and on related political, economic, and social subjects in northern and central Europe.

In 1808 Robinson also went to Spain for six months to report the Peninsular War, in which British forces were engaged with the French in Portugal and Spain from that time until 1814 under the command of Lieutenant General Sir Arthur Wellesley (later Lord Wellington).

Back in London in 1809, Robinson became the first "Foreign Editor" of the *Times*. As such, he engaged a number of "stringer" correspondents[2] to write from Spain during later phases of the Peninsular War, and also from several European cities, despite the shifting situation and the problems of communication during those war years. Robinson left the *Times* before the end of 1809 to pursue a career in law, but he is regarded as having taken the first step toward placing international news correspondence on a firm course of development, with the *Times* leading the way.

In France, at that time, only three Paris dailies had any importance. These were the *Journal de Paris,* which had an exceptionally large

---

2 The term "stringer," now long in standard usage, means a part-time, nonstaff correspondent writing for a newspaper or news agency. The term itself probably originated in the United States as weekly newspapers in small towns arranged for "country correspondents" to write letters, occasionally or regularly, reporting the "news" in nearby communities, where the newspapers also were delivered. The letters were written variously by the postmaster, a school teacher, the wife of a clergyman, a housewife, a retired person—someone familiar with the place and its people. To compensate the writer, the material used was clipped from the paper after publication, pasted together each month to form a column-width "string" to be measured, with the writer paid at so much per column inch for contributions. The system continues, but with "stringers" serving in more remote places for larger newspapers and for news agencies. Writing from state capitals, major cities, and cities of other countries, many of the "stringers" long have included professional journalists, perhaps writing for two or more papers, or even for two or more noncompetitive agencies, and being paid retainer fees and supplements for their services, rather than on the basis of a measured "string." As nonstaff writers, they are, nevertheless, known as "stringers."

circulation of 20,000 during the course of the French Revolution; the *Journal des Débats,* started in 1789; and *Le Moniteur,* an official paper, and one to which Napoleon himself sometimes contributed. With war in progress, neither Napoleon nor any other military commander, French or British, showed hospitality to newspaper representatives.

Typical was the experience of Peter Finnerty of the *Morning Chronicle,* who managed to join a British naval expedition moving against the French at Antwerp in 1809. When his presence became known to the Admiralty in London he was ordered home. At the Battle of Waterloo in June 1815, when British, Dutch, and Belgian forces engaged the French under Napoleon and brought about his ultimate defeat, no single press correspondent was present. It has been suggested that this may have been so because Lord Wellington, in command of the armies facing Napoleon, had been embittered against newsmen during the six years of the Peninsular War. So far as is known, Crabb Robinson was not at fault, but Wellington believed other writers, merely by references in their reports to uniforms and weapons, had revealed information endangering the security of his forces.

Such an attitude on the part of military leaders, combined with the limited press development and the restraints under which it operated, meant that the great events of these years were ill-reported. This was true of so potentially significant an event as the British navy's seizure in 1795 of the hundred-year-old Dutch colony at the Cape of Good Hope, on the southern tip of the African continent, lest it fall to the French, even then occupying Holland. It was true of the ceremony at Notre Dame in Paris in 1804 when Napoleon placed the crown upon his own head as Emperor of France, with Pope Pius VII in attendance; the same Pope was to excommunicate Napoleon five years later, and himself to be arrested in turn and held in exile at Savona and Fontainebleau until 1813. Similarly, only the most indirect reports appeared of the British naval victories in the Battle of the Nile in 1789 and the Battle of Trafalgar, with the death of Admiral Nelson, in 1805. Such great battles of the Napoleonic period as Austerlitz, Jena, and Wagram received no direct press coverage; nor did the invasion of Russia by a French army of 600,000 in 1812, or the retreat that followed, with Napoleon's eventual abdication in 1814 and exile to the island of Elba. Information appearing on these events came from indirect sources.

Napoleon returned from his exile at Elba to land in France again on

March 1, 1815, rallied his old army and sought to regain power. With no expectation of any such reappearance, representatives of Austria, Great Britain, Prussia, and Russia meanwhile had gathered at Vienna in September 1814 to reshape Europe after the disorientation caused by the French Revolution and the campaigns of Napoleon. The final treaties were signed June 9, 1815. Yet at that very time Napoleon was on the march again. Nine uncertain days followed until his defeat at the Battle of Waterloo on June 18 gave assurance that the Vienna decisions would become effective. Napoleon was imprisoned on the island of St. Helena, in the South Atlantic, and a new period in the history of Europe and the world began. Important as it was for the future, the vital Congress of Vienna went almost unreported by the press of any country, as did the Battle of Waterloo. It was still too early in the development of news gathering.

The press and the public were forced to endure delays in learning of the outcome of the Battle of Waterloo. Its result was not reported by any newspaper in London, only 240 miles away from the Belgian field of battle, until four days later; then the *Morning Chronicle* gave it first publication. Through those days London had been in a panic, with rumors circulating of a Napoleonic victory. But Nathan Rothschild, London member of that family banking house, equally represented in Paris, had received an earlier report, either by carrier pigeon or special courier, and had used his information effectively on the London Stock Exchange. Seven years later, when Napoleon died May 5, 1821, on St. Helena, that news did not reach Paris until July 6.

Such delays in news reporting, inevitable though they were at the time, could be serious. This was demonstrated again in 1815. The Anglo-U.S. War of 1812 had ended officially with the signing of the Treaty of Ghent on December 28, 1814. However, news of that event in the Belgian city did not reach the United States until February 1815 when a ship put into Charleston, South Carolina; and it was not known in New Orleans for another ten days. Yet a battle had been fought there on January 8, ten days after the war had ended in the ceremony at Ghent. The Battle of New Orleans, a victory for the United States, made a hero of General Andrew Jackson and helped propel him into the presidency from 1829-37. But the battle also resulted in 2,057 men being killed or wounded, most of them British, in a meaningless sacrifice.

As in Europe, so in the United States it was not quite time for the press to reach out with vigor to gather the news. The newspapers were still young, and the nation and its government were only beginning to take shape.

What had been thirteen colonies became thirteen states in 1783. Until 1789 they conducted their affairs under the terms of the Articles of Confederation, drafted in 1777 by the Continental Congress. It had become clear, soon enough, that this system was not going to work satisfactorily and in May 1787 a convention met at Philadelphia to draft a Constitution to serve as a basis for what became a federal or republican form of government. Completed in September, it was submitted to the states for ratification.

There followed a considerable debate. Alexander Hamilton, James Madison, and John Jay wrote a series of papers explaining and supporting the document, papers later known as the *Federalist.* They were published originally in the *New York Independent Journal,* a semi-weekly, in 1787-88, but were also reprinted in other newspapers and in pamphlet form. Ratification of the Constitution was completed late in 1788. The last Continental Congress named electors to choose a president and vice-president, and they named George Washington and John Adams.

In 1791 a "Bill of Rights" was added to the Constitution, the first ten amendments, all duly ratified. Of these, the first amendment, Article I, specified that "Congress shall make no law . . . abridging the freeedom of speech or of the press . . . ." This was the first legal assurance of such benefits anywhere in the world.

As with the government, changes were to occur in the press in the United States after 1783. The thirty-five weeklies existing then were to be augmented by others, and by dailies as well—all growing larger in size. Editors, rather than printers, became the dominant figures. Advertising content increased, bringing the financial means to permit staff additions and more effective news-gathering activities.

The press of the United States enjoyed certain advantages. It was not subject to any taxes on knowledge, such as still existed in Great Britain. Indeed, the founding fathers, Benjamin Franklin among them, with full recollection of earlier British restraints, not only gave the press assurance of freedom through the First Amendment, but soon authorized special low postage rates. This was based on a belief that the press was "the most important disseminator of intelligence among the people," and essential to their proper information as citizens of a new nation and a government dedicated to the principles of democracy, with supreme power vested in the people. For the same reason, there was an early emphasis on schooling.

Thomas Jefferson, author of the original draft of the Declaration of Independence, was one of the most eloquent advocates of a press that would be free from interference by government or any other institution. He had advanced the need for the First Amendment. His reasoning, widely influential, was set forth in a letter written from Paris in 1787, when he was serving there as United States minister to France. It was addressed to Edward Carrington, a Virginia member of the Congress. Often quoted in part, the more complete version follows:

> . . . The people are the only censors of their governors; and even their errors will tend to keep those to the true principles of their institution. To punish those errors too severely would be to suppress the only safe-guard of the public liberty.
>
> The way to prevent these irregular interpositions of the people is to give them full information of their affairs thro' the channel of the public papers, & to contrive that those papers should penetrate the whole mass of the people.
>
> The basis of our governments being the opinion of the people, the first object should be to keep that right; and were it left to me to decide whether we should have a government without newspapers or newspapers without a government, I should not hesitate to prefer the latter. But I should mean that every man should receive those papers & be capable of reading them. . . .

Jefferson had some second thoughts in later years, as he and his administration came under press attack, but he did not change his basic position. John Milton had written in the *Areopagitica* in 1644 that "though all the winds of doctrine were let loose to play upon the earth, so truth be in the field, we do injuriously by licensing and prohibiting to misdoubt her strength." So Jefferson, in the same spirit, said in his second inaugural address in 1805 that "since truth and reason have maintained their ground against false opinions in league with false facts, the press, confined to truth, needs no other legal restraint."

Among papers in some way noteworthy in the decades immediately following the Revolutionary War, the tri-weekly *Pennsylvania Evening Post*, established at Philadelphia by David Towne in 1775, became the first daily newspaper in the country on May 30, 1783. In a second pioneering move, Towne had the newspaper offered for sale on the street at a low price. A better Philadelphia paper was the *Pennsylvania Packet*, a weekly since 1771, which became the second daily in the country on September 21, 1784. Founded by John Dunlap, who was joined by David C. Claypool, it continued for more than fifty years as a respected paper under that name and, from 1796, as the *American Daily Advertiser*. When Washington left the presidency in 1797, the paper had first publication of the president's "Farewell Address," the text of which he gave personally to Claypool.

The first dailies in New York were the *Morning Post*, published from 1785 to 1792, and the *Daily Advertiser*, from 1785 to 1809. Baltimore had three dailies by 1800 and Charleston had two. In Boston, it was 1813 before the *Daily Advertiser* was established successfully.

The reason for daily publication, at the outset, was to provide wholesalers and merchants with shipping news, and to present advertisements for newly-imported merchandise. Generally dull reading except to the business community, they nevertheless presented news as well.

Other papers stressed political subjects. One such was the *New York Independent Journal*, which published the Federalist papers. Another was the *Gazette of the United States*, established in New York in 1789 even as the new constitutional government was formed there. Usually known more simply as the *United States Gazette*, it was almost official in support of the government and what were termed the Federalist views. When the government moved from New York to Philadelphia in 1790, the paper followed, and followed again to Washington in 1800, where it continued until 1847.

A second semi-official paper, the *National Gazette*, was established in Philadelphia in 1791, with the encouragement of James Madison and Thomas Jefferson, but it survived for only two years.

A paper taking a position in opposition to the Federalist party, as it had become, and therefore in opposition to Washington and Adams, was established in Philadelphia, the new capital, in October 1790. Commonly known as the *Aurora*, it was the creation of Benjamin Franklin Bache, grandson of Benjamin Franklin, whose death had occurred in the previous April. Bache, who died of yellow fever in 1798, was succeeded as editor by William Duane, who also married Bache's widow. He continued the paper in opposition to the Adams administration, and in support of the Democratic-Republican party, of which Jefferson was the leader.

A second Philadelphia paper giving its support to Jefferson was the *Independent Gazetteer*. Already well established in 1799, it was sold in that year by Joseph Gales, Sr., its second owner, to Samuel Harrison Smith, favorably known as a journalist and writer. Gales moved to Raleigh, North Carolina, where he established the *Raleigh Register*. He became mayor of Raleigh for nineteen years and state

printer for thirty. With the capital about to be moved from Philadelphia to Washington, Jefferson, vice-president under Adams, but even
then president-designate, urged Smith to move his printing office to
the new capital city. This he did, suspending the Philadelphia paper
and establishing the *National Intelligencer* in Washington as a
tri-weekly on October 31, 1800. It became the official voice of the
Jefferson administration, continuing from 1801 to 1809.

Smith retired in 1810, but the *National Intelligencer* was taken over
by Joseph Gales, Jr., who came from his father's paper in Raleigh,
along with William Winston Seaton, his brother-in-law. Gales and
Seaton made the paper a daily in 1813, and it gained an important
place among newspapers of the country, continuing until the Civil
War. Its political complexion changed in 1828, to support the Whigs,
but still later it became politically independent.

A substantial element in the importance attained by the *National
Intelligencer* was its full reporting of debates in Congress at a time
when no other permanent record of such debates existed. The official
Congressional Record did not appear until 1873, and until then the
government itself and the people of the United States were dependent
upon four Washington newspapers for reports of congressional
action—the *National Intelligencer* was the first to provide such
details.[3]

---

3   Until 1770 in England, British reporters were not permitted to report parliamentary
debates in detail. Only in 1803 was William Cobbett authorized to publish unofficial
summaries of those debates derived from verbatim accounts prepared by official
reporters, and not until 1909 were verbatim reports permitted in a Cobbett-established
volume long known as "Hansard," comparable to the *Congressional Record.*

Cobbett exercised an important influence on the press both in Great Britain and the
United States. As a youth, he had served in the British army, his regiment assigned to
Canada. In England in 1791, he failed in an effort to expose abuses in the army, and was
forced to flee to France. As war between England and France appeared likely in 1792,
he managed to reach the United States.

In Philadelphia, Cobbett taught English to French refugees from the revolution,
including the Duc d'Orléans, later to become King Louis Philippe (1830-48). He also
became a pamphleteer and then publisher in 1797 of a weekly, *Porcupine's Gazette.*
The title was derived from a pen name he used, Peter Porcupine, signifying the sharp
quills discharged at those of whom he disapproved. One such quill directed at Dr.
Benjamin Rush, a respected member of the community, brought a libel action decided
against Cobbett, with damages assessed at $5,000. He evaded this by returning to
England.

There, in 1800, he established a political weekly, *The Porcupine,* which was soon
replaced by *Cobbett's Weekly Political Register,* published from 1801 until his death in
1835. It was successful and influential, and brought him prosperity and reputation. But
it also brought libel suits. Cobbett was jailed during 1810-12, but managed to edit his
paper and produce pamphlets even in that period. He did the same during 1817-19 when

The three other Washington newspapers granted seats for reporters in both houses were the *United States Telegraph,* established in 1826, the *Washington Globe* (1830), and the *Madisonian* (1837). The *Intelligencer* and the *Globe* also published the debates separately in pamphlet or booklet form. For lack of a more official publication, all four papers received annual payments from the U.S. Treasury in return for such reporting and publication. Those payments totalled $330,000 in 1841.

Other reporters were able to hear congressional debates from the visitors galleries, but making notes there was neither easy nor approved.

Most of the general coverage of news in the capital, even beyond the House and Senate, was provided in the early years by reporters for the Washington newspapers. Their accounts were reprinted or rewritten by newspapers in other cities. Some reporters came to Washington from nearby Baltimore, and from papers in Philadelphia, New York, and other cities, but they came as visitors. Any such reporter, in addition to listening to debates in Congress, was free to visit with members of Congress, to enter the offices of various departments of government and talk with officials, and to go pretty much anywhere he wanted to go. Until 1841, however, the number of reporters in Washington was small. That year marked a change. Through the enterprise of the *New York Herald* and its publisher, James Gordon Bennett, facilities and rights were established in both houses of Congress and elsewhere for all *bona fide* reporters. It was another ten years at least before the four Washington dailies ceased to be almost the exclusive source of detailed information about debates in the Congress. But reporters from other cities began to be assigned permanently to the capital, and coverage grew from that time.

The major press developments after 1800, however, centered in New York, by then it was the largest city, with about 200,000 popula-

---

he took refuge in the United States to escape another possible prison term, conducting his affairs while living on a rented Long Island farm. He was prosecuted again in 1831, but escaped conviction, and in 1832 was elected a member of Parliament, serving until his death in 1835 at seventy-three.

From the time of his return to England in 1800, Cobbett also had published a number of well-accepted reference volumes. In 1803 he started a series of *Parliamentary Debates,* printed by Thomas Curson Hansard, who purchased it in 1812. *Hansard's Parliamentary Debates* became officially authorized in 1892, and was taken over entirely by the British government in 1909, published daily and weekly, with the previous summaries becoming full and verbatim reports. The name "Hansard" was dropped from the title at that time, but was restored in 1943.

tion. It was the busiest port, and commerce and banking were growing rapidly. Among eleven newspapers at that time, the leader in circulation was the *Mercantile Advertiser*, dating from 1792 as a weekly and as a daily from 1800. An emphasis on shipping and trade in most papers was somewhat balanced by the establishment in 1801 of the *New York Evening Post*. It was introduced as a Federalist paper, sponsored by Alexander Hamilton, and edited by William Coleman until 1829. After that it was owned and edited for more than four decades by William Cullen Bryant, remembered also as a poet. It continues to appear, now known more simply as the *New York Post*, the oldest existing newspaper in New York. A second surviving daily is the *Journal of Commerce*, established in 1827 by Arthur Tappan, a merchant. Soon taken over by experienced newsmen Gerard Hallock and David Hale, they made it an important paper.

In that same period, two morning dailies were established; the *Enquirer* in 1826 and the *Courier* in 1827. Combined in 1829 as the *New York Courier and Enquirer*, it was the paper of Colonel James Watson Webb, a veteran of the War of 1812. He made it one of the first truly enterprising newspapers of the United States in its coverage of national news. It continued under his vigorous direction until 1861. At that time, he was appointed minister to Brazil. His paper merged with the *New York World*, then recently founded.

The 'Human Interest Principle'

A major change in journalism, and one destined to have world-wide application, began inconspicuously in London in 1823. There on October 14 the *Morning Herald* published a short account of a case heard the day before in the Mansion House Court, commonly known as the Bow Street Police Court. Crime reports and police court cases had been reported in the newspapers before, but only if the cases were in some way important, and then treated with the utmost gravity. If persons entangled with the law were of low social status, or if the charges were trivial, little or no reference appeared in the press.

But John Wight (sometimes given as Wright), a reporter with experience in Birmingham, had recently joined the staff of the *Morning Herald*, and he ignored the precedent. His report from Bow Street, as published on that October day, was so unlike any previously coming from the courts that it is difficult to understand how it was permitted to appear. In a style somewhat reminiscent of the essays of Addison and Steele in the weekly *Spectator* more than a century earlier, or that of Charles Dickens a decade later, Wight wrote of the plight of ordinary persons brought before the court on minor charges.

He wrote other reports on other days, recounting the very human experiences, the remarks and emotional responses of humbly situated men and women charged with petty theft, with being drunk and disorderly, with involvement in loud quarrels in the night, and the like. Readers were told how these unfortunate and almost nameless individuals came to be in court, how they looked and acted, what they said, how they explained their problems or sought to excuse their behavior, what the arresting constable said, and what the judge said and did. The accounts involved both humor and pathos, and sometimes bathos; all were brief.

The interest of readers was caught by these vignettes of life in the city, so unlike anything appearing in any other newspaper. One reader called a story to the attention of another, and they shared an enjoyment of something quite different in print, and perhaps even felt some sense of identity with the persons figuring in the episodes reported. A quick reader response to the first such accounts caused comment and Wight was encouraged by the paper to continue them on a regular basis.[4]

Largely because of Wight's stories, the circulation of the *Morning Herald*, which had been only about 1,200 a day, moved sharply upward to 8,000 by 1829, second only to the *Times*, then leading among seventeen London dailies, with 10,000 in a city then of about two million. To assure his continued contribution to its new success, Wight was given an interest in the ownership of the paper. With its added revenue from circulation and from the increased volume of advertising that followed, the *Herald* also was able to extend and improve its general news content and it gained such respect and influence as to rival the *Times* in the 1840s.

What Wight and the *Morning Herald* had done was to discover the "human interest principle" for application in the selection and treatment of subject matter in newspapers and magazines. Even

---

4 Wight's stories were sufficiently popular to warrant the republication of many in the following year (1824) in a small book, *Mornings at Bow Street*. Interest survived and brought a new edition in 1875, illustrated with pen-and-ink sketches by George Cruikshank, a highly-regarded caricaturist and etcher.

readers of the most serious papers, such as the *Times,* and of those stressing business or politics, were attracted to the *Morning Herald* because it offered something refreshingly different, striking a new chord, bringing a sense of reality and emotion into the news. It was a welcome departure from the solemn and routine content of most publications.

The success of the *Morning Herald,* and the reason for it, did not go unnoticed. Some early attempts to imitate Wight's style of news coverage and writing failed to bring the same results, but nevertheless introduced new elements of interest in papers in England and other countries. But some notable successes were to follow application of the human interest principle. Among them were the *New York Sun,* established in New York in 1833, and two if its direct imitators, the *Philadelphia Public Ledger* (1836), and the *Baltimore Sun* (1837). Other imitators were the *New York Herald* (1835), and two papers in Paris, both started in 1836, *La Presse,* founded by Emile Girardin, and *Le Siècle,* by Armand Dutacq. Both Paris papers succeeded, with *Le Siècle,* in particular, soon attaining an unprecedented 38,000 daily circulation, and introducing the new style of journalism to France and the European continent.

The *New York Sun* appeared on September 3, 1833, almost ten years after the London *Morning Herald* had published Wight's first story. It was started by Benjamin Harry Day, a twenty-three-year-old Massachusetts-born printer, who had recently opened a shop in New York.

The *Sun* in its early editions was no more than a four-page folio, eight by eleven inches in size, two columns to the page. Although attractively printed, it in no way resembled any daily newspaper of the time. It was intended primarily to advertise Day's print shop, and made no pretense to being a newspaper in the accepted sense. It presented a miscellany of items, few more than two or three paragraphs in length, and selected only to provide entertaining reading; there was nothing whatever about politics, business, or shipping, and no editorial comment. It was offered for sale in the streets, then a common practice for newspapers in London, but not in New York. This made it convenient to buy, and the *Sun* was offered at one cent, as contrasted to six cents for other dailies.

Day was pleasantly surprised to find that his little paper was immediately received and enjoyed for itself. It was at least returning the cost of production, so he continued its publication. To add something to the reprinted miscellany from a variety of sources, Day had

George Wisner, an out-of-work printer, try his hand at writing the same sort of police court stories that Wight had produced in London. Whether either man was familiar with those stories is uncertain, but Wisner appears to have struck much the same note, and his stories were equally well received. They helped bring a following to the *Sun*. Its circulation grew, advertising came in unsolicited, the paper increased in size, and by 1835 it was returning a substantial profit.

As with Wight in London, Wisner was made a partner in the ownership of the paper, but for reasons of health he left New York in 1835.[5] He was succeeded as a staff member on the *Sun* by Richard Adams Locke, English-born, who had news experience both in London and with the *New York Courier and Enquirer*. In August 1835 Locke wrote a short paragraph for use in the *Sun* reporting the discovery of human life on the moon, as determined through the use of a new type of high-powered telescope set up in a South African observatory. He followed with other stories, going into considerable detail about life on the moon.

It was a complete hoax, but the reports had a quality of sober authenticity, with attribution to non-existent sources that sounded eminently responsible. The stories were widely accepted as true and generated great interest. There was no way to verify or disprove the reports by any prompt communication with South Africa or other sources cited. In the end, Locke himself "let the cat out of the bag," inadvertently, and the hoax was exposed by the *Journal of Commerce*. Meanwhile, the circulation of the *Sun* had climbed to 27,000 in 1836, larger than that of all other New York newspapers combined, and the largest for any newspaper in the world at that time.[6]

With its success, the *Sun* adopted the larger format of other New York papers and published a greater volume of material, including substantial news. Reader interest remained the first criterion in the selection of content. Day could scarcely believe in the success his paper had attained and, fearing the bubble would burst, he sold the *Sun* in 1837; the "silliest thing I ever did," he said later. The paper

---

5 George Wisner received $5,000 for his interest in the *Sun*. He settled in Michigan, where he later became a member of the state legislature.

6 The *New York Sun*, as it soon was retitled, retained a circulation leadership in New York and in the United States until the 1850s. It published a second hoax in 1844, an account written for the paper by Edgar Allen Poe about the flight of a "steering balloon" across the Atlantic from Wales to the South Carolina coast. Although this story was promptly reprinted by some other papers, it was quickly disproved, since South Carolina was more accessible than South Africa. The *Sun* cooly conceded that "the intelligence was erroneous."

continued under other ownership, becoming an excellent and more conventional newspaper.

The *New York Herald,* another paper making good use of the human interest principle, was James Gordon Bennett's third attempt in the publication of his own newspaper. He had failed with the *New York Globe* and the Philadelphia *Pennsylvanian,* although for reasons not entirely within his control. When he started the *Herald* on May 6, 1835, he was forty, thoroughly experienced, but with no more than $500 in capital. With dedication, he was to make the *Herald* a successful and leading newspaper.

If the human interest principle had been demonstrated originally in its application to minor police courts cases and subsequently to other relatively trivial subjects, Bennett showed how it might also be applied to matters of real substance. By special enterprise in news gathering and presentation, he showed how a newspaper could be printed at a reasonable price and be interesting and informative. With larger readership, the newspaper became an attractive medium for advertisers. The revenue received from the sale of advertising space enabled it to build a competent staff and to meet the costs of news gathering, locally, nationally, and world-wide.

Not every publication succeeded, even following the Day and Bennett formula, but enough did to bring "mass circulation" publications into existence on a modest scale. Not every newspaper aspired to a "mass circulation," for some preferred a policy which made small concession to "popular interest," and kept stress upon substantive affairs. The London *Times* is a prime example. Such "quality" newspapers thus stand in contrast to "popular" newspapers, with others occupying a middle ground, but all serving readers free to choose, where such a variety exists.

Newspapers leaning toward the "popular" side have been known to strive to win readers by resorting at times to "sensationalism" in the presentation of news. This was a criticism leveled at the *New York Herald* during its first years. Bennett placed such stress on a highly-personalized form of journalism between 1835 and 1840 that he earned, and perhaps deserved, the disapproval of many. But he also won readers. He stressed police court items in the manner of the *Morning Herald* and the *New York Sun.* But he went beyond that and was perhaps the first to report the news of crime itself, sometimes in a manner so frank as to shock many readers of the time. He was unabashed in writing of himself. As with the *Sun,* he published his own "wild animal hoax," a report that the animals in the Central Park Zoo had broken out and were a peril to all citizens. This he justified as a way of emphasizing the need for greater security measures in the zoo.

Beyond that, however, Bennett found ways to make interesting even such "dull" subjects as politics and finance. He established the axiom that "names make news," finding occasion to use as many names of local persons as possible, including the development of the "society column." There also was the axiom that "controversy makes news," and that also was made explicit. He developed the "interview" as a means to acquaint readers with interesting and important personalities and their ideas. He introduced the concept of the "columnist" as a writer of special personality and appeal, with something to say. He introduced the "Sunday newspaper" in New York, the first in the country, and viewed by some as most improper on the Sabbath.

In the years of his active direction of the *Herald* from 1835 to his retirement in 1866, Bennett was energetic in seeking news locally, nationally, and throughout the world. He found subjects of human activity previously ignored or slighted by the press, including sports, the theater, churches, social events, schools, organizations, weather, agriculture, and the special interests of women—so many that he was properly designated by one of his biographers as "the man who made news." His enterprise and originality made the *Herald* successful from the outset, increasingly respected after 1840, and gave it circulation leadership in New York and the United States in the 1850s.

The establishment of the human interest principle, and its successful application was reflected in the conduct and establishment of other newspapers. They did not necessarily make use of the police-court items, or pattern themselves after the *New York Herald*, but the element of interest was valued in news reports, in editorial columns, and in general content. It was demonstrated that a newspaper could be interesting, and yet thoroughly informative. Thus it was that in 1841 the *New York Tribune* appeared as a solidly made morning newspaper, founded by Horace Greeley, a printer. His paper became a highly effective and influential journal. He gained such respect as to become a serious candidate for the presidency of the United States in 1872, receiving nearly three million votes in a contest with President Ulysses S. Grant, then running for a second term.[7] Then in 1851 the morning *New York Times* was established by Henry J. Raymond,

---

7 The *Tribune* published some of the most effective human interest pieces, stories of episodes in New York by Solon Robinson, some republished in his *Hot Corn: Life Scenes in New York* (1854).

formerly an editor on the *Tribune,* along with George Jones, also formerly of the *Tribune,* and who had business experience. Edward W. Wesley, a banker, was a silent partner in the newspaper.

In England, too, the *Daily Telegraph,* established in London in 1855, provided an illustration of journalistic performance combining substance with interest. In Paris, in 1876, *Le Petit Parisien* was to do something similar.

The information revolution was advanced by the use of the human-interest principle in applications going far beyond the simple form originated by Wight. It was a revolution extending to the coverage of the news itself, which in turn affected the technology and the economics of publishing.

The Press Reaches Out

There was no shortage of news to be reported in 1800 and the years immediately preceding and following. But the problems of news coverage had not yet been solved. The press had attained a certain point of development in Great Britain, the United States, and in some other countries, but even at best few newspapers had enough qualified reporters to provide a thorough coverage of news sources in their own communities, much less beyond.

Delays in the movement of news subtracted from its value and its interest. Inevitable as they were, foreign reports were weeks and sometimes months old when received. Even national news moved slowly. When George Washington died at Mount Vernon on December 14, 1799, a Saturday, the news was published first in the nearby *Alexandria Times* on the following Monday. But nearly every other newspaper had to await the arrival of that Virginia newspaper, delivered by postriders, to learn of the event. It was not reported in Philadelphia until Thursday, in New York until Saturday, in Boston until Christmas Day, and in Cincinnati until January 7.

The population of the United States in 1800 was 5,308,483, and still concentrated along the Atlantic seaboard. Settlement was beginning to move westward, however, and in 1803 a vast area west of the Mississippi River was added to the national territory, acquired from France in the Louisiana Purchase. It was an area explored in 1804-05 by Meriweather Lewis and William Clark; commissioned by President Jefferson, they went as far as the mouth of the Columbia River on the Pacific Coast. But it was years before the people of the United States received any details of this important expedition.

In 1812 the United States became involved in war with Great Britain arising from seizures of U.S. ships and sailors to add strength to British forces then in conflict with Napoleon. With most British military effort concentrated in Europe, the United States had some successes at sea and in action against the British position in Canada. Indians gave support to the British in a number of places, including the Great Lakes section, where Detroit was captured and parts of Buffalo burned.

The abdication of Napoleon in April 1814 freed British troops and ships to cross the Atlantic. The capture of Washington followed in August, with much of the city burned, including the Capitol, the White House, and the office of the *National Intelligencer;* Baltimore was bombarded in September. The end of the Napoleonic wars removed the original reason for the 1812 conflict, and the war had become irrelevant. The British withdrew in October. A mutual willingness to negotiate brought the signing of the Treaty of Ghent in December, although the Battle of New Orleans was to occur in January 1815, because the news of the peace traveled so slowly.

The War of 1812 was almost as poorly reported as the American Revolutionary War and the Napoleonic wars, and for some of the same reasons. Facilities for news reporting had developed reasonably well in the Atlantic seaboard cities of the United States so that events centering there were adequately covered, but they were less promptly or well reported in other parts of the country.

This was exemplified in difficulties attending the reporting of battles with Indians in Indiana and Alabama, Florida and Georgia, and Illinois and Minnesota from 1811 to as late as 1862. Inadequate reporting was exemplified also in problems arising in Texas after 1830, when settlers in what then was Mexican territory began seriously to agitate for establishment of an independent state. A clash between settlers and Mexican troops in 1836 at the Alamo, an eighteenth-century mission-fort in San Antonio, with all 200 United States citizens killed, went unreported at the time. That loss was reversed some six weeks later in a victory for the settlers at the Battle of San Jacinto. They proclaimed an independent Republic of Texas, later recognized by the United States and annexed in 1845. These actions led to the U.S.-Mexican War of 1846-48. But again the San Jacinto battle and its early consequences were only reported considerably later.

The reporting of news between nations and continents was an even greater problem in the first years of the nineteenth century. It was dependent almost entirely upon the exchange of newspapers between cities and countries, with one paper reprinting or rewriting what appeared in another.

Contributing to the variety of information available through such exchange, new papers were added to existing papers in those decades. Among them, in Europe, were the *Kölnische Zeitung* of Cologne, established in 1804; the *Morgenbladet* of Christiania (Oslo) in 1814; the *Stockholms-Tidningen* of Stockholm in 1824; *Le Figaro* of Paris, and the *Journal de Gèneve* of Geneva in 1826; the *Handels-och Sjöfarts-tidning* of Gothenburg in 1832; *Le Siècle* and *La Presse,* both of Paris, in 1836; the *Nieuwe Rotterdamse Courant* of Rotterdam in 1843; and *Uusi Suomi* of Helsinki in 1847. Papers were appearing in Poland, Hungary, Rumania, Serbia, and elsewhere in Europe.

In the same general period, in other parts of the world, newspapers established included *El Telégrafo* of Buenos Aires in 1801, the first Argentine journal; the *Diário de Pernambuco* of Recife, the first in Brazil, in 1825; the *Jornal do Comercio* of Rio de Janeiro in 1827; *El Comerico* of Lima, Peru, in 1839; and others in Central and South America and the West Indies. The *Sydney Morning Herald* in 1831 became the first daily in Australia, and the *Melbourne Argus* appeared in 1846. The *Bombay Times,* started in 1838, became the important *Times of India.* The *Toronto Globe* began in 1844, and the *China Mail* of Hong Kong in 1845.

Newspapers, wherever published, benefited from technological advances during these years, and perhaps especially in the decade of 1820 to 1830.

Means were discovered to make paper of woodpulp, which was not as fine or long-lasting as paper made from rags. But wood was in far greater supply, the cost therefore was considerably less, and it was quite suitable for newspaper use.

Major improvements were made in the printing process, departing from the wine-press concept, unchanged in principle since the fifteenth century. The newer presses, sturdily built of iron and larger and steam-operated, produced newspapers more rapidly from a continuously running roll of paper, rather than hand-fed single sheets. The new presses printed both sides of the paper and cut it in one operation, although hand folding was still required. The type forms were still placed on a flat bed, but four to eight pages or more could be printed in one operation. Improved inks on a moving cylinder inked the type between impressions, and the paper was carried and brought against the type to produce a proper impression. Cheaper, better quality type could be cast automatically, but it remained necessary to set type by hand, letter by letter. Other production problems remained or would arise, but by 1840 to 1850 newspapers could be printed more expeditiously, more economically, and with more satisfactory results.

By definition, the function of a newspaper is to obtain and publish the news. For any newspaper, coverage of the news begins in its home community, whether that be a village or a great world capital. Whatever event is reported in any newspaper has originated in some specific community, first noted and, written by a reporter, and published by a newspaper in that community.

A nation and the world itself is the sum of such communities. The content of a newspaper on any day represents the sum of the efforts by reporters in numberless communities, supported by the efforts of editors and technicians advancing and processing their accounts from the point of origin to the pages of newspapers seen by readers in other communities, sometimes in many countries, and with publication in many languages. It is a complex cooperative undertaking.

The news concerns anything and everything having to do with people and events, issues and situations. A newspaper begins by reporting that which originates and relates to its own community. Some of that news, however, has a wider interest, and readers in that community also have an interest in events transpiring in other communities. So a winnowing and selective process takes place by which accounts are exchanged and some reach a world audience.

It is not the function of this book to discuss the coverage of news at the local level, important though it is, but rather to examine aspects in the exchange of information possessing wider interest and significance. The exchange of newspapers to make this possible was a vital element in the news process.

The time interval between the occurrence of an event and its publication elsewhere was determined by the distance between cities and countries over which newspapers had to be transported. It was affected by the conditions of that transport, proceeding at the speed of the horse and the sailing vessel, and shaped by the condition of roads, vagaries of weather, and incidents along the way. The breadth of the oceans, and the long sea routes meant especially long delays in the exchange of newspapers.

The sense of enterprise that became manifest in the London press shortly before 1800, with Perry of the *Morning Chronicle* in Paris, and with the *Times* appointing agents in Europe, attempting a cutter service across the Channel, and later sending Robinson to the continent, also appeared in the newly formed United States of America. Newspapers were reaching out for information beyond their own communities, with special purpose and intent to provide news more promptly and more fully to their readers.

Newspapers in port cities, first in the United States, and in England soon after, began to put forward an effort to hasten the receipt and publication of news by dispatching a representative to meet incoming ships in the harbor. The representative went aboard, obtained copies of newspapers brought from other ports, domestic or foreign, talked with the captain and some passengers to learn anything of interest they might have to communicate, and then returned bearing whatever he had obtained for prompt use in his newspaper.

This practice began in Boston, which was the first port of call in the United States for ships arriving from British and northern European ports. The practice appears to have been introduced by Benjamin Russell, founding editor in 1784 of Boston's *Columbian Centinel*. He went to the wharves to board ships as they arrived.

To gain added advantage in time, Henry Ingraham Blake, more commonly known as Harry Blake, representing the semi-weekly *New-England Palladium*, a paper started in 1793, began in 1804 to row out to an approaching ship and go aboard in advance of the mooring process.

In England, William Hunt, editor of the *Western Courier* at Plymouth, became the pioneer for the British press in the practice of meeting ships. This began about 1830, considerably after the method was well established at ports in the United States. Hunt also represented the *Daily News* of London, after its establishment in 1846, with his reports sent on to London by rail service. The practice of meeting ships also was extended to the ports of Bristol, Liverpool, Southampton, and London itself.

A significant adaptation of this system of news gathering, applying also to its dissemination, likewise originated in Boston. There Samuel Gilbert was proprietor of the Exchange Coffee-House, occupying space in a waterfront building of seven stories, then the tallest in the country. In a role somewhat comparable to that of Edward Lloyd in seventeenth-century London, Gilbert kept a file of all the newspapers he could obtain, foreign as well as domestic. He also maintained a Marine News Book, a ledger in which every sort of shipping information was entered. There were reference books available, and some periodicals.

All such material was kept in a "reading room" available to patrons of the coffee house—merchants, business men, ships' officers, and others. The Gilbert coffee house, existing from the late eighteenth century, was so useful as a center for news and general information that the Boston business community felt no urgent need for a local daily newspaper to supplement the existing weeklies. Even as dailies were appearing in other cities, the first two efforts failed in Boston in 1796 and 1798, and no daily succeeded there until 1813.

By 1811 Gilbert found that maintaining the Marine News Book was occupying too much of his time. He engaged a young man, Samuel Topliff, Jr., then twenty-two, the son of a sea captain and a sailor himself, as a clerk, and gave him charge of the news book. Topliff not only maintained that, but arranged to have a boat standing by at the wharf so that he might row out to incoming ships to obtain newspapers and information, as Blake continued to do. Further, Topliff arranged to have packets of newspapers addressed to him brought regularly from distant places, rather than depending merely upon the chance that some such newspapers might be aboard the ships. The Marine News Book became the Marine and General News Book as its scope was extended.

In 1814 Topliff bought the coffee house, changed its name to the Merchants' Reading Room, and conducted it until 1842. In those years, and especially after 1818, the reports available to the clientele gained depth and variety. What once had been retitled the Marine and General News Book now became Topliff's Private Marine Journal, maintained in what became seven ledgers. The newspaper and periodical files were extensive, the books more numerous and, after about 1830, it was the practice to charge "subscribers" an annual fee of $10 for full access to these sources of information. Topliff also arranged for letters from Europe to supplement what might be obtained from newspapers received, and those letters became part of the "General" news books. Topliff was himself in Europe in 1828 and 1829 and wrote letters from there.

By that time, it was usual for the Boston newspapers to look to Topliff's Reading Room as a source for local, national, and world news. Reports began to appear in newspapers in New England and in New York and Philadelphia, as well as Boston itself, with credit to "Mr. Topliff's Correspondent."

In all of this, Topliff might be regarded as the first special correspondent to report directly from abroad for the press of the United States, because of the use made of his letters from Europe in 1828-29 in a number of newspapers, even though the letters consisted largely of travel observations. And because of the use made of news reports obtained through the Reading Room, with due credit, over a period of about twenty-five years, Topliff also might be regarded as having been the proprietor of the first "news agency" or syndicate, such as it was, not only in the United States but in the world. Topliff's Merchants' Reading Room was copied in New York, Philadelphia, and elsewhere. His practice, and that of Blake and Russell, in meeting incoming ships also was matched. One of the most effective services of that sort was introduced in 1813 by Aaron Smith Willington, publisher of the daily *Charleston Courier* in South Carolina.

The procedure there was to have a coastal observatory hoist signals upon sighting an approaching ship. Willington or some staff member would be rowed out to get newspapers and interviews. Apart from coastal vessels arriving at Charleston, those crossing the Atlantic were mostly from western or southern European ports, including the Mediterranean; others came from Cuba and the West Indies, Central and South America, or even on return voyages from China. The first report of the Treaty of Ghent, ending the War of 1812, came by way of Charleston and was first reported in the *Courier*. That paper, like those in Boston, became a major source of world news, as reprinted or rewritten by other newspapers from copies received by post.

One of Willington's staff assistants in reporting what became known as "ship news" was a twenty-eight-year-old Scottish-born immigrant to the United States, James Gordon Bennett, who gained his first newspaper experience in Charleston in 1823-24. Bennett soon was to perform successfully as a reporter for the *New York Enquirer*, and for the combined *New York Courier and Enquirer* after 1829, and as one of the early correspondents for the New York press in Washington, prior to his own establishment of the *New York Herald* in 1835.

In New York, as well as Boston and Charleston, newspapers were sending men out in rowboats after 1827 to meet ships entering the harbor. The New York *Journal of Commerce* introduced a new element in 1828 by putting a sloop into service to meet the vessels near Sandy Hook, rather than waiting for them to move up the harbor. Harry Blake, although no longer young, came from Boston to manage this service for a time.

The New York papers were in sharp competition to obtain ship news. A semaphore system was set up to signal the approach of a ship, the "news boats" would race to meet it and later put into shore on Long Island. There mounted riders would receive newspapers and notes of information obtained and carry the material at the gallop to Manhattan and the printing offices.

After Bennett established the *New York Herald* in 1835, he applied lessons learned in Charleston and improved upon methods being used in New York. He had his sailing craft move out even beyond Sandy Hook to meet ships, and later used steam-powered boats to gain further speed. In some cases, the accounts of news obtained would be written and set in type aboard the news boat as it returned to Manhattan, with a galley or more of type taken immediately to the newspaper office, ready to be placed in the page form for use with the least possible delay.

The dissemination of news from the ports where it was received, or between the ports, was another matter. It was moved either by the existing postal service, meaning coaches or mounted postriders, or in some instances by "express," meaning a special mounted courier or relay. The same procedures were used in Great Britain and elsewhere. After about 1813 some coastal and river steamboats carried the mail, including dispatches and newspapers. Comparable use was made of rail service in England from 1825, in the United States after 1834, and in other countries later on.

Bennett, a leader and innovator from the time he established the *New York Herald,* introduced a rider-relay express service in 1838 to speed a two-way exchange of newspapers and dispatches between New York and Washington. Although not the first to do so, he also began the practice at that time of sending advance proofs of news material intended for use in the *Herald* to certain other selected newspapers in noncompetitive circulation areas for their free use; in return, however, they were asked to send to the *Herald* early news of their own cities and areas. This enriched the *Herald*'s news content.

Carrier pigeons had been used by the London *Times* as early as 1837 to move news from the European continent across the English Channel, an advance over the previous Channel cutter service. Carrier pigeons were brought into use in the United States in 1840, in a direct relationship to the methods used to obtain news from incoming ships. They added an element of speed to the distribution of that news.

Here, again, Bennett was much involved. The system was originated by Daniel H. Craig, then proprietor and editor of the *Boston Daily Mail,* and Craig was the key figure in what became a so-called "Pigeon Express." As ships westbound across the North Atlantic put in at Boston, Craig not only obtained the latest news from Europe for use in his own newspaper, but prepared reports on thin and light sheets placed in capsules attached to pigeons' legs, or beneath their wings. The birds then were released to fly to the roof of the *New York*

Herald building in New York, where lofts were maintained, and the news was published promptly in the *Herald*.

William H. Swain and his *Philadelphia Public Ledger* and Arunah S. Abell and his *Baltimore Sun* joined in this association. The same news reports therefore were moved by carrier pigeons from the *Herald* building in New York to Philadelphia and Baltimore. In return, pigeons released from the *Baltimore Sun* building carried news of Baltimore and nearby Washington north to Philadelphia, and so by relay to New York and Boston, with Philadelphia reports added by the *Public Ledger*. This system advanced the time of publication of news in New York and other cities by as much as three days, and all papers benefited from the exchange.

Papers in Boston other than the *Mail* also obtained European news from the arriving ships, and in New York the *Sun*, in competition with the *Herald*, formed its own associated group of newspapers, with its own carrier pigeon service. Those two New York papers, at least, were about evenly matched in their European reports. But that was not good enough for Bennett.

With the encouragement of the *Herald* proprietor, but equally for the advantage of his own paper competitive with others in Boston, Craig undertook further to expedite the receipt of European information. The westbound ships made their first landings at Halifax, Nova Scotia, before proceeding to Boston—and later to New York. Craig arranged to have a representative in Halifax board each mail ship upon its arrival there, taking aboard a basket of carrier pigeons.

In addition to receiving a special summary of news prepared by special arrangement in London or Liverpool just before the ship's departure from British shores, the representative would talk with officers and passengers, and then scan the London and European newspapers also brought especially for his attention. As the ship proceeded toward Boston, Craig's agent would write reports based upon the information so obtained, and the thin, closely-written sheets were placed in the capsules to be carried by the pigeons. Well in advance of the ship's arrival at Boston, the birds would be released to fly to the roof of the *Daily Mail* building. Craig then would supervise their use ahead of other Boston papers, and their dispatch to the *Herald* in New York, with other relays from there to Philadelphia and Baltimore. All four papers thus had a long lead over their competitors.

Those other papers sought to disrupt this service, even engaging sharpshooters to try to bring down the pigeons, but their efforts failed. Bennett boasted that the *Herald* always could beat the other New York papers in presenting European news, and usually it did so. Not even the appointment by the *New York Sun* of its own London agent in 1843, with an express rider to deliver the latest papers and dispatches to westbound ships just before their departure, was sufficient to beat the *Herald* at that time. Again, in 1846, success did not crown the combined efforts and substantial expenditures of rival papers in New York and other cities when they chartered a powerful tug to cross the Atlantic with what were intended to be the first reports on the decision of a court of arbitration meeting in London to act on the critical Oregon boundary dispute of that period.

The *Herald* may be credited, also, with opening the way for more effective coverage of the news from Washington. Bennett, who had written from there for the *New York Courier and Enquirer,* and also for the *Herald* itself, went to the capital in 1841 and organized a staff headed by Robert Sutton to serve his newspaper. He was able to break those arrangements favoring the *National Intelligencer* and other Washington papers so that *Herald* representatives also were able to provide direct coverage of sessions in Congress, as well as general news. Other newspapers then could not be denied equal rights, and Washington coverage was to grow from that period.

The *New York Herald,* in a further demonstration of enterprise, became the first newspaper in the Western Hemisphere to engage correspondents to provide special service from abroad. In so doing, it established a leadership long held among newspapers of the United States in the reporting of world news.

This began in 1838 when Bennett went to England, a passenger in the *Sirius,* the first commercial steamship in Atlantic service. The crossing took about two weeks, approximately half the time required by the fastest clipper ship. Bennett attended the coronation of Queen Victoria, who had succeeded to the throne the year before, and reported the ceremonies for the *Herald.* He engaged six experienced newsmen to write as stringers for his newspaper, from London, Glasgow, Paris, Berlin, Brussels, and Rome. The most experienced was Dr. Dionysius Lardner, already ten years in Paris for the *Morning Chronicle.* Following his return to New York, Bennett also arranged for stringers in Canada, Mexico, and the recently formed Republic of Texas.

Bennett made another visit to Europe in 1846-47 and wrote letters for the *Herald* about the serious economic and political trends on the continent—trends that were to lead to the "revolution" of 1848-49.

By that period, the *Herald* had stringers writing from various cities of the United States, as well as beyond its borders. California was a province of Mexico in 1846, with Monterey as its capital. Thomas Oliver Larkin, U.S. consul there, was also a stringer for the *Herald*. Even as citizens of the United States had moved into Texas, so a considerable number were established in California in 1846. Following the United States declaration of war on Mexico in May of that year, Larkin had news to report.

Captain John C. Frémont of the U.S. Army, who had been leading a surveying expedition since 1845, turned that expedition into a series of military actions, supported by settlers, and ranged from Monterey northward to Oregon. Settlers in Sonoma, encouraged to proclaim an independent Republic of California in June 1846 raised their own "Bear Flag." In July a U.S. naval detachment came ashore at Monterey and raised the American flag, proclaiming California a part of the United States. Naval action brought a seizure of San Francisco, a replacement of the Bear Flag at Sonoma with the American flag, and a seizure of Sutter's Fort on the Sacramento River. Mexicans in southern California drove out U.S. residents, but they were overcome in 1847 by a U.S. Army and Navy operation that established control there.

Apart from the war itself, Larkin may have been the first to report the discovery of gold in January 1848 at Sutter's Mill on the American River, forty miles from Sacramento. Publication of his letters on that subject in the *Herald,* after their slow return to New York, helped to start the California gold rush of 1849. Larkin was still in Monterey when California was formally ceded to the United States in February 1848 under the terms of the Treaty of Guadalupe Hidalgo, concluding the U.S.-Mexican War.

The *New York Tribune,* competitive with the *Herald* and *Sun* in the morning field, also began to reach out for news. Horace Greeley, founder of the paper in 1841, was to move about the country through three decades and to write extensively. It happened that Charles A. Dana, who had been city editor of the *Tribune* in 1847 and remained with the paper in major assignments until 1862, was in Paris, Berlin, and London between June 1848 and February 1849, a period when Europe was in the throes of political and social revolution. He wrote letters on the subject for the *Tribune,* and also for four other dailies in the United States. This may have been the first syndicated correspondence used by the press of the country, apart from the travel letters written by Topliff in 1828-29.

Margaret Fuller, a woman of scholarly attainments and views in advance of her times, much admired by Greeley, and a contributor to the *Tribune* from 1844, was married in Italy in 1846 to the Marquis Giovanni Angelo Ossoli. From Rome during the period of the 1848-49 revolution there, she both helped care for the wounded and wrote letters used by the *Tribune*. She and her husband and their small son were lost when their ship was wrecked en route to New York in June 1850. Although neither a staff member nor quite a stringer for the *Tribune,* she may have been the first woman to act as a foreign correspondent for any newspaper.

After 1850 the *Tribune* had four regular stringer correspondents in Europe, two in Canada, and others in Mexico, Cuba, and Central America. Its chief London stringer, beginning at that period and continuing for ten years, was Karl Marx, who was German-born, and had journalistic experience of a polemical variety in Cologne and Paris. Forced to depart both from Germany and France because of his political writings there during the revolutionary years, he had taken refuge in London in 1849. Dana had met Marx in Europe in 1848 and engaged him in 1851 to write a weekly letter from London for the *Tribune* on European political and economic subjects. For this he received five dollars per letter. It was at this time that Marx also was writing *Das Kapital* and other literature later accepted as communist doctrine. Friedrich Engels, also in London, sometimes would write Marx's weekly *Tribune* letter for him.[1]

Bayard Taylor, as a writer for the *Tribune* between 1844 and 1854, became perhaps the first *bona fide* staff correspondent to move about the world for any newspaper in the United States. A native of Pennsylvania, he became a printer's apprentice. At nineteen, having already published a small volume of poems, he went to Europe with an agreement to write travel letters for the *Saturday Evening Post* and the *United States Gazette,* both of Philadelphia, and for the *New York Tribune.* From 1844 to 1846, while studying in Germany, he also traveled in England, Scotland, France, and Italy, usually walking. He wrote of his observations for the three publications and in 1846 published a book, *Views Afoot,* which was well received.

Two years later, after experience on a small newspaper and writing

---

1 The *Tribune* purchased the *New York Herald* in 1924 and then became the *New York Herald Tribune.* A staunchly conservative paper through the years prior to its suspension in 1966, it was the target for some mild raillery in its later period for having helped, in effect, to finance Marx and Engels in producing what became the accepted testaments of world communism.

for magazines and newspapers in New York, he joined the *Tribune* staff in 1848 and made an adventurous expedition westward through unsettled country to California. There, in 1849, he reported on the California gold rush, as Larkin had done the year before, and his stories in the *Tribune* undoubtedly further stimulated that "rush," drawing 100,000 to California within the year.

In 1851 Taylor was in Europe again, writing for the *Tribune*. More important, however, he was the only news correspondent accompanying the U.S. East Asia Squadron in 1852-53, with Commodore Matthew C. Perry under instructions from President Fillmore to enter Tokyo Bay to try to open trade and diplomatic relations between Japan and the United States. This effort was made in July 1853, a first move to bring Japan into full and direct association with the world community of nations.[2] Taylor became the first U.S. correspondent to set foot in Japan, and perhaps the first western correspondent to do so. His reports to the *Tribune*, although greatly delayed in reaching New York, provided some of the earliest information about Japan and its people to reach a world audience.

With an unflagging interest in far places, Taylor moved on independently from Japan to China and India, and to the Middle East, Egypt, and Africa. While the London press by then was receiving reports from some of these areas, Taylor nevertheless was the first western correspondent in certain of the places visited, and one of the earliest in the others. Again, his reports provided new information about parts of the world still little known.[3]

As these advances within the press organization in the United States were taking place during the first decades of the nineteenth century, they were proceeding also in other countries, and notably in Great Britain. The return of general peace throughout Europe after 1815 at last made possible a normal resumption of trade, and the industrial revolution moved forward at a smart pace. The London press was poised to extend its service of information required to match the changing economy and social organization.

One of the evidences of enterprise was the presence of James Murray, formerly a parliamentary reporter for the *Times*, at the

---

2 Japan had extremely limited relations since the sixteenth century with Portuguese, Dutch, British, and Spanish traders and nationals.
3 From 1854, after leaving the *Tribune*, Bayard Taylor became a popular lecturer and wrote a number of books of travel, fiction, and poetry. In 1862 he entered the U.S. diplomatic service, serving first in the St. Petersburg legation. He was U.S. Minister in Germany at the time of his death in 1878.

Congress of Aix-la-Chapelle in 1817, where post-Napoleonic France, again under a Bourbon king, Louis XVIII, was "re-admitted" as a Great Power in Europe. Murray later went on assignments to Italy and Portugal, and in 1827 became the paper's foreign director, a position he occupied until 1835.

The *Morning Chronicle* arranged for a service of foreign reports that kept it in the leading position as a purveyor of international news until the 1840s. Most of the writers were stringers, but Dr. Dionysius Lardner, a resident staff correspondent in Paris in 1826, remained there for many years. The paper itself had changed ownership in 1821 upon the death of James Perry, its publisher since 1789. William Clement, succeeding him, was even then the owner of the *Observer*, established in 1792, and one of London's first and most successful Sunday newspapers, as it remains today.

The *Chronicle*, like the *Times*, was so serious a paper that it suffered somewhat from the new competition of the *Morning Herald*, made more entertaining through its introduction of the human interest principle. Three evening papers, or afternoon papers as variously called, also contested for readers. These were the *Sun*, established in 1792; the *Globe* (1803); and the *Standard* (1827).

The first sharp reduction in the taxes on knowledge in 1833 had the effect of encouraging the more general purchase of newspapers and the establishment both of newspapers and periodicals.

Among events in Great Britain prior to about 1850 reported in newspapers were the death of George III in 1820; the rule of his eldest son, George IV, from 1820 to 1830, with his attempt to divorce Queen Caroline; and the brief rule of his brother, William IV, from 1830 to 1837. He was succeeded by his eighteen-year-old niece. Queen Victoria ruled until 1901. Her marriage in 1840 to her first cousin, Albert of Saxe-Coburg-Gotha, who became Prince Consort, provided additional subjects in the news.

The press also gave attention to domestic problems arising from the industrial revolution, with crime, crowding, and social maladjustments in cities swollen by families working, or seeking work in mines and factories. The Peterloo Massacre of 1819 in Manchester was but one evidence of discontent and disorder that brought an end to the Tory regime in 1830, with a period of reforms following under a Whig government. The circumstances were complicated by the economic pressures following the Napoleonic wars, the progressive trend from the earlier agricultural economy to the industrial economy, and the Irish potato famine in 1846-48.

Farther afield, British interests in India were extended, and a position was established in China, with Hong Kong made a Crown Colony in 1842. Settlement was beginning in Australia and New Zealand; support was given to Greece in its attainment of independence from Turkey in 1831; and British forces were engaged in the First Afghan War in 1839-42. Britain, in 1815, had refused to become a party to the Holy Alliance of European powers, sponsored by Russia's Czar Alexander I, Prussia's Frederick William III, and Austria's Emperor Francis I.

British relations with Europe were close, however, with great concern for events on the continent. Among such events was the sponsorship by the Holy Alliance of a French invasion of Spain in 1823 to place Ferdinand VII on the Spanish throne. Following his death in 1833, there came the Carlist War of 1834-39 to determine succession to the throne, an issue never clearly settled until 1875. In France the death of Louis XVIII in 1824 brought his brother to that throne as Charles X. Troubles amounting to a new revolution led to his deposition in 1830, with Louis Philippe, the Duc d'Orleans, proclaimed as "citizen king" in a constitutional monarchy.

In 1848 all of Europe was caught up in still another revolutionary sweep that brought liberal reforms in many countries. That change began in France, with Louis Philippe forced to abdicate, and replaced after controversy and bloodshed by Prince Louis Napoleon, nephew of the former Emperor Napoleon. As president of a Second Republic, he survived a new series of internal changes culminating in a reversion in 1852 to a Second Empire. He himself then became Emperor Napoleon III, as he was to remain until 1870.

The revolution of 1848 had serious repercussions in Great Britain, but brought more direct changes in France, and in Germany, Austria, Hungary, Sardinia and the Italian peninsula, Spain, Holland, Denmark, and Sweden. Leaders of governments, shaken by public demands for freedom and opportunity, reinstituted press controls. This did not cause suppressions of newspapers, generally, or prevent the establishment of new papers or the attainment of strength and prosperity for some. But, almost by default, it left the British press, and some of the London morning dailies, most particularly, as nearly the only newspapers in a position to undertake coverage of news beyond the frontiers of their own countries.

The *Morning Post,* for one, sent Charles Lewis Gruneisen, previously known as a music critic, as its special staff correspondent to report the Carlist Wars in Spain. It later boasted that Gruneisen was "the first regular war correspondent for a daily paper" in that, unlike Crabb Robinson of the *Times* and some others who had written of the Peninsular War in Spain in 1808-09, he was actually on the battlefield.

Gruneisen, having transferred to the staff of the *Morning Chronicle* by 1845, accompanied Queen Victoria and Prince Albert on a visit to Germany in that year, and reported events associated with the journey. For the *Morning Post,* which continued to make some efforts toward foreign coverage, one writer in Europe in 1850-52 was Algernon Borthwick, son of Peter Borthwick, then owner of the paper. He returned to London in 1852 as managing editor of the *Post,* developed its foreign service to an important degree, succeeded his father in 1876 as proprietor of the *Morning Post,* and later was ennobled as Lord Glenesk.

The *Morning Chronicle,* in 1850, even with its leadership in foreign reporting by then yielded to the *Times,* still had stringers in a dozen European cities, and in New York, Bombay, Singapore, Alexandria, and Peking. This in itself was an indication of the manner in which a few newspapers were reaching out to far parts of the globe for current information.

Like the *Morning Chronicle,* the *Times* had been able after 1815 to appoint stringers in Europe and, before 1850, in more remote places, including India, China, and the United States. As a stringer in New York, Matthew L. Davis, of the *New York Courier and Enquirer,* wrote for the *Times* from 1840 until 1853.

The stringers for the *Times* and other newspapers were by then more than "agents" employed to forward newspapers. They provided original reporting from the cities and areas of their residence. By the 1840s, the *Times* began to take special pride in being able to claim "a priority of intelligence" from abroad, and made much of its "own correspondents." The paper sometimes was able to inform the British Foreign Office of developments in foreign countries before official dispatches reached London. This became the basis for a mutually useful relationship existing for a brief period between that newspaper and the British government.

The exchange of newspapers remained an important source of information for the London and British press, as it did in the United States. It required about two weeks to move newspapers and mail across the Atlantic after 1838, when the early steamships began to provide a regular service. But it still might have taken a week for some papers to reach London from European capitals.

For a London newspaper to receive newspapers or mail from

more remote parts of the world took much longer. From India, for example, where British interests had been important for many years, the time lag was nearly four months, assuming no added delays due to bad weather or accidents at sea; from China it would be more. There was no Suez Canal. The ships sailed from Calcutta, around the Cape of Good Hope, with a stop at Capetown, and on northward to Falmouth. An alternative routing for the dispatch of news, first used in 1834, was from Bombay and up the Red Sea to Suez, then by camel-carrier to Cairo and Alexandria, by ship again to Malta and on to Marseilles, from there by special courier northward across France to Boulogne or Calais, by packet ship across the English Channel to Folkestone or Dover, and by special train to London. This elaborate process cut the time to forty-seven days, at best.

The *Times* used both of these routings to obtain news from India, at a cost approximating £10,000 a year (nearly $50,000). Although proud to offer exclusive reports to its readers, occasionally utilizing carrier-pigeon service across the Channel after 1837, this expense induced the paper in 1840 to make its India dispatches available on a pro rata basis to its chief competitors, the *Morning Chronicle* and the *Morning Post*.

A problem arose at that time, however, when the French government, asserting the exclusive right to transmit mail within its own frontiers, objected to the use of private couriers by the *Times* to carry newspapers and dispatches from Marseilles to the Channel coast, and it intercepted and confiscated dispatches. Reminiscent of the controversy between the *Times* and the British General Post Office in 1793-1813, this action was to bring another change.

The *Times* altered the routing of its dispatches by sending them from Malta to Trieste or Dwino, on the Adriatic, rather than to Marseilles. From there they were carried northward by couriers across Austria, down the Rhine to Cologne, on to Ostend on the Belgian coast, and thence across the Channel, thus avoiding France altogether.

In a counter stroke, the French government for a time gave special concessions to the London *Morning Herald*, by then in sharp competition with the *Times*, to move *Herald* dispatches across France rapidly and at moderate cost. This proved of little effect, however, and by 1847 the *Herald* had joined with the *Chronicle* and *Post* as a member of the *Times* group, with France still bypassed. Even sharing the costs, each paper paid about £4,000 a year (more than $11,000) for the reports.

Proceeding toward the organization of a permanent foreign service, the *Times* named Andrew O'Reilly as Paris agent in 1840. He was not the paper's first Paris agent, but he presided over its first established office or bureau. In 1848 O'Reilly was followed in that position by J. B. O'Meagher, formerly a stringer in Madrid. Unlike O'Reilly, he was a writing correspondent. He began by reporting the 1848 revolution, and was to remain in Paris for the paper until his retirement in 1869. Henry Reeve and John Palgrave were assistants during those years.

At approximately the same time as O'Meagher began his assignment as a staff correspondent in Paris, T. M. O'Bird became the paper's representative in Vienna, and continued there until he retired in 1866. L. Filmore was named as the first full-time resident correspondent in Berlin. He was replaced in 1853 by G. B. Wilkinson, who remained until 1858. T. H. Hughes, in Lisbon in the late 1840s, was replaced by M. B. Honan, formerly a stringer in Oporto. Honan soon was moved to Rome, where he remained until leaving the paper in 1850.

Correspondents for the *Times,* as for every newspaper, remained anonymous figures so far as the reading public was concerned. Their names, or "by-lines," did not appear either at the beginning or end of their reports, dispatches or stories. Perhaps the only exception, at that time, was introduced by the *Constitutional,* a London daily making much of its political independence, which published only for ten months in 1836-37. With reporters in British cities and in Europe, it appended identifying initials to their reports, but not necessarily their own initials. The letters M.R.M. were attached to stories from Spain, for example, and T.T. to reports from Paris. T.T., in fact, was William Makepeace Thackeray, later to gain fame as a novelist, but then twenty-five and making a start in journalism.

Another newspaper appearing in London in this general period, but due for greater success, was the morning *Daily News,* begun in January 1846. Its first editor was Charles Dickens, already experienced as a reporter for the *Morning Chronicle,,* and just then entering upon his career as a novelist. Dickens soon retired from the staff, with direction passing to John Forster as editor and Charles Wentworth Dilke as manager. From the outset, the *Daily News* was well accepted, taking a liberal political position. It received reports from abroad, with a correspondent in Paris and agents in Madrid, Rome, Vienna, Berlin, and several other European cities. Mention was made of the arrangement by the *Daily News* with William Hunt, editor of the Plymouth *Western Courier,* to gather news by meeting incoming ships at that port. By his action, reports were received of events in the United States, Africa, Australia, and other far parts of the world, with that news hastened to London by rail, and by special train, when warranted.

By 1850 newspapers and news reporting had attained substantial development. In addition to those in London and New York, noteworthy developments also had occurred in France and Germany, but generally the press of Europe continued to lag, largely because of governmental restraints. In some other parts of the world the press was just making a start, or did not yet exist. Some reference still must be made to occurrences in the 1830s and 1840s, as relevant to an advancing service of public information, but the great advances in the press organization itself and in much of the technology of news communication was to come after 1850.

Time and Distance Overcome 8

Science and technology were to transform the world during the nineteenth century. The harnessing of the steam engine to a new variety of tasks seemed to stimulate the minds of men in many countries. Old ideas and new ones were brought together, in part because information was being exchanged more generally. They interacted and important results followed.

Steam power was applied to produce the locomotive in England in 1825, with railroads soon appearing also in France in 1827, and in the United States in 1829. A revolution in transport was on its way. The use of steam to propel small ships was not new in 1800, but the first ship crossed the Atlantic under steam and sail in 1819, and 1838 brought the first regular steamship service. From that time, such ships began to ply all the seas. The horse and the sailing vessel, formerly providing the best means of transport for people and goods, were superseded.

The elements of time and distance, for all previous generations, had separated peoples and delayed their awareness of events. An electronic revolution was to do as much as the revolution in transport to change all that.

The science of electronics continues to produce wonders touching every aspect of life. Applied to communications from 1837, it brought the telegraph and cable, the telephone and wireless, all by 1900, and so "put a girdle round the earth."

There had, of course, been earlier attempts to overcome distance as a barrier to communication. The "jungle telegraph" and smoke signals, runner-relays and rider-relays, carrier pigeons and flag signals all have been mentioned. But there was another transitional system.

In France, late in the eighteenth century, the Abee Claude Chappé proposed a mechanized semaphore system—an adaptation of the system of flag signals with a code devised, rather than the use of colored or patterned flags. Presented to the Legislative Assembly in Paris in 1792, it was put into operation in 1794, even in the midst of the French Revolution. The first message was moved on August 15 of that year, reporting a victory of French forces in Austria.[1]

The Chappé semaphore telegraph required the erection of posts at such intervals and on such heights or open ground as to make each post visible by telescope to the next in either direction. Those intervals averaged about fifteen kilometers (9.3 miles). Each post bore a crossbar with a pivoted arm at each end. Ropes and pulleys permitted the adjustment of the two arms to signify letters or words in the code system used.

The semaphore telegraph, by relay from post to post, made possible the transmission of a signal over a distance of 150 miles, for example, in about fifteen minutes. The total length of the message, naturally, would determine the over-all time for transmission in its entirety. As with flags, the system would not operate in a fog, but night transmission was possible by attaching lanterns to the signal arms.

This system was adopted in other countries. By 1825, with the Napoleonic period ten years ended and Europe at peace, all parts of France were in communication by semaphore. One of the longest spans over which it operated was between Paris and Toulon, on the Mediterranean coast, a distance of 475 miles, with 120 intermediate posts or stations by then relaying a signal in ten to twelve minutes.

An extensive network was operating in Prussia by 1832; in Russia, with 200 stations between Warsaw and St. Petersburg; in Belgium, Holland, Denmark, and Sweden; in Italy and in Great Britain. It was a system that continued to operate in some parts of Europe for more than sixty years, until supplanted by the "magnetic" or electric telegraph.

---

1 The semaphore telegraph was responsible for placing the word "telegraph" in the world's lexicon. It also was a word adopted as a name for some newspapers even before the electric telegraph existed: *El Telégrafo* of Buenos Aires appeared as early as 1801, the *Boston Telegraph* in 1824, and the *United States Telegraph* of Washington in 1826. Others using the word after 1844 included the short-lived London *Railway Telegraph* in 1846, a *London Telegraph* of 1848, surviving five months, and notably the *London Daily Telegraph and Courier* established in June 1855, with the title soon clipped to simply the *Daily Telegraph,* still in full vigor.

Scientists in England, the United States, Prussia, and other countries had been experimenting since early in the nineteenth century with the use of electricity as a means of creating and transmitting signals. Three men whose work bore fruit were Charles Wheatstone, a physicist, and William Fothergill Cooke, an engineer, both in England; and Samuel Finley Breese Morse, an artist of talent and a professor at the University of the City of New York (later New York University).

Morse was a man of many interests. In addition to art, he conducted experiments in chemistry, photography, and physics. It was in 1832 that he conceived an idea for what became known as an electromagnetic recording telegraph. He made the apparatus, had it working by 1836, demonstrated it at the university in 1837, and applied for a patent, which he received in 1844.

Morse's instrument sent a signal over a wire as an electric circuit was alternately closed and opened by the manual operation of a brass lever, or "key." When the key was depressed the wired circuit was closed, the electric current flowed from a battery and caused a small metal bar, or "armature," to be drawn sharply downward by magnetism to meet another metal bar; hence the name "magnetic telegraph" used at the time. As the key was released, breaking the circuit, the armature would return to its original position, touching an upper bar smartly. With the instrument housed in a small wooden box, serving as a kind of sounding board, each contact made by the armature with the metal bars, top and bottom, caused an audible metallic click. Further, at the end of the connecting wire, a similar instrument responded in the same fashion, with a double click as the key was depressed and then released. If the key was held down a trifle longer, and then released, the interval between clicks naturally was longer. Either instrument could signal, in turn, to the other.

The original Morse instrument was so constructed that, at the receiving end, the signal audible as short or long (delayed) clicks also could be recorded by pencil marks on a paper ribbon passing beneath the point of a pencil. If the key was held down very briefly, it would cause a short pencil mark to appear on the ribbon, or tape; if held down longer, the pencil mark would be longer. These marks were referred to as "dots" and "dashes." In either case, the interval was no more than a fraction of a second.

Morse worked out a code whereby each letter of the alphabet, numeral or punctuation mark, was indicated by a combination of dots and dashes, from one to six in number, but variously arranged. This became known as the "Morse code."

As the telegraph later came into general use, operators listening to the audible signals learned to "read" the dot-dash combinations and to transcribe the message directly at twenty-five or thirty words a minute. The operators devised a kind of code within the code so that combinations of letters and numerals conveyed words and even phrases, eliminating the need to send every letter of every word. The pencil-and-tape markings were abandoned as unnecessary.

Even as Morse was perfecting his telegraphic device in the United States, Wheatstone and Cooke were doing the same in England. They also demonstrated their own "magnetic telegraph" in 1837. Soon, they put into operation a "chronometric telegraph" along a mile and one-quarter of the London and Birmingham Railway line, between the Euston and Camden Town stations in London, using the steel rails rather than wires to carry the electrical impulses causing the signals to sound. In 1839 they installed the same system along the Great Western Railway line from London to West Drayton, about thirteen miles in the direction of Windsor. They devised their own code, to become known variously as the Continental, European, or International Code.

Morse, credited as the inventor of the telegraph, in applying for his patent in 1837, also requested Congress to provide funds to construct an experimental line. Ultimately, Congress voted $30,000 for that purpose in 1843, and a wire was strung between Washington and Baltimore, a distance of forty-four miles, parallel to the Baltimore & Ohio Railroad tracks. The installation was made under the direction of Ezra Cornell, a capitalist and business man of Ithaca, N.Y., who had become associated with Morse in 1842.

The Washington end of the line was in the Capitol itself. On May 1, 1844, it had been extended as far as Annapolis Junction, half way to Baltimore. It happened that the Whig Party national convention was meeting in Baltimore at that time. News was brought by train to Annapolis Junction that Henry Clay and Theodore Freylinghausen had been nominated as candidates for the presidency and vice-presidency. Alfred Vail, Morse's partner, stationed at Annapolis Junction, promptly telegraphed that information to Morse himself, at the Capitol. This would seem possibly to have been the first current news report ever to go by telegraph. It was not used by the press on that occasion, but caused lively comment in the Capitol.

Baltimore was the setting, about three weeks later, for the

Democratic party national convention. By that time, the telegraph line had been fully extended, and a series of reports about the convention were transmitted to the Capitol. On this occasion, the Washington *Madisonian* published a brief dispatch headed "Telegraphic News." The Washington *Globe* carried a report crediting "a Telegraph which is in operation between this city and Baltimore." By the time James K. Polk and George M. Dallas were nominated as the party's candidates there was great interest in the telegraph. The *National Intelligencer* and other papers applauded Morse and his invention for speeding the news. Its use at the very time both national conventions were meeting gave dramatic impact to what the *New York Tribune* called the "miracle of the annihilation of space."

In England, the first use of the Wheatstone-Cooke line for the transmission of news was noted by the *Times* in reporting the birth at Windsor Castle on August 8, 1844, of Queen Victoria's fourth child. By the following year, the telegraph lines had been sufficiently extended so that the Queen's address at the opening of Parliament was transmitted to cities throughout much of England, Scotland, and Wales. Several small telegraph companies were already in competition in Britain at that time, but they were merged in 1846 to form a single Electric and International Telegraph Company. Still others were formed later, all privately owned until 1870, when they were purchased by the British government, and domestic telegraph service was placed under the control of the General Post Office.

On the European continent, telegraph lines were projected from 1844, beginning in France, Belgium, and Prussia, and always controlled by governments, rather than private companies. Paris and Berlin were in direct telegraphic communication in December 1850. Lines reached from both those capitals to Vienna in 1854, and extended from there to Bucharest and the Black Sea coast by 1855. Constantinople, Rome, and St. Petersburg were brought into the growing telegraphic network beginning to form around the world.

In the United States, the original Washington-Baltimore line was made available in 1844 for use without charge, and so remained for almost a year, but little patronized. On April 1, 1845, it was put under the control of the Post Office Department. Then, on April 1, 1847, it was sold to the Magnetic Telegraph Company, organized by Morse himself. The company had established a line linking Newark, Philadelphia, Baltimore, and Richmond by early 1846, with the Baltimore-Washington link added in 1847. In the same period, another company, the New York and New England Telegraph

Company, had completed a line between Boston and New York. This permitted forwarding European news first received in Boston, and brought an end to the use of carrier-pigeon services as a means of speeding information to the New York papers under the system instituted by the *Boston Daily Mail* and the *New York Herald* in 1839. Papers using telegraphic news now commonly published the dispatches under some such line as "Latest Intelligence by Magnetic Telegraph."

Cities in the Middle West were joined by telegraph, beginning in 1847. Among many companies being formed, the New York and Mississippi Valley Printing Telegraph Company, incorporated in New York in 1851, planned lines linking Buffalo to St. Louis, by way of Cleveland, Columbus, and Cincinnati, and other links to New Orleans and Chicago. In 1856 the company name was changed, following mergers, to become the Western Union Telegraph Company. Ezra Cornell, former Morse associate, was the largest stockholder.[2] The first telegraph line on the Pacific Coast was a short wire from San Francisco to nearby Point Lobos, built in September 1853 to signal the approach of ships. Later in the year, however, other lines connected Sacramento, made the state capital in 1854, with the gold mining areas of central California. San Francisco and Sacramento were linked and, in the next few years, wires reached south from San Francisco to Los Angeles, north to the Oregon border, and east to Carson City in Nevada.

Not until October 1861 was a telegraph line completed across the prairies and mountains between the Mississippi River and the Pacific Coast, and not until May 1869 was the first transcontinental railroad line completed to link San Francisco to Salt Lake City, Omaha, Chicago, and the east.

Before the telegraph link was established in 1861, a pony express operated for sixteen months between St. Joseph, Missouri, and Sacramento. Mail was carried at five dollars an ounce when the service began, but was reduced to one dollar an ounce before it ended. In those months, more than 200 riders, using 500 horses, raced in relays east and west between 190 stations in an elapsed time averaging about ten days each way. William F. ("Buffalo Bill") Cody and James B. ("Wild Bill") Hickok were among the riders who braved

---

2 From 1862, Ezra Cornell was instrumental in founding an agricultural college at Ithaca, New York, his home, with an endowment of $500,000. It opened in 1868. He later contributed an additional $3,400,000 to what became Cornell University. Before his death in 1874 he also established the Cornell library in Ithaca, and brought railway service to the town.

Indians, wild animals, and hazards of weather and terrain, moving alone at night, as well as during the daylight hours. The service started April 3, 1860, and ended when the telegraph line was completed on October 24, 1861.

Bennett, always enterprising in seeking news for his *New York Herald,* had seized upon the telegraph as an aid to that purpose. He used it freely and continued to do so despite the substantial cost. Early and exclusive reports so obtained added to the reputation and readership of the paper.

During the first weeks of 1846, for example, the *Herald* spent $500 to receive the full text of a speech by Senator Henry Clay at Lexington, in his home state of Kentucky, on the pending Mexican War issue. Bennett arranged for a stenographic report, had it carried eighty miles by an express rider to Cincinnati, the nearest telegraph end, and wired to New York.

The telegraph line had not been completed farther south from New York than Richmond, Virginia, in the 1846-48 period of the U.S.-Mexican War. Bennett used it, however, to hasten the delivery in New York of war news carried by a relay of riders from New Orleans to Richmond. In the first two weeks of 1848, the decisive period of the war, the *Herald* spent $2,381 for war reports and others totalling 79,000 words received by telegraph.

The *Herald* was not alone among newspapers of the United States in using the telegraph. But its persistence in doing so virtually forced others in New York City to follow suit if they were not to suffer in competition. Editors and publishers in all cities were aware of the value of the telegraph as an aid in gathering news, but the costs were high. By 1861, however, the telegraph and railroad lines together were serving many parts of the country, and by 1870 the telegraph lines had brought virtually all parts of the United States and most of Great Britain and Europe into direct communication. Some parts of Latin America, Asia, the Middle East, and Africa also were joined.

The availability of telegraph service had a profound social significance. Prior to 1844, newspapers of importance were published almost exclusively in national capitals and seaport cities, places where news originated or was brought from elsewhere and therefore most promptly and fully available. Other cities and towns, even if they had newspapers, were out of the mainstream of affairs. Railroads helped to relieve that relative isolation, and brought in mail and other newspapers, but rail service often was slow and uncertain even as late as the 1880s.

Telegraph service sometimes was interrupted but, by contrast, it was extended more rapidly than rail service, and by 1870 it was possible for a newspaper in almost any town or city, certainly of North America and Europe, to receive and publish locally whatever was known at approximately the same time in the capitals and port cities.

The telegraph thereby brought the newspapers and residents of inland places into the mainstream of life. Where there had been no newspapers before, there was reason to establish them. A new vitality was added to existing newspapers. There was no essential reason why a "great" newspaper might not be published almost anywhere. The presentation of current reports received by wire also had the effect of stimulating special interest among the people in public affairs, helped toward the creation of an informed society, and built a sense of national unity.

The Cable
Closes
the Gap
The establishment and extension of telegraphic service opened the door for most peoples of the world to gain a vastly greater, and prompt understanding of their environment. But it was a Dutch door, so to speak, with the lower half still closed. That is, signals could not be dispatched across rivers, lakes, and oceans.

Wheatstone, Morse, and others learned very early that if telegraph wires were to be placed under water a superior form of insulation was the least that would be required. Beyond water damage, they would need protection against marine life, abrasion, ships' anchors, and dredging equipment. Such protective materials remained to be found. Pending that time, dispatches between Washington and New York, for example, had to be carried by messengers crossing the Hudson River by boat between Newark and Manhattan. There could be no wire connection across the English Channel between England and France, much less across the Atlantic or Pacific Oceans or other bodies of water.

A first partial solution of this problem came in 1849 with a wire put down beneath the waters of the Connecticut River at Middletown, Connecticut, as a link in a Boston-New York line. The wire was covered with gutta-percha, a resinous gum from trees found in Central and South America, but especially in Borneo, Sumatra, and Malacca. It provided excellent insulation, and was both water repellent and pliant. The Connecticut River was fresh water, however; the distance was not great, and the coating of gutta-percha provided no protection against other hazards.

Salt water was a greater problem. Wheatstone had drawn a plan as early as 1840 for extending a wire beneath the English Channel at its narrowest point of twenty miles between Dover in England and Calais in France. Such a wire, covered with gutta-percha, was put down in 1850. The heavy currents and the tides caused such abrasion that the insulation was rubbed off within twenty-four hours and the salt water caused the wire to lose its effectiveness as a conducting agent for the signals. Morse had a similar experience with a wire in New York harbor.

It was 1851 before a satisfactory protection was found for the underwater, or "submarine cable." A British-financed Submarine Telegraph Company had been formed in 1850 by John W. Brett. It was chartered also in France as the Société de Télégraphe Sous-Marin entre la France et l'Angleterre. Thomas Russels Crampton, an engineer acting for that company, oversaw the completion in September 1851 of a Dover-Calais line.

In this case, the wire was insulated again with gutta-percha, but armored with lead, in the form of a "cable." It cost £360 (about $1,750) for each mile, or £7,200 ($35,000) for the full length of the cable. Put into operation on November 13, 1851, it proved effective. This was the first step in establishing cable communications which were eventually to span the oceans in an augmentation of the telegraph lines over the land.

With the gap in communications thus closed, the cables were to draw nations and peoples closer in terms of mutual awareness. Government administration, commerce, and public needs and interests all were served. Newspapers at last were able to present truly current reports even from distant places, and to participate in a world-wide exchange of information.

The success of the 1851 Dover-Calais cable led to the placement of other British-financed and British-controlled cables. As with the telegraph, the technology of cable communication improved over the years. Other countries also entered into the extension of cables, but few were able to afford the cost of their placement over long distances. Also it would have been self-defeating to duplicate the cables over the same routes beyond a certain point. The result was that British interests not only were the first in the field of cable operation, but have remained most actively involved to the present time.

During the 1850s, in addition to the Dover-Calais line, two British cables were extended to Ostend, one to The Hague, two to Ireland, one to Denmark, and one to Sweden. British financing supported a 400-mile cable beneath the Black Sea in 1855 from Varna, Bulgaria, to Balaclava in the Russian Crimea, and from there to Constantinople. British interests laid cables in the Mediterranean in 1854 from Marseilles to points in Corsica, Sardinia, and the Italian peninsula, and then on to Algiers in 1860.

As early as 1845, John Brett, so soon to become involved in the establishment of the Dover-Calais cable, had proposed a system of cables to link British possessions around the globe. This necessarily would require a cable across the North Atlantic to Canada, if such a thing were possible.

In 1850 the Reverend John T. Mulloch of St. Johns, Newfoundland, had proposed in a letter published in the *St. Johns Courier* that a telegraph line already existing might be extended from Newfoundland by a cable to the mainland of Canada and the United States. News boats, he said, then might meet westbound Atlantic vessels as they passed Cape Race, Newfoundland, obtain the latest news from Europe and forward it from St. Johns by telegraph and cable to reach the press of North America as much as two days earlier than by waiting for the ships to reach Halifax, Nova Scotia, which was by then in direct telegraphic communication with cities in Canada and the United States.

Frederick N. Gisborne, manager of the telegraph lines in Nova Scotia, pursuing this same general concept, went to Newfoundland late in 1851. Because of the successful Dover-Calais cable, he gained official support from the Newfoundland government. He formed a Newfoundland Electric Telegraph Company, and found added financial support in New York. With that, he set out to arrange to have cables laid between Newfoundland and Prince Edward Island and on to New Brunswick, with telegraph connections from there to Nova Scotia and the United States. The effort was made in 1853, but the cable failed, presumably because the insulation or armoring was still faulty, and the company went bankrupt.

Undaunted, Gisborne went to New York early in 1854 to try to revive interest in his project. There he met Cyrus West Field, a native of Massachusetts, who had attained an early success and a fortune as a paper wholesaler, had "retired" at thirty-four, and had just returned from a visit to South America. Gisborne's proposal stirred Field's imagination to a point where he conceived the idea not merely for a Canada-Newfoundland cable, but for a cable that would span the North Atlantic.

The result was the formation by Field on May 6, 1854, of the New York, Newfoundland, and London Electric Telegraph Company, capitalized at $1.5 million, with most of the money raised in the United States. Peter Cooper of New York, a steel manufacturer, became president of the new company, and Field's brother, Matthew D. Field, was chief engineer. An association was formed with the heads of two of the regional telegraph companies then operating. These were James Eddy of the Maine Telegraph Company, and Hugh Downing of Philadelphia who controlled the New York & Washington Printing Telegraph Company, with wires covering much of New England. Out of this association came the formation of a new American Telegraph Company in 1855, with Cooper also becoming president of that company. It was to provide a link between the proposed North Atlantic cable, the New England telegraph lines (which it owned), and telegraph lines in Canada.

Meanwhile, Field went to London to arrange for the construction by British manufacturers of 2,300 nautical miles of cable.[3] There he also conferred with Brett of the Submarine Telegraph Company, who took some shares in the new American company; and he met with scientists and technicians who had experience in laying those cables already extended from British shores.

In the summer of 1855, accordingly, an attempt was made to put down a cable beneath the waters of the North Atlantic, to rest on an undersea plateau between Valentia Bay, Ireland, and Trinity Bay, Newfoundland. Added links were in prospect from there to Glace Bay, Cape Breton Island, and to Halifax, Nova Scotia, where connections could be made with landlines of the American Telegraph Company.

This first attempt failed, defeated by bad weather at sea and lack of experience in handling the long and heavy cable. In July 1856 a cable was laid successfully, however, from Newfoundland to Cape Breton Island, in an adaptation of Gisborne's plan, and on to Halifax. But for the North Atlantic cable itself, a new effort was required.

Field returned to London. A second company was formed in December 1856, this time under British control, but with Field as president. Known as the Atlantic Telegraph Company of Great Britain, it had support from both the British and U.S. governments. The second attempt to lay a cable over the same course was made in August 1857, when weather conditions were most favorable. On the sixth

---

3   A nautical mile is 6,080 feet, as compared to 5,280 feet in a land mile.

day, however, that second cable also parted and the end was lost at sea.

Once again, new financing was required for a third attempt. The company ordered an additional 700 nautical miles of cable, and on June 23, 1858, the third effort to conquer the Atlantic began. On this occasion, rather than starting from a shore point, two cable-laying ships met in midocean, spliced the ends of the cables and started away from each other. Four breaks occurred, but the ends were recovered, repairs made, and on August 4 the cable had been landed both in Ireland and in Newfoundland.

The signals were not strong, but formal messages of good will were exchanged between Queen Victoria and President James Buchanan on August 16 and 18, and duly published in the newspapers of both countries. Messages also were exchanged between the Mayor of New York and the Lord Mayor of London on August 22 and 23. A rate for the dispatch of commercial messages was announced at £2 a word (nearly $10 at the long-maintained exchange rate of $4.86 to the pound sterling).

The first news report by cable was moved eastward from New York and published in the London press of August 18. It reported a collision in American waters between the Cunard steamers *Arabia* and *Europe*. The first news moving westward appeared in the *New York Sun* of August 27, reporting a treaty concluded by Great Britain and France with the imperial government of China. A series of brief news items also reached New York on August 28, and some British government messages were cabled to Canada on August 31.

This transmission of messages beneath the broad Atlantic seemed almost unbelievable. President Buchanan himself hesitated, waiting a day before responding to Queen Victoria's greeting lest he find that he had been made the victim of a hoax. Some persons, unable to comprehend the principle of electrical communication, assumed that the cable worked like a giant bell-pull, with signals conveyed by jerking on one end or the other.

A public celebration marking the new and sudden adjacency of the Old World and the New World was scheduled to occur September 1 on both sides of the Atlantic. The signals passing over the cable often had been weak, and sometimes unreadable. Then, on September 1, virtually as the celebrations were in progress in London and New York, the cable went dead. The last flutter of a signal was heard on October 28, but that was the end. Nearly eight years were to pass before a new cable connection was established.

The near-success of the 1858 cable encouraged the American Telegraph Company to increase its capacity to handle the traffic anticipated when the next cable was completed. This it did by acquiring Morse's original Magnetic Telegraph Company in 1859, and also acquiring the New York and New England Telegraph Company lines formed in 1846 by F.O.G. ("Fog") Smith, a member of Congress who had turned to a pioneering development of the telegraph business. These acquisitions gave the American Telegraph Company connections extending from Nova Scotia to the Mexican border.

The fourth attempt to establish an Atlantic cable was delayed beyond what had been expected in 1858 and 1859 because the American Civil War (1861-65) made the enterprise impractical. The idea was by no means forgotten, however, and some extension of telegraph lines took place within the United States during those years. Notable was the completion of the line between San Francisco and the east, with transcontinental telegraph service introduced on October 26, 1861, when the war was in its early months.

Cyrus Field, whose concern for the cable had not cooled, went to London in 1862 to try to obtain new financing for the fourth effort. A third company was formed, the Telegraph Construction and Maintenance Company. Field also concluded an arrangement whereby the *Great Eastern,* a recently completed steamship of 25,000 tons, and the largest vessel built up to that time, would lay the new cable when the time was right.

The British press, like that of the United States, was fully aware of the value of the telegraph and cable in news gathering and dissemination and had used those facilities from the outset. Yet press enthusiasm was not unmitigated, the chief reservation being the costs involved. Indeed, Mowbray Morris, manager of the *Times,* in 1853 told G. B. Wilkinson, the paper's Berlin correspondent, that he would have preferred that the telegraph "had never been invented," and he later was to refer to the Atlantic cable as a "great bore." Morris understood, however, as did everyone else, that there could be no turning back to the horse express and the sailing vessel.

Undeterred by the war in the United States, British interests proceeded in the early sixties with telegraph and cable extensions. Most notable was the construction of a long, British-owned line establishing a direct overland link between London and India. Put into use March 2, 1865, it was operated by the Indo-European Telegraph Company, and included a cable from British shores beneath the

North Sea to Prussia, joining a telegraph line across Poland, Russia, and Persia to connect with India's government-owned line at that frontier, and so across India to Delhi, Calcutta, and Bombay.

Even in a United States at war, the Western Union Telegraph Company, a competitor of the American Telegraph Company, set out to match that company's prospective U.S.-Canadian-British-European communications tie. Its plan was to extend a telegraph landline from San Francisco northward through western Canada to Alaska, with a cable beneath the Bering Strait, and a landline across Siberia to St. Petersburg, where telegraph connections would be available to other points in Europe and beyond. Studies were made and approval was obtained in 1864 from the Canadian and Russian governments for this 7,000-mile communications link. George Kennan, manager of the Western Union office at Cincinnati, and an engineer, was sent to survey the route in Siberia. Construction of the line was started late in the spring of 1865, immediately after the American Civil War ended.

At almost precisely the same time, the arrangements Field had made in London in 1862 to resume work on the North Atlantic cable when the occasion became appropriate were put into action. In July 1865, three months after the war's conclusion, the Irish end of the fourth Atlantic cable was landed and the *Great Eastern* set off westward toward Newfoundland, paying out cable as she went. Once again there were difficulties caused by cable breaks and by failure of test signals sent back over the wire. Then, on August 2, the cable broke again; the end was lost at sea. It was hooked and partially lifted on August 11, but then this "1865 Cable," as it came to be known, was lost once more, and another year's effort ended in the fourth reversal since 1855.

Work went on, meanwhile, across the world in Siberia, with Kennan supervising the construction of the Western Union telegraph line.

A fifth attempt to span the North Atlantic at last brought success in 1866. But not before a fourth company was formed, the Anglo-American Company, with Field as its president. The three companies previously involved remained financially interested. The first of these, the New York, Newfoundland & London Electric Telegraph Company, still owned and operated the cable from Newfoundland to Cape Breton Island and the Nova Scotia-based telegraphic link to the Canadian and U.S. telegraph lines. The other two companies, the Atlantic Telegraph Company of Great Britain, which had managed to lay the nearly successful 1858 cable, and the Telegraph Construction and Maintenance Company that had almost completed the 1865 cable, both were represented also in the new Anglo-American Company. Additional stock in that company was sold to the public through the J. S. Morgan & Co. of New York, and also to private individuals in London.

During July of 1866 the Anglo-American Company, again using the *Great Eastern* to carry the drums of cable, at last laid 2,300 nautical miles of wire entirely without mishap from Valentia Bay in Ireland to Trinity Bay in Newfoundland. The first messages passed over the cable on July 26, 1866. These included news reports.

Moreover, on September 1, through the use of improved grappling equipment, the end of the lost 1865 cable was recovered from the ocean bottom, spliced, and landed September 8 at Heart's Content, in Trinity Bay, and also carried signals effectively.

So, eleven years after efforts had begun, and eight years after the brief success of 1858, two North Atlantic cables were placed in operation within six weeks and a permanent link established. The cables were sufficiently used, even at the high per-word rate, so that by 1870 Field was able to pay off all persons who had invested in the various companies, with the addition of 7 per cent on their funds. The Anglo-American Company, the ownership of which was primarily British, proceeded to maintain the cable service.

The completion and successful operation of the North Atlantic cables part of a newly formed Danish-own Union project for a land line from San Francisco to St. Petersburg by way of Alaska and Siberia. The project was formally abandoned by the company in March 1867. The enterprise, nevertheless, was a contributing element in the U.S. purchase of Alaska from Russia in that same year. That portion of the telegraph line already completed in Siberia was taken over and extended, still under Kennan's supervision until 1868,[4] to becomeed Great Northern Telegraph Company (Det Store Nordiske Telegraf-Selskab), with Russia's Czar Alexander II holding an interest.

---

4 George Kennan remained in Siberia until 1871, and returned there in 1885-86, but meanwhile was night manager for the New York Associated Press in Washington from 1877-85. Subsequently, he lectured, and wrote for the *Outlook* and *McClure's* magazines, including reports on the Russo-Japanese War in 1904-05. He received honors in Japan, and wrote several books prior to his death in 1923. His grandson, George Frost Kennan, active in U.S. diplomacy from 1927 to 1953, also spent many years in Russia, including a period as United States ambassador in 1952.

The Danish company had telegraph and cable rights in the Baltic and in Russia, and it also reached an agreement in 1871 with the Chinese imperial government to extend its St. Petersburg-Vladivostok line with cables to Shanghai, Amoy, the British Crown Colony of Hong Kong, a branch to Nagasaki, Japan, and spur telegraph lines in northern China to Tientsin and Peking. The ownership of the company was to be broadened by an agreement in 1896 whereby a British-owned Eastern Extension, Australasia and China Telegraph Company, Ltd., and the Chinese government became joint partners. The company had a virtual monopoly in its vast area of service.

In the North Atlantic, meanwhile, the Anglo-American Company laid a new cable in 1873. It supplanted the 1865 cable, which had developed faults. Still another cable was laid in 1874, and operated successfully until 1880, but with frequent interruptions after that. Other cables were laid as replacements or to accommodate a growing volume to traffic. Five cables owned by the company in 1910 were leased in that year for operation by Western Union, which had itself entered the cable field in 1873 in the Key West-West Indies area.

The Anglo-American Company had some competition after 1869 from a French-financed company, the Compagnie Française du Télégraphe de Paris à New York. It was organized in 1868 through the efforts of Paul Julius Reuter, British news agency proprietor, and Baron Emile d'Erlanger, financier of Paris and London, with funds raised by the sale of stock to various European banking houses. A cable was laid by the *Great Eastern* once again, over a distance of 2,584 nautical miles between Brest, on the Brittany coast of France, to the French-held island of St. Pierre, just south of Newfoundland, and so to Duxbury, on the Massachusetts coast, where a landing was made July 23, 1869.

The venture was opposed with some vigor by the Anglo-American Company, not only because of the competition it would offer, but because Reuter's participation in its development ran counter to assurances he had given Field in London in 1862 that he would support the prospective Anglo-American Company line by expending at least £5,000 a year for his news-agency dispatches. The controversy also reached congressional levels, centering on the right to land the cable at Duxbury. That landing was approved, however, partly because it had the support of the *New York Herald*. Four years later in 1873 that French cable was sold to the Anglo-American Company to help meet France's reparation payments to Germany following the Franco-Prussian War of 1870-71.

The broad extent of the British Empire afforded cable landing and message relay points throughout the world. With every incentive to extend communications facilities to advance the interests of the empire and of British commercial and press interests, and with the financial means to do so, British companies proceeded actively in cable development.

A Mediterranean cable was completed in 1869 linking the island of Malta to Alexandria, Egypt, a span of 900 nautical miles. This project was advanced by the Eastern Extension Telegraph Company, directed by J. Denison Pender, a Manchester merchant and member of Parliament who also had been concerned in the North Atlantic cable venture.

Pender directed two other companies. One, the British-India Submarine Telegraph Company, laid a cable from Suez, at the southern end of the Suez Canal, which had been opened for traffic November 17, 1869, to Port Sudan, on the Red Sea, at Aden. There it joined another cable, completed in 1870, beneath the Arabian Sea, from Aden to Bombay. Suez and Alexandria were linked to complete a line from Bombay to Malta. Another Pender company, the Falmouth, Gibraltar & Malta Telegraph Company, laid a cable between those three points and tied into the Eastern Extension line from Malta to Alexandria and beyond. The *Great Eastern* was engaged in several of these operations. On June 11, 1870, it became possible to send messages 6,000 miles between London and Bombay by direct cable connections. In 1872 these Pender companies were merged to form the Eastern Telegraph Company.

Between 1870 and 1873 cables were extended eastward from India by three companies, the British-India Extension, the Chinese Submarine Telegraph Company, and the British-Australia Company. In 1873, again through Pender's enterprise, those three companies were joined to form one, the Eastern Extension, Australasia and China Telegraph Company, Ltd.

The cables laid by those three companies, as merged in 1873, were based at Madras. From there one line went south to Colombo and Point de Galle in Ceylon. Another line was carried northward to Calcutta and on to Rangoon and Singapore, where a division occurred. One division continued eastward to Saigon and Hong Kong, which was reached in 1871, with an extension from there to Shanghai and to Tokyo by 1873, five years after Japan began its own internal telegraph system. The other division extended southward from Singapore to Batavia (now Djakarta) and to Port Darwin in northern Australia. There it joined a telegraph line stretching 2,000 miles to Adelaide, Melbourne, Sydney, and Brisbane, on the southern and eastern coasts. A cable link to New Zealand was completed soon after, thus bringing both Australia and New Zealand into the network by 1873-74.

British communications rights had been obtained in China in 1870. The Eastern Extension, Australasia and China Telegraph Company, Ltd., was to reach an agreement also in 1896 with the Great Northern Telegraph Company of Denmark, whereby the two companies became joint partners with the Chinese imperial government in communication in China.

From Madras, a telegraph line already existed in 1870 across southern India to Bombay, on the west coast, and there formed a connection with the Eastern Extension company cables reaching Aden and providing service to Alexandria and to London. That company also soon laid cables southward from Aden down the east coast of Africa to Zanzibar, Lourenço Marques, and to Durban by 1879, and on to Capetown by 1887. Then from Durban a cable was extended beneath the Indian Ocean to Perth, Australia, and to New Zealand.

Another British enterprise, the Western Telegraph Company, Ltd., ran cables down the west coast of Africa to Capetown, touching also at Madeira and the Canary Islands. The company obtained rights from the Brazilian government in 1873 and another cable, the first across the South Atlantic, was completed in 1874. It ran from England to Portugal to the African coast, and from Madeira and the Cape Verde Islands to Pernambuco (now Recife), on the Brazilian coast. Soon it was extended southward to Rio de Janeiro, São Paulo, Montevideo, and Buenos Aires. Telegraph service was available westward from there across the Andes to Chile and Peru on the Pacific coast of South America.

The British Western Telegraph Company cable also was extended northward from Brazil to the West Indies, and later to the Bahamas, Bermuda, and to Halifax, Nova Scotia, thus completing a circle of communication embracing both the North and South Atlantic ocean areas.

France was sufficiently recovered from the Franco-Prussian War by 1879 to permit entrance of two new French companies into cable communications between Europe, Africa, the West Indies, and South America. These were the Compagnie des Cables Sud-Americaine and the Compagnie Françaises des Cables Télé-graphiques.

A German company also entered into Atlantic communications, the Deutsche-Südamerikische Telegraphen Gesellschaft, A.G. Its cables ran from Emden, on the North Sea coast of Germany, to the Azores, with lines westward from there to New York, southward to Monrovia, Liberia, on the African coast, and from there across the South Atlantic to Recife, Brazil.

In the Western Hemisphere, a short cable had been placed in 1867 by the International Ocean Telegraph Company of New York between Key West, Florida, and Havana, Cuba. This cable was extended in 1870 to Jamaica and Panama, and also touched at Puerto Rico and Trinidad. Captain James Alexander Scrymser of New York had formed the operating company in 1865, but in 1873 he disposed of his interests to the Western Union Telegraph Company. When that company entered the cable communications field, supplementing its landline service in the United States, it set a precedent for its leasing in 1882 of the North Atlantic cables operated since 1866 by the Anglo-American Company.

Scrymser reentered the communications business in 1881, organizing a Mexican Telegraph Company and, later, a Central & South American Telegraph Company. The first of these put a cable into operation between Galveston, Texas, and Tampico and Vera Cruz in Mexico. The other company ran a telegraph line from Vera Cruz across the Isthmus of Tehuantepec to the Pacific coast, and a cable southward from there to El Salvador, Nicaragua, Panama, Colombia, Ecuador, and Peru.

United States-Mexican telegraphic communications had existed since 1851, but these new connections made it possible to communicate directly between the United States, Mexico, and the west coast of South America. In 1890 the cable was extended southward from Peru to Chile, and the purchase of the Transandine Telegraph Company in 1891 provided a link with Buenos Aires, on the east coast of South America.

This U.S.-Chile-Argentine connection was referred to as the "back-door cable." In 1917 the connection was extended northward from Buenos Aires to Rio de Janeiro. In December 1918, eight months after Scrymser's death, his companies were combined under the name of All-America Cables.

In the decades between 1850 and 1900 these various cables, and many shorter ones, were laid beneath the world's seas and oceans. The Pacific, between North America and Asia, was not spanned until 1903. But five of the world's continents—or six, including

Australia—were in direct communication even by 1874, and were knit ever more closely with the cable network augmented by telegraphic landlines.

Technology brought steady improvements in the equipment and methods of communication. Although telegraph messages were received audibly almost from the outset, signals sent over long lines and over ocean cables tended to fade with distance or to lack the strength to activate the sounder device at the receiving end. A system was devised whereby messages could be relayed, with renewed strength.

Sir William Thompson, using a marine galvanometer, also created a system whereby the electrical impulses caused a right or left deviation of a needle, along with a reflected ray of light, to convey a visible rather than an audible signal. The movement of the needle, and the length of time it remained stationary, left or right, represented a letter code similar to the audible dots and dashes of the code. Thompson further improved upon this system with a siphon recorder, or undulator, by which a stylus traced a line on a tape, with square-cornered hills and dales, wide or narrow, again representing the dot-dash code. This tape, passing before an operator, was "read" or decoded, with the hill-and-dale version of the dot-dash code translated into letters and words. An added advantage was that the tape was there to be "read" or rechecked, if necessary, whereas an audible signal vanished, unless repeated by special request. Among many other advances, it became possible through duplex and quadraplex systems to send two messages and then four at the same time over the same wire, allowing an increase in message volume without the expense of doubling or quadrupling the lines and equipment.

Neither telegraph lines nor cables ever have been entirely free from interruptions, failures, or damage. In some more remote parts of the world, telegraph lines have been cut by persons seeking wire for personal use, or out of ignorance or malice. They have been broken by storms or, even when armored and buried, have been severed by machines digging for construction or road repairs. Cables, although insulated and armored, may still deteriorate, particularly in salt water; they may be pierced by marine borers, abraded by the action of rough seas and tides and ice in combination with rough bottoms, reefs, and ridges; or they may be broken or damaged by underwater earthquakes, ships' anchors or trawling gear. A whale broke a U.S.-Alaska cable on one occasion, and a single earthquake in the Atlantic severed twelve cables in 1924.

It became the practice in the 1870s to lay cables in pairs, where financing and traffic volume justified the expense, so that if technical difficulties or a break put one cable out of service, the other might be used pending repairs. For the same reason, cables have been leased in pairs. Since the maximum length for efficient cable operations was long regarded as about 2,500 nautical miles, the usual practice was to route a long cable through island points where messages could be relayed with booster power or retransmitted entirely. This had made such islands as the Azores, Bermuda, Ascension, and Jamaica important cable stations in the Atlantic. The Hawaiian Islands, the Philippines, Guam, Yap, and the Fanning Islands serve the same purpose in the Pacific, as do others elsewhere.

Rates and Regulations

The message rates set for telegraph and cable communication were generally high from the outset and remained so until after about 1880.

The first telegraph line in the United States, as set up in 1844 between Baltimore and Washington under a special Congressional grant, was open for use without cost until April 1845. Then a rate of one cent for four characters was set. Thus one eight-letter word would cost two cents to transmit. As other lines were placed in operation in 1845 and 1846 by private companies offering a commercial service, the rate was set on a per-word basis, rather than on individual characters or letters.

The Boston-New York rate in 1846 was fifty cents for not less than ten words, or five cents a word. This came down to two cents a word for New York newspapers in 1848, after negotiation, but was four cents a word if two or more papers wished to share the same dispatch.

In general, as telegraph lines were extended, there was little uniformity in rates, little chance for negotiation, and each company charged what it could get. When telegraphic service began on the Pacific coast in 1853, for example, with only one company operating, the rate was one dollar for ten words between San Francisco and San Jose, only fifty miles away, or two dollars for ten words between San Francisco and Marysville, about 100 miles away. When the first transcontinental telegraph line went into operation in October 1861, originally as the Overland Telegraph Company, the rate was one dollar a word between San Francisco and Washington or New York. Later it became six dollars for ten words and seventy-five cents for each additional word, and remained so for several years. The cost for telegraphing the text of President Lincoln's message to Congress in 1862 from Washington to San Francisco was $600.

By 1870 one or two companies in the United States had agreed to set a special rate for press dispatches, lower than the regular rate, provided the dispatches moved during the hours of the night. Even so, it still cost ten cents a word between Boston and San Francisco, five cents between Boston and Chicago, and two cents between Boston and Washington. Reasonable uniformity in rates did not come until after the establishment of the Interstate Commerce Commission in 1887.

In European countries, where telegraph lines were owned by the governments rather than by private companies, rates were generally lower than in the United States, and the press sometimes received special concessions as well. A study of comparative rates in 1866, as made by Frederic Hudson, then managing editor of the *New York Herald,* indicated that a press telegram that would cost eighty-one cents in the United States would move for only three and one-half cents in Europe.

On the long Indo-European Telegraph Company line, completed between London and Bombay in 1865, a rate of ₤1 a word ($4.86) was set, with a minimum charge of ₤20 for twenty words ($97.20). This rate soon was reduced, but remained high enough to discourage anything more than moderate use of the line by the press. The cable line between London and Bombay, completed in 1870, was equally expensive to use, as were the extensions of 1872 and 1873 to Australia, China, and Japan.

When the short-lived North Atlantic cable of 1858 was opened the rate set for messages was ₤2 a word, or nearly ten dollars. The same rate was announced by the Anglo-American Company when the first permanently successful cable was completed in July 1866, and a minimum charge of ₤20 for (nearly $100) was specified, with ten words allowed at that figure. Even at that rate, 2,772 messages—government, commercial, private, and press—were transmitted during the first three months, the total wordage unspecified.

On November 1, 1866, four months after the cable opened, the rate was cut in half, to ₤10 for ten words, which was still a $48.60 minimum. With the first novelty gone, the traffic volume fell to an estimated 5 per cent of capacity, and on December 1 the rate was halved once again, to ₤5 for ten words, or $2.43 a word and $24.30 minimum. The volume remained small, but the cables nevertheless operated at a profit.[5] In September 1868 the rate was cut further to £3.7.6, a little over $16 for ten words, or about $1.60 a word.

The rates on all lines, telegraph and cable, were very considerably reduced, beginning especially in the 1880s. The higher rates prior to that time restricted the use made of the facilities by individual newspapers. Some of the more successful dailies of New York and London did use them, and news agencies as well, but they learned to write dispatches in the briefest possible form—in a manner that became known as "cablese" because of its word combinations and omissions. The full sense of the message was restored by editors at the receiving end. In this manner even long and complex reports could be presented to readers on the basis of relatively brief dispatches, at a saving in transmission charges and no loss of facts or accuracy.

As telegraph lines and cables were extended to carry messages across national frontiers, special arrangements also became necessary relative to the rates and the sharing of payments between the companies or governments over whose lines the messages passed, and sometimes as to the acceptability of messages for transmission. These became matters for international negotiation between governments and between companies and governments.

Originally, this was done through bilateral treaties, the first of which was concluded between Austria and Prussia in October 1849. It was immediately followed by treaties between Prussia and Saxony and between Austria and Bavaria. Next, representatives of these same four states met at Dresden in July 1850 and formed an Austro-German Telegraph Union, which held six conferences between 1850 and 1863. Five other central and northern European states became members: Hanover, Würtemberg, Baden, Mecklenburg-Schwerin, and Holland.

A group of western European states formed a similar organization, beginning with a treaty between France and Belgium in 1851. France then signed bilateral treaties with Switzerland in 1852, Sardinia in 1853, and Spain in 1854. In June 1855 representatives of these five states met at Paris and formed a West European Telegraph Union. Between 1855 and 1858 that Union held two conferences, and in 1860 Holland, Portugal, the Two Sicilies, and the Vatican joined the

---

5 In that same year of 1866, it was estimated that daily newspapers of the United States paid a total of $521,509 for telegraphic dispatches within the country.

group. Meanwhile, representatives of the two groups had met at Paris in 1852 to begin cooperative relations, and a conference at Brussels in 1858 was attended by representatives of Belgium, France, and Prussia.

The first international conference of real scope met in Paris in May 1865, by invitation of the French government, and a Paris Telegraph Convention was signed by representatives of twenty states. It created an International Telegraphic Union (ITU), and set up rules and regulations affecting telegraphic traffic in much of Europe, effective January 1, 1866. After this, the two regional groups lost importance and were dissolved in 1872, and the ITU became the chief regulatory body with reference to communication by telegraph between countries as well as by cable and telephone. It still exists, but known since 1932 as the International Telecommunications Union.

The conference agreed on periodic meetings to discuss matters of mutual concern and to revise regulations as required. The first such conference, officially the second ITU gathering, took place in Vienna in 1868. It approved the establishment of a permanent International Bureau of Telegraph Administrations supported by member governments and to be located at Berne, the Swiss capital. The name was changed in 1906 to the International Bureau of the ITU. After World II, the Bureau was moved to Geneva under the wing of the United Nations, whose European headquarters was established there, and where it continues to function.

A third ITU conference met in Rome in December-January of 1871-72, and a fourth at St. Petersburg in June-July 1875. The St. Petersburg Conference was extremely important. Earlier regulations and agreements were revised to bring new order into communications, and an International Telegraph Convention concluded there became the basis for the regulation of international communications in the years since, although with changes at subsequent ITU conferences meeting at intervals of five years, except as interrupted during World Wars I and II. The conference also may have been the first occasion upon which representatives of nations of the world, beyond Europe alone, came together. The objective itself was remarkable, non-political, and concerned with cooperative action looking toward an aspect of world order.

By 1875 most of the nations of Europe had joined the ITU. Most other nations were to join within the next decade or two to provide an almost 100 per cent representation. The ITU members are governmental rather than representatives of individual companies engaged in communications, and membership is voluntary. One of the prerequisites for association with the ITU until after World War II was that the communications facilities of the countries represented must be nationalized or, at least, be under complete government control. This circumstance did not exist originally in Great Britain and never has existed in the United States.

The British government assumed control of domestic telegraph lines on February 5, 1870, with private companies purchased from their owners at a cost of nearly £8 million under the provisions of the Electric Telegraph Acts of 1868 and 1869, and with direction of the lines placed under the British General Post Office. Even so, Great Britain did not join the ITU until 1878, although it had representatives at the St. Petersburg Conference of 1875 as observers.

The United States was not officially a member of the ITU until the regulations were modified after World War II, but it sent an observer to the St. Petersburg Conference of 1875, and to subsequent conferences. It did not participate officially in discussions, but its representatives took an unofficial part in the business of the conferences. It did not sign any conventions or agreements until 1932, but it paid a share in the cost of maintaining the ITU Bureau, and complied with most of the regulations.

The private companies doing business were bound to observe the rules and regulations generally agreed upon by the ITU, and beginning in 1885 also sent their representatives to the periodic conferences. This they were privileged to do after 1872, and they also participated unofficially in some discussions and negotiations.

The functions of the ITU were and are to assure fast and efficient international communication, to determine message-handling practices contributing to such service, to establish a fair basis for setting rates, to regulate the use of code whether as a means to assure secrecy or to reduce the costs of message transmission, and to fix arrangements for financial accounting.

The St. Petersburg Conference in 1875 agreed, among other things, that a press message might be handled at a rate below that set for a commercial message, especially if it were moved during the night hours from 6 P.M. to 6 A.M. when other traffic volume was lower. It would have no priority over a full-rate message, however. This was the beginning of an official "press rate," variously modified since then. Applied at first to the telegraph, it was extended to the cable after 1886, and subsequently to wireless and radiotelegraphic transmission. But no such special rates have been granted for use of the telephone.

Actual rate concessions for press messages were determined in practice by individual countries and companies, and were arrived at on the basis of competition and direct negotiation. In the United States, by 1880, for example, about 11 per cent of all telegraph messages were press messages, and this high volume earned a special rate. Between 1886 and 1914 the British Eastern Extension Company made progressive reductions in the press rate between London and Australia, with the 1886 rate then regularly about $2.28 a word set at about sixty-five cents for press dispatches, and the regular 1914 rate by then eighty-five cents a word set at thirty-eight cents for press use.

Some companies and governments not only set special press rates but granted certain rebates and showed favoritism to particular news agencies, newspapers, and sometimes even to individual correspondents. At times this was done to serve a special propaganda purpose. Such actions had no authorization from the ITU.

At an ITU conference in London in 1903, it was agreed that an unofficial rate in Europe would be 50 per cent of the regular commercial rate for night transmission; later even the night limitation was dropped. In the United States a domestic daytime press rate stood at one-third of the regular rate, and a night press rate at one-sixth of the regular rate.

Where a leased-wire arrangement existed, as for a news agency or for newspapers on particular circuits such as between Washington and New York, the word-rate had no meaning. Payment was based instead on a contract agreement providing for use of the wire at a monthly or annual rate, either on a twenty-four hour basis or for specified daily time periods. The number of words transmitted was irrelevant.

In many cases, even where a lower per-word press rate existed, but with full rate messages always taking priority in handling, newsmen often have chosen to file for transmission at the full rate, or even at a higher "urgent" rate to be assured of greater speed in the delivery of a dispatch.

The greatest volume of cable traffic always has been across the North Atlantic, and the heaviest portion of that has been westward, chiefly from London and Paris to New York. The $1.60 per word regular rate set in 1868 for that routing was cut to sixty cents in 1870. In 1884 it had been increased again, with a seventy-five cent per word press rate.

The Western Union Telegraph Company had leased North Atlantic cables from the Anglo-American Company in 1882. The six cables were paired, with two of the three pairs British-owned, the other pair

U.S.-owned, but all were operated by Western Union. Control of that company had been gained in 1881 by Jay Gould, a New York financier. He had negotiated the lease arrangement and also had been responsible for the increase in rates in 1884.

Three years before, in 1881, a new domestic telegraph company had been formed in the United States through the efforts of Elisha Gray of Chicago, a leader in telegraphic invention, and George D. Roberts of California. Known as the Postal Telegraph Company, it constructed lines from New York to Chicago and St. Louis, and soon added a connection to the Pacific coast by way of Canada, in collaboration with the Canadian Pacific Telegraph Company, a subsidiary of the Canadian Pacific Railway.

In the summer of 1883, Roberts persuaded John W. Mackay, who had made a fortune in silver in the Comstock Lode in Nevada, to take a financial interest in the company. Mackay bought one million dollars in Postal Telegraph stock and was made president of the company.

James Gordon Bennett, Jr., publisher of the *New York Herald* since his father's retirement in 1866, made his permanent home in Paris after 1877. He used the cables heavily for his personal business as well as for the newspaper. A man of strong prejudices, he disliked Jay Gould, and he foresaw the 1884 cable-rate increase and found it unacceptable. Bennett accordingly approached Mackay in November 1883 with a proposal that Postal Telegraph extend its service by establishing a cable connection to Europe. The result was that Mackay and Bennett formed the Commercial Cable Company, with Mackay providing 70 per cent of the capital and Bennett providing the rest, plus an assurance of considerable business for the company. A cable was completed in the summer of 1884 and a second in the autumn, linking New York to London and Paris.

A press rate of forty cents was announced, as contrasted to the seventy-five cent rate on the older cables. Western Union, however, matched the forty-cent rate. Commercial Cable thereupon cut its rate to twenty-five cents a word. Western Union countered again with a twelve-cent rate. Commercial Cable held to the twenty-five cent rate, however, and continued it to 1886, when a forty-cent rate was restored briefly. Western Union followed along in both instances.

Subsequent to an ITU conference agreement in Berlin in 1885, a new official North Atlantic press rate of ten cents a word was made effective in 1886, and that rate continued until 1916.

Internationally, cable rates remained more unstable and inconsistent than telegraph rates, despite agreements at various ITU conferences. Changes in rates and regulations have emerged both from ITU conferences and from radio conferences introduced after World War I, with complications arising from such items as government taxes, currency exchange rates, and blocked currencies. But continuous technical improvements in telegraphic and cable communications have commonly produced economies and greater effectiveness in news transmission and dissemination.

News Agencies and News Coverage 9

The telegraph, hailed as a miracle when its effectiveness was demonstrated in 1844, gained prompt recognition for its potential values in meeting a variety of human needs and requirements. The prospect of instantaneous communication over unlimited distances was a boon indeed.

Leaders in government, directors of industrial and business enterprises, editors; and publishers of newspapers were among those quick to see how the system might be used, with benefits to all. Railroads, by then functioning in many countries and penetrating into new areas, were early in utilizing the wires to advance the safety and efficiency of their operations. One result was that, in many cities and towns, the first telegraph offices were in railroad stations. The "telegrapher" also became a respected figure in his community.

With all this, entrepreneurs saw in the organization and provision of telegraphic service a new and profitable field for commercial exploitation. Where private companies were not so engaged, national governments constructed the lines and maintained the service. Together, these circumstances brought the telegraph into general service at an impressive pace. With cables added in the years after 1851, a world communications network was to be virtually complete by 1900.

Newspapers were prompt to use the telegraph, and so to present news reports from distant places without those intervals of time previously inescapable. News is a perishable commodity, at best, and to receive it by telegraph also was to provide a service appreciated by readers and of benefit to the newspaper itself. For these reasons, newspapers welcomed the telegraph, as they were to welcome the cable.

There was one great problem, however, more serious for newspapers than for any other users of the telegraph. That was the cost. The news never stopped. If a newspaper were to receive reports in any volume, the costs could be financially ruinous.

Some newspapers, more prosperous than others, were certain to use the telegraph rather freely. If even one newspaper used the telegraph to bring in the latest and most important information, any other was virtually compelled to do the same, or invite the loss of its readers to the paper offering the latest reports. Advertising patronage would follow the readers, thus depriving the newspaper of its only sources of revenue, and forcing it to suspend publication. Yet smaller newspapers, in smaller cities, even without local competition, were not sufficiently prosperous to afford any telegraphic service. Actually, the most prosperous papers sometimes incurred such costs that their business managers cried out in distress.

There was a related problem no less serious. Some daily newspapers had stringers or correspondents sending them reports by mail. Traditionally newspapers also had reprinted or rewritten news from other newspapers, received by mail. Usually, they came at no cost since newspapers found it mutually advantageous to "exchange" copies precisely so that they could obtain news in that way.

The existence of the telegraph tended to make these arrangements obsolete. Such material, received by mail, lacked the freshness and immediacy that now seemed necessary if "news" was actually to be new. Further, one newspaper might receive the same news by telegraph that another would otherwise have been able to publish only later, when received by mail, but now would hesitate to use. The logical solution would be for stringers to write and dispatch such news by telegraph, but news could originate anywhere. How many stringers would a newspaper need, and in what places, to cover all possibilities? Obviously, there was no answer to that question, and no end to the expense that certainly would be involved.

So it was that the appearance of the telegraph was not an unmitigated blessing for the newspaper press. The problems it brought were not to be solved overnight. But a solution did come in the formation of "news agencies," made both possible and necessary by the telegraph.

The function of the news agency[1] was to do what no one newspaper could do for itself in rounding up a complete report on the general

---

1   The terms "press association" and "wire service" have been used alternately. The first is misleading, because it is more properly descriptive of organizations of

news of the day to be delivered by telegraph to hundreds of newspapers at the same time. Doing business on such a scale, the agency could obtain the most favorable rates, and then divide the total cost by the number of newspapers served, and perhaps among other clients as well. Further, the costs could be scaled to the size, needs, and prosperity of the individual papers, usually hinging upon relative populations and circulations. An agency might be "cooperative," with costs shared by "member" newspapers assessed on a nonprofit basis. An agency might also be a privately-owned, commercial enterprise, perhaps conducted for profit. But if in competition with a cooperative, nonprofit agency, its charge for service almost necessarily would have to be close to the other. The quality and standards of service also had to be such as to satisfy its "members," "clients," or "subscribers."

An agency might be large, in the sense that it provided a service of news gathered from all parts of the world. They were to be few in number and, appropriately, were referred to as "world agencies." Most undertook only to report of news of their own countries and were therefore to be known as "national agencies." Some were specialized, concentrating on commercial news, on sports, or on diplomatic affairs.

Some agencies were granted subsidies by their governments, perhaps because it was necessary to enable them to exist at all for lack of sufficient financial return from the newspapers of the country, too few in number or lacking in prosperity. Agencies assisted by their governments, for whatever reason, were known, although usually without acknowledging the designation, as "official" or "semiofficial" agencies. The difference rested in the real or supposed obligation of the agency, in return for support, to respond to its government's guidance or direction in the selection and treatment of news reports distributed. There also were other special services for the press, such as commercial "syndicates," many of which were to gain great importance in the distribution, whether by telegraph or mail, of every sort of material, including news.

All of this was far in the future, however, for nothing of the sort existed in 1844 when the telegraph was introduced. When the news agencies began to appear they might be said to have represented a

---

newspapers themselves, such as the Inter-American Press Association. The second is not sufficiently specific since it could apply equally to a service providing only financial or commodity quotations, for example, in addition to which the transmission now may be by wireless or radiotelegraphy. The term "news service" is more acceptable, but still too general and implies no organization.

projection of undertakings previously described in such efforts as were put forward by the Fuggers, by Henry Muddiman, by Edward Lloyd, by the *nouvellistes* of Paris, and by Samuel Topliff of Boston. News agencies related also to the efforts of a M. Tansky, who prepared a Paris newsletter known as *Le Petit Papier*. It was a summary of European news used early in the nineteenth century as a basis for some accounts appearing in Paris and London papers, and perhaps for that special service of foreign news prepared by the British General Post Office in the period just prior to 1800.

The news agencies that were to meet those problems confronting the newspapers in 1844 appeared on the scene with due deliberation. Only five were operating in 1853, approximately ten years after the introduction of the telegraph. Others were to follow, but these first five were the Agence Havas, of Paris; the New York Associated Press; the Wolff'sche Telegraphen Büro, of Berlin; Reuter's Telegram Company, Ltd., of London; and the Agenzia Telegrafica Stefani of Turin.

The first of these agencies had its origin in a service started in Paris in 1832, before the telegraph existed, and then only incidentally directed at the press. It was established by Charles-Louis Havas. As it happened, the founders of two of the other four pioneer agencies, Dr. Bernhard Wolff and Paul Julius Reuter, received their first news training in his employ. These three men in particular were to set the pattern for news agency operation. Their influence and their news agencies were significant in shaping the service of information made available to the peoples of the world from that time to the present day.

The
Agence Havas   Charles-Louis Havas was born at Rouen, France, on July 5, 1783. His family background was Hungarian, where ,the name was Havache. Some member of the family, which was Jewish, moved to France in the late seventeenth or early eighteenth century and settled at Port-Audemer in Normandy, where the family name became Avas and where Havas's grandfather was born in 1717 and died in 1795. His father, born there in 1752, was educated at Caen and became a printer working in Rouen, chiefly with one of the early provincial dailies, *Le Journal de Rouen*. He changed the family named to Havas.

Charles-Louis Havas was privately educated, with emphasis on ancient and modern languages. As a matter of employment, however, he was attracted to the world of business and was so successful that in 1806, at twenty-three, he was in Nantes as a contractor for supplies to the French army. That army sent an invasion force into Portugal in November 1807, marking the beginning of the Peninsular War, and Havas was sent to Lisbon on official business, where he married and remained until 1809.[2] Back in France, he further prospered, established a bank, and moved to Paris. There he became a partner in the publication of the *Gazette de France,* then 180 years old and one of four Paris dailies permitted to appear at the time.

With the collapse of the Napoleonic regime in 1814 and its final defeat at Waterloo in 1815, Havas's fortunes also fell. He was obliged to start a new life to support his family and parents. During the next fifteen years he earned a precarious living by translating news reports and a variety of articles from foreign newspapers, periodicals, and specialized journals. These translations he offered for sale to French government offices and officials, embassies and legations, banks and business firms, and to such newspapers as the *Journal des Debats,* the *Moniteur Universel, Le Constitutionnel,* and undoubtedly to that newspaper, the *Gazette de France* (suspended in 1819), in which he once had an interest.

With the formation of the Louis Philippe government in 1830, many of those who had known favor under Napoleon were restored to positions of substance, and Havas found his own situation improved. Early in 1832, at forty-nine, he established the Bureau Havas. It was in the rue Jean-Jacques Rousseau, near the post office and near the Bourse, or stock exchange. This area was a center of commerce, a center for news, and a section of Paris in which a number of newspapers also had their offices. Here Havas was able to obtain foreign newspapers and periodicals promptly, make his selections and translations, have the hand-written items duplicated through a gelatin or hectographic process, and have copies carried by messengers to clients receiving his service.

Some Paris newspapers were among his subscribers, and he gained others among provincial papers, the reports going by post. Havas purchased two small rival press translation services, Degouve-

---

2 Because of this period spent in Portugal, some accounts have indicated that Havas was born there; others, that his parents came from there. Neither version is correct.

Denainques and Correspondance de Paris, gaining added clients and removing competition. In 1831 Adolph Garnier de Cassagnac, publisher of *Le Constitutionnel*, a Paris daily of some importance, had established a comparable service known as Correspondance Garnier. Havas had produced some material for its use, but in 1835 he absorbed it also as a part of the Bureau Havas, and added still another, the Bureau Borstein, in that same year.

Growing as it was, Havas reorganized his service toward the end of 1835. It was renamed the Agence Havas. This was to mark the formal date and beginning of the news agency that was to gain recognition as the first in the world, and one that continued actively for more than a century, until the World War II German occupation of Paris in 1940 made it impossible to function.

Havas recognized from the outset that the value of his service depended upon its prompt provision of news reports, many of which were derived from foreign publications. He arranged to receive, with the least possible delay, copies of newspapers from London, Brussels, Amsterdam, Berlin, Vienna, Rome, Naples, Madrid, St. Petersburg, and other European cities. In exchange, he provided those newspapers with news from Paris and France. He also began to provide special foreign reports for use by *Le Constitutionnel* and other newspapers, and notably in 1836 by the newly established Paris dailies, *La Presse* and *Le Siecle,* both of which soon attained substantial readership based upon their use of the human interest principle.

Until 1832 Havas had done all of his own translations, but as the service grew he engaged other translators. When his service had become the Agence Havas in 1835, and was gaining clients or subscribers, it became equally impractical to have copies for distribution prepared by hand in sufficient numbers within any reasonable time. Instead, he had the reports set in type in untitled sheets and copies printed for delivery by couriers in Paris and by mail elsewhere.

To supplement what might be obtained from foreign newspapers, and also to speed the reception of information, Havas engaged stringer correspondents in London, Brussels, Berlin, Vienna, Rome, Amsterdam, Madrid, and in other cities. Some of their reports were moved to Paris by semaphore telegraph.

All of this made the Havas service expensive to maintain. The agency had some 200 subscribers, and had gained a subsidy from the French government, but it was dangerously close to financial failure during the first five years of its existence.

In 1840, Havas undertook to use carrier pigeons to speed the news. The London *Times* had used pigeons in 1837 and continued to do so to move news across the English Channel from France. (The "Pigeon Express" had been started in the United States in 1839, and was operating effectively between Boston, New York, Philadelphia, and Baltimore.) Havas also arranged pigeon flights from London and Brussels to Paris and so was able to deliver to Paris afternoon papers news culled from London and Brussels newspapers of that same morning, and also to provide late financial and commodity market reports.

This improved service brought Havas additional clients both in Paris and in French provincial cities. It was the move that tilted the balance and placed the agency on the way to a solid success. By 1845 it had a near-monopoly on the distribution of foreign news in Paris and most of France, with local and national news reports also included in the service. Havas "sub-agencies" were established in that same year in London, Madrid, Rome, Vienna, Brussels, and even in New York. These were, in effect, bureaus or offices presided over by agents, each responsible for forwarding to Paris the news and the newspapers of the city and country.

Also in 1845, Havas used the first telegraph service in France—a line between Paris and Rouen. As the service was extended, he used it both to collect and distribute news. Paris and Brussels were linked by 1848, and by 1850 connections existed with Berlin, Vienna, Rome, and some other European cities. The completion of the first cable beneath the English Channel in 1851 put Paris in direct communication with London. Thus Havas became a telegraphic agency, with its service improved, and a means available to distribute reports to newspapers throughout France and beyond.

Havas retired at sixty-three in 1846 from personal direction of the agency. His sons, Charles-Guillaume and Auguste-Jean-Pierre, had been assisting in the work of the agency for several years. Auguste Havas succeeded his father as director, for Charles was not in the best of health and died in 1874.

The Agence Havas was firmly established by 1846, when Auguste became its managing director. An important change occurred in its internal organization in 1852, however, when it extended its operations as a news agency to enter into the business of advertising.

Those French newspapers receiving the Havas news service in the early 1850s had a competitive advantage, but the cost of the service was such that many papers did not feel able to afford it. No newspaper was larger than twelve pages in size, and none had a circulation in excess of 30,000. There were indications, however, that newspapers might grow larger because business and industry were discovering the value of advertising.

Aware of this trend, Mathieu Lafitte, former secretary-general of the Prefecture of the Seine (the area of Paris), had formed a business there to prepare advertising copy and to sell space in newspapers for the publication of the advertising messages. It was what now would be called an advertising agency, and he also was performing the function of an advertising representative for newspapers, although under a plan differing from modern practice.

Lafitte sought to lease, on an annual contractual basis, and at an agreed rate, one-third or one-quarter of the space in the third and fourth pages of newspapers. He then would undertake to sell that space to business firms for the publication of their advertising messages at whatever price he could arrange. He might profit additionally by preparing those advertising messages for them. Through the lease arrangement, newspapers were assured of a certain revenue. As a further inducement to make such an arrangement, Lafitte offered to the newspapers at no cost a daily *Bulletin de Paris* presenting items of foreign and domestic news for their use.

French newspapers unable to pay the price asked for the Havas news service, or unwilling to pay that price, or interested in a supplementary service, were attracted by the free service. With this double inducement, Lafitte established himself as the advertising representative of enough newspapers to return a certain profit and to have prospects of growth for his enterprise.

Auguste Havas regarded Lafitte's venture as seriously competitive, with the possibility that the *Bulletin de Paris* might develop into a fullscale, independent news agency. Charles Havas, although retired, continued to play an advisory role in the agency and was equally concerned. The two approached Lafitte with a plan of their own.

They proposed that the Agence Havas should make its news service available at no cost to the French provincial newspapers, then about 200 in number, with the understanding that those newspapers would make Lafitte their advertising representative, leasing space to him for resale. Lafitte's *Bulletin de Paris* would be suspended, relieving him of the cost of its preparation and distribution. Because the newspapers would be receiving a better news service, and at no cost, it was to be assumed that most of them would agree to the Lafitte advertising representation, thereby augmenting his income. With a better news service, the circulations of those newspapers might also be expected to rise, which would benefit them in terms of revenue, but also would benefit Lafitte further by supporting a higher rate to be charged advertisers for use of the space under his control. To compensate the Agence Havas for making its news service available, it was proposed that a percentage of Lafitte's return from the sale of advertising space be turned over to that agency.

Lafitte's business was young, as he heard this proposal, and his profits were modest. The number of papers he could expect to serve was limited. But with the leverage provided by the Agence Havas offering of a full and respected news service to newspapers at no cost, he believed that more papers would accept his representation, as was suggested. He believed they might presently include larger papers in Paris, as well as in the provinces, with their larger circulations commanding a higher rate for advertising.

For Havas, its principals believed that the revenue derived from Lafitte's sale of advertising space would represent a bonus, while removing a threat of competition. It seemed to them unlikely that any French newspaper could resist such a bargain in news service, and that the net return might be larger than the agency then received. It seemed, further, that the wider distribution of the Havas service also might impress the French government and bring an increase in the subsidy already granted to the agency.

With both parties seeing advantages in such an association, an agreement was reached on November 2, 1852. The Lafitte *Bulletin de Paris* was replaced by the *Correspondance Général Havas*. As anticipated, nearly all newspapers in France accepted the new arrangement, with Lafitte handling the sale of advertising space in certain of their pages. Some newspapers in Italy and Spain joined in the arrangement. And in due course, the French government subsidy to Havas was indeed increased.

The Agence Havas, performing its news function, and the Lafitte agency its advertising function, were to maintain at least a nominal separation until 1919, although with adjacent offices. The advertising agency proceeded under various names in those years, first as l'Agence Bullier, then successively as the Société Panis, Bigot et Cie.; Fauchey, Lafitte, Bullier et Cie.; Duport et Cie.; Lagrange, Cerf et Cie.; and as the Société Général des Annonces. Its business grew and the Agence Havas also extended its newsgathering activities, and added political correspondence, literary articles, short fiction, and serial novels (feuilletons) to its service. A need for more space for this total operation led to a move in 1870 from the original Havas location in the Hotel de Bullion, at 3 rue Jean-Jacques Rousseau, to 34 rue Notre Dames-des-Victoires, still close to the Bourse and to the offices of many Paris newspapers. There the business was conducted until 1896, when another move was made to 13 Place de la Bourse, still near the original location.

The agency went through important changes in the half-century following its assumption of a double role in news and advertising. Certain of these will be described in their proper context in later pages. As a news agency, it extended direct coverage to Latin America, beginning in 1860, to most parts of Europe in the late 1870s, and to some other parts of the world. It became a key member of the Ring Combination, as examined in later pages. The agency also passed through a critical period at the time of the Franco-Prussian War of 1870-71, but soon regained full strength.

Auguste Havas retired from the direction of the agency in 1873, when he was fifty-nine, and was succeeded by Jacques-Edouard Lebey, who had been instrumental in developing the advertising aspect of the business since 1852. Lebey was to head the agency in both of its functions until 1897. He was followed by Charles Lafitte, son of Mathieu Lafitte, founder of the advertising service in 1850. He was to be managing director until his death in 1924. Meanwhile, Charles-Louis Havas died in 1858, in his seventy-fifth year; Auguste Havas retired in 1873, and his brother, long inactive, died in 1874. Neither left heirs.

Any possible vestige of Havas family control in the agency ended in 1879 when the private company was purchased by Baron d'Erlanger, a Paris banker with international interests. He also bought control of the Fabra news agency in Spain. It had been jointly owned since 1870 by Havas and the Reuter agency of London, but now operated as Havas Fabra until 1893, and under other names until 1926, when it was sold to a Spanish banking group. The Agence Havas itself was reorganized by Erlanger, incorporated (societé anonyme) with a capitalization of 8.5 million francs (then about $1,666,000), and with 17,000 shares of stock offered at 500 francs each, but largely held by Erlanger himself. Thus the Agence Havas entered the twentieth century as one of the great news agencies of the world.

Except for the Agence Havas, there was no other effective news agency in the world prior to 1848. The cost of using the telegraph and cable facilities during the 1845-55 period made news agencies an economic necessity. What one newspaper could not afford to do alone, a news agency could do by dividing the cost among many newspapers.

In the development that took place, the second news agency of the world had its beginning in 1848 in New York. The newspapers of that city, as of others, had been confronted with the problem of telegraphic news costs. The *New York Herald* and the *New York Sun* each had formed its own relationship with newspapers in Boston and other cities since 1839 in the conduct of pigeon-news expresses. Those relationships had been extended during the U.S.-Mexican War of 1846-48, and included use of the telegraph. All of the New York dailies by then were forced to give serious thought to what threatened to become a matter of economic survival.

Telegraphic costs were an important issue, but one easier of solution was the expense of meeting ships entering New York harbor to obtain news. That race had lost much of its meaning with European news reaching New York from Boston by carrier pigeon since 1839, and by telegraph since 1846. Some cooperative arrangements to cover ship arrivals had existed since 1827, but most papers still maintained their independent services. By 1848, however, all six dailies recognized the practice as an expensive and needless duplication of effort. The *Sun, Herald, Tribune, Journal of Commerce, Courier and Enquirer,* and *Express* then formed a Harbor News Association, dividing the cost of running a single news boat to meet incoming ships, and also engaging agents at Boston, Halifax, and Liverpool to expedite the service of European news. From that date, and with that organization, the second news agency is recognized as having begun, and was the origin of the present-day Associated Press.

The second step in that organization was, in fact, directed at the issue of telegraphic costs, and brought the formation in 1850 of the Telegraphic and General News Association of New York. Its function was to arrange for the transmission of news by telegraph from Boston, Washington, and other cities to the same six morning dailies—seven after the establishment of the *New York Times* in 1851. The agency paid for the one transmission, with copies delivered to the member newspapers, each to pay its share of the total cost, plus whatever small supplement might be necessary to maintain the service. In Washington, Lawrence A. Gobright, an experienced reporter, was engaged as a correspondent; a bureau was established at Albany, the state capital; and staff or stringer correspondents were added in some other eastern cities. No one paper received an exclusive report, or could expect to publish a report in advance of other papers. But the cost of telegraphic news was brought within the means of all. This was the essential purpose and value of a news agency wherever located, and an assurance of prompt reports reaching the public.[3]

In 1856 the New York newspapers agreed to a merger of the Harbor News Association and the Telegraphic and General News Association. Together, they became the General News Association of New York, and a year later, more simply, the Associated Press. But even that title was modified in 1858, becoming officially the New York Associated Press. That name was to stand until 1893.

The first two administrators of the NYAP and its parent organizations were men who had acted previously as independent "telegraph reporters," conducting limited regional telegraphic news services of their own. These men were Dr. Alexander Jones in New York, and Daniel H. Craig of the *Boston Daily Mail*. Craig was identified with the earlier "pigeon-express," in Boston. They became the first "agents" or general managers of the New York organizations— Jones from 1848 to 1851, and Craig from 1851 to 1866.

The Telegraphic and General News Association had been spending $40,000 to $50,000 annually for telegraph service in the years 1851

---

3 Newspapers in all cities, New York included, had fought great inconsistencies in the rates and policies of the various private companies. The *New York Tribune*, for example, had attempted to establish an arrangement by which it would share the costs of transmission with another paper, both using the same report. This plan was rejected by the telegraph company, which insisted that, even sharing the dispatch, each paper would be expected to pay the full rate. Another company made no such objection. Thus, a Pittsburgh paper estimated its cost for a long report from Harrisburg at $16; a message of the same length transmitted from Boston to New York, about the same distance, would have cost $330. Apart from the cost differential, this also meant that readers in the area served by the second company were likely to be far better informed.

The effectiveness of the Telegraphic and General News Association in correcting such a situation in New York was that it could present a solid front, representing all of the city's papers, rather than just one or two, in dealing with private telegraph companies. The association also considered entering the telegraph business itself. This suggestion alone put it in a bargaining position, with the companies prepared to accept the arrangement formerly denied whereby a single dispatch, at the regular rate, could be distributed for use by other newspapers at no additional cost.

through 1855. It sometimes paid double the regular rate to assure uninterrupted handling of messages and to assure them priority over other messages filed for transmission at the regular rate. At the time of its reorganization in 1856, as the General News Association, an agreement was reached with the Western Union Telegraph Company, recently formed at Rochester, N.Y., by Ezra Cornell in a merger of thirteen small companies. The agreement called for priority handling of news dispatches in New York state, through the Great Lakes area, including Chicago, and as far south as St. Louis. It also granted favorable rates and other concessions, in return for which the NYAP specifically agreed to abandon any idea of entering the telegraph business itself.

Under its briefly used Associated Press designation in 1857, a contract for an exchange of news was signed with the Reuter agency of London, the world's fourth such organization when formed in 1851. This contract added European reports to the service, although those reports were necessarily late because they had to be carried by ship across the Atlantic until cable communication was established in 1866. At the same time, the exchange arrangement was carrying news of the United States to London.

As the New York City newspapers were proceeding with the organization of an agency to meet their needs, newspapers in other areas were equally concerned with telegraphic costs. They formed their own regional groups in the Middle Atlantic states, in New England, and in New York state. It was the existence of a New England Associated Press and a New York State Associated Press that induced the New York City newspapers to abandon the 1857 designation of "Associated Press" within the year, and to become the New York Associated Press in 1858. The difference, although slight, was intended to reduce a possible confusion arising from similarity of names.

The NYAP was distributing a substantial report by that time. Its location in New York City was an advantage, for it was the leading port and business center, where considerable news originated. The New York City newspapers, as a condition of membership, also made their own news available for general distribution by the NYAP. The NYAP, further, had its own representatives in Washington, Albany, and elsewhere, and was receiving European reports through Reuter. Recognizing the superiority of this total NYAP service, newspapers in other cities, or their regional associations, were not long in seeking an arrangement whereby they might share in those reports. The NYAP responded by agreeing to provide the full report on a fee basis, with the provision that it have a reciprocal right to reports appearing in the newspapers served.

The result was that soon the NYAP service was being used by newspapers throughout New England and New York state, in Philadelphia, Baltimore, Washington, Pittsburgh, Charleston, Atlanta, New Orleans, and other cities. Further, in 1862, a new regional association was established, the Western Associated Press, centering in Chicago. It also formed a contractual arrangement with the NYAP, whose service thereby went to newspapers in Chicago itself, in Cincinnati, St. Louis, Detroit, Milwaukee, and other cities of the Midwest.

The New York Associated Press was absorbed in 1893 by the Associated Press of Illinois, an outgrowth of the Western Associated Press, and embracing the other former regional associations, including the more recently organized Southern Associated Press, based in Atlanta. There were complex reasons for this change, to be examined later, along with further complexities that resulted in the replacement of the Associated Press of Illinois in 1900 by the present-day Associated Press, a New York corporation, with headquarters in New York City.

Wolff'sche Telegraphen Büro

The third telegraphic news agency in the world was formed in Berlin in 1849 by Dr. Bernhard Wolff. Born in Berlin on March 3, 1811, and a member of a family of culture, he studied medicine. His earliest journalistic-related work was in the translation of medical writings. He was skilled in languages and had an interest in finance. Utilizing his linguistic talents, he went to Paris when he was thirty-six and served as a translator during 1847 and part of 1848 in the growing Agence Havas.

In April 1848, following two months of serious disorders in Paris marking the beginning of the 1848 Revolution which extended to most parts of Europe, Wolff returned to Berlin, where he was favorably known, and became editor of the *National Zeitung*. Less than a year later, he established an agency to gather and distribute commercial information. Reflecting Wolff's interest in finance, the service began January 11, 1849, and was called the Berlin Telegraphische Anstalt.

As the name indicates, he used the telegraph lines then being extended in Prussia and beyond to serve subscribers, who were bankers, stock and produce brokers, and businessmen in Berlin and other cities. He applied some of the practices he had observed while with the Havas agency.

Wolff discovered that he was in competition with a number of small local services in Hamburg, Bremen, Frankfort, Dresden, Leipzig, and in Berlin itself. Within the next decade, he was to absorb most of them. In 1855 he took the important step of adding political and general news to what, until then, had been exclusively a service of commercial information. With this, he extended that service increasingly to newspapers. In 1859, he formed an arrangement for an exchange of news with the Agence Havas and with the Reuter agency, by then well established in London and already exchanging news with Havas and with the New York Associated Press. This arrangement enriched the service of all four agencies and, later, also the Agenzia Telegrafica Stefani which had been formed in Turin in 1853, and in 1861 joined in an exchange relationship with Havas.

With these various developments, the Berlin Telegraphische Anstalt underwent reorganizations by which it became known first as the Wolff'sche Telegraphen Büro, then as the Telegraphisches Korrespondenz-Büro B. Wolff, and finally as Wolff's Telegraphisches Büro (WTB).

One of the larger services absorbed by the Wolff agency was the Continental Telegraphen Gesellschaft of Berlin. It was to continue within the Wolff organization, its name preserved, as the Continental Telegraphen Compagnii, and as the Conti-Nachrichten Büro (CNB). The combined agencies were reorganized in 1865, gaining Prussian government financing, and known as Wolff's Telegraphisches Büro-Conti Nachrichten Büro (WTB-CNB).

In practice, the Wolff agency or WTB, undertook to gather and distribute a service of world news in Germany and in other countries, with subsidiary agencies controlled in some of those countries. The CNB operated only within the German frontiers, gathering and distributing national news, with its reports available to the WTB for incorporation, so far as deemed appropriate, in its world service.

Wolff retired as managing director of the combined agencies in 1871, when he was sixty. An associate, Richard Wentzel, assumed direction at that time, to be followed by Dr. Heinrich Mantler from 1887 until his retirement in 1932.

The fourth news agency of importance was formed in London in 1851 by Paul Julius Reuter. He was the third son of Samuel Levi Josaphat, provisional Rabbi of Kassel, capital of the Electorate of Hesse-Kassel, centrally located in the grouping of Germanic states of the early nineteenth century. Born in Kassel July 21, 1816, Reuter's name then was Israel Beer (Ben) Josaphat, with variations sometimes given. As a youth, he became a clerk in a private bank conducted by a cousin in nearby Göttingen, and he continued in banking in Berlin in 1840 to 1845.

There, in 1844, when he was twenty-eight, he was baptized a Christian, adopting the name of Paul Julius Reuter (pronounced Royter). In 1845 he married and left banking to become a partner in a book publishing firm, Reuter & Stargardt.[4] In March 1848, the demands for liberal reforms that had brought violent outbreaks in Paris the previous month were echoed in Berlin. The climate became so uncomfortable that Reuter and his wife left there and moved to Paris, although that was no more peaceful a city, nor would it be for three or four years. In Paris, Reuter became a translator in the Agence Havas, perhaps as a direct successor to Wolff, who had returned to Berlin at about that time, and possibly even through his intervention. He was to remain with the agency only a few months, but it was his introduction to the news business, as it had been Wolff's.

Early in 1849, Reuter and his wife attempted to establish their own service of commercial information in Paris. With the benefit of his experience in banking, Reuter extracted material from French publications and from others for translation into German, and sent handwritten copies to possible clients in the Germanic states. The effort failed and, in the summer of 1849, Reuter and his wife left Paris and its political disorders. He found employment in a bank in Aachen (Aix-la-Chapelle) at the Belgian-Prussian border.

Reuter's experience both in banking and, briefly, in news work of a sort induced him to attempt another service of commercial and financial information in Aachen. With Europe shaken by the revolutionary popular demands for change, political and economic tensions were high. Financial matters and business trends were of urgent importance to bankers, investors, and merchants. Both the

---

4   The Reuter & Stargardt firm continued in Berlin until forced to suspend during the National Socialist regime in the 1930s, but resumed business in Hamburg after World War II.

Havas and Wolff agencies were giving special attention to such subjects, and Reuter undertook to do the same in Aachen and its vicinity. He called his service an "Institute."

Completion of a Prussian state telegraph line from Berlin to Aachen on October 1, 1849, enabled Reuter to receive financial and commercial reports and prices from Berlin. These he made available, for a fee, to bankers and merchants in Aachen and presently added information received by railway mail service from Cologne, Antwerp, Amsterdam, and Brussels, cities where he also found clients for his service.

Early in 1850 a telegraph line was completed between Paris and Brussels. But there remained a gap of about 100 miles between Brussels and Aachen, where the telegraph line from Berlin ended. The fastest train then required nine hours to cover that distance. But carrier pigeons could fly between the cities in two hours. Reuter conceived the idea of using that method, as Havas had done ten years before to bring news to Paris. He arranged with Heinrich Geller, an Aachen brewer, baker and pigeon breeder, for the use of forty birds, and he engaged an agent in Brussels.

Using the pigeons, Reuter improved his service. When the Brussels stock exchange and produce markets closed in the afternoon, and after the last Paris market quotations had reached Brussels by telegraph, these reports were written on tissues in duplicate copies and placed in silk bags fastened under the wings of three pigeons which were then released to fly to a dovecote atop the Geller house in Aachen. Three pigeons were used to assure that at least one would arrive, or that one might outspeed the others. The reports were recovered and copies made for distribution to subscribers by messenger, along with reports received by telegraph from Berlin, and by rail from Cologne, Antwerp, and Amsterdam.

Reuter presently formed a working arrangement with Havas and Wolff. Reports received in Aachen by telegraph from Berlin and by rail from the other cities were forwarded by pigeon to Brussels for clients there, and sent on to Paris by telegraph for Havas. Those messages received from Paris and Brussels, reaching Aachen by pigeon flights, along with Cologne, Amsterdam, and Antwerp reports, were forwarded to Berlin by telegraph for Wolff. At the same time Havas and Wolff were making their reports available to Reuter for use in his service.

Reuter conducted his Aachen Institute service for eight months, achieving a modest success. In that period, however, telegraph lines were being extended to include Cologne, Antwerp, and Amsterdam, among other places, and by December 1850 the last link in a direct Paris-Berlin wire was completed. Toward the end, he was using horses over a remaining five-mile interval, rather than pigeons, to move his reports.

It had been obvious from the start that Reuter's service could not survive the inevitable advance of the telegraph. In expectation of the telegraph's completion, he also had been advised to undertake the establishment of a comparable commercial news service in London, where none existed. Accordingly, after making further inquiries, Reuter closed his Aachen Institute in the summer of 1851 and went to London.

Reuter's move was well-timed. In London, on October 10, 1851, he established what was called, quite simply, "Mr. Reuter's Office," in two rooms in the Royal Exchange Building, with the Stock Exchange, banks, brokerage houses, and many leading business firms in the immediate neighborhood. About a month later, on November 13, the first cable was placed in successful operation beneath the English Channel from Dover to Calais, with ties both to the British telegraph lines and to the lines being extended on the European continent.

Reuter, now thirty-five, had some capital derived from his Aachen venture. There he also had developed an organization of stringer correspondents who could continue to send him information from the continent, using the new cable for urgent reports. He had established friendly relations with Havas and Wolff. He had a certain reputation that enabled him to make an agreement with the London Stock Exchange to provide it with the earliest quotations from the exchanges on the European continent. He was given a privileged status in the London exchange, with access to information originating there. British banks, brokerage houses, business firms, traders, and merchants became subscribers to his service, then providing two reports each day.

When he began in London, Reuter prepared the service personally, but he soon required assistance as he also required more space and would move to larger quarters. His first employee was an office boy, John Griffiths, twelve years old; in 1865, Griffiths was to become secretary of Reuter's Telegram Company, as it then became known. Others were added to the staff, and Reuter's former Aachen correspondents or agents forwarded commercial information from Paris, Brussels, Berlin, Amsterdam, Antwerp, Cologne, Vienna, Athens, and other European centers of trade and commerce. He established offices at Calais and Ostend on the French and Belgian Channel coasts to speed his service. He himself became the agent for financial and business groups on the continent, and provided them with information from London and other centers.

Sigismund Engländer, a refugee from Austria in 1848 after participating in revolutionary activities there, had worked with Reuter in the Havas office; he now became General Agent in Europe for the new Reuter service, and was to play an important role in developing that service through its first forty years.

The Reuter service expanded steadily, and its reputation grew. In time, Reuter arranged to receive reports from India, the Straits Settlement, Java, China, and elsewhere in the Far East, to be brought by ship and other transport to Suez and Marseilles and transmitted from there by wire and cable to London, or later by cable from India and beyond, as service became available. In 1856 he arranged for an exchange of reports with Havas and Wolff, later formalized in 1859. In 1857 he also arranged to provide reports by steamship delivery to the New York Associated Press, receiving its report in return. A Reuter agent was sent to New York in 1858 to select and process the NYAP report for return to London, and a NYAP agent was in London from 1866 when the Atlantic cable became operative.

Even in Aachen Reuter had planned to expand his commercial news service to include political and general news, but the time then was not appropriate in view of the certainty that his Institute would become the victim of the telegraph's advance. In London, however, Reuter soon approached the *Times*, as the daily of greatest prestige, with an offer to provide commercial reports and, on later occasions, with an offer to provide general news reports. The *Times* always refused. By then, leading London dailies had their "own correspondents" providing reports from other cities and countries. They were unwilling to exchange the advantage of such "exclusive" reports for a service provided by Reuter that would be common to all who subscribed, and a service that Reuter also would want credited to his name. Even if less costly, as originally offered, they also feared it might become actually more costly, once they had committed themselves to use it, while possible curtailing their own services.

Persistent in his effort, however, Reuter in 1858 persuaded James Grant, publisher of the London *Morning Advertiser,* then second only to the *Times* in circulation, to give the Reuter service a trial for general news for two weeks at no cost, but on the understanding that if the service proved satisfactory it would be continued at £30 a month (about $145). The *Advertiser*, had a small service of its own, costing it about £40 a month.[5] With Grant's acceptance in 1858, and his continued use of the Reuter service, other London dailies also agreed to receive it on the same trial basis. Only the *Times* held out.

Mowbray Morris, manager of the *Times*, since 1851 had rejected Reuter's repeated offers of service, and was supported in this refusal by John Walter II. Neither saw advantage in replacing or even supplementing the *Time's* own exclusive reports, which had contributed to its circulation leadership of about 60,000, far in excess of any other paper.

In August of 1858, however, even before the *Morning Advertiser* began to receive the Reuter service, Morris was tempted to modify his earlier objections. This was when the North Atlantic cable began to operate. Morris felt that a cabled Reuter report on the American "money market" each day would be an acceptable economy. The *Times* would have to pay £2 a word (nearly $10) for messages from its New York agent. Reuter could pay that rate and still realize a profit by selling the same dispatch to various clients at five shillings a word (about $2.50), as he agreed to do. He further agreed to halve that amount for the *Times* if the paper would credit the Reuter service for the report as published. This would mean a substantial saving for the *Times* over a period of time. The value of an "exclusive" financial table, purely routine, seemed a too-expensive luxury, by contrast. The failure of the new cable on September 1, however, made the issue suddenly irrelevant, and Morris's moment of temptation passed; the matter was dropped.

Before the end of the year, however, with virtually all other London newspapers receiving the Reuter general news service, Morris and the *Times* at last relented and agreed to receive the service. Even so, the *Times* used it as rarely and inconspicuously as possible, viewing it primarily for reference and as a protective backstop on its own reports.

For Reuter, the introduction of the general news service in 1858 marked the beginning of a great advance for his agency, and one that was to find reflection in other agencies, with benefits in world news coverage. The commercial and financial service was also continued at full strength, remaining a part of the total offering to the present time.

The agency was to be reorganized to match its growth, becoming a

---

5 Like the *Times*, the *Advertiser* is a paper surviving to the present day, although itself much changed in character. No longer a general newspaper, it is the organ of the Society of Licensed Victuallers, known as the *Morning Advertiser & Licensed Restaurateur*.

limited liability company on February 20, 1865; what had been "Mr. Reuter's Office" then became Reuter's Telegram Company, Ltd. The agency entered directly into the extension of telegraph and cable facilities in some areas. Offices or "bureaus" were set up in Europe and beyond, with staff correspondents and stringers engaged. Reuter conceived and brought into effect an exchange of news not only between his own agency and the Havas and Wolff agencies but with others throughout the world. Started in 1870, this exchange became known as the "Ring Combination." It made a world news service available to the peoples of nearly all lands.

Reuter directed the agency until his retirement in 1878, and was succeeded by his eldest son, Herbert, then twenty-six. Reuter had been ennobled in 1871 as Baron Julius de Reuter by the Duke of Saxe-Coburg-Gotha. His title was given recognition in 1891 in Britain, of which he had become a citizen, and upon his death at Nice in 1899, Herbert de Reuter succeeded to the title. He directed the agency until his death in 1915. This ended the family connection with the agency. A reorganization followed by which it became Reuters, Ltd.

Agenzia Telegrafica Stefani

The fifth news agency in the world, and the fourth in Europe, was formed by Guglielmo Stefani in 1853 at Turin, ancient city of Piedmont and capital of the province of Torino in northern Italy. Piedmont itself was a part of the Kingdom of Sardinia, dating from 1720, and was, with the areas of Savoy, Nice, and Liguria, administered from Sardinia.

Stefani, born in Venice on July 5, 1819, entered journalism after study at the University of Padua, and became director of the *Gazzetta Piedmontese* in Turin. With the support of Count Camillo Benso Cavour, a leading political figure active in the Italian unification movement, Stefani formed the news agency bearing his name. It provided telegraphic reports to newspapers in Piedmont and in the adjacent states of Savoy and Lombardy. With the Count of Cavour as prime minister in the government of the kingdom from 1851 to his death in 1861, Stefani was well informed, and his agency also was in a position to report the war of 1859 in which France joined with Piedmont against Austria.

By coincidence, Count Cavour died on June 6, 1861, and Stefani died five days later. It is possible that Stefani's widow directed the agency for several years after his death, until their sons, Girolamo and Guerrini, were able to assume that responsibility, and to conduct the agency from 1870 to 1881. In 1861, following Stefani's death, an agreement had been concluded with the Agence Havas for an exchange of news, and the Stefani agency also soon added agents in Rome, Naples, and other cities of the Italian peninsula to strengthen its news coverage. A second agreement was concluded with the Havas agency in 1867 by Stefani's widow and his eldest son, Girolamo, extending the association by fifty years to 1917, with Havas exercising considerable influence in the direction of the Stefani agency.

Even though the capital of a unified Italy was moved to Florence in 1865 and to Rome in 1871, the Stefani agency headquarters remained at Turin until 1881. It was moved to Rome in that year, and Ettori Friedlander assumed its direction for the next eighteen years. The agency never attained the importance of the other four noted in these pages, but it became a substantial national agency reporting the news of Italy to the Italian press and making it available to Havas in exchange for a general world report.

The Stefani family concern with the agency vanished after 1881, and it was virtually a subsidiary of the Agence Havas until the Fascist government under Benito Mussolini established control in Italy in 1922.

National Agencies Multiply

Newspapers did not develop at an equal pace in all countries. Government restrictions, economic circumstances, and varying standards of education and literacy slowed or even prevented growth in a number of areas. The costs and complexities of extending telegraph and cable facilities were elements affecting the situation. So were civil disorders and wars.

From 1853, when the Stefani agency was established, no other news agency of importance was formed until 1860. Within the next decade, however, a dozen agencies appeared, and nearly as many more by 1900. Some became "national" agencies serving most of the newspapers in about ten countries, stressing news of those countries, but receiving world reports from some one of the "big three" agencies—Havas, Wolff, or Reuter. Others were regional or specialized agencies. More than half of those agencies formed between 1835 and 1900 continue to exist today, although some under a modified name or form. The first of the national agencies to be formed after 1853 was the K. K. Telegraphen Korrespondenz-Büro of Vienna which was established in 1860. As with most agencies, whatever the full name, it was commonly referred to by a short title, also used as an identifying logotype attached to its news reports. Thus the Austrian agency was more simply known as "Korrburo." It was an official agency of the Austro-Hungarian government, serving the press in both parts of the dual empire.

It was noted that Wolff, in establishing his agency in Berlin in 1849, was to purchase a number of small local services in various cities of Prussia and adjacent states even before 1860. Such local services, usually concerned with financial and commercial matters, also existed in Holland before and after 1860 under the names of Vas Dias and Belifante and Delamar. The first two became subsidiaries of the Delamar agency of Amsterdam, conducted by Alexander and Herman Delamar.

Among the agencies formed in the 1860s offering something more than commercial information and providing telegraphic service, the first in chronological order following the Korrburo was the Herold Depeschen Büro of Berlin. It was established in 1862 as a privately owned enterprise and provided reports to newspapers in Prussia and other Germanic states.

Four other Berlin agencies appeared. One was the Continental Telegraphen Gesellschaft—known later as the Continental Telegraphen Compagnii, and as the Conti-Nachrichten Büro, and by its logotype as the "CNB." This was the agency combined with the Wolff agency in 1865, and its name preserved in a joint operation. The three other Berlin agencies, all established in 1868 and privately owned, were the Korrespondenz Hofmann, Bösmans Telegraphen Büro, and the Büro Louis Hirsch.

Reference has been made to regional associations formed in the United States in the 1850s, in New England and New York state, and to the making of contractual arrangements to receive and distribute NYAP reports. A third such regional association was organized in Chicago in 1862—the Western Associated Press (WAP)—to serve newspapers in the middle western states. Its importance grew after 1867, and by that time a fourth association, the Southern Associated

Press, based in Atlanta, was in operation also. All were receiving reports from the NYAP, including the Reuter service, and were contributing their own reports in partial exchange.

In London, an agency known as the Central Press of the United Kingdom was established in 1863. In 1871 it was acquired and transformed by William Saunders, a member of Parliament, to become the Central News (CN), a privately owned agency. Reorganized again in 1880, it was made a limited company, providing a report of limited scope, but touching upon both national and international subjects.

A Spanish journalist, Nilo Maria Fabra y Deas, established a private agency in Madrid in 1865. Known as the Centro de Correspondencia, its name was changed in 1867 to the Agencia Telegrafica Fabra (Fabra). It operated as a national agency serving newspapers in Madrid, Barcelona, and other cities in Spain. In March 1870 an agreement was signed between Fabra, Havas, and Reuter by which the Spanish agency became known as Havas-Reuter. In 1879 it came under the full control of the Agence Havas, known first as Agence-Havas, Madrid, and then as Havas-Fabra, with the service extended to Portugal. In 1893 its name was changed once again to the Agence Espagnol et International. Fabra y Deas, founder of the agency, who retained an interest in its direction, died in 1903. It continued to operate as a subsidiary of the Agence Havas until 1926, although reverting in 1919 to its earlier name of Agencia Telegrafica Fabra, with the "Fabra" logotype restored.

News agencies were established in three Scandinavian countries in 1866 and 1867, with news exchange arrangements between them. The first of these was formed in Denmark in 1866 by E. N. Ritzau. Known as the Ritzaus Bureau (Ritzau or RB), it was privately owned and based in Copenhagen, and provided a general news report to dailies in its own country, bolstered by an exchange arrangement first with Reuter and after 1870 with Wolff, which also had a small interest in the agency. Commercial reports went to the Royal Exchange and to business firms in Denmark. Reports were added through bureaus in Hamburg and in Newcastle, England.

In Norway, then in a union with Sweden, but still with its own entity and government, the Norsk Telegrambyrå (NTB) was set up at Christiania (later Oslo) in 1867 as a national agency by A. H. E. Fich, a Dane, who had been one of Ritzau's associates. The Wolff organization had an interest in the agency.

In that same year, the Svenska Telegrambyrå (ST) was established in Stockholm with Wolff support. It continued until 1921, then merged with other smaller agencies formed to become the Tidningarnas Telegrambyrå (TT), a cooperative but nevertheless semi-official agency controlled by the daily newspapers of Sweden.

Two privately controlled telegraph companies in Great Britain, both established in 1846, were the Electric Telegraph Company and the Magnetic Telegraph Company. Beyond conducting a normal telegraph business, each had undertaken to provide a news service and found clients among most of the provincial newspapers then appearing. After Reuter had established his office in London in 1851, and entered the general news field in 1858, he sold a service to what by then was known as the Electric and International Telegraph Company for distribution to provincial dailies.

There was considerable dissatisfaction with these services on the part of the newspapers, however, because of delays, inaccuracies, and high rates; even the Reuter service was lacking in British news originating outside of London itself. At the same time, there was some question in the government as to whether telegraph service in Great Britain should be conducted by private companies or should be placed under government control, as in the countries on the European continent. The International Telegraphic Union had agreed that any country, to have a voting membership in that organization after January 1, 1866, should control if not own the communications facilities within its frontiers. Accordingly, the British postmaster-general arranged in 1866 for a study looking toward the possibility of making all domestic telegraph facilities the property of the British government.

If such a change were to occur, it clearly would mean the end of any provision of news service by a private telegraph company to the newspapers. Considering the dissatisfaction of the provincial newspapers with the service as provided, there was reason for their editors and publishers to consider some alternative means of news service which was better. Among the provincial newspapers, the *Manchester Guardian* was one of the more prosperous, enterprising, and respected. Established as a weekly in 1821, it had become a morning daily in 1855, when the taxes on knowledge were largely removed. Its proprietor was John Edward Taylor, son of the paper's founder. He brought a number of other provincial papers together in an informal agreement by which they would cooperate to gather news throughout the British Isles, including London, and distribute it for their own use. This service began in 1865 and was designated as the Press Association (PA).

The study projected by the postmaster-general in 1866 brought a

recommendation from the commission favorable to British government control of the telegraph lines. In 1868 and 1869, as a result,
Parliament voted the Electric Telegraph Acts, authorizing the
government to purchase all such lines from their private owners, with
control then to be vested in the British General Post Office. The
transfer of ownership was to take place early in 1870, with the
government paying nearly £8 million ($38,880,000) for the lines, on a
generous estimate of value.

With ample time to prepare for this change, the Press Association,
already operating on a tentative basis, was organized officially in 1868
as the Press Association, Ltd. It was to be a nonprofit, cooperative
agency to gather and distribute news for the provincial press, with its
headquarters in London. On the day in February 1870 when the
General Post Office took charge of the telegraph lines, the PA was in
full operation.

An agreement had been made with the Reuter's Telegram Company whereby the Press Association had an exclusive right to distribute the Reuter service to British newspapers outside of London.
There Reuter provided its service direct. At the same time, the news
of the British Isles, as gathered by the PA through its member papers, was made available to Reuter for distribution to papers in
London, to its clients outside the United Kingdom, including the
NYAP, and for exchange with Havas and Wolff.

For a time, the Press Association maintained a subsidiary agency,
the London News Agency (LNA), to provide provincial papers with
news of London and of parliamentary and government activities.
This was soon abandoned, however, with the PA London bureau
providing that coverage. The service of the Press Association
became highly developed in the decades following, and its relationship to Reuter became increasingly close.

Still another British news agency was formed in 1872. This was
the Exchange Telegraph Co., Ltd. (Extel), set up in London to
distribute stock exchange quotations, telegraphically reproduced in
offices by means of a machine devised in the United States by
Thomas A. Edison and Frank L. Pope, and introduced into Great
Britain in 1869. Exchange Telegraph later extended its service to
include a limited presentation of general news, sports news, and
foreign reports, and it continues to operate.

The New Zealand Press Association (NZPA) was formed in 1878
as a national cooperative agency, with headquarters in Wellington.
The Agence Fournier was formed in Paris in 1879 as a specialized

agency to distribute financial and business news to the French press and to business offices. The Ungarische Telegraphen Büro (UTB), began operations in Budapest in 1881 as a branch of the Vienna-based K. K. Telegraphen Korrespondenz-Büro, occupying an official position in the Austro-Hungarian government service to the Hungarian press.

Four other agencies were formed in Europe during the late years of the 19th century. The Agencia Mencheta (Mencheta) was established in Madrid in 1882 by Francisco Peris-Mencheta. It was a privately owned specialized service chiefly concerned with sports reports, and still exists.

Finland, then a grand duchy with some independence under the wing of Czarist Russia, gained an agency in 1887. Because of more than six centuries of earlier Swedish rule, with Finnish as the second language despite the nation's Russian connection, the agency bore a combination Finnish-Swedish designation, and put out a report in both languages. This agency, the Suomen Tietotoimisto-Finska Notisbyran (STT-FNB), was a national cooperative based in Helsingfors (later Helsinki).

Switzerland, a trilingual country, gained a national news agency in 1894, although smaller local and regional services had existed earlier. With headquarters in Berne, the capital, the agency name was used in the three languages of the Swiss confederation, French, Italian, and German: Agence Télégraphique Suisse (ATS), Agenzia Telegrafica Svizzera (ATS), and Schweizerische Depeschenagentur (SDA). In 1899 it absorbed the Agence Berne, its only competitor, and became a joint stock company owned by the Swiss press.

In 1894, also, there was established in St. Petersburg the Rossiyskoye Telegraphnoye Agentsvo, or Russian Telegraph Agency (RTA or Rosta). It was controlled and its service distributed by the Wolff agency, which had been serving Russian newspapers in a direct fashion for at least two decades. In 1902 a second Russian agency was formed to specialize in financial and business reports. Known as the Torgova Telegraphnoye Agentsvo (TTA), or Commercial Telegraph Agency, it was subsidizied by the Russian imperial government, but also received reports from Wolff. In 1904 these two agencies were combined to form an official Russian governmental agency. This was the Sankt-Petersburgskoye Telegraphnoye Agentsvo (SPTA), or St. Petersburg Telegraph Agency. Jointly directed by the Ministries of Foreign Affairs, Interior, and Finance, it continued to receive a world news report through Wolff.

The first news agency in Japan, or any other Asiatic country, was formed in Tokyo in 1886 to serve that country's press, which had been developing since about 1870. With cable service reaching Japan in 1873, Reuter undertook to provide a world news service, but it remained a mail service for some years because the Japanese press was not then prepared to meet cable costs. The first national agency, Shimbun Totatsu Kaisa (Newspaper Service Company), provided no world reports in 1886. Two years later, it was merged with a small, recently formed agency Jiji (Current News), specializing in political news. The combined services were known as Teikoku Tsushin-sha (Empire News Agency), which had official status.

Latin America was late in developing news agency service. The first was the family-owned Agencia Noticiosa Saporiti (ANS). It was established in Buenos Aires in 1900 to serve provincial newspapers in Argentina.

*The Creation
"Ring of the
Combination"*

The Reuter service was well established in Great Britain by 1865. Personally enterprising and constantly encouraged by his European representative, Sigismund Engländer, to extend coverage and service, Reuter began at that time to offer his news and commercial reports to possible subscribers in Belgium, Holland, Denmark, the Germanic states, and Austria. In this, he met with some success.

Reuter also wanted to have a cable of his own from England across the North Sea to serve subscribers in those parts of northern and central Europe. Offices were to be established in Berlin, Vienna, and elsewhere. The Indo-European Telegraph Company line also was to go into operation in March 1865, and Reuter saw the prospect of a service to and from India and perhaps other parts of the Far East and the Middle East.

The Germanic states of central Europe had not yet been unified, and George V of Hanover, ruler of one of those states with a frontier on the North Sea, promised Reuter the right to land a private cable from England on Norderney Island, just off the coast, with the Hanover government providing a cable spur and telegraph connection from there to the capital city of Hanover, and also to Hamburg, Bremen, and Kassel.

To finance such a cable, Reuter needed additional capital. This he obtained by converting his service into a limited liability company. It was the occasion for that reorganization by which "Mr. Reuter's Office" on February 20, 1865, became the Reuter's Telegram Company, Ltd., capitalized at £250,000 ($1,215,000), representing 10,000 shares at £25 each, with £80,000 realized by the sale of shares. Of this, £65,000 went to Reuter for the business he had built. A board of directors was named, including Reuter himself as managing director. The new company took over the existing Reuter service in this technical reorganization, including the concession from the Hanover government.

The new Reuter's Telegram Company, Ltd., and the Hanover government signed an agreement on November 16, 1865, formalizing the Norderney Island cable concession and the proposed telegraph extensions. It also gave Reuter the right to establish an office in the city of Hanover, with the right to conduct both a news business and a private communications service over the cable. That cable was completed in September 1866, running from Lowestoft, on the English coast, to Norderney Island, and telegraph and cable communications were opened on October 3, 1866.

A complication arose, however, after the Hanover government had concluded its agreement with Reuter in November 1865. Count Otto von Bismarck, prime minister since 1862 in the Prussian government under Wilhelm I, had been the moving figure in a plan to form a unified Germany, with Prussia exercising administrative power over the states and principalities of central Europe. In an alliance with Austria, military action in 1864 had resulted in the surrender by Denmark of the duchies of Schleswig and Holstein. They became the joint possessions of Austria and Prussia, with Austria administering Holstein and Prussia administering Schleswig. It did not suit Bismarck's purpose, however, to have Austria occupying an area adjacent to Prussia, and he found a pretext to draw Austria into a brief war in 1866. With Prussia victorious, Holstein also was gained for Prussia and became part of a North German Confederation that included Hanover as well.

Two elements now threatened Reuter's plan to extend his agency service to subscribers in northern and central Europe, with Hanover as his base of operations. One was that Hanover had cast its lot with Austria in the 1866 war and, perforce, had become a part of the North German Confederation to be administered by Prussia. This meant that the Prussian government was in a position to cancel the agreement made by the Hanover government with Reuter, if it wished to do so. The second element arose from the fact that Dr. Wolff had been aware since 1865 of Reuter's intent to enter into competition for clients in an area of Europe where his own agency was active, or might logically become active. He took prompt action to protect his position and by 1866 had established a possible barrier to Reuter's invasion of the territory.

The Wolff agency by 1865 was sixteen years in existence and favorably regarded in Berlin. Through the intermediation of an associate, Richard Wentzel, Wolff gained the support at that time of the Prussian government. A government loan of 300,000 thalers (about $215,000) was granted to the Wolff agency, and an additional 200,000 thalers (about $143,000) to the associated Conti-Nachrichten Büro.

The funds were provided through the Bleichröder Bank in Berlin, a Rothschild-connected enterprise acting regularly for the government and for King Wilhelm I personally. The loan to Wolff carried a provision requiring the reorganization of the Wolff-CNB agency as a limited stock company, much as the Reuter agency had been reorganized. Dr. Wolff continued as managing director, but the reorganization had the effect of placing the actual ownership of the agency primarily with the Bleichröder Bank, although two other banking firms participated. The bankers, then and later, acting on behalf of Wilhelm I and then Wilhelm II, regarded their general relationship to the agency as in the nature of a "sacred duty, not as a business," according to Dr. Edgar Stern-Rubarth, editor of the agency in later years.

From 1865, the banks and the agency alike were responsive to suggestions from the Prussian government and from the German imperial government that followed in 1871. This meant that the Wolff-CNB agency had an official status. In return, it was given information first, or exclusively, and was obliged at least not to counter the government or any official policy. It also received preferential rates on the German state telegraph lines, and enjoyed the right to use a special code for the transmission of financial and market reports.

Despite the prospective competition the Reuter agency might offer the Wolff-CNB agency, the Prussian government did not cancel Reuter's Norderney cable and telegraph concession in 1866. It did, however, demand a new agreement. There was to be no Reuter office in Hanover, and Reuter representatives were discouraged from taking up permanent residence in German territory with a view to seeking and serving clients. The special Reuter wire connecting with the

Norderney cable also was to terminate in Berlin, rather than in Hanover, and the Prussian government contracted to use it for communication with London. With these modifications, the Norderney connection opened on December 31, 1866.

Between that time and 1870 Reuter went ahead with his plan to seek subscribers to his service and was bold enough to do so even in states of the new North German Confederation. In that his success was limited; he found he was operating at a loss in most places by reason of the Prussian government support going to the Wolff agency. The same was true in Austria, where the Korrburo benefited equally from a close relationship with that government.

In Hamburg and also in Bremen, however, Reuter established a solid position. Both were old Hanseatic League ports, cherishing traditions of independence. Neither was inclined to look favorably upon the growing Prussian domination in Germany. Hamburg had held status as a "free city" since the sixteenth century, with its own constitution, and had long been a great center of trade. Five daily newspapers served the city, among them one or two of the best then appearing in Europe. All five became subscribers to the Reuter service. In Bremen an arrangement was made for a news exchange with a small local agency, which in turn served the Bremen newspapers. No objection had been raised to Reuter's offices already established in Berlin, Frankfurt, and Vienna for the *collection* of news, and this enabled him to produce for his subscribers, wherever located, a better service of commercial information and general news from those cities than was available at the time through any other source.

When the Ritzau agency was established in Denmark in 1866, even as the Norderney cable was in process of construction, Reuter had arranged for an exchange of news, to the profit as well as advantage to Reuter. In Holland Reuter purchased control of the Delamar agency of Amsterdam in about 1867, with the Vas Dias and Belifante subsidiaries included. This gave him an outlet for his service in that country.

The Norderney cable venture was a success, for within a year after the service began it was returning £2,000 a month in revenues, and produced a profit for three years. Under the provisions of the Electric Telegraph Acts, the British General Post Office took over direction of the domestic telegraph lines in February 1870, and also purchased the cable for £726,000, as against its original cost of £153,000. It remained available, of course, for agency use.

Reuter's expectation that the Norderney cable might be useful in a tie to the Indo-European telegraph line to India already had proved correct. Operative in 1865, the India connection had given Reuter reason to send a young staff member, Henry M. Collins, to open an office in Bombay in 1867. With cable connections also established with India in 1870, and extended in the next three years to China, Japan, and Australia, Collins opened agency offices and service in many Asian cities and remained in Sydney as Reuter's manager for Australasia for twenty years. Reuter thus was established in Asia and the Pacific.

When a cable connection was established between London and Alexandria in 1869, Reuter had sent a Mr. Virnand to set up an office there and in Cairo. He was to report upon the opening of the Suez Canal in November, and to remain as a correspondent. Another move in 1869 was an agreeement between Reuter and Havas by which they set up a common office in Brussels, with suboffices in Antwerp, Ghent, and Bruges, and joined in the provision of news service to the Belgian press. In 1870 they also joined in an agreement with the five-year-old Fabra agency of Spain, whereby that agency was operated for the next nine years under the name of Havas-Reuter.

Reuter had an extraordinary vision bearing upon opportunities in the news agency field. With his own highly successful agency located in London by 1865, he was aware of the advantages that were his by reason of the great flow of information into London, a center of empire and of world trade. With a special interest in commerce, he was aware of the prospective extension of British cables. He reasoned that if he could use them to maintain and advance his lead in the business of gathering and distributing commercial and general information internationally, he might gain something approaching a monopoly in the world news business.

Sigismund Engländer, Reuter's representative on the European continent and aware of his ambition to occupy such a world position, had urged him from the outset to protect his flanks lest competition arise. Reuter was not deaf to this advice, nor was he idle. He had established news-exchange arrangements with Havas and Wolff in 1856, and formalized them in 1859. He had established an exchange arrangement with the NYAP in 1857, with the Reuter service through that association serving newspapers in the United States and Canada. The Norderney cable venture, the efforts to extend service to newspapers in northern and central Europe, the dispatch of Collins to Bombay and Virnand to Egypt, and the arrangements with Havas in Belgium and Spain all tended to bolster his agency's strength.

Against all that, however, Engländer reminded Reuter that the Agence Havas had established an office in Rio de Janeiro in 1860, and was looking toward Latin American coverage and news distribution; that it had established a relationship with the Stefani agency in Italy, had attained a strength through its advertising agency subsidiary, and had French government support.

Perhaps Reuter did not have to be reminded of those developments. He certainly did not need to be reminded that Dr. Wolff had reacted vigorously to his attempt to extend the Reuter service to subscribers in Hanover and other areas that Wolff might reasonably have regarded as his own. Although Wolff gained Prussian government support, Reuter had emerged better than he might have dared to expect.

Another circumstance at the same period also invited his consideration. In the United States, the regional Western Associated Press had gained strength since its formation in 1862, and in 1866 had sought a more favorable relationship with the NYAP. Although this circumstance will be examined more fully in its proper context, the relevant point here affecting Reuter was that the NYAP rejected the WAP proposals. The WAP thereupon undertook to operate independently. In losing the Reuter service provided through the NYAP, it arranged to receive a world service through the Wolff agency, beginning in December. The Wolff service was moved over the new Atlantic cable, then five months in operation. Reuter countered by providing a more comprehensive service to the NYAP, also by cable. The WAP and the NYAP settled their differences in January 1867, the improved Reuter service then became available again to the WAP, and it ceased to receive the Wolff report. Reuter was led to recognize, nevertheless, the vulnerability of his agency to such competition.

It had become clear that Wolff and Havas could act to curb the extension of Reuter service to other countries, as Wolff had done in the German states by invoking government support, both political and financial; and that either one might extend its own service, as Wolff had so recently done briefly in the United States by invitation, and with Havas undertaking to move into South America and Italy. Neither did Reuter's then tentative position in India and Egypt mean that Havas or Wolff might not make their own entrances into that part of the world if it pleased them to do so. Further, other news agencies were being established. Reuter had reached an agreement with one, the Ritzau agency in Denmark, and also with the Delamar agency in

Holland. But there was the possibility that some new agency, perhaps with a government subsidy, might also become competitive.

In the light of his own ambitions, and considering the limited compass for the growth of his own agency within the British Isles alone, Reuter considered how he might improve his prospects while blocking, or at least containing, possible competition. By 1869 he was ready with a plan.

The Havas and Wolff agencies, at that point, were the only two with the organization and financial weight to rival the Reuter agency. Reuter's concept was that the three might divide the world among themselves, with each to have the exclusive right to "exploit" its own territory. Each would be free to gather news through its own effort in any part of the world. But for the sale and distribution of news each would be limited to its own designated territory, and neither of the other agencies would be authorized to distribute news there.

Within its special territory, each agency might serve any subscriber or client, which could mean sale of its news service to individual newspapers. If a national news agency existed in a country within that territory, the sale would be to the agency, under a contractual arrangement. The agency would receive the report for distribution to its own member papers. The national agency would gather the news of its own country both by direct effort and by receipt of news gathered by its subscribing newspapers. This total service, incorporated in its own report, also would be made available under the contract for delivery to that "world" agency—Reuter, Havas, or Wolff—from which it received service. The national agency would also pay a "cash differential" to the world agency in recognition of the fact that the service received from the world agency was greater in volume than the national report provided in exchange, more costly to gather, and would not otherwise be available at all.

Each of the world agencies, receiving reports from the newspapers or national agencies served, would incorporate that material in its own report, thus enriching the report delivered to subscribers in all parts of its territory—including a number of countries. That same total report would go to each of the other two agencies within the "big three." By this interchange, a complete world report would be made available for distribution by each of the three agencies, and each could properly be called a "world" agency.

The base rate set for the sale of service, and the "cash differentials," scaled to the size and means of the national agencies served, would presumably return a net profit to the world agencies. Each presumably would grow financially stronger, and be respected for the quality of its service and sufficiently entrenched to be safe from competition from other agencies.

This was Mr. Reuter's plan. He had to persuade Bernhard Wolff and Auguste Havas to join with him in the undertaking. He began by going to Berlin to present the plan to Dr. Wolff. Even though the two had been in what seemed to be a growing competition since 1865, with each making some progress, Reuter was in a good position to negotiate, if that seemed necessary. The Wolff agency at that time would be able to contribute news from central Europe, Austria, Norway, and Sweden, but not much else. Reuter, by contrast, could provide news from Great Britain and the British Empire, from the United States, and from India and Egypt. He occupied a position in Denmark and Holland, had formed an association with Havas in Belgium, had his own reports coming from Berlin and other German cities, and also was established in the provision of news to newspapers in Hamburg and Bremen.

Wolff agreed to become a party to the plan Reuter put forward. A general agreement was reached, subject to approval by Havas, on the territories in which each of the agencies would have its "rights." An understanding was reached that Reuter would leave central and northern Europe exclusively to Wolff, withdrawing from Hamburg and Bremen when his contracts with papers there expired, and transferring to Wolff his agreement with the Ritzau agency in Denmark. Reuter would retain his position in Holland, however, and also continue with Havas in Belgium.

Reuter then proceeded to Paris. He felt less personal warmth toward Auguste Havas than toward Dr. Wolff, and even less toward his associate in the direction of the Agence Havas at that time, Charles Emard. They were nevertheless in amicable alliance in Belgium, and the discussions in Paris were as successful as they had been in Berlin.

The result of these various negotiations was an agreement between the Reuter, Wolff, and Havas agencies following the general plan conceived by Reuter. It was to become effective in January 1870. Later referred to as a "treaty," it was a contractual arrangement to which national agencies also became parties.

The association of agencies, ultimately to include about thirty, was to be variously known as the League of Allied Agencies (les Agences Alliées), as the World League of Press Associations, as the National Agencies' Alliance, and as the Grand Alliance of Agencies. In the view of some, it was a "cartel," which suggested that its influence on world opinion was shaped by governments to suit their own purposes. Most commonly, it was referred to simply as the "Ring Combination."

The basic contract, as drawn in 1870, set the "reserved territories" for the three world agencies. Each agency made its own separate contracts with the national agencies or other subscribers within its own territory. Provision was made for a few "shared" territories in which two, and sometimes all three agencies had equal rights. The basic treaty was subject to periodic review and renewal, usually every ten years. Changes and modifications were made on some such occasions with reference both to the reserved and the shared territories.

In practice, the Reuter agency tended to dominate the Ring Combination. Its influence was greatest because its reserved territories were larger or of greater news importance than most others. Reuter also had more staff and stringer representatives throughout the world and so contributed more original news to the pool. As Reuter had foreseen, British control of more than half of all cable lines in the world made London itself an unmatched news center, further enhanced by British commercial, financial, and empire activities.

The exchange nevertheless gave strength to all three agencies, as Reuter also had anticipated, and contributed immeasurably to the volume and quality of information available to millions of person in all parts of the globe.

By the terms of the original 1870 agreement, and with notations of some modifications, the division of the world into three "reserved territories" for distribution of news was as follows:

Reuter's Telegram Company, Ltd.

Great Britain and the British Empire, with Canada yielded in 1893 for direct service through the Associated Press of Illinois, and the Associated Press after 1900.

The United States until 1893, when service was handled through the API and the AP after 1900, distributing the Reuter reports.

Holland; the free city of Hamburg until yielded to Wolff in 1872, but with some service continued to 1900; Belgium, shared with Havas until 1920, when a new Agence Télégraphique Belge, formed as a national agency, bought the Reuter-Havas interest; Spain, shared with Havas in 1870-79 through control of the Fabra agency; Greece and Turkey, shared with Havas and Wolff until 1914; Greece, shared with Havas from 1914 to 1918; Greece and Turkey, shared with Havas from 1918.

Egypt and the Sudan from 1890, when yielded by Havas; the Belgian Congo (now Zaire), shared with Havas from formation in 1885 to 1920; British Empire areas in Africa.

China, Japan; Indo-China until yielded to Havas in 1890; British Empire areas in Asia and the Pacific; Persia and mandated areas in the Middle East from 1920.

South America, shared with Havas from 1871 to 1890; Mexico and Central America, shared with Havas, and shared with the API from 1893, the AP from 1900, along with West Indies.

Agence Havas

France and French overseas possessions in Africa, the Pacific, and the West Indies. Mandated areas in Middle East from 1920.

Belgium and the Belgian Congo, shared with Reuter until 1920, then served by Havas through new Belgian national agency (see above); Italy until 1922 through relations with Stefani agency; Spain, shared with Reuter from 1870 to 1879, through Fabra control; then Spain and Portugal until 1926 through that control, and later by contract; Switzerland; Greece and Turkey, shared with Reuter and Wolff until 1914; Greece, shared with Reuter from 1914 to 1918; Greece and Turkey, shared with Reuter from 1918; Russia, shared with Wolff from 1894 to 1914, then by Havas alone until 1917. (See Wolff for 1920 sharing.)

Egypt and the Sudan until 1890, when yielded to Reuter; Angola, Libya, Eritrea, and Italian Somaliland (now Somali Republic).

Indo-China from 1890, when yielded by Reuter.

South America, shared with Reuter from 1871-90, then by Havas alone until 1918, when Associated Press shared; Mexico and Central America, shared with Reuter, with API and then AP sharing equally from 1893.

Wolff's Telegraphisches Büro

Prussia, the North German Confederation and south Germanic states and principalities, or the German Empire, as it became in 1871; German colonies and possessions, as later added in Africa and the Pacific, until 1918.

Austrian-Hungarian Empire; Austria and Hungary separately after 1918; Denmark, yielded by Reuter in 1870; the free city of Hamburg after 1872, as yielded by Reuter; Norway and Sweden, Russia until

1914, shared since 1894 with Havas; Greece and Turkey, shared with Reuter and Havas until 1914; Turkey alone from 1914 to 1918; Poland, Rumania, Bulgaria, shared with Havas after 1918, along with new Baltic States, Czechoslovakia, and Yugoslavia, from 1920.

The Ring Combination was shaken at the very outset by the Franco-Prussian War of 1870-71. This broke the exchange relationship between the Havas and Wolff agencies, and placed the Havas agency in administrative and financial difficulties that threatened its survival. It did survive, but European political maneuverings threatened the Ring Combination in the late 1880s. Both of these crises will be examined in other pages.

Correspondents Take the Field   10

Events do not occur in a vacuum. Whether taking place in the life of an individual or a nation, an event has roots in the past and casts a shadow on the future. It may be an event of concern only to a few; but it may also be an event, or series of related events, of interest and importance to millions throughout the world, and conceivably bearing upon the lives of later generations.

Events obviously make news. For reasons already explored, the development of the press as an information medium was slow. Its very existence represented a great advance, and evidence of special enterprise in news gathering had appeared in the period just before and after 1800. Even then and for some time to follow many events were unreported, poorly reported, or reported very late. It was not until the decade of the 1840s that a truly substantial advance began in press performance and development.

The change then grew out of the needs of the industrial revolution, with an easing of government restraints upon the press. Better newspapers available at a lower price, and newspapers made more appealing by a broader concept of the news and applications of the human interest principle, brought a greater readership. Larger circulations, with a consequential growth in advertising volume, brought a prosperity enabling some newspapers to afford larger staff organizations to gather and process the news. The very important introduction of telegraphic and cable transmission of news, which brought a sense of immediacy and freshness to reports, permitted the growth of newspapers in cities and towns wherever located. News agencies aided in the further gathering and distribution of information.

From the 1840s, therefore, reporters, stringers and correspondents became increasingly active. This activity began in the newspaper's own community, then nationally and progressively in foreign fields. The national and foreign activities were sponsored chiefly by some London and New York morning dailies. With rare exceptions, it was not until the 1870s that some newspapers in other countries began to show any comparable enterprise. News agency services drew heavily upon the newspapers for their own distributed reports.

The world was largely at peace after 1815, until the mid-1840s. Then the U.S.-Mexican War of 1846-48 occurred, the "revolution of 1848" affected most of Europe, the Crimean War of 1853-1856 followed, and a brief Italo-Austrian War of 1859. The clash, suspense and violence of these wars received close press attention.

Newspapers had not been able to provide effective coverage even of the Napoleonic wars of 1803-15, to say nothing of earlier conflicts, but some now were prepared to attempt such reporting. From that time, the attention given by the press to the coverage of wars, and the attention given in literature to the activities of "war correspondents," became somewhat misleading. It would almost seem to suggest that war was the "main" news, with more substantive matters relegated to a positon of relative unimportance, and that war correspondents were virtually the only newspaper correspondents.

Neither of these suggestions is valid. Almost coincidentally with the war coverage beginning in the 1840s, other correspondents were beginning to move about the world in increasing numbers and were establishing themselves as staff or stringer representatives in various capitals, with their reports occupying space in the newspapers. But it is true, nevertheless, that the press was to give prominent display and much effort to the reporting of wars.

It could not properly have been otherwise, since the press by then was at last in a position to provide coverage. However regrettable, wars occurred, and they had importance. They affected the lives of many and the public needed to be informed of the issues and events. The press was the only means of conveying the information. For the press and for the correspondents it was a difficult, costly, and hazardous responsibility, performed with varying degrees of success.

Ironically, the necessities of war reporting seem almost always to have brought advances in the standards of general news reporting that might not otherwise have occurred, or would have been delayed. Reporters acting as war correspondents learned hard lessons, some of which were to improve the coverage and writing of news in times of peace. The urgency of war coverage forced the press to act with little concern for expense, which brought advances in technology and communication that had lasting benefits. The drama and suspense of war advanced the readership and circulation of newspapers, helped establish the "habit" of newspaper reading, and so brought to the press a greater prosperity, with a new cycle of growth translating into a still better service of public information.

In all this, beginning in the 1840s, newspapers gained such general acceptance, so firm a position economically, and such influence that doors were opened more freely to them and to their representatives in the pursuit of news.

*The U.S.-
Mexican War,
1846-48*

Without discounting earlier press efforts to extend and improve its coverage of events at home or abroad, a new era in the reporting of national and world affairs may be said to have begun at the time of the U.S.-Mexican War of 1846-48. The reporting of that war, while suffering from some of the defects of the past, did accelerate the transmission of information, provided some lessons in coverage, and established a cooperative effort between newspapers on a scale that had not existed before. These gains contributed toward the formation of the New York Associated Press, a larger cooperative venture, and one of permanent value.

The seeds of the war were planted in 1821. Mexico gained its independence from Spain in that year and became the Republic of Mexico. The northern boundary of its territory, deriving from the Spanish conquest and claims dating from the sixteenth century, stood near the forty-second parallel, running eastward from the Pacific, approximately at the present-day California-Oregon border, through the Great Salt Lake and beyond. The boundary then turned generally southeast to the Gulf of Mexico at a point about 200 miles west of New Orleans.

One of the early acts of the new Mexican government was to grant a right to Stephen Austin, a resident of Missouri, to settle with a group of U.S. citizens in an area designated by the Mexican republic in 1824 as the State of Texas.

The U.S. settlement was made and other settlers followed. They became restive under Mexican restrictions—one a prohibition against slave-holding. The United States government offered without success to buy the area from Mexico. From 1833 relations between U.S. settlers in Texas and the government of Mexico became increasingly tense. An armed clash at the Alamo in San Antonio in 1836 was a defeat for the settlers, but they were victorious at San Jacinto a month later. In 1837, led by Sam Houston, they declared Texas an independent republic—the "Lone Star State"—and petitioned Washington for its annexation to the United States.

Annexation was a controversial issue for both Mexico and the United States, but in March 1845 the Congress voted its approval. Mexico immediately broke off diplomatic relations, and both countries soon had troops on the opposite sides of the Rio Grande River. Negotiations proceeded, with the United States seeking the purchase, also, of California and New Mexico territory, but was rebuffed, and Mexico reaffirmed its right to Texas. A skirmish between Mexican and U.S. troops near Matamoras in April 1846 led to a U.S. declaration of war in May. Military and naval action followed, with U.S. forces moving into California as well as Mexico itself. The campaigns continued through 1847.

United States troops entered Mexico City in September 1847. Tentative peace negotiations began at that time. A new Mexican government took office in January 1848, a peace treaty was signed at Guadalupe Hidalgo in February, ratified in May, and made effective in July. By its terms Mexico relinquished all claims to Texas north of the Rio Grande, and ceded California and New Mexico territories to the United States, a total area of more than a million square miles. The United States was to pay $15 million to the Mexican government, and adjusted claims of Mexican citizens to the amount of $3,250,000.

The possibility of the war had existed since 1836, when the settlers had unilaterally proclaimed the independence of a Republic of Texas. James Gordon Bennett recognized the volatile situation and arranged in 1838 for stringers to serve the *New York Herald* in Mexico City and in the new town of Houston, then the designated capital of the Texas republic (the capital was moved to Austin in 1846.) Thomas Larkin also was a stringer in Monterey, California, in 1846-48. Bennett was in Europe during much of 1846 and 1847, but he had arranged in advance with the *New Orleans Picayune*[1] for a

---

1   The *New Orleans Picayune* was established as a daily in 1836 to serve a port city then of about 45,000 population. It took its name from a coin used during the time of the Spanish presence in the area (until 1801), and worth about six cents, the price of the

special service of news to be forwarded to New York from that U.S. city closest to the scene of any conflict that might occur between Texas and Mexico, or the United States and Mexico.

To this extent, the *New York Herald* was prepared to provide special reports of the Mexican war when it began in 1846, and so also was the *New Orleans Picayune*. The *New York Sun* later formed an association with the *New Orleans Crescent*. The *Philadelphia North American*, founded in 1839, and the *Boston Journal*, founded in 1833, were both successful newspapers, and became associated with the *New Orleans Delta*. Two other New Orleans dailies, the *Tropic* and the *Bee* also covered the war when it began. The *New York Herald* extended the news-exchange arrangement it had had in the conduct of the "Pigeon Express" since 1839 with the *Boston Daily Mail*, the *Philadelphia Public Ledger*, and the *Baltimore Sun*; those papers shared in the cost of the special war service, and the *New York Journal of Commerce* was added to the group. The *New York Sun* association with the *New Orleans Crescent* was shared with the *Charleston Courier*.

Nearly a score of correspondents were involved in the coverage of the war. While the reports usually were not notable for volume, speed of delivery or quality, the general coverage still was to mark a great advance over the reporting of any previous war or revolution.

As the war began, Kendall of the *Picayune* was the first correspondent in the field, attached to the U.S. Army forces under General Zachary Taylor, and he remained in Mexico throughout the war. He was present during the major engagements at Monterrey, where he captured a Mexican flag, at the Battle of Buena Vista, at the capture of Vera Cruz by General Winfield Scott, and he was wounded during Scott's invasion of Mexico City.

The Mexican press, scarcely developed at the time, provided no direct coverage of the war, and the only correspondents in the field were representatives of U.S. newspapers. Kendall unquestionably was the most effective. His reports were numerous, informative, well-written, and accurate. He has been called both "the first American war corespondent" and the first "modern" war correspondent.[2]

---

paper. Its founders were George W. Kendall and Francis Lumsden. Kendall, dominant in the paper's establishment and in its almost immediate success, was a New Hampshire-born printer, with experience in New York and Washington. He also knew Mexico, but none too pleasantly, having been captured there while on a trading expedition about 1840, and held prisoner for several months in Mexico City under harsh conditions.

2 Both references have been contested on the basis of various interpretations. There

The names of three other memorable correspondents emerged in Mexico during the war. James L. Freaner of the *New Orleans Delta*, signing his dispatches "Mustang," was writing also for the *Philadelphia North American* and the *Boston Journal*. William C. Toby, also a correspondent for that Philadlephia paper, produced a small paper of his own in Mexico City during the period of its occupation by U.S. troops, from September 1847 to June 1848. Lumsden of the *Picayune* was also in the field.[3]

Three aspects of coverage in Mexico are noteworthy. The daguerreotype process of photography had been developed successfully in France in 1839. New as it was, several photographers used the process to produce "tintypes" of war scenes, a first effort of its kind. There was no way then to reproduce them in any printed form, nor was there any public display of the views, so far as is known. Some remain in archives and have been reproduced since, but with no reference to the names of the photographers.

Another "first" in a war situation appears to have been the publication of an army newspaper, the *American Flag*, produced at Matamoras on the Rio Grande River opposite Brownsville, Texas, which was headquarters for the U.S. Army in 1846 as the war began. The paper became a source of information for some correspondents.

The third element in coverage was the organization of a system for moving correspondents' reports from Mexico to New Orleans, and

---

had been Isaiah Thomas's eye-witness report of the Battle of Concord during the American Revolution, as published in his *Massachusetts Spy* of Worcester. During the War of 1812 an account of the Battle of New Orleans had been written by James M. Bradford, former editor of the *New Orleans Gazette,* and founding editor of the weekly *Time Piece* of St. Francisville, Louisiana, in which his report appeared. Neither of these men was a special correspondent, in the same sense as Kendall or some others. Thomas was in Concord by chance on the day of that engagement, and Bradford was a soldier at the time he wrote.

The *Morning Post* of London had claimed the distinction of the first modern war correspondent for Charles Lewis Gruneisen, its special staff correspondent reporting the Carlist War in Spain in 1837. Even though Crabb Robinson, for the *Times,* and other correspondents had written even earlier of the Peninsular Wars in Spain in 1808-09, the *Post* contended the Gruneisen was the first correspondent actually "in the field" and therefore the first "war correspondent."

The *Times* was to call its staff correspondent, William Howard Russell, the "first and greatest war correspondent" because of his reporting of the Crimean War during 1854-56. He was in the field and he performed with high distinction, but he was not the "first" war correspondent, since both Gruneisen and Kendall certainly preceded him. He may have been the "greatest" in the period prior to about 1860, but not necessarily thereafter, for other correspondents demonstrated their own talents.

3 Letters from soldiers addressed to their families sometimes were used in newspapers appearing in their home towns or cities.

from there to New York and other cities of the United States. The most effective use of the system was that by which Kendall's dispatches were forwarded to New Orleans and sent on to the *New York Herald,* adding to that newspaper's reputation for news enterprise.

Kendall's dispatches were carried by riders to Vera Cruz or Port Isabel on the Gulf coast, and moved from there to New Orleans by ship. This came to be known as "Kendall's Express" and proved generally reliable, although some riders were ambushed and killed, and it was expensive to maintain. Other New Orleans papers used a similar system with their own riders, even though the dispatches might then be carried to New Orleans in the same vessel. On one occasion, Kendall chartered a special steamship from Vera Cruz to New Orleans at a cost of $5,000.

Copies of Kendall's dispatches, as used in the *Picayune,* were carried north by a "Great Southern Daily Express," organized by the *New York Herald* with costs shared by the associated newspapers. The express used sixty fast horses in a rider-relay from New Orleans to Richmond, Virginia, setting out, not "daily," as the name implied, but when dispatches arrived. The relay ended at Richmond because by 1846 the telegraph had been extended to that city. A spur also existed from Richmond to Baltimore and to Washington. From Baltimore the messages moved northward to Philadelphia and Newark—to be taken by messenger from there by ferry across the Hudson River to New York City, and then forwarded by wire to Boston.

This routing cut twenty-four to forty-eight hours off the ten days then usually required for mail carried by postriders from New Orleans to New York, and at least another day for delivery in Boston, thus saving as much as seventy-two hours. Because of delays between Mexico and New Orleans, however, there still was a lapse of two to five weeks before news of events in Mexico could appear in New York and the other cities of the north.

The enterprise of the *New York Herald,* in its association with the *New Orleans Picayune,* was nevertheless such as to enable those newspapers and the related group to publish reports from the Mexican front from one to five days ahead of their competitors.

The *New Orleans Delta-Philadelphia North American-Boston Journal* dispatches moved up the Mississippi and Ohio rivers to Cincinnati, and eastward from there by telegraph. The *New Orleans Crescent-New York Sun* routing involved a rider-carry between

Mobile and Montgomery, Alabama. This saved a day over regular mail delivery, but still failed to match the *Picayune-Herald* system.

The *Herald* received reports on the California aspects of the war through its stringer in Monterey, Thomas Oliver Larkin. They were even later in reaching New York than the reports from Mexico. Since no other New York paper was equally represented in California at the time, the *Herald* still led with exclusive accounts.

In its leadership, the *New York Herald* sometimes published Mexican war reports before the War Department in Washington had received its own dispatches on the same actions. This irked the department and, to avoid possible repercussions, the *Herald* arranged to have copies of its dispatches forwarded to the department from Baltimore. Even with that, when the Treaty of Guadalupe Hidalgo concluding the war was signed on February 2, 1848, the *Herald* published the terms of settlement before they were officially announced in Washington. The *Herald*'s capital correspondent, then John Nugent, was summoned before a senate committee for questioning on how the paper had obtained the information. His responses were such that he was cited for contempt.

The Crimean War, 1853-56

The Crimean War arose out of a controversy between France and Russia over custody of the "Holy Places" in Palestine. Russia also sought a protectorate over the Orthodox Christian churches in Constantinople, and brought pressure on the Turkish government by occupying principalities in the Danubian area then counted as Turkish territory. The dispute escalated, with Turkey declaring war on Russia in October 1853, battling Czarist forces in parts of southern Europe, and suffering a serious loss when naval vessels and transports were destroyed in the Black Sea in November.

France's Emperor Napoleon III, partly to win favor with the clerical element in his country, sent a French fleet to the Black Sea to give support to Turkey, and persuaded Great Britain to do the same, as well as to join France in a declaration of war on Russia in March 1854. In September Anglo-French forces were landed in the Crimea, with an attack directed at a Russian defensive position at Sebastopol. Battles followed there, at the Alma River, Balaclava, and Inkerman, and continued until December 1855. Sardinia (Piedmont) had joined in the Anglo-French-Turkish alliance in January 1855.

The death of Russia's Czar Nicholas I in March 1855, a disposition on the part of his successor Alexander II to make peace, and an Austrian threat in December 1855 to enter the war if Russia persisted in its refusal to accept peace proposals advanced at a Vienna conference by France and England the previous year, brought a Russian agreement to yield. A peace treaty was signed at Vienna in February 1856. It was a victory for the alliance, and especially for France and Great Britain, with both Russia and Turkey making concessions, but with Turkey establishing more amicable ties with the western European powers.

This confrontation, as contrasted to the somewhat individualistic coverage of the U.S.-Mexican War, brought the first grouping of news correspondents on overseas assignment, whether in war or peace. In that, it made press history, as well as political history. It was a strange grouping, as compared to some later occasions, in that the correspondents were almost exclusively representatives of London publications, even though five nations were involved in the war. Seven London publications were represented, but more correspondents served the *Times* than any other, and the most noteworthy accounts appeared in that newspaper.[4] The first artist-correspondents appeared in overseas reporting, and photographers were present again.

The chief correspondent in the field for the *Times* was William Howard Russell, then thirty-three, already experienced, and about to become the first "big name" in international news reporting. A native of Ireland, Russell had written for the *Times* since his student days at Trinity College, Dublin, in 1841. He had reported the Irish potato famine in 1845-46, became a regular member of the paper's staff in 1848, was a parliamentary reporter, and gained his first experience as a war correspondent when he accompanied the Danish army in July 1850 during the early phase of Denmark's contest with Prussia and Austria over the disposition of the duchies of Schleswig and Holstein.

Following the British declaration of war on Russia in March 1854 in support of Turkey, Russell sailed with a detachment of troops bound for Malta. He had expected then to return to England. In Malta, however, he received instructions from the *Times* to stay with the

---

4 The *Times* by 1854 led all other newspapers in the world in original coverage of international news. It also led in daily circulation in Great Britain, and possibly in the world, with 55,000. This was more than three times the circulation of the next four London papers combined. These were the *Morning Advertiser*, with 6,600; the *Morning Herald*, down to 3,500; the *Morning Post*, with 3,000; and the fading *Morning Chronicle*, with 2,500.

troops and proceed with them to the Crimea. Landing there in September, he remained through the war.

During the next fifteen months Russell gained a personal reputation beyond that of any journalist previously engaged in international reporting, and his work also enhanced the reputation of the *Times*. Some of his battle accounts, although prepared under great stress, were vividly descriptive, and some of his phrases passed into the language, notably a reference to "the thin red line" of British infantry at Balaclava in October 1854. A report of "the charge of the Light Brigade" in the same battle inspired Alfred Tennyson's poem bearing that title.

Other Russell reports revealed such inefficiency in British army direction, supply, and equipment as to bring about the fall of the Aberdeen government in Britain, and a reorganization of the War Office. His accounts of great casualties and of the poor care given the sick and wounded among the troops so moved Florence Nightingale, then twenty-five and superintendent of a London nursing home, that she organized a volunteer nursing group, gained the opportunity to go to the war zone, and there arranged suitable medical care and hospital facilities.[5]

Russell's exposure of army blundering, while it possibly saved the situation, antagonized British commanders in the Crimea and irritated the War Office in London. He was accused of providing information useful to the enemy, was denounced by some as being nearly treasonous, and even Queen Victoria and Prince Albert were critical. In the field, he was denied courtesies and facilities that might logically have been accorded a correspondent for an important newspaper covering his country's army in a critical war. He was denied information, kept at arm's length, so far as possible, and was accorded prejudicial treatment in the matter of getting his reports back to London in situations where the army controlled communications. His position might have been even worse if he had not received strong support from the *Times* itself, and from John Delane, its editor.

Lord Raglan, commander of the British forces in the Crimea until his death in June 1855, had been with Lieutenant General Sir Arthur

---

5 Florence Nightingale's accomplishments during the war gained her fame and respect, permitting her to proceed in what became a revolution in hospital and nursing practices, the establishment of training schools for nurses, world-wide advances in sanitation and public health progrs, and, indirectly, brought the International Red Cross into being through the Geneva Convention of 1864.

Wellesley (later Lord Wellington) in the Peninsular War in Spain in 1808, and later at Waterloo in 1815. Raglan shared Wellington's prejudice against all correspondents, as conceived in Spain, and would have nothing to do with them in the Crimea. Raglan's successor, General Sir William Simpson, carried on this same prejudice. He called correspondents "the curse of modern armies," and spoke specifically of the "low and groveling correspondents of the *Times*."

Whether this latter slur included Russell cannot be said, but the leading historian of the Crimean War, A. W. Kinglake, who had himself been with the British army during that war, was to take quite a different view. In his history of the war, he gave high praise to Russell, to the *Times*, and to Delane. Had it not been for Russell's fortitude, ability and ingratiating personality, in Kinglake's retrospective analysis, essential facts might never have become known, nor corrective action taken in time to bring victory rather than defeat in the war. Credit also was given to the sturdy support given Russell at home by his editor, and to the prestige of the *Times* itself.

Even though Russell has received most attention from writers and historians for his work during the war, others were actively engaged, faced the same problems and prejudices. Except for Gruneisen in Spain in 1837, and the few reporting the U.S.-Mexican War, they were the first war correspondents. With no precedents or accepted practices attaching to their presence in a theater of war, they were almost entirely on their own, forced to find their own food, shelter, transport, and means of communication.

When the war was declared in 1853, the *Times* had Dr. Humphrey Sandwith, a practicing physician, serving as a stringer in Constantinople. He was soon followed by John Barklay and a Captain Twopenny until March 1854, and then by Thomas Chenery, a young barrister. Chenery's reports reinforced Russell's as an influence in bringing Florence Nightingale and her nurses to the war area. Frederick Hardman, formerly in Madrid for the *Times*, succeeded Chenery in Constantinople in 1855. Ferdinand Eber, who had left Hungary, his native country, after playing an active part in the 1848 revolution there, had been writing for the *Times* from Athens; he joined Russell in covering the war in the field. Andrew Archibald Paton, formerly writing from Hungary, also was in the field briefly. Henry Stowe, who did commendable work, died of fever, one of the first casualties of war correspondence. A second victim was Lieutenant Charles Naysmith, an officer of the East India Company's

Bombay Artillery, but on leave in the Mediterranean as an observer with the Turkish army. He also wrote for the *Times* until killed during the defense of the fortress of Silistria, on the Danube. T. M. O'Bird, Vienna correspondent since 1848, remained there, but produced reports relevant to the war, and also helped facilitate communications between the war zone and London.[6]

For other London publications, one of the first correspondents to arrive in the Crimea was Edwin L. Godkin of the *Daily News*. Irish-born, like Russell, but only twenty-three, he remained throughout the war. Again, some of his reports reinforced Florence Nightingale's determination to undertake her mission in the war area. The *Morning Post* was represented by George Alfred Henty, barely twenty-two, who arrived early. The *Morning Herald* sent Nicholas A. Wood, and writers were present also for the *Morning Chronicle*, the *Morning Advertiser*, and the *Standard*. An average cost for maintaining a correspondent in the Crimea is estimated to have been close to £200 a month (about $972); some were there briefly, others for the year or more of the conflict.[7]

The *Illustrated London News* had been established in 1842, something of a departure in journalism. A weekly, in a format almost more akin to a magazine, it combined news with sketches and drawings illustrating some of the matters referred to in the news accounts. Attaining success, it was to be imitated by other illustrated news publications in England and other countries. Among the London illustrated papers, it was the most durable, and still exists. Several, however, were to be regularly represented by artist-correspondents on the news fronts of the world. This began in the Crimean War, with the *Illustrated London News* served by J. W. Carmichael and William Simpson in the Crimea itself, Samuel Read in Constantinople and on the Black Sea, and Joseph A. Crowe, son of the *Daily News* correspondent in Paris, as a writing correspondent only.

Another aspect of news pioneering, was the presence of three photographers, Roger Fenton and James Robertson, both British,

---

6 Among these correspondents for the *Times*, Barklay later wrote for the paper from Bucharest. Chenery was to become editor of the *Times* from 1878-84. Hardman and Eber both were to have long careers with the paper.

7 Among these latter correspondents, Edwin L. Godkin went to the United States in 1856, immediately after the war, and made it his home. There he served as *Daily News* correspondent, established *The Nation* in 1865 as an important weekly of opinion, and was editor of the *New York Evening Post* from 1883 to 1900. Henty reported other wars through 1876, and from that time until his death in 1902 he was the author of some eighty books, mostly adventure stories for boys based largely upon his own observations of war.

and Charles Langlois, French. Of the three, Fenton is chiefly remembered. Also a painter, and representing Messrs. Agnew & Son, art dealers of Manchester, he arrived at Balaclava in March 1855. He carried elaborate and bulky equipment about the war zone in a horse-drawn cart fitted up as a "darkroom." As with Robertson and Langlois, Fenton's efforts went almost unnoted at the time, aside from later displays of his photos in Manchester and some other British cities. Because of the technical limitations then attaching to photography, the views were static, reflected little of the realities of the war, and were seen by few persons. There is no record that they were used by artists as a basis for sketches to be converted into woodcuts for use in the illustrated publications.

Readers of the London press were best informed about the Crimean War as it proceeded. The peoples of the other four countries involved in the war fared far less well. For France, *Le Moniteur* of Paris, as an official government paper, had Alfred Kanouy in the Crimea, but only to forward official reports. Whatever was published in France was based almost entirely upon such reports.

In Russia, the limited and severely controlled press presented reports only as officially received and prepared. However, news of some actions in the war did appear earlier in Russian newspapers than in some others, because direct telegraphic communication existed between the Crimea and St. Petersburg. The people of the Sardinia-Piedmont kingdom were little informed. General La Marmora, commander of its forces in the Crimea, barred correspondents from his area altogether. In Turkey, the press scarcely existed.

What the people of the United States and other parts of the world may have learned about this remote war almost necessarily came from the *Times,* or possibly from one of the other London papers, as reprinted or rewritten from copies received belatedly by mail delivery.

Even for those London papers, the news was slow in arriving. One of the major problems for the British correspondents was arranging to get their reports back to London, not to mention sketches for the *Illustrated London News.* They did some pioneering of their own in this essential aspect of international reporting.

When the shooting began in 1854, the telegraph line providing a connection with London reached only as far south in Europe as Vienna. It required ten days to two weeks for messages to move from Balaclava to London. They were carried overland by courier and by ship up the Danube to Vienna. By 1855 the telegraph had been extended from Vienna to Bucharest and on to Varna, Bulgaria, on the

Black Sea coast. From there, a 400-mile British-controlled cable was laid to reach Sebastopol and Balaclava. Constantinople also was connected to Balaclava by a British cable, and messages moved from there to London by way of Varna and Vienna.

As the telegraph line was extended eastward to Bucharest and Ruschek, on the Bulgarian frontier, it became possible to get a message to London in about seventy hours. This became twenty-four hours when the connection reached Varna, and considerably less when the cable tie was made to Balaclava. The rate was high, however, and military demands for use of the line commonly delayed the transmission of press reports. It was understandable that the military should have priority in the use of the communications facilities. British army displeasure with Russell, however, denied him the use of the Balaclava-Varna cable under any circumstances. That denial did not continue indefinitely, perhaps because of pressure from the *Times* itself. While it did exist, Russell forwarded his dispatches by steamer from Balaclava to Varna, to be telegraphed from there.

In his assessment of Crimean War coverage, Philip Knightley, in *The First Casualty*, quotes Godkin, one of the correspondents, in later judging its most important results, so far as the press was concerned, as, first, the creation of the "special correspondent," and second, bringing about a recognition by government officialdom that the press and the people had a direct interest and concern in public affairs no longer to be disregarded. Thus, the war introduced the advance guard of a first generation of professional correspondents, and it brought press and public alike to a new point of awareness.

New Frontiers of Coverage

The decade preceding the Crimean War had been enormously important in advancing the service of the press. It had brought the telegraph and cable, and the first of the news agencies. It brought new readership and economic strength to some newspapers. It brought a beginning of active world reporting on the part of a few dailies. The coverage given the U.S.-Mexican War and the Crimean War was evidence of change.

The decade following the latter war brought further advances. Greatly significant was the virtual end of the taxes on knowledge in Great Britain in 1855. This permitted the sale of newspapers at a price more attractive to the general public, encouraged their reading, and the establishment of new publications. Thus, in that same year, the

London *Daily Telegraph* was founded. It was destined for vigorous growth. The first dailies appeared outside of London, including the *Manchester Guardian*, a weekly since 1821, the *Scotsman* of Edinburgh, a weekly since 1817, the *Liverpool Daily Post*, the *Sheffield Daily Telegraph*, the *Birmingham Post*, and a score of others, either converted from weekly publication or started anew.

Among the news agencies, Wolff, which had specialized in financial and commercial information since its formation in 1849, moved into the field of general news distribution in 1855. The Reuter agency, founded in 1851, followed the same course and added general news to its service in 1858. In the United States, the New York Associated Press, which had begun as the Harbor News Association in 1848, assumed that name ten years later.

Already a leader in news enterprise, the *Times* maintained its lead after the Crimean War. It had its staff and stringer correspondents deployed in Europe since 1848. It had a stringer in Washington as early as 1840, and in 1854 engaged J. C. Bancroft Davis, an attorney formerly attached to the U.S. Legation in London, as a stringer in New York. In that same year Meredith Townsend became a stringer in Calcutta. Indeed, by 1860 the *Times* claimed more than a dozen correspondents in foreign places "from Calcutta to San Francisco."

It was natural that the *Times* should have kept William Howard Russell busy on assignments, in view of his success in the Crimea. The fighting had ended there late in 1855 and, after returning to London, Russell went to Moscow in 1856 to report the ceremonies marking the coronation of Alexander II. Sutherland Edwards reported the event for the *Illustrated London News*. Russell remained to write a series of articles about various cities in Russia and on the life of the country with which Britain had so recently been at war. In doing so, he also became perhaps the first foreign correspondent to write from Russia.

Later in the year, Russell rejoined his family in London, and was widely honored for his work in the Crimea. He received an honorary LL. D. from Trinity College, Dublin, his alma mater, and afterwards was commonly known as "Dr. Russell."[8]

---

8 William Howard Russell received many honors for later exploits as a journalist through 1884. He established a periodical, the *Army and Navy Gazette* in 1860, and edited it for many years. He was knighted in 1895. He served as a member of Parliament. Following his death in 1907, he was commemorated with a memorial bust in the crypt of St. Paul's Cathedral, an area now surrounded by memorials to other British news correspondents distinguished for their accomplishments, some killed in the line of duty. It is here that Russell is identified as the "first and greatest" of war correspondents.

In December 1857 Russell went from London to India. Townsend returned to England from Calcutta in 1856, subsequently becoming owner of the *Spectator,* a weekly magazine of opinion. By then, however, the *Times* had James A. Stanton in Bombay, while Joseph A. Crowe had succeeded Townsend in Calcutta, headquarters for the British East India Company, then exercising control over much of India. Crowe, who had represented the *Illustrated London News* in the Crimea, remained in India for the *Times* until 1859. He was there during the Sepoy rebellion in May 1857, when native troops in India's northwest provinces mutinied against the East India Company command. It was in part to report the aftermath of this event that Russell arrived in India in December and remained more than a year.

During that time he reported disorders following the mutiny, and changes by which the administration of the country was transferred to the British Crown in 1858 from the East India Company, after 250 years of control. His dispatches during that period cost the paper about £5,000 (more than $24,000).

Russell and Crowe returned to England at almost the same time in 1859. Crowe proceeded to Vienna, but Russell remained in London. He returned to India in 1875, accompanying the Prince of Wales (later Edward VII) as his private secretary; having also previously accompanied the Prince on a visit to Egypt in 1868, and having been in the United States and Canada in 1861-62, and on other assignments.

Two other *Times* correspondents who had been in the Crimea, Eber and Hardman, were on assignments in Europe after the war, with Eber in Austria in 1859, and Hardman accompanying a Spanish expedition to Morocco. One of the paper's leader (editorial) writers, George Wingrove Cooke, was sent to Algeria in 1856, and in the following year to China, where he had spent some time as a younger man. Back in London in 1860, he was replaced in China by Thomas William Bowlby. Reporting an aspect of the T'ai P'ing rebellion in October, when French and British troops occupied Peking in retaliation for a seizure of foreign diplomats, Bowlby was captured and killed by slow torture. Added to the two losses in the Crimean war, he was the third *Times* casualty. Except for the visit of Bayard Taylor of the *New York Tribune* to Japan and China in 1853, Cooke and Bowlby were the first western correspondents to undertake reporting from the Far East beyond India.

Another unprecedented expedition by *Times* representatives occurred in 1856 when no fewer than five visited the United States, including the editor, John Delane, accompanied by Robert Lowe, a leader writer, and Laurence Oliphant, later to become Paris correspondent for the paper. The others were L. Filmore, formerly Berlin correspondent, and Thomas Gladstone. The first four conducted news inquiries in New York, Washington, and other cities in the East. Gladstone, however, went as far west as Kansas territory and wrote a series of articles about the controversy in that area between free-soiler and pro-slavery groups over whether slavery should be accepted locally. It was an issue involving the "Pottawatomie massacre" of five pro-slavery settlers in May of that year by order of John Brown, an abolitionist.

The Reuter agency also soon made a place for itself when it introduced its general news service in 1858. Operating as a commercial service since 1851, it already had benefited through its exchange arrangement with the Havas and Wolff agencies, and it had a half-dozen representatives in European cities. Engländer, in Paris, was in the confidence of the secretary to France's Emperor Napoleon III, and gained exclusive and early information from that source.

Reuter was neither an official nor semiofficial agency, but it worked in close harmony with the British government. Information deemed important was sent by Reuter, immediately, by special courier to the appropriate officials of government and, at times, to the Prince of Wales and to Queen Victoria herself. This brought reciprocal benefits to the agency. The queen conceived great trust in its reports and a respect for Reuter. For some months, in this period of the late 1850s, Reuter was able to obtain through the Foreign Office copies of government dispatches from India.

In its service to newspapers, clerks, or "manifolders," in the London office made copies of news reports for distribution by messengers. By 1860, the service was going to newspapers outside London by telegraph and to Ireland by cable. Agents also had been added in India, South Africa, Australia, and the United States. Where the Reuter service had been offered to the London morning dailies in 1858 at an introductory rate of £30 a month, or £360 a year (about $1,750), that rate was increased, even as the *Times* had anticipated when Mowbray Morris agreed reluctantly to receive it. In 1868 the rate was to stand at £1,000 a year (nearly $5,000) for each London morning daily, although only one-quarter that amount for evening papers, and with negotiable charges for provincial dailies.

The position of the press in France was difficult during the period of the Second Empire (1851-70). The government of Napoleon III maintained a control and censorship. This applied also to the Agence

Havas, which became in effect an official or semiofficial agency. As such, it received a government subsidy and favorable consideration in the use of the government-controlled telegraph lines. It began to make occasional efforts to provide direct coverage of some events, and in 1860 opened an office in Rio de Janeiro, with an agent to forward newspapers and reports to Paris. A reciprocal distribution of a Havas report began in South America.

The Havas agency was well established at the time of the Crimean War, but had taken no part in its coverage, even though France was deeply involved. It was no more active in reporting the Austro-Italian War of 1859.

The Austro-Italian, or Austro-Piedmont War, grew out of the revolutionary movements of 1848-49 in Europe. But it was a war deliberately provoked by France's Emperor Napoleon III, who was much given to international intrigue, and by Count Cavour, prime minister of the split state of Piedmont-Sardinia, who also had supported the formation of the Stefani news agency in Turin in 1853. The object of the intrigue in this case was to end Austrian influence in the Italian peninsula and effect a unification of the Italianate states. Napoleon III triggered the war by calculated remarks to Austria's ambassador in Paris in January 1859, and by a speech to the French Legislative Assembly in February. Military action did not begin until April 29, when Austrian forces invaded Piedmont, and ended with a July armistice and peace agreement, also maneuvered by Napoleon but unsatisfactory to Cavour. Austria was curbed, but it cost Piedmont control of the areas of Savoy and Nice, which became French, and it led to events that placed French troops in Italy until 1870. The war led to the formation of a Kingdom of Italy in 1861, although full unification was delayed until 1870. Apart from the April invasion and the July armistice, the major events of the brief war itself were the Battle of Magenta on June 4 and the Battle of Solferino on June 24.

In general, the war was not well reported. Napoleon III later remarked that the battles were described as if they were circus performances. Correspondents were few, mostly inexperienced, and barely tolerated by the military. The Piedmont-Sardinia government created a kind of information bureau, but it was ineffective. General La Marmora, the military commander, who had barred correspondents from his area during the Crimean War, threatened to hang any correspondent found in his camp. The Stefani agency, although based in Turin and backed by Cavour, was no more than an official channel for government-approved reports going to papers in northern Italy.

French military advisers virtually barred Edmund Texier, of *Le Siècle*. The Paris government put out its own reports, distributed by the Agence Havas, which was not otherwise represented. Nor were the Reuter or Wolff agencies.

Correspondents with the Austrians were dependent for information almost entirely upon what appeared in the official *Wiener Zeitung*.

So far as is known, the only French press representative in the field in this general period was Charles Emile Yriarte, an artist-correspondent for *Monde Ilustré*, an illustrated weekly of which he was to become editor in 1864. He had been in Morocco with a Spanish military expedition, the same one that Hardman of the *Times* had accompanied. Yriarte also reported a campaign in Sicily in May 1860, but it was unrelated to the war with Austria which had ended. It was part of a guerrilla campaign led by French-born Guiseppe Garibaldi, a "patriot" in the cause of Italian unification in the long period from 1848 to 1870.

Almost by default, as in the Crimea, the chief reports of the 1859 war itself were produced by British correspondents. For the *Times*, Joseph A. Crowe in returning from India had joined the Austrians almost immediately and witnessed the Battle of Solferino from that side. Ferdinand Eber, like Crowe, a veteran of the Crimea, witnessed the war from the Piedmont side. He became so personally involved, however, that he later accepted a commission in the volunteer forces led by Garibaldi, even as he continued to write for the *Times*. Two new correspondents were added to the *Times* service on the Piedmont side, Henry Wreford, who was British, and Antonio Gallenga, an Italian. Gallenga was to remain in the *Times* service in various assignments until his death in 1886.

Mrs. Jessie White Mario, an English woman married to an Italian, became a stringer in Italy for the *Daily News* from 1857 until 1860. She reported aspects of the war, and so may have become the first woman war correspondent. Frank Vizetelly was an artist-correspondent in those months for the London *Illustrated Times*, established in 1855 as another of the illustrated papers appearing at that period.[9]

---

9 The *Illustrated Times* was edited by Henry Vizetelly, father of Frank. The paper did so well that it was purchased not later than 1865 by the older *Illustrated London News* to remove it from the field of competition. Henry Vizetelly then was made Paris correspondent for the *Illustrated London News*. He and his son, Frank, were the first of a family of artist-correspondents of that name serving actively with various British publications through most of the second half of the century.

The *New York Times,* established in 1851, had two stringers in Paris by 1859—Dr. W. E. Johnstone, who wrote under the name of "Malakoff," and Frank Boott Goodrich, who signed his contributions "Dick Tinto." Henry J. Raymond, editor of the paper, and one of its founders, was in Europe in 1859. He and Johnstone, along with Frank Vizetelly, of the London *Illustrated Times,* witnessed the Battle of Solferino from the Italian side. Raymond managed to get an account back to New York and into print ten days before any other appeared in the United States. He may also have become the first U.S. correspondent to report directly as an eye-witness on a military action in Europe.

One other U.S. press representative in Italy at this approximate time was Thomas Nast, an artist, who did sketches of the 1860 Garibaldi campaign in Sicily for the *New York Illustrated News* and for the *Illustrated London News.*[10]

Apart from the coverage of the three wars in Mexico, the Crimea, and Italy between 1846 and 1859, the same years brought the beginnings of a consistent and substantive reporting of political and economic matters in such centers as London, New York, Washington, Paris, Vienna, and Rome, and even in India. They were formative years for five news agencies and for the communications facilities. It was a time during which newspapers increased in numbers, illustrated periodicals appeared, and photography entered the field. Some dailies, operating with new freedom and enterprise, gained in readership and attained a certain prosperity and influence.

Events of the next decade, the 1860s, were to receive considerably more press coverage, with the press itself entering upon a new era.

---

10 Nast arrived in Sicily from England after producing there for *Frank Leslie's Illustrated Newspaper* of New York sketches of a heavyweight fight in which J. C. Heenan ("The Benecia Boy"), an American, battled to a forty-two round draw with Tom Sayers of England, the heavyweight champion, and so became joint-champion.

The Winds of Change

The 1860s was a decade of fundamental change, largely shadowed by disorder and warfare. It began with the American Civil War of 1861-65. The Austro-Prussian War against Denmark at the same time was followed in 1866 by a war between those former allies as a prelude to the Franco-Prussian War of 1870-71.

The press had much to report in those years. In France, however, it was under restraint where the various intrigues of Napoleon III were concerned. In Prussia, Otto von Bismarck, as chancellor, was equally involved in his own intrigues, and contrived to manipulate the press in his own country and others to serve his purposes.

The British press, the most advanced in the world, reported the death of Prince Albert in December 1861, a victim of typhoid at age forty-two. A great series of social reforms occupied the Disraeli and Gladstone governments. There were problems in Ireland. There was great concern about the British position in China; the impact of the American Civil War on the British economy; the opening of the Suez Canal in 1869; critical events in Europe; and matters of the empire: the new power of the Crown in India, the settlement in New Zealand and Australia (where gold had been discovered) and in the African Cape Colony (where diamonds had been found), the establishment of union and dominion status in Canada in 1867, the addition of the Northwest Territories in 1869, and the breakout of an Indian rebellion in western Canada.

Italy had become a kingdom in 1861, with Victor Emmanuel II, former king of Sardinia-Piedmont, on the throne, first in Turin and then in Florence. An alliance with Prussia during the Austro-Prussian War of 1866 gained Venetia and Lombardy for Italy. Continuing guerrilla activity by Garibaldi in support of full Italian unification brought French troops into Italy to defend Rome and the papal states against seizure. They were only withdrawn when Napoleon III was faced with the prospect of war with Prussia in 1870. Full Italian unification followed and Rome became the capital.

An insurrection in Spain in 1866 led to the departure and deposition of Queen Isabella II in 1868, with a contest for the throne following and no permanent solution reached until 1875.

These were only some of the problems and issues figuring in changes receiving press attention in the 1860s.

The American Civil War, 1861-65   The United States of America by 1860 had become a nation of thirty-three states. Since 1789, when George Washington had become the first president in the constitutional government, the land area had increased from 867,980 square miles concentrated along the Atlantic seaboard to 2,973,965 square miles extending from the Atlantic to the Pacific, with continental limits much as at present. The population of 3,929,625, shown by the first census in 1790, had become 31,443,321 in 1860.

For all those years, the first concern was to assure the stability and safety of the new nation. For some fifty years prior to 1860, considerable news attention had gone to the advancing settlement of areas west of the Appalachian Mountains, and after about 1850 to settlement west of the Mississippi River. The country was primarily agricultural, and such industry as existed was chiefly in the northeastern states, where most of the major cities also were located. New York, the largest, had a population of 813,669 in 1860.

Apart from westward growth and economic stability, a further related matter of serious concern within the country was the issue of Negro slavery. Since about 1820, it had been an issue of growing importance.

The first slaves, twenty in number, had been brought to the American colonies in August 1619 by a Dutch ship arriving at Jamestown in Virginia colony. By 1790 the first census counted 697,624 slaves. They were in all thirteen states of that time, except Massachusetts, but most were in the South, serving as plantation workers and house servants.

Antislavery sentiment, growing in the world, brought a British ruling in 1807 holding the slave trade to be illegal. Such sentiment existed in the United States as well, and it was legally possible for a slave owner to grant freedom to any slave, as some did. An Act of Congress also made the slave trade and importation of slaves illegal in the United States after January 1, 1808. Illicit trade continued, however. The census of 1810 showed more than a million slaves in the United States, and the 1860 census counted 3.5 million, along with almost a half-million "free Negroes."

Sentiment for freeing the slaves had found expression since the discussions in the Continental Congress in 1776 relating to the Declaration of Independence. Slavery had been made illegal throughout the British Empire by 1833, in the French colonies by 1848, and in the Latin American republics by 1850. But representatives of the southern states insisted that slaves were required if their agricultural economy was to function at all.

The "abolitionist cause" grew strong, and a Quaker-originated "underground railroad" operating from 1804 to 1860 helped to move an estimated 40,000 to 100,000 slaves to "freedom" in Canada. Prominent in the abolitionist effort after 1820 were William Lloyd Garrison, publisher of the *Liberator* in Boston from 1831, the Reverend Elijah Lovejoy, publisher of the *Observer* in St. Louis (killed in 1837 by a mob at Alton, Illinois), and John Brown, a Mayflower descendant, active for abolition from 1856 in Kansas and later at Harper's Ferry, Virginia. There he was captured in 1859, convicted of treason, murder, conspiring with slaves and other rebels, and was hanged. Harriet Beecher Stowe's 1852 novel, *Uncle Tom's Cabin*, portrayed the plight of the slave, and sold more than a million copies within a year.

Basic in shaping events to come, however indirectly, was the invention of the cotton gin in 1793 by Eli Whitney. A native of Massachusetts and recent graduate of Yale, he was invited to spend some time on a Georgia plantation, where he observed the slow process by which seed was manually separated before the cotton could be baled. Possessing a knack for mechanics, he devised a machine to perform the same task. Using it, cotton could be produced fifty times faster, and his device revolutionized the South. Cotton soon far surpassed tobacco, sugar cane, and rice as the profitable crop. A "Cotton Kingdom" resulted, with new acreage planted, and the product shipped to mills in New England and in Great Britain, where textiles had become so important a product of the industrial revolution. A record 5,387,000 bales of cotton were produced in the South in 1859, but this was possible only because slaves were available to work in the fields.

A second factor of importance in developments after 1850 was the prospective settlement of the great land area west of the Mississippi River and the possible extension of slaveholding to that area. A tacit agreement had existed since 1802 that, as states were admitted to the Union, an equal balance would be maintained between slave states and free states. The Missouri Compromise of 1820, envisioning eventual settlement of the West, had drawn a line marking off southern areas as slave states and northern areas as free soil.

The passage by Congress in 1854 of the Kansas-Nebraska Act, looking toward settlement of that territory, brought the issue to a crisis point. Free-soilers and states-righters favoring slaveholding, clashed in Kansas in 1855 and 1856. Violence became so general that the area became "Bleeding Kansas," and the issue was not finally settled until 1861, when Kansas was admitted to the Union as a free state.

Meanwhile the controversy had escalated. In the Dred Scott decision by the United States Supreme Court in 1857 it was ruled that Scott, a slave who had been freed, still had no right to assert his freedom in court or elsewhere. The Court lost prestige as a result of the decision, and the case became a highly devisive issue. The Supreme Court, at the same time, had found the Missouri Compromise of 1820 to be unconstitutional, with the inference that slaveholding was acceptable in any prospective state if its residents so wished.

The issue was injected into the presidential campaign of 1856—James Buchanan, favoring noninterference with slaveholding, was elected in a contest with John C. Fremont, who disapproved the extension of slavery. The issue was raised again by Abraham Lincoln, speaking in Springfield, Illinois, in June 1858, when he referred to a "house divided," and contended that the United States must become either all slave or all free, and preferably the latter, if the government was to "endure permanently." It became a subject discussed in the Lincoln-Douglas debates—seven meetings between August and October 1858. As a candidate for the presidency in 1860, Lincoln was regarded in the South as unfavorable to the extension of slavery and was therefore solidly opposed in that part of the country, with support going instead to Stephen A. Douglas, whose views on slavery, although somewhat equivocal, seemed more acceptable.

By 1860 there were fifteen slave states and eighteen free states, which would become nineteen with the admission of Kansas to the Union in January 1861. The population of the slave states was 8,100,000. Of these, only about 350,000 owned slaves; fewer than

8,000 owned fifty or more, and 2,292 were large planters, with 100 slaves or more. A minority in the total population, these were the men and families of wealth and influence. They, above all others, wished to maintain the institution of slavery, and were desirous of extending their holdings to the new lands in the West.

Arguing the right of state sovereignty, or states rights, in support of slavery, and viewing the prospect of the early accession to power in Washington of a party and president "whose opinions and purposes are hostile to slavery," South Carolina in December 1860 proposed secession from the Union as a response to Lincoln's election.

By February 1861, South Carolina had been joined by six other southern states in voting to secede, citing Northern aggression against their "domestic institutions." In convention at Montgomery, Alabama, representatives of the seven states formed the Confederate States of America. A constitution was drafted resembling that of the United States, but with slavery recognized and protected. To avoid offending opinion in Great Britain and France, the importation of slaves was prohibited. Jefferson Davis of Mississippi, a planter and slaveholder, was elected as provisional president, and the convention members as a provisional congress, pending elections held in November 1861, when the arrangement was regularized.

When Abraham Lincoln was inaugurated on March 4, 1861, it was as president of a dis-United States. He spoke carefully and acted cautiously, more concerned with restoring the Union than with interfering with slavery in the states where it existed. Just over a month later, however, on April 12, a Confederate bombardment of Fort Sumter, a federal fort in the harbor at Charleston, South Carolina, brought the beginning of the Civil War.

Four other southern states, including Virginia, unwilling to secede earlier, joined the Confederacy in April and May. The capital of the Confederacy was then to be at Richmond, and Robert E. Lee, declining Lincoln's invitation to take command of the Union forces, instead took charge of Virginia's forces and ultimately of all Confederate forces.[1]

---

1 The Confederate States of America, in order of their secession, were South Carolina, Mississippi, Florida, Alabama, Georgia, Louisiana, and Texas. Joining in April and May, after the bombardment of Fort Sumter, were Virginia, Arkansas, Tennessee, and North Carolina, in that order. Of the fifteen slave-holding states, four did not secede. These were Delaware, Maryland, Kentucky, and Missouri. A large section of western Virginia was opposed to secession, and, in June 1861, formed its own separate government, became West Virginia, and was admitted to the Union June 20, 1863, in the midst of the war, as the thirty-fifth state.

The eleven Confederate states were matched against twenty-three northern or Union states, including the four that had been among the slaveholding states. In terms of population and manpower, there were twenty-two million on the Union side as against eight to nine million on the Confederate side, of whom about three and one-half million were slaves. The North also had far more industry and resources to support the war to preserve the Union, but the South was strong in morale, and could muster nearly as many men into service because the slaves could carry on in agriculture. The Confederate states also had the advantage of interior lines, and believed they could wear down the Union forces. Aware of the importance of their cotton to Great Britain, they counted on support from that direction, and from France as well.

Whatever the expectations, the Civil War was relatively long. In the matter of press coverage, it was the most thoroughly reported war to that period. It received attention, particularly from correspondents for newspapers in the North, but less actively so for newspapers in the South. Some representatives of the British press, and a few for European newspapers, reported aspects of the war. There were numerous eye-witness accounts of battle. Considerable use was made of the telegraph. There was more careful planning and larger expenditures than had ever gone before into the gathering and distribution of news—whether in time of war or peace. Lessons were learned and practices introduced that were to be applied in later years. A number of correspondents were to earn personal reputations through their exploits, and some were to put their experience to account on other battlefields in other wars, or in general news administration.

When the war was in progress, with the United States divided, another hazard arose when a coalition of British, French, and Spanish forces landed troops in Mexico in 1862, at a time when Mexico itself was in political upheaval. The pretext for the landing was that Mexico owed European creditors more than $82 million. The real reason was that France's Napoleon III sought to establish a French position in Latin America. Ignoring the Monroe Doctrine of 1823, specifying that the American continents no longer were to be considered open for future colonization by European powers, he reasoned that a Confederate victory could suit his purpose. He therefore aided the South with ships built in French shipyards, among other things.

The British and Spanish reached an agreement with the Mexican government and soon withdrew their troops and ships. French troops remained, however, and entered Mexico City in June 1863. Protests from the United States were ignored. In furtherance of his plan, Napoleon III conspired to establish the Archduke Maximilian of Austria—a brother of Austria's Emperor Franz Joseph—as "Emperor" of Mexico. He assumed the throne in April 1864. When the Civil War ended in a Union victory in 1865, Napoleon III yielded to demands from Washington and French troops were withdrawn in 1867 from Mexico. Maximilian, unable to maintain his position without French support, was forced out and executed soon after. Benito Juarez, president of the republic at the time of the French intervention, resumed office.

Great Britain was interested in the American Civil War for other reasons. Its textile industry placed great dependence upon a steady supply of cotton from the southern states. That supply was obstructed by a Union blockade of southern ports intended not only to prevent the export of cotton but, even more, to prevent British arms and assistance—and French as well—from reaching the Confederate states. Neither the British government nor its people supported the institution of slavery, but there was a substantial sentiment sympathetic to the Confederacy. It has been estimated that the well-being of 20 per cent of the British people was adversely affected by the wartime interference with the delivery of cotton, and that the British economy was considerably hurt by its lack, even though new supplies were obtained in Egypt. As in France, ships for the Confederacy were built in British yards.

In November 1861, the U.S. Navy sloop San Jacinto halted the Trent, a British mail packet, eastbound on the Atlantic, and removed James M. Mason and John Slidell, Confederate envoys bound for London and Paris. This action came close to bringing Great Britain into the war on the side of the Confederacy. The tension was relieved when Lincoln acted to release the Confederate emissaries.

With these circumstances, the British press was generally favorable to the Confederacy. For the *Times,* the most respected and influential newspaper, partiality to the South and opposition to the North shaped general policy as set by John Walter III, proprietor since the death of his father in 1847; by John Delane, the editor, who had visited the United States in 1856; and by Mowbray Morris, general manager, who had been born in the West Indies and was a supporter of slavery. Some British journalists appear to have accepted bribes from representatives of the Confederacy to write and publish material amounting to propaganda in support of the South.

Only one London newspaper, the *Daily News,* took a balanced position on the war.

The *Times,* as the first foreign newspaper to give any sort of consistent attention to events in the Western Hemisphere, was also the first to send a special correspondent to report on the critical situation existing in the United States before the war began. This was no less a personage than William Howard Russell, celebrated for his coverage of the Crimean War, and for his work in India and elsewhere.

Russell arrived in New York in March 1861. Cordially received, he was immediately in demand as a speaker. Proceeding to Washington, Russell met President Lincoln, only recently inaugurated. Lincoln politely remarked that "the London *Times* is one of the greatest powers in the world—in fact, I don't know anything which has much more power, except perhaps the Mississippi."

Touring the southern states, Russell saw slave markets in operation. These created in him a sentiment favorable to the North in its opposition to slavery. At the same time the Confederate States of America had been formed, and he concluded that the spirit of the South was too strong to permit any restoration of the Union, even should the North emerge victorious in a war. It was a view he was to change somewhat later, to the dismay of the *Times.*

Russell was back in Washington when war actually began on April 12, and he remained there until August. His dispatches were moderate and perceptive, more favorable to the North than to the South. But he was present July 21 in the field at Bull Run, near Washington, the scene of the first major battle, and was forced literally to flee when Union forces broke before a Confederate onslaught. His account of the action occupied seven columns in the *Times* of August 6. It was far from complimentary to the Union Army and did not spare critical references to reports in northern newspapers tending to hide the gravity of the Union defeat.

There was great interest in the United States as to what Russell, an experienced war correspondent, would have to say about the Bull Run engagement. When copies of the *Times* reached New York late in August, his account was widely republished, quoted and commented upon. It aroused much resentment. Coupled with the unsympathetic editorial position taken by the *Times* with reference to the Union cause, and with other evidences of British sympathy for the South, it made Russell suddenly unpopular in New York and Washington, where he now was referred to scornfully as "Bull Run

Russell." Handicapped in his news work by reason of this attitude, Russell went to Canada and remained there through the winter. He returned to Washington on March 1, 1862, but was denied permission to go again into the field with the Union armies. He sailed for England on April 4 and did not return.

J. C. Bancroft Davis, after seven years as the *Times* correspondent in New York, resigned from that position in December 1861. Charles Tuckerman, also an American citizen, replaced him briefly. Then Charles Mackay, former contributor to the *Illustrated London News,* who had visited the United States in 1857, was sent from London to take the post. To report from the South, the *Times* managed to get Francis (Frank) Lawley, formerly on the staff of the British Minister in Washington, to return to America as a correspondent in Richmond. He wrote some reports from there in the summer of 1863. For reasons of health, he soon retired officially, but remained in the South until the end of the war and did contribute occasional letters. The paper had another correspondent in Richmond in 1864, a Mr. Alexander, possibly P. W. Alexander, formerly of the *Savannah Republican.* Their reports were transmitted to London by way of the French consulate in Richmond and the Paris office of the *Times.*

Antonio Gallenga, a correspondent for the *Times* since 1859 in his native Italy and elsewhere, was sent to the United States in 1863 to report the war from the North. He did not remain long, however, which meant that the *Times* was chiefly dependent upon Mackay. His reports were consistently unfriendly to the Union side. This was pleasing to the management of the paper until the war ended in a Union victory, whereupon he was dismissed. Louis John Jennings, who had been correspondent for the *Times* in India since 1860, held the New York post from 1865 to 1867, then was replaced in turn by Joel Cook, an American citizen and a former Civil War correspondent for the *Philadelphia Public Ledger.*[2]

Edwin L. Godkin, who had written for the London *Daily News* during the Crimean War, had taken up residence in the United States in 1856, but was in Paris during most of the first year of the Civil War

---

2 Louis John Jennings joined the *New York Times* in 1867, and became its editor until 1876. Returning then to England, he served later as member of Parliament, during which time he also wrote for the *New York Herald.*

Joel Cook remained as stringer correspondent for the *Times* from 1867 to 1907, writing both from New York and Philadelphia. During those years, he also was a member of the *Public Ledger* staff. He served two terms in Congress from 1907 until his death in 1910.

as a correspondent for the *New York Evening Post.* Back in the United States in 1862, Godkin served as a stringer for the *Daily News* until the end of the war, but did not go into the field. In keeping with the liberal policy of that paper, his reports were the most consistently favorable to the Union cause to appear in the British press.

The *Daily News* was represented in the South for about three years by Frank Vizetelly, who had served as an artist-correspondent for that paper during the Austro-Italian War of 1859. He took many personal risks, including running the Union blockade to make a round trip to London in 1864, and witnessed several important engagements. He sent both reports and sketches to London by way of Richmond. Some of his sketches were intercepted at sea and appeared in *Harper's Weekly* of New York. Because they were taken as contraband of war, neither Vizetelly nor the *Daily News* had any recourse.

The *Daily Telegraph* published some war reports by George Augustus Sala and Edward James Stephens Dicey; both made the journey from England and wrote from the North. Dicey also wrote for *Macmillan's Magazine* and the *Spectator,* both London publications.

George Alfred Lawrence, intending to write from the South for the *Morning Post,* entered the country by way of New York, but was arrested while trying to reach the Confederate lines. The *Morning Herald* had some accounts from Samuel P. Day, who was with the Confederates.

Miscellaneous reports appeared in the Paris press, some by Frederick Gaillardet, editor of the French-language *Courier des États-Unis* of New York, writing for *La Presse* and *Le Constitutionnel.* Michel Chevalier, an economist, wrote from New York for *Le Journal des Débats.* Georges Clemenceau wrote from Richmond for *Le Temps* at the war's end.[3]

The most consistent reporting of the war for the British press was provided through the Reuter news agency. Many of those reports also appeared in French, German, and Italian newspapers by reason of the exchange between the Reuter, Havas, and Wolff agencies, and their various connections with other smaller agencies.

When the Civil War began in April 1861 Reuter sent James McLean

---

3 Arriving in the United States late in 1865, Georges Clemenceau remained until 1868, teaching at a girls' school in Stamford, Connecticut, while also writing for *Le Temps.* Premier of France from 1917-20, he also was active as an editor.

to New York as agent. He arranged to receive information through the New York Associated Press and other sources, including some reports from the South. Summaries of news were prepared, and a schedule set up by which such dispatches, along with clippings and copies of newspapers would be placed aboard every mail steamer outbound from New York for England. The fastest crossing, from New York to Southampton, then required eleven days; other ships took fifteen or sixteen days.

Because of British interest in the war, both Reuter and the *Times* chartered fast boats to meet the incoming ships off Southampton Water to receive their special dispatches, which were tossed overboard in watertight metal cylinders or canisters affixed to wooden floats, with phosphorus flares added at night so they could be seen. These were caught up in nets at the end of poles by news boats. On shore, the dispatches were telegraphed to London.

Reuter kept staff men on duty in London to receive reports by day or night. The news was forwarded promptly to all subscribing newspapers, and also went forward by wire and cable to the Havas agency in Paris and the Wolff agency in Berlin for further distribution.

Two British telegraph companies at that time still were attempting to combine their communication services with services of news to the provincial press, as described earlier. The Magnetic Telegraph Company and the Electric Telegraph Company were, to this extent, in competition with Reuter. Both had cable connections from Ireland to Scotland and England, and wire connections to London. Rather than wait for the arrival of mail steamers from the United States at English ports, these companies arranged for tenders to go out from Roche's Point, near Cobh (or Cork), off the Irish coast, and there pick up canisters containing dispatches and newspapers for which they had arranged. From Roche's Point, the news was telegraphed to Cork and on to London for delivery to subscribing newspapers several hours before the Reuter dispatches, or others, became available through Southampton.

Reuter met this competition by gaining permission to run a private telegraph line between Cork and Crookhaven, some sixty miles westward on the southern Irish coast, and ninety miles sailing distance from Roche's Point. Two German engineers were engaged to extend the line with the greatest secrecy, and a small tender and three-man team based at Crookhaven soon was moving out to intercept approaching mail steamers at this westernmost point off the Irish coast. Canisters containing McLean's dispatches were recovered off Crookhaven and the reports telegraphed directly from there to Cork and London. This enabled Reuter to regain his lead, with messages now reaching London eight hours ahead of any others. Success in providing news of the Civil War brought prestige to the Reuter service. The number of subscribers increased, despite higher charges. There was criticism also, but on two occasions Reuter gained special acclaim.

The first occurred early in 1862 when the agency led with information ending a critical situation—the commissioners of the Confederate government, Mason and Slidell, after having been forcibly removed by Union naval action from the British mail ship Trent the previous November, had been released on order of President Lincoln. This message reached Mr. Reuter on a Sunday, and he took it at once to Prime Minister Palmerston. At the same time, he obtained a personal interview with the prime minister for use with the news report as published in the newspapers of Monday morning.

The second notable Reuter success came just after the end of the war when the agency was able to provide Great Britain and all of Europe with the news of President Lincoln's assassination a full week before any other report reached Europe. This was made possible when McLean, in New York, obtained an account of the shooting and related events, based on direct coverage by Lawrence Augustus Gobright, Washington representative of the New York Associated Press. McLean then hired a special tug to pursue an outbound mail ship already at sea, overtake it, and toss the news canister aboard.

Most of the news of the Civil War, as reported in Europe and other parts of the world, was based upon accounts published in the press of the United States, and particularly the press of the North, since the flow of news was primarily through New York. Such few correspondents as reported from the South, referred to newspapers available there.

It has been estimated that about 300 ''specials''—as reporters or correspondents covering the Civil War were called—went into the field at some period during the four years of the fighting. With the few exceptions noted, all were representatives of the domestic press, North and South, but most of them, by far, were with the Union armies of the North.

For that large group, the War Department in Washington requested that the accounts published bear the names of the writers as a means of fixing responsibility for any breaches of security. The result was that individual writers became widely known by name, or known by initials or pen names. The names or initials usually were appended to the reports, rather than surmounting them. This was perhaps the first general departure from reportorial anonymity.

The press in the Confederate states operated under extreme difficulties. Many papers were forced to suspend simply for lack of print paper.[4] A heavy censorship was imposed, and correspondents rarely were permitted to accompany army units. Such news as was published came largely from official releases, from editors or reporters visiting various headquarters, or from letters written by soldiers, some of whom had been newsmen before they donned uniforms.

A Press Association of the Confederate States (PACS, or PA, as it was more commonly known) was formed in Augusta, Georgia, in February 1862. Directed by J. S. Thrasher, it served some forty-eight southern newspapers. Among the very few names to emerge among correspondents reporting the war for Confederate papers, A. J. Riddle was one; others were George W. Bagby and Samuel C. Reid, Jr., writing for several papers.

Matters of military security and censorship were important in the North as well as in the South, partly because newspapers were smuggled across the lines in both directions throughout the war. In Washington, Secretary of War Edwin M. Stanton and Secretary of State William H. Seward both undertook to establish certain censorship regulations and to control what was transmitted by telegraph. These efforts had only limited effect, but army commanders in the field themselves demanded that correspondents accept certain restrictions in return for facilities and assistance extended to them.

Major General George B. McClellan, in command of the North's Army of the Potomac in 1862, was perhaps most successful in his understandings with correspondents. General William T. Sherman, on the other hand, had trouble with some who revealed information improperly, as he believed, and his attitude was not improved by one report that he was insane. He was hostile to all "specials," and in 1863 even proposed that Thomas W. Knox of the *New York Herald* be hanged. General Henry W. Hallock expelled some thirty correspondents from his camp in Mississippi in 1862, and one who protested was put in detention. General Ambrose E. Burnside ordered William

---

4   More than a dozen Southern newspapers produced editions printed on the reverse side of wallpaper. An 1863 copy of the *Vicksburg Daily Citizen,* so published, later was reproduced as a curiosity of the war.

Swinton of the *New York Times* to be shot, but General Ulysses S. Grant, as commander-in-chief, interposed.

The correspondents with the Northern armies were loyal to the Union cause and discreet in what they reported. But since no clear statement on censorship existed and since individual commanders set their own rules, correspondents were obliged to find sources of information and develop such methods as they could to obtain news, and to write as they deemed prudent. Even so, some information appeared in print that could have aided the Confederate side. There also were cases in which a spirit of enterprise, or even carelessness and irresponsibility, led corrrespondents to report matters at least unwelcome and sometimes personally embarrassing to commanders.

Correspondents for the *New York Herald,* the *New York Tribune,* and the *New York Times* were reporting from the Southern states when the first shots of the war were fired at Fort Sumter. Regarded then as spies, they were in immediate personal danger. A *Tribune* man was arrested at Charleston, near Fort Sumter, and a *Times* man narrowly escaped hanging at Harper's Ferry. A mob at Richmond also tried to hang a *Herald* man, but failed. Two *Herald* men, one at Charleston and the other in New Orleans, contrived to reach Northern lines only at considerable risk. Other representatives were in North Carolina, Florida, Alabama, Arkansas, and Texas.

The most effective coverage of the war was provided by the *New York Herald.* James Gordon Bennett, its publisher, had foreseen this war, as he had foreseen the Mexican War, and the *Herald* sent out more "specials" than any other one newspaper. In addition to permanent correspondents already in Washington, Chicago, St. Louis, and Cincinnati, and the men it had sent to Southern cities early in 1861 on what became hazardous missions, some forty *Herald* men accompanied the Union forces even as the war began, and as many as sixty later were in the field at one period.

The army made no essential provision for news correspondents, so those *Herald* men requiring it were equipped with their own field outfits, including horses, tents and provisions, and sometimes covered wagons. Because the *Herald* paid its men better than others, and also gave them bonuses for exclusive and superior reports, it had a choice from among the best. It even managed to get some reports from behind the Confederate lines. Frederic Hudson, managing editor, later estimated that the total coverage had cost the paper more than $500,000—a very substantial expenditure at that time. One *Herald* correspondent was killed, three died of illness or hardship, several were wounded, and several captured.

Among *Herald* men who attained particular distinction was Charles Henry Farrell, who had been in New Orleans when the war began, but managed to get to the Union lines. Later, he reported the Battle of Antietam Creek (1862), Grant's attack on Vicksburg (1863), and the surrender of Confederate commander General Robert E. Lee to General Grant at Appomattox Court House in Virginia, marking the end of the war on April 9, 1865.

Another *Herald* man was Bradley S. Osbon. Originally with the *New York World*, he was aboard a U.S. naval vessel in Charleston harbor on April 12, 1861, and wrote an eye-witness account of that day's Confederate attack on Fort Sumter, the first action of the war. Joining the *Herald* staff later, Osbon accompanied several naval expeditions, including that in which Admiral David G. Farragut directed action that won Union control of the mouth of the Mississippi and of the city of New Orleans in 1862. His account, occupying three pages in the *Herald*, was the longest battle report yet published in the United States. An artist as well as a writer, he provided sketches, which were reproduced as wood engravings to illustrate his account.

Henry Villard was another *Herald* correspondent in the first period of the war. Born in Germany, Ferdinand Heinrich Gustav Hilgard was well educated; when eighteen he came to the United States in 1853 and settled in Springfield, Illinois. There he changed his name to its simpler form, studied law, and entered the practice. He also wrote from the Illinois state capital for the *Chicago Tribune*, the *Cincinnati Commercial*, and other newspapers. Among other things, he reported the Lincoln-Douglas debates in 1858, and the 1860 Republican national convention in Chicago, where Abraham Lincoln was nominated for the presidency.

Villard already had become acquainted with Lincoln, also a resident of Springfield and also practicing law there after service in the Illinois state legislature (1834-41) and as a member of Congress (1847-49). He reported aspects of the campaign leading to Lincoln's election in November 1860, and provided the only report of Lincoln's address to his fellow-townsmen as the president-elect was about to leave for Washington for his inauguration in March 1861. These reports appeared in the Chicago and Cincinnati papers which Villard represented and in the *New York Herald*, and were sent to the New York Associated Press for wider distribution.

Villard followed Lincoln to Washington as representative of the *New York Herald*. He reported the inauguration and was in the capital when the war began in April. Like William Howard Russell, he witnessed the first Battle of Bull Run in July and produced a memorable account for the *Herald*. The paper used only part of it, however, for fear of causing a public panic because of the Union defeat.

Shortly after Bull Run, Villard formed a small syndicate of his own, the first of its kind, not as a news agency but as a special service from Washington offered to newspapers. It began by providing reports from the capital to five newspapers, presumably those for which he had written before, including the *Herald*. This continued only briefly, because in 1862 Villard became chief war correspondent for the *New York Tribune*, which he was to serve well thoughout the remaining years of the war.[5]

For the *New York Herald*, Dr. George W. Hosmer provided the first and most detailed account of the Battle of Gettysburg (1863). George Alfred Townsend, signing his reports "Gath," produced a notable report of the Seven Days Battle in Virginia (1862), occupying five pages in the *Herald*. William Young and F. G. Champan were with the Army of the Potomac and contributed excellent accounts of action. William F. G. Shanks was with Brigadier General Don Carlos Buell's Army of the Ohio (1861-62), and E. D. Westfall reported in 1863 the Battle of Chattanooga (Lookout Mountain).

Sylvanus Cadwallader ("Cad") first represented the *Chicago Times*, but later was the *Herald* correspondent at General Grant's headquarters, where he became a close friend and confidant of the Union commander. The *Herald* led all other papers with reports on the Battles of Shiloh (1861) and Yorktown (1862). Captain David P. Conyngham, with Major General William Tecumseh Sherman in the advance through Georgia to the sea in 1864, wrote extensively for the *Herald*.

The *New York Tribune* was second only to the *Herald* in the quality of its war reports. Its editor and founder, Horace Greeley,

---

5 After the war, from 1866 to 1868, Henry Villard was in Europe as a free-lance writer. At the same time, he was drawn into a study of the financing of banks and railroads. Returning to the United States, he became an active participant in such enterprises and made a fortune, notably through association with the Northern Pacific Railway, of which he was a director; and the General Electric Company, which he helped establish. In 1881 he purchased a controlling interest in the *New York Evening Post* and *The Nation*. Upon his death in 1900 control of the newspaper and the weekly magazine passed to his son, Oswald Garrison Villard. Edwin L. Godkin, who had founded *The Nation* in 1865 and also had been editor of the *Evening Post* since 1882, continued as editor of both publications until his own death in 1902. Oswald Garrison Villard retained control of the *Evening Post* until 1918 and of *The Nation* until 1940. He died in 1949.

exerted considerable influence on public policy and thinking through his editorials, as he had done for many years before the war, and continued to do later.

The *Tribune* had fifteen to twenty "specials" in the field. One of the first was Albert D. Richardson, who risked his life traveling through the southern states in the spring of 1861, getting his reports back to New York in cipher. Later, he wrote eye-witness accounts of a number of battles. Along with another *Tribune* man, Junius Henri Browne, he was captured by the Confederates at Vicksburg. Both escaped and reached northern lines with personal stories to write.

George W. Smalley, a young Boston lawyer when the war began, became a *Tribune* "special" and its chief correspondent in the first months of the war. He earned acclaim for an eye-witness report of the Battle of Antietam (1862), which he carried from the Maryland battlefield to New York, traveling by horse and train and arriving in time to enable the *Tribune* to appear the following morning with the first news of the engagement, a six-column story regarded as one of the best battle accounts of the entire war.

Smalley was made a member of the *Tribune* staff in New York soon after Antietam. Henry Villard suspended his recently established Washington syndicate, and took his place as chief correspondent with the Army of the Potomac. He provided an eye-witness report of the Battle of Fredericksburg (1862), a Union defeat; was present at the Battle of Lookout Mountain (1863), and was with Grant at the Battle of the Wilderness (1864).

Henry E. Wing, a youthful *Tribune* "special," also was present at the Wilderness battle. He carried the first news of that Union victory to an anxious Washington, long beset by reverses, and was hurried to the White House to give the details to President Lincoln personally. The President was so moved by the reassuring news that he is said to have kissed Wing on the forehead.

Homer Byington, a member of the *Tribune*'s Washington staff, produced an exclusive report of the first day's action in the Battle of Gettysburg (1863). Samuel Wilkeson, chief Washington correspondent for the paper, also was at Gettysburg and wrote his report while beside the body of his son, killed in action there.

James Redpath, Scottish-born, but a resident of the United States since his youth, had written letters to the *Tribune* from the southern states before the war, and in Kansas had interviewed John Brown as he acted there in the free-soil cause. This has been called by some the first real newspaper "interview," although others credit Bennett and the *Herald* as having used the method earlier. Redpath may have been the first to use that precise word, however, to describe the meeting. He remained with the *Tribune* throughout the war, including coverage of the march of General Sherman's forces across Georgia to the Atlantic coast (1864).[6]

James Robert Gilmore was still another *Tribune* wartime "special." Charles A. Page, with the paper from 1862 through 1865, also produced some notable accounts, including a report of President Lincoln's funeral in 1865.

The *New York Times* had as many as thirty-four men in the field during the war, with two in the South just before the clash at Fort Sumter. Henry J. Raymond, cofounder and editor, who had reported the Battle of Solferino in 1859, was another observer of the Battle of Bull Run, like Russell and Villard. He was present with James B. Swain, the paper's Washington correspondent, and he wrote the account of the Union defeat appearing the *Times*.

William Conant Church, who had been publisher of the *New York Sun* in 1860, took charge of the *Times* coverage at the outset of the war. He also established the *Army and Navy Journal* as a personal venture in 1863. Other *Times* correspondents included Frank B. Wilkie, who signed his reports "Galway," George F. Williams, Major Ben F. Truman, William Swinton, and Lorenzo L. Crounse. Both Swinton and Crounse were with the Army of the Potomac. It was Swinton who ran afoul of General Burnside and was saved from possible execution by General Grant's intervention. Crounse reported the surrender of General Lee in 1865.

Among other correspondents in the field for the northern press, Charles Carleton Coffin represented the *Boston Journal,* signing his reports "Carleton." Except for periods of home leave, he served throughout all four years of the war, perhaps the only correspondent to do so, and distinguished himself by his unsparing effort and the accuracy of his battlefield reports.

The *New York Evening Post* had Walter F. Williams as one of its "specials" and also used Coffin's reports in New York. Edmund

---

6 After the war, James Redpath established the Redpath Lyceum Bureau in Boston in 1868 and conducted it until 1875 as perhaps the first lecture bureau in the United States. Later, however, he wrote again for the *Tribune* from Ireland in 1879 and 1881, primarily on the Land Question, involving absentee ownership of land and houses, with agitation to improve the position of the people through the Irish Land League, headed by Charles S. Parnell and Michael Davitt. This resulted in the Land Act of 1881, passed by Parliament in a step toward Home Rule in Ireland and the establishment of the Republic of Ireland.

Clarence Stedman, later to win a reputation as a poet, was a special for the *New York World* at the Battle of Bull run (1861) and throughout most of 1862. Joel Cook and John Russell Young represented the *Philadelphia Public Ledger,* and Uriah Painter, the *Philadelphia Inquirer.* Cook was to become correspondent for the *Times* of London after the war, and Young was to become a correspondent for the *New York Herald.*

For papers in the Midwest, Whitelaw Reid, as city editor of the *Cincinnati Gazette,* chose to go into the field for his newspaper. Writing under the name of "Agate," he produced a graphic account of the Battle of Shiloh (1862). Soon after, he became Washington correspondent for the paper, but returned to the field to report the Battle of Gettysburg (1863).[7] The *Cincinnati Commercial* had two specials reporting the war, Murat Halstead, later to become editor of the paper, and James R. McCullagh, later publisher of the *St. Louis Globe-Democrat.*

Other western papers involved in war coverage included the *Chicago Times,* with Warren P. Isham in the field, and also Sylvanus Cadwallader ("Cad") until he joined the *New York Herald* staff. The *Chicago Tribune,* whose great growth began at this time, with Joseph Medill as a partner in ownership since 1855 and as editor-in-chief in 1863-66, had twenty-nine specials, including George P. Upton, Richard J. Hinton, and Albert H. Bodman. The one far-western newspaper represented was the *Sacramento Union,* with Noah Brooks, originally of Boston, serving in the field from 1862-65. Writing also from Washington, he was well acquainted with President Lincoln.

The New York Associated Press war coverage centered in Washington, supervised by Lawrence Augustus Gobright, chief correspondent there for the agency since 1850. He organized a considerable group of specials to go into the field. Most of them were relatively inexperienced, however, and poorly paid at ten to twenty-five dollars

---

7 While in Washington, Whitelaw Reid established a reputation, along with friendships, that led to his joining the staff of the *New York Tribune* in 1868 as the "first writing editor," or chief editorial writer, even though Horace Greeley was still active. In 1873, the year following Greeley's death, Reid became owner of the *Tribune.* After 1888 he was primarily in diplomacy, representing the United States as minister to France and ambassador in England, and otherwise on foreign assignments virtually to the time of his death in 1912. Others directed the paper, including his son, Ogden Mills Reid, who succeeded to ownership. The *New York Herald* was merged with the *Tribune* in 1924, and the *New York Herald Tribune* continued until 1966, with Reid family members involved to the time of the paper's suspension.

a week, out of which they were expected to buy feed for horses supplied to them. Perhaps this explains why no correspondent for the NYAP attained distinction. The one outstanding accomplishment was that of Gobright himself, a week after the war ended, in reporting the assassination of President Lincoln.

In addition to newspapers and news agency correspondents in the field, as many as a dozen artists were producing sketches and drawings for such publications as *Harper's Weekly* and *Frank Leslie's Illustrated Newspaper*. Sometimes they worked underfire. One was Thomas Nast of *Harper's*, who also did some well-received oil paintings of war subjects.[8] Another was Winslow Homer, later to gain a reputation as a watercolorist, but who was with *Harper's* from the inauguration of Lincoln to the end of the war. Chiefly with the Army of the Potomac, most of his sketches were of camp life, but he did oils as well, and established himself as one of the foremost artists of his time. Edwin Forbes, later known as an etcher and painter, was an artist for *Leslie's*. Frank Vizetelly, as noted earlier, was an artist-correspondent for the London *Daily News,* working in the South.

Following in the wake of those anonymous daguerrotype photographers during the Mexican War, and of Roger Fenton and others during the Crimean War, most satisfactory photographs were made during the Civil War. The photographers included Mathew B. Brady and several assistants. Other war photographers were Timothy O'Sullivan, Alexander J. Gardner, and Lamont Buchanan. O'Sullivan had three cameras destroyed on the battlefields. Gardner was present at the Battle of Gettysburg, and Buchanan's photographs were made on the Confederate side of the lines.

Brady is the best remembered photographer of the war. Greatly successful as a portrait photographer since 1844, he spent nearly $100,000 of his own money to go into the field, and to send out others to make pictures of men, forces, and events from the time of the Battle of Bull Run through the surrender at Appomattox. His wagons full of

---

8   Reference has been made to Thomas Nast's earlier work in England and Sicily in 1859-60, and of his association with *Harper's Weekly* from 1862 to 1902. During those years, his cartoons and caricatures were influential in driving the corrupt Tammany Hall ring out of power in New York in 1871-72, and sending its director, William Marcy ("Boss") Tweed to jail—a campaign in which the *New York Times* also played a major role. In the years between 1871 and 1895, Nast created the lasting cartoon symbols for Tammany Hall, a tiger; the Republican party, the elephant; the Democratic party, the donkey; and also the familiar Santa Claus image. Appointed U.S. consul at Guayaguil, Ecuador, in 1902, he died there a few months later at sixty-two, a victim of yellow fever.

bulky equipment became familiar sights in areas of war, known to many as the "Whatsit Wagon" or the "Whatizzit Wagon." His photos of Abraham Lincoln were among the greatest, and his portrait of General Robert E. Lee at Appomattox also was to become memorable.[9]

As with those photos made during the Mexican and Crimean wars, there was no means to reproduce the photos of the Civil War at the time, though they since have become a part of the published history of that war. Some were used by artists, however, to prepare sketches for wood cuts for use in *Harper's Weekly* and other illustrated publications, and occasionally in newspapers. Maps produced from woodcuts also were used to illustrate reports of the war.

Correspondents, photographers, and sketch artists all faced personal risks and endured hardships during the war. At least one was killed, some were wounded, many fell ill, and some died, and a considerable number were taken prisoner.

George Alfred Townsend, correspondent for the *New York Herald,* built a home after the war on South Mountain in Maryland, the scene of the Battle of Antietam in 1862. He called his estate "Gathland," derived from the name "Gath," with which he had signed his war reports. There he also had built a fifty-foot arched and turreted stone memorial of his own design bearing the names of 151 war correspondents, both Union and Confederate, together with a laudatory "War Correspondents Ballad" of his own composition. Completed in 1896, the memorial and the estate were accepted in 1904 by the United States government on behalf of the National Parks Service as a part of the Antietam battlefield domain, and named Gathland State Park.

So far as the press content was concerned, the war years were not exclusively a matter of reporting battle action. There was much else to report. In October 1861, for example, the last link in a coast-to-coast telegraph line was completed. The Trent affair arose in November. In 1862 the French move into Mexico began, and was a subject of continuous concern. In May 1862, Congress passed a

---

9   The financial return from his efforts were so slight that Mathew Brady was virtually bankrupt, and his health also suffered. Many of his plates of the war years were lost or broken in the period from 1865 to 1874, and those remaining were auctioned in 1874. Some were purchased by the U.S. War Department for $2,800. Congress also voted him a grant of $25,000. He continued as a photo portraitist after the war, but less successfully, and died at seventy-three in the alms ward of a New York hospital in 1898.

Homestead Act that was of great importance in advancing the settlement of the country, entitling any citizen or an immigrant intending to become a citizen to acquire 160 acres of the public domain at $1.25 an acre after living on the land for five years. A Department of Agriculture was established, and a Bureau of Printing and Engraving.

President Lincoln signed two bills in July 1862 that were to prove important. One led to the incorporation of the Union Pacific Company, federally subsidized, to build a railroad from Nebraska to Utah that became the major link in the first transcontinental line completed in 1869. The other bill, the Morrill Act, provided for grants of public land to states for the establishment of agricultural colleges. This resulted in the formation, beginning in 1864, of "land grant" colleges in most states, some now major universities.

Three war-related events included the use of a balloon by Thaddeus Lowe in 1862 to photograph Confederate emplacements near Richmond, the development of the machine gun by Richard J. Gatling, and the drafting of the Emancipation Proclamation specifying the abolition of slavery, officially announced January 1, 1863.

The year 1863 brought the formation of West Virginia and its admission to the Union as the thirty-fifth state, and the formation of the territories of Idaho and Arizona. The first national conscription act in March was followed by antidraft riots in New York in July, with more than 1,000 persons killed or wounded, and the *New York Tribune* and Horace Greeley himself as special targets. In November, President Lincoln dedicated a national cemetery on the former battlefield at Gettysburg with a brief address that became a classic, but was virtually ignored at the time.

Lincoln was re-elected in 1864 to a second term as president. Nevada was admitted in that year as the thirty-sixth state, and Montana territory was formed. An Act of Congress provided a new spur to immigration. Wartime action at sea saw the first successful use of a submarine by the Confederates in Charleston harbor, but also the loss of the Confederate cruiser Alabama off Cherbourg. There was an attempt by Confederate agents to burn New York City in 1864, and a cloak-and-dagger mission by Horace Greeley to discuss possible peace negotiations with Confederate representatives in Canada. Lincoln met Confederate commissioners aboard ship in Hampton Roads, Virginia, in February 1865.

That year brought Lincoln's second inaugural in March, the surrender of the Confederates at Appomattox on April 9, the shooting of the president at Ford's Theater by John Wilkes Booth on April 14 and his death on April 15, with Vice-President Andrew Johnson succeeding to the presidency. Jefferson Davis, the Confederate president, was arrested May 10 at Irwinville, Georgia.

The days immediately following the war brought the worst ship disaster ever to occur in the United States when the steamer *Sultana*, carrying Union soldiers freed from Confederate prison camps, exploded on the Mississippi River April 27, with the loss of 1,700 of 2,300 aboard. The Ku Klux Klan, formed in Pulaski, Tennessee, near the year's end, was balanced by the adoption of the thirteenth amendment to the Constitution abolishing slavery. The opening of the Union stockyards in Chicago, already a railroad center, foreshadowed the growth of that city.

Other indications in 1862 of developments to come, while not necessarily reflected in the news during the war years, included a Sioux Indian uprising in Minnesota, with 350 whites killed; the opening of the first "department store" in New York City; and the formation of a partnership by a twenty-three-year-old Cleveland man named John Davison Rockefeller to refine oil recently discovered at Titusville, Pennsylvania.

In 1863 a thirty-three-year-old tailor in Sterling, Massachusetts, Ebenezer Butterick, tried to sell some dress patterns cut out of heavy paper and within fifteen years was selling patterns throughout much of the world. A National Academy of Sciences was chartered in Washington by Congress to advance the interests of science. At the same time a boy of sixteen named Thomas A. Edison was earning his living as a telegraph operator at Mount Clemens, Michigan, even as an infant named Henry Ford first saw the light of day on a farm near Dearborn, twenty-five miles away; and Samuel D. Goodale of Cincinnati patented a stereoscopic device that made people in pictures seem to move.

In 1863, also, William Bullock in Pittsburg patented a system for the use of a large roll of paper with the printing press to permit its continuous operation; and in 1864 George Presbury Rowell in Boston formed the first successful advertising agency. In New York, John Pierpont Morgan, twenty-seven, was a member of Dabney, Morgan & Company, a financial firm; while in Pittsburgh a man named Andrew Carnegie, twenty-nine, born in Scotland and a former telegraph operator, but then a Pennsylvania Railroad employee, introduced sleeping cars. He also bought a farm near Oil Creek, Pennsylvania, where oil had been found.

Among persons more widely known in 1865 than some of those mentioned were Mark Twain (Samuel Clemens), who won a large reading public with a story of "The Celebrated Jumping Frog of Calaveras County"; Walt Whitman, a male nurse in Washington during the war, who published *Leaves of Grass*; James Russell Lowell, Henry Wadsworth Longfellow, Petroleum V. Nasby (David Ross Locke), Josh Billings (Henry W. Shaw), Mary Mapes Dodge (*Hans Brinker: or, the Silver Skates*), Mrs. Henry Wood (whose *East Lynne* had sold a million copies), and Louisa May Alcott, just then coming into prominence.

There were others known during the war as writers, actors and actresses, artists, figures in sports, or prominent for other reasons. Among them were John Greenleaf Whittier, Herman Melville, Oliver Wendell Holmes, Charles Farrar Browne, Edward Everett Hale, David Belasco, Augustin Daly, and Adah Isaacs Menken. Others were James McNeill Whistler, George Inness, Edward P. Weston, Al Reach, Henry Ward Beecher, Clara Barton, and Francis Parkman.

In summary, a great deal was going on in the United States even as the war proceeded, and much of this was reflected in the press. At least three such things advanced by the war—photography, objective news writing, and cooperative news gathering—brought changes in the information process in the United States and throughout the world.

Photography as a Medium of Information

The presence of a few photographers in camps and on battlefields during the Civil War served as a reminder to alert members of the press that another means for vivid supplementation of prose was at least potentially available—lacking only a means to reproduce the photos in print. Photography already had advanced in quality since its practical beginning some twenty years earlier, and could be expected to become an important adjunct to the developing press system.

A public appreciation of pictorial treatment of the news had been demonstrated in the success of illustrated periodicals in a number of countries. Photography and photographs would be a clear advance over the wood engravings used in such publications, and occasionally in newspapers, and was indeed something to be nurtured and used as an added means of recording and providing information.

Photography, believed to have been given that name in 1839 by Sir John F. W. Herschel, British scientist and photographer, is commonly regarded as having had its real beginning in 1824, even though preceded by earlier experiments. Joseph Nicéphore Niepce of Paris, a chemist, seeking an improved process for making lithographic plates, worked with a camera obscura, itself dating in earliest form at least from the eleventh century. It was possibly used in England for photographic experiments conducted by Thomas Wedgewood in 1794 and by Sir Humphrey Davy soon after.

Niepce, working in 1824 with his elder brother, Claude F. A. Niepce de Saint-Victor, a physicist, succeeded in obtaining permanent impressions on a sensitized metal plate of views seen through the camera obscura. In 1829 he formed a partnership with Louis Jacques Mandé Daguerre, an inventor and theatrical scene painter in Paris. They worked together to improve what Niepce called a "heliography" process.

After the death of Niepce in 1833, Daguerre continued to work independently to increase the sensitivity of the metal plate to light. In January 1839 he was able to demonstrate a process that permitted clear and permanent pictures to be made on thin, silvered copper plate by camera exposures of from two to forty minutes. The brilliance of the object photographed governed the time required. This process was demonstrated and explained by Daguerre to the Paris Academy of Sciences later in 1839. Recognized as important, the right to use the process was purchased from Daguerre by the French government so that it might be placed in the public domain for general use and development.

The process was put to use with improvements and variations in a number of countries. William Henry Fox Talbot in England, for one, produced sensitized paper to receive the image. Claude Niepce, Joseph's brother, found a means of sensitizing a glass plate, or negative, from which prints could be made. Frederick Scott Archer, also in England, devised a wet collodion process in 1851 that was laborious and complex but yielded better negatives. It was a favored process until an improved dry plate was introduced in 1878 by Charles Bennett, reducing the time of exposure to one-tenth of that previously required, and simplifying the entire procedure.

Improved paper for printing the image transferred from the plate came after 1879. Cameras were improved with better lenses, and more easily tranportable. The great development giving the camera world-wide use came after 1889. George Eastman of Rochester, New York, a manufacturer of dry plates, and Thomas A. Edison—already known for many inventions and then experimenting in his New Jersey laboratory with motion picture photography—produced and manufactured sensitized film—a thin, flexible transparent sheet of cellulose acetate available in various sizes or in rolls. The film could be used in still cameras, or for motion picture photography as evolved after 1890 in France by Charles Pathé, and others in England, as well as by Edison. Advances then came rapidly after 1900.

Promptly after Daguerre's public demonstration of his "perfected" system of photography in 1839, he began to receive visits in Paris from those wishing to acquaint themselves with the new process. Among them were Samuel F. B. Morse and a young assistant in photographic experiments in New York, Mathew B. Brady. Morse, then forty-eight years old, had already filed a patent application in Washington in 1837 on his electric telegraph, and was waiting for Congress to act on his request, made at the same time, for funds to construct an experimental line.[10]

Back in New York in 1840, while proceeding with his development of the telegraph and waiting for Congress to vote funds for the experimental line, Morse and Brady set up the first apparatus in the Western Hemisphere to make daguerrotype photographs. They had added assistance from John W. Draper, a professor of chemistry at the university, who also had worked with Morse on the problems of telegraphy. When Congress at last appropriated $75,000 in 1843 for construction of the telegraph line between Washington and Baltimore, to be completed in 1844, Morse gave his whole attention to that project, and afterward to the development of the Magnetic Telegraph Company.

Brady, no longer able to work with Morse, set up his own photographic studio in New York in 1845, when he was twenty-one. Specializing in portraiture, he gained quick success. Later, he added a studio in Washington, and he also made portraits in London. Before the Civil War began in 1861 he had experimented with tinting, had produced portraits on ivory, had gained many awards for his work,

---

10   F. B. Morse was a man of many talents, rather like Leonardo da Vinci of four centuries earlier. Telegraphy was not his first interest, nor photography. Following graduation from Yale in 1810, he studied painting in England and was successful in that medium and in sculpture. He organized what became the National Academy of Design in New York in 1825, served as its president for sixteen years, and was a professor of art in the University of the City of New York. At the same time, he was deeply interested in "natural philosophy," chemistry, physics, and electricity. This spurred his invention of the telegraph. But he also conducted experiments in photography, and this interest induced him to go to Paris to meet with Daguerre.

and had accumulated a fortune. The "fortune" was lost through his largely uncompensated activity in making what amounted to a photographic record of the war. He was forced to close his New York studio, but did manage to continue in Washington. Between 1844 and his death in 1896, Brady photographed thousands of persons, including every president of the United States from John Quincy Adams, the sixth president, to William McKinley, the twenty-fifth, with the one exception of William Henry Harrison, who died after only one month in office. Brady might have escaped the financial difficulties that plagued him during the last thirty years of his life if there had been any demand for his photographs during the war or afterward—or a way to reproduce them in print.

Niepce himself, in addition to his experiments in photography, had made the first photoengraving in 1824, and Talbot, in England, had produced a plate upon which photographic images could be etched. It was 1873 or 1874 before Carl Klic, a Bohemian, developed a process by which an image could be transferred to a copper plate and etched into that plate in intaglio form. With the plate placed on a flatbed press and inked, and by using paper of a superior quality and exercising the greatest care, the image or photograph could be reproduced.

This was a great stride forward, but the process was not suitable for use by newspapers or magazines, by then produced on presses operating at high speed and printed on relatively rough paper made from wood pulp. For such use, any illustrations continued to be made by artists, possibly working from photographs, but with their drawings converted to hand-carved woodcuts. If large and elaborate illustrations were to appear, they were carved in squared-off sections by several artisans to speed completion, with the sections then assembled as the page was made ready for the press.

After 1888, using an acid process, it became possible to make zinc etchings of line drawings, maps, diagrams, and charts, which eliminated the need for hand-carved wooden blocks. A photoengraving process introduced in 1886 permitted satisfactory reproduction of photographs, if the printing was done on a flatbed press operating at moderate speed and using a good quality paper—a process used by magazines with increasing success. But it was 1897 before photographs could be reproduced on rough paper in newspapers, and be printed on high-speed rotary presses requiring the use of stereotype plates. It was, therefore, only shortly before the first years of the twentieth century that photographs began to appear in newspapers. They were seldom well reproduced, nor would be for many years.

The increased use of the telegraph for news purposes during the four years of the Civil War put newspapers and news agencies to considerable expense. In earlier times, before the existence of the telegraph had made speed a virtue and a competitive necessity, with reports from distant places delivered by mail, a reporter had more time to contemplate and to write his story. With a good story to tell, he might go on at some length and, if able, produce a minor or even major literary classic. By the standards of the period, this sometimes meant reports replete with fine phrases, florid description, and subjective comment. If the correspondent was writing a political report, he felt justified in presenting issues and personalities with all the flair likely to be appreciated by his editor and his newspaper, with due regard for that paper's dedication to a particular party, candidate, or issue.

With telegraph transmission rates what they were, however, this kind of writing became a luxury few newspapers cared to afford, whether to be paid for directly or through news agency service. Brevity now became important as a matter of economy. Plain facts took precedence over gems of thought, adjective-studded digressions, and personal opinions. The more concise the report, the more quickly it could be transmitted; the clearer the subject matter became, the better the reader would be informed, and the more likely he would be to read the entire report.

Reporters covering the war still produced long stories when the occasion demanded it, although those stories did not necessarily go over the telegraph lines. But brevity was increasingly demanded by editors, with a stress on facts, and the "specials" learned to comply. If this was expected of war reporters, it also was expected of reporters covering news in the home community as well, if only as a matter of consistency.

The new journalistic style required, first, what became known as a "summary lead." That is, the leading paragraph, in a sentence or two, and without preliminaries, presented the essential facts of the particular event being reported. It told What happened, Where it happened, When it happened, Who was involved, and Why or How it happened. Sometimes the "What" came first, sometimes the "Who," or whichever was the most interesting or important element. But the five "Ws" and the "H" were the building blocks for the lead.

Such a summary lead might provide all the information required to tell the story. But if it seemed necessary to enlarge upon these basic facts, or to add details, as was usual, those details could follow in the "body" of the story. Often three paragraphs to a story were enough, but as many paragraphs might follow as were warranted by the subject: with consideration of the time available for writing and transmission to meet the deadline, of costs of transmission, of "reader interest," and of the space available.

In writing the "body" of the story, the new style required that the elements or details adhere to facts only, as in the lead, and that they be presented in an order of diminishing importance. This made it possible for an editor, faced with considerations of time or limited space in the edition of the paper being prepared, to trim the body of the story by cutting from the bottom, even to the point of retaining only the summary lead, but with readers still provided the essential information.

This manner of telling a story not only meant an economy in telegraph costs, as contrasted to what they would be if the earlier discursive style were used, but it was a novelty. It added point, interest, and clarity; it permitted a quick reader understanding, and found general favor. Editors liked it not only as an economy, but because the new style resulted in better writing and more accurate writing. Such stories required less time to prepare for publication and solved some problems of finding space for others.

With its stress on facts, this style of writing became known as "objective" reporting, as contrasted to the opposite "subjective" form. The subjective form might be interesting, but in it the writer's views, personality, judgment, and opinions might obscure basic facts, with no way for a reader to be sure where fact and opinion overlapped, or where fact might have been canceled.

The objective style of reporting became doubly important during the Civil War, and even essential, because of the coincidental growth of news agency service. Indeed, the special problems of the news agency were as important as a desire to control telegraph charges in making objectivity an accepted rule in news writing from this period to the present in all countries where the information function of the press is respected. While a reporter might write a report that would be acceptable to his own newspaper, a news agency report on the same subject, going to scores of newspapers, might be wholly unacceptable to some. The individual newspapers could have special views on political issues, controversial subjects, and even on what might seem quite routine matters. Editors could object to what they deemed partisan, prejudicial, or inaccurate, and to words and phrases considered pejorative or misleading. Since the news agency existed to serve all member or subscribing newspapers, it was obliged in its reports to take a careful middle ground, concentrating on demonstrable facts. The objective style of writing was the answer.

If an individual newspaper wished to take a position on any subject so reported, to interpret or comment, whether in a partisan spirit or in a soberly responsible and reasoned advocacy, that it was its right and privilege. But, with objectivity governing news presentation, it was to be done only in its editorials, or in special signed articles or "columns," with readers presumably aware that this was opinion, open to free acceptance or rejection.

Taken together, the elements of news reporting relating to brevity, fact, and objectivity, as applied both to news agency accounts and to staff-written stories, became an article of faith in the publication of responsible newspapers in the United States from the time of the Civil War. Given an equal stress on accuracy, the public was provided with a more reliable service of current information.

It has become fashionable in recent years to question the reality of objectivity in news reporting and writing, to speak of a "new journalism" allowing and justifying a permissive return to subjectivity. The argument is that it is not possible for a human being to view a subject or write of it without the subtle influence of some element of personal background and experience. This, it is contended, is bound to determine how a reporter "sees" a subject, and therefore what is selected for emphasis in writing a summary lead, in what he judges to be more or less important and selects or rejects, or assigns priority, for mention in the body of the story.

This concept cannot be wholly dismissed. But the same could have been said before the objective style proved its value. It does not follow that a newsman need not even try to be fair and balanced, or accurate, as the other argument might suggest. It does not follow that his integrity as a representative of the public at the source of the news may properly come second to his personal beliefs, instincts, and emotions, much less to his prejudices. It does not justify his imposition of his personal views on others, perhaps in the guise of facts, or taking refuge in the ancient question, "What is Truth?"

There is such a thing in news writing as "factual interpretation." As a concept of more recent decades, this did not go unchallenged when first introduced. It was viewed by some as a dangerous departure from orthodox objectivity. As properly applied by a professional journalist, however, it holds no threat; rather the opposite. It means only an inclusion of added facts to give background and perspective to a report, still factual and objective.

But to reject the basic concept of objectivity can only invite a reversal of hard-won advances in the presentation of information. It is significant that the greatest scorn is heaped upon the concept of objectivity by those autocrats and dictators of the world who use information as a tool to manipulate people and events to suit their own purposes.

To argue further that objectivity is impossible of attainment is an irresponsible rationalization for refusing even to attempt to find the facts, for denying the need to try to be honest, and for excusing if not justifying partisanship, prejudice, and intolerance. Granted that the reality of objectivity requires a certain mental self-discipline on the part of the newsman, this does not mean that it is any the less earnestly to be sought. It has been done; therefore it can be done. The mark of the professional, for the reporter and the editor, is his ability to make the appropriate discounts to prevent his personal views from distorting his performance in the provision of information to the people. His mission is to inform as well and as truly as possible.

Objective handling of the news in the press of the United States, purposefully undertaken in the 1860s, set a pattern for the press of other countries. Its adoption elsewhere was not immediate, and is far from universal even today. Yet the advance did follow in much of the world, with readers better informed as a consequence.

Cooperative News-Gathering The WAP Takes a Lead

When the Civil War began in 1861, the New York Associated Press was distributing a news report to the seven New York City morning dailies sponsoring it,[11] including a world service received belatedly by ship from the Reuter agency of London.

The NYAP was making its service available to other newspapers, on a contractual basis, and to regional associations in New England, New York State, and the Middle Atlantic states.

Settlement in what then was the "west"—now the Midwest—had been growing, and daily newspapers were well established in such cities as Pittsburgh, Cincinnati, St. Louis, Chicago, Detroit, Cleveland, Milwaukee, St. Paul, and Omaha.

The war held great importance for the people of that middle-western area. Its newspapers gained greatly in readership. Some sent

---

11   There actually were seventeen dailies in Manhattan at this time—afternoon papers among them—and three others in Brooklyn.

"specials" to accompany the Union forces, and all wanted prompt news reports. This latter urgency brought the formation of a new regional association in 1862, the Western Associated Press (WAP), based in Chicago. It sought and obtained the service of the NYAP. Thomas W. Knox became it own representative at NYAP headquarters to prepare from the total NYAP-Reuter file those dispatches to be telegraphed to Chicago for distribution to member papers. Knox was an experienced newsman, a correspondent in the field for the *New York Herald* during the first year of the war, and he remained in New York for the WAP through its remaining years.

As a condition of membership in that association, WAP newspapers shared their own local news, including all that they received or originated individually. This material went also to the NYAP as a part of the exchange arrangement attaching to that relationship. Neither the WAP nor other regional associations were wholly pleased with the NYAP service. They felt the reports were being written primarily for the seven New York City dailies forming the core membership, without sufficient consideration for the interests of newspapers and readers elsewhere in the country. They regarded the rates as somewhat excessive, and the general attitude of the NYAP as arbitrary and unsympathetic to the needs and circumstances of other papers receiving the service.

So long as the war was in progress, the regional associations hesitated to express their discontent beyond a certain point lest they be deprived entirely of the NYAP service. In November 1866, however, with the war more than a year past and with the first successful North Atlantic cable in operation and the recovered 1865 cable as well, the Western Associated Press, by then the strongest of the regional associations, presented several proposals to the NYAP.

The WAP proposed that it should provide the NYAP with extended news reports from the Midwest, Southwest, and Pacific Coast in exchange for NYAP reports from the East, from Canada, and from the rest of the world as received through Reuter. It proposed that the WAP and NYAP should share equally the costs of news telegraphed from that portion of the country west of the Mississippi River and of news received from Europe by cable or otherwise. It proposed that the WAP should cover the news of congressional activities in Washington, with the NYAP continuing to cover other news sources in the capital. It proposed that the WAP make its own arrangement for telegraphic transmission of news between New York and Chicago, and that the NYAP do the same with reference to the eastward transmission between Chicago and New York. The WAP announced that it intended to get news wherever and however it could, and not necessarily from the NYAP alone. In general, the WAP proposed an equal and cooperative relationship, rather than a continuation of the arrangement whereby it was no more than a client of the NYAP, and that new financial arrangements should be made on that basis.

Some members of the NYAP, aware of changes that had taken place in other parts of the United States, were prepared to give greater consideration to the needs and interests of those growing newspapers of the country and to the WAP proposals. Daniel H. Craig, former publisher of the *Boston Daily Mail* and general agent or manager of the NYAP since 1851, was among those who took this view.

The core member papers of the NYAP saw it differently, however, including papers of such prestige at the *New York Herald* and *New York Tribune*. The NYAP, like the WAP, required that member papers receiving news from their own sources should make that news available to other member papers. Since this would require the *Herald* and the *Tribune* to share news they now were beginning to receive from Europe by cable, at great expense to themselves, they saw no justice in asking that they make a free gift of such news to other papers. On this issue, particularly, the NYAP rejected the WAP proposals.

In the course of the discussions, Craig had placed himself in such a position, by reason of his support of the WAP proposals, that he was "discharged by unanimous vote of all the members" of the NYAP. James W. Simonton of the *New York Times,* a former San Francisco newspaperman and former Washington correspondent, was appointed to succeed Craig as general agent for the NYAP.

The directors of the Western Associated Press, following the rejection of their proposals, authorized an independent program to gather and exchange news. Craig joined with the WAP to assist in that program. He first formed a company in New York called the United States and Europe Telegraph News Association, backed by Western Union, and controlling its own extensive domestic telegraph network. The WAP signed a contract with the new organization and broke off relations with the NYAP. Craig also became "General Agent" or manager of the WAP. He arranged to receive a cabled report of world news from the Wolff agency of Berlin, channeled through his new Telegraph News Association in New York and forwarded by Western Union to the WAP in Chicago for distribution to its member papers. Craig also attempted, with some success, to divert other regional clients of the NYAP to the WAP.

The New York Associated Press, in a counter move, sent Alexander Wilson to London in December 1866 to open the first transatlantic bureau serving any Western Hemisphere news agency. His main task was to go through the Reuter file each day and make a selection of material to be cabled to New York for distribution to members and clients of the NYAP, including the regional associations in New York State and New England, and one established in Atlanta, the Southern Associated Press.

The NYAP and WAP together soon were spending as much as $2,100 a week for European cable dispatches, with payments going partly to Reuter and partly to Wolff. Since this involved a duplication of subject matter, it was wasteful as well as costly. After only three weeks of such rivalry, the NYAP showed a disposition to make some concessions and on January 11, 1867, the two associations reached a new agreement, with cable costs reduced to about $800 a week by using the Reuter service only.

Under this arrangement, the WAP was to pay the NYAP 22 per cent of the cable costs, not to exceed $150,000 a year, and also to pay 20 per cent of the cost of California and trans-Mississippi news delivered in Chicago. That far-western news, along with news gathered by the WAP in the Midwest through its member papers, was to be delivered to an NYAP agent in Cleveland or Pittsburgh at the expense of the WAP. All remaining costs, including coverage of Washington news, were to be borne by the NYAP.

At the same time, the NYAP agreed to divide the territory so that the WAP had a monopoly on news gathering and news distribution in that part of the country west of the Allegheny Mountains and north of the Ohio River. The NYAP retained its own separate arrangements with the three other regional groups in New York State, New England, and the South, westward to New Orleans. The newspapers of the United States thus were being served, in effect, by five news associations working in a joint and cooperative relationship. With this new arrangement, Craig was retired from his briefly held position as general agent of the WAP, and his United States and Europe Telegraph News Association also ceased to exist. Craig himself continued in the communications field, however, associated with Ezra Cornell in his extensive telegraph company activities, including majority control of Western Union.

George B. Hicks, an experienced telegrapher, replaced Craig as general agent for the WAP. Two years later, in 1869, he was succeeded in turn by William Henry Smith, founder in 1867 of the *Cincinnati Evening Chronicle,* who began a tenure of twenty years with the agency. The WAP and NYAP operated in an harmonious relationship for a quarter century. Indeed, when Simonton retired as general agent of the NYAP in 1881 for reasons of health, William Henry Smith became general agent for both associations, and continued in that dual role through 1892.

In 1872 the NYAP expended more than $200,000 for cable reports distributed by then to 200 dailies in the United States, including members of the WAP group. In 1880 cable costs ranged from $300 to $500 a day, and sometimes rose as high as $2,000 a day. The European and world report of the Reuter agency was the basis for this service available through the Reuter-NYAP contract. The Havas and Wolff services, delivered to Reuter in London and augmented after 1870, became a part of the total service. Alexander Wilson, in London for the NYAP, and his successor, Walter Neef, selected whatever they wished from that total service at the Reuter headquarters, which also received NYAP reports.

The Western Associated Press, while receiving the Reuter service through the NYAP, soon sought to supplement it by establishing its own stringer correspondents in London and in Liverpool to cover and speed British and European news. By 1891 it also had stringers locally employed in Paris, Rome, and Berlin, with others elsewhere by 1892. It is fair to assume that those WAP representatives depended heavily upon the newspapers in the European capitals as a major source for their reports.

The WAP also looked in new directions. Charles Sanford Diehl, formerly of the *Chicago Times,* where he made a reputation covering the Indian Wars in the plains states in the seventies and early eighties, was made a member of the WAP Chicago headquarters staff. In May 1887 he was sent to open a bureau in San Francisco. Diehl regarded his area of coverage as including all of the far-western states, and also as extending westward into the Pacific. He not only reported news arriving by ships putting in to San Francisco, but one of his first acts was to go himself to Hawaii to cover a revolt against the rule of Queen Liliuokalani, who was deposed in 1893. His reports, reaching the telegraph end in San Francisco, and widely distributed, turned the attention of the press and people of the United States to the Pacific area for almost the first time.

In 1889 Diehl sent John P. Dunning to the Samoan Islands to report a controversy over their control between Germany, Great Britain, and the United States—ten years later the islands came under the protection of the latter. While there, Dunning witnessed one of the most violent hurricanes or typhoons ever to strike the South Seas—one that took many lives and wrecked three U.S. naval vessels, and one British and one German, all anchored in Apia harbor. Because of a lack of cable facilities in the Pacific, the March 16 storm was not reported in the United States or elsewhere until April 13. It then was the subject of the longest account to be telegraphed up to that time from San Francisco eastward across the continent, and was reprinted by newspapers in other countries, including the London *Times,* which had praise for its style. Two years later in 1891, Dunning was in Chile for the WAP, the only U.S. correspondent to report a civil war then in progress.

Meanwhile, in 1875, the NYAP set up the first leased wire telegraphic news circuit in the United States, linking New York, Philadelphia, Baltimore, and Washington. It soon was carrying 18,000 to 20,000 words a day at a considerable saving because of the leased wire arrangement, with a contract payment based on time of use rather than on words transmitted. A second leased wire opened in 1884 reached Boston and a New York-Chicago line also served WAP members. By 1891 the NYAP-WAP leased wires were operating coast-to-coast to provide a rapid, assured and more economical service of information to the newspapers and the people of most of the United States.

The subsequent development of the Western Associated Press, and its relationship to the New York Associated Press is reserved for later examination. What had been established long before 1891, however, was the advantage of a cooperative exchange between newspapers of local reports to enrich the total service of the news agency structure.

In summary, the significant element in the advancement of public information stemming from the American Civil War and its aftermath is that the war itself and related needs and influences gave a new strength and maturity to the press organization in the United States in the approximate period between 1861 and 1875. It had overtaken the older and more advanced British press—or more specifically the London press—in its improved capacity to report current affairs, and in the quality of some of its newspapers and periodicals. Prior to 1860, certain London newspapers had set standards and devised methods adapted by most other newspapers in the world. Some such standards and methods now were contributed by the press of the United States, and were accepted and adapted by the press of other countries, including that of Great Britain.

This two-way Anglo-U.S. exchange became clearly operative by 1871. Press advances in other countries, so far as they occurred, were to come later, but usually followed precedents and practices originating first in Great Britain, in the United States, and to some extent in France. The press in each of these countries set its own pattern, exemplified in matters of physical appearance, as well as in content.

The distinctive physical characteristic of a British newspaper was its use of the first and last page for advertising, with the facing center pages free of advertising—one the important "leader" page and the other the "main news" page. The French and U.S. papers used page one as a main news page—often with a greater headline display than was used on the main news page of a British newspaper—and in some cases carried small advertisements. The British and U.S. papers presented the news in a generally objective manner, but the French papers often permitted opinion, policy, and polemics to enter into the news. These "patterns" were never without exceptions, and they were modified after 1900, but until that time they were at least typical.

Prussia, the Press and a Shrinking World

The focus of press attention shifted back to Europe after the conclusion of the American Civil War in 1865. For the people and press of the United States, the last five years of the 1860s included a special interest in events relating to "reconstruction," looking toward a restored unity within the country. There also was the advancing settlement of the West, the purchase of Alaska from Russia in 1867, the effort to impeach President Johnson, the presidential campaign of 1868, and the inauguration in 1869 of Ulysses S. Grant as the eighteenth president of the United States.

Of interest and importance to the United States and Great Britain, but to other countries as well, was the successful completion of the North Atlantic cable in 1866, and the recovery and equally successful operation of the 1865 cable. It was a great occasion when that first permanent North Atlantic cable went into operation on July 26, and doubly gratifying when the second cable became effective on September 8.

With the North Atlantic cable at last functioning, the Western

Union Telegraph Company soon halted its effort to extend a telegraph-cable connection between San Francisco and St. Petersburg, by way of Alaska and Siberia. The Danish Great Northern Telegraph Company salvaged much of that line in Siberia before the end of the decade. Western Union itself gained a complete national telegraphic wire system in the United States in April 1866. The Indo-European Telegraph Company line had started operation in March 1865, and London and Alexandria were linked by cable in 1869, the year the Suez Canal opened.

News agency developments in the decade included the Havas entrance to Latin America in 1860. The Reuter agency undertook service in northern and central Europe until Reuter himself established the basis for the Ring Combination, begun in January 1870. The same years brought eleven new agencies into existence.

Reference has been made to Napoleon III and France in the 1859 conflict between Austria and Piedmont, with the beginning of an Italian unification; to the Austro-Prussian alliance by which the duchies of Schleswig and Holstein were separated from Denmark in 1864, with Prussia then administering Schleswig and Austria dominant in Holstein; and to the desire of Bismarck to bring about a confederation of Germanic states and principalities under Prussian direction.

In 1865 these latter elements came together in a direct relationship. Bismarck and Napoleon III met at Biarritz, France, in October. Bismarck found the Austrian position in Holstein quite intolerable since it represented an Austrian enclave in what should, in Bismarck's view, be Prussian territory. He had contrived to turn his former alliance with Austria into a tense relationship, and a war between the two countries was more than a possibility. At Biarritz, Napoleon was offered inducements to assure France's neutrality, with prospects of French territorial control in Rhineland areas in return. His influence also was invited to bring Italy into an alliance with Prussia against Austria. Austrian-controlled Venetia was to be Italy's reward, assuming a Prussian victory.

With Napoleon's agreement, an alliance between Prussia and Italy was formed. Napoleon was privately convinced that Austria would be the victor in a Prussian-Austrian war. In June 1866, accordingly, he reached a secret understanding with Austria, again assuring French neutrality if war occurred, but with an agreement that Austria would cede Venetia to Napoleon, win or lose, while any changes a victorious Austria might wish to make in the Germanic states would have Napoleon's approval. Further, it was agreed that a French-controlled buffer state might be created along the Rhine, even as Bismarck had hinted, to provide security for France.

As Napoleon was building his bridges in Austria and Italy, the Austrian governor of Holstein summoned the local legislative body to discuss the future of the duchy. Bismarck, who had been seeking a pretext since April to make war on Austria and seize Holstein, now asserted that the governor's action violated an earlier agreement for the joint Austrian-Prussian administration of the territories, and made this a reason to send Prussian troops into Holstein. Austria responded by making for its own military intervention. Wilhelm I of Prussia, with Bismarck's urging, proclaimed that Prussia had no option, other than war, if unity were to be established in Germany.

The Germanic states did not all agree with Bismarck, and some found the Prussian presumption of leadership objectionable. Thus, Hanover, Bavaria, and Saxony, three of the larger states, sided with Austria. Italy itself sided with Prussia, both because of its traditional differences with Austria, and because it had Venetia to gain in its own plan for unity.

The Austro-Prussian War began on June 16, 1866. It continued only seven weeks, with the actual fighting ending early in July in a victory for Prussia. Peace was restored by a treaty signed in Prague on August 23.

The military engagements occurred in Hanover, Bohemia, Italy, and in the Adriatic. Italy was defeated by the Austrians but, as an ally of Prussia, it did gain the Venetian area and adjacent Lombardy—a further step toward peninsular unity. French troops shortly moved into the papal states, however, to protect Rome from seizure by Garibaldi in his independent campaign to complete Italy's unification.

Meantime, Napoleon failed to get his Rhineland buffer state, as he believed he had been promised by Bismarck, as well as by the Austrians. But Bismarck got a North German Confederation, formed in 1867, which included Hanover as well as Schleswig and Holstein. Opposition in the south German states continued to block his desire for a wholly unified Germany.

The press of Prussia, Austria, France, and Italy reported the war, but not in a manner to enlighten readers. The news agencies of those countries stood in an official or semi-official relationship to their governments. Bismarck was notable for a skillful use of the press to advance his own designs. No more than perhaps six or eight dailies in the four countries had attained the strength or prosperity to enable them to undertake anything approaching original coverage of the news. Only a few had any correspondents in other capitals, and if any had correspondents in the field their names appear to have been lost.

The more highly-developed daily newspapers of London again showed enterprise in reporting the Austro-Prussian War. Five put men in the field. It also was at this time that the press of the United States began to establish staff correspondents in Europe, rather than relying exclusively upon a few stringers, occasional visits by editors or writers, or the reports provided through Reuter. The extension of telegraphic communications in Europe encouraged coverage, and the beginning of North Atlantic cable communication on July 26, a month before the war was ended by treaty, spurred the press in London and New York to action.

When the war began on June 16, the London *Times* sent experienced war correspondent William Howard Russell to accompany Austrian forces. He wrote an eye-witness report of the key battle, occurring July 3 around the Bohemian villages of Königgrätz and Sadow, with more than a half million men engaged, and resulting in a stunning Prussian victory. He had C. B. Brackenbury as an assistant. Henry Hosier, a British army captain, was with the Prussians for the *Times*. This was the only battle action reported, although Italian forces were defeated by Austrian in two encounters in the south, and there had been early action in Hanover.

Other London newspapers were represented in the field. George Alfred Henty moved with Italian forces allied with the Prussians. He represented the *Standard,* started in London in 1827 as an evening paper, but converted to a morning daily in 1857. The *Pall Mall Gazette,* only established in 1865, had Henry Mayers Hyndman with the Italians. Edward Dicey of the *Daily Telegraph* was with the Austrians. The *Daily News* had Frank Vizetelly with the Austrians and Hilary Skinner with the Prussians.

This representation, although small, foreshadowed a circumstance that was to become increasingly common, both in war and peace, whereby many of the same correspondents appeared and reappeared as their presence was required by events, but sometimes for different publications. In this instance, Russell and Henty had reported the Crimean War, but with Henty then writing for the *Morning Post.* Vizetelly had been a correspondent for the *Illustrated Times* during the Austro-Italian War of 1859, but now wrote for the *Daily News,* as he had during the American Civil War.

For the U.S. press, the *New York Herald,* leading in news enterprise, came under the active direction of James Gordon Bennett, Jr., in 1866, when his father, the paper's founder, retired at seventy. The younger Bennett, then twenty-five, was to continue his father's policy of emphasizing the news, including world reports, without counting the cost. One of his earliest acts was to assign one of the paper's Civil War correspondents, Colonel Finlay Anderson, as representative in London.

The *New York Tribune* at that time had two stringer correspondents in London. One was Karl Marx, as previously noted, and the other was Moncure D. Conway, an American. When the war began in June the *Tribune* also started two staff men on the way from New York to London. Both were experienced Civil War correspondents—George W. Smalley and Henry Villard. It was intended that they should report the new conflict, but even before they reached London the war had ended in an armistice on July 22. The nearest thing to war coverage that either man was able to provide was a newsworthy interview Smalley obtained with Count von Bismarck in Berlin. Villard remained in Europe as a free lance-writer and student of finance in Berlin, which led him into a new career.

After the Prussian victory was established so quickly, to the surprise and alarm of much of Europe, King Wilhelm of Prussia announced the proposed formation of a North German Confederation of twenty-two small states under Prussian domination. This was a great step toward Bismarck's program for a union of Germanic states.

The new North Atlantic cable had gone into successful operation on July 26, 1866, and James Gordon Bennett, Jr., directed Colonel Anderson in London to cable the full text of King Wilhelm's pronouncement. It appeared in the *New York Herald* of August 1, transmitted at a cost of $6,720. That cost was shared with two other New York papers which also used the dispatch. On the same day, the *New York Tribune* published its first cable dispatch from "Our Own Correspondent in London." It was based upon a brief message from Smalley, but cost some $235 at the original London-New York cable rate of £2 a word.

With the war at an end, there were other subjects for attention. Bennett spent £1,000 ($4,850) to cable from London a full account of a prizefight between Jem Mace and Joe Coburn, the current British and U.S. heavyweight champions. Early in 1867 he informed Field of the Anglo-American Company, operating the cable, that he was prepared to sign a contract to pay $3,750 monthly for an assured connection on cable messages to and from London for the *New York Herald*. On several occasions during the first five years after the Atlantic cable service began, the *Herald* paid in excess of £1,000 in London for the transmission of single messages.

Newspapers and news agencies alike, stimulated by the availability of telegraphic and cable services, reexamined their methods of reporting, both nationally and internationally.

Smalley of the *New York Tribune* was among newsmen who recognized that information was going to move in greater volume. Upon his return to New York from London in the autumn of 1866, he recommended to the *Tribune* that it open a bureau in London, and that the bureau be placed under the direction of an editor or correspondent possessing full authority to direct all news-gathering operations for the paper on the European continent. This was a new concept in editorial administration.

Even then the *Tribune* had stringers in London, Paris, Berlin, Rome, Madrid, Vienna, Athens, Constantinople, and St. Petersburg. The *New York Herald* was very similarly represented, as was the London *Times*. Some other London and New York dailies were represented on a smaller scale, and so were a few newspapers on the continent. In all such cases, however, authority for the direction of such representatives was exercised through the paper's home office. For Smalley to propose otherwise meant a departure from existing practice. Although he had not intended it or desired the bureau for himself, he was persuaded to return to London in the spring of 1867 to put the plan into operation for the *Tribune*, and to begin what became a quarter-century of residence there.

Bennett of the *New York Herald* scoffed at the *Tribune*'s action, regarding it as a division of authority in the conduct of a newspaper, but he was to adopt the method for the *Herald* later, when its value was demonstrated. It was to become the general practice for U.S. newspapers as their coverage of European affairs developed. Sometimes Paris was made the administrative center, but usually it was London because of superior communications facilities centering there, more extensive sources of news,' and fewer complications arising from language differences. Paris was favored, however, by many newspapers of Europe and Latin America.

Smalley's return to London in 1867 was well-timed because, before the Franco-Prussian War began in 1870, he had his bureau so well organized that the *New York Tribune* led all newspapers in the coverage of that important conflict. He also had been able to establish favorable arrangements for handling cable messages promptly, at rates still high ($1.60 a word to New York after September 1868), but a fraction of what they had been in 1866.

Because the *Tribune* was an original member of the New York Associated Press, Smalley had access each day to Reuter reports, and knew what was being transmitted to New York for the NYAP and available to the *Tribune*. Thus he was able to avoid needless and costly duplication in his own messages and could direct his efforts instead toward a more specialized coverage of particular stories with more background. This set the pattern to be followed by special correspondents for newspapers. They left the more routine and general coverage to agency correspondents and bureaus, and concentrated upon the more important subjects of the day.

When the Franco-Prussian War began, Smalley also was able to form a working alliance with the *Daily News* of London whereby dispatches written by correspondents for either newspaper were shared with the other, to the enrichment of both. A comparable arrangement was extended to the *Pall Mall Gazette*. This was the first arrangement of such a nature between newspapers published in different countries. It set another precedent, one that proved of mutual advantage in this instance, and one adapted by other newspapers.

Smalley's experience as a correspondent during the Civil War, and his familiarity with the objective style of news writing was to give further advantage to the *Tribune* during the Franco-Prussian War, and, by example, to bring change and improvement to the press of Great Britain and the European continent.

Broad Perspectives: A New Era 12

The decisive Prussian victory at Sadowa in 1866 and the formation of the North German Confederation marked the beginning of a new era in Europe. A further victory in the related Franco-Prussian War of 1870-71 brought that era into full being. It meant the end of the Second Empire in France, and the beginning of the Third Republic. It resulted in the formation of a Germany dominant on the continent and with overseas territories added in 1884 in Africa and the Pacific. The impact of these events was to be nearly as important as the industrial revolution in reshaping the world.

Changes came not only in Europe, but in the opening of the interior of Africa. In the United States, there was a beginning of industrialization and the settlement of the western territories. In India, China, and Japan, there were changes, and closer relations with the western world. Noteworthy events occurred in Canada, Australia, New Zealand, in areas of the Pacific, and in Central and South America. Exploration and archeological ventures extended horizons, and advances occurred in education, science, and technology. With all of this, the face of the world was transformed in the three decades between 1870 and 1900.

These developments provided the subject matter for news, and the press organization was occupied in reporting on an ever-broader stage with a growing professional competence. The Ring Combination was in full operation. Telegraph lines were further extended, cables brought most parts of the world into direct communication, and costs were generally reduced, with special press rates and leased wire arrangements encouraging the transmission of news in greater volume. There were wars and military expeditions to be reported, but a vast amount of substantive news as well.

The decade of the 1870s brought the telephone into the communications network, with progressive advancement in quality and service. The typewriter was in general use. Newsprint made from woodpulp, rather than rags, added to its availability and reduced its cost. Improvements were made in the printing process, with presses operating at greater speed, and automatic typesetting added before the end of the century. Newspapers became larger, more numerous, more prosperous, more informative, and more interesting. Readership grew accordingly. Weekly and monthly periodicals added another dimension to public information. Photography and photoengraving also advanced and motion picture photography was beginning. By 1900, wireless transmission of messages became possible, though still imperfect.

The advances may be said to have begun in 1870, at the time of the Franco-Prussian War.

The Franco-Prussian War, 1870-71

Count Otto von Bismarck as chancellor of Prussia under King William (or Wilhelm), successful in creating the North German Confederation in 1866, undertook to bring in the four south German states of Baden, Württemberg, Bavaria, and Hesse-Darmstadt to make a united Germany. They were persuaded to join a customs union and a customs parliament, but continued to oppose full union with Prussia.

Bismarck believed the southern states might agree to join in a general union if they had reason to suppose that France was to gain a buffer state in the Rhineland, infringing upon some part of their own territory. This Bismarck also opposed, even though he had hinted at some such arrangement in his meeting with Napoleon III at Biarritz in October 1865. That, however, had only been to gain assurance of France's neutrality in the prospective war with Austria. Once that war was over and won, he blocked Napoleon's every effort to attain any Rhineland territory or, alternatively, to make Luxembourg or Belgium a part of France.

The only other circumstance that would induce the southern German states to join in full union with Prussia, in Bismarck's view, was a war in which France attacked Prussia and so raised the prospect of a forced cession of Rhineland territory in event of victory. He was equally convinced that France itself would not agree to the inclusion of those south German states in a union short of a war in which Prussia emerged victorious. He therefore saw such a war as inevitable and even essential to his plan for a unified Germany.

Napoleon III had seemed to agree with Bismarck's proposals at Biarritz, but then had entered into secret agreements with Austria in 1866, in the personal belief that Austria would defeat Prussia in a long and exhausting war, with France gaining a position of strength. He was shocked by the brevity of the war and by Prussia's victory. He was outraged and humiliated by Bismarck's obstruction of his territorial designs in 1867. Further, he was alarmed by the prospect of a united Germany as a powerful central European nation, and as a threat to France. He saw a war with Prussia as inevitable, and perhaps necessary, if such a union was to be prevented.

Thus both Bismarck and Napoleon III, each for his own reasons, began preparations for war. Prussia already had a strong military force, but it was further strengthened. Napoleon sought a military alliance with Austria and Italy, but neither country was prepared to join in a such an alliance. Austria saw the issue as strictly between France and Prussia. Italy felt it had been betrayed by Napoleon in 1859, and also insisted that French troops would have to leave Rome, where they had been since 1867. Napoleon nevertheless persuaded himself that he would have the support of both countries if war with Prussia occurred.

Bismarck's problem was how to make it appear that France was the aggressor in the war, if there was to be a war, so that the four southern states would indeed rally to his banner. In this, a secondary but not unrelated issue played into his hand. A revolution in Spain in 1868 left that country without a monarch. Acting in great secrecy, Prussia backed the candidacy of Prince Leopold of Hohenzollern-Sigmaringen, a German principality. Leopold was prepared to accept the throne, and the Spanish Cortes was about to vote on the matter. That prospect became known, and raised an alarm in France lest a German ruler in that neighboring country pose a danger.

Prussia's King William was at Bad Ems, a German spa, in July 1870. On instructions from Napoleon III, Count Vincent Benedetti, France's ambassador in Berlin, followed him there to make a request that Prince Leopold's name be withdrawn from consideration in Madrid. King William responded to Benedetti's request in a friendly manner, but made no promises. In the normal course of affairs, a telegram went to Bismarck, in Berlin, informing him of what had transpired at Bad Ems.

Bismarck found in this telegram his opportunity. Using excerpts from the original, he prepared a shorter version that gave the impression the king had rejected Benedetti's request, had insulted him in the process, and seemed to indicate a severance of diplomatic relations between Prussia and France. Through the semi-official Wolff agency, Bismarck released this "Ems telegram" for publication. It was a distortion, deliberately contrived, but it had the intended effect.

There is reason to believe that Napoleon might have taken France into war with Prussia even without the Bad Ems telegram as a pretext. But it did become a pretext, and France declared war on July 19. This suited Bismarck's purpose in having France appear as the aggressor, driving the south German states into alliance with Prussia and the North German Confederation, resulting in a permanent union.

The Franco-Prussian War began July 19, 1870, and continued until May 10, 1871. It ended in a Prussian victory and the formation of the German Empire. Napoleon III was himself captured during the Battle of Sedan on September 2, and held prisoner until the end of the war. The French Empire ended with his departure.

The ten months of the war brought a series of battles: one at Wörth early in August 1870, one at Gravelotte on August 18, one of the great battles of history at Sedan on September 1 to 3, the surrender of Metz on October 27, moves on Strasbourg and Nancy, and a long siege of Paris extending from September 19 to January 28, 1871.

During that period, revolution broke out within Paris, where a temporary government was established. At the same time, a provisional French government was formed at Bordeaux, a safe sanctuary in the south of France. Prussian troops did not enter Paris until March 1, and civil strife did not end there until May 28.

With the end of the empire, the French Third Republic was formed at Bordeaux, and a preliminary treaty of peace was signed between Prussia and the new Republic at Versailles on February 26. Bismarck signed for Prussia and Adolphe Thiers, acting as president of the Republic, signed for France. At that time King William of Prussia was proclaimed Emperor Wilhelm I of a united German Empire. A final treaty of peace was signed at Frankfurt on May 10.

By the terms of the peace, France was forced to yield to Germany the eastern border province of Alsace and a portion of the adjacent province of Lorraine, with Metz included. France also agreed to pay reparations of five billion gold francs (about $1 billion). Prussian troops were to remain in occupation in parts of France until full payment was made.[1] The reparations payment demanded, considered huge at the time, was made sooner than had been expected, and German troops were withdrawn from France in September of 1873. The country also suffered economically in terms of men and property, and the loss of Alsace and Lorraine rankled until they were recovered after World War I.

The war was reported more thoroughly than any previous European conflict. British correspondents had been alone in the field at the time of the Crimean War, and almost alone in the Austro-Italian and the Austro-Prussian War, but the press of a half-dozen countries was represented during the Franco-Prussian War.

The Havas and Wolff agencies tended to take official reports from their governments as a basis for accounts distributed, with a minimum of direct coverage. Because their two countries were at war a direct exchange of news, such as had existed from 1859, was necessarily suspended. Each continued to exchange news with Reuter, however, which resulted in an indirect exchange since the Reuter service, incorporating their reports, reached both. But the Havas service was greatly disrupted by the war.

At first, the French government announced that no war correspondents would be permitted with its forces in the field. Bismarck, confident of Prussia's readiness for the war, and believing press coverage would be advantageous to his purpose, took the opposite position, and France felt obliged to modify its own press policy. It was agreeed that French correspondents might move in the war zone and observe action, but they were still to be barred from accompanying the armed forces and, for a time, were barred from headquarters. The government also established an official news bureau at the Ministry of the Interior in Paris, but it was of small value and largely ignored by the press.

It may be that among French dailies *Le Gaulois,* recently established in Paris, had more men reporting the war than any other; twenty-six were listed in the London *Publishers' Circular* of September 1870. Emile Cardon of that paper, and Henri Chabrillat of *Le Figaro,* were captured by the Prussians at the Battle of Wörth, but were released. Edmund Texier wrote for *Le Siecle,* as he had attempted to do in Piedmont in 1859. G. Jennerod wrote for *Le Temps,* and Jules Clarétie for *Opinion Nationale.*

---

1 To help meet the payment, the first French North Atlantic cable, completed in 1869, was sold in 1873 to the Anglo-American Company.

The Prussian government was more cooperative with the press, both of its own and of neutral countries. The *Frankfurter Zeitung* had Ludwig Holthof with troops at Metz and Hermann Voget at Nancy. Theodor Curti, that paper's correspondent in Paris when the war began, remained there, surprisingly, even throughout the long siege and afterward, but had no means of transmitting reports. The *Kölnische Zeitung* had Hans Wachenhusen at the front and also received reports in Cologne from at least six others: Julius von Wickede, Theodore Fontane, Dr. George Horn, A. Petermann, a Herr Kayssler, and a Herr Pietsch.[2] These two leading German dailies, with some correspondents serving in European capitals, built reputations during the war which were enhanced in later years. *Die Grenzboten* of Leipzig also was represented at the war front by Gustas Freytag—later of the *Kölnische Zeitung*. The *Staats Zeitung*, an official Prussian government paper, was granted certain advantages and presented some of the first and best reports, a number of them prepared by a young Dr. Hassell.

Austria's interest in the war was intense, and Arnold Wellmer was one correspondent in the field for the *Neue Freie Presse* of Vienna. Correspondents also were active for *La Stampa* of Turin; for the *Indépendance Belge* of Brussels; and for Spain's *Diario de Barcelona*, which was represented by Nilo Maria Fabra, founder in 1865 of the Spanish news agency bearing his name.

The neutral press was able to have correspondents in both camps during the war, and the reports so provided by special correspondents for the British and U.S. press were generally the most satisfactory of the period. The Reuter agency depended heavily upon Sigismund Engländer, who had a roving commission. It received reports from George Douglas Williams, who had joined the London staff in 1861, had served in Italy and elsewhere in Europe, and was in Paris. The Havas and Wolff reports reached the agency under the established exchange arrangement.

The London *Times* with its great prestige, was served once again by William Howard Russell, now forty-nine years old, accompanying Prussian forces. He is said to have been grandly equipped for a war of movement, with three saddle horses, two carriage horses, a courier, a

---

2   An incidental point of some concern in news reporting through the years, and in reconstructing the personnel engaged in that reporting, was the manner in which names were used. The Anglo-American press has been punctilious about the use of full names. The European press tends to use one initial and sometimes the surname only, commonly omitting other identification relating to occupation, title, age, and address.

groom of livery, a coachman, a wagonette, a brougham, and a luggage wagon. By reason of his personal reputation and that of the *Times* itself, and his standing as the "dean" of correspondents, he was granted every courtesy. He also had assistants, one a retired British officer, Colonel Christopher Pemberton, who was killed at Sedan, and A. B. Kelly, and others.

Even though he produced some excellent reports, Russell was outdone by some younger correspondents. He also was made a target of satire in his own country by Matthew Arnold in an essay suggesting that he suffered from a sense of over-importance. Published after the signing of the preliminary peace treaty at Versailles in February 1871, it presented an imaginary picture of an occasion where

> . . . Dr. Russell was preparing to mount his war-horse. You know the sort of thing—he has described it himself over and over. Bismarck at the horse's head, the Crown Prince holding his stirrup, and the old king of Prussia hoisting Russell into the saddle. When he was there, the distinguished public servant waved his hand in acknowledgement, and rode down the street, accompanied by the *gamins* of Versailles, who even in their present dejection could not forbear a few involuntary cries of '*Quel homme!*' Always unassuming, he alighted at the lodging of the Grand Duke of Oldenburg, a potentate of the second or even the third order, who had beckoned to him from the window. . . .[3]

The *Times* also had Charles Austin with the French forces at Metz in October 1870. He was in Paris later, during the siege. E. S. Dallas and the English-born Vicomtesse de Peyronnet also wrote for the paper from that city, so far as they were able, during the period of its encirclement.

Frederick Hardman, in the service of the *Times* since the Crimean War, had gone to Paris in 1869 to replace J. B. O'Meagher upon his retirement. He remained as long as the French government was there, and returned from the south of France with the new Republican government in May 1871. In Bordeaux during the war period, Hardman was not well and the paper was actively represented there by Laurence Oliphant, who had also written for its columns from the United States in 1856. In Paris early in 1871, after the siege had ended, but prior to Hardman's return, Oliphant engaged as an assistant Henri de Blowitz, Bohemian-born but long a resident of

---

3 Matthew Arnold, *Friendship's Garland* (London, 1871), pp. 111-12.

France. He was to be a member of the *Times* foreign staff stationed in Paris for the next three decades.

The *Daily Telegraph* had become an important competitor of the *Times,* particularly since its absorption of the *Morning Chronicle* in 1862 and the suspension of the *Morning Herald* in 1869, both previously active in the reporting of foreign news. Among correspondents for the *Daily Telegraph* during the war, John Merry LeSage, later to become the paper's editor, led all others with his account of the Prussian army entrance into Paris on March 1, 1871. William Beatty Kingston, the paper's Berlin correspondent, was first with the terms of the surrender of Paris. Felix Whitehurst, who had become the paper's first Paris correspondent in 1864, remained there throughout the war and was afterwards joined by James Macdonell and J. Hall Richardson.

George Augustus Sala, who had represented the *Daily Telegraph* briefly in the United States during the Civil War, and Francis (Frank) Lawley, who wrote for the *Times* at that period from the Confederate States, both wrote war reports for the *Daily Telegraph*—as did Lord Adare, with the Prussians toward the end of the conflict. He was notable for traveling about the war area in a carriage drawn by a particularly fine pair of horses. Moncure D. Conway, who represented the *New York Tribune* in London, wrote primarily for the *Daily Telegraph* during the Franco-Prussian War. Both papers, however, used a vivid eye-witness report he produced of the Battle of Gravelotte.

Two other London dailies presenting war reports were the *Daily News* and the *Pall Mall Gazette.* Both were associated in those efforts with the *New York Tribune* through arrangement conceived by Smalley of the *Tribune,* and worked out originally with John R. Robinson, manager of the *Daily News,* and Frank Hill, its editor.

During the early months of the war, particularly, *New York Tribune* correspondents produced some outstanding battle reports used also by the *Daily News.* Smalley had assigned Joseph Hance, the *Tribune's* Berlin correspondent, to accompany Prussian forces. A. M. Chamerauzan remained in Paris for the paper throughout the war and M. Mijanel followed the French in the field.

Holt Whyte, a youthful Briton representing both the *Tribune* and the *Pall Mall Gazette,* was with the Prussians at the Battle of Sedan when Emperor Napoleon III surrendered personally to King Wilhelm and Bismarck. Whyte rode his horse across the battlefield, and across Belgium to Brussels, where his account, including its reference to the surrender of Napoleon III, was rejected for telegraphic transmission as too improbable. Whyte promptly rode on to Ostend and proceeded to London, with his account published there two days before any other appeared.

Gustav Müller, an American attached to the Prussian army hospital service, had an arrangement to write for the *New York Tribune*. He too made his way to London to provide an early, remarkable, and moving report of the Battle of Metz and the surrender of that city to the Prussians on October 28. Following its publication in London by the *Daily News*, and its transmission to New York, it was republished by the *Times*—a tribute in itself. It was characterized later by Archibald Forbes, one of the most distinguished of correspondents, as "the greatest journalistic *coup* of our time on this side of the Atlantic."

Archibald Forbes was the particular star of the *Daily News* team of correspondents during the war. Forbes had been a soldier himself. He enlisted in the British Royal Dragoons in 1859 at the age of twenty-one, moved to do so after hearing a lecture by William Howard Russell, whose reports of the Crimean War he had read in the *Times*. While in military service, Forbes began writing for the London *Morning Advertiser*, and so successfully that, following his period of enlistment, the paper sent him to report the early weeks of the Franco-Prussian War. He was with the Prussians at Gravelotte and Sedan, and wrote a notable report of Sedan and the surrender of Napoleon III, which he witnessed. As Prussian forces then deployed for an advance on Paris, the *Advertiser* recalled Forbes to London, prepared to let its Paris correspondent report the anticipated attack on that city.

Forbes thereupon offered his services to the *Times*, without success, and then to the *Daily News*, which accepted and sent him to France again. He was slightly wounded late in October during the Battle of Metz, and nearly lost a leg from gangrene, but he recovered and returned to action to report the siege of Paris. He was the first correspondent to find a way into the city after its capitulation on January 28, 1871. Later, he reported the triumphal return of Prussian troops to Berlin in June. This was the first of several war assignments that Forbes carried out between 1870 and 1880. His name became bracketed with that of Russell as among the great war correspondents, and the two men became friends and mutual admirers.

Like Russell, Forbes later wrote his memoirs, in the course of which he speculated, with tongue in cheek, about "the attributes that

ought to be concentrated in the ideal war correspondent.'' In his
Memories and Studies of War and Peace (1895), he concluded that
such a correspondent

> ought to possess the gift of tongues . . . have the sweet angelic
> temper of a woman, and be as affable as if he were a politician
> canvassing for a vote; yet, at the same time, be big and ugly enough
> to impress the conviction that it would be highly unwise to take any
> liberties with him. He . . . should be able to ride anything that
> chance may offer, from a giraffe to a rat; be able to ride a hundred
> miles at a stretch, go without food for a week if needful, and
> without sleep for as long; never get tired . . . and be able at the end
> of a ride . . . to write round-hand for a telegraph clerk ignorant of
> the correspondent's language, at the rate of a column an hour for
> six or eight consecutive hours; after which he should, as a matter of
> course, gallop back to the scene of action. . . . He should be a
> competent judge of warfare, conversant with all military opera-
> tions . . . have supreme disregard for hostile fire when duty calls
> upon him to expose himself to it; . . . have a real instinct for the
> place and day of an impending combat . . . have an intuitive
> perception of how the day hath gone; be able to discern victory or
> defeat while as yet, to the spectator not so gifted, the field of strife
> seems confusion worse confounded; and so . . . to ride off the
> earliest bearer of the momentous tidings. . . .

"Alas!" he concluded, "There never was such a man as I have
ideally depicted, and there never will be such a man." Yet, actually,
in the course of his own experience Forbes demonstrated many of
those qualities which he satirized.

Other members of the *Daily News* organization during the
Franco-Prussian War included Henry Labouchere (''Labby''), recently become one of the proprietors of the paper, and also a member
of Parliament. He was in Paris when the siege began in September
1870 and remained there throughout the period of more than four
months. He wrote letters signed discreetly merely as ''H.L.'' and
dispatched by an uncertain balloon service. Some reached London
for publication there and in the *New York Tribune,* and all later were
brought together in Labouchere's informative *Diary of a Besieged
Resident.*

Hilary Skinner, who had covered Denmark's vain effort to save the
provinces of Schleswig and Holstein from Prussian aggression in

1864, as well as the Austro-Prussian War of 1866, again represented the *Daily News* in 1870-71, this time with the Prussian forces as they moved across France.

Four members of the Vizetelly family were engaged in coverage of the war, three of them writing for the *Daily News*. A fifth member, Frank Vizetelly, who had reported the Austro-Italian War, the American Civil War, and the Austro-Prussian War, was absent from the field on this occasion. His father, Henry Richard Vizetelly, in Paris for the *Illustrated London News* since 1865, remained there through the siege, transmitting some material by balloon post. His youngest son, Ernest Alfred Vizetelly, was also the youngest correspondent, at seventeen, as a writer and artist for the *Daily News* and also for the *Pall Mall Gazette* and the *Illustrated London News*. Another son, Edward Henry Vizetelly, wrote for the *Daily News* and the *New York Times*. A nephew, Montague Vizetelly, in the field for the *Daily News* with the French, was captured.

Nicolas Thiéblin, although French, knew English well and covered aspects of the war for the *Pall Mall Gazette,* writing under the name of "Azamat Bartouk." As with correspondents for the *Daily News,* some of his reports also appeared in the *New York Tribune.*

The *Standard* of London, was represented again by George Alfred Henty, and also by John Augustus Shea. T. Farman, who had replaced Hely Bowes as Paris correspondent in 1867, remained there through the war to begin an assignment of forty years in that capital. Sydney Hall, an artist for the *Graphic* of London, was with the French army in the early period of the war; he was arrested by the Prussians on suspicion of being a spy, but was released.

The *New York Herald* was listed in the *Publishers' Circular* of London as having twenty-four correspondents in the field, but only three are mentioned in the literature of the war. These were British-born H. Findlater Bussey, who wrote also for the *Times* and for the *Daily News;* John P. Jackson, Paris correspondent, with the French army; and Januarius Aloysius MacGahan, a young Ohioan who interrupted studies in Berlin to accompany the Prussian forces through the occupation of Paris. MacGahan produced some good accounts, and so began a relatively short but distinguished career as a correspondent first for the *Herald* and later for the *Daily News.*

The *New York Times* attempted to report the war, but was handicapped because it chose to direct its coverage from Paris, which was so soon under siege. The *New York World,* established in 1860 and absorbing the old *Courier and Enquirer* in 1861, was capably edited at this time and received some war correspondence from a Mr. McLean, with the Prussians. Frederick Gaillardet, editor of the *Courier des États-Unis,* French-language paper in New York, who had written of the American Civil War for the Paris press, now wrote from Paris for his own paper. His letters, so far as they were available by balloon post during the siege, were used in translation by other newspapers in the United States.

The coverage of the Franco-Prussian War was important not only in itself, but in that it set new standards both for war reporting and for news reporting in general, perhaps most particularly in Europe. It established the practice of using both telegraph and cable facilities regularly to speed the news in greater volume, despite the costs. By Smalley's enterprise, and stemming largely from his experience as a Civil War correspondent, an objective style of news writing was introduced to Europe, with an emphasis on brevity, speed, and accuracy, rather than on subjective description and comment, such as had been common in the British and European press, and in the United States prior to the Civil War.

A special need for brevity of writing arose to get the news out of besieged Paris by balloon post and carrier pigeon. Some sixty-four balloons left Paris during more than four months when it was surrounded by Prussian troops. In addition to pilots and nearly 100 passengers, they carried more than three million letters, no one of which could weigh more than three grams (one-tenth ounce). The balloons were released in the dark of moonless nights, when the Prussians would have difficulty seeing them and shooting them down. Even so, some fell into Prussian hands, some were lost as sea, and some drifted as far as Norway.

Carrier pigeons also were used to carry messages, flying between Paris and Tours, westward beyond the occupation zone. One account says 363 pigeons were used in the service, though how they were moved into Paris is not clear. Messages were handled through the post office at a rate of fifty centimes (ten cents) a word, without guarantee of arrival. The messages were commonly in cipher to permit more information to be conveyed. But they had to be in French, limited to twenty words, and written on paper so thin that about 200 such messages could be placed in a quill attached to the leg of a single bird, or to the tail-feathers. Later in the siege, longer messages were photographed on thin films of collodion, lighter than paper, to be enlarged upon receipt so that they could be read and forwarded in the manner of a telegram.

Any news message sent out of Paris by either means must necessarily have been very brief. Realistically, if correspondents depended upon French authorities supervising the services to accept messages for transmission, they had to expect those messages to be examined prior to dispatch and never sent at all unless completely satisfactory in subject matter. For that reason, Labouchere of the *Daily News*, and some others, were able to make private and personal arrangements by which longer and more informative messages were smuggled out by pilots or passengers in the balloons.

Neutral correspondents were relatively free of official censorship on either side during the war, but some were roughly handled as suspected spies, especially in Paris. They endured hardships, perils, and deprivations, including dire shortages of food and medical supplies in besieged Paris. A number were wounded, including Forbes and Oliphant; some were captured, and Pemberton, of the *Times*, was one of several killed during the ten months of war. For Prussian and French newsmen there was somewhat less freedom. The Prussian press was at the disposition of that government during the war, and the French press was under heavy censorship, hardly able to appear at all in besieged Paris.

The war reports by the more successful correspondents, and Smalley's personal role in organizing coverage, drew special praise from A. W. Kinglake, a contemporary British historian. In his view,

the extraordinary triumphs of European journalism at the time . . . were due, in no slight degree, to the vigor, and the enterprise that were brought to bear on the objects from the other side of the Atlantic. The success of the 'partnership for the purpose of war news' which had been formed between the *Daily News* and the *New York Tribune* was an era in the journalism of Europe, though not in that of the United States, where the advance had an earlier date, deriving from their great Civil War.

In an obvious reference to Smalley, Kinglake also wrote several years later that

I cannot speak of the *New York Tribune* without thinking of one of its conquests achieved in another direction. . . . Years ago it established in London a kindly, highly gifted correspondent, whose charming house has done more than the stateliest embassies could well have achieved toward dispersing old, narrow pre-judices, and creating and maintaining good-will, affection, and friendship between the two great English nations.[4]

The costs of covering the Franco-Prussian War were high, largely because of telegraph and cable tolls. The *Daily News* paid about ₤1,200 ($5,832) a month for telegrams alone. The *New York Tribune* cable tolls amounted to $4,000 for a single four-day period, and its total communications costs for ten months of war coverage exceeded $125,000. The public response to the joint enterprise of the two newspapers was demonstrated, by an increase in the *Daily News* circulation from 50,000 to 150,000 during the war, and the *Tribune* also gained, though less dramatically.

James Grant, publisher of the London *Daily Advertiser,* wrote that war coverage increased that paper's operating costs by ₤8,000 to ₤10,000 (up to $48,600), with special correspondents being paid ten guineas a week (about $50), and as much again for expenses. Comparable costs for the *Times* correspondents were ₤30 to ₤40 (up to $194) a week. The New York Associated Press cable charges from London to New York were about ₤3,500 ($16,890) for the period between July and October of 1870, with a charge of ₤818 ($3,975) on one day alone. Messages costing ₤30 to ₤75 ($145 to $364) a day were common, and occasionally reached ₤100 ($486).

From the beginning of telegraphic communication, newspapers had been seeking ways to reduce those costs, as well as cable costs. Whatever economies had been achieved came through direct negotiation with a telegraph company, or because of competition between companies seeking business. During 1870-71, however, such competition hardly existed outside of some parts of the United States.

---

4   George W. Smalley, in London for the *New York Tribune* from 1867 to 1895, returned to New York as a correspondent there and in Washington for the *Times* of London in 1895-1906, when he retired. He returned to England to spend the last years of his life, dying in London in 1916, aged eighty-two. An account and appraisal of his career is presented by Joseph J. Mathews in *George W. Smalley, Forty Years a Foreign Correspondent* (1973).

Elsewhere, governments owned the lines, or there was no competition, as was the case with the North Atlantic cable. Nor were special "press rates" authorized by the ITU until 1875.

Telegraph operators had devised a code for their own use and convenience,[5] but newspapers had failed to establish any such code or cipher for news transmission. At the time of the Franco-Prussian War, the best a newspaper or news agency correspondent could do to save transmission costs was to omit non-essential words and phrases from his disptach. Since every word bore a charge, this could mean a considerable saving. News reports were transmitted, therefore, lacking articles, prepositions and conjunctions, omitting full names and titles of persons regularly in the news, omitting information already known from previous reports. Punctuation marks were not transmitted in any case, and the word "stop" for a period, "query" for a question mark, or "comma" would be omitted unless essential for clarity.

Using this method, a relatively few words transmitted could become several hundred in a full text, when processed by a skilled editor at the receiving end. The more so, if background material drawn from previous reports or from the files was added, or material forwarded in advance by mail, when circumstances permitted. This might seem to have been a mild fraud perpetrated upon readers, since the published account would appear to have been transmitted in its entirety, bearing a "dateline" to indicate the city from which it came. It was not a fraud, however, in the sense that readers were in any way misinformed. It was rather a measure of practical economy, and a method long used.

In 1875 the International Telegraph Conference, meeting at St. Petersburg, authorized the establishment of lower "press rates" for news messages transmitted over telegraph or cable lines. This permitted further economy. In 1879, Walter Polk Phillips, then a telegrapher for the New York Associated Press, patented an

---

5 It was the telegrapher's "OK," meaning "correct" or "all right," that put a new term into the language, produced "FYI," meaning "for your information," and established the use of "30" to signify the end of a message or a news story. An operator in the United States would hear his call, in the dot-dash code, usually with two letters representing the name of his city, as NY for New York, BH for Boston, and WX for Washington. He would respond with "GA," meaning "go ahead." With such letters and numbers, operators "talked" among themselves over the wire.

elaborate code and "dictionary" incorporating many of the abbreviations and shortcuts used by telegraphers in the United States.[6] The Phillips Code, as it was called, soon had its counterpart in Europe. Charges were computed, however, upon every word of the text as fully reconstructed after telegraphic dispatch.

With cable costs higher than domestic telegraph charges, and with the volume of cable news sharply higher during and after the Franco-Prussian War, the press devised its own system, somewhat comparable to the telegraphers' codes. One word, as transmitted, became two or more as reconstructed at the receiving end. Used almost exclusively for cable transmission, it became known as "cablese." Combined with the word omissions already established, it meant a further economy.

For example, in a later period, a message might be written in the following form by a correspondent in Berlin, as part of a lead for dispatch:

> Cumcrisis impending governmenters upset secretest council exstatesmen proexamine emergency measures reichstagward subguard downlay program . . .

Put into proper form by an editor in New York, and with omitted words also inserted, the fourteen "words" transmitted became forty-three, to appear as follows:

> BERLIN.—With a crisis impending in Germany over the nation's currency situation, members of the government today set up a secret council, composed of leading statesmen, to examine possible emergency measures. They proceeded to the Reichstag, under guard, to lay down the program. . . .

No dictionary of cablese ever was prepared, but the usage was well understood. It was used not only for news reports, but also for "service messages," queries, comments, instructions, and informative messages passing between home office and correspondent, or between bureaus.[7]

---

6 Examples included such usages as "potus" (president of the United States), "scotus" (Supreme Court of the United States), "sot" (Secretary of the Treasury), "cgal" (congressional), "kfc" (conference), "unxl" (unconstitutional) "fapib" (filed a petition in bankruptcy).

7 Other examples of cablese would be "smorning" (this morning), "omniagreed" (all agreed), "unagreement" (no agreement), "ungo" (will not go), "downhold" (hold down), "Parisward" (going to Paris), "exlondon" (left London), "protreaty" (favored the treaty).

The Franco-Prussian War had far-reaching results. Most important, in its ultimate meaning to the peoples of the world, was the emergence of the German Empire. Also important was the final unification of Italy, and the establishment of the French Republic. The impact of the war upon the press likewise was considerable.

The Ring Combination had been formally established on January 1, 1870, with the Reuter, Havas, and Wolff agencies undertaking a division of the world for distribution of their services in designated territories, and for an exchange of news. The effectiveness of that combination was threatened by the outbreak of war in July. Any direct exchange between the Havas and Wolff agencies was immediately interrupted. With Paris under siege from September until May 1871, the headquarters office of the Havas agency was isolated. For this reason and because much of France was under German occupation, the advertising division of the agency was inoperative. Havas representatives had accompanied the French government to Bordeaux, but the facilities for handling news there were limited, and the press itself, as well as telegraphic service, was disrupted in much of the country. Under these circumstances, the ten months of the war so weakened the Agence Havas that even after peace was restored in 1871 there was some possibility that the agency might collapse.

The Havas and Reuter agencies had been operating jointly in Belgium since 1869. In 1870 they had joined to conduct the Fabra agency in Spain, under the name of Reuter-Havas. Serious thought was given to the sale of a large share of control in the weakened Havas agency to Reuter so that it might be saved, but no such sale was to occur, and Havas did survive, but largely through Reuter assistance and support. The two agencies collaborated closely from 1871 to 1876 and, in some respects, until 1890.

Havas was able, by June 1871, to resume operations in France in both its news and advertising divisions. Its news exchange with Wolff was renewed. It resumed relationships in those areas specified in the Ring Combination agreements of 1870, including its association with the Stefani agency in Italy, and with Reuter in Belgium and in Spain.

Highly significant was the Reuter aid which began immediately in 1871 to help Havas sustain its still tentative efforts in South America, begun in 1860 with an office in Rio de Janeiro. Reuter now provided financial assistance, sharing half the cost of developing coverage and distribution of news to such clients as Havas served from that office in Brazil.

The British-owned Western Telegraph Company, Ltd., was at that time projecting what was to become the first South Atlantic cable. Running from British shores to Recife (Pernambuco), Brazil, by way of Portugal and the Portuguese Madeira Islands, the line was completed on August 1, 1874. A spur line was added from Recife to Rio de Janeiro.

A Havas agent, a M. Ruffier, represented both Havas and Reuter in Rio de Janeiro, with the agency designated as the Agencia Telegraphica Reuter-Havas. The first newspaper client became the *Jornal do Comercio* of Rio de Janeiro. A Reuter agent, Walter F. Bradshaw, represented both agencies at Valparaiso, Chile, where *El Mercurio* became a subscriber to the service by means of a trans-Andean telegraphic connection to Buenos Aires. Cable connections were extended southward from Rio de Janeiro to Montevideo and Buenos Aires, with *El Telégrafo,* in the Uruguayan capital and both *La Prensa* and *La Nación,* in the Argentine capital, becoming subscribers to the world news service provided. Ruffier and Bradshaw also began to return reports on South American events to Europe.

As the South Atlantic cable began operation in 1874, the Agence Havas established its first bureau in London, directed by Elié Mercadier, who had conducted a carrier-pigeon service for the agency in Paris during the war. He was assisted by a M. Harel. The London bureau was designated as "Amsud," a cable name for "South American bureau." It received reports from South America and processed them for the service. In return, it dispatched a world report to South America.

The original cable rate between Rio de Janeiro and London was forty French gold francs a word ($8). This rate was maintained until 1882, when it was reduced to seventeen gold francs ($3.40). By that time, the rate between London and New York was $1.60 a word, and special press rate of ten cents a word was set after 1886. The South Atlantic rate also came down, but remained higher than the North Atlantic rate. The rate difference tended to restrict the exchange of information to and from South America.

The Havas agency, in addition to its almost enforced association with Reuter, went through administrative changes after the Franco-Prussian War. Its founder, Charles-Louis Havas, had retired in 1846 and died in 1858. His son, Auguste Havas, who had directed the agency since 1846, retired in 1873, although only fifty-nine. The management passed to Jacques-Edouard Lebey, director of the advertising division of the agency, introduced in 1852. Prominent in the new administration were Lebey's son, Edouard (Léon) Lebey, one of his friends, Henri Houssaye, and Elie Mercadier, then in London as director of the "Bureau Amsud."

By 1876 the worst of the crisis facing both France and the Agence Havas, as a result of the war, had ended. Havas and Reuter signed a new contract on May 20, 1876, concluding what had amounted to a brief fusion of the agencies. Havas again proceeded independently. Its South American service was now conducted under the name of "Agencia Havas," with both the former Agencia Telegraphica Reuter-Havas and the Bureau Amsud names dropped.

The Havas news service was extended beyond anything previously attempted, with staff correspondents assigned to various capitals. Mercadier gave special attention to this development. In July 1876, he turned over direction of the London bureau to Harel, his assistant, and went personally to St. Petersburg, Berlin, Vienna, Bucharest, and Constantinople to establish bureaus. He covered the Congress of Berlin in 1878. Between 1880 and 1890 he arranged for correspondents in Tunis, Cairo, Alexandria, and Algiers. The first correspondent in the Far East was appointed at Saigon in 1883, with a stringer at Tonkin. In 1894 Mercadier was back in St. Petersburg to sign a treaty with the newly formed Rossiyskoe Telegraphnoye Agentsvo (Rosta), or Russian Telegraph Agency, sharing Russia with Wolff for the provision of a world news report.

These various arrangements brought into the Havas service such correspondents as Léon Pognan, originally in Bucharest; a M. Dumontel-Lagreze, the first appointee in Saigon; Georges Fillion, followed him in 1884, but later served in Berlin and Vienna; Georges Vayssié, an Arab, in Cairo and other Mideast and North African areas. Gaston Chadourne was in Athens and then became the first Havas correspondent in Rome, where he remained for sixteen years. A. M. Guillerville followed Fillion in Berlin from 1890-1905, and then Chadourne in Rome. André Meynot was in Berlin from 1905, and in other major assignments; and a M. Giaccone was in St. Petersburg shortly after 1900.

Meanwhile, in South America, Bradshaw remained in Valparaiso as Reuter correspondent until 1882, but was replaced by Arturo Salazar, who represented both Havas and Reuter and remained until 1895. Bradshaw later was to succeed John Griffiths as secretary in London of the Reuter Telegram Company, Ltd. Even though the Havas service operated independently in South America after 1876, the new contract signed with Reuter at that time provided for a sharing of the Latin American territory. Correspondents serving both agencies were named in 1882 at Montevideo and Buenos Aires.

While the Agence Havas was extending its news coverage after 1876, a major change in the agency organization occurred in 1879. Control was purchased by Baron Emile d'Erlanger, banker of Paris and London, who had been associated with Baron Reuter in the construction of the 1869 French North Atlantic cable. In this sale, the last financial interest of the Havas family in the agency vanished, and Henri Houssaye attained a part ownership. His nephew, Charles Houssaye, also in the agency service, directed the South American service, based in Buenos Aires, from 1902.

In acquiring control of the agency, d'Erlanger also bought the Fabra agency in Spain, which had been operating under the name of Reuter-Havas since 1870. It now became Havas-Fabra from 1879 to 1893, then the Agence Espagnol et Internationale.

Lebey, managing director of the Agence Havas from 1873, continued in that position until 1897. He was succeeded by Charles Lafitte, son of Mathieu Lafitte, founder of the advertising agency with which the news agency became associated in 1852. Lafitte served as managing director for twenty-seven years, and as president of the board of directors.

The Havas agency, having survived the financial crisis arising from the Franco-Prussian War, was the target almost twenty years later of a related political intrigue that might have had serious results had it succeeded. In Germany, Bismarck, still the "Iron Chancellor" at seventy-two, had been dismayed by France's quick recovery from the war, the vigor of its economy by the 1880s, and the political strength of the new republic in Europe and overseas. He was disturbed both by a surviving French hostility toward Germany, and a French military activity that he considered alarming.

Experienced in maneuvering the press to suit his purposes, Bismarck viewed the Agence Havas as having contributed to anti-German sentiment in France and elsewhere, and to advances in the French position that he viewed as dangerous to Germany. He conceived the idea of using the Wolff agency as a pawn in a scheme to undo the Havas influence. He found support for his plan in Italy.

Relations between France and Italy had deteriorated following France's occupation of Tunis in 1881. Italy was concerned both by what it regarded as a trend toward French imperialism and by a fear that Rome might be lost to Italy by action of powers supporting the

Pope, who had lost control there in 1870. In its own interests, Italy had joined with Germany and Austria in a Triple Alliance in 1882 by which it was assured support against any military action by France. But the Italian government, then headed by Premier Francisco Crispi, also wished protection against a use of the news as distributed by the Havas agency, with French government support, and further aided by Havas control of the Stefani agency, to help attain political ends by influencing and shaping public opinion. This was what became known in Europe as "tendentious news." Italy's Premier Crispi, in these circumstances, fell in with Bismarck's designs to curb Havas.

The Ring Combination had become fully effective by 1882. The Havas agency was at full strength after the 1879 reorganization. In Germany, Dr. Wolff had retired in 1871 and died in 1879, at age sixty-nine. Richard Wentzel, succeeding him as director of the Wolff-CNB agency, was almost obliged to bow to Bismarck's objective because the agency stood in a semi-official relationship to the government.

Bismarck's plan took shape in 1887. In that year Crispi visited Berlin and Vienna with a proposal that the Wolff agency, the Korrburo of Austria, the UTB agency of Hungary, and the Stefani agency of Italy should join to form a new organization to be known, in its English-language version, as the Agencies of the Triple Alliance Powers. This would remove Wolff and the other three agencies from the Ring Combination, along with other national agencies within the Wolff territory, and might be expected to clip the Havas power in Europe.

But what of Reuter? If Reuter could be induced to join in the purposed new agency alliance it would curtail Havas very seriously indeed. Wentzel was urged by Bismarck to extend the invitation to Reuter. He went to London and met with Herbert de Reuter and also with Baron de Reuter, retired, but still active in agency affairs. He sought to persuade them to join the Wolff-oriented group.

The Reuter agency at that time was under some financial pressure, and was feeling competition from the Central News and Exchange Telegraph agencies. It had ended its association with Havas in Spain. It was aware that Havas now would prefer to have South America as an exclusive territory, with Reuter withdrawing. France had established a political position in Indochina, which was part of Reuter's exclusive territory in the Ring Combination, and Havas also was showing an interest in that area. The Reuter general service was proceeding at a moderate pace, while Havas was extending its news coverage with some vigor, as well as its advertising business. It was, in summary, a period when Reuter was feeling some unrest about its status as a world agency.

The time also was near for renewal in 1890 of the Ring Combination treaties, and Reuter had no clear assurance that Havas was prepared to renew the treaties, or to do so without asking changes unwelcome to Reuter. Bismarck undoubtedly was aware, through Wentzel, that the treaty-renewal date was approaching, and took that as a reason for making his own move in 1887. Wentzel may well have played upon this also, and upon Reuter's problems, in his London conversations.

Reuter was in a delicate position. It could not abandon Havas, but neither was it certain what Havas was planning. Reuter therefore made a cautious agreement with the Wolff agency, a so-called "offensive-defensive" alliance, providing for joint action if Havas declined to renew the "big three" treaty in acceptable form in 1890. Even that agreement was revised in 1889, in a somewhat firmer style, between Wolff, Reuter, Stefani, the Korrburo of Austria, and UTB of Hungary.

In the end, however, the Bismarck-Crispi design failed, and the tentative agreements proved meaningless. The Agence Havas was too-well established. Its financial interest in the Stefani agency of Italy was solid, with the support of the French government to back it, if necessary, and the power and revenue attaching to its advertising subsidiary gave it added substance. Yet there was no need to invoke these elements, because Havas was quite prepared to renew the "big three" alliance when the time came. There were changes, but they were acceptable to Reuter.

In 1890, therefore, Wolff as well as Reuter joined again with Havas in the signature of a new treaty, for another ten years. Havas emerged stronger than ever. It was by the terms of this treaty that it did gain South America as an exclusive territory, and also Indochina. But Havas yielded its position in Egypt, which became exclusive Reuter territory. Havas retained control of Stefani and Fabra, but continued to share Belgium and Central America with Reuter. The Austrian and Hungarian agencies continued as before, strictly national agencies within Wolff's exclusive territory.

Even as the new treaties were signed, Bismarck, who had been so eager to strike both at France and at the Agence Havas, was the victim of his own broad intrigues and ambitions. Wilhelm I, king of

Prussia and emperor of Germany, whom Bismarck had served since 1862, died in 1888. His son, who became Frederick III at age fifty-seven, lived only three months, succeeded in turn by his son, Wilhelm II. Two years later, in March 1890, differences with the new emperor resulted in Bismarck's forced resignation. In Italy, Crispi also was forced from power ten months later.

The period between 1871 and 1890, when Havas and Reuter worked together in Latin America, was also a time when cable communication and telegraphic communication increased in that part of the world, and when the press of the area gained in importance.

Although the first Havas office had been at Rio de Janeiro in 1860, and the first South Atlantic cable landing had been in Brazil in 1874, Buenos Aires became the center for South American news coverage and distribution after about 1882. One reason was that the trans-Andean telegraph lines also reached Buenos Aires from Chile and Peru; it therefore was a more convenient communications center. Another reason was that two remarkable morning dailies were by then established in Buenos Aires. Not only were they Havas clients, but they were good sources of news for use by Havas in preparing its South American report for return to London and Paris. Unrest in Brazil also contributed to the move to Argentina—the Brazilian empire established in 1822 came to an end in 1889 and was succeeded by a republic.

The two Buenos Aires newspapers were *La Prensa,* begun in 1869, and *La Nación* in 1870. Both were conceived in the image of the London *Times,* but they developed their own special characters, to become among the best newspapers in the world and among the most prosperous. Both used the telegraph from the outset. They seized upon each advance in communications methods, and were enterprising in seeking news. Even before the existence of the South Atlantic cable, *La Prensa* was the first daily in Latin America to publish a report of the Prussian victory at Sedan in 1870 and the capture of Napoleon III, setting a precedent in news leadership it was to retain through the years without consideration for costs.

In the absence of a national news agency in Argentina, or any other Latin American country, *La Prensa* engaged stringers in various cities and towns (eventually to number about 2,000), with branch offices in larger places, to provide a national news report. *La Nación* had a similar organization with about half as many stringers. Both papers later engaged stringers in Rio de Janeiro, Montevideo, Santiago, Lima, and other Latin American capitals. Both sent staff members to Europe on special missions and, much later, established resident correspondents in Paris, especially, and in London and New York, with stringers in Madrid, Rome, Berlin, and elsewhere. On a limited scale, they were to make their news reports available by syndication to other newspapers in Argentina. Even in the earlier years, as this system was beginning, the news so obtained was of value to the Havas and Reuter representatives in Buenos Aires in preparing their dispatches to London and Paris, which became a part of the world service distributed through the Ring Combination.

The first of these dailies, *La Prensa,* was directed until 1898 by its founder, Dr. José Clemente Paz, who lived until 1912. From 1898, the paper was directed by his son, Don Ezequiel Paz, until his retirement in 1943.

The founder of *La Nación* was Dr. Bartolomé Mitre, born in Buenos Aires in 1821, son of an Argentine military leader. In his youth, he edited *El Mercurio* in Valparaiso, Chile, during 1848-49. Returning to Buenos Aires in 1852, he was himself a military leader in the unification of what then were the United Provinces, and he became president of the united Argentine Republic from 1862-68. In 1870, when he was forty-nine, he established *La Nación.* It gained immediate recognition as a newspaper of quality. As with *La Prensa,* it has been continued by members of the family. Well before Dr. Mitre's death in 1906, at eighty-five, direction had been vested in the hands of his grandson, Don Jorge Mitre, who continued through World War I, followed by his sons, Luis and Emilio Mitre.

Both *La Prensa* and *La Nación* set the highest standards of quality and responsibility in matters of news reporting, editorial leadership, and advertising content. They made no concessions to popular interest, but nevertheless became circulation leaders—a rare circumstance for a newspaper treating public affairs in so serious a fashion, while reflecting credit also upon the taste and intelligence of the citizens of Argentina. The papers became "models" for the press of other countries of Latin America and, in due course, were honored internationally.

The two papers were much alike in content and appearance. But *La Prensa* gained special recognition as a "paper of record," and for contributions beyond its immediate news and editorial function that made it something of an "institution." This latter character arose from a precedent established by Dr. Paz whereby a generous proportion of its substantial profits was to be devoted to the support of services benefiting the nation, the community, and worthy individuals.

Such services, introduced over a period of years, included: (1) a free medical, surgical, and dental clinic, headed by a distinguished medical man, offering advice and treatment by the most skilled specialists; (2) a free legal consultation service, staffed by the best legal talent, for persons of limited means, with necessary documents prepared without cost; (3) an agricultural consultation service to provide free advice and guidance, with a staff of experts in charge; (4) a music conservatory which offered free, complete education in a three-year course to worthy applicants, and which also provided public concerts; (5) a splendid library of 90,000 volumes and an information service open to the public without obligation; (6) an Institute of Popular Lectures, for free weekly addresses during six months of each year by national and world authorities; (7) a postal service whereby a letter addressed to anyone in Argentina and sent in care of the paper would be forwarded if the address could be obtained; (8) literary prizes, and a prize of 1,000 pesos (nearly $1,000) to the person who proved he had taught the greatest number of illiterates to read during the year; (9) a free employment service.

For the people and press of Latin America, as in the United States, historical and cultural ties meant that interest in world news developments was primarily in affairs in Europe. The direct cable connection with Europe supported that flow of news. The British cable of 1874 was joined in 1879 by a new French cable across the North Atlantic, with a spur to Brazil, and by a new German cable from Emden to the Azores, to Monrovia, on the African coast, and from there to Recife, Brazil. The dependence of the Latin American press upon Havas for world service was another reason little other than European news reached those papers.

In the years between 1870 and 1900 the more important newspapers so served began with *La Presna* and *La Nación* in Buenos Aires. Others included *La Capital* of Rosario, established in 1867, *Los Andes* of Mendoza (1882), and *El Día* of La Plata (1884), all in Argentina. Dailies in Brazil included the *Diario de Pernambuco* of Recife (1825); the *Jornal do Comercio* (1827), the *Jornal do Brazil* (1891), and *A Noticia* (1894), all of Rio de Janeiro; *O Estado do São Paulo* (1875) and the *Diario Popular* (1884), both of São Paulo. In

Chile, the most important papers were *El Mercurio* (1827) and *La Unión* (1885), both of Valparaiso.[8] A Santiago edition of *El Mercurio* was added in 1902.

In other countries,the papers of importance were *El Día* (1886) and *La Tribuna Popular* (1879), both of Montevideo, Uruguay; *El Comercio,* established in Lima, Peru, in 1839 by José Antonio Miró Quesada, as an informative and respected paper; *El Espectador,* established at Medellin, Colombia, in 1888, but later moved to Bogotá; and two English-language dailies at Georgetown, British Guiana, the *Evening Post & Sunday Argosy* (1880) and the *Chronicle* (1881).

Central America and the West Indies were areas shared by Reuter and Havas, even after 1890. Newspapers of some importance there before 1900 included the *Diario de la Marina,* Havana, Cuba (1832), and several papers in Mexico City. These latter included *El Noticioso* (1894); *El Imparcial* (1896), a government sponsored newspaper; *El Mundo,* soon to follow but retitled as *El Heraldo,* and published by Rafael Reyes Spindola; and *El Siglo II* (1898), published by Plutarco Elías Calles, later to become president of Mexico (1924-28). With Cuba under Spanish administration until 1898, and with Porfirio Diaz heading a dictatorial government in Mexico f49.   1876 until 1911, the press in those countries did not operate freely.

The news flow between South America and Europe meant that any mutual awareness of events in North and South America depended upon the indirect exchange through Havas and Reuter. There was scarcely any departure from this procedure until the 1920s and, more particularly, the 1930s. Shipping and mails also moved on the same triangular course between North and South America, usually by way of British ports.

There were some direct relations, however, between the United States and Mexico and Cuba. The first telegraph line linking Mexico

---

8   The press had its effective beginning in Chile in 1813, with the appearance in Valparaiso of the weekly *La Aurora de Chile.* The printing press used, along with type and equipment, had been brought from the United States in 1811 through the initiative of Jose Miguel Carrera, a leader in the movement to gain independence from Spain, and with the assistance of Joel Poinsset, U.S. cônsul at Valparaiso. Four experienced printers also came from the United States to help set up the printing office and produce the paper.

and the United States went into operation in 1851. A cable was laid between Key West, Florida, and Havana in 1867, extending to Puerto Rico, Trinidad, Jamaica, and Panama by 1870. British cables linked points between Buenos Aires and Halifax, Nova Scotia, including the West Indies, the Bahamas, and Bermuda in the later 1870s and 1880s. Reference has been made also to cable and telegraph links established in the period from 1881 to 1891 between the United States and Central and South America, including the "back-door" cable.

There was no national news agency in Latin America until 1900, when the Agencia Noticiosa Saporiti was formed in Buenos Aires, and then only as a small privately-owned service to provincial papers in Argentina.

So far as is known, no Latin American journalist visited the United States in his professional capacity until after 1900, and only two journalists from the United States went beyond Mexico in that same period. One such journey was especially important. William E. Curtis, of the *Chicago Record,* in 1888 visited Central and South America and produced a series of articles, written upon his return, that were serious and well researched. They contributed to an awareness in the United States of matters of concern to the countries of the Western Hemisphere.[9] The second exception came in 1891, when John P. Dunning, of the Western Associated Press, provided direct coverage of civil war in Chile.

In the United States a merger of the New York Associated Press and the Western Associated Press in 1893 to form the Associated Press of Illinois (API) was followed by an amendment of the Ring Combination agreements under which the API was permitted to

---

9 Out of William E. Curtis's visit and reports emerged a Washington conference in the winter of 1889-90, with an International Union of American Republics formed by the representatives of the participating countries. It was agreed that a permanent bureau should be established in Washington to gather and distribute commercial information for the benefit of all states of the Western Hemisphere. This became the Bureau of the American Republics, with Curtis as its director. A second meeting, a Pan-American Conference, met in Mexico City in 1901-02. It was there agreed that the Washington bureau should be made permanent and its functions extended. In 1910 it became known as the Pan-American Union and a building was erected to house it, with three-quarters of the cost covered by a gift from Andrew Carnegie. Pan-American Conferences followed in various capitals, and in 1948 the Pan-American Union became the Organization of American States (OAS), one of the more important international organizations.

share Mexico and Central America with Reuter and Havas, and also to share Canada and the West Indies with Reuter, while handling distribution of the Reuter service in these areas.

One further change came as a result of the Spanish-American War of 1898. With Cuba and Puerto Rico lost by Spain, the API gained a position there formerly held by Havas, by reason of its control of the Fabra agency in Spain. But until World War I, Havas maintained an exclusive position in South America.

Other Continents: New Technologies 13

The decade of the 1870s was a kind of watershed as between the dark ages and an enlightenment. For all the advances since 1800, the pace suddenly increased, bringing almost the entire world into perspective within approximately another three decades.

Latin America came into a new relationship with other nations, and almost coincidentally, Africa, Asia, and Australasia were brought into the world community. The great spaces of the western part of the United States also were on the way to settlement.

The United States and the Indian Wars

Many years were required for the United States to recover from the effects of the Civil War. The issues were reflected in Washington and in state and national political campaigns. All of this made news. By 1866 the continental United States was served by telegraph, and the North Atlantic cable became operative. In 1867 Alaska was purchased, Mexico again became a republic with the removal of Maximilian as emperor, and Canada gained Dominion status.

The population of the United States, 38.5 million in 1870, grew to become nearly 80 million by 1900, partially accounted for by nearly 12 million immigrants in those years. What had been thirty-seven states became forty-five. Railroad lines had been built throughout the West since 1869, when the first transcontinental connection beyond the Mississippi was completed. Many colleges and universities were established under the provisions of the 1862 Morrill Act providing land grants for that purpose. There was a great growth of public interest in sports, the theater, and literature.

On a less pleasant note, much of the central area of Chicago was destroyed by fire in 1871, and there were two severe financial crises in 1870 and 1873. At the same time, the Centennial Exposition in Philadelphia in 1876 was reflected in a national jubilee. There were constructive developments in industry and commerce, immigration was changing the nation, cities were being lighted by gas and electricity. All of these made news.

A subject of major concern during these years was the settlement of the West, from the Mississippi River to the Pacific Coast. The Homestead Act of 1862 had opened the way for many persons to acquire land. Grants were given to the Northern Pacific, the Union Pacific, and the Kansas Pacific railroads, and soon to the Great Northern and the Atchison, Topeka, and Santa Fe to extend their tracks westward, with adjacent lands opened for settlement. The prairies were taken over as open range for the raising of cattle. Trails became roads, telegraph lines were put through, farmers and sheep herders moved in, fences went up, towns grew, newspapers were established, territories became states, and settlement proceeded at a mounting rate.

This appeared to be progress. But it did not seem so to those Indian tribes that had, for unnumbered generations, used these same western lands for hunting, a source of food, and as a center of their very existence. They did not welcome this invasion, with the slaughtering of millions of buffalo and the closing of areas that had been theirs to roam. Neither was it welcomed by other Indians already shifted from eastern areas to the open lands of the West, and now again under pressure to move.

Settlers arriving from Europe in the "new world" had been in conflict with the Indians from the beginning. A first treaty to assure peace between them was concluded in Massachusetts in 1621, but the first "massacre" of white settlers occurred in 1622 near Jamestown in Virginia. From that time, conflicts occurred wherever Indians and white settlers were in any sort of relationship. Treaties brought peace, but the treaties were broken as regularly as they were made, usually by the whites.

A government Department of Indian Affairs, formed in 1834, had no solution for the clashes that occurred with Indians in the western lands. In March 1871 an Indian Appropriation Act nullified all treaties previously made. The Indians became "national wards," to be settled on "reservations" where they might live—unless the reservations also were made subject to change. Indians often wandered from the reservations, and Indian "wars" became persistent in the West after 1860.

The Indian Wars, through that period of approximately thirty years (1860-90), actually were more in the nature of guerrilla campaigns in which settlers defended themselves as best they could against unpredictable attacks. United States military units either defended a position or pursued the "savages," as they were commonly termed, who had attacked settlers or travelers, or had left the reservations.

There had been nearly twenty clashes between Indians and settlers or cavalry units in the 1860s, from Minnesota to Arizona. The decade of the 1870s was crucial, however, with more than twenty battles, as Indians fought for land and rights that always had been theirs. The odds were too great and, in the end, they lost.

The settlement of the West was proceeding at that time, and commanders of Union forces in the Civil War were assigned to the frontier to keep the Indians under control. General Winfield Scott Hancock, in St. Louis, took charge of the area of Kansas, Nebraska, and southwestern Missouri, and General Philip H. Sheridan was in Oklahoma. General William T. Sherman and others became involved.

Press coverage began. A few correspondents were with the Hancock and Sheridan commands in Kansas and Oklahoma in 1867-68. Others joined a Peace Commission of which General William T. Sherman was a member. From April to October of 1867 that Commission sailed the Missouri and Platte Rivers, or used the Union Pacific Railroad, seeking sites for Indian reservations.

Reporters with Sheridan included William Fayel of the St. Louis *Missouri Republican,* Henry Stanley of the St. Louis *Missouri Democrat,* Theodore R. Davis, an artist-correspondent for *Harper's Weekly,* and DeBenneville Randolph Keim of the *New York Herald.* All wrote from Sheridan's headquarters, chiefly at Camp Supply, Oklahoma. They wrote many "sidebar" stories, not about the "war," but about the areas in which they were moving. Their reports went by military courier service, and then by mail, rather than by telegraph.

Events covered from the Sheridan headquarters were few. Most important was of a battle at the Washita River, some seventy miles south, in which the 7th Cavalry under General George Armstrong Custer fought the Cheyennes in November 1868.

Keim remained with Sheridan through 1869. Stanley, Fayel, and Davis, seeking more activity, had joined the Peace Commission in 1867. Stanley, writing for the *Missouri Democrat*, also had become a stringer for the *New York Herald*, the *New York Tribune*, the *New York Times*, the *Chicago Republican*, and the *Cincinnati Commercial*. He produced considerable copy on frontier matters, as well as about Indian affairs, and was one of about ten journalists who reported a meeting between the Peace Commissioners and Indians at Medicine Lodge Creek, Kansas, in October. His last dispatch was written from Omaha on November 21, 1867. With winter then setting in, and action unlikely on the plains, Stanley left for New York and new activities that were to take him to Europe.

In the chronology of the Indian "troubles," reservations had been designated for the various tribes after 1868. But members of those tribes did not always remain in their assigned areas, and in 1872-73 a group of about 160 Modoc Indians terrorized and killed some settlers in southern Oregon and northern California. More than 130 members of the U.S. Army were killed in trying to capture the renegades. A Peace Commission, headed by General E. R. S. Canby, ultimately was able to meet repeatedly with representatives of the Indians and supposedly was nearing a settlement. Then, at a meeting in April 1873, the Indians suddenly attacked the members of the Commission, killing Canby and another member, the Reverend Dr. Eleazur Thomas; a third, Lieutenant William F. Sherwood, died of his wounds.

This resulted in a long campaign to capture the Indians, whose leaders were hanged months later. This entire long conflict was reported, among others, by Robert D. Bogart and H. Wallace Atwell of the *San Francisco Chronicle;* by Alex McKay of the *Yreka Union,* near the scene of the action; by S. A. Clarke, a newsman from Salem, Oregon, also representing the *New York Times;* and by Edward Fox, sent west as a "special" by the *New York Herald.* Only three foreign reporters gave any direct coverage to the Indian wars through the thirty years, and this was the first such occasion. William Simpson, an artist for the *Illustrated London News*, and a veteran of Crimean War coverage, was briefly present.

The most active and significant period of the Indian wars came in 1875-81. General George Crook in 1875 was given command of the Department of the Platte, embracing the entire north central plains area, with his headquarters in Omaha. He had prewar experience with the Indians in the Pacific Northwest, and had returned to that section from 1866-72. General Philip H. Sheridan by then was in command of the Department of Missouri, and Brigadier General Alfred Terry directed action in the Department of Dakota, based in St. Paul. General Custer was constantly in the field with the 7th Cavalry.

The Indians had been moved onto reservations in the plains areas, as elsewhere, but enough remained unwilling to give up their freedom to hunt and move about as they pleased to cause repeated "incidents." It was the army's mission to find them and return them to the reservations, peacefully if possible. A special irritant arose in the Black Hills of the Dakotas. A treaty of 1868 had made that area strictly Indian territory. But a Custer expedition of 1874 confirmed the existence of gold there, and hundreds of men moved in seeking riches, and moved on to Montana where other gold deposits existed.

When it seemed impossible to halt the new "gold rush," the government tried to buy the Black Hills from the Sioux Indians, but they insisted that the 1868 treaty be observed. With President Grant's approval, it was privately agreed, however, in November 1875, that gold-seekers might go into the Black Hills and that the Indians should move out by January 31, 1876. The winter weather made it impossible for them to do that, even if they had wished, and in March 1876 General Crook sent troops to begin forcing them out. Sheridan and Terry sent other forces in from the south and east. The Indians resisted, and a series of battles occurred in 1876 through 1879, mostly in a 200-mile square in Wyoming and Montana.

The Battle of Rosebud, in southern Montana, on June 17, 1876, brought forces under General Crook into combat with Sioux and Cheyenne Indians. It was probably the biggest battle of the wars, with perhaps 1,300 men under Crook matched against possibly twice as many Indians. The battle went on for almost six hours, and might have continued, but the Indians withdrew, not because they were defeated but because they were "tired and hungry," as it was said later. The casualties were not great.

A more serious confrontation came a few days later about twenty miles northwest of Rosebud on June 25. This was the Battle of Little Big Horn. A regiment under General Terry's command approached a Sioux encampment of about 4,000. The twelve companies of the 7th Cavalry were maneuvered in three columns. Custer, with five companies, was in the middle. Vastly outnumbered, he and all of his 264 troopers were killed. It was the greatest Indian victory.

A winter campaign followed in 1876-77, with General Crook reorganizing for a Powder River Expedition, with about 1,800 men moving between November and March, still in the same Wyoming-

Montana area. By February, Indians were surrendering, and others escaped into Canada, including the Sioux leader, Tatanka Yotanka, otherwise known as Sitting Bull.

Almost as this plains area became peaceful, the Nez Percé Indians of Idaho, unwilling to go onto reservations, tried to join the Sioux. Led by Chief Joseph, they moved through the Yellowstone area, recently made a national park, and northward through Montana, almost to the Canadian border. Along the way, on a 1,700-mile trek, the Indians repeatedly defeated or eluded contingents of the U.S. Army under General O. O. Howard of the Department of the Columbia. They were ultimately defeated at a four-day Battle of Bear Paw Mountains in December 1877 by infantry forces under Colonel Nelson A. Miles.

Another clash involved the Ute Indians in Colorado in the fall of 1879. An army unit was ambushed near the White River, with its commander, Major Thomas T. Thornburg, among those killed. This brought a relief force south from Rawlins, Wyoming, in October, and the Indians were defeated.

By 1880 most of the Indians were on reservations. The Apaches held out in the Southwest, however, until forces under Brigadier General Miles imposed control in 1886.

The last major confrontation occurred in South Dakota in 1890-91. Sitting Bull, the Sioux chief, had returned from Canada to the United States in 1879, under an amnesty granted by the government, and had settled at the Standing Rock Reservation in the southern part of North Dakota. The Indians were on the move in that area in November 1890, and some were seized by the 7th Cavalry in December, placed in camp at Wounded Knee, and ordered to surrender all arms. Instead, they fired upon the troopers, and a battle of several hours followed. Lest Sitting Bull, then fifty-six, stir a wider uprising, an order was issued for his arrest on December 14. Whether he resisted is not clear, but he was killed. General Indian casualties at Wounded Knee included 145 killed and thirty-three wounded, women and children among them. This became known as a "massacre," although thirty U.S. troopers also were killed and thirty-four wounded. Other Sioux attacks followed in the next few days, but were put down, with the Indians returned to the reservation by early 1891. Indian revolts against their limitation to reservations were to occur as late as 1915, but the Wounded Knee clash is commonly regarded as marking the end of the Indian wars.

Detailed accounts of the wars and their press coverage have been told by participants and by at least two later historians, Oliver Knight and Elmo Scott Watson.[1] The wars were reported by writers for newspapers, including especially the *St. Louis Democrat,* the *Bismarck Tribune,* the *Omaha Herald,* and the *Chicago Times.* Other papers in Chicago, Cincinnati, and New York arranged for stringers on the frontier, but the *New York Herald* was notable in sending correspondents to the area.

There were twenty-five or thirty correspondents active in the 1870s and 1880s, some briefly but others for long periods. They moved by rail where possible, and used the telegraph. But much of the time they were riding horses or mules, and were far from any telegraph point. It was a hard and dangerous assignment but, so far as is known, only one correspondent was killed. Many were able to write eye-witness accounts, directly and accurately reported, sometimes telegraphed but often in longer letters carried by couriers and scouts. Some military officers also wrote for newspapers. On a few occasions, correspondents were able to talk with the Indians, but most reports were produced without access to the Indian side of the story or a sure knowledge of Indian casualties.

The Battle of Rosebud received direct coverage by five correspondents, later to report other battles. One was John F. Finerty, twenty-nine, of the *Chicago Times.* Irish-born, he was a member of a New York regiment during the Civil War, and a Chicago newspaperman after 1868. He was in the thick of the action from 1876 to 1879. Reuben Briggs Davenport, twenty-four, of the *New York Herald,* was in the Indian campaigns from 1875 to 1881. Robert E. Strahorn, twenty-four, of the Denver *Rocky Mountain News,* writing under the name of "Alter Ego," also was a stringer for the *Chicago Tribune, New York Times, Omaha Republican,* and the *Cheyenne Sun.* Thomas C. MacMillan, twenty-five, Scottish-born, represented the *Chicago Inter-Ocean.* Joe Wasson, somewhat older and experienced in newswork on the Pacific Coast, represented the *Alta California,* the *Philadelphia Press,* and the *New York Tribune.*

These men and two others were present with Crook and Terry forces at the time of the Little Big Horn battle. One of the two new correspondents was Jerome B. Stillson, thirty-six, of the *New York Herald,* a former Civil War correspondent, Washington correspondent, and managing editor of the *New York World.* The other was

---

1 See Oliver Knight, *Following the Indian Wars; The Story of Newspaper Correspondents Among the Indian Campaigners* (1960), with bibliography; John F. Finerty, *War-Path and Bivouac* (1890). See also *The American Heritage Pictorial Atlas of United States History,* Hilde Heun Kagan, ed. (1966), pp. 242-61, with special attention to maps, pp. 246-49; and *Webster's Guide to American History* (1971), pp. 720-25.

Mark Kellogg, a former telegrapher and assistant editor of the *Council Bluffs Daily Democrat* in Iowa. He was equipped and sent out as a representative of the *Bismarck Tribune* in North Dakota, writing under the name of "Frontier." C. A. Lounsberry, an officer during the Civil War, had founded the Bismarck paper, and was a stringer for the Western Associated Press. A wartime friend of General Custer, he might have accompanied the Crook expedition, but named Kellogg instead. Kellogg also became a stringer for the *New York Herald* and the *Chicago Tribune*.

Kellogg was the only one of the seven correspondents to accompany Custer's five companies in the Little Big Horn area, and was the only correspondent to lose his life in the Indian Wars. The disaster that had overtaken the Custer detachment was only discovered later in the day by others in the Terry command. Kellogg had been long enough in the field to have written many stories for the Bismarck, New York, and Chicago papers, and he had written some copy even about the day's events before he was killed. This, and other notes, were found with his body.

The news of the Little Big Horn "massacre" of June 25 did not become known to any newsman until July 1, when W. H. Norton of the *Helena Herald* learned of it. He was in the field, and what he wrote had to be carried 180 miles by courier to reach Helena on July 4. Through the efforts of a military scout, the news had reached Bozeman, however, on July 3, and the *Bozeman Times* published an "extra." The news was telegraphed from there to Salt Lake City. The telegraph eastward from Bozeman and Helena was out of order, and the news only reached Bismarck on the night of July 5 by steamer bringing wounded up the Missouri River. Published there on July 6, telegraphers were busy for forty-three hours sending official dispatches to Washington as well as news reports to Chicago and New York, where the first accounts appeared in papers of July 6 and 7. Lounsberry sent bulletins to the *New York Herald*, followed by a full story, including separate material Kellogg had prepared. That entire account ran 18,000 words and cost $3,000 in telegraph charges.[2]

The Indian victory at Little Big Horn resulted in an intensified army effort to place the Indians under control. At least four new correspondents joined to provide coverage. They were Charles Sanford Diehl of the *Chicago Times*, Barbour Lathrop of the *San*

---

2 Much to C. A. Lounsberry's annoyance, the *Herald* and the *Chicago Tribune* each claimed Kellogg as its "own correspondent." Bennett, of the *Herald*, sent $500 to Kellogg's two daughters living in LaCrosse, Wisconsin.

Francisco Evening Bulletin, James J. O'Kelly of the *New York Herald,* and James William Howard of the *Chicago Tribune.*

Diehl, only twenty-one, nevertheless had seven years of experience in news work in Illinois. He was taken in tow by Stillson of the *New York Herald.* Both reported the long Nez Percé pursuit. As that neared its end, they went together into Canada with a Peace Commission headed by General Terry, organized at the suggestion of the Canadian government to help get the Indian refugees out of Canada, and to talk with Chief Sitting Bull as part of the effort. Terry's own attempt to do so failed to produced anything useful, and Finerty, of the *Chicago Times,* was unable to talk with the Chief at all. Stillson and Diehl, however, had a long joint interview with Sitting Bull on October 17. Having returned to Bismarck, Stillson prepared a report that occupied more than a page in the *Herald* in November, along with a map of the Little Big Horn battlefield; Diehl's version of the interview appeared in the *Chicago Times.*

Diehl, Lathrop, O'Kelly, Howard, Finerty, and other correspondents were occupied until 1879 writing of the Nez Percé migration, aspects of settlement, and the clash with the Utes in Colorado. Lathrop, thirty, a Virginian and Harvard-educated, was an experienced newsman. O'Kelly, thirty-one and Irish-born, had served in the French Foreign Legion in North Africa and also in Mexico in 1863, and had been in the French army during the Franco-Prussian War. With the *Herald* since 1872, he had entered Cuba in 1873 to interview leaders of the revolutionary element seeking independence of Spain. Howard, writing under the name "Phocion," had published papers in Kentucky, served in the Civil War, entered news work in Chicago in 1866, and had represented the *Tribune* in Sioux territory prior to his return.

When the Ute Indians attacked the White River Indian Agency in Colorado in September 1879, Major Thornburg led an expedition from Rawlins, with Finerty riding with it. When Thornburg was killed, and Colonel Merritt led a relief force south from Rawlins, two new correspondents were with him—John C. Dyer of Denver, representing the *New York World* and *Chicago Tribune,* and W. P. Boardman of the *Denver Tribune.* The *New York Herald* had no correspondent nearby at the time, but Stillson, who had returned to Washington in 1878 as the paper's correspondent there, happened to be accompanying President Hayes on a western trip, and the *Herald* reassigned him to the Ute story. He wrote from Rawlins, rather than from the field. A few months later he died in Denver.

As the last campaign seemed to be developing in South Dakota in November 1890 an entirely new group of correspondents gathered. They were about twenty in number, but only three actually saw any action. These were Charles W. Allen, of the *New York Herald*, Will Cressey of the *Omaha Bee*, and William F. Kelley of the *Lincoln State Journal* in Nebraska. Frederic Remington, known as an artist of "the west," was present for *Harper's Weekly;* and Mrs. Teresa Howard Dean of the *Chicago Herald* wrote as a woman "war correspondent." The Chicago *Times, Tribune,* and *Inter-Ocean* also were represented, as were the *Omaha World-Herald, St. Louis Post-Dispatch. St. Paul Pioneer-Press, New York World,* and the New York Associated Press.

Of the three foreign correspondents to write of the Indian wars, two did report something of the South Dakota campaign. One was A. K. Zilliacus, representing a European newspaper not specified. John Merry LeSage of the London *Daily Telegraph,* later editor of that paper, obtained an interview with Sitting Bull, although precisely when and where is not clear.

The correspondent group covering the major period of the wars between 1867 and 1879 was small but quite remarkable, judging by their later experiences. Diehl became assistant general manager of the Associated Press, and then owner-publisher of the *San Antonio Light.* Finerty became a congressman, representing a Chicago district. MacMillan became a member of the Illinois state legislature, serving both in the House and Senate. He was also an active leader in public affairs. Wasson made a fortune in mining in California, served in the state legislature, and became a U.S. consul in Mexico. Lathrop inherited a fortune and turned it to the advancement of a program of research and experimentation in plant and seed importation that brought great benefits to agriculture. Strahorn became a railroad and utilities director in the Pacific Northwest.

Davenport established the *New Haven Morning News* in Connecticut, was an Associated Press correspondent during the Spanish-American War, a foreign correspodnent for the *New York Times,* and an editorial writer for the *New York Herald* Paris edition from 1920 to his death in 1932. Howard continued in Chicago journalism as a political writer. Keim became a Washington correspondent for the *New York Herald*. During three years of Civil War coverage, he had established such good relations with General Grant that he was always welcome at the White House. He usually visited informally with the president on Sundays—the only correspondent on such terms with Grant. The president sent him on confidential missions abroad, during which times he also was able to write for the *Herald*. O'Kelly returned to Ireland, served for many years as a member of Parliament, and also was a correspondent for the London *Daily News* in the Sudan in 1885 when Khartoum was under attack.

Stanley went directly from coverage of the Indian wars to serve the *New York Herald* abroad. He attained fame as a correspondent in Africa, which he helped open to the world.

Stanley and Africa

Henry Morton Stanley, as he became known, was baptized John Rowlands in Denbigh, Wales, where he was born in 1841. When he was six years old his unwed mother, a domestic servant, was no longer able to arrange for his support and he was placed in the St. Asaph Union Workhouse at Denbigh. There he remained for ten years, and received whatever formal education he was to have.

There are several versions of his life at this period. One that seems acceptable is that he was released from the workhouse when he was sixteen to instruct younger children at Mold, Flintshire, close to Denbigh. A year later he went to Liverpool, and, in December 1858, shipped as cabin boy in the Boston-registered packet boat *Windermere*. The voyage took the ship to New Orleans in 1859. There Rowlands, now a deckhand, jumped ship, sought work, and was befriended by a well-established cotton broker, Henry Hope Stanley, a native of Cheshire, England, near both Liverpool and Denbigh.

Recently widowed, Stanley gave the boy his name, with the intention of adopting him, although he never did so formally. They traveled together in the South as father and son. Differences arose between them, however, and the cotton broker placed the boy, now known as Henry Stanley, on a friend's plantation in Arkansas, while he himself went to visit a brother in Cuba.

By then it was 1861. The usual story is that Henry Hope Stanley died either in New Orleans or in Cuba before he could legalize the adoption of Rowlands. Evidence indicates, however, that he returned to England for the period of the Civil War, but came back to New

Orleans after the war, and lived there until his death in 1878.[3] Although they never found each other again, Rowlands apparently regarded Stanley as his "father" and used the name Henry Stanley. At a certain point, he began to experiment with middle names and initials, and by about 1870 he settled upon Henry Morton Stanley as the name he was to use.

Young Stanley soon became dissatisfied with life and work on the Arkansas plantation. Nearly twenty, he took his few possessions and walked forty miles to Cypress Bend, Arkansas, where he found work as a clerk in a general store. In May 1861, with the Civil War begun, Arkansas joined the Confederacy. Although Stanley had no personal interest in the issues of the war, he was a young man of military age, and he felt the social pressure in the community that led him to sign up for service. In August he left Little Rock as a member of the Sixth Arkansas Regiment of Volunteers. In April 1862, engaged in the Battle of Shiloh, in western Tennessee, he was slightly hurt, captured, and sent as a prisoner of war to Camp Douglas near Chicago.

The war situation was such that he was freed after two months, on the agreement that he would join the Union forces. With no emotional commitment to either side, he accepted the opportunity to become a member of the First Regiment of the Illinois Light Artillery. Later, in camp near Harper's Ferry, Virginia, he became ill, was hospitalized and then discharged. He became a harvest worker in Maryland, regained his strength, made his way to Baltimore, worked on an oyster schooner, and then signed on a sailing vessel for Liverpool. Poorly received at his home in Denbigh, he returned to sea, sailing in merchant ships in the Atlantic and the Mediterranean.

Back in New York in October 1863, Stanley worked in a law office, copying documents until mid-1864. For some unexplained reason, he chose to re-enter the war in July, signing on for three years in the navy. By December he was a ship's clerk aboard the Union frigate Minnesota, standing off Confederate-held Fort Fisher, at Wilmington, North Carolina. The ship was involved in two actions against the fort, was somewhat damaged in the second in January 1865, ana moved to Portsmouth, New Hampshire, for repairs. There,

---

3   Henry Morton Stanley himself presented several versions of his early years. During his lifetime, he wrote extensively, including seven books—one an autobiography. He also has been the subject of more biographical books and articles than any other correspondent. It remained for Richard Hall to conduct the most complete research, and his book, *Stanley: An Adventurer Explored* (1975), is by far the most accurate and informative account of ：is life and experience.

in February, Stanley and a very young shipmate, Louis H. Noe, of Sayville, Long Island, both deserted. Noe, suddenly alarmed at what he had done, and under pressure from his family, promptly re-enlisted, under an assumed name, in the Eighth New York Mounted Volunteers. Stanley stayed in New York, found work, and began to take an interest in journalism.

The war ended in April, and Stanley was in St. Louis by June. There he persuaded the *Missouri Democrat* to hire him as an "attaché." This gave him status as a free-lance representative, or stringer. It was his first newspaper connection. He wanted to explore the West, and went on to Salt Lake City and San Francisco, then back to Denver and Central City, later to Omaha, back to St. Louis, and then to New York again by June 1866. He supported himself during these months in a variety of jobs, but he also had adventures. He wrote for the paper in St. Louis, too, and discovered that he had some talent. Now twenty-five, he conceived the idea of "writing" his way around the world. He had kept in touch with Noe, now seventeen and out of the army, and persuaded him to join in the world venture, and also persuaded Noe's parents to approve his going.

The two left Boston in July, bound for Turkey, working as ship's hands to pay their way on an old three-master. The voyage took fifty-one days. Their intent was to go on to China and return by way of the Pacific. As it turned out, they began by exploring Turkey, had a series of misadventures, were robbed, beaten, and nearly killed, and turned to the U.S. minister in Constantinople for financial assistance.

Stanley wrote some stories on the basis of their experiences, but he and Noe were back in New York by February 1867, about six months after they left—following another visit in Denbigh and a stop in London, where Stanley met with Colonel Finlay Anderson, the *New York Herald* representative, perhaps to ask for a job.

Failing that, Stanley proceeded immediately from New York to St. Louis again, where the *Missouri Democrat* sent him as a staff reporter to cover the Missouri state legislature in Jefferson City. There he remained from February to April of 1867, attempting also to lecture on his adventures in Turkey, but with little success. It was in April that Stanley set out on the Hancock-Sheridan campaign to control the Indians in Kansas and beyond. He was now on a salary of $15 a week, and had his own horse. Reference already has been made to his activity in reporting the Indian "wars" between April and November 1867.

Those months marked a turning point in Stanley's life and career. From an adventurer and *poseur* of questionable behavior and no clear purpose, he was, by the end of 1867, at twenty-six, a considerably self-reliant journalist of some experience, growing competence, and judgment. He had written fully and regularly of the frontier and its problems, and with considerable understanding of the Indians' plight. In competition with journalists from a dozen other papers, he had been writing not only for the *Missouri Democrat,* but for the *New York Herald* and other papers. His reports were personal and subjective, but that style was still acceptable in mail copy, and what he wrote was interesting by those standards.

When the travels and meetings of the Peace Commission ended in November, and the approaching winter made it certain that there would be no major Indian activity until spring, Stanley conceived the idea of returning to the Middle East as a reporter, properly accredited by an established newspaper. He sought such a position with the *New York Tribune,* perhaps aware of Smalley's current efforts for that paper in London, but this was denied him. He went to New York, however, and in December 1867 obtained an interview with James Gordon Bennett, Jr., who had only assumed direction of the *New York Herald* the year before, when his father retired. They were of exactly the same age, and Stanley, having been writing as a stringer for the *Herald,* asked Bennett for an assignment abroad for the paper.

By offering to pay his own way to London, Stanley persuaded Bennett to agree that he might go to Abyssinia (Ethiopia) as a correspondent for the *Herald.* He would join a British army expedition due to leave Bombay under General Sir Robert Napier (later Lord Napier of Magdala) to attempt the rescue of the British consul, Captain Charles Cameron, and about sixty other British officers, missionaries, and civilians who had been kept as chained captives for some years in the mountain fortress of Magdala, prisoners of Abyssinia's King Theodore. Stanley was assured that if he did well on the assignment he might expect to be put on the *Herald* list of permanent correspondents.

He departed for London, where he presented credentials from Bennett to Colonel Anderson. Then Stanley proceeded to Suez, where he made private arrangements with the chief of the telegraph and cable office for priority handling of his messages to London and New York. At Aden he joined the Napier expedition coming from

Bombay and went on with it to Annesley Bay, in the Red Sea, where a landing was made in January 1868. Magdala, 420 miles from the coast, was reached in April. The fortress was stormed and destroyed, the captives were freed, and King Theodore killed himself.

The arrangements made earlier at Suez for priority handling of his dispatches now paid dividends. Stanley's reports were the first to reach London and New York. Further, a break occurred in the cable immediately after his dispatches had gone through, and no other accounts could be moved for a considerable time. This made his success even greater, especially since correspondents with the expedition included such veterans as George A. Henty and Frederick Boyle, both of the *Standard*, Charles Austin of the *Times*, Lord Adare of the *Daily Telegraph*, and a representative of Reuter. It assured Stanley's place as a *New York Herald* correspondent.

For some months following, Stanley had a roving commission that took him about the eastern Mediterranean, to Spain, and then to London. There he was instructed to return to Aden and await the arrival of a Scottish missionary and explorer, Dr. David Livingstone, who had gone to Zanzibar in 1866 and on into Africa in the latest of several journeys since 1840. He was expected at Aden early in 1869. After waiting there for weeks, however, with no word from Livingstone, Stanley was sent to Spain again. There he remained from March until October to report on disorders following the removal of Queen Isabella from the throne the previous year.

In October 1869, Stanley was summoned to Paris to see Bennett, who revived the Livingstone matter. He instructed Stanley to go first to Egypt to report the prospective opening of the Suez Canal, and to cover several other stories in that part of the world. Then, if Livingstone still had not returned, Stanley was to go to Africa himself and "find Livingstone."

Stanley was described as being, at that time, "a husky, medium-sized young man with penetrating black eyes, a swarthy, determined face, and a piratical mustache." He left Paris a few days after his meeting with Bennett and did not return to Europe until the summer of 1872—missing the entire period of the Franco-Prussian War. He did report the opening of the Suez Canal on November 17, 1869, and went up the Nile in a party of seventy invited by the Khedive of Egypt. He reported the excavation of antiquities in Jerusalem, went to Constantinople and through the Middle East, and arrived in Bombay on August 1, 1870. Dr. Livingstone still had not been heard from and Stanley, accordingly, was to start for Africa by ship from Bombay to Zanzibar. But no such ship was to sail until October, so Stanley covered stories in India.[4]

It was December 31, 1870, when Stanley at last reached Zanzibar. An additional three months was required to organize an expedition to move into the interior of Africa where Livingstone might be found, or some word of him obtained. Stanley had an unlimited expense account from Bennett and the *Herald* and, by then, it also had been arranged that the costs would be shared by the *Daily Telegraph*. By the spring of 1871, when Stanley led his expedition to the African continent, there was a common belief in London that Dr. Livingstone had died, since nothing had been heard from him for four to five years. Bennett did not share that opinion, however, and Stanley's assignment remained unchanged.

After months of difficulties and perils, by good fortune Stanley and his expedition found Livingstone at Ujiji, on the shore of Lake Tanganyika, on November 10, 1871. Stanley's greeting, "Dr. Livingstone, I presume," was to become a kind of jocular byword in later times but, as originally spoken, it was an almost prayerful end of a long and arduous journey. The missionary-explorer, then fifty-eight years old, had had many problems in his explorations and was not well, but he was neither lost nor dead.

Stanley remained with Livingstone from November 1871 until March 1872, joining him in some further explorations, and learning much of his previous findings. The two men became great friends and Livingstone later referred to Stanley as his "good samaritan," and as a man whose conduct was "beyond all praise."

Returning to Zanzibar by the late spring of 1872, in a fifty-four-day journey, Stanley organized and dispatched a new party to carry urgently needed supplies to Livingstone, who chose to remain at Ujiji. Stanley himself then returned to Paris and London with full reports, including letters from Livingstone for delivery, and with much new information about the interior of Africa, then unmapped and unknown.

---

4 It is possible that Stanley's assignment to Africa might have been changed even at this late period. DeB. Randolph Keim, *New York Herald* correspondent during the Civil War and the early period of the Indian wars, became Washington correspondent for the paper in 1870. He was very close to President Grant, who sometimes sent him on special missions. Oliver Knight, in his *Following the Indian Wars*, indicates (p. 321) that at a time when Keim was in Ceylon on such a mission, probably in 1870, even as Stanley was in Bombay, Bennett wrote to Keim asking him to go to Africa to seek Livingstone. The letter failed to reach him, and Stanley went, as Bennett had proposed in 1869.

On behalf of the *Daily Telegraph,* co-sponsor of the expedition, John Merry LeSage of that paper and Dr. George W. Hosmer, successor to Anderson as London representative of the *New York Herald,* informed of Stanley's return, met him at Marseilles and accompanied him to London. Aside from what they wrote, no detailed reports about Stanley's expedition appeared until after he reached London. His long accounts of the African journey and of Livingstone and his work then appeared in the *Daily Telegraph* and the *New York Herald.* They were widely read and much quoted and commented upon in many countries, and brought personal fame to Stanley, who was called upon to lecture in England and the United States. They brought prestige to both newspapers, and were re- printed in book form.

Stanley returned to Africa in 1873-74, representing the *Herald* as a war correspondent. Since 1807 the African Gold Coast, on the Atlantic seaboard (now part of Ghana), had been under British protection. Disorders among the Ashanti tribesmen in 1824-27 had been ended by a British military expedition, but new disorders brought a second expedition in 1873, with General Sir Garnet Wolseley in command. On this occasion, the British fought their way into Kumasi (or Coomassie), the Ashanti capital, and an uneasy truce was concluded in February 1874.

Other correspondents with the expedition included Henty and Boyle of the *Standard,* whom Stanley had known on the Abyssinian expedition in 1868 (Henty since had covered the Franco-Prussian War); William Winwood Reade of the *Times,* known also as a novelist; Colonel J. F. Maurice, assistant military secretary to General Wolseley but also writing for the *Daily News;* and Melton Prior, artist-correspondent for the *Illustrated London News,* on his first war assignment of many that were to occupy him for more than thirty years, to the time of the Balkan War of 1912.

Stanley returned from the Gold Coast to London in March 1874. There he learned of the death of Dr. Livingstone in Africa on May 1, 1873, about a year after they had separated. Livingstone's remains were returned to London in April 1874 and buried in Westminster Abbey on April 16. Stanley was present as one of those doing him honor. During more than thirty years in Africa, Livingstone had traveled over about one-third of the continent, and had contributed an enormous amount of knowledge concerning its geography, ethnography, flora, and fauna.

As a friend and admirer of Livingstone, and by reason of an interest he now possessed in Africa, Stanley wished to return there to carry forward explorations required to advance understanding of the continent. Bennett of the *New York Herald,* and Edward Levy-Lawson (later the first Lord Burnham) proprietor of the *Daily Telegraph,* again joined, along with others interested in Africa, to finance a second expedition. On this occasion Stanley was to be in Africa from October 1874 until August 1877, concerned strictly with exploration.

Again marked by hazards and hardships, and almost constantly racked by fever, Stanley's new discoveries nevertheless had the long-term result of opening up equatorial Africa. Among other things, he verified the source of the Nile and he traced the Congo River from its source to its mouth in the Atlantic. No day-by-day reports emerged, but when Stanley's carefully prepared articles began to appear in the two newspapers late in 1877 they were to spur the dispatch of more missionaries to Africa and also to stimulate important political developments. Stanley gave Bennett's name to an African mountain peak that he had been the first white man to see— Mount James Gordon Bennett—and also to a river. So many honors were conferred upon Stanley after the second expedition, however, that Bennett was offended and, when the correspondent visited New York to lecture he was slighted both by Bennett and the *Herald* itself. On the same occasion, he was made the target of ungenerous and undeserved abuse by the *New York Sun,* then in great rivalry with the *Herald* in the morning newspaper field.

The second expedition marked the end of Stanley's activities as a correspondent, but not of his preoccupation with Africa. King Leopold II of Belgium persuaded him to lead a third expedition to that continent in 1879-84, resulting in the formation of the Congo Free State in 1885 as an area under Belgian control. In 1887-89 Stanley led a fourth expedition that was to result in the establishment of British control in East Africa.

By 1889 Bennett had recovered his sense of proportion with reference to Stanley, and he commissioned Edward Henry Vizetelly, experienced as a British correspondent since the time of the Franco-Prussian War, to go to Zanzibar to await the explorer's return from the interior of the continent. Indeed, Vizetelly's instructions were to go to the continent himself when information reached Zanzibar that Stanley was approaching the coast and to meet him, learn the details of his latest findings and rush the reports to New York, using the cable by then serving the east coast of Africa. Vizetelly was in competition on this assignment with Thomas Stevens, also in Zanzibar, a representative of the morning *New York World,* under the vigorous direction of Joseph Pulitzer since 1883 and in sharp rivalry with the *Herald.*

The two men had a wait of six months. In the end, Vizetelly was successful in meeting Stanley and getting a 1,400-word exclusive dispatch to New York, at a cable cost of $3,500, for first publication in the *New York Herald* on December 5, 1889.[5] James Creelman, Canadian-born newsman then representing the *Herald* in London, also met Stanley at the Italian port of Brindisi, midway on his return journey, to obtain further information.

Honored and already long accepted as an authority on Africa, Stanley was consulted by leaders of government and business. He was renaturalized as a British subject in 1892, and was a member of Parliament from 1895 to 1900. He made a fifth and last visit to Africa in 1897, and in 1899 was knighted, becoming Sir Henry Morton Stanley. He had suffered from repeated fevers and illness during his African journeys and had aged greatly. He died in London in 1904, aged sixty-three.[6]

The success of the first two Stanley expeditions into Africa, so largely concerned with exploration and providing information on a little-known part of the world, brought credit as sponsors to the *New York Herald* and the London *Daily Telegraph.* It may be assumed that public appreciation of these ventures had a part in inducing Bennett and Levy-Lawson, publishers of the two papers, to sponsor later expeditions also intended to broaden knowledge of the world.

---

5 Edward H. Vizetelly was rewarded for his early and exclusive report with a bonus of £2,000 (nearly $10,000). He had been very much on the move since reporting aspects of the Franco-Prussian War for the London *Daily News* and the *New York Times.* He had reported a Turkish-Serbian war in 1876 and the Russo-Turkish War of 1877-78, both for the London *Standard.* He had also written for the *Glasgow Herald,* had established and written for the weekly *Cyprus Times* in 1881, and had written for the *Bombay Gazette,* the *Egyptian Gazette,* and the *Times of Egypt.* The Zanzibar assignment, however, ended his wanderings and also ended his active news work. Following that exploit, he lived quietly in Paris and then in London, where he died in 1903.

6 Stanley's autobiography, substantially edited by his widow, was published in 1909. The Richard Hall biography, published in 1975, is far more accurate and complete. Stanley's expeditions in Africa have been retraced on three occasions, first by Charles Wellington Furlong, in the early 1930s; then by his grandson, Richard Morton Stanley, in 1957; and by Thomas Sterling, whose book contrasts and comments upon the Africa of Stanley's time and that of 1960.

The *Daily Telegraph* in 1872-73 sent George Smith, noted British Assyriologist, to Ninevah, where he directed excavations bearing upon the biblical story of the flood. The paper also aided an expedition led by Sir Harry Hamilton Johnston to Mount Kilimanjaro, Africa's highest mountain, in 1884-85. Further, it backed another African expedition in 1899-1900, a trek from the Cape of Good Hope northward to Cairo, under the leadership of Lionel Decla.

Following his own interests, Bennett meanwhile turned to a support of Arctic exploration. In 1875 he backed an expedition under Captain Allen Young seeking a "Northwest Passage" through the northernmost waters of North America into the Pacific. To report the venture for the *New York Herald*, J. A. MacGahan was with the ship.

The Young expedition failed of its objective, but Bennett backed another in 1879-81 directed toward reaching the North Pole, and expending $340,000 in the effort. The ship bearing the members of the expedition sailed from England through the Straits of Magellan, northward to San Francisco and through Bering Strait. In June 1881 it was caught in Polar ice and sank. Half of the twenty-four members of the group were lost, including Jerome J. Collins, a *Herald* reporter who had given nearly three years to the assignment and finally gave his life. Survivors of the disaster found refuge on the Lena delta, off Siberia. John P. Jackson, then in the paper's Paris bureau, was sent with money and supplies to Irkutsk, and on by sled to the delta, and returned with the refugees from there to St. Petersburg.

This did not end Bennett's concern with Arctic exploration. He backed two attempts by Commander Robert E. Peary to reach the North Pole, with William Henry Gilder accompanying him as a *Herald* reporter. In 1908, when Peary sought his support again, however, Bennett refused. He had contributed $25,000 to an expedition led by Dr. Frederick A. Cook, who subsequently claimed to have reached the Pole, a claim later disallowed. With Bennett's refusal to back him, Peary had turned to the *New York Times* which contributed $4,000 to his venture and was rewarded by having first and full rights to publication of Peary's own story of his successful expedition, the first to reach the North Pole.[7]

---

7 The *Herald* persisted in supporting Cook's claim until it was discredited, officially.

The Reuter's Telegram Company, Ltd., as officially known since 1865, was far more active than the Havas and Wolff agencies after 1870 in extending its service, and was the moving force in the Ring Combination. Under the agreements governing that combination, Reuter had exclusive rights to distribute its world report in Asia and the Middle East. To this, Egypt was added in 1890. British Empire points also were part of Reuter's territory, which included Australasia (Australia and New Zealand), as well as India and Hong Kong, among other areas in the East.

The Reuter strength in these areas followed the extension of telegraph and cable lines. Telegraph lines, almost all of which were government-sponsored, were operating within parts of most countries of the East by 1870. British enterprise in the development of world communication lines exceeded that of other countries. The British-sponsored Indo-European landline telegraph between India and the Prussian North Sea coast had gone into operation in 1865. The cable had been extended from British shores to Alexandria, Egypt, by 1869, to Bombay in 1870, and other cables had been extended from Madras to Ceylon and from Singapore to Australia and New Zealand by 1873, and also to Hong Kong, Shanghai, and the Japanese coast. Connections were made in China in 1896 with a spur of the Great Northern Danish-owned line across Siberia to Russia and other points in Europe.

With Henry M. Collins assigned as Reuter's representative in India in 1866, an office in Bombay was established and stringers engaged in Calcutta, Delhi, Madras, and Karachi, and also in Ceylon, both at Colombo and at Point de Galle. The chief Reuter clients at first were the British East India Company and merchants, bankers, and traders. The first newspaper to receive service was the Colomnbo *Ceylon Observer,* but subscribers increased among newspapers and others in India. As the cable was extended, Collins arranged for stringers at Rangoon, Singapore, Hong Kong, Shanghai, Yokohama and, in another direction, at Batavia, Sydney, and Wellington. His own headquarters was at Sydney from 1878 until 1898.

India had been important to the British economy since the East India Company established a position there in 1610, with headquarters in Calcutta. It became a ruling power in India after 1757, and remained so until 1858, the year after the Indian mutiny. At that time the administration of India was transferred to the British crown and Queen Victoria became Empress of India in 1877. Calcutta remained the capital of British India until 1912 when Delhi was selected as the site of a new capital.

A progressive growth of British trade, military, business, missionary, educational, and administrative concern with India, especially after 1800, brought a great influx of British residents, and a press development followed. Although printing had begun in India in the sixteenth century, the first newspaper appeared only in 1780, in Calcutta, and in English. By 1880, a number of newspapers of some importance were appearing. These included *Samachar Darpan* of Calcutta, the first vernacular paper, started in 1818; the *Times of India,* begun in Bombay in 1838; and the *Amrita Bazaar Patrika* of Calcutta, dating from 1860. This third was a bilingual Bengali-English daily, becoming strictly an English-language paper in 1878, and attaining the largest circulation in the country at that period.

Other papers, all in English, included the *Hindu* of Madras, begun as a weekly in 1873, but an important daily in 1889; the *Statesman,* begun in 1875 in Calcutta; the *Civil and Military Gazette* of Lahore, and the *Pioneer* of Allahabad, with both of which Rudyard Kipling later was to be identified; the *Indian Daily Mail* of Calcutta; and the *Tribune* of Ambala, begun as a weekly in 1881, but later a respected daily. Most of these papers received the Reuter service.

Literacy was limited in India, and a variety of languages complicated the problem of publishing vernacular newspapers. The large population nevertheless justified the production of newspapers, small though they might be, appearing weekly, in many cases, rather than daily. They were published not only in Bengali in the Calcutta area, but in Hindi, Gujarati, Urdu, and other languages. Some Indian publishers owned both vernacular and English language papers, and publishers of British newspapers sometimes owned vernacular newspapers. In nearby Ceylon, the *Ceylon Observer* had been established in 1834, and the evening *Times of Ceylon* began in 1846, both at Colombo.

With the East India Company and other British business interests looking farther eastward, both before and after the extension of the cable, other English-language newspapers also were established.

The first real newspaper in China, the *Canton Register,* was started in that port city in 1827 by James Matheson. In 1841 Great Britain, by treaty with the imperial Chinese government, acquired the island of Hong Kong at the mouth of the Pearl River. In 1843 it became a British Crown Colony. The *Canton Register* was moved there at the time, retitled the *Hong Kong Register,* and continued until 1859. A weekly *China Mail,* established at Hong Kong in 1845 by Andrew Shortrade, became a daily in 1876. Both added vernacular editions.

In other treaties, between 1842 and 1860, the British gained rights to trade and reside in five ports: Canton, Shanghai, Amoy, Foochow, and Ningpo. Rights were extended later to Tientsin, Hankow, and Peking, along with the right to travel in China. As the century advanced, these rights were extended to all other nations and their peoples, and a system of extraterritorial rights was recognized by treaty, permitting foreigners in China to maintain their own courts to handle cases involving foreign nationals and their interests, and to enjoy certain other privileges. The treaties became the basis for the establishment of an "International Settlement" in Shanghai, and a "French quarter"; of a "French Concession" in Tientsin, a comparable foreign enclave in Hankow, and a "Legation Quarter" in Peking, the capital. In such areas, the entire administration was in the hands of foreigners, and the Chinese government had no jurisdiction.

It was in the period from 1842 that English-language newspapers began to appear in cities of China where foreigners were permitted to live. Papers in other languages came later. In such places the first vernacular papers of China also appeared. Although perhaps Chinese-owned, they usually were registered at a foreign consulate, with a foreigner named as managing director. Thus "flying the foreign flag," as the phrase went, they were protected from Chinese government interference under the treaties.

In Shanghai's International Settlement, the *North China Daily Herald* began as a weekly in 1850. A supplement added later, called the *Daily Shipping and Commercial News,* became so important that in 1864 the *Herald* and its supplement were combined to form a new paper, the *North China Daily News.* The first important vernacular paper in the Settlement was established in 1872 by Frederic Major, a British tea merchant. Known as the *Shun Pao* (Shanghai Gazette), it was a weekly, became a daily within three months, and attained great success. In contrast, most vernacular newspapers in China at that time presented mostly trivia and gossip, and were published in a few hundred copies.

Editors of English-language papers in China acted as stringers for London dailies. They were dependent for what they printed largely on London and world reports taken from newspapers reaching them months after publication.

The London *Times* had been the first western newspaper to send a special resident correspondent to China—George Wingrove Cooke from 1857-60, followed by Thomas William Bowlby, who was killed. Bayard Taylor, writing for the *New York Tribune*, had been briefly in China in 1854. Valentine Chirol was in China for a time in 1875 for the London *Standard*.

The telegraph was moving messages within parts of China by 1873 and cable connections with Europe were established. Not only did Reuter then gain stringers in Hong Kong and Shanghai, but it was able to deliver news reports, although at great cost.

Japan was not in the mainstream of world affairs until after 1853, or more accurately, until after 1868. Portuguese traders and Jesuit missionaries were the first persons of the western world to establish relations with Japan in the sixteenth century. With bases also at Goa in India, in Ceylon, and at Macao in China, the Portuguese were permitted one trading base in Japan at the port of Nagasaki.

Navigators of the Dutch East India Company established a position at Batavia (Djakarta) in Java in 1602. Trading from that base, a relationship with Japan began in 1609. In 1647 the Portuguese were forced out and replaced at Nagasaki by the Dutch. By the eighteenth century, other Europeans also were permitted to live there, and to trade, but rarely go beyond. Not until after 1853, when the U.S. naval squadron under Commodore Perry visited Japan with an invitation to enter into trade with the United States, did normal relations begin between Japan and other peoples of the world. Bayard Taylor of the *New York Tribune*, with the Perry squadron, went ashore and was almost certainly the first news correspondent to see more of Japan than might have been visible at Nagasaki.

Meanwhile, in Batavia, the Dutch were sufficiently settled by the eighteenth century to establish a number of small newspapers, including the *Batavaise Nouvelles* in 1744, followed by the *Batavaische Courant* in 1816, which became the *Javasche Courant* in 1828 and continued for more than a century.

The Dutch East India Company, with rights in Nagasaki, was requested by the Japanese shogunate, certainly before 1800, to prepare an annual report on events in the rest of the world. In 1861, with a new spirit stirring in Japan, this annual report became a monthly publication. It was called the *Batavia Shimbun* (Batavia Newspaper) because, although actually prepared in Nagasaki, the contents were derived from the Batavia papers.

From 1862 to 1864 the *Batavia Shimbun* was prepared by Hikozo Hamada, sometimes credited with having introduced "modern" journalism to Japan. As a young man, he was a sailor. His ship was wrecked off the coast of Japan in 1850, perhaps in a storm, and he was picked out of the water by an American sailing vessel bound from China to San Francisco. Arriving in California (then only just admitted as the thirty-first state in the Union and in the midst of the gold rush) Hamada learned English, received some education, acquired the name "Joseph Heco" or "Joseph Hikoza," and even was naturalized as a citizen of the United States. In 1853 he returned to Japan with Commodore Perry's naval squadron, possibly as an interpreter, and remained there.

Having observed the press in the United States, and having become bilingual, Hamada became active in preparing news reviews for the Japanese government and also in preparing the monthly editions of the *Batavia Shimbun*. Up to that time, the people of Japan had had no source of general information except the kawara-ban prints displayed by shops, and the "yomiuri" sold by street vendors.

In Nagasaki, an English-language paper called the *Shipping List and Advertiser* had been established in 1861; later, it was moved to Yokohama and continued under the name of the *Japan Herald*. But there was no general newspaper in Japanese. Hamada and two friends, Ginko Kishida and Senzo Homma, therefore undertook to publish a paper intended for general distribution. Known simply as the *Shimbunshi* (News), the first issue appeared in March 1864. It consisted largely of material translated from foreign newspapers and publications. After the tenth issue, however, it was suppressed by the government. Hamada soon returned to the United States, and Kishida went to China.

The Meiji era began in Japan in 1868—"Meiji" being the year-name, and meaning "Enlightened Government," a reference to a reformist view then gaining support in the country. It was a name selected to apply also to the reign of a new emperor, Mutsuhito, who had succeeded to the throne in 1867. Although then only fourteen years old, he reigned for forty-five years, until 1912, during which time Japan emerged from isolation, developed industry and trade, and gained recognition as a world power. The capital had been moved in 1603 from Kyoto to Yedo, and in 1868 Yedo was renamed Tokyo, or "Eastern Capital."

Opportunities for development of the press advanced as the new era began, and schooling and literacy also developed. A new ordinance in 1868 established laws to govern a press that scarcely existed at the time. Amendments were added in 1873 and in subsequent years. Telegraph lines began to operate in 1869, and a

Shanghai-Nagasaki cable was laid in 1871. In 1873 Japan was brought into cable connection with Europe. For Reuter, Collins established an office at Yokohama, and branch offices were opened in Nagasaki and Tokyo.

The first modern-style vernacular newspapers of general circulation appeared in 1872. There were three; all in Tokyo. The first was foreign-sponsored, but began with Japanese government support. Known as the *Nisshin Shinju-shi* (Chronicle of Ever-New Facts), it was established by F. da Roza, possibly of Portuguese heritage, with John Reddie Black, an experienced British newsman, as editor. It was a paper of merit, stressing current news, and might have continued successfully had not an 1874 amendment to the 1868 press law specified that foreigners could not conduct vernacular papers. Even though da Roza had government support originally, he was obliged to suspend the paper.

The second paper started in 1872 was the *Hochi Shimbun* (News), originally known as *Yubin Hochi* (Postal News). Designed for easy reading, it became a successful, popular newspaper, through changes of ownership.

The third paper proved the most important. This was *Nichi-Nichi* (Today-Today, or Day-to-Day). Started as a daily in February 1872 by Genichiro Fukuchi, an educator, it was edited by Ginko Kishida, a former associate of Hamada, returned from China. John Reddie Black also was active in its production. Like most successful Japanese newspapers to follow, it had support from at least one prominent government official who used the paper to advance his own interests, as well as support from a major business group.

The *Nichi-Nichi* demonstrated enterprise. It presented current news at a time when that was still a novelty in Japan. It was the first paper in Japan to subscribe to the Reuter service, and it was the first to publish reports from its own representatives outside the country. This began in a small way when Prince Tonomi Iwakura went on a mission to the United States and Europe in 1872-73, with about fifty in his party, "to study the institutions of civilized nations" and also to explain conditions in Japan with a view to establishing formal diplomatic and trade relations with other countries. Whether from a correspondent with the party or from a stringer, at least one report was published describing the mission's presence in Salt Lake City. In 1874 when Japanese forces landed in Formosa, following the murder there of a Japanese seaman whose vessel had been wrecked off the shore, Kishida himself accompanied the expedition and wrote reports for the paper.

Five other vernacular dailies were established in Japan during the 1870s. The *Yomiuri* (The Call) of Tokyo, taking its name from the generic name of the news sheets produced earlier as block prints, was established in 1874. Written for easy reading, like the *Hochi Shimbun*, it succeeded.

In 1876 the *Osaka Nippo* was established in that seaport. It was purchased in 1888 by Hikoichi Motoyama, an industrial leader, its name changed to the *Mainichi Shimbun* (Daily Newspaper), and became one of the most successful and important newspapers.

Two business dailies were established in 1876 in Tokyo, and both became important. One was the *Nippon Keizai Shimbun* (Japanese Economic Newspaper). The other, the *Chugai Shogyo* (Journal of Commerce) was sponsored by the Mitsui industrial group.

The fifth daily, which also became successful and important, was the *Asahi* (Rising Sun). It was established at Osaka in January 1879 by Ryuhei Murayama. A Tokyo *Asahi* was added in 1888.

Other newspapers were established in Tokyo and other cities during the 1880s, and the first news agency in Asia was formed in Tokyo in 1886. This was the Shimbun Totatsu Kaisa (Newspaper Service Company). A second agency, Jiji (Current News) was formed in 1887 or early 1888, and the two were merged in 1888 to form the Teikoku Tsushin-sha (Empire News Agency), which had official status and remained a national agency until 1927.

Two English-language newspapers were operating in Japan in the 1870s. The first was the *Japan Herald* of Yokohama, deriving from the *Shipping List and Advertiser* as originally established at Nagasaki in 1861. The other was the *Tokyo Times,* established in 1877 by Edward Howard House. He was its editor until 1880. Then and perhaps as late as 1901, the year of his death, he also was a stringer in Japan for the *New York Herald,* the *New York World,* and the Associated Press.[8]

In establishing the first Reuter bureau in Japan in 1873, Henry M. Collins, managing the agency's far eastern affairs from Bombay, engaged the first stringer at Yokohama. Except for stringer reports from House and one or two others, most of the news of Japan

---

8 Edward Howard House, a native of Boston, had been part-owner of the *Boston Courier* in 1854. He also was a staff member of the *New York Tribune* and the *New York Times,* and collaborated with Dion Boucicault in writing plays for the New York stage. He went to Japan in 1870, and taught English for several years at the University of Tokyo. Also a musician, he prepared and conducted the first orchestral concerts to be given in Japan, conducted the imperial court orchestra, and received high government honors prior to his death at sixty-five.

reaching the world between 1873 and 1894 came through Reuter. The news of the world reaching the press of Japan was also provided by Reuter.

The cost of the Reuter service was high because of cable charges, and few Japanese newspapers felt able to afford it in the first years. John Griffiths, as secretary of the Reuter agency, had developed a coding system for telegrams, a means for transmitting news in volume with the greatest economy of words. This permitted Reuter to make use of "omnibus" messages including reports of many events to be sent to subscribers in Japan and other far places with speed and economy. And there was a mail service as well. The "omnibus" system also enabled staff and stringer correspondents to send their reports to London. After 1875 the introduction of "press rates" for transmission permitted further economies.

Australia and New Zealand, like Japan, were brought into direct contact with the world after 1873. Pending his own permanent residence in Sydney five years later, Collins placed his brother there as Reuter's agent, and another agent was named in Wellington to handle the business in New Zealand.

The press then was not highly developed in either area. The *Sydney Morning Herald* had become the first daily in Australia in 1831. The *Melbourne Argus* was established in 1854. They were sufficiently prosperous by 1873 to appoint a representative to serve them both in London. From late that year, he undertook to prepare cable reports based on material selected from the complete Reuter file at the headquarters office. This arrangement set a precedent by which Australian newspapers were regularly to have their own staff members in London. The same procedure was adopted by the newspapers of New Zealand through the formation of a New Zealand Press Association in 1878, with that agency also represented at Reuter headquarters.

At the outset, in 1873 and 1874, the cables to the Sydney and Melbourne papers averaged only forty words a day, in a condensed form that translated into considerably more copy than the words suggested. Even that limited service, at the rate then applying, cost the papers about £2,000 (roughly $10,000) a year for the communications charges alone. Again, the introduction of "press rates" in 1875 helped reduce charges, and further reductions in the regular rates after 1876 helped even more. There was another problem, however, in that the cable between Java and Port Darwin sometimes was out of service for ten to twenty days at a time.

Among other newspapers operating prior to 1880 were the Melbourne *Age*, the *Sydney Evening Post*, the Wellington *Evening Post*, the *New Zealand Herald* and the *Auckland Star*, both of that city, and the New Plymouth *Taranaki Daily Herald*.

By 1880, or before, Asia and the Pacific had joined in the world news flow, particularly through Reuter and its use of the new cables. The same was true for Latin America, largely because of the efforts of the Havas agency. Africa had ceased to be an unknown continent. The United States was nearing full settlement from coast to coast. Europe had recovered from the Franco-Prussian War, but had suffered from other violence. The public was better served by the press than ever before, and technological developments promised still better service.

The Telephone and Press Technolog

World communications advanced enormously in the decade of the 1870s. Reference has been made to the extension of telegraph lines and cables linking all continents by 1874. The decade brought the telephone into existence. The typewriter became available as an instrument destined to change the business and social structure, and was adapted also to news and communications uses. New experiments brought a beginning of wireless telegraphy by the end of the century, introducing still another dimension in communication.

Mention has been made of that most important meeting of the International Telegraphic Union at St. Petersburg in 1875. It established basic regulations for the conduct of telegraph and cable business across national frontiers, and gave the first official recognition and authorization for special, lower "press rates," which encouraged greater news exchange.

In 1874, a Universal Postal Union had been established, with headquarters at Berne, Switzerland, to bring a new uniformity and efficiency to the international movement of the mails. Coming at a time when railroad and steamship services also were being extended, added advantage was to follow in the transport of people and of goods, including newspapers and periodicals, books and general information.

Science and technology contributed important improvements during the 1870s in press operation, including photography and photoengraving, and the manufacture of paper from woodpulp.

The telephone provided the first means for the transmission of voice over distances. It was originally demonstrated in 1876 by Alexander Graham Bell. Approaches to the idea had been made in England by Dr. Robert Hooke as early as the sixteenth century, and by Sir Charles Wheatstone in the nineteenth century. And the development of the idea owed something to Charles Bourseul of France; to Phillip Reis of Germany; and to C. G. Page, Elisha Gray, Amos E. Dolbear, and Daniel Drawbaugh, all of the United States. But Bell's patent, upheld by the courts after long litigation, won him the distinction of being known as the inventor of the telephone.

Scottish-born, Bell had reached Boston by way of Canada. There, in 1871, when he was twenty-four years of age, he began to instruct deaf children in lip reading. In 1872 he opened a school for training teachers of the deaf, and in 1873 he became a professor of vocal physiology at Boston University. His interest in means by which sounds might be transmitted to the deaf led to his invention of several devices, the telephone among them. He was assisted by Thomas A. Watson, an able machinist who also worked with electricity, particularly with application to the telegraph. Bell also obtained advice and encouragement from Joseph Henry, one of the pioneers in telegraphy in the United States.

Bell's first application for a patent on his telephone device was filed in Washington February 14, 1876. The first successful transmission of voice over the instrument occurred March 10, when Bell was able to summon Watson from an adjoining room with the words so often quoted, "Mr. Watson, come here! I want you." He was to exhibit the invention at the Philadelphia Centennial Exposition in the summer of 1876. Visiting his parents in Brantford, Ontario, later in the summer, he tested the instrument over a distance of eight miles.

Gardiner G. Hubbard, a Boston attorney whose deaf daughter, Mildred, Bell had helped and was to marry in July 1877, had been interested in the telegraph and he gave Bell support in his telephone experiments. He arranged for Bell to give lecture-demonstrations of the telephone in New England during the winter of 1876-77. Watson remained in Boston on those occasions, and part of the demonstration was a telephone conversation between Bell, wherever he might be lecturing, and Watson, with the connection made over existing telegraph wires.

The first of these lectures was in Salem, Massachusetts. After the lecture, Henry A. Batchelder, a reporter for the *Boston Globe,* used the instrument to telephone an account of the lecture and demonstration from Salem to A. B. Fletcher in the newspaper office in Boston. The account was published in the *Boston Globe* of February 13, 1877, under a headline: "Sent by Telephone; The First Newspaper Dispatch Sent by a Human Voice Over the Wire."

Through the further efforts of Hubbard, and with his legal guidance, a Bell Telephone Company was established on July 9, 1877. By the end of that year it was estimated that 2,600 telephones were in use. The first telephone exchange was opened by the company in New Haven, Connecticut, on January 28, 1878, and in February the New England Bell Telephone Company was formed as the first of many regional subsidiaries of the parent Bell Telephone Company. In the spring of 1878 Hubbard engaged Theodore N. Vail, a cousin of Alfred Vail, who had worked with Morse on the telegraph, as manager of the Bell Telephone Company. The manufacturing of the instruments was assigned to the Western Electric Company, established a few years earlier in Chicago by Elisha Gray, an inventor in the communications field, under the original name of Gray & Barton.

Meanwhile, Bell had gone to England with his bride in the summer of 1877. There, under the sponsorship of Sir William Thompson (later Lord Kelvin), whose interest in the North Atlantic cable had been important, Bell demonstrated the telephone to Queen Victoria and others. In 1878 he returned to demonstrate the instrument publicly both in London and Paris. The first telephone exchange in London was opened in 1879, public service began in Paris in 1881, and telephone systems using the Bell patents were installed throughout Europe in the years following. The first telephone line between any two countries joined Paris and Brussels in 1887, and Paris and London were in telephonic communication in 1891 by means of a special cable beneath the English Channel.

In the United States, the Bell Telephone Company was reorganized in 1879 as the National Bell Telephone Company, and again in 1880 as the American Bell Telephone Company. Technical improvements relating to power, wire quality, and character were made in the telephone transmitter and receiver by Thomas A. Edison, Emil Berliner, and others.

An important new subsidiary entered the field in 1885 when the American Telephone & Telegraph Company was formed to construct and operated long-distance lines for the Bell company. Circuits were established between Boston and New York and Washington, with the first telephone in the White House installed during the first administration of President Grover Cleveland (1885-89). New York and Chicago were linked in 1892, and eastern Canadian cities were joined to those in the United States.

In Europe, a Berlin-Amsterdam circuit went into operation in 1896, and Paris was linked both to Berlin and Frankfurt in 1900. By that time there were 227,000 telephones in operation in the United States, and thousands more elsewhere in the world. Michael Pupin, Serbian-born U.S. scientist, helped to make longer circuits possible by devising a method to boost signal strength along the wire's length, but it was only after 1900 that further technical advances made really long lines possible for telephonic use.

As the telephone was being developed and put to use, among other things, for news purposes, improvements also were being made in the transmission of telegraphic and cable signals.

Even as early as 1853, a means was devised to send two messages over the same wire simultaneously without one interfering with the other. This was known as the "duplex" system by contrast with the "simplex" system, where one message moved. In 1874, Edison produced a "quadraplex" system permitting four messages to move over the same wire simultaneously, two in each direction. Years later, in 1915, this was to be increased to eight messages by a "multiplex" system introduced by Western Union. Each such advance was adapted to the cables and to the telephone lines. Better materials, better design, better insulation of the wires, and improved methods to amplify sound were to bring progressive advances in the reliability and speed of wired communication.

The accuracy and speed of such communication was advanced, too, by the development of automatic printer systems and automatic sending and relay devices, ending exclusive dependence on manual operation of the key and the audible reading of the code signals, even though that method was to continue in use, under certain circumstances, for many years.

Sir Charles Wheatstone, working on the telegraph in England, had patented a device in 1838 to turn the code signals received on his chronometric telegraph of 1837 into the form of printed letters. Other automatic printing devices were produced in France, Germany, and the United States. Alexander Bain in Scotland introduced automatic sending and relay of messages with a device invented in 1847 or 1848. This consisted of a mechanism that responded to audible letter code signals by punching holes in a paper tape as it moved through the machine, with the pattern of the holes representing the letter. The same punched tape then moving over a sending instrument permitted electrical impulses to pass through the perforations and over the line to a receiving point, where again the audible signals were repunched on a new tape. Improvements have been made in the equipment, but this remains the essential method for automatic message transmission and relay, with various combinations of five holes representing each letter or figure. Moreover, a message sent from one point may be received at any number of other points simultaneously, given the proper wire connections.

Further, to record messages so transmitted in something like typewritten form at the receiving end, early machines were devised in the United States by Royal E. House and David E. Hughes. The Hughes machine, the better of the two, was produced in 1855, and improved by George W. Phelps. Daniel H. Craig, then general manager of the young New York Associated Press, urged its adoption by that agency and by the telegraph companies. It actually was used more in Europe than in the United States because of patent complications.

An improved machine was produced in England by Wheatstone in 1872. His was both a sending and receiving device, and also provided for the automatic punching of a new tape at a relay point on a long line, with the message forwarded without human intervention, and with renewed impetus. At the receiving end, adapting the system pioneered by Sir William Thompson and by Alexander Bain, and known as a siphon recorder or undulator, a stylus passed over a tape to form square-cornered hills and dales representing the dot-dash code, readable by an operator for conversion into text, even though not readable in itself in the form of actual letters and words, as with the Hughes machine.

Stock market and commodity market reports began to be distributed in the markets themselves, and to brokers, bankers, and others, in visual and readable form in 1866, using a device operated by telegraphic impulse. In 1867 this was improved upon, with the quotations printed on a running paper tape. A Gold and Stock Company was formed in New York to provide this service, and was made a subsidiary of Western Union soon after 1870. Edison and Frank L. Pope devised a tape machine used in the process. The system was made available in London in 1872 through the newly formed Exchange Telegraph Company, Ltd.

As an aid to rapid and legible writing of a conventional sort, as in general correspondence, Christopher Latham Sholes (who had been city editor of the *Milwaukee Daily Sentinel*), with Carlos Glidden and Samuel W. Soulé also of Milwaukee, devised a machine in 1867 that operated effectively. This was the first practical typewriter. Improvements followed and commercial production began in 1873 by E. Remington & Sons, small arms manufacturers at Ilion, New York. The machine was revolutionary in the business world, in which women as typists were employed for almost the first time. It was to become generally used in newspaper and news agency offices after about 1880, and also was adapted to electrical communications, first by telegraphers, who used the typewriter to put the audible dot-dash signals into written form and, after 1912, in teleprinter circuits permitting the automatic distribution of messages and news reports.

Looking to the mechanical and production problems of the press, the decade of the 1870s marked a turning point between methods differing only in degree from those devised by Gutenberg and other printers of his time, and methods that still may be termed "modern."

The flatbed press of the fifteenth century had been enlarged and improved, and was operated by steam power, but the process of printing was essentially the same. Most newspaper circulations remained small, by present standards, but some exceeded 85,000 a day. It was scarcely possible to produce more than 10,000 copies of a four-page paper in an hour on any press in 1870. Yet many papers appeared in at least eight pages, twelve pages was a common size, and some were larger. It was possible to print four pages at a time, two on each side of a sheet. But the sheets were hand fed into the press.

Even assuming that two or three presses were used, the sheets then had to be assembled and folded by hand. In the circumstances, production of a daily paper of any size and circulation required hours of work by pressmen and assistants, and the demand for papers sometimes tended to outrun the supply. Even for a morning paper, with the hours of the night used for production, it might be difficult to have the papers ready for delivery on time.

The cost of presses was high; labor and the newsprint added to the expense of production. With daily editions of tens of thousands, the type itself suffered wear and had to be replaced as often as four times a year, again at considerable cost.

The answer to this complex problem began to appear in the 1870s. For one thing, experiments in progress since 1800 brought an acceptable quality of newsprint made from woodpulp rather than rags, and was far more plentiful and much less expensive. Further, the paper previously available only in sheets was produced in rolls, could be run through a press in a continuous sheet or "web," printed on both sides as it ran, and cut automatically as it emerged. It was referred to as a "perfected" newspaper. The hand assembly and folding of separate sheets was still required, but. the printing process was speeded.

The answer to the need for greater speed, and also to the problem of type wear, came with the development by R. Hoe & Company, New York, of the rotary press in 1871. Described as "the first roll-fed continuous printing rotary press with gathering and distributing cylinder," it was used originally in London by *Lloyd's Weekly Newspaper* in 1874, then by the *New York Tribune,* and eventually by newspapers throughout the world.

The 1871 model permitted the production of an eight-page paper ready for hand folding at a speed exceeding that of other presses. A "double perfecting" press in 1874 permitted the production of a twelve- or sixteen-page paper, and an automatic folding device was added. A "double supplement" press in 1882, a "quadruple" press in 1887, and an "octuple" press in 1895 each increased production, with the 1895 press turning out 48,000 papers of sixteen pages in an hour—and further improvements were to come. The added speed still did not necessarily keep pace with rising circulations, but the answer to that was for a newspaper to install two or more presses.

An essential element in the operation of the rotary press was the "stereotype plate," semi-cylindrical in form to fit the press cylinder. It was a plate cast in lead from a mold of one page of type, and was a precise reproduction of that page. The plate was clamped securely on one half of a cylinder on the press. A second plate bearing a cast of another page was clamped to the other half of the cylinder. The 1871 press had two cylinders, each bearing four such plates, permitting the printing of one eight-page paper with each turn of the cylinders. The plates were inked by rubber rollers as they turned. The 1874 press was built to accommodate sixteen plates, and each improved model handled more.

The flatbed press had operated from a page of type resting on the bed of the press, secure in a metal frame, or "chase," and the paper brought in contact with its inked surface, pressed upon it with a rubber roller cylinder. In 1845 a means was devised to clamp the type on the surface of a cylinder, then inked and brought in contact with the paper. This required that the type be so secured that it would not loosen and fall out. In a rotary press, operating at far greater speed, that could hardly have been avoided. The stereotype plate provided the solution.

The stereotype process required that the original page of type be overlaid with a "flong," or sturdy sheet somewhat like paper maché, and commonly referred to as a matrix or "mat," itself overlaid with a "blanket" and then subjected to brief, firm, and uniform pressure by a steam-operated mechanism. This transfered an exact impression of the type to the mat. The mat then was placed in a drier to be shaped in semi-cylindrical form, and next in a casting-box of the same form, with molten lead alloy metal forced in to form a plate reproducing the type in relief form. That plate, cooled by water injection, with its edges shaved, emerged ready to be clamped on the press.

Despite the apparent complexity of the process, a page plate could be produced in hardly more than a minute. Two or more plates of the same page could be produced for use on different presses to speed the total production of an edition. The plate, new and sharp, produced a clear printed impression, and could be remelted and the metal used again. The original type, subjected to pressure only briefly in making the mats, suffered little wear, was available for later use, and the need for frequent type replacement was ended.

The stereotype process, in its essentials, had been used in London in the printing of books as early as 1816, and experiments in its use by newspapers had been conducted in London, Paris, and New York from 1852. It was slow and costly, however, until the need for its use on the rotary press led to new methods of production. The use of the plate had advantages, also, in permitting greater flexibility in page design and general makeup. Freed of the restrictions of column rules, more effective headlines and advertising layout added variety, interest, and attractiveness to newspapers.

For all newspapers, however, at least two other production problems remained. One involved the use of illustrations, and the other the need to put all text matter into type manually, letter by letter, and then redistribute that type so that it might be reused. Skilled as compositors were, this was a slow and laborious process that delayed production, particularly as newspapers grew larger, and required the employment of many men.

Since the earliest days of the press, illustrations had been reproduced from hand-carved wooden blocks used as insets with advertising, as cartoons, as maps, and as diagrams, and sometimes in a news
context. The first departure from this procedure had originated in
Paris in 1859, permitting the transfer of line drawings to zinc plates,
so treated that acid ate away the metal while leaving the lines
standing high to receive ink in the printing process and reproduce
the drawing. Such "zinc etchings" were being used in newspapers in
the 1870s, and by the 1880s artists were producing line. drawings of
photographs to be so reproduced. These were more satisfactory
than wood engravings.

Efforts had been made at least as early as 1824 in England to
produce engravings of photographs, but it was 1873 or 1874 when
Carl Klic developed a process to transfer a photographic image to a
copper plate suitable for reproduction under carefully controlled
circumstances. At about that same period, in 1878, Frederic E. Ives,
working on photographic processes at Cornell University in Ithaca,
N. Y., began experiments that led by 1886 to the making of
"halftones," or plates suitable for reproduction through the printing
process.

The Ives process involved rephotographing a photograph through
clear plate glass on which lines were etched to form a closely
cross-hatched pattern or "screen." With the screen intervening, the
original photo was reproduced on a sensitized thin plate of copper,
subsequently treated and put through an acid bath to produce an
engraving or "cut." The acid ate into or cut the metal where the
lines on the screen criss-crossed the photo, leaving the rest slightly
higher, to take and hold ink in the printing process to follow. The
result was referred to as a "cut."

Viewing the cut itself through a magnifying glass, the picture was
revealed as a pattern of dots, the surviving high points on the plate.
For the darker portions of the photo, the dots were close together,
more widely separated for the middle tones, and absent in the white
portions. Scarcely visible to the eye, the dots took the ink and gave
the printed picture an appearance almost equal to the original in
clarity. It is a process still in use, although improved.

The number of lines on the plate-glass screen may vary. For the
most perfect reproduction, that number should be from eighty to 400
lines to the inch, both vertically and horizontally. In practice, the
number is rarely above 200 lines. To produce a satisfactory picture
from a halftone so made required careful printing on a flatbed press,

using paper of the highest quality, calendered to make it smooth and glazed. Periodicals using such paper were able by the 1870s to publish excellent reproductions of photographs.

The coarser paper used by newspapers, whether rag or woodpulp, could not reproduce photos made with such a screen. The stereotyping process and the speed of the rotary presses were further obstacles. By using a screen of forty to sixty lines, however, it became possible to obtain fairly satisfactory newspaper reproduction of photos by the 1880s. With further improvements, some newspapers were using them regularly by the 1890s, and most were doing so after 1900.

The second problem that of finding a means to set type by some mechanical means, had stirred many inventive minds. Forty patents had been granted in the United States alone before 1884, and more in other countries, for machines to be used in composition. It remained for Ottmar Mergenthaler, a German immigrant to the United States in 1872, to produce the first machine to satisfy the requirement. This he did in 1884, after having given the problem his concentrated attention since 1876.

Trained as a watchmaker, Mergenthaler found employment in Washington, D.C. Then eighteen, he was occupied for the next four years in keeping the clocks and bells in good operating order in government buildings, where he also improved the signal service apparatus. But he had become interested in the development of a machine to set type. In 1876 he moved to Baltimore, commissioned by a manufacturer of scientific equipment to give all of his time to that effort. As he proceeded, he also received financial support from three newspapers, the *New York Tribune,* the *Chicago Daily News,* and the *Louisville Courier-Journal.* In 1884 he produced a machine. By then he was in business for himself, with at least one other invention to his credit, and he patented the typesetting machine in his own name.

With further improvements and some useful additions by Philip T. Dodge and others, the first of the machines went into operation in the office of the *New York Tribune* in 1886, another soon went to the *Chicago Daily News,* and no less than fifty-five were in operation in 1887. It was adopted throughout the world, with 3,000 in use by 1897. At the time of his death in 1899, Mergenthaler had factories producing his machine in England and Germany, as well as in the United States.

The Mergenthaler machine was known as the "Linotype" because it set type line by line, cast in lead, and operated through a keyboard comparable to that of a typewriter. The setting proceeded more rapidly than would have been possible for any hand compositor to match. It provided also for a variety of type faces and sizes. Since every line was freshly set, the type always was clear and sharp, and it ended the need to re-sort type. Once used, the metal was remelted to be used again. The lines themselves could be handled with an ease and confidence and speed exceeding anything possible with handset type.

Improvements were made in the Linotype through the years, and new models and developments continue to appear, in step with changes in publishing. Other machines also appeared in various countries. One was the Lanston Monotype, patented in the United States in 1887 by Tolbert Lanston, casting single letters, rather than lines of type. It was used more for magazine and book work than by newspapers. Another was the Intertype, comparable to the Linotype, sponsored by Herman Ridder, publisher of the New York *Staats-Zeitung,* and first put to use in 1913.

Headlines and much advertising display copy continued to be handset until after 1906, when Washington I. Ludlow and William A. Reade established the Ludlow Typograph company, with the "Ludlow" then available as a device to permit casting larger type units for such purposes.

These advances in communications and in the printing process, occurring or beginning in the 1870s and combined with the increasingly vigorous coverage of news, made for an extraordinary decade.

The Correspondent in War and Peace   14

Incredible as it may seem, the many events and developments of the 1870s already described by no means complete the story of press activities in that busy decade.

Problems in Spain received press attention, as did a related episode in Cuba. There were two wars bearing upon Turkey's position in southern Europe, and military expeditions in parts of Asia and Africa. Highly significant also was a lively new enterprise by individual newspapers and news agencies in the appointment of their "own correspondents" in greater numbers in more countries. Out of this came a special emphasis on professional standards and practices contributing to a quality and consistency in news reporting extending to the present day.

Some reporters seemed to be occupied almost exclusively with wars, or incidents of violence. At the same time, at least as many were concentrating on news of substance, or "hard news," relating to national and world politics, diplomacy, public administration, economics, finance, and social problems, and perhaps to matters of science and the arts. While some of these reporters might be drawn into the other areas of war and violence, their more usual concerns kept them in the capitals of the world and their sources of information were quite different. Generally, they were able to go about their business in an almost routine fashion, like any professional person.

Spain, Cuba, and the Balkans

The disorders in Spain that had taken a few correspondents to that country in 1868 and 1869 continued until 1876. Queen Isabella, who had occupied the throne since 1833, fled to France in September 1868, and was declared deposed. A provisional government directed the affairs of the country until December 1870. At that time, the throne was accepted, somewhat unwillingly, by the Duke of Aosta, son of Victor Emmanuel II, king of Sardinia-Piedmont and of a semi-unified Italy. He was crowned in 1871 as Amadeo I.[1]

Amadeo I ruled for only two years. In 1873, with his own approval, the first Spanish Republic was formed and he abdicated. Even as this occurred, Don Carlos (Carlos Maria de los Dolores de Borbón), who was directly related to former Spanish monarchs, claimed the throne as Carlos VII (Charles VII). Supported by monarchists both in Spain and in France, he made a determined effort to establish his right, and Spain was involved in a civil war from 1873 to 1876. At the end of that time, Carlos was forced to take refuge in France, but the Spanish republic again became a monarchy, with a son of Isabella proclaimed as King Alfonso XII. He ruled until 1885.

Correspondents entering Spain to report the Carlist War of 1873-76 encountered dangers arising not only from a confused battlefield situation, but because both Republicans and Monarchists tended to view them as spies. Some were seized and jailed, without much recourse, and some were threatened with execution.

Among correspondents braving such hazards were Antonio Gallenga for the *Times;* Edmund O'Donovan for the *Daily News;* George Augustus Sala for the *Daily Telegraph;* John Augustus O'Shea for the *Standard;* two artist-correspondents, Melton Prior for the *Illustrated London News,* and Frank Vizetelly for the *Graphic;* Archibald Forbes for the *Daily News;* Henri Houssaye for the Agence Havas; Cecil Buckland, a British newsman, for the *New York Times;* and Januarius Aloysius MacGahan for the *New York Herald.* Buckland was one of the correspondents to be jailed for a time, and MacGahan was another. The latter was condemned to death and saved only by the intervention of the United States ambassador to Spain.

The disorders in Spain had their repercussions in Cuba. The deposition of Isabella II failed to bring reforms there, and a revolutionary movement seeking independence from Spain began. It continued from 1868 to 1878, and was revived in 1895. In October 1873 a Spanish gunboat in Cuban waters captured an American-registered

---

1 Prussia had supported Prince Hohenzollern-Sigmaringen for appointment to the Spanish throne, and he had accepted, but was not confirmed by the Córtes because of objection by France and Napoleon III. This matter had provided the pretext for the Franco-Prussian War.

steamer, the *Virginius,* carrying arms and supplies to the Cuban revolutionaries. A filibusterous ship, it was illegally flying the American flag. The execution by Spanish authorities in Cuba of some of the ship's passengers and crew, including eight U.S. citizens, brought a brief threat of war between Spain and the United States. Julius Chambers and Ralph Keeler covered the story for the *New York Tribune.* Keeler disappeared without a trace. MacGahan of the *New York Herald* was in Cuba also on the story.

It was after reporting the "Virginius affair" that MacGahan went to Spain for almost a year. In 1875 he was assigned to accompany the Bennett-sponsored expedition seeking a Northwest Passage, but was back in Europe in 1876.

In the south of Europe in 1870, the Turkish Empire, although reduced in size from its greatest extent in the sixteenth century, still controlled much of the Balkan area. Serbia, which had had effective independence of Turkish rule since 1830, had been making concerted efforts since 1860 to unite the Balkan states and drive Turkey out of that part of Europe. Turkish troops had bombarded Belgrade, the Serb capital, in 1862, but on June 30, 1876, Serbia, in alliance with neighboring Montenegro, declared war on Turkey, hoping for Russian support. That did not come, and by September 1 Serbia conceded defeat. Turkey refused to grant an armistice except under excessive terms. To forestall a possible general war in Europe, British influence brought a settlement at a London conference in December. It counted as a Turkish victory, but solved no problem in the Balkans.

This brief conflict in 1876 was a prelude to recurrent troubles that were to draw correspondents to the Balkans repeatedly until the beginning of World War I in 1914. Indeed there had been troubles in the Balkans for many years preceding, but the 1876 clash was the first to receive effective press coverage. About twenty correspondents reported the campaign, some with the Serbs and others with the Turks. Two were killed.

Archibald Forbes, respected for his coverage of the Franco-Prussian War for the *Daily News,* represented that paper again,[2] as did Hilary Skinner and Edmund O'Donovan. George A. Henty again represented the *Standard,* but was on his last news assignment prior

---

2 Since the Franco-Prussian War, Archibald Forbes also had gone to India in 1874, and returned there in 1875 to report a tour by the Prince of Wales (later Edward VII), in a party also including William Howard Russell for the *Times,* Henty for the *Standard,* Drew Gay for the *Daily Telegraph,* and others.

to turning to a career as a writer of fiction. Edward Henry Vizetelly also represented the *Standard*. Frederic Villiers, for the *Graphic,* was on the first of many assignments that were to keep him busy as an artist-correspondent on world news fronts until 1916.

William J. Stillman was the only U.S. correspondent in the field. A native of Schenectady, New York, he had been United States consul in Rome and then in Crete from 1861 to 1869. In that year he became Vienna correspondent for the *New York Tribune*. He began also to write for the *Times,* and switched from the *Tribune* later in 1876 to represent the London paper in Vienna.

Gaston Lemay wrote for a Paris newspaper, and a M. Grignau for the Agence Havas. The group reporting the campaign also included a correspondent for a Moscow newspaper, possibly the official *Moskovski Vedomosti* (Moscow Gazette).

The Russo-Turkish War (1877-78)

The same dissatisfaction with Turkish rule that had motivated Serbia was felt keenly in Bulgaria. Demonstrations there in opposition to Turkey in May 1876 had brought terrible retribution. Even before the Serbian-Turkish War began, rumors had been circulating in Constantinople about the harsh measures taken. Thousands of Christians were said to have been massacred, and entire villages burned.

Edwin Pears, stringer correspondent in Constantinople for the *Daily News,* reported these rumors for the information of editors in London. The British government, friendly toward the Turkish government, with which it had been allied during the Crimean War, chose to dismiss the rumors as unsubstantiated. British officials were aware that the Russian government remained hostile to Turkey, with which it had been twice at war since 1800, and had been restrained with difficulty from supporting Serbia in its conflict with Turkey. The London government feared that the rumors about mistreatment of the Christians in Bulgaria, if given credence or publicity, would be seized upon by Russia, acting as defender of the Christian faith, to attack Turkey again. In this London also saw the possibility that Russia might at last gain a long-desired, ice-free port in the Mediterranean, and even pose a threat to the British line through the Suez Canal to India and China. For these reasons, British officials, hoping to halt talk of any Bulgarian atrocities, belittled the unconfirmed reports.

It happened, however, that J. A. Mac Gahan was in London in June 1876 after his assignment with the *New York Herald*-sponsored Young expedition to the Arctic. He heard the rumors of Bulgarian massacres. Bennett of the *Herald,* was in London also, and Mac-Gahan asked the publisher to let him go to Bulgaria to investigate. Bennett rejected the idea, and what began as an amicable conversation between the two men, both in their early thirties, became a violent quarrel.

Mac Gahan left the *Herald* bureau, where the meeting had occurred, and walked to the *Times* offiice, intending to seek the opportunity to go to Bulgaria for that paper, but he was turned away. He then went to the office of the *Daily News,* and made the same proposal to Frank Harrison Hill, its editor, that he had made to Bennett. He was promptly engaged, severed his relations with the *Herald,* and set off for Bulgaria.

Mac Gahan had been with the *New York Herald* since 1870. A native of New Lexington, Ohio, he had been studying in Berlin when the Franco-Prussian War began, but abandoned his books to become a correspondent for the *Herald.* Accompanying the Prussian army, he did well covering the move through France and reporting disorders in Paris in 1871.

After the war, he went to the Crimea for a holiday. There he became friendly with members of the Czar's court, summering at Yalta. He returned with some of them to St. Petersburg, and covered several stories in Russia. Later, in Paris, he was to marry a member of Russia's "lesser nobility" whom he had met at Yalta.

Mac Gahan was in Russia again in 1873. During that summer a Russian military expedition advanced into Turkistan, in central Asia, captured the Khiva khanate on the banks of the Oxus River, and made it a part of Russian territory (now Uzbekistan).

Denied the right to accompany the Russian forces, Mac Gahan nevertheless followed them, at every sort of personal risk, taking with him only a Tartar interpreter. They went by horse-drawn wagon, and often on foot, for more than a thousand miles, much of the way across trackless desert, and sometimes pursued by Cossacks. The journey required more than a month.

Reaching Khiva, the daring of Mac Gahan's exploit so excited the admiration of the Russian command that he was permitted to remain and report the ultimate surrender of the Khan Mohammed Rakhim Kuli, who was forced to become a vassal of Russia. He further established and extended friendships among the Russians and became a particular friend of General Mikhail Dimitrovich Skobeloff, a relationship that was to stand him in good stead four years later during the Russo-Turkish War.

Mac Gahan was back in the Western Hemisphere at the end of 1873. He went to Cuba to report the "Virginius affair," to Spain in 1874-75, and on the Young expedition to the Arctic in 1875. His quarrel with Bennett in the summer of 1876, and his switch to the staff of the *Daily News* was so timed that he did not join in reporting the Serbian-Turkish War, where the paper was well represented by Forbes, Skinner, and O'Donovan. But he did go to Bulgaria.

In a series of reports written in July and August 1876, based on personal observation and inquiry, Mac Gahan more than substantiated the earlier rumors of Turkish atrocities. Brilliant and circumstantial, their content aroused indignation in England, and had the effect of reversing the previous official dismissal of the first reports from Bulgaria. At the same time, they did give Russia's Czar Alexander II the very pretext Britain had foreseen. War was declared on Turkey in April 1877, in the name of civilization and Christianity, without mention of Russia's interest in access to the Mediterranean.

The Russo-Turkish War of 1877-78 saw some eighty news correspondents in the field at one time or another. Some were with the Turkish forces or in Constantinople, but most were with the Russians. Following the procedure in vogue for coverage of a war of movement since the time of the American Civil War, each correspondent was outfitted with a wagon containing such supplies as he might need, several wagon horses and saddle horses, and two or more servants or drivers or couriers to provide assistance. Funds were carried, usually in gold, to pay cash for telegraph tolls, which were about 1 shilling 6 pence (36 cents) per word to London from Bucharest, Rumania, the nearest telegraph point. There the Russians maintained a censorship. The correspondents, in a departure from past practice, were assigned numbers, wore badges of accreditation at the outset, and then armbands. They were placed on their honor not to reveal information of potential value to the enemy, and were required to arrange for copies of their newspapers to be sent to Russian headquarters for later inspection. During the course of the war, some were warned about the content of their dispatches, and Frederick Boyle of the *Standard* was expelled from headquarters, with accreditation withdrawn.

On the Turkish side, regulations existed also. Antonio Gallenga, in Constantinople for the *Times* since 1875, was expelled during the war. In a period when military officers of other countries attached to warring forces as observers still were permitted to write for the three British officers with the Turks forwarded dispatches to the *Times*. Sigismund Engländer, for Reuter, was in Contantinople, and engaged W. H. G. Werndel as an assistant.

The *Daily News* led all others in its reports, as it had led among British and European newspapers during the Franco-Prussian War. MacGahan was in St. Petersburg when the war began and accompanied the Russian armies, although under difficulties because of a broken foot. He had the advantage, however, of his personal friendship with General Skobeloff, dating from Khiva in 1873.

Archibald Forbes, also with the Russians for the *Daily News,* was on equally good terms with General Ignatieff. Forbes and MacGahan, along with Frederick Villiers, artist-correspondent for the *Graphic,* on his second war assignment, witnessed a number of key engagements of the war. These included a futile Russian assault on Plevna on July 31, 1877, but also a Russian victory at Schipka Pass late in August. Some of Forbes's dispatches ran as long as 8,000 words, delivered to the telegraph in Bucharest only through the greatest of personal exertions, and at a cost of $2,280 for sending so long a report. The Czar, first learning of the Schipka victory through Forbes's story, awarded him the highest Russian decoration for personal bravery. Nor did MacGahan spare himself, winning great respect and affection from all whom he met.

Despite regulations, *Daily News* correspondents organized a system to evade the Russian telegraph censorship at Bucharest. It involved a pony express service, with eight men and eight horses, to carry dispatches from Bucharest over the Carpathian mountains to Kronstadt (Brasov), some eighty-five miles away, in neutral Austria. In practice, however, this system was used only once and was hardly necessary because the Russian censorship was not severe, in addition to which the *Daily News* occupied a favorable position because of the MacGahan-Forbes friendships with the two Russian army commanders.

In the early months of the war, the *Daily News* exchanged its dispatches with the *New York Herald,* which was represented in the combat area by John P. Jackson, who had been in Paris for that paper, and by Francis D. Millet, a sketch artist later to become known as a painter. After the exchange arrangement expired in September 1877, Millet joined the *Daily News* staff, while also doing sketches for the *Graphic,* and he received honors for bravery from

Russia and Rumania alike for his battlefield work. Other *Daily News* men included Edmund O'Donovan on the Turkish side, and Francis A. (Frank) Scudmore.

The correspondent group also included Melton Prior for the *Illustrated London News,* Frank le Poer Power for a Dublin newspaper, and three men for the *Daily Telegraph*—William Beatty Kingston with the Russians, and Drew Gay and Campbell Clarke reporting the Turkish side from Constantinople or in the field. William J. Stillman came from his regular post in Vienna to write for the *Times.* Joseph L. Stickney, a U.S. Navy officer, wrote for the *Chicago Tribune.* John A. Cockerill, later to become executive editor with Joseph Pulitzer's *St. Louis Post-Dispatch* and *New York World,* wrote for the *Cincinnati Enquirer,* of which he had been managing editor.

The Russian press had some representation at the front, but names of newspapers and correspondents do not appear in the available literature of the period. The Wolff agency in Germany was providing service to Russian newspapers at the time, but if Wolff had a correspondent in the field his name has not survived. Neither is there evidence of any Reuter agency representative providing direct coverage of the war. Léon Pognon, Bucharest correspondent for the Agence Havas was active, along with stringers engaged to assist him. He was seriously wounded, but recovered. Camille Barrère, later to have a career as a French diplomat, represented a Paris newspaper at this time, and a Herr Von Huhn, writing for the Cologne *Gazette,* was another member of the press group. It was the first occasion on which the press of so many countries were represented in the coverage of any one event.

In December 1877, Turkey appealed to the European powers for mediation, with a view to ending the war. This appeal failed, largely because it was rejected by Bismarck. In January 1878 Turkey therefore appealed directly to Russia for an armistice, which was concluded at the end of that month. The Russians then held lines just outside Constantinople and in so strong a position that Great Britain felt compelled to make a show of force on behalf of Turkey to protect what it conceived to be its own interests.

The Treaty of San Stefano in March restored peace. By its terms, Turkey granted independence to Serbia and Montenegro. Rumania was to be independent, but was forced to yield Bessarabia to Russia, which also gained some former Turkish territory, a right to occupy

Bulgaria for two years, plus a large indemnity from Turkey. Certain secret agreements followed in May and June by which Great Britain sought to safeguard its position. Most important, a Berlin Conference was called to meet in mid-June, attended by representatives of Germany, Austria, Belgium, Britain, France, Italy, and Turkey.

That Congress of Berlin, lasting a month, was one of the great events of the decade. It ended Turkish power in southeastern Europe and brought about a redrawing of frontiers. Despite earlier conferences of importance—such as the Congress of Vienna in 1814-15—it was the first international gathering to receive extensive press attention. It did not bring permanent peace to the Balkans area, and it did not give Russia free access to the Mediterranean, but it did create alliances and tensions that were to shape the course of European affairs beyond World War I.

One of the circumstances relating to the coverage of the Berlin conference was the publication in the *Times,* in advance of its official release, of the full text of the Treaty of Berlin. A copy of that document had been obtained from a delegate to the conference by Henri de Blowitz, Paris correspondent of the *Times* and a specialist on European affairs, then in Berlin to use his expertise as an observer and reporter. Donald Mackenzie Wallace, St. Petersburg correspondent for the *Times,* also in Berlin to contribute to the coverage, and working with Blowitz, had taken the copy of the treaty out of Berlin sewed in the lining of his coat, carried it to Brussels, and on to London for publication.

MacGahan probably would have been present at the Berlin conference for the *Daily News,* but with the signature of the peace terms, and with the Russian forces then cose to Constantinople, he had gone to that capital. There he learned that a friend, U.S. Navy Lieutenant Francis V. Greene was suffering from typhus, and he undertook to help care for hi. MacGahan was none too well himself. Hardships endured during the war had weakened him, and he fell victim to the same disease and died in Constantinople in June 1878, shortly before his thirty-fourth birthday. He was buried at nearby Pera. By request of the Ohio legislature, his body was returned to the United States in 1884, transported aboard a U.S. Navy ship, laid in state in New York's City Hall, and reburied at his birthplace, New Lexington, Ohio. His only son unveiled a monument to his father at the cemetery there in 1911. He also was commemorated in Bulgaria for many years with an annual Requiem Mass.

The movement of correspondents continued through the 1870s and 1880s. Affairs in Europe, India, China, Africa, and the United States all received direct attention from the British press, still the most highly developed and most enterprising.

Late in 1878, accordingly, several British correspondents went to report the Second Afghan War. The first war affecting British interests in that part of the world had occurred in 1839-42, but the press was not then prepared to provide direct coverage. Whatever appeared came from the official *London Gazette,* based upon information drawn from British government sources in London. In the second war, which continued for three years, Great Britain sought to avenge violence directed at representatives of the crown, but also to safeguard India against Russian infiltration from Khiva and neighboring Afghanistan. On this occasion, the British press was prepared to provide direct coverage.

Archibald Forbes, who had suffered in health as a result of the rigors of Russo-Turkish War coverage, even as MacGahan had suffered, nevertheless went to report the campaign for the *Daily News.* He remained briefly, and then proceeded to India and Burma to produce other reports. Frederic Villiers again covered the war for the *Graphic,* and Harry Williams was present for Reuter. A brother of George Douglas Williams, who became chief editor of that agency in 1880, he was the second member of a family to be identified with Reuter. Another brother, Valentine Williams joined the staff later.

A Zulu war in Natal in 1879 was reported by a slightly larger British press contingent. Forbes hastened from Southeast Asia to Africa and, typically, became the star performer. Also present were Melton Prior for the *Illustrated London News,* Charles Fripp as an artist for the *Graphic,* a writer for *Le Figaro* of Paris, and William Howard Russell, representing the *Daily Telegraph,* rather than the *Times,* with which he had so long been identified, because the *Times* had arranged to send Francis Francis.

Forbes won special distinction in the Natal War by his report of the British capture of Ulandi, the Zulu capital. This story he managed to put on the cable to London and the *Daily News* after a hazardous twenty-four horseback ride over 120 miles of unmapped country to Landsmann's Drift, and then another 170 miles in thirty-five hours to the port of Durban, the cable point. There he also mailed sketches by Prior, making it possible for them to appear in the *Illustrated London*

News a week ahead of any other illustrations from the war front.[3]

Edmund O'Donovan, a colleague of Forbes and Mac Gahan in the coverage of the Russo-Turkish War for the *Daily News,* but with Turkish forces rather than Russian, started on a journey, after that war, in 1878 to report on the situation in central Asia. An almost unknown part of the world, it was potentially important because of Russia's move into the area, and because of British concern lest its position in India be affected by this approach toward neighboring Afghanistan.

O'Donovan, Irish-born and adventurous, traveled for three years in the area. His experience, often marked by peril and hardship, was in some respects comparable to that of Stanley's in Africa, and even more like Mac Gahan's approach to Khiva. Mac Gahan had entered Turkoman territory from the north. O'Donovan entered from the south and made his way to the Merv Oasis, about 300 miles south of Khiva, and just above the northern border of Afghanistan. There he remained for six months, under curious circumstances in which he was half captive and half honorary member of the rulii group. When at length he was able to return to Engliand at the end of 1881, his reports in the *Daily News,* his lectures, and a book providing information on the remote area all aroused great interest.

Thus, the decade of the 1880s brought an increase in the number of correspondents, their wider distribution in the world, and a growing volume of news. Enough staff and stringer correspondents for newspapers and news agencies of various countries were established in Paris by 1879 to warrant the formation there of an organization to which all were expected to belong. This was the Syndicale de la Presse Etrangère (Council of the Foreign Press). In London, also a

---

3 For both William Howard Russell and Archibald Forbes, this was a last working field assignment. Russell had been busy since the Franco-Prussian War as editor of the *Army and Navy Journal,* which he had purchased in 1864. He also had traveled about Europe on a number of assignments taking him to major capitals where he wrote descriptive reports of such events as the Vienna World's Exposition in 1873, and a European tour by the Shah of Persia in that year. His reports appeared in the *Times* and were widely reprinted. In the Natal, Russell then fifty-nine years old, was injured. He was an observer of the British campaign in Egypt in 1882. He was knighted in 1895. To his earlier work, he added a number of books, before his death in 1907 at eighty-seven.

Forbes was only forty-one at the time of the Natal campaign, but his health deteriorated in part because of the hardships he had endured as a correspondent in the field. He lived quietly in England, lecturing and writing, in the twenty years remaining to him.

Foreign Press Association was established in 1888. Comparable organizations were formed later in Rome, Vienna, Berlin, and other capitals.

These were more than "clubs" or social organizations, although some had that character, too. Basically, however, they were professional groups concerned with the problems and conditions confronting correspondents in their relationship with the government of a country in which they worked. They need to establish full accreditation with that government and its officials so that their *bona fides* were clear as they approached news sources in or out of the government, and so that their right might be recognized by telegraph and cable offices for the dispatch of messages at press rates. There were positions to be established with reference to taxes, travel, office space, insurance, the employment of assistants, telephone service, money transfer, mail, living conditions for themselves and their families, schooling for their children, and other matters. The professional organization could help in such matters by speaking for all correspondents with some authority.

On the social side, such an organization also had value. Through luncheon or dinner meetings, it enabled correspondents to know one another as they worked in a foreign environment, and to develop helpful cooperative relationships. Further, by extending hospitality to officials and personalities of the country, and by inviting them as guests and speakers at luncheon meetings and annual banquets, the correspondents extended their news sources, grained useful information, and understanding.

A correspondent concerned with substantive matters needed to acquaint himself with the capital and country in which he was working. This required reading and travel and as many friends and acquaintances as he could make in diverse fields of activity and knowledge. For the best results, it meant that he needed to become thoroughly familiar with the spoken and written language of the country.

As international reporting became increasingly important, from about 1870, it became common for correspondents to remain in a capital for from ten to forty years. While some were natives of the country, particularly as stringers, most newspapers maintaining foreign representation preferred to have their own nationals serving abroad on the theory that they would have a better understanding and write of what readers would need to know and want to know.

A time came, however, when some editors and publishers believed that if a correspondent remained too long at one post he tended to become almost more a native of that country than of his own, to lose perspective, and to lose freshness and enthusiasm in his approach to the news. This view became common enough so that, at present, it is exceptional for a correspondent to remain more than three years, or six at most, in the same capital. This policy has some merit, but it also means that the correspondent, in moving to a new post must begin again to learn about a new country and often a new language.

The growth in the number of correspondents reporting the news from world capitals had the advantage of producing a more thorough coverage. But it also had a certain negative result. Government officials, bankers, and other leading personalities within a country or capital had been willing to receive and talk with individual correspondents, providing them with useful background information. These officials, and others, discovered by the 1880s and 1890s that the numbers of correspondents requesting such meetings tended to encroach seriously upon the hours remaining to conduct the affairs of government or business.

Even with only a few correspondents present in a capital, there had been some discrimination in receiving certain of them, while excluding others. Representatives of newspapers of special prestige or viewpoint might be received, others not. Certain correspondents might be dealt with more frankly than some others. But with the new demands on time there also developed a tendency to give preference to a correspondent representing a news agency—usually Reuter, Havas, or Wolff, or the national agency of the country—on the theory that the agency report would reach all newspapers, no newspaper would lack for information, and the official would save time. This procedure naturally was satisfactory to the news agencies, but far from pleasing to individual newspapers or their correspondents, editors, and directors. A newspaper such as the London *Times,* by then accustomed to having its own correspondent receive special attention, and with its prestige deriving in part from that circumstance, felt its position of leadership in serious news reporting threatened by the very suggestion. The *Times* was not alone among newspapers viewing the prospect with concern.

Without denigrating the news agencies or their correspondents, many thoughtful persons, whether in or out of journalism, also felt that to restrict the opportunity of highly-qualified newspaper correspondents to deal directly with officials and other news sources on terms of mutual respect would deprive the public of a healthy diversity of reports. For reasons already discussed, a news agency was obliged to report current factual information and, at that period, omit background interpretation, even though also factual. This might mean the news agency would merely report what its representative was told, which could be a bland policy statement, self-serving, possibly misleading, or even untrue. A newspaper correspondent, by contrast, would be able to put a statement in perspective. He would not have to stop with what he was told, but might seek other sources to provide supplementary information. Also, there was an awareness that some news agencies were "official" or "semi-official," with all that might mean in the shading, omission, or even distortion of reports on sensitive subjects.

In practice, the channeling of information exclusively through news agencies did not occur. A compromise solution was arrived at over the years, and modified as seemed necessary. Officials and others continued to see newspaper correspondents when that seemed mutually desirable. Some scheduled meetings, or "conferences," to meet with accredited or visiting correspondents. Special "press officers" were appointed, perhaps with assistants, to speak for officials or others, to meet with newsmen individually or in groups to respond to questions, and to make themselves available at almost any hour, both directly and by telephone. Much of this evolution was reserved, however, for the years after 1900 and later.

The experienced correspondent, even talking personally with a government official, or with any other source, does not accept everything he hears as necessarily a full, reliable, or even truthful statement. He retains a cautious skepticism, and does what he can to double check statements or published "releases" against other sources. He is wary of information volunteered or "leaked" to him, or others, on whatever pretext. It is part of his responsibility to evaluate such material in terms of reliability, accuracy, and purpose.

The indirect contact with news sources, through press conferences, press officers, or public relations officers, while not wholly to the liking of correspondents or the media, at least has the effect of placing the correspondent in a position perhaps freer than he would be following a direct conversation with an official. He is under no restraint in pursuing the subject further to provide a more balanced or interpretative treatment. This a newspaper correspondent can do, and is expected to do, within the bounds of accuracy and fairness. That option was less open then to the news agency correspondent, whose first concern was expected to be with the facts of the day and of the moment. Each form of news reporting is valuable in its way, and the two together provide a useful service to the public.

One of the few occasions prior to the twentieth century when any considerable number of correspondents gathered to report an event other than a military campaign occurred in May 1883, when Russia's Czar Alexander III was crowned in Moscow. Most were correspondents normally on permanent assignment in the capitals of European countries. The ceremonies naturally were reported by the press of Russia, limited though it was in extent and freedom. But representatives were present for the press of Germany, Austria, France, Great Britain, and the United States. Charles Lowe, Berlin correspondent for the *Times* since 1870, and George Dobson, St. Petersburg correspondent, represented that paper. Lowe was the only British correspondent admitted to the rather small Cathedral of the Assumption, traditional scene of Russian coronations.

George Augustus Sala had gone to St. Petersburg in March 1881 to report the funeral of Alexander II, killed by terrorist bombs, and returned in 1883 for the *Daily Telegraph*, along with John Merry LeSage. Alfred Thompson represented the *Daily News*, Charles Marvin, the *Morning Post*, and a Mr. Baddeley, the St. Petersburg correspondent for the *Standard*, wrote for that paper. William Simpson, whose experience had begun in the Crimean War, and who had been an observer of the Modoc Indian War in California in 1873, was again an artist-correspondent for the *Illustrated London News*, with Frederic Villiers present in the same capacity for the *Graphic*. John P. Jackson of the *New York Herald*, formerly correspondent in Paris, but then in St. Petersburg, was the only U.S. correspondent present, and another of the few newsmen in the cathedral. Elie Mercadier represented the Agence Havas.

New Balkan troubles, with brief wars between Greece and Turkey in 1886 and Bulgaria and Macedonia in 1888, received only slight press attention, while a British military campaign in Burma in 1885, leading to the annexation of Burma to India, drew no correspondents into the field. These events were reported by newspapers in the nearest capitals, but chiefly on the basis of official reports. Whatever reference to the actions appeared elsewhere came through news agency services.

Events in China during the 1880s were dealt with by stringers in Peking and in Hong Kong. The country was so large that even though some telegraph service existed, and railroads began to provide service in the Tientsin-Peking area, no organization existed to report the general news of the country. Yellow River floods in 1887, for example, took perhaps a million lives, and famines following affected more than twelve million persons. But this was scarcely known at the time. There was no effective vernacular press to report the news in China. For the rest of the world, the news came late. What was reported seemed almost beyond comprehension and, in that period, seemed to have no direct meaning for persons of different cultures, thousands of miles removed.

Somewhat the same could have been said of a war involving Chile, Bolivia, and Peru in 1879-84. What the Agence Havas transmitted to Europe was not given much space or prominence in the newspapers on that continent. Even the Second Afghan War of 1878-79, with British troops victorious and taking control of the Khyber Pass, although given some direct coverage, was too far away to gain great attention in the London press. German moves into Africa and the Pacific in 1884, and of concern to British interests, proceeded with such deliberation as to receive only rather routine treatment in the press. The same was true of the extension of French colonial interests in Africa and the Far East in those years. This was almost reminiscent of France's move into Algeria, Morocco, and Tunis in the 1830s. Since the press at that time was still undeveloped, it is not surprising that little was reported on the action. Yet, as late as 1885, on the occasion of a Franco-Chinese War, the French press was less informative on the matter than the British press, and even that treatment was low key.[4]

The Indo-Chinese "war" resulted in France establishing a colonial position in Southeast Asia. France had taken an interest in the area at least since 1858, and had infiltrated and fought to gain control of it. The Agence Havas had named its first agent at Saigon in 1883, and had a stringer at Tonkin. Victory in a localized war with China in 1883-85 confirmed French control. Campaigns around Tonkin and Huê in 1883 were reported for *Le Figaro* of Paris by Pierre Loti, as he later became known under his pen name as author of many stories dealing mostly with the East. At the time of the campaign, he was a lieutenant in the French navy, Louis Marie Julien Viaud. Georges

---

4 The French press was subject to government restraint even after the Franco-Prussian War, in spite of laws purporting to assure it freedom. With some exceptions, newsmen lacked professional standing. This was never more dramatically illustrated than when Camille Fancy, writing from Morocco for several Paris dailies, was executed there in 1881 by order of the French military command, accused of having revealed information judged to have made him guilty of treason. So far as is known, this is the only instance of a correspondent being executed, by official order, until the Nazi government exercised control in Germany during World War II.

Fillion was sent by Havas to report from Indo-China in 1888-90, and in 1890 Reuter yielded that area to Havas as an exclusive territory within the Ring Combination agreement. French reporting was limited, perhaps in part because the Saigon-Paris communication rate was about $1.90 a word. The best reports of the 1883-85 campaign itself came from Archibald Ross Colquhoun of the *Times,* who was normally stationed in Peking, but who also moved about Asia.

The extension of coverage in the 1880s established a momentum within the press organization that was to accelerate in the decade of the 1890s, and beyond. It brought more intensive and wide-ranging coverage of issues both of peace and of war. The British press organization maintained its position of leadership in world reporting, but was joined by that of the United States. Increasingly, the press of other countries was represented also.

These joint efforts were brought to bear on a series of events, including a long period of British political and military involvement in Egypt and the Sudan from 1881 to 1899, a significant Sino-Japanese clash in 1894, and a new conflict in the Balkans in 1897. There followed the Spanish-American War of 1898 and its aftermath in the Philippines, which drew the United States into the world community as never before; the South African War of 1899-1902, when British forces contested with the Boers for control of the tip of the continent; new trouble in China in 1900; and the Russo-Japanese War of 1904-05, which brought Japan into the world community.

Adding other events of those decades, the position of man by 1905, and that of the press, was almost incredibly different from what it had been a century before.

The British Press Organization

Certain London morning newspapers in the nineteenth century were the first in the world to demonstrate special enterprise in reporting the news. Among news agencies, Reuter was preeminent.

The *Times* by 1870 was commonly regarded as the best newspaper in the world, respected equally for its news content and for its informed editorials or "leaders." Although a quality newspaper, making no concessions to human interest appeal, it led all British newspapers in circulation. Two of its most active competitors had recently vanished, the *Morning Chronicle* in 1862 and the *Morning Herald* in 1869.

The Times *as a Standard-Bearer*

John Walter III was proprietor of the *Times* from 1847 until 1894, when he was succeeded by his son, Arthur Fraser Walter. John Delane was editor until he retired in 1877 and was succeeded by Thomas Chenery. Mowbray Morris, manager of the newspaper, died in May 1874. John Cameron MacDonald, long with the paper, succeeded him.

One of MacDonald's first acts as the new manager of the *Times* was directed toward an even greater improvement in the service of information from the European continent. Anticipating an increase in the volume of news to be transmitted, and with communication rates in mind, he arranged for a leased wire and cable connection between Paris and London, with extensions to Berlin and Vienna, which previously had transmitted messages to London through an office established in Brussels as early as 1860.

Under the new system, a correspondent in Rome would telegraph his message to Paris for relay over the leased wire. The Constantinople correspondent would telegraph through Vienna, the Hamburg correspondent through Berlin, and correspondents in those capitals would forward their own and other dispatches to Paris, for transmission to London. Correspondents and stringers in the Far East and Australia would send their reports to Calcutta, and on to London by way of the Indo-European Telegraph Company landline, with a special low rate for Sunday transmission. A special rate also was arranged in the late 1880s for dispatches sent from Egypt, while correspondents in Canada and the United States could use the North Atlantic cable at new and lower rates established in 1886.

All of this, combined with salaries and office and travel expenses for more correspondents, put a financial burden on the *Times* during the 1870s and 1880s. Finances might have become easier, with increased circulation and advertising revenue accruing to so prestigious a paper, had not the *Times* also been subjected to a crushing additional expense of more than £ 200,000 (nearly $1,000,000) during the 1880s because of a libel action brought against it by Charles S. Parnell, Irish political leader and head of the National Land League of Ireland. He had been accused by the *Times,* editorially, of having had a part in crimes committed by Irish extremists battling for land reform in that country. The loss of the case placed the paper under severe economic hardship from which it did not fully recover for more than twenty years.

To the credit of the management, however, it recognized that the *Times* had grown great largely because of its substantial home and foreign news reports. To curtail such services, even for reasons of economy, would hurt the paper perhaps beyond recovery, it was reasoned, and such action therefore was avoided. Indeed, the *Times* staff of correspondents and leader writers was improved and maintained at the highest level.

This was considered doubly essential to the continued success of the paper because, even though some earlier competitors had vanished, other morning papers, notably the *Daily News* and the *Daily Telegraph,* had so advanced in quality as to rival the *Times* in some respects, and even overshadow it on occasion.

The *Times* therefore built upon its early representation in foreign capitals, as well as upon its strong home coverage. A concession of some financial benefit was made in the decade from 1894 to 1904 whereby the *Times* foreign reports were made available on a contract basis to certain non-competitive papers outside the British Isles, including the *New York Times*, the *Chicago Tribune*, and *Le Matin* of Paris. This returned up to $3,500 annually from each subscribing newspaper. To save costs, some limitations were placed on the use of telegraph and cable by correspondents who were to use the mails for less timely reports, although never on important dispatches.

The *Times* had established its first permanent foreign bureau or office in Paris in 1848, with J. B. O'Meagher in charge of gathering and speeding information until 1869. L. Filmore was in Berlin in 1848, G. B. Wilkinson in 1853, and Frederick Hardman in 1858. In 1866, when Berlin was still the Prussian capital, the paper's second permanent bureau was opened there, with Dr. Carl Abel, himself a Prussian and a great linguist, serving as correspondent until 1878. He had responsibility for covering the news of all of northern Europe, including the Scandinavian countries and Russia.

Staff correspondents and stringers wrote for the *Times* between 1848 and 1870 from Vienna, where T. M. O'Bird was already established at the time of the Crimean War and remained until his retirement in 1866; from Constantinople, where Dr. Humphrey Sandwith was a stringer, although replaced when the Crimean War began; from Madrid, where Hardman had his first assignment with the paper in 1854; from Athens, where Ferdinand Eber, a Hungarian, served in 1853. Reports came from Rome, Alexandria, and even New York, where J. C. Bancroft Davis became a stringer in 1854, followed by Charles Tuckerman, and Charles Mackay.

Members of the London staff sometimes went abroad on short journeys, and wrote of what they observed. This had been the basis for the beginning of overseas reporting for the *Times* when Henry Crabb Robinson went to Hamburg and Stockholm in 1807 and to Spain in 1808, following which he engaged the paper's first stringers. In 1856, John Delane, the editor, Robert Lowe, a leader writer, L. Filmore, formerly in Berlin, Laurence Oliphant, and Thomas Gladstone all visited the United States.

The great upsurge in coverage of international affairs by the *Times* began after the Crimean War. Reference has been made to the movement, just after that war, of William Howard Russell to Russia and India; to Meredith Townsend, James Stanton, and Joseph A. Crowe, all in India; to George Wingrove Cooke, in

Algeria and China; and to Thomas William Bowlby, also in China in 1860.

The paper had George Finlay in Athens from 1864 until the early 1870s. He was replaced by Charles Ogle. Louis John Jennings, who had been in India since 1860, became New York correspondent in 1867, replacing Mackay, and was replaced in turn by Joel Cook, a former Philadelphia newsman with Civil War experience. O'Meagher, in charge of the Paris bureau since 1848, retired in 1869, and was replaced by Hardman. Almost constantly ill after 1870, Hardman spent considerable time in Italy and in the south of France. Laurence Oliphant, meanwhile, was the acting correspondent in Paris until 1873, when he resigned to take up permanent residence in the United States.

Shakespeare Wood was in Rome for the paper from 1872 to 1884. He was followed by Antonio Gallenga, an Italian national in the paper's service since 1859, but with experience in Constantinople, Madrid, and elsewhere. Gallenga's death in Rome in 1886 was to bring William J. Stillman from Vienna, where he had served for ten years, and where he was succeeded by James Brinsley Richards. In Berlin, Dr. Carl Abel, correspondent there since 1866, was succeeded in 1878 by Charles Lowe.

From China, the *Times* had received reports from correspondents since 1857. Consistent and substantial coverage in China only began in 1883, however, when Archibald Ross Colquhoun began more than a decade of service in Peking, ranging also over other parts of Asia. Alexander Michie, editor of the *Eastern Times* at Tientsin, was a stringer from 1885 to 1891.

In Japan, the first regular reports came from Captain Frank Brinkley, proprietor and editor of the *Japan Mail* at Yokohama, who wrote from there for the *Times* from 1892 until his death in 1912. Irish-born, Brinkley had gone to Japan in 1867 with a detachment of guards for the British legation. He made himself an authority on Japan, married a Japanese in 1878, and ultimately was honored by the Japanese government, ranking among the 300 highest personages in the country. He received a government subsidy for the *Japan Mail,* an English-language paper established in Yokohama, in 1881, and was an adviser both to the Japanese Foreign Ministry and to the Nippon Yusen Kaisha steamship line. He asserted that his editorial independence was in no way compromised by these benefits and associations. Some, however, regarded him as a consistent defender and apologist for all things and all policies relating to Japan.

Among a number of quite fabulous characters attached to the *Times* staff was Walter Burton Harris, correspondent in Morocco from 1887, shortly after he left Cambridge at twenty-one, until his death at Tangier in 1933. For most of those forty-six years he was recognized as an authority on the area of the world where he had elected to make his home. Like a number of *Times* correspondents, he became involved in matters of British foreign policy to a degree that earned him a position of importance considerably beyond that which might have been his, even as a highly knowledgeable correspondent for a leading newspaper.

Another man of distinction in the *Times* service was Donald Mackenzie Wallace, who joined the paper in 1877 when he was thirty-five years old. He had been educated at the universities of Glasgow, Edinburgh, Berlin, Heidelberg, and the École de Droit in Paris. From 1869 until 1875 he had lived in Russia, was fluent in Russian, German, and French, and in 1877 had published a book, *Russia,* which was immediately recognized as a remarkable analysis of that country. Logically, the *Times* assigned him to St. Petersburg as a correspondent. He had been there hardly a year, however, when the Russian government expelled him. This was the first such action against a *Times* correspondent since Gallenga had been expelled from Constantinople in 1875. The paper was indignant. It refrained from naming a new St. Petersburg correspondent for several years. Instead, it depended upon a member of an English family long resident in the Russian capital, George Dobson, who provided "occasional correspondence," but without identifying himself as being with the *Times.*

Wallace, meanwhile, went briefly to Berlin to assist in covering the 1878 Congress of Berlin, following the Russo-Turkish War, and then to Constantinople, where he remained as correspondent until 1884. There he became almost as much a diplomat as a newsman. His talents were such that when Lord Dufferin, the British ambassador to the Turkish Porte, became Viceroy of India in 1884 he invited Wallace to accompany him as private secretary. It so happened that Wallace had been ordered out of Turkey at that same time, even as he had been ordered out of Russia six years before, and he accepted Dufferin's invitation, leaving the *Times*— temporarily, as it turned out. Wallace remained in India for five years, with Lord Dufferin and with his successor, Lord Lansdowne. In 1887, while there, he was knighted for his role in supporting British interests in India, becoming Sir Donald Mackenzie Wallace.

A major change occurred at the *Times* in 1890. John Cameron MacDonald had died in 1889, and Charles Frederick Moberly Bell succeeded him as manager, and soon became managing director, a post he was to occupy until his death in 1911.

Bell, born of British parents in Egypt in 1847, but educated in England, had returned to Egypt in 1865. In 1866 he was named as agent or correspondent for the *Times* at Alexandria, and continued as such until 1873, at a time when Alexandria had become the midway point on the new cable link between London and Bombay. In 1873 he entered private business in Egypt and also became one of the founders and proprietors of the *Egyptian Gazette,* established at Alexandria in 1880. From 1873 until 1882 his brother, John Scott Bell, occupied the Alexandria post for the *Times,* but in 1882 Moberly Bell resumed that post and continued until he was summoned to London by John Walter III to succeed MacDonald.

The fortunes of the *Times* were at a low ebb when Bell assumed his responsibilities in 1890, shortly after the loss of the Parnell libel suit. Because of the importance of the paper's exclusive service of news from abroad, Bell regarded the foreign department as holding a key to the solution of the problems he had inherited. He felt that it required even greater strength and also special direction by a man of exceptional qualifications.

Sir Donald Mackenzie Wallace had returned from India in 1889, and Bell invited him to rejoin the *Times* as its Berlin correspondent in 1891. This Wallace declined, but he accepted a newly created position as "Foreign Assistant Editor," which meant that he became director of the paper's foreign department in London. It was a new title for a position occupied since 1884 by Edward Cant-Well, previously with the London *Standard* and later a correspondent for the *Times* during the first part of the Egyptian-Sudan campaigns from 1881 to 1883.

For the eight years from 1891 to 1899, Bell and Wallace worked together to strengthen the *Times.* It cannot be said that they repaired the paper's financial situation, which only improved with its sale in 1908 to Lord Northcliffe. They did, however, strengthen the foreign service, which had been languishing.

Evidence of a need for improvement in the foreign service existed in the desertion of one or two correspondents to other newspapers, and in some resignations prior to 1890. Clear opportunities had been missed, somewhat earlier, to acquire the services both of Archibald Forbes and of J. A. MacGahan; both had been turned away when they sought places on the *Times* staff in 1870 and 1876, respectively, and subsequently brought distinction to the *Daily News*.

Bell and Wallace together engaged new correspondents and instructed all of them through letters and memoranda that presented some of the earliest coherent statements for guidance in serious reporting of international news. Considering also the caliber of correspondents forming the *Times* staff, these instructions set, or synthesized standards accepted by the best professionals of all media since that period.

For example, to a newly appointed correspondent, Bell wrote:

The duties we expect from our correspondents are:

(1) The transmission of all authentic news of importance without regard to any particular view which may be entertained by the correspondent personally, or to any particular policy which may be advocated by the paper.

(2) The transmission of any explanation or rectification of that news which may have been given you by any person of authority, and this more particularly if the person desiring to make such explanation or rectification holds views contrary to those expressed by yourself or advocated by the paper.

(3) The transmission of your own appreciation of the situation, well founded and without any personal prejudice.

In one word, *The Times* desires to give equal publicity to every view of any important question, and in the public interest is glad to have any information or correction of information from any person in a position to give it. But it asks no favour, and its opinion, expressed in its leading articles, is formed on the judgment of the editor alone, based on such information as he possesses from his correspondents and other sources without regard to any personal consideration.

To a war correspondent Bell wrote in 1894: "Get us early and trustworthy information," but "better twice late than once wrong." Where there is doubt, he advised, "guard your statement with reserve, giving, where you can, authority." Also, he said:

. . . gain the confidence of the people with whom you have to deal, and never be tempted to betray confidences for the sake of scoring a success. In unimportant matters there is no good being lavish

with telegrams. In really important matters telegraph freely. . . .
Write letters when you can, try to make them a consecutive history
of events. . . . Remember that telegrams are for facts; appreciation
and political comment can come by post. . . . Remember that a
correspondent must keep his sympathies under control. You are
not a partisan in the war, but a recorder of it. We are historians, not
history makers. . .

To another correspondent, he wrote a reminder in 1900 that:

. . . every corresponaent who is worth his salt occasionally hears
confidentially information which he is not at liberty to publish.
That he is given such information is a proof that he is trusted, and
that is the very first quality that we want in a correspondent. A
more difficult question arises when a correspondent gets some
information in the ordinary course—that is, *not* confidentially—
and on going to obtain confirmation of it is asked to treat it as
confidential—that is, not to telegraph it. Here, of course, there is
no obligation to refrain from communicating it.

Bell took the view that "the position of a correspondent is nearer
akin to that of a judge and jury than that of counsel, and the more
impartial you show yourself, the more weight will be attached to your
conclusions."

Both Bell and Wallace supported the paper's correspondents if
they came into conflict with officials of the countries to which they
were assigned, insisted that they be treated with proper respect, and
resisted efforts sometimes made by governments to expel
correspondents—almost invariably because they were reporting facts
unwelcome to the officials of that government. In this, they continued
the tradition already set by two of the paper's greatest editors,
Thomas Barnes and John Thaddeus Delane.

Relations between the *Times* and the Reuter agency were sensitive
for reasons already indicated. The paper expected its "Own Correspondent," wherever located, to provide factual reports on all matters
of importance at least equal to anything Reuter might provide, and
often to go beyond that by providing an interpretation—what Bell
called an "appreciation" of the subject.

One correspondent was told that "for all ordinary events of small
importance trust to Reuter; in times of crisis or importance ignore
Reuter." The correspondent's problem was to guess what Bell or
Wallace might regard as a time of "crisis or importance." If he

guessed wrong, he would hear about it, as one correspondent did when he failed to telegraph a full account of a particular event because he sought to avoid what seemed to him the needless expense of duplicating what he knew the Reuter correspondent would send. Bell reproved him, saying:

> The fact that *The Times* had to fall back on Reuter was mentioned with surprise by the weekly papers, by the evening press, and by correspondents abroad. . . . Reuter is doing his utmost to improve his service everywhere, and unless we improve ours it will result in our being no better off than our neighbour in spite of much larger expense. Reuter is sure soon to try to get an increased subscription from us. We are anxious to be in a position to say that we can do without him, but we certainly cannot if, in a place where we have a special correspondent, we still have to use Reuter's copy.

To help improve the quality of the *Times* service, Wallace gave special attention to organizing a strong reference library or intelligence department (ID), as it was known in the office. It was designed for the special assistance of leader writers, but also was available for the use of writers and subeditors in the preparation and verification of copy and the addition of background information.

The direct Bell-Wallace association continued until 1899, at which time Wallace took charge of editing the ninth and tenth editions of the *Encyclopaedia Britannica,* then a *Times* enterprise undertaken with a view to improving the paper's financial situation. Wallace later performed other missions for the paper, and also for the British government and Crown, continuing almost to the time of his death in 1919.

He was succeeded as foreign assistant editor of the *Times,* or as foreign editor, as the title became, by Valentine Chirol, whose qualifications and career bore a certain resemblance to Wallace's, and whose importance in the paper's advancement was virtually as great.

One of Bell's early acts after asssuming the management of the *Times* had been to dismiss Charles Lowe as correspondent in Berlin. He left that post on June 30, 1891, after about thirteen years. Lowe brought suit against the paper for damages and wrongful dismissal. He lost the case, but aired his protests in an autobiography, *Tales of a 'Times' Correspondent* published many years later, in 1927. In it he expressed special resentment toward Bell, whom he had long outlived, but still referred to as a "burly bully," a "truculent fellow," a man of "flagrant defects and blemishes," a "strong but heartless, vain, ambitious, and unprincipled . . . upstart," and as a "Levantine-minded mis-manager of *The Times*" who ended "by financing *The Times* out of the Walter family altogether"—the latter a reference to the 1908 sale of majority control to Lord Northcliffe, three years before Bell's death.

Bell had offered the Berlin post to Wallace, but when he declined James Brinsley Richards, Vienna correspondent for the previous six years, was transferred to Berlin on January 1, 1892. William Lavino, in Vienna for the *Daily Telegraph,* was engaged to replace Richards there. Four months after moving to Berlin, Richards died. This was the point at which Chirol was brought to the *Times* staff, assigned to Berlin.

Valentine Chirol, then forty, had been educated in France and Germany, had been a member of the British Foreign Office staff, but also had been a correspondent for the *Standard,* with service in China, India, the Near and Middle East, and the Balkans. He was Berlin correspondent for the *Times* from 1892 to 1896.

Across the world, the Sino-Japanese War of 1894-95 affected British interests in China and, because Chirol had been there for the *Standard,* Wallace encouraged him to go there again from Berlin to report the war situation. Chirol did so, also stopping briefly in Egypt. In Berlin again for a few months after that war, he returned to China in 1896, to remain a year, with no intent to return to Berlin.[1]

Returning from China in 1897, Chirol was a leader writer for the *Times* until 1898, at which time he became assistant to Wallace in the foreign department of the paper. With Wallace's relinquishment of that post in 1899, Chirol succeeded him and exercised an important influence in shaping the paper's foreign service until his retirement in 1912. Chirol was knighted at that time, becoming Sir Valentine Chirol. From 1912 to 1916 he was a member of a Royal Commission on Indian Public Services, but also returned to the Foreign Office staff in 1914 to serve through World War I. In the years between that time and his death in 1929 at seventy-seven, he wrote a number of authoritative volumes on India, Egypt, the Middle East and Asia, and two autobiographical books.

---

1 Valentine Chirol had become *persona non grata* in Berlin just before his departure in 1896 because of his accounts of a telegram sent by Kaiser Wilhelm II in January of that year to Paul Kruger, president of the Boer South African Republic, and hinting at German support for the Boers in the conflict with the British that was to lead to the South African War.

With Chirol's general absence from Berlin after 1894, that post had been filled by Charles G. Earle, who had become his assistant there in 1893. Earle was then only recently graduated from Oxford and, when Chirol left for China in April 1896, Wallace wanted an older and more experienced man in Germany. Upon Chirol's advice, he offered the position to George Saunders, who had represented the *Morning Post* in Berlin for nine years. Saunders accepted, but his commitment to the *Morning Post* meant that he could not assume active duty for the *Times* until the end of the year. He continued in that post until 1908.

Earle, who might have remained in charge in Berlin at least until Saunders was ready to take over, became ill and died. Again, upon Chirol's recommendation, cabled from China, a temporary appointment was given to another young Briton, Henry Wickham Steed. Like Earle, he had been a student in Berlin when Chirol first met him in 1892. He spoke both German and French. By 1896 he had some experience as a correspondent for Central News, and the *New York World* had just offered him a post as its Paris correspondent.

To persuade Steed to remain in Berlin for the *Times,* Wallace agreed to send him to Rome after Saunders took charge. Steed accepted, replaced Earle in Berlin and, with Saunders established, he went to Rome in March 1897 as assistant to Stillman, correspondent there since 1886. Three months later Stillman retired at sixty-nine, and then made his home in London until his death in 1901. Steed served as Rome correspondent from 1897 to 1902. He then became Vienna correspondent until 1913.[2]

When Steed left Berlin in 1897, Saunders gained as an assistant still another young man recently down from Oxford, Dudley Disraeli Braham. He soon left Berlin, however, to become the *Times* correspondent in St. Petersburg. There he remained until 1903, when he was expelled, as Wallace had been a quarter-century earlier. Charged with "hostility to the Russian government and invention of false news," his offense apparently was a critical reference to Russian policy in the Kishinev massacres of early 1903, in which thousands of Jews were killed.

---

2 By that time a leading authority on European affairs, Henry Wickham Steed, was named foreign editor of the *Times,* following Chirol. He delayed his return from Vienna to London for a year. In 1919 he became editor of the *Times.* On leaving the paper in 1922, he still had more than two active decades before his death in 1956. He served variously as a magazine editor, lecturer, radio commentator for the British Broadcasting Corporation on world affairs, wrote articles for syndication, and several books.

Again, the proud *Times* resented the expulsion of its correspondent and did not name another for three years. It did so then only after receiving assurances at high diplomatic levels that the charges against Braham had been withdrawn and that the new appointee would be completely welcome. That new man, assuming his post in 1906, was Robert Wilton, who had been writing from St. Petersburg for the *Glasgow Herald*—although unofficially for the *Times* as well. Braham, meanwhile, became a leader writer in the London office of the *Times,* with an emphasis on foreign affairs.

When Bell and Wallace entered upon their administrative duties at the *Times* in 1890 and 1891, the particular star of the paper's foreign service was Henri Stefan Opper de Blowitz, Paris correspondent since 1875, and to continue in that post until 1902.

Already one of the most widely-known and influential journalists in 1890, Blowitz had been born December 18, 1825, at or near the Blowsky chateau, in the region of Pilsen, Bohemia. One version of his name is that he adapted it from the name of the chateau, and amended it later to " De Blowitz." His mother's name was Opper, or Oppert. One jibe was to refer to him as "Opper von Nowitz," since "Blowitz" (or Blowsky) was a place name rather than a family name. His father is said to have encouraged the youth to travel in Europe. When financial reverses affected the family, young Blowitz settled in France. He became a professor of foreign literature and of German at Angers or Tours, and certainly later at Marseilles.

In Marseilles in 1870, and already forty-five, Blowitz became acquainted with Louis Adolphe Thiers, a native of that port city who was an historian and already experienced in French political and administrative affairs. During the Franco-Prussian War, Thiers sought to bring a return of peace in Europe, and became the first president of France's Third Republic.

With an instinct for politics, and possibly acting as an emissary for Thiers, Blowitz entered Paris as soon as communications were opened in January 1871, following the wartime siege of the city. At a friend's home there, he met Laurence Oliphant, acting as chief correspondent for the *Times* in the absence of Hardman. Oliphant invited him to become an assistant. While Oliphant covered events in Paris, Blowitz reported from Versailles, where the preliminary treaty of peace was signed in Februrary 1871, and where the new French government was established. At that time, Blowitz also became a naturalized French citizen.

Because of his friendship with Thiers, Blowitz was able to obtain prompt and reliable information. This was an advantage to the *Times,* although both Oliphant and Hardman sometimes suspected that he was acting primarily in the interest of Thiers. Nevertheless, Hardman's continuing ill health gained Blowitz a permanent place in Paris for the paper. When Oliphant retired in 1873 to take up residence in the United States, Hardman resumed active direction of the Paris bureau, with Blowitz as an assistant, and Charles Austin as a third member. Following Hardman's death in 1874, Blowitz was placed in charge, and on February 1, 1875, he was named officially as Paris correspondent.

During the period when Thiers was president until May 1873, Blowitz's connections with his office and also with members of the diplomatic corps in Paris had enabled him to obtain a number of exclusive stories for the *Times,* and he demonstrated his value in other ways. This association continued after Marshal Marie Edme Patrice Maurice De MacMahon, the Duke of Magenta, succeeded to the presidency and served until 1879. And it remained so under governments following.

Blowitz never was modest about his own accomplishments, and a pun based upon the phrase "Blowitz own horn" had quite a vogue at one time. Nevertheless, he did have the patience and talent to develop sources, not only in France but in many parts of Europe, that produced useful information, often in advance of events. This, combined with his general enterprise and an amazingly retentive memory, helped to advance the reputation of the *Times.* His claim to having helped avert a new Franco-German war in 1875, as advanced in his autobiography, *Memoirs of M. de Blowitz* (1903), has been generally rejected, but one of his achievements was to obtain in advance the text of the treaty signed at the Congress of Berlin in 1878, after the Russo-Turkish War, for first publication in the *Times.*

Blowitz exerted great influence editorially on the foreign policy positions taken by the *Times* itself for more than a decade, and especially during the latter part of the period during which John Cameron MacDonald was manager of the paper, with Thomas Chenery as editor. Bell and Wallace sought to modify that influence, but it remained important virtually up to the time of Blowitz's retirement in 1902. He had a part, also, in bringing to the foreign staff a number of correspondents who were to add distinction to the paper.

The official history of the *Times,* as prepared by Stanley Morison, with staff aid, and published in five volumes (1935-52), takes a mixed view of Blowitz. It gives him credit for certain abilities and accomplishments, but also indicates shortcomings and notes that his enormous self-esteem irritated many, including Germany's Chancellor Otto von Bismarck and his son, Count Herbert Bismarck. It is Morison, presumably, who observes dryly that his "inexhaustible fluency enabled him to write dogmatically on all subjects, all men, all countries, and all events, including some events that never happened."

The *Times* history then goes on to say of Blowitz that:

> In the course of time his curiosity outstripped his sense of accuracy and his personal vanity his sense of discretion. . . .
>
> Unlike his colleagues, he loved to write as one human being to be read by other human beings. Even in its palmiest days popular journalism never produced a more brilliant master. Blowitz also had more serious claims. He possessed a thorough understanding of the internal politics of France. . . . Colour fascinated him. Lacking convictions of his own, he inclined to adopt those of one party or another, and, over all, he felt the temptation to study his audience and their wishes. Herein lay the secret of his methods as a journalist.
>
> If Blowitz was so often first with the news, it was not due simply to the unscrupulousness of his methods, but their resourcefulness. He was unrivalled in his day for appreciation of speed and journalistic tactics. Blowitz never wasted discretion upon news that could be obtained without it. He knew how to secure confidences; he ever had something to give in exchange for news. He got it from everywhere. Blowitz . . . regarded Paris as a vantage point for observing not France only but the whole of Europe. Blowitz's wide surveys were a regular feature of *The Times*. The material upon which they were based came from a network of friends in all European capitals to whom he was in the habit of sending bits of news. . . .
>
> At the time of the death of [Thomas] Chenery [editor of the *Times* from 1878 to his demise in 1884] Blowitz was without a rival. . . . He possessed the liberty to publish statements about any and every aspect of European politics, and his views were regularly supported in leading articles. When his judgments were departed from he felt justified in complaining. He was, moreover, consulted when difficulties arose in the choice of representatives abroad.

Whatever may have been Blowitz's faults, the prestige of the *Times* in international news reporting, and especially European reporting, was sustained in part by his activities in a period otherwise difficult for the paper. Even Bell and Wallace, with their distrust of him, did not entirely curb his influence. When he retired in 1902 he had been Paris correspondent for the paper for twenty-eight years. Then unwell, he died in 1903 at seventy-eight years of age. He had assistants in Paris, the last of whom was William Norton Fullerton, an American, who had joined the bureau in 1891 and remained until 1909.

Bell approved the establishment of a new post in the *Times* foreign staff organization in 1892. This was at Sofia, capital of Bulgaria. The Balkans previously had been covered from Vienna and from Constantinople. The major curtailment of Turkey's control in southern Europe followed its defeat in the Russo-Turkish War of 1877-78, and agreements reached at the Congress of Berlin in 1878.

Vienna and Constantinople remained important as news centers. But James David Bourchier was placed in charge of *Times* coverage from Sofia, and remained there until World War I. Irish-born, a former teacher and a classical scholar, he had suffered a hearing loss and had been in Vienna since 1888 seeking medical aid. Appointed to the Sofia post, despite this handicap, and on the basis of some journalistic assignments in Vienna, he soon was on friendly terms with virtually every leader in the Balkans. Even as Bourchier went to Sofia, William Lavino took the Vienna post, as Richards went from there to Berlin to succeed Lowe. Bourchier worked in cooperation with Lavino and also with Steed, who followed in the Vienna post from 1902 to 1913.

From Sofia, Bourchier covered not only Bulgaria, but Rumania, Serbia, and Greece. He had several assistants through the years, one of the first being H. A. (Howell Arthur) Gwynne, who served the *Times* in Rumania until he joined the Reuter organization in 1893. Bourchier himself was to build a reputation as an authority on the Balkans, and served the *Times* well. He remained there until Bulgaria allied itself with Germany and Austria in 1915, during World War I.

Another important addition to the *Times* foreign organization occurred in 1895 when Dr. George Ernest Morrison was engaged as a permanent staff correspondent in China, succeeding Colquhoun at Peking. An Australian by birth, and a medical doctor, Morrison was widely traveled, adventurous, and physically strong. Then thirty-three, he had completed a 3,000 mile journey through the interior of China and had written a book, *An Australian in China,* on his experiences and observations. In London to complete arrangements for its publication, he met Bell, Wallace, and other *Times* staff members, and was invited to return to China to represent the paper. He accepted, going by way of Burma and Siam, and served the *Times* in China until 1912. He gained a reputation as an authority on the country, becoming known as "China Morrison," and in 1912 became adviser to the first president of the new Republic of China, Yuan Shih-k'ai, serving until Yuan's death in 1916.

Morrison's reports from China were supplemented by accounts from Hong Kong by Thomas Cowen, whose career also included the establishment of the *Manila Times,* the *China Times* of Tientsin, and service on the staff of the *Japan Times* of Tokyo. T. H. Whitehead also wrote from China as a stringer, and in the late 1890s David Fraser was engaged as a staff correspondent at Shanghai. He remained for a decade in China.

Between 1892 and 1894 the *Times* also received some correspondence both from China and from the Middle East written by George Nathaniel Curzon. He became Lord Curzon following service as British undersecretary of state for foreign affairs (1895-98), viceroy and governor-general of India (1899-1905), and secretary of state for foreign affairs (1919), among other offices. It also will be remembered that Valentine Chirol absented himself from his Berlin post in 1894-95 and again in 1896-97 to write from China for the paper.

The first woman to be employed by the *Times* in a major editorial capacity was engaged in 1890. Flora Louise Shaw, previously with the *Pall Mall Gazette,* became head of the *Times* colonial department, which was distinct from the foreign department. As part of her work, she traveled to Australia, South Africa, Canada and the Klondike in 1890-92. She was in South Africa again in 1895, and remained with the paper until her marriage in 1902 to Colonel Sir Frederick Lugard (later Lord Lugard), who had military service in the Sudan in 1884-85, experience as a colonial administrator, and later became governor of the Crown Colony of Hong Kong (1907-12), and a member of the Privy Council.

Captain Francis Younghusband was engaged as a correspondent to serve from 1887 to 1895 both in India and South Africa. Edmund Powell was correspondent in Capetown. Auguste Couvreur, a Belgian statesman, also was stringer correspondent in Brussels until his death in 1894, when he was succeeded by his wife, Jessie Charlotte Huybers Couvreur, born of a Belgian father and an English mother. She was the second woman to write from abroad for the *Times.*

George W. Smalley, after nearly thirty years as head of the *New York Tribune* bureau in London, joined the *Times* in 1895 to return to the United States as the paper's correspondent there, first in New

York and later in Washington. He served until his retirement in 1906, and then returned to London to live until his death in 1916 at eighty-three.

Leopold Charles Maurice Stennett Amery, who had written from the Balkan area for the *Manchester Guardian* and the *Edinburgh Review* early in 1898, shortly after he left Oxford, was engaged by the *Times* later in that year. He was sent to Crete and then was made an assistant to Chirol in the foreign department in London. So began a decade of service to the paper, including an assignment to Berlin in 1899 and then to South Africa, where he directed the paper's coverage of the South African War from 1899 to 1902. Subsequently he edited *The Times History of the South African War*. Elected to Parliament in 1911, he left the paper for a distinguished career in government service.[3]

As new head of the foreign department in 1899, Chirol engaged William Francis Hubbard as chief correspondent for Spain and Portugal, with headquarters in Madrid, while A. W. Peterson acted as correspondent in Lisbon. Blowitz's retirement as Paris correspondent in 1902 brought a staff switch, with Lavino moving from Vienna to Paris, Steed from Rome to Vienna, and Hubbard from Madrid to Rome.

The *Times* service of foreign news, long respected, became almost a model of excellence during the period when Bell managed the paper from 1890 to 1911. He died at his desk. The particular merit of the service attached to the caliber of the correspondents and to their highly informed reporting of political, economic, and social subjects centering in the major capitals and nations of the world.

Wallace was one of the mainstays of that service. Others contributing included Chirol, Steed, Harris, Blowitz, Bourchier, Morrison, Saunders, and Amery. Their distinction was evidenced by the careers of some in activities apart from those directly relating to the *Times* itself, or even following their association with the paper. Yet, as correspondents, they tended to remain anonymous figures to readers of the paper, however well they might be known to leaders of government, and others, in the capitals where they served, and to some informed persons in Great Britain.

---

3 Following World War I, Leopold Amery held appointments as first lord of the admiralty, secretary of state for colonies, for dominion affairs, and for India and Burma.

The *Times* had great prestige and influence during those decades and performed a notable news and editorial service, despite its financial problems and some personal differences within the organization. No other newspaper or periodical at that time, anywhere in the world, had a staff of reporters and correspondents so large, so generally well-qualified, or so widely distributed. This, however, is not to say that other newspapers were without merit.

Other British
"Special"
Correspondents

In the late years of the nineteenth century the *Daily Telegraph* was as active as any other newspaper in Great Britain, aside from the *Times,* but the *Daily News* rivalled them both on occasion.

The *Daily Telegraph* had been growing in importance since its establishment in 1855. In 1862 it absorbed the *Morning Chronicle,* a former leader. It made an appeal to the public by reason of a lower price and because of an unusually strong general news coverage, domestic as well as foreign, with less stress than some on relatively dull political and economic subjects, and a less partisan editorial position than characterized some others. Like the *Times,* although on a more limited scale, it also made an effort to report world news through its own correspondents, supplementing the Reuter service.

A Paris office was established by the *Daily Telegraph* in 1856, and a column of information was soon appearing each day dealing with aspects of life in that capital. Not until 1864, however, was Felix Whitehurst named as the first permanent staff correspondent there. He remained until 1880, aided during the Franco-Prussian War and later by James Macdonnell and J. Hall Richardson. Richardson also acted as a stringer for the *Philadelphia Press* in the United States. Campbell Clarke, formerly a British Museum librarian, in Constantinople for the *Daily Telegraph* during the Russo-Turkish War, followed Whitehurst in Paris, remaining from 1880 until his death in 1902. He was knighted in 1897.

The *Daily Telegraph,* late in 1857, also began to publish a weekly letter from Canada, prior to the laying of the Atlantic cable. In the same period, occasional letters appeared from Australia under the curious heading "Steam Intercourse With Australia," and also from New Zealand, with accounts of the Maori war there at that time.

These letters necessarily arrived by ship, hence the "steam inter-course" reference, and were also late in appearing. The paper nevertheless used the telegraph more freely than many others, and also the cable when it became available, both of which contributed to its advance in public favor.

George Augustus Sala, although always a contributor rather than a staff correspondent, wrote regularly for the *Daily Telegraph* almost from the time of its establishment in 1855 until 1893, signing his reports "G.A.S." He was a great traveler and a lecturer as well as a writer. One of the few British correspondents in the United States during the Civil War period, he was there again in 1879-80 on a coast-to-coast journey, and made a third trip later. He had reported aspects of the Italian unification campaigns in 1858-61, was in St. Petersburg to report the funeral of Czar Alexander II in 1881, and in Moscow in 1883, along with John Merry LeSage, to report the coronation of Alexander III. He visited nearly all parts of Europe and many parts of the world, wrote fluently on almost any subject, and was much admired by journalistic aspirants in Great Britain.

Edward Dicey, a lawyer and scholar, helped report a part of the American Civil War, covered the Schleswig-Holstein conflict be-tween Denmark and Prussia in 1864, and the brief Austro-Prussian War of 1866. Francis (Frank) Lawley, former *Times* correspondent in the Confederate States during the Civil War, helped cover the Franco-Prussian War for the *Daily Telegraph*. So did LeSage, who also went to cover the Egyptian-Sudan campaign in the fall of 1882, aspects of the Indian wars in the United States, and other assign-ments, and later became editor of the paper to complete a sixty-year association extending from 1863 to 1923.

The interest of the *Daily Telegraph* and its publisher in casting light on global subjects was demonstrated in its co-sponsorship, along with the *New York Herald,* of Stanley's first two expeditions to Africa in 1871-72 and 1874-77, along with its sponsorship of other expeditions in Africa and the Middle East.

William Beatty Kingston became Berlin correspondent for the paper in the 1860s and remained there for more than ten years. From Berlin he covered all of central Europe, and spent considerable time in Vienna. He reported the Franco-Prussian War from the Prussian side, and the Russo-Turkish War from the Russian side. A tall and vigorous man, and an able correspondent, he had the respect if not the liking of Bismarck, who tried on one occasion to have him expelled from Berlin because he had been too successful in countering the chancellor's use of the press to serve his own purposes. Intervention by the British Foreign Office blocked that expulsion effort. Kingston had some of the quality of Blowitz in his mastery of European affairs.

Edwin Arnold, who had been principal of the Deccan College, at Poona, India, joined the *Daily Telegraph* in 1861 and remained with it for more than forty years. Chiefly a leader writer, and an editor handling foreign dispatches, he sometimes went on foreign assignments. A poet as well, he was knighted in 1888, and from that time until 1904, when he died, he traveled widely, twice to the United States, but especially to Japan and elsewhere in Asia.

Drew Gay, an early correspondent for the paper, was in Constantinople for a long period before, during, and after the Russo-Turkish War. He also helped report the Egyptian-Sudan campaign, as did Godfrey Langdon, Hector Macdonald, and the experienced John Merry LeSage. While in Egypt in 1882, LeSage hired Bennet Burleigh, then with Central News. Burleigh remained with the *Daily Telegraph* for more than twenty years—through the Russo-Japanese War—chiefly as a war reporter.

Burleigh was another adventurous person. Scottish by birth, he had served in the Confederate army during the American Civil War as "Capt. Bennet G. Burley." He was wounded and captured, but escaped. After the war he worked for the *Houston Telegraph* in Texas, where he gained his first news experience, and only returned to the British Isles in 1878. In 1881 he became a correspondent in Egypt for the Central News until his transfer to the *Daily Telegraph*. He remained in Egypt and the Sudan through the entire period of that campaign, from 1881 to 1898, except for a brief visit to Greece during the Greco-Turkish War of 1897-98.

Never a favorite with other correspondents because of a rough manner, and an aggressive and individualistic pursuit of news, Burleigh nevertheless was much respected. He wrote vividly and well, although some credit for the effectiveness of his published reports, bearing his "B.B." initials at the end, has been attributed to sharp editing by Edwin Arnold in the London office.

In Egypt, Burleigh duplicated some of the feats performed on other battlefields by Archibald Forbes, making hard and dangerous rides to get his dispatches to the telegraph ahead of competitors. He was wounded at Khartoum in 1885. Like Forbes, also, he received mention in official dispatches commending his courage and personal services. Some have professed to see Burleigh, Forbes, and Melton

Prior, individually or in combination, as prototypes of the artist-correspondent known as "Dick Helder," main character in Rudyard Kipling's *The Light That Failed* (1899).

One of the most remarkable correspondents for the *Daily Telegraph* or any other newspaper was Dr. Emile Joseph Dillon, who joined the paper's staff in 1866 and remained with it until 1914. Based in Russia during those years, but also roving far afield, he was another who resembled Blowitz in that his news concern extended throughout Europe. He had wide sources of information; but he had special talents as well.

Of Irish-English ancestry, Dillon had studied as a young man at the School of Oriental Languages in St. Petersburg. He became "one of the greatest philologists of the age," in the judgment of Harold Herd, historian of British journalism, and also had a masterful grasp of international affairs. He became a professor of comparative philology at the University of Kharkov, wrote regularly for two Russian newspapers, and had edited the *Odesskia Novosti* at Odessa for about a year when he was persuaded to join the *Daily Telegraph*. He was then thirty-one years old.

Although St. Petersburg became his place of residence, and Russian affairs the subject of most of his correspondence, it was understood that he might travel wherever on the continent he wished in following his concerns for news. Lord Burnham, proprietor of the *Daily Telegraph,* in a centennial account of the paper's history in 1955, said of Dillon:

> As a roving correspondent he somehow always contrived to arrive in a capital the day before trouble broke. His enemies said that the value of his intelligence system and his news sense were proved when without warning Cherif Pasha he cancelled his arrangement to accompany him on the Brussels carriage drive when the attempt was made on his life.
>
> His knowledge of the Chancelleries of Europe and their occupants was extensive and peculiar. He was on close personal terms with most of the leading politicians of the continent. . . . His knowledge of the men and the issues made him an invaluable interpreter of the tangled international politics of the years before the first World War.

Dillon also had what Lord Burnham called "a 'cloak and dagger' complex, and disguise had a fascination for him." In the critical political situation existing in the 1895 period between Turkey, Armenia, Greece, and Russia, Dillon at times moved about in Armenia variously disguised as a Cossack officer, a Kurdish chief, or a Turkish woman. On those occasions he was reporting Turkish atrocities in the area. As his stories began to appear in the *Daily Telegraph,* the Grand Vizier of Turkey requested that the British ambassador in Turkey order Dillon out of the area, and the matter reached the House of Commons in London. But Dillon left Armenia only when he was ready to do so.

His resort to disguise was used again, shortly afterwards, as the Greco-Turkish War was in progress during 1897-98. An insurrection in Crete, fomented by Greeks seeking to annex the Turkish-held island, brought on the war. Dillon was able to go to Crete to report the preliminaries, despite an official Turkish ban on travel. He went disguised as a monk, assisted by the Russian consul-general, a former school friend, and lived with the insurgents favoring Greek control of the island.[4]

The *Daily News* had reported events with such enterprise as it could afford from about 1850 to 1870. It then attained recognition by its excellent reports of the Franco-Prussian War, in an association with the *New York Tribune,* and the special contributions of Archibald Forbes and Henry Labouchere.[5] Then and later under the editorial direction of John R. Robinson (later Sir John Robinson) and Frank Harrison Hill, the *Daily News* successfully reported the Russo-Turkish War, with Forbes and MacGahan adding to the paper's lustre.

Other British newspapers presenting reports from their own correspondents in major capitals and at scenes of war and crisis during the 1870-1900 period included the *Morning Post,* the *Manchester Guardian,* and the weekly *Illustrated London News.* Of shorter life, there also were the *Standard,* the *Pall Mall Gazette,* and

---

4   Dillon also wrote a series of articles revealing harsh prison conditions in Russia itself. These were published in the London *Fortnightly Review* under the name of "E. B. Lanin."

5   Henry Labouchere, a man of many talents, became one of the proprietors of the *Daily News* in 1868, and conducted his own successful weekly, *Truth,* in London, after 1877. As a young man, leaving the university, he had gone to the United States before the Civil War, traveled about the country for two or three years, some of the time as a member of a circus. Then, as a member of the British diplomatic service, he was posted to Russia, Prussia, Sweden, Italy, and Turkey. In England again in 1864, then thirty-three, he learned the ways of the financial world, gained a seat in Parliament, and turned to journalism.

the weekly *Graphic*. The *Daily Mail,* only established in 1896 by Alfred Harmsworth (later Lord Northcliffe), soon attained quick success as a popular paper.

The Reuter agency was considerably preoccupied after 1870 with giving form to the Ring Combination, and playing its own part in that system of world news exchange. Its first task was to help restore the Agence Havas to economic stability after the setback experienced by the French agency as a result of the Franco-Prussian War.

From 1865 when the Indo-European Telegraph Company line was activated, and from 1869 when British cables were extended to Egypt, India, China, Japan, Australia, New Zealand, and intermediate points, Reuter also was deeply concerned with news gathering and news distribution in those areas, and later to both coasts of Africa as cables were extended to them.

Paul Julius Reuter, founder of the agency, retired in 1879, but continued in an advisory capacity almost to the time of his death in 1899. The active direction from 1878 was in the hands of Herbert de Reuter. John Griffiths was secretary from 1865 until succeeded in 1882 by Walter F. Bradshaw, who had been in Valparaiso since 1874. George Douglas Williams, with the agency since 1861, had served in Italy and in Paris, and also had helped train Herbert de Reuter. In 1880 he was appointed chief editor, a new post, and one he occupied until 1902, doing much to give character, solidity, and scope to the service.

Sigismund Engländer, representing Reuter himself on the continent from the time the agency began in 1851, retained a roving commission and acted as consultant until the 1890s. The elder statesman or *doyen* among the agency's correspondents, he brought others into its service, while serving personally for considerable periods in Paris, Constantinople, Berlin, and Vienna.

While in Constantinople, Engländer engaged W. H. G. Werndel as an assistant in 1877. Werndel served for twenty-five years as the agency's correspondent in Turkey. He became an expert on the Middle East and the Balkans, and then served in Geneva after World War I, covering the League of Nations and completing a half century with Reuter. Werndel had been joined in Constantinople in 1888 by

Fergus Ferguson, who was also to remain with the agency for fifty years in the Balkans, Egypt, and the Middle East. He succeeded Werndel in Geneva in 1932.

Virnand, who had become the first Reuter agent in Egypt in 1869, was based in Alexandria, the cable point. He remained there until the 1880s, when he was succeeded by Joseph Schnitzler. In that same decade, David Rees joined the staff, was based in Cairo, and became an expert on Egypt.

Henry M. Collins, who had played so active a role in the extension of the Reuter service in the Far East between 1866 and 1878, became general manager for Australasia in the latter year, with headquarters in Sydney, where he remained until 1899. Then, until 1902, he became general manager for South Africa.

Another Reuter correspondent of long service, M. J. M. Bellasyse, had become general agent in Capetown, South Africa, in 1861. When the first European cable connection was made in that part of Africa at Durban in 1879, Bellasyse made his headquarters there until 1887, when that east coast cable end was extended to Capetown. He then was made general manager for South Africa, a position he held until succeeded by Collins.

Bellasyse had been obliged to divide his time between Capetown and Johannesburg after the discovery of gold in the Transvaal in 1886. To assist in the coverage of news from that part of the South African Republic, or Transvaal, William Hay Mackay had been appointed as a correspondent in Pretoria, its capital, in 1884. There he remained until 1902, so well-established and respected that he was not even requested to leave the Boer capital during the Boer War of 1899-1902. Mackay had a young assistant from 1896 to 1899, Roderick Jones, who was to become general manager of Reuter in 1915, and its principal proprietor.

In the United States, James McLean was appointed as Reuter's first general agent in 1861, sent from London to represent the agency as the Civil War began. He served well, and brought distinction to the agency by providing the first report to reach London and all of Europe of the assassination of President Lincoln in 1865. In about 1868, however, he was dismissed by Reuter for sending a highly-exaggerated report of a tidal wave said to have swept over Tortola, one of the British Virgin Islands, with several hundred persons reported to have perished. From that time until 1893 stringers provided most of the Reuter reports from the United States. Then, however, S. Levy Lawson, long a member of the London staff, took charge in New York for the agency until after World War I.[6]

The first permanent Reuter bureau in Berlin was established in 1891, headed by E. A. Brayley Hodgetts, formerly in St. Petersburg as a correspondent for the *Graphic*. He was succeeded a few years later by Austin Harrison.

H. A. Gwynne, in Bucharest as assistant to Bourchier, correspondent for the *Times* in the Balkans, transferred to the Reuter staff in 1893, and was sent to Egypt and the Sudan, where fighting was in progress, then to report the Greco-Turkish War of 1897, and to Cuba in 1898 to report the Spanish-American War. He went to South Africa as an active correspondent during the South African War of 1899-1902. Subsequently, Gwynne became editor of the London *Standard* in 1904, and in 1911 began a long association with the *Morning Post* as editor of that London daily.

Another correspondent who remained long with Reuter was Edward John Buck. He was political correspondent in India in 1897 and continued there until his retirement in 1935, after thirty-five years with the agency. He became an authority on India and was knighted in 1929.

In India also, Lionel James, an indigo planter, joined the Reuter organization at twenty-four and in 1895 accompanied an expedition sent to relieve Chitral, capital of a state in northwest India then under siege in a dispute over a succession to the throne and the establishment of a frontier with Afghanistan. He became personally involved in the fighting. On that occasion he also wrote for the Bombay *Times of India,* and for the *Englishman* of Calcutta. He served the agency in the Sudan in 1898, reporting the fighting in progress there, but later transferred to the *Times,* with which he was to have active experience through the Russo-Japanese War of 1904-05.

Even as the Reuter service was extended and improved, the agency was plagued by financial problems and by special pressures that resulted in the difficulties of the decade of the 1880s being carried over into the 1890s. By 1880 the agency was encountering competition from two of the smaller British agencies. Central News, formed in 1863 as the Central Press of the United Kingdom, had come under new ownership in 1871, had entered the telegraphic news field, had

---

6 S. Levy Lawson is not to be confused with Edward Levy-Lawson, later Lord Burnham, proprietor of the *Daily Telegraph*.

some correspondents abroad, and had become fast and active. The Exchange Telegraph Company, formed in 1872 primarily to report stock and commodity prices and financial news—which had been Reuter's original specialty and continued to be an important part of its service—gained an exclusive right to representation on the floor of the London Stock Exchange, providing a strong general commercial service. It also developed a service of sports reports that was well received, plus a limited telegraphic service of general and foreign news reports.

Beyond that, Reuter was hard pressed to meet unusual costs of reporting wars and crises in the Balkans, the Far East, and in Egypt and the Sudan. It had asked the London papers to accept a rate increase for service "in time of war or prolonged political disturbance." In 1885 most of the morning papers agreed to do so, recognizing the need, but that was not soon enough to save the Reuter Telegram Company from the necessity of informing its stockholders in 1884 that, for the first time, no dividend was to be paid.

Newspapers and magazines making a deliberate "popular" appeal to a new generation of semi-literate readers to build circulations intended to attract advertisers and generate profits were succeeding both in England and in the United States after 1880. To entice readers, they departed from patterns of substantial news and information and from considerations of accuracy and truth to present stories of crimes and scandals, the more sensational the better; reports of disasters and accidents of special violence, riots and disturbances, oddities of nature and of human behavior, short or long items of "human interest," and whatever else might capture interest or stir the emotions. Even some sober and established newspapers, observing the public response to this material, were tempted to use some of it as a stimulus to circulation.

To provide a special service of meeting the obvious appetite for such reports, a new London agency was formed in 1889 by Davison Dalziel, owner and publisher of the respected London morning *Standard*. The agency bore his name, Dalziel. In its establishment, he had financial support from the United States. Indeed, it was from the United States that much of the material came, a circumstance that was to help implant an impression in British minds during the next several years that the United States was a strange and dangerous place, peopled by eccentrics and marked by odd and violent events.

Surprisingly, considering its staid character, the *Times* gave its support to the Dalziel agency, and encouraged other newspapers to subscribe to the service. This was not because the *Times* approved of the sensationalism and trivia, or the distortion of fact and blatant emotional appeal forming the substance of the Dalziel output. The *Times* never used the material, which did not measure up to its standards. Nor did any other quality newspaper in the British Isles.

The *Times* support of the Dalziel agency seemed rather to be a move intended to curb Reuter's strength. It was a move quite deliberately taken by Moberly Bell, only recently named as manager of the *Times,* and was in the spirit of Mowbray Morris's consistent refusal to subscribe to the Reuter service when it began in 1851, and to use as little of it as possible after 1858 when he reluctantly accepted it. The *Times* also had refused in 1884 to agree to any rate increase, as requested by Reuter.

The Reuter agency did, in fact, feel the added pressure of competition from the Dalziel agency. The Dalziel service was bought and paid for by many London and provincial newspapers, even when they had no intention of using its material. The competition was such that Reuter, with the urgent advocacy of Engländer, felt compelled to meet it in some degree. Thus in December 1890 Reuter announced a "Special Service" to be available to those who might wish it, at an extra charge, consisting of "human interest" stories of a type not previously included in the Reuter service, and produced by its own staff through extra effort and expense. Even the *Times* subscribed to this supplementary service, although again without using much of it.

The two services, Dalziel and the Reuter "Special Service" continued, with Dalziel prospering, until 1895. Toward the end of that five-year period, however, it had become clear that much of the Dalziel output was pure invention, with no basis in fact, and that some of the rest was rewritten from the Reuter service, but still with little concern for accuracy. With this fact demonstrated, the Dalziel agency lost subscribers, the *Times* dropped its support, and the agency ceased to exist. Reuter then also suspended its "Special Service."

The contest had been costly for Reuter, however, and the agency had been concerned, in the same period, with a new problem involving the pirating of its regular dispatches, not only by Dalziel, but by nonsubscribing newspapers in England and elsewhere. To halt this practice further costs were added. The period ended with the Reuter service back on a normal course and even with a pleasant benefit in that the total experience had in fact given the service a somewhat brighter and more readable content and style, with no harm to its reliability.

Another crisis had arisen in the 1880s that was worrisome and might have become serious in a variety of ways. This related to an effort by Germany's Chancellor Otto von Bismarck and Italy's Premier Francesco Crispi to undermine the position of the Agence Havas and to draw Reuter into the plan through the formation of a new agency combination involving Wolff, the Austrian Korrburo, UTB of Hungary, and the Stefani agency of Italy. This attempt, and its ultimate failure, has been described. For the period from 1887 to 1890, however, it placed Reuter in a difficult position, ethically, and created uncertainties about the future of the Ring Combination.

The Agence Havas had its own problems in the 1870s and 1880s, even after recovering from the difficulties engendered by the Franco-Prussian War, including a reorganization in 1879, but it was at full strength in 1890.

The Wolff agency was the least enterprising of the "big three." It had the support of the German government. but relatively weak support from the German press itself, and its "exclusive territory," limited to parts of Europe only, made it less profitable. Its foreign agents or correspondents were hardly more than those in Paris and London who did little except select what might be desired from the Havas and Reuter services. It had so little news to exchange that it actually paid a differential to Reuter, even as it received differentials from national agencies in its own territory.

The Havas agency and the Wolff agency alike received financial aid, or subsidies from their governments and therefore were commonly referred to, whether properly or not, as "semi-official" agencies. Havas denied that its subsidy made it in any sense "official." It asserted that its grant from the government was only to cover the cost of providing special service to its colonies, especially in Africa, where no payment for service could reasonably be expected from the small and generally unprofitable newspapers then appearing there, and where French government officials needed a service of current information. This same view would have applied to its service to Southeast Asia after 1890.

The Reuter agency, although on consistently good terms with the British government, never received any financial support from that source. Contrary to assertions sometimes made, it never was an "official" agency of the British government, or even a "semi-official" agency. The only possible basis for such a belief might have rested in the fact that Reuter and Havas alike received £1,000 (about $5,000) from the Khedive of Egypt annually between 1875 and 1900 to cover the cost of transmitting certain dispatches from London or Paris to Cairo. The viceroy of India paid Reuter the transmission costs to cable some of his formal addresses to London, and Reuter also received grants from the British government in payment for news services to the outposts of the empire. These payments, however, were in the nature of business subventions to meet communications costs, and not necessarily related to the matter transmitted. For all else, the agency was obliged to finance its own undertakings.

Reuter financed its service from fees paid by subscribing newspapers and clients at home and abroad, and from payments made by the national agencies under contracts providing for cash differentials between the world service received and the limited national reports provided in partial exchange. This included a cash differential from the Press Association within Great Britain itself.

Substantial additional revenue was provided, however, by banks and business houses and stock and produce brokers, both in England and other countries, receiving Reuter's commercial and commodity reports, always an important part of the service. In 1891 Reuter instituted a telegraphic money transfer service between London and Australia, and a private telegram service as well, using an elaborate code system that permitted economies with no loss of accuracy in transmission. An "advertisements branch" also was established in Sydney, patterned somewhat after the advertising division within the Havas agency. It seemed to be successful, and inspired a similar venture in London. This required extra capital, but the venture was a failure, resulting in a substantial loss and contributing to an inability, again, to pay any agency dividends for 1893 or 1894.

The situation was saved by a fortuitous upsurge in the profits from the telegraph remittance subsidiary in Australia, heavily patronized by reason of speculation at the time in gold mining shares there and in South Africa. The remittance business continued so profitably that in 1912 a "Reuter's Bank" was established in London, becoming the British Commercial Bank in 1914, but World War I brought the suspension of both the bank and the remittance business.

In the period between 1895 and 1900, however, Reuter was stronger than at any previous time, and more effective in its news function than any other existing agency. At the turn of the century, the strength and prestige of Great Britain and the British Empire were at a high point. In this, the Reuter agency shared, even though it was then under heavy new expense in reporting the South African War of 1899-1902. On this occasion, however, subscribers made no objection to a special wartime rate increase, and Reuter carried forward into the new century in full vigor.

Press Organization in the United States 16

The settlement of the United States, from coast to coast, was virtually complete by 1890. The population was just short of 63 million and would be 76 million by 1900. More than 1,600 daily newspapers in 1890 became more than 2,200 by 1900.

The most enterprising newspapers, in the sense that they reached out in direct coverage of news beyond their immediate areas to Washington and abroad, were some in New York City. By the 1890s comparable enterprise was being shown by newspapers in Chicago.

Except for such limited efforts as were made by a few dailies to obtain reports from other countries, world news reports reached the papers of the United States primarily by way of the Reuter agency through its contractual relationship with the New York Associated Press and the secondary relationship between the NYAP and such regional agencies as the Western Associated Press.

The Newspapers

The *New York Herald,* which had led in aggressive news gathering since 1840, was never more successful than in the decade from 1873 to 1883. Don Seitz, biographer of the Bennetts, described it as "probably the most profitable and potentially the most powerful newspaper in the world" at that time. Until the late 1890s, the most satisfactory service of world news available in the United States was provided by and through the *Herald.*

James Gordon Bennett, founder of the *Herald* in 1835, contributed in many ways to the advancement of journalistic practice between that time and his retirement in 1866. James Gordon Bennett, Jr., succeeding to the direction of the paper, proceeded in the same spirit of enterprise. From 1877 he lived chiefly in Paris and conducted his business from there. In addition to the morning *Herald,* he established the New York *Evening Telegram* in 1867, and a Paris edition of the *New York Herald* in 1887. The Paris *Herald* survived the earlier *Galignani's Messenger* (1814-1904) and a number of other English-language papers, and continues today as the *International Herald Tribune.*

The younger Bennett, able though he was, was an eccentric and unpredictable man, as many had reason to know.[1] Only because he had a thoroughly professional staff was he saved from the consequences of some of his more egregious errors of judgment and behavior. Even though a number of individuals were denied mention in the *Herald* because they had offended Bennett in some way, and even though he had what he called his own "foreign policy" for the paper,[2] the *Herald* was kept to a course dedicated to substantial news reporting. It was generally fair as well as fulsome in its presentation of national and world news, and reasonably nonpartisan by the standards of the time in its political stance.

Among staff members, ample reference has been made to Stanley and MacGahan, active during the 1870s. Colonel Finlay Anderson was sent to London for the paper when the North Atlantic cable went into operation in 1866. He was succeeded there in 1870 by Dr. George W. Hosmer, a former *Herald* Civil War "special." John P. Jackson was in Paris with French forces during the Franco-Prussian War, and throughout the Russo-Turkish War. He also served as foreign editor in New York, but was no desk-bound editor, going at

---

1   For example, his jealousy and disregard of Stanley, after his second expedition to Africa, and his quarrel with MacGahan have been noted. Another was his treatment of Charles Henry Meltzer, the *Herald* music critic, who wore his hair long and refused to cut it to suit Bennett's taste. Bennett suspended him as critic, sent him as a correspondent to St. Petersburg, to Berlin, then back to New York, and discharged him. Meltzer sued and was awarded damages, but Bennett was fully prepared to afford his gesture. See also Richard O'Connor's *The Scandalous Mr. Bennett* (1962).

2   Bennett's view was expressed in these words: "My attitude on foreign affairs is often called changeable, and is, I believe, frequently misunderstood. It is simply this: If a nation is friendly to this country [the United States] I wish the *Herald* to be friendly to that nation, but if a nation shows an unfriendly policy I wish the paper to adopt an unfriendly tone. This may not be patriotism but it is the course I wish the paper to follow."

times to London, Berlin, St. Petersburg, Paris and elsewhere. Because he lived too well in Paris to suit Bennett, he lost favor, and John Devoy succeeded him as foreign editor.

John Russell Young, a Civil War reporter who became managing editor of the *New York Tribune,* was with the *Herald,* from 1869 to 1882, during which time he reported from European capitals, and also accompanied former President Grant on a world tour in 1877.[3] Edward Howard House was a stringer for the *Herald,* among other papers, in Japan from 1874-76, while also editing the *Tokyo Times.* James Gilder also spent some time in Asia for the paper. Stephen Bonsal, who probably had the longest career as a *Herald* correspondent, journeyed to many parts of the world for the paper between 1885 and 1919, although with interruptions after 1893, when he held posts in the U.S. diplomatic service, was an officer in the army during World War I, and interpreter for President Wilson during the peace conference. He later wrote a Pulitzer prize-winning book, *Unfinished Business, Paris-Versailles, 1919* (1944).

Reference has been made to Bennett's association with John W. Mackay in 1883 in establishing the Comercial Cable Company, and so bringing a sharp reduction in North Atlantic cable rates. Mackay also financed the establishment in Paris in 1884 of the French-language paper *Le Matin,* which became a mass circulation daily published until World War II. It was edited during its first two years by Samuel S. Chamberlain, who had been with the *New York Herald* from 1875-79, with the *New York World* from 1879-80, the *New York Evening Telegram* from 1881-83, and identified with the newspapers and magazines published by William Randolph Hearst from 1886 to 1909.

When Bennett established the Paris edition of the *New York Herald,* its first editor was Julius Chambers, previously a reporter for the *New York Tribune,* but then managing editor of the *Herald* in New York from 1886-87. He was succeeded by William C. Reick. In 1889 Bennett undertook to establish a London edition of the *Herald,* with Reick transferred from Paris, and assisted by James Creelman, a member of the *Herald* organization from 1887 to 1893. The London edition failed to gain a place for itself and in 1890 Ralph D. Blumenfeld, of the *Evening Telegram,* was assigned to London

---

3   Young was appointed U.S. minister to China from 1882-85, and became librarian of Congress from 1897 until his death in 1899.

specifically to suspend the paper. He then remained there through 1892 as correspondent for the *Telegram*, and returned in the same capacity from 1894 to 1900.[4] Joseph V. Snyder also was in the London bureau in 1898.

The *New York Tribune* had provided excellent coverage of the Franco-Prussian War and was highly respected. Whitelaw Reid, publisher since 1873, was so involved in diplomacy from 1889 to his death in 1912, serving as envoy to France and Great Britain during most of those years, that the paper was operated under a "regency," and suffered in enterprise.

Its Washington coverage was adequate, and its own reports from Europe came from a limited number of correspondents directed from London by George W. Smalley until 1895. He was succeeded by Isaac N. Ford, who had been in the New York office since the 1870s.

Joseph Hance had continued as *Tribune* correspondent in Berlin for some years after the Franco-Prussian War, Henry O. D. White was in Constantinople from 1872 to 1892, Clarence Cook was in Paris, and William J. Stillman in Vienna from 1869 to 1876. Julius Chambers, a local reporter for the paper for some years after leaving Cornell, became a roving correspondent in the United States, and also moved between London, Paris, Havana, Madrid, Washington, and other places before joining the *Herald* in 1886.

The *Tribune* had British-born Frederick Cunliffe-Owen as foreign editor in New York from 1889 to 1898. From 1890 he also wrote a weekly column concerned chiefly with the affairs of the European royalty and nobility, which he signed "By the Marquis de Fontenoy." Used by the *Tribune* and syndicated to other newspapers in the United States, it was continued until 1913, when its writer retired.

The *New York Sun,* owned and edited from 1868 by Charles A. Dana, formerly of the *Tribune,* became noted for its local news reporting and exceptional writing by a group of talented staff members. William Mackay Laffan, as co-owner and publisher, in 1887 brought about the formation in that year of the *Evening Sun,* which became successful and profitable. He also succeeded to ownership of the *Sun* papers upon Dana's death in 1897, and formed the Laffan News Bureau.

---

4 Blumenfeld had been in London originally in 1887, sent by the United Press of that period, to report Queen Victoria's golden jubilee. Leaving the *Herald* in 1900, he became associated with the London *Daily Mail* and, after 1902, with the *Daily Express,* where he continued as an executive until his retirement in 1933.

The *Sun,* morning and evening, depended chiefly upon agency reports for its national and world news. There were some departures from this policy, however, beginning particularly in the 1880s. In 1878, Hungarian-born Joseph Pulitzer, with experience in news work in St. Louis, provided some correspondence while on a journey to Europe. Stoddard Dewey, going to Paris in the 1870s following his graduation from Harvard, wrote as a stringer for the *Sun,* thus beginning a lifetime of Paris news work, although mostly for other papers.

Arthur Brisbane, then only twenty-one, but already two years with the morning *Sun,* went to London as its correspondent in 1884-88, and then became editor of the *Evening Sun.* From London, the *Sun* also used articles by T. P. O'Connor, who had founded the evening *Star* in 1888. He was a member of Parliament, and also wrote for papers in St. Petersburg and in Italy. Frank Marshall White also served in London, and there were stringers in Berlin and elsewhere.

Henry R. Chamberlain became a particularly valuable correspondent in London, serving from 1892 to 1905. He was a careful reporter, had the confidence of statesmen and diplomats, and managed the London office of the Laffan News Bureau after 1897.

Julian Ralph, one of the morning *Sun*'s ablest reporters, covered the Sino-Japanese War in 1894, and Richard Harding Davis, of the *Evening Sun* staff, became a correspondent of even greater note, although not for the *Sun.*

The *New York Times,* strongly established in the 1870s, was respected for its exposure in 1870-71 of William M. ("Boss") Tweed and his Tammany Hall $200 million swindle of New York City and its taxpayers. Much of the editorial power in the campaign was provided by British-born Louis J. Jennings, editor from 1869 to 1871, and former correspondent for the London *Times* in India and then in New York. It was in this campaign that *Harper's Weekly* and its cartoonist, Thomas Nast, played an important part. The paper also had an arrangement in those years by which it was able to use material produced by the London *Times,* including reports by William Howard Russell, who moved about Europe at that period.

In 1884 Harold Frederic, former editor of the *Albany Evening Journal,* became the *New York Times* representative in London, where he remained until his death in 1898. He did a weekly cable letter, processed the service of the London *Times* for use in New York, and sometimes traveled and wrote from the continent. Another weekly letter was received from Paris.

Apart from that, however, the 1880s and 1890s were a difficult financial period for the *New York Times*. George Jones, the last of its founders, died in 1891, and the paper faced vigorous competition in the New York morning newspaper field, first from the *New York World*, under the direction of Joseph Pulitzer from 1883, and then from the *New York Journal*, under William Randolph Hearst after 1895. Economic strength only began to return to the paper after its purchase in 1896 by Adolph S. Ochs, then thirty-eight, publisher of the *Chattanooga Times*.

The *New York World*, established in 1860, but in financial difficulties in the 1870s, was revived after its purchase in 1883 by Pulitzer, by then publisher of the *St. Louis Post-Dispatch*. The *World* sent Ballard Smith to London, briefly, and also was represented there by Tracey Graves and by David Graham Phillips, later known as a novelist. In 1899 a British newsman, John H. Touhy, became the paper's London representative, to serve until 1922.

The *World* made at least one gesture toward special coverage abroad in 1889 when it sent Thomas Stevens to Zanzibar to meet Henry Morton Stanley on his emergence from Africa after his fourth expedition. But he was out-maneuvered by the *New York Herald* representative, Edward Henry Vizetelly. In 1896 the paper also sought to engage Henry Wickham Steed, then in Berlin, as its Paris correspondent, but lost him to the London *Times*.

The *World* developed a strong national and Washington coverage. Its one notable success in what might be called international correspondence in that period occurred in 1889 when it sponsored an attempt by a woman reporter on its staff, Elizabeth Cochrane (later Mrs. Robert Seaman), to better the fictional record of Phileas Fogg in circling the globe in eighty days. Jules Verne's novel, *Around the World in 80 Days*, had been serialized in 1872 in *Le Temps* of Paris, with book publication in that same year. It had been converted into a play in 1880; the novel still had a vogue, and the *World* sought to exploit it as a circulation feature.

Elizabeth Cochrane had entered newspaper work in Pittsburgh in 1885 at the age of eighteen, when women rarely served as daily newspaper reporters. She demonstrated her competence, however, and in 1886 the *Pittsburgh Dispatch* permitted her to spend six months in Mexico investigating corruption in government, conditions in prisons, and the position of the peons. With that experience, she managed to persuade Pulitzer to hire her as a *World* staff member.

Again she proved her talents as an investigative reporter, able to cope with difficult situations, and produce readable and informative stories. By doing so, she helped break down barriers that had kept women out of the newspaper business.

In November 1889, Miss Cochrane began her round-the-world adventure, taking the same eastward course as Phileas Fogg had followed in the Verne story, although with New York as her point of departure. Even pausing to interview Jules Verne in Paris, she was back in New York in just over seventy-two days. Her reports were printed in the *New York World,* as they were received, under the name of "Nellie Bly," a pen-name used since her Pittsburgh days, and borrowed from the Stephen Foster song. The stories appeared irregularly, built up a public interest and suspense, were widely reprinted, and brought her home to a great civic welcome. They also helped the *World* circulation.[5]

The *New York World,* under Pulitzer, had been converted from a failing newspaper in 1883 to the newspaper of largest circulation in the United States by 1895, and had become perhaps the most profitable newspaper in the world, surpassing the *Herald.* Between 1895 and 1898, however, it became involved in a contest to hold its circulation leadership, and modified its standards to meet competition from the *New York Journal.*

The *New York Morning Journal* had been established in 1882 by Albert Pulitzer, a brother of Joseph Pulitzer, but was sold in 1894 to John R. McLean, publisher of the *Cincinnati Enquirer.* He found it was losing money and promptly resold it in 1895 at a bargain price to William Randolph Hearst, then thirty-two, successful as publisher of the *San Francisco Examiner* and looking for a New York paper.

Hearst called the paper simply the *New York Journal.* From San Francisco, he brought Samuel S. Chamberlain, formerly of the *New York Herald,* as editor. With several million dollars in resources, derived from a family interest in the Homestake gold mines in South

---

5 If an imaginary Phileas Fogg had circled the globe, a real William Perry Fogg, writing for the *Cleveland Daily Leader,* had made a more leisurely trip in 1870-71, shortly before the Jules Verne story had appeared—possibly establishing the idea in his mind. The real Fogg had gone in the opposite direction, from the United States to Japan, China, India, Egypt, Europe, and New York, with letters written en route and appearing in the Cleveland paper.

Dakota, he outbid other newspapers for those he wanted for the staff organization. These included Arthur Brisbane, who had moved from the *Sun* to the *World;* James Creelman from the *Herald;* Julian Ralph from the *Sun*, and Richard Harding Davis, formerly of the *Evening Sun*, but then editor of *Harper's Weekly*. An *Evening World* had been established in 1887, so Hearst established an *Evening Journal* in 1896. Both papers published elaborate Sunday editions.

A revival of the insurgent campaign in Cuba to gain freedom from Spain occurred in 1895, and Hearst seized upon it as a subject for special attention, supporting the cause of independence. To protect its position, the *World* did the same, and both papers resorted to sensationalism in the choice and even invention of subject matter, in writing style, and in typographical display. The excesses have commonly been regarded as a major contributing cause of the Spanish-American War of 1898. The war was brief, however, and with its end the *World* reverted to a more serious and responsible style of journalism that was to mark its future years.

Pulitzer himself, nearly blind and then totally blind from 1889 to his death in 1911, was rarely in New York, but nevertheless kept a firm hand on the paper, aided by a number of secretaries.[6] His personal interest went to substantive news and an editorial page presenting sound guidance. The paper provided good reports from Washington and some foreign reports, with Louis Seibold notable among several writing from the capital and from abroad. The *World* was not, however, to develop any consistent international reporting of its own until the period of World War I.

The *Journal,* in addition to its activity centering on Cuba in the 1895-98 period, also made special arrangements to report on foreign events, including the Greco-Turkish War in 1897, and the South African War in 1899-1902. The morning *Journal* was renamed in 1901 as the *New York American,* while the *Evening Journal* continued as the *New York Journal*. Hearst added other newspapers to his group. He owned six in 1905: the original *San Francisco, Examiner,* the *American* and *Journal* in New York, the *Chicago American,*

---

6 Pulitzer had been elected to Congress in 1884, but resigned before the end of his term.

established in 1900 as an evening paper, with a morning *Examiner* added in 1902, and a Boston evening *American* founded in 1904.[7]

The *New York Press* was established in 1887, and was a morning paper of some merit. Frederick Palmer became its London correspondent in 1895, beginning for him a long career, chiefly as a war correspondent.

The *New York Evening Post,* the oldest existing newspaper in New York (now the *New York Post*), was founded in 1801, and gave serious attention to public affairs but, as is generally the case with afternoon newspapers, made little effort to gather news abroad. William Cullen Bryant, its editor from 1829 to 1878, now mainly remembered for his poetry, made six journeys to Europe during those years, and wrote numerous and lengthy letters of some substance for publication. The paper provided some direct coverage of the Spanish-American War, but beyond that depended largely upon news agency service for its world reports.

The *Chicago Tribune,* the *Chicago Record,* and the *Chicago Inter-Ocean,* all morning publications, and the evening *Chicago Daily News* were the first inland daily newspapers in the United States to undertake direct staff or stringer correspondence abroad.

The *Chicago Tribune,* established in 1847, had provided active coverage of the Civil War, had grown strong, and in 1898 sent Henry Norman to London as its correspondent, sharing his services with the *New York Times.* It made staff assignments for coverage of the Spanish-American War, both in Cuba and in the Philippines.

The *Chicago Record,* founded in 1881 by Victor F. Lawson, was published in association with the *Chicago Daily News,* an afternoon paper established in 1876 by Lawson, in partnership with Melville E. Stone. Active though he was in the Western Associated Press, Lawson was prepared to supplement the news agency service by having writers for his own newspaper undertake some original coverage beyond the national frontiers. Where other papers in the United States sponsoring any such coverage looked to Europe, the *Record* sent William E. Curtis to Central and South America in 1888; Omar

---

7 Hearst himself was elected to Congress from a New York City district in 1902, and re-elected in 1904. He aspired to the presidency of the United States as a Democratic party candidate in 1904, but failed of nomination, and was defeated for the governorship of New York State in 1906. He had been narrowly defeated for mayor of New York in 1905, was defeated in another campaign for that office in 1909, and in 1910 was defeated as a candidate for the lieutenant-governorship of New York State.

Maris to Alaska in 1896 and to the Klondike in 1897; Trumbull White to Australia and New Zealand in 1897; and Curtis, along with William Sumner Harwell, to Europe, at last, also in 1897, but with attention directed to Sweden, until then a journalistically neglected part of the world for visiting reporters.

Correspondents for the *Record* also went on special journeys to London, Paris, Peking, and Tokyo. Although not engaged for any great length of time in these ventures, they, along with coverage of the Spanish-American War, gave the *Record* by 1900 one of the better international news-gathering organizations. Lawson sold the *Record* in 1901, but he retained its still-young foreign service, transferring it to his *Chicago Daily News*. Even though an afternoon paper, the Daily News provided a world report equal in quality to almost any morning daily.

The *Chicago Inter-Ocean* was not able to approach the *Tribune*, the *Record*, or the *Daily News* in quality or news-gathering enterprise, and it was to vanish in 1914. Established in 1865, and undergoing a change of ownership in 1897, it was represented that year, during the Greco-Turkish War, by a young man named Percival Phillips, formerly a reporter on the *Pittsburgh Press*, and who was to have a long career as correspondent with London newspapers.

As the New York and Chicago papers were developing coverage abroad after 1870, James E. Scripps and his half-brother, Edward W. Scripps (from 1873), were developing the *Detroit News*, the *Cleveland Press*, and the *Cincinnati Post*—all afternoon papers. Associated with them in these ventures was their sister, Ellen Browning Scripps.

On three occasions between 1881 and 1889 Ellen Scripps accompanied her brothers on extended travels. With Edward, she was in Europe and North Africa in 1881-83, in Mexico, the southern states, and Cuba in 1884-85, and with James in Europe again 1887-89. Both before and after these journeys, she prepared regularly a column of "miscellany," short filler-paragraphs, and brief items, strong in reader-interest, for use in the Scripps newspapers. Throughout the journeys with her brothers she wrote and mailed further miscellany, but also many longer articles based upon inquiries, observations, and interviews in the areas visited. Descriptive, informative, and sometimes news-related, they bore her initials, "E.B.S."

In the provision of these longer reports through a period of five years or more, Ellen Browning Scripps became another of the early women correspondents for the press. Along with her "miscellany," her reports also represented the beginning of the Newspaper Enterprise Association (NEA), as formally organized under the proprietorship of Edward W. Scripps at Cleveland in 1902, and still operating as a major newspaper syndicate. Scripps became, also, the proprietor of the world's first "group" of newspapers, and founder of the United Press Associations (UP) in 1907—one of the great world news agencies, now the United Press International (UPI), by reason of a reorganization in 1958.

The daily newspaper press had developed greatly in the United States by 1890, with established papers grown larger, and new papers founded in many cities. There were by then some stringer correspondents in the United States for the foreign press, and correspondents or stringers abroad for some newspapers of the United States. But the major exchange of news between the United States and the rest of the world continued to be through Reuter and the Ring Combination in an exchange with the New York Associated Press, and involving the NYAP contractual ties with the regional associations in the United States. The distribution of national news depended upon that same system.

The strongest of the regional associations, the Western Associated Press (WAP), with headquarters in Chicago, had been operating on an equal footing with the NYAP since 1867. With the settlement of the country growing on both sides of the Mississippi River, it was natural that newspapers in that section should look to the WAP for service. As it happened, however, the WAP had become as dictatorial in its dealings with newspapers as the NYAP had been in its earlier relations with the WAP and other regional groups.

A newspaper holding a "membership" in the WAP, as a cooperative association, was recognized as having an exclusive right to receive and use the agency service in its own area. That membership was a powerful advantage in any competitive situation. A member could object to service being made available equally to a nonmember paper or to a new paper in its community. In such case, its own prior right was recognized. This made it difficult or even impossible for a new daily newspaper to obtain a service of telegraphic news in any community in which a "member" paper already appeared. Although other press services might exist, and some did, they were small, and none was able to offer any telegraphic or world service.

In 1882, however, a group of five newspapers in Boston, Philadelphia, New York, Chicago, and Detroit, unable to obtain service from the NYAP, WAP, or other regional agency, formed a new agency known as the United Press. This was itself an outgrowth and combination of certain of the earlier, small associations, some dating from 1869. The new agency was established in New York City as a privately owned enterprise for the distribution of news on a commercial basis to any who might wish to buy the service.[8]

The United Press was headed by Francis X. Schoonmaker, formerly with one of the earlier small agencies, the National American Press Company, formed in 1877 in Philadelphia, but forced to suspend because of communications rate increases. Direction of the new United Press soon passed to one of its incorporators, Walter Polk Phillips, a former telegrapher and inventor of the Phillips Code, who had moved from positions on newspapers to become assistant general manager of the NYAP in 1875, and director of its Washington bureau from 1878 to 1882.

Aware that the United Press would require a world news service if it were in any way to match the NYAP-WAP service, utilizing the Reuter reports, Phillips formed the Cable News Company. It was a subsidiary of the United Press, although it purported to be independent, and Schoonmaker was placed in charge. This company arranged to receive a limited world news report from Central News (CN) of London, and also, by some accounts, from the Louis Hirsch Telegraphisches Büro of Berlin. Those agencies were completely independent of the Ring Combination.

The Cable News Company sold its foreign reports to the United Press. The company also prepared a slightly different version of the same report, after 1883, and offered it for sale as a supplementary service to newspapers receiving the NYAP or WAP report.

The new United Press, providing a national report along with foreign reports, prospered to such an extent that by 1885 it had three leased wires distributing 17,500 words daily to newspapers in seventeen cities. In 1886 the wire was further extended from Chicago to San Francisco.

---

8 This United Press (UP), as formed in 1882, continued only until 1897. It is not to be confused with the United Press Associations (UP), as formed in 1907, or with the United Press International (UPI), formed in 1958 when the United Press Associations purchased the Hearst-owned International News Service (INS), dating from 1909.

The Western Associated Press directorship was not deceived by the claim of the Cable News Company to independence of the United Press. It objected when some WAP members began to buy that company's "supplementary" news service in 1883, viewing such action as a sort of disloyalty to the WAP and also as contrary to the terms of membership. Some publishers and editors in the WAP group were puzzled, further, by what seemed to them to be an abnormally rapid growth of the United Press. A quiet investigation accordingly was undertaken by a committee headed by Victor F. Lawson, publisher of the *Chicago Record* and *Chicago Daily News*.

Several years of discreet inquiry were required to gather and verify the essential facts. By 1892, however, it was clear that, since 1884, a few members of the NYAP and a few members of the WAP were aiding the rival United Press, to their own financial advantage, while at the same time—intentionally or not—undermining the NYAP-WAP.

By secret agreement, the NYAP-WAP conspirators were passing over to the United Press all news reports gathered by their own newspapers, reports which should have become the exclusive property of the NYAP or WAP. They also were passing along world reports based on the Reuter service. Schoonmaker, of the Cable News Company, was found to be on the conspirators' payroll. Both the Cable News Company's own reports and the pirated Reuter reports were being combined and rewritten to make a good United Press world news service. Prepared at a moderate expense for cable charges, with nothing whatever for the Reuter report, it could be sold at a rate below that which the NYAP and WAP were required to charge to cover original costs. This helped explain the growth of United Press membership that had baffled Lawson and others in the WAP.

Meanwhile, the burgeoning United Press was reorganized in 1887 to permit the agency to extend its activities. One action also was to send a member of its staff, Ralph D. Blumenfeld, formerly of the *Chicago Herald,* to London in 1887 to report the ceremonies surrounding the Golden Jubilee of Queen Victoria's reign. Later, it was to send Louis H. Moore to Moscow to report the coronation of Czar Nicholas II in 1896.

Stock in the United Press, secretly acquired by the NYAP-WAP conspirators, promised to bring them substantial personal gain through an expansion of the agency planned as an essential part of the 1887 reorganization. Ironically, in view of the reason for its formation in 1882, that plan authorized the reorganized agency to limit its membership, just as the NYAP and WAP had done, and continued to do. But the United Press now hoped to gain added revenue from NYAP-WAP members by agreeing *not* to provide service to competitive papers in their circulation territories.

Even as this went on after 1887, the NYAP itself was being further weakened from within because of a running conflict with the Western Union Telegraph Company, where Craig, the NYAP's former general manager, who was dismissed in 1866, and then briefly directed the WAP, was in a position of authority. More significant, on that score, Ezra Cornell had died in 1874, and Jay Gould, gaining control of Western Union after 1880, manipulated telegraph and cable rates to the general disadvantage of the press organization. The *New York Sun* and the *New York Tribune,* founding members of the NYAP, also withdrew from that membership in 1892 and joined the United Press. It developed that they were among the conspirators. The NYAP was languishing so seriously by that time that the United Press was discussing taking over its assets, including its contract with Reuter.

At this critical point members of the Western Associated Press and of the New York Associated Press, now enlightened and disillusioned, determined upon a reorganization and merger of both agencies to eliminate the conspirators. The solution they saw was to form a single new association, freed from all taint of the conspiracy now revealed, and one to be completely national in character. The three other major regional associations, equally dismayed by the plight of the NYAP, with which they also were allied, joined in the new effort. These were the New York State Associated Press, the New England Associated Press, and the Southern Associated Press.

Out of this arrangement developed the Associated Press of Illinois, which was chartered in that state. By a majority of its membership vote, the old New York Associated Press ceased to exist on December 31, 1892, with most of its newspapers and most of its staff joining the Associated Press of Illinois (API). The Western Associated Press took parallel action, as did the other three regional associations. Thus, the Associated Press of Illinois replaced those five agencies. Its headquarters were in Chicago, and its service began January 1, 1893. William Henry Smith, who had been general manager of the joint NYAP-WAP group since 1881, was continued temporarily as general manager of the new association.

Once the Associated Press of Illinois had been formed, Lawson and his associates both in the W AP and N Y AP were able to move in a forthright manner denied to them so long as the conspiracy had been obscured. A first need was to assure a continuation of the relationship with the Reuter company for the receipt of a world news service. With the aid of William Henry Smith and through William Neef, London agent for the NYAP-WAP, the new situation in the United States, and its background, was made known to Herbert de Reuter.

At the same period, William M. Laffan of the *New York Sun*, one of the prime conspirators, and a large shareholder in the United Press, was seeking to persuade Reuter to transfer the service contract to that agency. Neef was more persuasive, however.

In early March, Melville E. Stone accepted the general manager-ship of the Associated Press of Illinois, supplanting Smith. Stone had been associated with Lawson in the conduct of the *Chicago Daily News* from 1876 to 1888, but had been in the banking business since that time. Now persuaded to return to the news field, he went immediately to London to see Herbert de Reuter, and the agreement Neef already had reached with Reuter was confirmed. A ten-year contract was signed by which the Associated Press of Illinois took over the NYAP right to distribute the Reuter service in the United States. It was to make its own service available to Reuter in exchange, and also to pay a cash differential of $17,500 annually.

Under the new contract, Reuter also granted the API the right to distribute the Reuter service in Canada, in Alaska, and in the Hawaiian Islands.[9] The API further was granted the right to share Mexico and Central America with Reuter and Havas for the distribution of news. Other extensions were to be approved in later years, but the extensions of 1893 were such that what previously had been recognized as the "big three"—Reuter, Havas and Wolff—were now sometimes referrred to as the "big four." In terms both of news distribution and contribution of news, the API gained new status in the Ring Combination.

---

9 In practice, most newspapers of Canada had been obtaining their world news through the United States, and this circumstance was only given formal recognition through the new contract. Canada, as a Dominion in the British Empire, was nominally within the Reuter reserved territory, as established under the Ring Combination. No national news agency existed there until 1903, when the Canadian Associated Press was formed, supplanted in 1917 by the Canadian Press (CP), later to become a member of the Ring Combination.

The Associated Press of Illinois, formally recognized as a non-profit, cooperative agency owned by its member papers, represented a new corporate form. The former NYAP and WAP rule on exclusivity of membership was adopted by the API.

The United Press continued after the formation of the API, with its own considerable newspaper membership. Deprived of access to the Reuter service, however, the UP report was so far inferior to that of the API that the agency lost ground. As contracts with newspapers expired few were renewed. By late 1895 the UP was reduced to outright pirating of dispatches from the API.[10] The UP loss of clients continued and on April 7, 1897, it halted all service and ceased to exist.

The conspirator newspapers in the NYAP and WAP had been denied membership in the API. Such newspapers, along with those denied service by the United Press itself after the 1887 reorganization, plus those that dropped out voluntarily after 1892, and those remaining when the United Press suspended in 1897 were now faced with a difficult problem. They had nowhere to turn for a world news service, or even a national service.

Laffan, of the *Sun,* undertook a sort of last-ditch fight against the API. Since about 1880 the *Sun* papers, morning and evening, had developed a small group of correspondents and stringers. Chamberlain, in London, provided a well-tailored report drawn from London and European newspapers, benefiting also from the five-hour time difference between London and New York.

With the suspension of the United Press, the *Sun* engaged more correspondents, and a Laffan News Bureau was established in 1897. It offered the entire *Sun* home and foreign service to any newspapers wishing to subscribe. The bureau continued until 1916, seven years after Laffan's death.

Meanwhile, Edward W. Scripps, publisher since 1878 of afternoon newspapers in Cleveland, Cincinnati, St. Louis, San Diego, and other cities, had formed two small services of his own. Scripps could have had WPA or API membership for some of his papers, at least, but declined because those services were designed primarily for

---

10 To demonstrate that this practice was going on, the API on one occasion inserted in a dispatch from India a reference to an imaginary person named "Siht El Otspueht." The UP distributed a rewritten version of the story, using the same name. The API promptly pointed out that the name, spelled backward, really read "The UP stole this."

morning papers and because he also objected to some of the bylaws. His papers stressed local news, obtained by staff efforts, with limited attention to national and world news, and they were successful. Milton A. McRae, associated in the direction of the *Cincinnati Post,* took over active management of most Scripps papers after 1890, with Scripps himself in semi-retirement, although still involved. He had a certain personal preference for the United Press, so long as it existed. He did not join it, but some special dispatches for his newspapers were sent over its wires.

Scripps foresaw the end of the United Press in 1897, and a Scripps-McRae Press Association was formed in January of that year to provide telegraphic news reports to the Scripps papers in the Middle West. A Scripps News Association also was established on the Pacific Coast to gather and distribute news for his papers there. At the same time, another group of newspapers in the East formed the Publishers' Press Association in 1898. These three associations subscribed to the Laffan report at $200 a week. The three also exchanged news, thus producing a national service available to any newspaper. In 1904 Scripps bought control of the Publishers' Press Association, and in 1907 he merged the three services to form the United Press Associations (UP) and put it on the way to becoming one of the major world news services. Again, it must be emphasized that the Scripps-sponsored UP had no relationship whatever to the former UP of 1882–97.

Meanwhile, the Associated Press of Illinois made steady gains after its formation in 1893. It was to meet a new challenge, however, not unrelated to the Laffan vendetta. The *Chicago Inter-Ocean,* a member of the API, was sold in November 1897 to a group headed by Charles T. Yerkes, a Chicago utilities operator, whose methods had outraged citizens. He was opposed by all the city newspapers, and bought the *Inter-Ocean* to gain at least one friendly voice.

To edit the *Inter-Ocean* under its new management, George Wheeler Hinman was brought to Chicago from the staff of the *New York Sun.* Hinman directed editorial attacks at Lawson and his papers, and at the API, of which Lawson then was president. Hinman also subscribed at once to the full service of the Laffan News Bureau for the *Inter-Ocean.* This was contrary to regulations approved by the membership of the API, which judged the Laffan service to be "antagonistic." The result was that the *Chicago Inter-Ocean* was suspended from membership in the API in 1898 and denied its service.

Hinman and the *Inter-Ocean* had anticipated this move and promptly obtained an injunction in Illinois courts restraining the API from stopping the news report. Further, the court was asked to deny the right of the API to bar its members from subscribing to other services, including that of the Laffan News Bureau. The court also was asked to deny the right of the API to withhold news service from any newspaper wishing to receive and to pay for it.

The API defense was based on its status as a nonprofit, cooperative organization. As such, its operating costs were borne on a pro rata basis by member papers, with due allowance for variations in size and circulation. Apart from the world report received from Reuter, its news was gathered by member papers themselves and exchanged, or was gathered by correspondents engaged and paid by the organization to serve it as staff or stringer representatives. Its members determined the conditions under which it was operated.

The member papers of this cooperative association were required to vote upon the applications of new papers for membership. As with the WAP, any member newspaper had the privilege of protesting approval of an application for membership submitted by another paper in the same city, and such a protest normally would be supported by other members. This was held justified on the grounds that the service possessed a commercial value in a competitive situation. Denials of membership also were deemed reasonable because many new papers were short-lived and the policy, even in a noncompetitive situation, was to wait until a paper gave promise of survival before being accepted into membership. Some papers, further, were editorially irresponsible, financially weak, and had no substantial news to contribute to the general membership. In these circumstances, the API contended, it had a right to limit its membership to newspapers demonstrably worthy, and also to set regulations—such as that relating to the Laffan News Bureau—on the basis of a majority agreement by members.

This contention of the API was upheld in the circuit court and in the appellate court. On behalf of the *Inter-Ocean*, however, Hinman appealed to the Supreme Court of Illinois. That court, on February 19, 1900, some two years after the case had been opened, reversed the decisions of the lower courts and ruled against the API and in favor of the *Inter-Ocean*.

The charter under which the API had been set up in 1892 as an Illinois corporation had stated one of its possible purposes as being "to erect, lease, or sell telegraph or telephone lines." It never had acted to do so, but the Illinois Supreme Court, in its ruling, took the position that the possibility, as so authorized, gave the association the character of a public utility. By that interpretation, it was held legally obligated to provide a service of "information and news, for purposes of publication," to any newspaper wishing to purchase it, without distinction. This decision invalidated any limitation on membership.

The court also held that any provision denying the right of members to purchase another service was in restraint of trade, and so null and void. This ruled out any ban by the association on the *Inter-Ocean* subscription to the Laffan News Bureau service. The court also ruled that the *Inter-Ocean* must be restored to membership in the API, left free to subscribe to the Laffan service, and was to be paid $40,500 by the API.

Since this was a decision of the highest court of the state in which the API had been incorporated, there was no possibility of a further appeal by that agency to the United States Supreme Court. The *Chicago Inter-Ocean* not only applied for reinstatement, but now sought to put the API into a receivership preliminary to reorganization. It also brought suit against the agency for losses it claimed to have sustained, over and above the $40,500 award, during the period since 1898. Other newspapers that had previously been denied service also demanded admission to the association.

The membership of the Associated Press of Illinois met in Chicago on May 18, 1900, to discuss what was to be done in the face of this decision. Lawson declined re-election as president, and Stone resigned as general manager. Charles Knapp, of the *St. Louis Republic,* was elected to replace Lawson as president, and Charles Sanford Diehl, by then assistant general manager, replaced Stone as manager.

The API directors, and many members felt that the court ruling requiring an open membership would destroy the chief advantage of an exclusive and comprehensive news service available to the limited membership, especially in competitive situations, which were numerous at that time. It was learned that New York State had a law permitting the establishment of nonprofit, cooperative associations allowing both a limitation of membership and the maintenance of regulations supported by vote of the membership. The law had been drafted and approved to meet the needs of social clubs, charitable organizations, and other groups not formed "for pecuniary profit." The API already was a cooperative organization not formed for pecuniary profit, and the New York law seemed to meet the requirements for a continued limited membership provision and for member-approved regulations.

The result was that a new organization was incorporated under the laws of New York State, effective on May 22, 1900. Known more simply as "The Asssociated Press," its certificate of incorporation was signed by the publishers of six newspapers. The provisions were slightly more liberal than those of the Associated Press of Illinois, but still retained limitations on membership. Melville E. Stone was recalled and designated as General Manager and Frank B. Noyes, president of the *Washington Star,* was chosen as president. Stone sent out invitations to membership, received prompt responses and, before the end of the year, 700 newspapers had accepted, including the members of the former API, except for the *Inter-Ocean.*

On September 1, 1900, the membership of the Associated Press of Illinois held its last meeting in Chicago and voted formally to disincorporate. The last API news reports went out over the wires on September 3. On September 4 the service of the new Associated Press (AP), as incorporated in New York State and with headquarters in New York City, was distributed over the same network, with 9,345 miles of leased wire by day to serve afternoon papers, and 20,467 miles at night to serve morning papers in the United States and Canada. It included the Reuter world news service, as before, and was handled by the same staff, to reach virtually the same membership. The new AP purchased the property and business of the API, which ceased to exist, officially, on September 30, 1900.[11] This change over from API to AP was contested on legal grounds by Hinman of the *Chicago Inter-Ocean* and others, but the action was upheld.

The Associated Press soon began a development, including appointment of resident correspondents in world capitals after 1902, that was to make it one of the great world news agencies, rather than merely a national agency. By the time Melville E. Stone retired as general manager in 1921, it had attained that status.

---

11 Because of the nature of the New York law under which it was incorporated, originally intended for social clubs among other organizations, the AP sometimes was referred to jocularly as "The Fish and Game Club."

New Events,
New "Powers," and a New Century

The years between 1880 and 1900 brought important changes in the world. The press shared in those changes, contributed to them, and reported them.

The spotlight shifted widely. It shone on Great Britain, as a center of empire, with political and military involvement in Egypt and the Sudan from 1882 to 1899, and in South Africa from 1899 to 1902. It was on Germany and France, both reaching for spheres of influence in Africa, Asia, and the Pacific. It touched the Balkans, again, with Greece and Turkey at war in 1897.

But the spotlight turned to the United States, then beginning an industrial growth, and at war with Spain in 1898. These developments were accompanied by an extension of the nation's interests beyond its own frontiers to the West Indies, to the Pacific and Asia, and to an unsought assumption of a new role as a "world power."

The spotlight rested also on China and Japan, both responding to the impact of the western world on their ancient cultures. Again, the press became involved in reporting a Sino-Japanese War in 1894, a crisis in China in 1900, and a significant clash in 1904-05 between the small island empire of Japan and the vast continental empire of Russia. The outcome was fateful to both countries and to the world. Japan, like the United States, gained status as a "world power," even as the fuse was set that was to bring a revolution in Russia hardly more than a decade later.

All of these developments were of major concern to the press through a period of twenty to twenty-five years. The British press, well-organized in 1880, became vastly more so. The press of the United States made a great advance, entering upon world coverage as never before. The French press, for the first time, gained real freedom in 1881. There and in Germany, Austria, and Italy some newspapers of merit developed. This was true also in Japan. The peoples were well served by some newspapers in Holland, Denmark, Norway, Sweden, Canada, Australia, New Zealand, Argentina, Brazil, Chile, and India. Government censorship often interfered seriously with press growth and performance in some other countries—Russia as a prime example. Illiteracy was a restrictive influence throughout many regions. Over great areas, also, such daily newspapers as existed were small in size, lacking in revenue, and often poorly produced.

The World Press and Wireless Communication

The world population had grown from about 906 million in 1800 to approximately 1.6 billion in 1900. The prognosis for the press and public information was favorable. One element making it so was the interest taken by the people in the publications available to them; rising circulation figures made that obvious. Another was the growing availability of educational opportunity, promising new generations of informed and competent citizens. A third element was the advance of science and technology, including that relating to communication itself.

Telegraph and cable networks, and telephony, well-established by the 1890s, were remarkable enough. Scientists had been experimenting for years, however, on what seemed to the layman the complete impossibility of communicating over distances even without wires. But by 1900, wireless telegraphy became a reality.

Scientists contributing to this new miracle included Morse and Bell, inventors of the telegraph and telephone. Others were: Pupin, Edison, Joseph Henry, and Nikola Tesla—all in the United States; James Clerk-Maxwell, Michael Faraday, A. W. Heaviside, Sir William Preece, Sir William Crookes, and Sir Oliver Lodge—all in Great Britain; Heinrich Hertz and C. A. Steinheil—German physicists; A. S. Popoff of Russia; and Andre Marie Ampère and Edouard Branly of France.

It remained, however, for Guglielmo Marconi, son of an Italian father and an Irish mother, to find the practical application of known principles by which a dot-dash code might be transmitted over distances without dependence on a wire. This he did on his father's estate near Bologna in 1895, when he was twenty-one.

Earlier experiments, among other things, had produced a method by which electric sparks might be induced to jump across a gap from one coil to another at the speed of light. Marconi, using a long antenna or aerial, and with a ground connection, was able to project the electric impulse, or electro-magnetic wave caused by such a spark, to carry a dot-dash code message over the distance of a mile and one-quarter. The oscillatory currents from the spark were there received by a "coherer" or detector, making and breaking a contact in synchronization with the dots and dashes of the spark, and thereby activating a sounder key, or a coil or diaphragm on a telephone headset.

On June 2, 1896, in Great Britain, Marconi received the first patents on wireless telegraphy. He continued his experiments in Italy and in England, where he worked with Preece and Lodge to find ways to extend the range of the signals and improve reception. On July 20, 1897, Marconi formed the Wireless Telegraph and Signal Company, and the first station for sending wireless signals was erected that year at The Needles, west of the Isle of Wight in the English Channel.

The first use of wireless for news purposes, or for any practical purpose, occurred in July 1898 when the annual Kingstown Regatta took place off the Irish coast. The Dublin *Daily Express* arranged to have reports of the progress of the race sent by wireless from a ship following the racing craft to a receiving instrument on shore, and then relayed to the newspaper office by telegraph. Marconi himself directed the experiment, which enabled the Dublin paper to publish the earliest accounts of the event.

As London correspondent at the time for the *New York Herald,* Milton V. Snyder called the Kingstown experiment to the attention of Bennett, known as an avid yachtsman. Bennett responded by arranging for Marconi to visit the United States in 1899 and to be paid $5,000 for a similar coverage for the *Herald* of the America's Cup Race, off Sandy Hook. The Associated Press of Illinois also arranged with Marconi to receive reports of that race from a second following vessel, at an expenditure of $25,000. The payments helped Marconi finance his continuing experiments.

The coverage of the America's Cup Race was less successful than that of the Kingstown Regatta because the signals from the two following vessels, broadcast on the same wavelength, set up an interference and were unreadable by the shore-based receiving sets. The result was that neither the *Herald* nor the API derived any value from their attempts to provide early reports of the race.

These trials demonstrated that the wireless signals radiated in all directions from the antenna and lost strength as they traveled, so the range was limited. It was learned, too, that signals carried better in the dark hours of the night or when the sky was overcast, but faded in the sunlight or when the sky was clear. These were difficulties to be overcome.

Meanwhile, Marconi cooperated with Lloyd's of London to develop communication between ships, and from ship-to-shore, thus establishing a basis for increased safety at sea. The first instance of a ship in distress receiving aid through the use of wireless signals occurred on March 3, 1899, in British waters, and the practice of equipping vessels with wireless began in that year.

A Marconi International Marine Communication Company was formed in 1900, with shore stations established. Marconi's Wireless Telegraph and Signal Company, as formed in 1897, also was reorganized in 1900 as the British Marconi Wireless Telegraph Company, with James A. Fleming as its chief engineer. A more powerful transmitting station was built at Poldhu, on the Cornwall coast in England, to conduct experiments in transatlantic communication.

These experiments began in 1901, with the Poldhu station undertaking to communicate with a station set up at St. John's, Newfoundland, and another later at Glace Bay, Nova Scotia. The first faint signals were heard at St. John's on December 21, 1901. The Reuter, Havas, and Stefani news agencies experimented with the use of wireless in 1901 and 1902. It was December 1902 before the first complete messages were transmitted between Poldhu and Glace Bay, and then only at night, when the signals gained strength.

A Marconi Wireless Telegraph Company of America was formed in 1901, with a station constructed on Cape Cod at Wellfleet on the Massachusetts coast. In 1903 news messages were sent experimentally, for a brief period, from the Wellfleet station to Poldhu for publication in the *Times* of London. Under favorable conditions, the transmission could be received on a siphon recorder at a rate of 150 words a minute. But weak or uncertain signals continued to make long-distance wireless communication difficult for some years, and it was 1907 before transatlantic transmission became reasonably satisfactory.

It was possible, earlier, to send wireless messages between ship and shore, and to relay messages from one ship to another. This method enabled the Marconi organization, in another experiment, to provide a service of brief news items to ships at sea in 1904, and some Atlantic liners presented passengers with daily news sheets mimeographed or printed on board.

The great development of wireless communication came in the first decades of the twentieth century, and became the basis for radiotelegraphy, radio broadcasts of voice and sound, radiotelephony, phototransmission, television, and satellite transmission of voice, sound, and pictures.

Egypt and the Sudan, 1882-99

British military campaigns in Egypt and the Sudan through the years from 1882 to 1899 bracketed other events, including a Sino-Japanese War from 1894-95, military actions in Crete, India, and Madagascar, the Greco-Turkish War in 1897, and the Spanish-American War of 1898. All received direct press coverage in a notable extension of enterprise. The complex situation in Egypt and the Sudan was the first of these matters to demand attention.

The power of Turkey in Egypt ended after 1841. Mohammed Said, the khedive or governor from 1854 to 1863, supported liberal reforms, established relations with European powers and began a modernization of the country. This was carried forward by Ismail, khedive from 1863 to 1879. Steps were taken to suppress slavery, schools multiplied, agriculture advanced, and a great program of public works was undertaken. Railroads and telegraph lines were extended, cable connections established, and the Suez Canal opened in 1869.

Egypt was prosperous in the 1860s as British textile manufacturers turned to it for cotton supplies not then available from the United States because of the Civil War. But the khedive had borrowed heavily, at high interest rates, from Great Britain and France to finance the public works program. The national debt had become so great by 1875 that the khedive sold the controlling shares in the Suez Canal Company to the British government. British and French officials were appointed to exercise control over the country's finances. Egypt won a war with Ethiopia in 1875-79, but this did nothing to restore the financial situation, and discontent resulted in the deposition of the khedive in 1879 and his replacement by his son, Tewfik.

Discontent continued, an anti-foreign sentiment arose, and a strong nationalist movement developed in 1881, with army support. The khedive, under pressure, appealed to France and Great Britain for aid. In response, British and French naval squadrons appeared at Alexandria in May 1882. Riots in that city were fatal to about fifty Europeans. The port was bombarded by the British and troops were landed, with another force sent to protect the Suez Canal. Cairo was occupied in September.

In the general rebellion against the Cairo government, the Mahdi Mohammed Ahmed of Dongola sought to win control of the Sudan and ports on the Red Sea. The very large Sudan area had been conquered by Egypt in 1820-22, the objective then being to find gold and obtain slaves. The British now recommended that Egypt withdraw from the Sudan. General Charles Gordon, popularly known as "Chinese Gordon" because of successes in campaigns in China in 1860-64, but with experience also in Egypt, was sent in 1884 with a force to evacuate the Egyptian garrisons in the Sudan. From Khartoum, he attempted to negotiate with the Mahdi. The Mahdi paid slight attention, continued with his own campaigns and in January 1885 took Khartoum, killed Gordon, and massacred the garrison. A relief expedition sent from Cairo arrived too late.

Meanwhile, some order had been brought into the Egyptian financial situation and the conduct of the Suez Canal. But France, which had been an increasingly reluctant participant, withdrew at the end of 1882, and pursued a policy sometimes contrary to British interests. Great Britain had concluded by 1887 that it must remain strongly represented in Egypt.

Abbas Hilmi II, who became khedive in January 1892, resented the British presence. A clash of wills led to an assertion of full British authority in January 1893, with the military forces of occupation increased. By 1896, the British also had reconsidered the need for control of the Sudan, judging it important as relating to an assured Nile water supply, vital for agriculture in Egypt. They were aware, too, that the French were moving upon the Sudan from the southwest, by way of the Congo and Central Africa, where they had by then established a colonial position.

In those new circumstances, General Sir Horatio Herbert Kitchener (later Lord Kitchener) undertook the reconquest of the Sudan in 1896. Dongola was taken in September and the advance proceeded, although with great deliberation. The decisive battle occurred at Omdurman in September 1898, and Khartoum was retaken.

The Kitchener forces then advanced to Fashoda (now Kodok), on the Nile, where French forces were found in occupation. This was a new crisis. The British insisted that the French should leave the Sudan, which they did, under threat of war, but with an Anglo-French hostility created that was not eased until 1904. An Anglo-Egyptian Sudan was formally established in January 1899.

This sequence of events between 1882 and 1899 was reported by correspondents for the British press, almost exclusively. It was not war reporting alone, since it had political and economic aspects as well. British concern with Egypt rested largely upon the protection of the Suez Canal as a "lifeline" to India, China, and the Pacific, and on its key position in cable connections between British shores and Asia, Australasia, and the east coast of Africa. Concern extended to the position of Turkey in the area, and to Russian and German aspirations in the Mediterranean and Middle East and their possible encroachment upon British interests in India, as well as to the French and German positions in Africa. Quite apart from the coverage of military action, these were continuing subjects for the British press and, indeed, for the press of other countries.

The Reuter agency was represented in Egypt by Joseph Schnitzler, with headquarters in Alexandria. Fergus Ferguson, moved from Constantinople to Cairo for Reuter at this period. Georges Vayssié represented the Agence Havas. Charles Frederick Moberly Bell represented the *Times* in Alexandria from 1882 until 1890, when he was called to London to become managing director of the paper. Edward Cant-Well, formerly of the *Standard*, was in Cairo for the *Times* for several months before moving to London in 1884 as head of the paper's foreign department. Frank le Poer Power, who had reported the Russo-Turkish War for a Dublin newspaper, went to Egypt in 1883 with Edmund O'Donovan of the *Daily News* to collaborate with him on a book, but he was to succeed Cant-Well as correspondent for the *Times*. It was in 1890 that Egypt became an exclusive territory for the distribution of the Reuter service, with Havas withdrawing in exchange for exclusive rights in Indo-China.

The disorders in Alexandria in 1882 made that port city a hazardous place in which to work. Schnitzler moved to Cairo, but certain news operations had to continue at Alexandria because it was the cable head. Most of the military operations were in the Sudan, however, with two periods of particular action, the first from 1883 to 1885, and the second from 1896 to 1898. For the press, as for the military command, they were difficult campaigns, hard and dangerous to report, with six correspondents killed and others wounded. They also were costly, with cable charges at fifteen shillings (about $3) a word to London at the regular rate, although the press rate was lower.

The Sudan campaign began with the Battle of El Obeid in November 1883 when an Egyptian force of 10,000 under British command was annihilated by forces under the Mahdi. This battle received no direct press coverage. When General Gordon led his forces to Khartoum in 1884, however, he was accompanied by a considerable group of correspondents.

Gordon knew the area well. He had administered the Sudan and the upper Nile area in 1874-76 and, after an interval in Cairo, again in 1877-79. He had been recalled to London at that time, and his return to the Sudan in 1884 actually came too late to repair the damage that had been done during his five-year absence. Nor did he receive the support he required either from Cairo or London. The Mahdi's attack on Khartoum came in January 1885 and besieging dervishes overwhelmed the inadequate defense forces in bloody fighting. A relief force under General Garnet Joseph Wolseley, commander of the successful expedition against the Ashantis in the Gold Coast in 1873-74, arrived two days after the city had fallen, with Gordon and many others dead.

Among correspondents reporting the Khartoum campaign, five were killed. They were Edmund O'Donovan of the *Daily News,* Frank Vizetelly of the *Graphic,* Frank le Poer Power of the *Times,* John Alexander Cameron of the *Standard,* and St. Leger Herbert of the *Morning Post.* Two were wounded—Bennet Burleigh of the *Daily Telegraph* and Melton Prior of the *Illustrated London News.* James J. O'Kelly, of the *Daily News,* missing for a month, reappeared.

The campaign did not end with the disaster at Khartoum. The surviving forces under Wolseley engaged the dervish army in June and killed the Mahdi. A sixth correspondent was lost in this period—British-born Hubert Howard, writing for the *New York Herald.*

These six correspondents killed in the Sudan were later to be commemorated in the crypt of St. Paul's Cathedral in London, which also shelters the bust of William Howard Russell and memorials to other British correspondents who became casualties in later wars.

From 1885 to 1896 a frontier between Egypt and the Sudan was maintained by dervish forces under the Khalifa Abdullah el Taashi, successor to the Mahdi. With the British campaign to recover the Sudan, under forces commanded by Kitchener between 1896 and

1899, a new period of difficulty arose. In the final year of the conflict, an Anglo-Egyptian army attack was directed at Omdurman, on the west bank of the Nile, opposite Khartoum, and very slightly north. A large city today, it was hardly more than a village in 1898, but a center from which the dervish army had moved against Khartoum, and a place where European captives of that action were held prisoner. The battle there was the decisive victory for Kitchener's forces. The Khalifa was pursued farther south, defeated, and killed.

The correspondents reporting this aspect of the war included Burleigh and Prior, witnesses of all the battles in which British troops were engaged in Egypt and the Sudan between 1882 and 1898. Other correspondents arriving for the 1896-98 campaign included Lionel James of Reuter, formerly in India; H. A. Gwynne, also for Reuter; George Warrington Steevens of the *Daily Mail*; and Winston Churchill for the *Morning Post*.

Churchill, then twenty-four, was an officer with the Twenty-first Lancers serving in cavalry action near Omdurman. It was the third occasion on which he had written for a newspaper while on military assignment. Commissioned at Sandhurst in 1895, he had become a member of the Fourth Hussars. While on leave in that same year, he had visited Cuba as an observer of Spanish military action against local insurrectionists seeking independence from Spain, and he wrote of his observations for the London *Daily Graphic*, established in 1890 and unrelated to the illustrated weekly *Graphic*. Assigned to India in 1896-97 with the Thirty-first Punjab Infantry, active in the Malakand and Tirah expeditions on the northwest frontier, he had written for the *Daily Telegraph*—his articles signed "From a Young Officer"— and he also wrote as a war correspondent for the *Pioneer* of Allahabad.[1]

The campaign of 1896-98 proceeded slowly, in part because Kitchener moved at a pace determined by the construction of a railroad to move men and supplies southward. Until the Battle of Omdurman on September 2, 1898, there were only two military engagements, one in August 1897 and the other in April 1898.

---

1 George Warrington Steevens had been in India for the *Daily Mail* at the same period. On the basis of his experience in India, Churchill wrote the first of many books, *The Story of the Malakand Field Force* (1898). The second related his experiences and observations in the Sudan, *The River War, an Historical Account of the Reconquest of the Soudan* (1899). In Egypt, Steevens wrote an article about Churchill himself. Titled "The Youngest Man in Europe," it predicted a bright future for the young officer-correspondent.

Schnitzler, in a letter to the Reuter London office at the time, remarked that "The work of the war correspondent appears to be journalism no longer, but simply horsemanship." The same comment, reflecting the need to get about an area and to carry dispatches back to a telegraph point, might have been made at least as early as the American Civil War.

Among other correspondents covering the Egyptian-Sudan action were such veterans as LeSage and Drew Gay of the *Daily Telegraph,* Villiers of the *Graphic,* and Harry H. S. Pearce and J. C. Chapman, both of the *Daily News.*

The youngest correspondent was an adventurous Australian of eighteen, John Revelstoke Rathom, writing for the *Melbourne Argus.*[2] Others present included Henry Spencer Wilkinson of the *Manchester Guardian,* Charles Williams of Central News, Philip Robinson of the *Daily Chronicle,* and Ernest W. Bennett of the *Westminster Gazette.* The only representation for the press of the United States was by John Foster Bass for the *Chicago Record,* beginning a long career.

The Egyptian and Sudan campaigns, and the circumstances underlying military action, were of special concern to the British public. But the drama of some of the episodes, particularly the loss of Khartoum in 1885, its reconquest in 1898, and the confrontation at Fashoda, captured world attention.

Incidental to the first part of the campaign was an advance in news communication. The Reuter agency in London made use of the telephone to relay reports on Khartoum in 1885, and the arrival of the relief forces. This news, as it reached the Reuter office, was telephoned to the Press Association, with the Press Association also telephoning the bulletins to provincial newspapers. It was perhaps the first such use of the telephone for news dissemination.

---

2   Rathom later made a career in the United States. He was a correspondent for the *Chicago Herald* during the Spanish-American War in 1898, going later as a member of expeditions to New Guinea and Alaska. Back in Chicago, he became managing editor of what by then had become the *Chicago Record-Herald.* In 1910 he became managing editor of the *Providence Journal* in Rhode Island, and then its editor and general manager, and a director of the Associated Press. He also was a stringer for the *Daily Telegraph* and wrote for other newspapers and periodicals prior to his death in 1923.

China and Japan held news interest and importance by 1890 for certain persons in European countries and in the United States. Trade and finance, missionary and educational concerns had established ties drawn closer by the improved communication and transportation facilities. Special attention turned to the area when China and Japan went to war in 1894.

Imperial China, for some years, had been seeking to make Korea (or Chosen) a dependency and a buffer against possible aggression by Japan. For its part, Japan had recognized the independence of Korea, even though its government was weak and corrupt. To bolster that government, while undertaking to advance its own position there, China had sent several military expeditions into the country, a peninsula extending southward from its own Manchurian province. Japan also had been encouraged by other Korean elements to assist in that country's development. China and Japan had been in conflict there in 1884-85, but both had withdrawn.

An insurrection in Korea early in 1894 brought an appeal from Korea's King Kojong for Chinese aid, and a small force was sent. In accordance with the 1885 agreement, China informed Japan that these troops were being sent. Japan, without invitation, sent a larger force to Korea, also calling for reforms in the government. The insurrection was promptly at an end in Korea even as Chinese forces moved in. China was prepared to withdraw, but Japan insisted that the reforms should be made first. Over this issue hostilities arose and the Japanese attacked the palace in Seoul, seized the king and declared war on China on August 1, 1894.

Battles were fought at Ping-yang, near Port Arthur, and at Weihaiwei, with both the Chinese army and navy destroyed by February 1895. A treaty of peace in April gave Japan control over Formosa and the adjacent Pescadores Islands, the Liaotung peninsula in Manchuria, and the right to occupy the port of Weihaiwei, pending China's payment of a large indemnity. The independence of Korea also was recognized.

The war was short, but it was the first in Asia to receive press coverage. Japanese correspondents moved outside the boundaries of their own country for the first time, except for the token coverage of the 1874 Formosa incident. At least four newspapers were represented, *Jiji Shimpo*, *Hochi*, and *Kokumin*, all of Tokyo, and *Mainichi* of Osaka. In China, the vernacular press was as yet undeveloped.

Coverage for the world press was provided by stringers and a few special correspondents, but they were not permitted with the Chinese forces, and Japan did not make their work easy. They therefore reported largely from Tokyo, Peking, and Tientsin, utilizing such limited sources as were available. Correspondents were present at Port Arthur in December, however, and observed a Japanese massacre of the population.

Reuter had stringers in Peking and Tokyo. For the *Times,* Archibald Ross Colquhoun was staff correspondent in Peking, Thomas Cowen of the *China Times* in Tientsin was stringer there, Captain Frank Brinkley and a Colonel Palmer both served the paper as stringers in Tokyo. Valentine Chirol, Berlin correspondent for the *Times,* made a special journey to China, where he had been earlier for the *Standard.*

For the *Graphic,* Frederic Villiers, following a visit to the United States in 1893-94, hastened to China. James Creelman, formerly with the *New York Herald* in Paris and London, arrived as a correspondent for the *New York World.* Stephan Bonsal arrived for the *Herald and Julian Ralph for the New York Sun,* the latter on his first assignment outside the United States.

As the Sino-Japanese War was drawing to a close, attention turned to Russia. There Czar Alexander III, whose coronation had been reported in 1883 by a small group of correspondents, died November 1, 1894. He was succeeded by his son, who became Nicholas II. His coronation at Moscow in May 1896 was carried out with great ceremony. But on this occasion about 300 correspondents were present. It was the largest concentration of newsmen ever assembled up to that time to report a single event, whether in war or peace, and also represented a national diversity reflecting growing attention to international affairs.

Villiers, who had reported the coronation of Alexander III thirteen years before, again represented the *Graphic.* Wallace, head of the *Times* foreign department, who had started his journalistic career in 1877 as that paper's St. Petersburg correspondent, was present. British-born Aubrey Stanhope wrote for the *New York Herald.* Edwin Arnold, scholarly veteran of the *Daily Telegraph,* wrote for that paper and also for the *New York Herald.* Dillon, the *Daily Telegraph*'s Russian correspondent, was in the group. The Associated Press of Illinois had Oscar Watson in Moscow, and the United Press, nearing its inglorious end, sent Louis H. Moore.

One of the younger generation of correspondents in Moscow was an American, Richard Harding Davis. He was to become a colorful and almost fabulous journalistic figure in the next two decades, a symbol for many Americans, at least, of what a "foreign correspondent" should be. Already known in the United States as a writer of news, magazine articles, fiction and books, and as an editor, Davis, then thirty-three, arrived in Moscow designated as "high commissioner" for the *New York Journal.* This pretentious title sometimes was used at that period to give a semblance of diplomatic status to a working reporter on a foreign assignment. Whether it was the title, or Davis's personal appearance and manner—handsome, well-dressed, arrogant or charming, as suited the occasion, and always enterprising—he was one of only eight correspondents admitted to the small Church of the Assumption, within the walls of the Kremlin, to witness the coronation ceremony. One other American correspondent was admitted and, ironically, it was Moore of the UP, rather than Watson of the more important API.

Davis was one of the first successful journalists and "personalities" engaged by William Randolph Hearst to gain public attention and readership for the *New York Journal.*[3] His first assignment was what later would be called a "sidebar" story on the drama and color surrounding the Yale-Princeton football game of 1895. His second assignment for the *Journal* was the coverage of the Moscow coronation.

In addition to the ceremony itself, there were colorful events and pageantry to report. One such event turned to tragedy when great crowds, gathered to receive traditional commemorative bounties granted by the new czar, were so poorly directed that 3,000 persons literally were crushed to death in the streets.

Immediately following his Moscow assignment, Davis went to Budapest for the *Journal* to cover that city's millennial celebration, along with other correspondents. He then went to Cuba to cover the

---

3 Davis had started his journalistic career on the *Philadelphia Record* in 1886 at twenty-two, moved to the *Philadelphia Press* later in the year, and to the New York *Evening Sun* in 1889, hired by Arthur Brisbane as a reporter. Within a year he had established a reputation through a series of features for the paper, and through the first of a spate of short stories for *Scribner's* magazine. From December 1890 until 1894, he was editor of *Harper's Weekly,* and from 1892 to 1896, two years after resigning his editorship, he traveled in Europe, Central America, and elsewhere writing for the magazine on topical subjects, and turning his experiences and his fancies into books of personal narrative and short stories.

unrest there, as local insurrectionists sought to free the island from Spain's control. This was a matter given special emphasis by the *Journal,* but Davis also wrote of what he observed for *Harper's Weekly.* Shortly afterward, he was in London, along with Mark Twain—both writing for the *Journal* of Queen Victoria's Diamond Jubilee ceremonies of 1897.

Archibald Forbes, living quietly in London from 1880 to the time of his death in 1900, is said to have opened many a conversation with the remark that "There'll be trouble in the Balkans in the spring." Frequently enough, there was, whether in the spring or the summer. It had been true in 1876 and 1877—with Forbes himself present—in 1885, 1886, and 1888. It was true in 1897, as it would be on later occasions.

The Greco-Turkish War of 1897 occurred after revolutionists in Crete, restive for a year or more in their opposition to Turkish rule there, sought to put the island under Greek control. It was to report those events that Dillon of the *Daily Telegraph* moved about in Crete at this period, sometimes in disguise, as mentioned earlier, to avoid Turkish control and censorship. It was in support of the revolutionists that Greece declared war on Turkey, and a five weeks' conflict (April 17 to May 21) ended in the defeat of the Greek forces.

A considerable group of correspondents covered the brief war. They were with both armies. Most represented the British press, as in virtually every previous war situation. But the *New York Journal* had more representatives than any other one newspaper or news agency. It was evidence of the growth and enterprise of the press of the United States to find four of its newspapers represented. In addition to some veterans of war coverage, there were a number of men new to the craft who would see other wars.

In charge of coverage for the *New York Journal* was John Foster Bass, a Chicagoan who had started his international news reporting activity accompanying British forces in Egypt in 1894. He also had been in Crete prior to 1897 to report on the earlier insurrections there. In those ventures, he was acting for the *Chicago Record,* but then was engaged by Hearst to represent the *Journal.*

Not only was Richard Harding Davis to accompany Greek forces for the *Journal* and the London *Times,* but so was another "name" writer engaged by the *Journal.* This was Stephen Crane, author of *The Red Badge of Courage* (1895), the well-received and classic story of the Civil War. Crane also wrote for the *Westminster Gazette* of London. A friend, Cora Taylor, accompanied him on this assignment, and even signed two or three dispatches for the *Journal*, using the pseudonym "Imogene Carter," although it is possible that Crane was the true author.

Two other *Journal* correspondents were present, both among Hearst's acquisitions from other papers—James Creelman, formerly of the *New York Herald* and, more recently, the *New York World*, and Julian Ralph of the *New York Sun*. Both had been among those reporting the Sino-Japanese War of 1894. Creelman had been in Russia and Cuba since that time, and Ralph had been in London for the *Journal* since 1895.

Ralph accompanied the Turkish army, and Creelman was with both the Turks and the Greeks. While with the Turks, Creelman took a photographer with him, for it had at last become possible to reproduce photographs in newspapers. While with the Greeks, he spent some time with King George.

For the *New York World*, Sylvester Scovel was on his first war assignment, as was Davis for the *Journal*, and Frederick Palmer, then twenty-four, and London correspondent since 1895 for the *New York Press*. A fourth newcomer to war reporting was Percival Phillips, then only twenty, and formerly of the *Pittsburgh Press*. He was a free-lance writer or stringer for the *Chicago Inter-Ocean*. Both Palmer and Phillips were to continue for many years as correspondents, especially in wars, with Phillips becoming identified with the British press and receiving a knighthood for his service with the *Daily Express* during World War I.

For the British press, professional war correspondents were in the field again. They included Prior of the *Illustrated London News;* Francis A. (Frank) Scudmore of the *Daily News;* and Villiers representing the *Standard*, rather than the *Graphic*, on this occasion. W. T. Maud represented the *Graphic*.

Dillon of the *Daily Telegraph* has been mentioned. Bennet Burleigh, also of the *Daily Telegraph*, who was in Egypt and the Sudan at this period, spent most of the five weeks' war with the Greeks, as a change from the Sudan.

For the *Times*, James David Bourchier, resident Balkan correspondent, normally based at Sofia, moved to Athens for the war period. Clive Bingham was with the Turks for the paper. With the Greeks, in addition to Davis, there was Edward Frederick Knight, an adventurer who had been traveling about the world since 1870. He began writing for the *Times* in 1891, reporting a British military expedition in Kashmir, and also had reported the French seizure of the island of Madagascar in 1895.

The *Daily Mail,* only started as a London morning paper in 1896 by Alfred Harmsworth, also was represented.[4] In creating a staff for the *Daily Mail,* Harmsworth engaged George Warrington Steevens, described as one of the most brilliant young men of his generation at Oxford. He might have become a classical scholar, but elected journalism instead, and went to the *Pall Mall Gazette* in 1893 and moved to the *Daily Mail* when it was established in 1896.

Steevens was sent to the United States to report the McKinley-Bryan presidential campaign of that year. In 1897 he wrote from Germany. To report the Greco-Turkish War, he was attached to the Turkish forces—his first war assignment. He went next to India, later in 1897, to report the expeditions on the northwest frontier, where he met Churchill. Both were in the Sudan for the Omdurman campaign of 1898.

For the *Daily Chronicle,* Henry W. Nevinson, with the Greeks, was on his first foreign assignment. Charles Williams, formerly in Egypt for Central News, represented the paper with the Turks. The *Chronicle,* dating from 1877, attained some distinction from the 1890s onward. In 1896 it paid Dr. Fridtjof Nansen £4,000 ($19,440) for exclusive publication of that Norwegian explorer's personal account of an 1893-96 expedition seeking to reach the North Pole.

John B. Atkins, later the chief biographer of William Howard Russell, was present during the Greco-Turkish War for the *Manchester Guardian.* William Miller represented the *Morning Post,* for which he was to write later from Rome for many years. W. Kinnaird Rose, H. A. Gwynne, W. H. G. Werndel, and Fergus Ferguson reported the war from both sides for the Reuter agency. The latter three also were in Egypt and the Sudan, both before and after the Greco-Turkish War.

Even though Greece and Turkey were the adversaries, there seems to be no record of newspapers of either country having had

---

4 As with Hearst and his *New York Journal,* Harmsworth (later Lord Northcliffe) made the *Daily Mail* the first of the British "popular" daily newspapers. Both were aggressive papers in matters of news coverage at home and abroad, in editorial policy, and in attaining the million mark in circulation. Harmsworth already had made a success with a weekly publication, *Answers to Correspondents,* started in 1888, and with the London *Evening News,* purchased in 1894 and converted from near-failure to prosperity. Both men added newspapers and periodicals to their holdings.

representatives in the field. Their newspapers were not strongly developed at the time, and it may be assumed that whatever they published was provided from official government sources, or came from Havas and Reuter, which shared both countries for the distribution of news.

Oddly, no German, Austrian, or Italian correspondents appear to have been present in the field and, less surprisingly, no Russian journalist. For the French press, however, Pierre Mills wrote for the *Journal des Débats*. The Agence Havas received reports from Gaston Chadourne, its Athens correspondent, who also moved with Greek forces, and from a M. DuBois, its Vienna correspondent, who went to Constantinople to report from the Turkish side.

The French press, with more freedom and enterprise since 1881, and with the Agence Havas increasingly active, still did not match the British press, even in areas where French interests were greater. This had been illustrated in Indo-China in 1885, with Archibald Ross Colquhoun of the *Times* providing better coverage than Havas or any Paris newspaper. It was illustrated again in 1895 when French forces moved into Madagascar.

That large island off the east coast of Africa had been a French naval base and a protectorate since 1642. The French military invasion of 1895 made it a colony of France—until 1960, when it became the independent Malagasy Republic. French correspondents accompanied the 1895 expedition, but were poorly equipped. They refrained as a matter of economy from using the telegraph or cable, and depended on Havas to provide basic news accounts. Finally they left the expedition altogether, after a dispute with the French commander, General J. C. Duchesne, and returned to France before the military objective had been attained. In this situation, the only correspondent who remained to the end of the 1895-96 campaign was a Herr Wolff, representing the *Berliner Tageblatt*. His reports were of good quality, but the best general accounts were provided by British correspondents, especially Edward Frederick Knight of the *Times*.

A number of the larger Paris dailies acting individually at this period in the 1890s innovated a system of *grand reportage* that had importance and was adopted and adapted elsewhere. Under this system a qualified member of a newspaper's staff would make a thorough investigation of some particular subject, area, or country. He was under no pressure to meet a deadline, and his investigation or research might take any form suitable to the need, with whatever travel might be required. Only after he had completed his investigation would he begin to write. Thus there never was any question of daily reports or the use of telegraph, cable, or even mail. What resulted was a series of well-researched articles, substantive in character, and of such quality as often to warrant later republication in book form.

This was a system used then and later by such Paris dailies as *Le Temps, Le Journal des Débats, Le Matin, Le Petit Parisien, l'Echo de Paris, Le Journal, Le Petit Journal,* and others. It was a system adopted by some newspapers in other countries, particularly in Europe. It was a forerunner of "team reporting" by some newspapers of the United States in the mid-twentieth century, with two or more correspondents collaborating on a major subject requiring investigations in various countries. It also had its obvious relationship to what became known later as "depth reporting," with writers going thoroughly into the background and meaning of a topic.

The decade of the 1890s closed with two major military campaigns, the Spanish-American War of 1898, and the South African (or Boer) War of 1899-1902. Echoes of the Sino-Japanese War of 1894-95 also were to relate to a "Boxer" rebellion in China in 1900-01 and to the Russo-Japanese War of 1904-05. A significant legal issue in France, the Dreyfus trial of 1899, was another event that occasioned world interest.

It was a period that marked a kind of transition between two generations of newsmen, those who had pioneered and those who were to carry forward the process of public information. It also brought new place-names, or datelines, into the consciousness of readers, and extended their mental horizons. At the time, stress may have seemed to go to "more wars," but much else was reported. For those with the wit to see it, significance attached to many such reports.

The Spanish-American War and the Philippines (1898-1903)

The Spanish-American War and its immediate aftermath had the effect of shaking the government and people of the United States out of what had been an almost exclusive, although understandable, preoccupation with domestic interests. At the same time, it established the United States in the eyes of the world as a nation suddenly become a first-class power. It stimulated a far greater attention by the press of the United States to international affairs, and resulted in more attention being given to the United States by the press of other lands.

The West Indies had been important to the United States from colonial times, figuring in trade and commerce. The activity of pirates in the area was a serious problem for many years, combatted by British and U.S. naval forces. The Monroe Doctrine of 1824 was relevant, as was the presence during the Civil War of French troops in Mexico and the establishment of Maximilian as a puppet emperor there from 1864–67.

A potentially serious situation also arose in 1896 over the establishment of a proper boundary line between British Guiana and Venezuela. When it appeared that Great Britain was inclined to make territorial demands upon Venezuela, President Grover Cleveland invoked the Monroe Doctrine and some alarm arose lest the United States and Great Britain be brought into armed conflict. The *New York World* undertook to smooth relations between the two countries, and was credited with helping to solve a delicate problem. The *New York Journal* managed to obtain in London an advance copy of the arbitration treaty ending the dispute in 1897, and published it ahead of ratification by the two governments.[5]

Spain's great colonial empire in the Western Hemisphere was virtually ended in the 1820s, but Cuba and Puerto Rico remained under the Spanish flag. A revolt there in 1868 had been followed by twelve years of guerrilla warfare. A critical incident of that period had been the seizure by a Spanish gunboat in 1873 of the filibusterous ship *Virginius*.

A new insurrection occurred in 1895, accompanied by a proclamation of independence. Spanish forces under General Valeriano Weyler used harsh measures to put down that rebellion. It was at this time that Winston Churchill visited Cuba. He was then twenty-one, recently out of Sandhurst, a junior officer in the British Fourth Hussars, and present as an observer with Spanish forces. He wrote also for the *Daily Graphic* of London, in his first experience as a newspaper correspondent.

---

5 A second and comparable crisis was to arise in December 1902 over a failure of Venezuela to pay certain debts owed to Great Britain, Germany, and Italy. Those countries established a naval blockade off the Venezuelan coast, bombarded Porto Cabello, sank and seized Venezuelan ships, seized the custom houses, and threatened an occupation of the country. No occupation occurred, however, and a settlement was reached in February 1903.

The interest of the people of the United States in Cuba mounted from this time, for the island was only ninety miles off the tip of Florida. There was sympathy for the Cubans themselves in their aspirations for independence, and an emotional resentment over reports of Spanish brutality. Such reports were provided in full measure, and with considerable sensationalism, by the *New York Journal,* recently purchased by Hearst, and by Pulitzer's *New York World.* The two morning papers were in sharp competition as the *Journal* sought to take circulation leadership from the *World.* Both exploited the Cuban confrontation to a degree that made Hearst and Pulitzer targets of criticism, but both papers nevertheless succeeded in winning a readership that put them over the million mark at times—a record. Their reports were widely quoted, creating a national sentiment favorable to Cuban independence and hostile to Spain.

Probably the first representative of the *New York Journal* sent to Cuba was Frederick Lawrence. Richard Harding Davis was present late in 1896 and, again, early in 1897 as among his first special assignments for the *Journal.* He was also writing for *Harper's Weekly.* Others of the first *Journal* correspondents were Charles Michelson, already experienced as a San Francisco newsman, and Frederic Remington, an artist. It was Remington who reported in 1897 that there seemed to be no war in Cuba at the time, and proposed leaving. Hearst responded in a much-quoted telegram: "Please remain. You furnish the pictures and I'll furnish the war." Karl Decker, George Eugene Bryson, and Grover Flint also wrote from Cuba for the *Journal* before the war began. Ralph D. Paine wrote both for the *Journal* and for the *Philadelphia Press.*

The *New York World* had Sylvester Scovel in Cuba, and also received reports from William S. Bowen, James Creelman, and Howard Clemens Hillegas, all between 1895 and 1898. The *New York Herald* was represented by Stephen Bonsal in 1897, and George Bronson Rae was there in the 1896-97 period. William Francis Mannix, writing under the name of "William G. Leonard," served both the *New York Times* and the *Philadelphia Press.*

The Havana correspondent for the Associated Press of Illinois was F. J. Hilbert, present throughout the critical years before the war. The *Chicago Record* undertook a sober coverage of Cuban affairs, beginning in 1897, with Crittenden Marriott in Havana, and with Trumbull White, William E. Curtis, Charles M. Faye, and British-born Charles E. Crosby all engaged in the service. Crosby was killed in March 1897, and Curtis and White soon left on other assignments.

The Spanish administration in Cuba was offended by reports appearing in the press of the United States during the 1896-98 period, and particularly by some in the *New York Journal* and *New York World,* both of which did, in fact, commit serious offenses against accuracy and fairness. A reward of $10,000 was offered for the capture of Scovel of the *World.* He was seized and held for several weeks, but was released following a demand by the U.S. Senate that he be freed.

Decker of the *Journal* was expelled from Cuba in 1897 on orders of General Weyler, but not before he had "rescued" Evangelino Cisneros, youthful niece of Salvador Cisneros Betancourt, leader of the Cuban insurrectionists. In a well-publicized exploit, Decker spirited her out of the country to New York and used her story, highly illustrated and sensationalized, to dramatize the plight of Cubans under Spanish rule.

On February 15, 1898, at a time when feeling in the United States already was high against Spain and her policy in Cuba, the U.S. battleship *Maine* exploded in Havana harbor, under mysterious circumstances, with a loss of 258 lives. Hilbert, as API correspondent in Havana, gave the disaster direct and prompt coverage. The occurrence further inflamed sentiment in the United States. Pressures were such that, in April, Congress recognized Cuba's independence and demanded that Spain give up the island. Spain rejected the ultimatum and broke off diplomatic relations with the United States. In support of its demand, Congress on April 25 declared war on Spain.

Meanwhile, U.S. naval and military forces had been mobilized and deployed against Spanish-held Cuba and nearby Puerto Rico. Halfway around the world, in the Philippine Islands, a quite separate native revolt against Spanish rule, in effect there since 1571, had occurred in 1896-97, led by Emilio Aguinaldo. Spain also held the island of Guam in the Western Pacific.

Most of the decisive action occurred in Cuba and Puerto Rico during June and July of 1898. An armistice came in August, and the war ended with the signature of the Treaty of Paris on December 10. It was a brief war, with actual conflict concentrated chiefly in two months of the seven during which it was officially in progress. With 300,000 men engaged on the U.S. side, there were only 385 battle deaths, and 1,662 wounded. Apart from ship losses, Spanish casualties were lighter. The greatest threat to life was yellow fever, which accounted for most of the 2,061 nonbattle deaths.

Short as it was, the war was reported by approximately 500 press correspondents, far more than were present on any previous occasion, in war or peace. It also was an expensive war to report.

Because the destruction of the battleship *Maine* in February 1898 made it seem likely that war would follow—as it did in April— newsmen began to move toward Cuba.

Among them were British correspondents. As neutrals, they were able to enter Cuba itself. Edward Frederick Knight of the *Times,* remained in Havana throughout the war. Poultney Bigelow, an American, also wrote for the *Times,* although not from Cuba itself. Others in Cuba at some time for the British press included John B. Atkins of the *Manchester Guardian*; George Lynch of the *Daily Chronicle*; Charles E. Hands, in the first years of a long career with the *Daily Mail*; Seppings Wright, an artist for the *Illustrated London News*; and A. Maurice Low (later Sir Maurice Low), recently appointed as U.S. correspondent for the *Morning Post,* and one of the first British correspondents to take up permanent residence in Washington, where he was to remain for many years. Coverage for Reuter was organized by S. Levy Lawson, in charge of that agency's New York bureau, and H. A. Gwynne was present briefly. But Reuter depended heavily upon its exchange arrangement with the Associated Press of Illinois, which reported the war intensively.

Those aspects of the war centering in Washington and Madrid, as capitals of the belligerent countries, were reported by resident correspondents. A censorship was in effect in Washington and in the prospective battle areas from the time the *Maine* was destroyed until the end of the war, but it presented no great problem. Madrid, however, was under heavy and effective censorship. The Agence Havas, which then also owned the Fabra agency of Spain, known at the time as the Agence Espagñol et International, provided reports from Madrid not only to its subscribing papers in France and parts of Europe, but to the press of Latin America. The Havas service went to Reuter, and the Reuter reports reached the United States through the Reuter-API association.

Correspondents in Madrid for Havas, for Reuter, for the *Times,* and for other British and European newspapers sometimes undertook to evade the Spanish censorship. British correspondents, in particular, engaged couriers to take some dispatches by hand across the border to Biarritz or Bayonne in France, whence they could be telegraphed to Paris or London without censorship. This arrangement cost as much as $2,000 a week, but the expense was shared by the U.S. press as a means of obtaining news from Spain.

As the demands of war coverage had on other occasions added new dimensions to general reporting, so the Spanish-American War may be said to have added photo-journalism, the motion picture, and magazine journalism as aids in providing a more complete understanding of events.

The half-tone process for making cuts had been sufficiently advanced to permit the reproduction of photographs in newspapers, and the correspondent group included two or more photographers. One was British-born James H. (Jimmy) Hare, who represented *Collier's* and began an active experience on various war fronts. There also was at least one motion picture photographer, J. C. Hemment of the *New York Journal*—a distinct "first" in war reporting. Some recent motion pictures had been made in the United States and Europe of events in the news, but there was as yet no means of exhibiting films to the public. And, even though there had been artist-correspondents representing periodicals on the war fronts since the Crimean War, this was the first occasion when writing correspondents were present for general magazines.

The war had interest for the people of the United States for reasons already cited, but also because sentiment had been stirred by the destruction of the battleship *Maine*, and perhaps because there had been no war directly affecting the country for a generation—not since the Civil War ended in 1865. Indeed, by some interpretations, the national unity it engendered helped to heal the breach between North and South remaining from that war. Also, there were no defeats, no long casualty lists, no huge national costs, no stalemates, and no damage done within the United States itself to detract from what Elmer Davis later characterized as "a glory story." It also was called "the most convenient war ever fought" because it was relatively near at hand, short in duration, and limited in its demands upon men and materials.

The chief problem for the press was one of communications and expense. The cables touching Cuba had been cut when the war began. Once action started in June, fast tugs were engaged as dispatch boats to ferry correspondents to the areas of conflict, and to rush their dispatches to the nearest telegraph or cable points. Such points included Key West, Florida, where messages could be telegraphed to

New York, Chicago, or elsewhere; Kingston or Port Antonio, in Jamaica; St. Thomas, in the Virgin islands; or other West Indies ports where cable transmission was available. From Jamaica the dispatches went to Halifax, Nova Scotia, for relay by telegraph to New York and then to all parts of the United States and Canada, or by cable to London, for relay to Europe and Latin America and Asia. Or they might reach New York by cable by way of Panama, Mexico, or Texas.

The owners of the tugs asked $5,000 to $6,000 a month for the use of each vessel. The *New York Journal* at one time had ten under charter at a total cost of $1,500 a day. The Associated Press of Illinois had four, and the *New York World*, the *New York Herald*, and the *New York Sun* each had from two to six. In addition to the lease cost, there were insurance fees amounting to as much as $2,200 a month on each tug, and there were substantial coaling charges.

To send a news dispatch by telegraph from Key West to New York cost about five cents a word. More reports appear to have gone by cable, however, at from fifty cents to $3.25 a word, depending upon distance and urgency. Payment commonly was demanded in gold, meaning that correspondents had to be adequately supplied in advance and, indeed, burdened with funds in that form.

The most expensive dispatch probably was one directed to the Associated Press of Illinois reporting the destruction of the main Spanish fleet, under Admiral Cervera, during an attempt to escape from the harbor of Santiago on July 3, virtually ending Spanish rule in Cuba. Sent from Kingston to New York at the urgent rate of $1.67 a word, it cost $8,000. The *New York Herald* received a dispatch on the night of July 3 reporting the same event. Running 3,000 words, filed at Port Antonio at $3.25 a word, double the commercial rate to assure immediate handling, it cost $6,500. The API commonly sent 2,000 to 6,000 words a day, and some papers received up to 5,000 words a day, which would cost about $250 even if only sent from Key West to New York by telegraph.

Adding the salaries of as many as twenty correspondents for a single paper—and one estimate was sixty or seventy for the *New York Journal*—the costs of coverage were even higher. The *Journal* is estimated to have spent $500,000 to report the short war, which was as much as the *New York Herald* had spent to produce the best coverage through four years of the Civil War. The API spent $284,000, and the *New York World*, the *New York Herald*, and the *New York Sun* were estimated to have spent $250,000 each, or more.

For the *New York Journal*, William Randolph Hearst himself, then thirty-five, was present in Cuban waters and later in Cuba to direct writers, artists, and photographers for his paper.

The *Journal* group included James Creelman, who had reported the Sino-Japanese War for the *New York World,* but had switched to the *Journal* to report the Greco-Turkish War. It included Frederic Remington, who also served *Harper's Weekly;* J. C. Hemment, pioneer newsreel motion picture cameraman; Charles Michelson, Edward Marshall, Julian Hawthorne, John Barrett, Alfred Henry Lewis, H. G. McNichol, and George Coffin. In August, Stephen Crane, who had been with the *New York World* from April to July, rejoined the *Journal*, for which he had written during the Greco-Turkish War.

Marshall lost a leg in the war. Creelman was shot in the arm during an assault on a Spanish position near El Caney on July 1. Taken to the rear, the story is that Hearst appeared beside him, equipped with pencil and notebook, took down Creelman's account of the action as he dictated it, and carried the story to the coast where one of the tugs rushed it to Jamaica for dispatch.

The Associated Press of Illinois provided a consistent coverage of the Cuban campaign under supervision of Charles Sanford Diehl, assistant manager. It was characterized later by Melville E. Stone, the general manager, as the agency's "first notable achievement."

Among a score of correspondents for the API were John P. Dunning, who had reported the disastrous Samoan hurricane in 1889 for the Western Associated Press and also had reported the Chilean Civil War in 1891; Oscar Watson, who had reported the coronation of Czar Nicholas II in Moscow in 1896; and Reuben Briggs Davenport, who had reported the Indian wars for the *New York Herald*.

Other API correspondents included Elmer E. Roberts, later to serve the Associated Press in Europe for a quarter-century; Howard N. Thompson and British-born W. A. M. Goode (later Sir William Goode), both destined for important European assignments, and Goode later for a British diplomatic career. Still others were A. W. Lyman, George E. Graham, Harrison L. Beach, Alfred Cecil Goudie, Harold Martin, Nathaniel C. Wright, Albert C. Hunt, J. B. Nelson, and Arthur W. Copp. Beach was seriously wounded during the fighting, but recovered. Lyman died of yellow fever.

Goode was aboard Admiral William T. Sampson's flagship, the *New York*, when the Spanish fleet was destroyed. 'Graham was aboard Commodore Winfield Scott Schley's battleship during the same action.

Edward L. Keen was on assignment to report the war for the Scripps-McRae Press Association formed in 1897. Keen was beginning a lifetime of news activity, primarily in Europe, in the service of the Scripps enterprises.

The *New York World* war staff was directed by Henry C. Cary. It included Scovel, described as a "special commissioner" for the paper. Captured before the war and held for several weeks by the Spanish administrators of Cuba, because of reports he had written that offended them, Scovel also offended the U.S. military leadership. He attempted to punch General William R. Shafter in the nose at the time of a U.S. flag-raising ceremony following the surrender of Santiago on July 17, because Shafter refused to permit him to be included in the official victory photograph.

Other *World* correspondents in Cuba included Louis Seibold; George Bronson Rae, who had been there for the *New York Herald* before the war; Ralph D. Paine, also in Cuba before the war for the *New York Journal* and the *Philadelphia Press*; Stephen Crane, until he returned to the *Journal*; Percival Phillips, who had his baptism of fire during the Greco-Turkish War; and Francis H. Nichols and Adolph Koeble.

The *New York Herald* staff was in charge of Howard K. Mumford and Harry Brown. It included Davis, also writing for the London *Times*, as he had during the Greco-Turkish War, and for *Scribner's* magazine. Others representing the *Herald* included Francis D. (Frank) Millet, artist, who had represented the *Herald*, and also the *Daily News* and *Graphic* of London, as early as the Russo-Turkish War of 1877-78; Stephen Bonsal, with Balkan and Sino-Japanese War experience; and Walter Scott Meriwether, Robert E. Livingston, Nicholas Biddle, and Ernest McReady.

Davis, along with Biddle, Stephen Crane, and Hare, the photographer, were witnesses of the charge of the "Rough Riders" at San Juan Hill, on July 1. Colonel Theodore Roosevelt played a part that was to give him a prominence leading indirectly to the presidency of the United States three years later. Davis also covered the campaign in Puerto Rico in late July and August.

The *New York Sun* coverage was directed by Wilbur J. Chamberlin, with Harold M. Anderson, Dana Carroll, and Walstein Root among members of his staff. Henry M. Armstong and Acton Davies represented the *Evening Sun*. Chamberlin witnessed the surrender of Santiago to General Shafter on July 17.

The *New York Evening Post* was represented by John Foster Bass, formerly on the *Journal* staff in the Greco-Turkish War; Albert Gardner Robinson, Franklin Clarkin, and "E. G. Bellairs" (a pseudonym). It provided a limited but good report. Bass was to return to the *Journal* to report the post-Cuba campaign in the Philippines.

The *New York Tribune,* which had shown so much enterprise during the Franco-Prussian War nearly thirty years before, had almost no direct coverage of the Cuban war. The *New York Times* was only emerging from a period of financial stress and not yet sufficiently vitalized to permit any direct war coverage, except as provided by Mannix, writing also for the *Philadelphia Press.* Both New York papers depended upon reports by the Associated Press of Illinois.

The *Chicago Record* had a staff of about twenty correspondents, directed from Key West by Trumbull White, who had been in Cuba for the paper in 1897, and returned after an assignment that took him to Australia and New Zealand. His wife, Katherine White, served as a nurse on a Red Cross steamer, and also acted at times as a correspondent, notably at Siboney, near Santiago, during the July action there. Other *Record* staff members were Malcolm McDowell, Henry Barrett Chamberlin, Kennett Harris, W. A. Varty, Jr., Daniel Vincent Casey, Howbert Billman, and William Schmedtzen, an artist. Even with only one dispatch boat, the paper scored well.

The *Chicago Tribune* sent Charles M. Pepper to Cuba. He had been in the Hawaiian Islands between August 1897 and early 1898, when the people of the islands indicated their desire for annexation to the United States as a territory, an action formalized in 1900. Pepper was joined by H. J. Whigham, a British-born newsman, who was wounded; Richard Henry Little, who was to have a long career with the paper; and Willis Gordon Oakley.

James O'Donnell Bennett represented the *Chicago Journal* at this time, but later served for many years in Washington for the *Chicago Tribune.* John Rathom wrote for the *Chicago Herald.* Frank Collins, in Cuba for the *Boston Journal,* died of yellow fever, as did Lyman of the API.

Magazine representatives in Cuba included Hare, a photographer for *Collier's Weekly*, with George Parsons as an assistant; Casper Whitney and British-born James Burton, a photographer, both for *Harper's Weekly*; and Frank Norris, a novelist, writing for *McClure's* magazine; and Davis who wrote for *Scribner's.*

Two women, other than Mrs. White, were accredited as correspondents: Mrs. Josephine Miles Woodward of the *Cincinnati Commercial Gazette,* and Mrs. Blake Watkins of the *Toronto Mail and Express.* They served only briefly, and Mrs. Watkins did not get beyond Key West.

Although the conclusive engagements of the Spanish-American War occurred in Cuba and surrounding waters, the first clash was in the Philippines on May 1, 1898. Seven ships of the U.S. Asiatic Squadron, under Commodore George Dewey ordered from Hong Kong, sailed into Manila Bay and put ten ships of the Spanish fleet out of action. Combined with the success of the Aguinaldo forces, it ended Spain's control of the Philippines.

War had been declared on April 25, and there had not been time for correspondents to reach the Philippines from the United States. By chance, however, three correspondents were able to join Dewey's squadron in Hong Kong, and they witnessed the Manila encounter. One was Joseph L. Stickney, a former U.S. Navy officer, who had written for the *Chicago Tribune* during the Russo-Turkish War of 1877-78, and later had become naval affairs editor for the *New York Herald.* He happened to be in Japan when war was declared. The others were Edward W. Harden of the *Chicago Tribune*, and John T. McCutcheon, a political cartoonist for the *Chicago Record.*

Harden and McCutcheon had sailed from Baltimore in January as guests aboard a new U.S. revenue cutter, the *McCulloch,* being delivered from the builder for service on the Pacific Coast. The voyage was to be a kind of holiday for the two Chicago journalists. Since the Panama Canal did not yet exist, the vessel set its course around the world by way of the Atlantic, the Mediterranean, the Suez Canal, and Singapore, and then was to cross the Pacific. The trip was rough and slow to Malta. There news was received of the destruction of the battleship *Maine.* At Singapore the cutter received orders to proceed to Hong Kong, rather than crossing the Pacific, and to attach itself to Dewey's squadron.

By the time of arrival in Hong Kong, the crisis had reached such a point that Harden made arrangements to act as correspondent for the *Chicago Tribune* and for the *New York World* to report any action in which the Asiatic Squadron might become involved. McCutcheon also received cabled instructions from the *Chicago Record* to file dispatches. From Tokyo, Stickney, as a former naval officer, meanwhile cabled Dewey to volunteer his aid, with assurances that he would send no reports to the *New York Herald* without approval, and Dewey agreed.

As the Asiatic Squadron left Hong Kong April 28, bound for the Spanish-held Philippines, Stickney was aboard Dewey's flagship, the *Olympia,* while Harden and McCutcheon remained aboard the *McCulloch.* The three were the only press representatives to witness the Battle of Manila Bay on May 1. The Spanish naval vessels and shore batteries were put out of action within a few hours. The city could have been taken, but Dewey lacked the manpower to hold it. He therefore established a blockade, which continued for three months, pending the arrival of U.S. transports bearing army units. Meanwhile, Manila remained peaceful, largely because the rebel forces under Aguinaldo had the situation in hand, were in contact with Dewey, and were backed by the guns of the U.S. ships. The city itself was not formally occupied until August 13, a day after an armistice ended the war on all fronts, including Cuba, Puerto Rico, Guam, and the Philippines.

Because of their presence with the fleet in Manila Bay, the three correspondents had a tremendous eye-witness story to report, but no immediate way to get it out. The Spanish governor general at Manila had denied Dewey the use of the cable, and Dewey therefore ordered it cut. Just before this was done, however, the British consul general in Manila had reported to London on Dewey's success, and from London the Exchange Telegraph (Extel) had put out a brief bulletin. This appeared in the London newspapers of May 2, and also in the United States and elsewhere. But details were lacking, and nothing further was available from Manila, or from any other source, for almost a week.

Ships at that time were not wireless-equipped, and the *McCulloch* was ordered to Hong Kong to carry messages from Dewey for transmission from there by cable to Washington. The cutter made the 640-mile voyage to arrive on the afternoon of Sunday, May 8. The three correspondents were aboard and had prepared their dispatches.

In the race for precedence, after landing, Harden reached the cable office first and sent a thirty-word bulletin to the *New York World* at the urgent rate of $9.90 a word, followed by an 800-word message presenting more details and dispatched at the regular rate of $1.80 a word. Copies were to be delivered to the *Chicago Tribune,* which Harden also represented. Stickney filed a bulletin at the urgent rate to the *New York Herald,* followed by a more detailed story filed at the press rate of sixty cents a word for night transmission. McCutcheon filed a bulletin at the regular rate, followed by 600 words at the press rate, both directed to the *Chicago Record*, followed in turn by a 4,500 word skeletonized follow-up cable sent at the press rate, but still at a total cost of $2,700.

The time differential between Hong Kong, New York, and Chicago, complicated by the date change at the international date line in the mid-Pacific, and affected by newspaper deadlines and relations between newspapers themselves, all combined to bring some strange reversals in the actual use of these reports, and illustrated one of the problems of handling global news, whether in times of war or of peace.

Harden's "urgent" message to the *New York World* quite properly arrived in the United States ahead of other reports. Because of the time differential and the international date line, although it was filed in Hong Kong probably at about 5 P.M. on Sunday, May 8, it reached the *New York World* office at 5:30 A.M. on Saturday, May 7. Transmission and delivery were prompt, but at the time the bulletin was received that Saturday morning edition of the *World* was already off the press, and no report appeared.

The *Chicago Tribune* had received a copy of the Harden message at approximately the same time it had reached the *World*. Located in the Central time zone, rather than the Eastern zone, Chicago had the dispatch at 4:30 A.M. their time. That was still late for publication in the Saturday morning paper, but James Keeley, managing editor of the *Tribune*, recognizing the importance of the dispatch, remade page one to use Harden's bulletin in the final edition of Saturday morning. This was the first published report of the Manila Bay action. Harden's 800-word dispatch following with more details, sent at the regular rate, did not arrive in time for Saturday morning use in either paper.

McCutcheon's sixty-word bulletin, sent at the regular rate, and the 600 words sent at press rate, and both filed in Hong Kong slightly later than Harden's "urgent" bulletin, nevertheless arrived at the *Chicago Record* office at 5:30 A.M., Chicago time, on Saturday. This was too late to use, for the Saturday morning paper was off the press by that time. The only alternative at that hour would have been for the *Record*—as for the *World* in New York with Harden's report—to produce an "Extra," but neither paper did so.

Since Victor Lawson owned both the morning *Chicago Record* and the afternoon *Chicago Daily News*, it might have seemed reasonable to use McCutcheon's reports of so important an event in the afternoon paper on Saturday. There was a standing rule, however, that neither paper used matter intended for the other, so they did not appear in the *News*. Further, the *Record* was a six-day morning paper, producing no Sunday edition, which meant that McCutcheon's bulletin and follow-up story could not appear in the *Record* until Monday morning, May 9, almost two days after its receipt and a full day after Harden's complete story addressed to the *Chicago Tribune* certainly would have appeared in that paper's Sunday morning edition.

More complicated still, the *New York Journal* had an arrangement whereby it shared all its own dispatches with the *Chicago Record*, including reports from Cuba, and could in turn use those war reports received by the *Record*. The *Journal* did have a Sunday morning edition, and it received permission from the *Record* to use McCutcheon's story in New York on Sunday, May 8. The 600 words McCutcheon had filed in his follow-up report were rewritten and expanded by James Creelman in New York to make a none-too-accurate 3,500-word story.

The *Chicago Tribune*, which also had its own arrangement with the *New York Journal*, was authorized to use McCutcheon's story intended for the competing *Record* in its own Sunday morning edition in Chicago, along with Harden's full story, which also appeared in the Sunday *New York World*.

Stickney's dispatch to the *New York Herald*, sent from Hong Kong at least in part at the "urgent" rate, as was Harden's, failed to reach New York in time for use on Saturday morning, but the full dispatch did appear in the *Herald* on Sunday morning. This meant that the three New York papers, the *World*, the *Journal*, and the *Herald*, had extended accounts of the Manila Bay occurrence in their editions of Sunday morning, May 8, and the *Tribune* used two of those accounts in Chicago.

The *Chicago Record* of Monday morning, May 9, used McCutcheon's second story presenting the details of the engagement, with his 4,500 words expanded to 6,000 words. The same edition at last presented his original report, minus the Creelman touches. McCutcheon himself received an offer from Hearst to represent the *Journal* in Manila, but he chose to remain with the *Record*.

After two days in Hong Kong, Harden, McCutcheon, and Stickney returned to Manila aboard the *McCulloch,* and remained for some months in the Philippines.

When transports arrived in Manila from the United States in June, they brought correspondents as well as troops. Later ships brought some reporters who had covered the Cuban phase of the war, and even the South African War.

Correspondents arriving late in June included Oscar King Davis for the *New York Sun* and the Laffan News Bureau, and also representing *Harper's Weekly.* Davis (not to be confused with Richard Harding Davis, to whom he was unrelated) was on his first foreign assignment in a long career spent mainly in Washington. He arrived in Manila aboard the U.S. cruiser *Charleston,* which had taken control of Guam on June 20, en route from the U.S. Pacific Coast. The Spanish commander there, lacking communications facilities, was not even aware that a war was in progress, and the island was wholly lacking in defenses.

Frederick Palmer also was aboard the *Charleston.* He had been covering the gold rush in the Klondike, which had started in northwestern Canada in 1897 and was still in progress. Palmer was now writing for the *New York World* and *Collier's Weekly.* He returned to New York in 1899 with Dewey, by then promoted to rear admiral. Other arrivals included John Fay, *Chicago Tribune;* David Morris, Associated Press of Illinois; and Martin Egan, *San Francisco Chronicle.*

Veterans of the Cuban campaign, reaching the Philippines in August, included John P. Dunning, API; Edward L. Keen, Scripps-McRae Press Association; Richard Henry Little, *Chicago Tribune*; George Bronson Rae, *New York World*; James Creelman, *New York Journal*; John Foster Bass, also for the *Journal* again, although he had written for the *New York Evening Post* in Cuba; and Stephen Bonsal and Francis D. Millet for the *New York Herald.* Millet was also writing for the London *Times* and sketching for *Harper's Weekly.*

Spanish rule ended officially in the Philippines following the signature of the Treaty of Paris on December 10, 1898. The cable, meanwhile, was restored to operation. The people of the islands had welcomed the Spanish defeat, and aided materially in its accomplishment. Now they were concerned, lest the United States should impose its own control, and so destroy their hopes of independence. On January 10, 1899, accordingly, Aguinaldo, as the leader of the Philippines independence movement since 1896, issued a proclamation declaring that the fight for independence would continue.

This marked the beginning of a period of guerrilla warfare, with the first clash between Aguinaldo's independence fighters and U.S. Army forces occurring in Manila on February 5. Conflicts continued in the Philippines until 1903, although a civil government was set up under United States direction in 1902.

The period between 1899 and 1903 produced problems of censorship, which grew increasingly sharp. Among those who remained to cover some part of the fighting and political adjustments were McCutcheon, Dunning, Keen, Little, Bonsal, Creelman, Bass, Davis, Palmer, and Morris.

Keen, of the Scripps-McRae Press Association, switched to a related Scripps' enterprise, the Publishers' Press Association, which had its headquarters in New York. He was the first to report the capture of Aguinaldo on March 23, 1901, by U.S. forces under General Frederick Funston. An important story because it signaled the end of the guerrilla action, Keen filed 600 words to New York at the urgent rate of $5.40 a word from Manila, for a total cost of $3,240. This stood as a record cost for a single dispatch until 1923, and also provided a noteworthy "beat," reaching readers in the United States even before War Department dispatches reached Washington on the matter.

Morris, of the API, moved on to China in 1900, but returned soon to Manila as publicity adviser to William Howard Taft, who was sent to the Philippines by President McKinley. Taft became the first civil governor from 1902 to 1904.[6]

Other later arrivals of correspondents in Manila included Harold Martin, Associated Press (as the API became in 1900). He had been in Cuba, and remained in Manila for two years. Others arriving were Robert M. Collins, also of the Associated Press (later active with the agency in Japan and Europe); and William Dinwiddie, *New York Herald*, who became an islands administrator during the first year of occupation, but then went to report the South African War for the *Herald*.

---

6 In 1904 Taft became secretary of war in President Theodore Roosevelt's cabinet, with an interval as provisional governor of Cuba in 1906. He followed Roosevelt in the presidency by election in 1908.

The Spanish-American War, in its total effect, stirred the press of the United States to greater activity in handling news, introduced true mass circulations, gave life to magazines in their attention to current news subjects, brought an advance in news photography, and introduced motion picture photography as an adjunct to news reporting.

Havana and Manila remained as news centers receiving staff or stringer coverage. Elmer E. Roberts continued in Havana for the API for seven months after the war. He was followed by Howard N. Thompson until 1902 for the Associated Press. Malcolm Mc Dowell of the *Chicago Record* remained for a time, and the *New York Sun* had O'Neill Sevier in Santiago. The number of correspondents in Manila was even greater because of the continuing military action there, but some moved to China and Japan in 1900-01.

The South African War (1899-1902)

The area about the Cape of Good Hope, at the southern tip of the African continent, had been colonized in 1652 by settlers from Holland, and became the Cape Colony, with Capetown as its capital. The settlers were referred to as "Boers," the Dutch word for "farmers," which most of them were. It was controlled by the Dutch East India Company until that company went bankrupt in 1794, and Holland itself was politically disrupted and then overrun by the forces of revolutionary France and later by the armies of Napoleon. England, at war with France, and also under authorization by Holland's exiled prince of Orange, occupied the Cape Colony in 1814 as a wartime naval maneuver.

Holland had become allied with France in the period of the Napoleonic wars, and the British conquered all of the Dutch colonial empire of the time. In the postwar settlement at Vienna in 1814-15, most of that territory was returned to Holland, but the British retained part of Dutch Guiana in South America, and also retained the Cape Colony. Twenty years later, between 1835 and 1838, many of the descendants of the original Dutch settlers, objecting to the British administration, made a Great Trek northeastward and formed two separate, but adjacent independent Boer republics. One was the Orange Free State, with Bloemfontein as its capital. Beyond that was the South African Republic, also known as the Transvaal, with Pretoria as its capital.

From the Cape Colony, the British also extended their authority eastward to the area of Natal, a separate colony under British administration, with the port of Durban as its capital on the east coast. This was enlarged by the annexation of Zululand in 1887, an area adjacent to the Transvaal where the British had conducted a military campaign in 1879.

Relations between the British and the new Boer republics were variable for some years, but in 1854 Great Britain recognized the independence of the Orange Free State and, in 1880, of the Transvaal, although with some conditions attached.

The British press extended its coverage to South Africa beginning in 1861. At that time the Reuter agency appointed Irish-born M. J. M. Bellasyse as representative at Durban, but moved him to Capetown in 1876. The first African cable connection with London, established at Durban in 1879, was extended to Capetown in 1887. Reuter established William Hay Mackay as correspondent in Pretoria in 1884. Bellasyse was named as Reuter's general manager for South Africa in 1887 when the cable reached Capetown, a position he retained until 1899.

German moves into Africa had aroused British concern in 1884-86, for they took over areas of the west coast and, in the east, regions that Stanley had explored between 1871 and 1874. By 1896 there already was tension enough in South Africa between the British and the Dutch of the two Boer republics. Discovery of gold in the Rand district of the Transvaal, near Johannesburg, in 1886 led to worsening relations. Foreigners, moving into the Transvaal in great numbers in search of gold, British among them, turned Johannesburg from a mining camp into a rapidly-growing town.

The British administration in Capetown demanded that those arriving in the Transvaal be granted equal treatment with the Boer residents of the republic. This demand was resisted, and the Orange Free State allied itself with the Transvaal in opposing the British demands. The differences became personified in Cecil John Rhodes, prime minister of the Cape Colony from 1890 to 1896, and Paul Kruger, president of the Transvaal from 1883 to 1900.

Rhodes, a native of England, spent most of his life in South Africa and was largely responsible for its settlement and development under British control. Advised as a youth of seventeen to seek a better climate, he arrived in Natal in 1870, and joined an elder brother already engaged in cotton raising. In that same year, diamonds were discovered in the Kimberley fields in the Cape Colony. The brothers hastened there, met with quick success, and both became millionaires within two years.

Between 1873 and 1881 Rhodes moved back and forth between Africa and England. In addition to obtaining both B.A. and M.A. degrees at Balliol College, Oxford, he explored areas of southern Africa, and gained a vision of British development of the continent. By 1890 his efforts had brought large new areas into British control, including Bechuanaland, northwest of the Dutch republics, and an even larger area north of that, which became known as Rhodesia. He augmented his interest in diamonds with goldmining interests. Since 1881 Rhodes had been a member of the Cape Colony Assembly. His goal was to make the African continent British "from the Cape to Cairo," with a proposed merger of Dutch and British interests. His actions as a "benevolent dictator," backed by his enormous wealth, made him an important and powerful figure from 1881 until his death in 1902, and especially so when he was prime minister from 1890 to 1896.

Kruger, twenty-eight years older than Rhodes and often in conflict with him, had been born in the Cape Colony. Although living in the Transvaal since boyhood, and commandant of the forces of that republic from 1864, he also worked in British government service until 1878. From that time, however, his over-riding concern was with the independence of the Dutch republics. He was in an unending controversy with the British in the Cape Colony and with Rhodes and his plans. He was as interested in extending Dutch, or Boer influence in Africa as Rhodes was in extending British influence. He was president of the Transvaal from 1883 until 1900, when Pretoria was captured by the British. He then left the country for Switzerland.

Both Kruger and Rhodes made tactical mistakes, especially after 1890. Kruger tried to interfere with normal trade and commercial relations between the Transvaal and the Cape Colony, contrary to an agreement of 1884, but felt obliged to yield when it appeared British military force might be invoked. He also was prepared, in later years, to accept support from Germany, which had ambitions on the African continent. This solidified British opposition in Capetown and in London.

Rhodes, in addition to pressing for Boer acceptance of British advances in Africa, even at the cost of their own independence, was moved also by his personal interests in gold mining. Thus in 1895, at a time when he was prime minister of the Cape Colony, he encouraged a revolutionary movement in Johannesburg. The object was to help the non-Boers there win rights equal to those of the Boers themselves. This led to the "Jameson Raid" which backfired and forced Rhodes to resign as prime minister.

A friend of Rhodes, Dr. Leander Starr Jameson, was chief of the British South Africa Company's interests north of Bechuanaland and the Transvaal. That territory had been developed through the efforts of Rhodes between 1889 and 1895 and was named after him. Jameson organized a group of 500 mounted men, recruited from among the British South Africa Company's own troopers. They rode into the Transvaal and to Johannesburg on December 29, 1895. Their purpose was to give armed support to what had become a numerically larger foreign element in the gold-mining center, to stage a planned uprising against the Boers, to seize control of Johannesburg, and to enforce the demand for equal rights. The foreign group was not prepared when the troopers arrived, and the entire plan failed. After four days, the Jameson party surrendered to the Boers, who had been prompt to contest their presence and purpose in the area.

The failure of the Jameson effort forced Rhodes to resign as prime minister in the Cape Colony, although any complicity he might have had in the Jameson raid was unclear despite an investigation conducted by the House of Commons in London. He was succeeded by Sir Alfred Milner (later Lord Milner), who was sent from London to repair the situation and to serve as high commissioner and governor of the Cape Colony from 1897 to 1905.

Milner tried to negotiate with Kruger to win concessions, at least, for foreigners in the Transvaal. Kruger refused any such compromise, and his government in the Transvaal also issued an ultimatum in October 1899 demanding the withdrawal of British troops from the Transvaal frontier. This withdrawal did not occur, and the Transvaal, with the active support of the Orange Free State, moved troops into Natal and the Cape Colony, beginning a war between the Boers and the British that continued until the end of May 1902.

British newspaper correspondents began to visit South Africa during the critical years of the 1890s. Among them for the *Times* were Miss Flora Louise Shaw, colonial editor; Captain Francis Younghusband, who had written for the paper from India while on military service there; and Edmund Powell. Others were Frederic Villiers of the *Graphic*, and J. A. Hobson of the *Manchester Guardian*.

Bellasyse, Reuter's general manager in Capetown, was frequently in Johannesburg because of its growing importance. Henry M. Collins, veteran of the Reuter service and general manager for the agency in Australasia for the preceding twenty years, set out for London in 1899, but by way of Capetown, where he remained from April until August of that year to examine agency affairs. When the war began in October, Collins returned to Capetown, replacing Bellasyse in charge of agency business there.

Visiting correspondents, especially, were almost certain to seek interviews with Rhodes and with Kruger. The three *Times* correspondents mentioned, however, were regarded by the Boers as sympathetic to the Rhodes plan to extend British influence in Africa and, after the Jameson raid, they were accused, along with the *Times* itself, of having encouraged that raid and the intended Johannesburg revolution. An examination of the entire situation by a Select Committee of the House of Commons continued in London for months, with Flora Louise Shaw as a chief witness.

Considerable sympathy for the Boers and for Kruger, personally, existed in several countries, including Germany. After the Jameson raid, Kaiser Wilhelm II, who had succeeded to the throne in 1888, addressed a telegram to Kruger congratulating him and his people for "repelling with their own forces the armed bands which had broken into their country, and maintaining the independence of their country against foreign aggression."

In London the Kaiser's message was taken to mean that Germany might support Kruger and the Boers with arms, if asked. Throughout the South African War, the German press further reflected hostility toward Great Britain. This seemed the more serious because the most critical press voices were those of the *Norddeutsche Allgemeine Zeitung* of Hamburg, regarded as reporting official views; and the *Kölnische Zeitung,* known to be close to the German Foreign Ministry.

The South African War began in October 1899 when the Boers laid siege to the cities of Mafeking and Kimberley, both in the British Cape Colony, and to Ladysmith, in the British colony of Natal. The three cities were surrounded, and the Boer campaign went successfully for the first several months. Meanwhile, British troops were en route from Great Britain under the command of Field Marshal Lord Roberts, with Major General Lord Kitchener as his chief-of-staff. They arrived in the Cape Colony in December, were ready for action by February of 1900, and the Boer successes were soon reversed.

The Boer siege of Kimberley was ended February 15, Ladysmith was relieved on February 28, and Mafeking on May 17. British forces occupied Johannesburg on May 31 and Pretoria on June 5. By the autumn of the year the Boers were reduced to guerrilla fighting. Field Marshal Roberts felt free to return to England, with Kitchener continuing as British commander. Kruger, the Boer leader, fled to Europe in October, leaving Louis Botha in command. In July 1901, Botha met with Kitchener to discuss peace, but no agreement was reached, and the war dragged on into the spring of 1902.

By May of 1902, however, the Boers abandoned hope of winning, and met with the British at Pretoria to begin six weeks of negotiations. In the Treaty of Vereeniging, signed May 31, 1902, the Boers renounced the independence both of the Transvaal and of the Orange Free State, and both were placed under British administration. Not until 1910, however, was the situation sufficiently healed to permit the formation of the Union of South Africa, embracing all four provinces, the Cape Colony and Natal included, and with the former Boer commander, Louis Botha, as the Union's first prime minister. By that time, both Rhodes and Kruger were dead. Rhodes died in 1902 near Capetown, and Kruger in 1904 in Switzerland.

When the war began, Reuter and the *Times* were best prepared to provide news coverage, with representatives already in South Africa, whereas most other correspondents were obliged to travel from London or elsewhere, and were not familiar with the area and its problems when they did arrive.

Reuter, during the two and one-half years of the war, had about 100 staff and stringer correspondents at work in South Africa, with at least thirty-seven actively in the field. Two were killed. The agency's correspondents were trusted by both sides, and the entire world press depended greatly upon the Reuter reports. The agency gained added prestige, but was subjected to heavy expense. Because he was regarded as being too sympathetic to the Boer position, Bellasyse, general manager of the South African service since 1887, and correspondent there since 1861, was retired in November 1899, a month after the war began. He was replaced as general manager by H. A. Gwynne, who was in the field at times and rated as the agency's principal correspondent. Collins, in Capetown, supervised general administrative operations. Following Gwynne as chief correspondent in the field was J. de Villiers Roos, who later became auditor-general in the government of the Union of South Africa.

Among other Reuter correspondents, William Hay Mackay, in Pretoria since 1884, was permitted to remain in that Boer capital throughout the war, although his reports were subject to censorship. It was through Mackay's enterprise and ingenuity, nevertheless, that

Reuter was able to provide an exclusive report of the relief of Mafeking on May 18, 1900, the day after the seven-months' siege of the city by the Boers came to an end. The Boers themselves had given Mackay the information, but believed the censorship would prevent him from getting the news out. Mackay, however, rushed his dispatch to the frontier between the Transvaal and Portuguese East Africa (Mozambique), where he gave it, along with £5 for his trouble, to the engineer of a train about to leave for Lourenço Marques, on the east coast. The engineer is said to have carried the message inside a luncheon sandwich to avoid possible detection, and then delivered it himself to the Eastern Telegraph Company's office in the coastal city for cable transmission to London.

The public demonstrations in London, upon receipt of the Reuter report were of such enthusiasm as to add the word "mafficking" to the language, derived from "Mafeking," and meaning "to celebrate hilariously." It was not until two days later that official messages arrived from Mafeking itself, confirming the freeing of the city, but it was a tribute to Reuter that neither Queen Victoria nor any government official or other person questioned the accuracy of the earlier agency report. A sad aftermath, however, was that Mackay later became one of the two Reuter corrrspondents to be killed in the war. James Innes Calder was the second.

Another Reuter correspondent who gained distinction during this period was Roderick Jones. British-born, and in the Transvaal as a youth, he had worked for the *Pretoria Press* and the *Pretoria News* before he was eighteen, at which time he became an assistant to Mackay. Very shortly after, in January 1896, he was the only correspondent given permission by Paul Kruger to talk with Dr. Jameson following his capture in the attempted raid on Johannesburg. Jones later joined the Reuter bureau in Capetown, where he also worked for the *Cape Times*. He accompanied British forces under Field Marshal Lord Roberts in 1900.[7]

Colonel Robert Stephenson Smyth Baden-Powell had first served Reuter in 1890 at a time when he was an officer in the British expedition that settled Rhodesia. During the South African war, in

---

7 Jones went to Reuter headquarters in London in 1902, after the war, but was back in Capetown from 1905 to 1915 in charge of the agency's interests in Central and South Africa. In London again in 1915, he became managing director of the agency in 1916, succeeding Herbert de Reuter. He was knighted in 1918.

command of the British forces within the besieged city of Mafeking,[8] but still acting for Reuter, he seems to have had no trouble getting reports out for the agency.

For the *Times,* William Flavelle Monypenny, who had been an assistant to George Earle Buckle, editor of the paper, was in Capetown when the war began. An early arrival, also, was Leopold Charles Maurice Stennett Amery, formerly an assistant to Saunders in the Berlin bureau. He assumed direction of the paper's coverage throughout the period of the war. When Amery took charge, Monypenny joined the British armed forces and was in Ladysmith during the months it was under siege.[9]

Other *Times* correspondents operating under Amery's direction during the war included Lionel James, formerly of Reuter; Angus Hamilton, Percival Landon; William Burdett-Coutts, a member of Parliament; and Bron Herbert (later Lord Lucas). James was one of the correspondents to be bottled up at Ladysmith. Knightley, the best press historian of the war, credits Burdett-Coutts with a notable series exposing inadequate treatment of the sick and wounded.[10] As comparable reports at the time of the Crimean War brought Florence Nightingale and others to the scene, so a volunteer group moved from Great Britain to South Africa to provide assistance. Among them was Lady Randolph Spencer Churchill, mother of Winston Churchill, then also in South Africa.

Correspondents for some other British newspapers, and a few for the press of other countries arrived in Capetown to report the war.

The *Daily Telegraph* sent Bennet Burleigh, who joined the forces of Field Marshal Lord Roberts in the campaign against Pretoria,

8 Phillip Knightley, in *The First Casualty* (1975), portrays Baden-Powell as inept both as a military strategist and as a correspondent. After the war he established the Boy Scout and Girl Scout organizations, and received a peerage in 1929 as Lord Baden-Powell of Gilwell.
9 Monypenny remained in South Africa for a time after the war as editor of the *Johannesburg Star.* In 1908 he became one of the directors of a new company formed to operate the *Times* under the proprietorship of Lord Northcliffe. Leopold Amery remained with the *Times* after the war, returning to London, chiefly as a leader writer, but also as author of a *Times*-sponsored *History of the South African War.* He might have succeeded Chirol as head of the foreign department in 1912 had he remained, but he became a member of Parliament in 1911, and later was secretary of state for the dominions and colonies.
10 See Philip Knightley, *The First Casualty,* p. 74. Knightley reports that 14,000 of the 22,000 British war deaths were attributable to sickness. He also notes that Rudyard Kipling took personal action in the matter and that a Parliamentary inquiry followed.

which began on June 5, 1900. Burleigh also made an adventurous horseback ride, somewhat in the Forbes tradition, through Boer territory in mid-May of 1902 to get news past the censor that peace was imminent.

Another *Daily Telegraph* representative was Percy S. Bullen, who had written from Paris, Berlin, and Rome, and later was correspondent in the United States for thirty years. Ellis Ashmead-Bartlett, beginning a long news career, and Robert McHugh also were in South Africa for the paper.

The *Morning Post* was represented by Edward Frederick Knight, who had served the *Times* during the French move into Madagascar in 1895, during the Greco-Turkish War in 1897, and in Cuba in 1898. He also wrote for the *New York World*. Knight was shot while with Lord Metheun's forces during an engagement near Belmont, in the critical Modder River area in February 1900, and his arm had to be amputated at the shoulder. This did not end his career as a correspondent, however, for he was to report the Russo-Japanese War of 1904-05 for the *Post*. Prevost Battersby, military writer on the paper's London staff, was sent to South Africa to replace him. F. D. Baillie was early in the field for the paper. John Stuart, another of its correspondents, was caught in the siege of Ladysmith. A third, George Alfred Ferrand, was killed.

Still another *Morning Post* correspondent was Winston Churchill, then twenty-four, who already had experience as a correspondent in Cuba, India, and the Sudan. A civilian correspondent on this occasion, rather than an officer, and unusually well paid, he was captured near Ladysmith on November 15, 1899, by Louis Botha, then a Boer private. Botha was soon to advance to the rank of general, succeed Kruger as the Boer commander by 1901, and to serve as prime minister of the Union of South Africa from its formation in 1910 until his death in 1919.[11]

Following his capture, Churchill was imprisoned with about fifty others at Pretoria in mid-November of 1899. On December 12, acting with great audacity, he escaped. With a Boer offer of £25 outstanding for his recapture, dead or alive, Churchill made his way without map or compass across 300 miles of unmarked territory and reached sanctuary in Portuguese East Africa. There he arrived December 20

---

11 During those latter years Botha also was commander of combined Dutch and British forces invading German Southwest Africa during World War I, receiving that colony's surrender in 1915; and he signed the Treaty of Versailles, ending World War I, on behalf of the Union of South Africa, in the last year of his life.

at the port of Lourenço Marques and proceeded by ship to Durban. His capture had been widely publicized in Great Britain. The details of both the capture and escape in his own reports to the *Morning Post* gained him a fame contributing to his later political career, beginning with his election to a seat in Parliament in 1900.

In Durban, Churchill rejoined the army as a lieutenant in the South African Light Horse regiment, participating in the relief of Ladysmith in February 1900 and in the taking of Pretoria in June. He also continued to write for the *Morning Post,* although by special permission, since a new regulation denied British soldiers the right to act also as correspondents, as some had done at least since the period of the Crimean War.

The *Daily Mail,* by 1899 successfully on the road as a popular newspaper, undertook to cover the South African War with much the same vigor as had been displayed by the *New York Journal* in its coverage of the war in Cuba. As with the *Journal,* the circulation of the *Daily Mail* was to touch the million mark.

S. J. Pryor, an assistant to Alfred Harmsworth, the paper's proprietor, organized a special war service in South Africa. Its correspondents and special writers included George Warrington Steevens, Charles E. Hands, Frederick Slater Collett, Edgar Wallace, and two Americans, Julian Ralph and Richard Harding Davis.

Steevens, after covering the Omdurman campaign in the Sudan in 1898, had been assigned to report the second Dreyfus trial in Paris in 1899 before proceeding to South Africa. That trial was an event of world interest. It had grown out of the arrest in 1894 of French Army Captain Alfred Dreyfus. Tried in secret at that time and convicted on a charge of selling military information to Germany, he was stripped of all rank and honor and sentenced to life imprisonment on Devil's Island, off the coast of French Guiana in the Caribbean.

In 1898, however, the case was revived, largely because Emile Zola made it the subject of a novel, *J'Accuse,* originally appearing as a *feuilleton* in the Paris newspaper *l'Aurore.* Zola indicated that Dreyfus had been the victim of an army conspiracy based, at least in part, on the fact that he was Jewish. Zola also produced evidence that the victim was innocent of the charges brought against him. The result was a long legal contest, extending through much of 1898 and part of 1899. On this occasion, Dreyfus was pardoned, which was interpreted as exonerating him of all earlier charges—an exoneration made official in 1906—and as an indictment of the military clique responsible for the original action. Not only was it a dramatic trial, but the case caused deep political and social rifts in France, with Zola himself under such pressure that he took temporary refuge in England.

The trial, especially during its closing weeks in 1899, received extensive coverage. In addition to Steevens, correspondents included Henri de Blowitz of the *Times*; Ernest Smith, then Paris correspondent for the *Daily News*; Dr. Emile Joseph Dillon, who came from St. Petersburg for the *Daily Telegraph*; and Henry J. Middleton of the Associated Press of Illinois, who was regarded as having done particularly well in handling the complexities of the story.

After the Dreyfus trial ended in September 1899, Steevens went on to South Africa for the *Daily Mail*. There he added to his reputation as an able writer and corrrespondent. He had the misfortune, however, to become one of the correspondents trapped in Ladysmith from late October 1899 until late February 1900. The promise of a brilliant career as a journalist was cut short when, partly for lack of proper food and medical supplies in the besieged city, Steevens died of enteric fever in January 1900. He was only thirty years old.

Charles E. Hands, who had covered the war in Cuba for the *Daily Mail*, was wounded in the campaign to relieve Mafeking in May 1900. Edgar Wallace, a former soldier, who had become editor of the Johannesburg *Rand Daily Mail,* served Reuter early in the war, and then became a correspondent for the London *Daily Mail*. Subsequently better known as a writer of popular fiction, he gained professional acclaim by getting the news to London, despite the censorship (as Burleigh also had done), that the Treaty of Vereeniging, ending the war, was about to be signed. His report appeared in London forty-eight hours ahead of the actual signature on May 31, 1902.

The *Daily Mail* had two resident stringers in Mafeking. One, Lady Sarah Wilson, an aunt of Churchill's, remained throughout the seven months' period. The Mafeking siege was not so tight as at Ladysmith or Kimberley. A Mr. Hellawell, carried dispatches out quite regularly, but ultimately was captured and held prisoner at Pretoria.[12]

Frederick Slater Collett, one of the *Daily Mail* correspondents, was killed. Julian Ralph, London correspondent for the *New York*

---

12 Other correspondents in Mafeking, aside from Baden-Powell, also the commander, were Angus Hamilton, the *Times*; F. D. Baillie, the *Morning Post*; E. G. Parslow, the *Daily Chronicle*; Emerson Neilly, the *Pall Mall Gazette*; and Vere Stent, Reuter. J. E. Pearson, also of Reuter, paid a brief visit to Mafeking.

Journal, represented that paper in South Africa, as he had during the Greco-Turkish War. But he also wrote for the *Daily Mail* until he was succeeded by Wallace. Ralph returned to London, where he died in 1903.

Richard Harding Davis wrote for the *Daily Mail*, while also representing the *New York Herald*. Davis arrived in Capetown in February 1900, accompanied by his wife—perhaps the only occasion when a war correspondent took his wife with him on an assignment.[13] Mrs. Davis remained in Capetown in the first weeks, but later went with her husband to Pretoria. Davis himself, at the outset, reported the campaign that brought the relief of Ladysmith, and was twenty-four hours ahead of all others with news of the freeing of the city on February 28. Later, as a neutral, Davis was able to enter the territory of the Boers, with whom his personal sympathies rested. He wrote from there in such a vein as to compromise his later reception in London. He and Mrs. Davis were in Pretoria as British forces under Field Marshal Lord Roberts approached, but left before the city was taken on June 5, and were back in New York by late summer.

Dr. Arthur Conan Doyle, known for his Sherlock Holmes stories, and Rudyard Kipling, also by then widely known as a writer, were both in South Africa. Kipling became associated with an army newspaper, *The Friend*, published at Bloemfontein. Harmsworth offered him £10,000 (nearly $50,000) to write of the war for the *Daily Mail*, but he declined.

Among other correspondents for the British press were a number of veterans of war coverage beyond those already mentioned. The senior of them all was Melton Prior of the *Illustrated London News*, who had been active since 1873. Frederic Villiers, active since 1876, represented the *Graphic* and the *Daily News*. Harry H. S. Pearce, active since 1883, and A. G. Hales, an Australian, also represented the *Daily News*. Henry W. Nevinson of the *Daily Chronicle*, and William T. Maud of the *Graphic*, had covered the Greco-Turkish War of 1897.

John Black Atkins of the *Manchester Guardian* was another who had reported the Greco-Turkish War, but he also had been in Cuba during the Spanish-American War. George Lynch of the *Daily*

---

13 There had, of course, been other women war correspondents, and at least three husband-and-wife teams were to serve jointly during World War II. Mrs. Davis was not a correspondent.

Chronicle, also formerly in Cuba, was the only correspondent who managed to get out of Ladysmith during the siege. One version of his escape, possibly apocryphal, was that he rode out at night on a horse painted a khaki color on the side that might be visible to any watching Boers.

British correspondents also included Robert Mitchell and William Maxwell (later Sir William Maxwell), both of the *Standard*; Edward Daniel Scott of the *Manchester Guardian*; Ernest Smith of the *Daily News*, formerly in Paris, and also a reporter at the Dreyfus trial; Lester Smith, an artist for the *Illustrated London News*; Harold Ashton, representing both the London *Morning Leader* and the evening *Star;* Joseph Smith Dunn and Robert Beresford, both for Central News; and Alfred Julian Adams of Exchange Telegraph.

The British Empire press was represented for the first time in a war coverage, if one excepts Rathom's brief presence in the Sudan. Among those in South Africa were William John Lambie of the *Melbourne Age*, who was killed; Horace H. Spooner of the *Sydney Evening News*, also killed, and Donald Mc Donald of the *Melbourne Argus*.

Correspondents for the press of the United States, in addition to Ralph and Davis, included Richard Smith and George Denny for the Associated Press of Illinois. Howard Clemens Hillegas, who had been in Cuba, wrote for the *New York World*, which was also served by Knight of the *Morning Post*. Others were William Dinwiddie of the *New York Herald*, who had been in the Philippines, and Hugh Sutherland of the *Philadelphia North American*. John T. McCutcheon, after writing from the Philippines for the *Chicago Record*, proceeded to South Africa in the spring of 1900 and, like Davis, also went into the Transvaal to see something of the war from the Boer side, and to interview Kruger.

The only known correspondents for the non-Anglo-Saxon press during the war were Reginald Kann, representing *l'Illustration*, the Paris weekly illustrated magazine, and Colonel de Villebois-Mareuil, a member of the Boer army, writing for *Liberté* of Paris until he was killed in action. There was little organized effort to make photographs for the press during the war, although photos were made and used.

The most critical situations during the war related to the Boer sieges of Mafeking, Kimberley, and Ladysmith, the campaigns to relieve them, and the British drive on Pretoria. Mafeking was under the longest siege, but the most desperate situation was that of Ladysmith, surrounded from November 2, 1899, until February 28, 1900, with food virtually unobtainable for troops or civilians, and with medical supplies and other requisites in equally short supply. It was there that Steevens of the *Daily Mail* died of illness, and where, apart from the escape of Lynch, at least eight other correspondents were trapped. They included Nevinson and Lynch of the *Daily Chronicle*, Maud of the *Graphic*, Stuart of the *Morning Post*, Pearce and Smith of the *Daily News*, Maxwell of the *Standard*, Prior of the *Illustrated London News*, and James of the *Times*.

These men made great efforts to get dispatches out of the besieged city. They could use a British army heliograph service, but only thirty words a day were allowed any one paper or service. This limitation induced correspondents to try to hire Kaffir runners to try to get through the Boer encirclement at night with longer dispatches. Steevens and Prior paid a runner £70 (more than $400) to take that risk. The price asked by runners was as high as £100 (nearly $500), which tended to discourage use of that method, even assuming that correspondents had such funds with them or that runners were willing to chance the effort at all.

Thirteen correspondents lost their lives during the war. They were Steevens of the *Mail;* Mackay and Calder of Reuter; Lambie and Spooner of the Australian press; Adams of the Exchange Telegraph; Dunn of Central News; Collett of the *Daily Mail;* Ferrand of the *Morning Post;* Mitchell of the *Standard;* Parslow of the *Daily Chronicle;* and Scott of the *Manchester Guardian*. Maud of the *Graphic* died at Aden in 1903, but his death was attributed to hardships suffered at Ladysmith.

These men are memorialized in the crypt at St. Paul's Cathedral, London, along with victims of the Egyptian-Sudan campaigns, and of later wars. Beyond the fatalities, thirty-seven other British correspondents were wounded, including Knight and Hands, and a number were captured, including Churchill, who escaped, and Hellawell. The only known casualty among non-British correspondents was Colonel de Villebois-Mareuil of the Paris newspaper *Liberté*.

China Again, and the Russo-Japanese War (1904-05)

After the Japanese victory in the Sino-Japanese War of 1894-95, an anti-foreign sentiment developed in China. It was fanned by extremist secret societies that formed a league, the *I Ho Ch'uan*, literally "Fists of Righteous Harmony," freely translated as the "Boxers." It was dedicated to driving foreigners out of China, and undoing western influences on the rise there since the sixteenth century and particularly since about 1840.

Riots and violent incidents directed against foreign residents and establishments led the governments of several nations with commercial, missionary, and educational interests in China to demand that the imperial Chinese government suppress the Boxer group. When this was not accomplished, military action was taken through the joint efforts of eight governments. British, French, United States, Japanese, Russian, and German forces were in China between June and August of 1900. Tientsin was captured in July. About 18,000 troops fanned out to assist missionaries and others under siege, and to move into Peking where mobs had attacked foreign legations and killed a number of persons, including Baron Klemens von Ketteler, the German minister to China. A peace protocol was signed in September 1901, by which time the Chinese imperial family itself had been out of Peking for more than a year, established at Sianfu, in Shensi province.

These events during the summer of 1900 brought to China a number of correspondents who had been in the Philippines. Among them were Frederick Palmer, for the *New York World* and *Collier's Weekly*; Stephen Bonsal for the *New York Herald*; Oscar King Davis for the *New York Sun* and the Laffan News Bureau; Robert M. Collins and David Morris for the Associated Press; and Martin Egan, who had represented the *San Francisco Chronicle* in the Philippines but went to China also for the Associated Press. The AP was represented further by Charles E. Kloeber, recently manager of the agency's Washington bureau. Ralph D. Paine, who had reported the Cuban campaigns during the Spanish-American War, was present again for the *Philadelphia Press*.

Dr. Robert Coltman, recently engaged in China for a growing *Chicago Record* service, covered the Boxer trouble from the outset in Peking. Thomas F. Millard, beginning a life-time career in China and Japan, represented the *New York Herald*. Welsh-born Willmott Harsant Lewis (later Sir Willmott Lewis), who had completed his formal education at Heidelberg and the Sorbonne, and had recently become editor of the *North China Daily News* in Shanghai, also wrote for the *New York Herald*, beginning a career that was to culminate in an assignment in Washington for the London *Times*.

Joseph Medill Patterson, representing the *Chicago Tribune*, was in China on his first journalistic assignment. The son of R. W. Patterson, then publisher of the *Tribune*, and grandson of Joseph

Medill, for many years editor and publisher of that newspaper prior to his death in 1899, young Patterson was still a student at Yale and on his summer vacation. Some years later he became joint proprietor of the *Tribune*.

For the British press, George Lynch of the London *Daily Chronicle*, veteran both of the Spanish-American and South African Wars, traveled 300 miles to reach the nearest telegraph point with the first report of the capture by the allied forces of Tientsin, and then returned to march with the troops to the relief of Peking. Dr. Emile Joseph Dillon of the *Daily Telegraph* journeyed from St. Petersburg by way of the Trans-Siberian Railway, then in about the third year of its operation, to accompany the international expeditionary force that moved on Peking. Dr. George ("China") Morrison, the *Times* correspondent in Peking since 1895—like Dr. Coltman of the *Chicago Record*—produced eye-witness accounts of the Boxer attacks on the legations. Morrison was wounded and erroneously reported to have been killed.

The French press received reports from Gaston Chadourne of the Agence Havas, a veteran of Greco-Turkish War coverage in 1897 and later in Rome for the agency. He accompanied French troops from Marseilles to Tientsin and on to Peking, and he remained to cover other news subjects in the Far East before returning to Paris in 1901 by way of Canada and the United States. Pierre Loti (Louis Marie Julien Viaud), a novelist, who had written for *Le Figaro* of Paris from Indo-China in 1883, when serving as a lieutenant in the French navy, wrote again for *Le Figaro* of the Boxer campaign.

Luigi Barzini of Milan's *Corriere della Sera* returned substantial reports to Italy, on the first of a number of war assignments covered with distinction.

The hazards and difficulties of this campaign were considerable, and it was expensive to cover, both in matters of transportation and communication. Dispatches were moved to Europe and the United States from Shanghai, Tientsin, and Peking by way of the Great Northern Telegraph line across Siberia. The regular rate from China to London was $1.62 a word, and $1.72 to New York.

Some of the correspondents who reported the Boxer rebellion remained in the Far East, or returned there during the Russo-Japanese War of 1904-05. They joined others to cover that ninth armed conflict in a decade and the third major war since 1898.

The roots of the Russo-Japanese War sprang from the results of the Sino-Japanese War of 1894-95. Even though Japan had won that war, it was deprived of the fruits of victory when Russia, France, and Germany—all with interests in China—made clear they would use military force, if necessary, to bar Japan from Manchurian territory and from the port of Weihaiwei, even though those benefits had been granted in the treaty of peace signed with China in 1895.

Great Britain, whose interests in China were greater than any other foreign power, did not join in this protest. Indeed, in 1902 an Anglo-Japanese treaty established a situation wherein Britain stood in nonmilitary alliance with Japan.

While Japan was denied a foothold in Manchuria, Russia's desire for an ice-free port on the Pacific, and one to serve the needs of the Asiatic part of the realm, led to an arrangement with the weakened Chinese imperial government whereby Russia was granted a twenty-five-year lease of Port Arthur and the Liaotung Peninsula extending to it from Manchuria, with the adjacent port of Dairen leased in the same fashion. A branch of the Trans-Siberian Railway, known as the South Manchurian Railroad, was extended to Port Arthur from the Siberian port of Vladivostok, 600 miles to the north, where winter ice was a problem.

Since Japan had hoped to exploit the Manchurian area, and had been barred from doing so in part by Russian objection, and also had been denied the use of the port of Weihaiwei southward across Korea Bay from Port Arthur, the alternative development benefiting Russia did not please Tokyo. Then, in 1903, Russia also moved forces into the Korean Peninsula. Again, Japan had been denied the right to do that very thing in 1895 by Russia, France, and Germany. Since Japan had been financing Korean development and sending in settlers, it had added reason for objecting to Russia's action and lodged strong complaints.

After five months of diplomatic negotiations in 1903-04, during which Japan tried without success to get Russia to withdraw its forces from Korea, the talks were broken off. The Japanese attacked the Russians at Port Arthur on February 8, 1904, and declared war on February 10.

The war was conducted both at sea and in Manchurian territory, including the Liaotung Peninsula, with complete and final victory for Japan in May 1905. The decisive encounters did not occur until early in 1905, however. The Japanese took Port Arthur on January 1, 1905, defeated Russian forces on land in a three-week battle at Liao-yang, south of Mukden, between February 20 and March 15, and destroyed the Russian fleet in Tsushima Strait, between Japan and Korea, on May 27-28.

By invitation of U.S. President Theodore Roosevelt, a peace conference met in August 1905 at Portsmouth, New Hampshire, where a treaty was signed in September, with ratification following in October. By the terms of the treaty, Japan took over the Russian lease at Port Arthur, gained control of the southern half of the Russian island of Sakhalin, directly north of Japan, and was recognized as having special interests in Korea. Japan was to make it a dependency in 1906, and proclaim its annexation in 1910.

The world, through the eyes of the press, was watching the negotiations of 1903-04. There was a considerable sense of sympathy with Japan in what seemed a David-and-Goliath confrontation with the power of Russia. As the possibility of a war arose, some correspondents started early for Japan, and the actual outbreak in February 1904 brought a mobilization of correspondents for its coverage. About 200 representatives of the world press, and especially of the Anglo-American press, were in the area before the conflict ended. Many had reported the Spanish-American and South African Wars, the Philippine and Boxer campaigns, and some had reported earlier wars. And new correspondents also appeared.

The Japanese press, which had shown growth since the Sino-Japanese War, was well represented, with correspondents for its newspapers, especially *Asahi, Mainichi,* and *Jiji,* permitted where others were not. The Russian press, by contrast, had few correspondents.

Because Germany and France had interests in the Far East, some writers were present from those countries. Italy was also represented.

China had not developed a vernacular press in any way equal to that of Japan, but there were a few representatives from that country. This was notably so for the Shanghai *Shih Pao* (The Eastern Times), newly established in 1904 and of brief importance, with correspondents for a few years in London, New York, and other capitals outside China.

Most of the correspondents made Tokyo their goal, arriving as promptly as transportation facilities permitted. A considerable group was with the Russians, however, moving from St. Petersburg by way of the Trans-Siberian Railway, and remaining on the Asian mainland.

In Tokyo, at least a score of correspondents were kept waiting four months after the war began, until after both land and naval action had occurred. Only after June 1904 were some permitted to move to areas of relative activity in Manchuria. Even then, they were controlled, conducted in small groups and never permitted nearer than about three miles on any approach to the front lines. Thus they lacked the freedom of movement some had known in covering other wars, and they were under a more severe censorship than had existed on any previous occasion. A number became so frustrated and irritated by the delays and obstructions that they departed.

Frederic Villiers of the London *Graphic,* with long experience, observed that the correspondents accredited in Tokyo commonly worked in groups and kept close together, "not out of affection for each other's society, but to keep watch upon one another and to jump the news if possible." This conduct applied since the Franco-Prussian War, but with the difference that in Tokyo they watched one another not so much to avoid being beaten by a competitor on a story as to be sure that no one would be favored over another in opportunity to get to the scene of action.

The war set at least two new records for press coverage. It was the first occasion for the use of wireless as a means of transmitting dispatches from observers on the scene of action, or near it. It also was the most expensive war to cover, up to that time, in part because of high costs for dispatches directed to London or Paris, New York or San Francisco. One estimate placed the total expenditure for reporting the war of about fifteen months duration, in which the action concentrated chiefly in the last five months, at something in excess of $10 million, with three-quarters of that cost borne by the Anglo-American press.

A third special element figuring in the coverage was that the first transpacific cable had been completed in 1902 by British interests, and a second had been completed in 1903 by U.S. interests.

The first cable was the joint property of the governments of Australia, New Zealand, Great Britain, and Canada. It ran from the Canadian port of Vancouver to Sydney and Brisbane, by way of Fanning Island, Suva, and Norfolk Island, with a spur from Norfolk Island to Auckland, New Zealand. A connection already existed, established in 1873, linking Tokyo and London, with ties to Shanghai, Hong Kong, Singapore, Colombo, Calcutta, Bombay, and Alexandria, and with cable and telegraphic spurs by way of Singapore and Batavia to Darwin, Sydney, and Auckland, where ties were made to the new transpacific cable to Vancouver. A Tokyo-Shanghai-St. Petersburg-London communications link also existed by way of the Great Northern Telegraph Company line across Siberia.

The second transpacific cable provided a link between San Franciso and Manila and from there to the Asian mainland and Japan by existing British cables. John W. Mackay of the Postal Telegraph-Commercial Cable Company, operating a North Atlantic cable since 1883, had organized a Pacific Cable Company preparatory to extending a line across that ocean. He died in July 1902, but his son, Clarence W. Mackay, took over management of the companies. In December 1902 the shore end of the new cable was landed in San Francisco and extended from there to Honolulu, to Midway Island, Guam, and Manila, where the connection was made July 4, 1903. All of these were U.S.-controlled landing points: the Hawaiian Islands a territory of the United States since 1900; Midway claimed by the United States in 1867; and both Guam and the Philippine Islands having come under the U.S. flag as a result of the Spanish-American War in 1898.

Cable service from Manila to Hong Kong already existed in 1903 over facilities of the British-owned Eastern Extension Company, with other British lines fanning out to points on the China coast, to Japan and elsewhere in the Far East. After July 1903 a direct Pacific cable connection existed between San Francisco and Asian cities. The Vancouver cable provided a second means for direct communication between the west coast of North America and points in Asia.

In addition, a spur line was completed in 1904-05 between Guam and Yokohama, by way of the Bonin Islands, even as the Russo-Japanese War was in progress. This was accomplished in great secrecy at the explicit request of the Japanese government, lest Russian naval forces should cut the other cables from the China coast and so isolate Japan for communications purposes. This never happened, and the war ended with the spur completed by the Pacific Cable Company, with Japanese participation.

The rate on the new U.S.-owned Pacific Cable Company line between San Francisco and Tokyo, by way of Manila, was $1 a word. Telegraph charges at press rates between San Francisco and New York, or intermediate points, were added, plus another ten cents a word from New York to London, if messages were to be routed that way. The rate from Shanghai to London by the Great Northern Telegraph Company line across Siberia, lower than by the British cable via India, was $1.62 a word, with the additional ten cents a word if London to New York transmission were added.

The use of wireless as an aid to covering the war was a concept developed by the *Times* and implemented by Lionel James, one of the first special correspondents to arrive in Japan. He had been in the Balkans after returning from South Africa and his entrapment at

Ladysmith. When Russo-Japanese negotiations were nearing their end, with no evidence of agreement, he started for Japan by way of New York.

Considerable technical progress had been made in the use of wireless since 1895, when Marconi first introduced it. Marconi himself, with James A. Fleming and C. S. Franklin of the British Marconi Company, Reginald Aubrey Fessenden, Canadian-born engineer with the Westinghouse Electric and Manufacturing Company of Pittsburgh, and Dr. Lee DeForest, who had been working on communications devices in the United States since 1901, all had contributed improvements.

Fessenden produced devices for the better reception of signals, and DeForest had devised a new type of vacuum tube signal detector. By his persuasion, the Publishers' Press Association had used his equipment to report the 1901 America's Cup Race off Long Island. The results were hardly more satisfactory than those trials made during the 1899 races, with signal interference still a problem—this time between the DeForest equipment and that again provided by Marconi for use by the Associated Press. The problem was somewhat relieved in 1902, with Marconi, Fessenden, and DeForest all reporting U.S. Navy maneuvers off the Connecticut Coast, and then in 1903 when its use during the America's Cup Race of that year was at last quite successful.

Meanwhile, the *New York Times* had concluded a contractual arrangement on September 2, 1901, with the London *Times* providing for an exchange of news and special correspondence—an arrangement that continued until World War I. Both papers also were directly interested in the experiments being conducted by Marconi to bridge the Atlantic by wireless between England and Nova Scotia. The first news message to go in that fashion, moving eastward across the Atlantic, was a twenty-five word dispatch sent on December 26, 1902, by Dr. George E. Parkins (later Sir George Parkins), stringer correspondent for the *Times* in Toronto.

DeForest had organized an American Wireless Telegraph Company in 1901 to produce and market wireless equipment incorporating certain of his inventions, and he reorganized it in 1902 as the American DeForest Wireless Company. In 1904 he constructed wireless stations in Florida for the U.S. Navy at Pensacola and Key West, in Cuba at Guantanamo Bay, in Puerto Rico, and in the Panama Canal Zone, newly under U.S. control and with construction of the canal about to begin.

Lionel James in New York, familiar with developments in wireless communication, and with the approval of the *Times,* was prepared to charter a small vessel equipped with a wireless transmitter. This he purposed to operate in or near the war zone, if war came. The vessel would have its own communications system, with messages to be sent to a shore station in neutral China for relay to London, all without censorship. James had authority to make these arrangements, and a DeForest wireless system was shipped aboard the liner *Siberia,* leaving San Francisco bound for Hong Kong, Shanghai, and Yokohama. He was one of a number of correspondents sailing, along with technicians, to install and operate the wireless.

At Hong Kong, James chartered a 1,200-ton steamer, the *Haimun,* and had the transmitter installed. He arranged to have a receiving station set up at Weihaiwei, on the China coast, with David Fraser, correspondent for the *Times* at Shanghai, in charge. American wireless operators were aboard the *Haimun* and at the shore station. James arranged to have a Japanese naval officer join him aboard the *Haimun* both to clarify points that might arise in the news and to facilitate the handling of dispatches, uncensored though they might be, without giving unnecessary offense to the Japanese government. By this time, war had been declared.

While other correspondents were awaiting permission from Japanese authorities to leave Tokyo, the first message went out by wireless from the *Haimun* to the China shore station on March 14, 1904, and others followed, even though no substantial actions had as yet occurred. The *New York Times,* by reason of its arrangement of 1901 with the *Times,* was sharing the cost of James's enterprise and receiving the dispatches he sent.

Almost immediately after these messages began to move, the United States minister in Tokyo, probably acting in response to complaints entered by U.S. correspondents bottled up there, and concerned about competition, protested to the Japanese Foreign Ministry that favoritism was being shown to the *Times* and the *New York Times* in the arrangements involving the *Haimun.* The Foreign Ministry, however, disclaimed any responsibility or authority in the matter.

Aboard the *Haimun,* in the Yellow Sea, James was able to gather information on naval actions, including the sinking by a mine off Port Arthur of the Russian flagship *Petropavlosk* in April, with Admiral Makaroff aboard. He was able to report also the Japanese naval blockade of Port Arthur. At the same time, Fraser, in China, was able to report the landing of Japanese forces in Manchuria. The paper also had Dr. George Ernest Morrison in Peking and Thomas Cowen in Tientsin, both able to report other aspects of the war. In Tokyo, further, the *Times* was represented by a Captain Colquhoun of the Australian navy—not to be confused with Archibald Ross Colquhoun, *Times* correspondent in China in earlier years—and by U.S.-born Harold George Remington, formerly of the Paris edition of the *New York Herald,* who covered some of the late action of the war.

Early in June 1904, after about three months in service, the *Haimun* was obliged to cease operations, partly because of protests by Russia, but more because of objections at last raised by the Japanese military and naval staff. The experiment had produced some good reports beyond those noted, including accounts of the Japanese occupation of Dairen on May 30 and the beginning of the siege of Port Arthur. It was expensive coverage, and Moberly Bell, general manager of the *Times*, later observed ruefully that the costs amounted to about £2,000 (nearly $10,000) per month, and that the messages received averaged about £1 ($5.86) a word in actual expense, as compared to the $1.62 Shanghai-London rate by Great Northern Telegraph.

Other small craft were used to help report the war, but without wireless equipment, and more in the manner of the tugs engaged during the Spanish-American War. Paul Cowles, Pacific Coast superintendent for the Associated Press, sent to direct operations for the agency, shocked the AP management by asking for $80,000 "to buy a yacht." The *Genbu Maru* was, in fact, purchased and provided a means of reporting naval engagements and also carrying dispatches to Chefoo, on the China coast, whence they were sent along to Shanghai and on to the United States without censorship. This system was used until the war ended.

Ernest Brindle, a correspondent in China for the *Daily Mail,* and Stanley Washburn, son of U.S. Senator William Drew Washburn of Minnesota and acting as correspondent for the *Chicago Daily News,*[14] each chartered a dispatch boat. Brindle, aboard the *Chefoo,* tried to enter Port Arthur to cover the war from the Russian

---

14 The *Chicago Record,* Victor Lawson's morning paper, had been sold in 1901 to the morning *Chicago Times-Herald.* The *Record*'s foreign service was retained by Lawson at the time of the sale and made part of his evening *Chicago Daily News* organization.

position there, but was turned back. This effort cost the *Daily Mail* about £1,000 (nearly $5,000) before it was abandoned, and netted little or no news. The *Daily Mail* also had E. J. Harrison and Tom Clarke as correspondents. Harrison was in Tokyo, where he was to remain until 1913 for the *Mail* and also for the *New York Herald*. Clarke, then a young member of the staff of the *South China Morning Post*, recently established at Hong Kong, also wrote for the *Chicago Tribune*, but later had an extended career with the *Daily Mail*, mainly in London.

Washburn, of the *Chicago Daily News*, chartered the *Fawan* as a dispatch boat and operated it for about four months, facing hazards and meeting adventures, but realizing small return on the investment. Its chief value proved to be in ferrying John Foster Bass, then directing the *Daily News* war coverage. He witnessed the conclusion of a long Japanese land and sea operation bringing the Russian surrender of Port Arthur on January 1, 1905. Having observed the action from a position aboard a British cargo ship, he then moved aboard the *Fawan* to Chefoo to file his report.

Correspondents on shore in Manchuria reported land battles in February and March 1905 ending in Russian defeats, with some vivid accounts emerging. The end of the war came in May when a Russian fleet, bolstered by ships sent from the Baltic to the Far East,was almost entirely captured or sunk in the Tsushima Strait. The threat of disorders in Russia itself after the loss of the fleet led the Czar to accept mediation, even though the war continued through July, with the Japanese establishing control in Korea and occupying Sakhalin.

In proportion to the effort, expense, and numbers of correspondents deployed to report the war, the results were not impressive. Restrictions on their movements and the strict censorships, imposed by both belligerents, made the correspondents' tasks difficult, and the volume and quality of reports suffered through no essential fault of their own.

Lewis Etzel, an American reporting for the *Daily Telegraph*, was killed in Manchuria. Henry J. Middleton of the Associated Press, sent from the Paris bureau by way of St. Petersburg, died of illness in June 1904 near Liao-yang, then Russian headquarters in Manchuria. Nicholas E. Popoff, a Russian-born correspondent for the Associated Press, who signed his dispatches "Kirilov," was seriously wounded while with a Russian battery during the Battle of

Liao-yang in August 1904, regarded by some as the greatest battle since Sedan in 1870.[15]

Richard Henry Little, who had been in Cuba and the Philippines for the *Chicago Tribune* during the Spanish-American War, and who returned to that paper for a long career, primarily in the home office, represented the *Chicago Daily News* in the Russo-Japanese War. Attached to Russian forces, he was captured by the Japanese in Manchuria and held for five weeks. Francis McCullagh, also with the Russians for the *New York Herald* and the *Manchester Guardian*, was captured at Port Arthur and taken to Japan as a prisoner of war. Returning later to Russia, he represented the same two newspapers there during the Russian Revolution in 1917.

Melton Prior, artist-correspondent for the *Illustrated London News*, arrived in Tokyo early. He was dean of the press corps, with experience dating from the Ashanti campaign of 1873-74, and this was his last assignment. Frederic Villiers, artist-correspondent for the London *Graphic*, also in Tokyo, was a close second to Prior in terms of experience, having started in the Serbian-Turkish conflict of 1876.

Correspondents present, and already schooled in war coverage, beyond others already mentioned, included Bennet Burleigh of the *Daily Telegraph*; Edward Frederick Knight of the *Morning Post*, minus an arm lost in the South African war; Richard Harding Davis for *Collier's Weekly*; James H. (Jimmy) Hare, news photographer for *Collier's* and for the London *Sphere,* a weekly established in 1900; Frederick Palmer for *Collier's* and the *New York World*; Stephen Bonsal, William Dinwiddie, Thomas F. Millard, and Willmott Harsan't Lewis, all of the *New York Herald*; Oscar King Davis for the *New York Sun* and the Laffan News Bureau; Charles E. Hands and F. A. McKenzie for the *Daily Mail*; Percival Phillips for the *Daily Express*; William Maxwell for the *Standard*; Reginald Kann of *l'Illustration* of Paris; Luigi Barzini of the *Corriere della*

---

15   An unverified story is told of another Russian correspondent, Kraievsky by name, writing for the *Russkoye Slovo* of St. Petersburg. He is said to have posed either as British or American, calling himself "Colonel Palmer," and to have managed to enter Japan by way of the United States. Russian though he was, he is believed to have remained for two months, interviewing prominent Japanese, visiting troops and military installations, taking pictures, and then returning to the United States to do his writing. If true, he may have been engaged in espionage. It has been suggested that he may have been in Japan earlier, from 1885 until about 1894, also as a "Colonel Palmer," and acting as a stringer for the London *Times*. The *Times* did have stringer of that name in Tokyo at about that time.

Sera, Milan; and John T. McCutcheon, formerly of the *Chicago Record,* but a political cartoonist since 1903 for the *Chicago Tribune,* who made a quick trip to Japan as an artist-correspondent for that paper.

Reuter, with bureaus both in Tokyo and St. Petersburg, as well as in China, had correspondents present on both sides. The Agence Havas had Georges de LaSalle with the Russians. Martin Egan, formerly in the Philippines and China, was chief of the Associated Press bureau in Tokyo, with Robert M. Collins as an assistant. Both were in the field at times with the Japanese. Howard N. Thompson, AP correspondent in St. Petersburg, was with the Russians in Manchuria for a limited period, but returned to the capital. He was replaced by Henry J. Middleton of the Paris bureau, who died in Manchuria. Other AP men were George Denny, Frederick McCormick, W. Richmond Smith, Christian Hagerty, and Nemirovich Danchenko, a Russian, who produced a notable report on the capture of Port Arthur.

Jack London, already possessed of a reputation as a novelist, was in Japan on special assignment for the *New York Journal,* an afternoon paper since 1902. London's reports also went to other Hearst-owned papers, by then seven in number, plus two monthly magazines.

John Fox, Jr., also a novelist, was present as a writer for *Scribner's* magazine of New York. Edwin Emerson, who had written for *Leslie's* and *Collier's* during the Spanish-American War and later from Latin America, represented *Collier's.* Also serving *Collier's* were Richard Harding Davis, Frederick Palmer, and James H. Hare, a photographer. George Kennan, once with the Western Associated Press and the supervisor from 1865-68 for the construction of telegraph lines in Siberia, later a part of the Great Northern Telegraph Company facility, was a writer with the Japanese for *Outlook* magazine and witnessed the siege of Port Arthur.

Other newspaper correspondents reporting the war included Ellis Ashmead-Bartlett for the *Daily Telegraph,* who had reported the South African War; Gerald Morgan, representing both the *Daily Telegraph* and the *New York Tribune*; John T. Swift, Tokyo correspondent for the *New York Sun* and the Laffan News Bureau; Maurice Baring of the *Morning Post,* and John G. Hamilton of the *Manchester Guardian,* both with the Russians in Manchuria; two Paris journalists, a M. Recouly of *Le Temps,* and Ludovic Naudeau of *Le Petit Parisien,* who produced a notable report from Port

Arthur in 1905; and Captain Nicholas Klado of the Russian navy, who produced at least one excellent dispatch for *Novoe Vremya* of St. Petersburg.

The offer of mediation in the war by President Theodore Roosevelt, accepted by Czar Nicholas II early in June 1905, and then by the Japanese, brought a beginning of negotiations at Portsmouth, New Hampshire, on August 9 and signature of a peace treaty on September 5, with its terms favorable to Japan, the victorious party.

The conference was attended by only two correspondents possessing any direct or even remote experience with the war itself. They were Howard N. Thompson, Associated Press representative in St. Petersburg, who had been briefly at the Manchurian war front; and Dr. George Ernest Morrison, correspondent for the *Times* in Peking.

Dr. Emile Joseph Dillon, *Daily Telegraph* correspondent in St. Petersburg, accompanied the Russian delegation. En route to New York, he had a shipboard interview with Count Witte, Russian foreign minister. The text was sent by wireless to London by relay between four ships at sea, in another forward step in the technology of news communication.

Sir Donald Mackenzie Wallace, with previous experience in St. Petersburg, made the journey to Portsmouth for the *Times*. George W. Smalley, then in his last months as correspondent for the *Times* in Washington was present. A considerable number of other Washington correspondents also attended the conference, among them James T. Williams and R. O. Bailey, both of the Associated Press. The AP was further represented by Salvatore Cortesi, its Rome correspondent, and by its general manager, Melville E. Stone.

Stone had become acquainted with Count Witte and Baron Rosen of the Russian delegation while in St. Petersburg on agency business in 1903. At Portsmouth, he also became acquainted with three Japanese leaders, Barons Komura, Takahira, and Kaneko. Two Tokyo newspapers, the *Asahi* and the *Nichi Nichi,* and the St. Petersburg *Novoe Vremya,* had reporters present.

The conference brought together a group of journalists concerned with high politics and diplomacy rather than action, color, and personalities, and their reports were appropriately sober. This was something of a departure and foreshadowed substantial press attention to subjects of international significance in the years ahead.

The Spanish-American War had established the United States as a recognized world power. The Russo-Japanese War had done the same for Japan. These two wars, along with the campaigns in the Sudan, South Africa, the Philippines, and China in the years between 1898 and 1905 were a violent introduction to the twentieth century. But the violence was misleading, since it obscured great constructive advances occurring in the same years and reported also by the press. The capacity of the press to report the events both of war and of peace, and on a truly global scale, had been demonstrated by these very events. This in itself, and within the context of these pages, was evidence that some light and enlightenment had come to mankind.

The people of the world, well-served by the information media, were aware of new forces stirring to justify a sense of optimism as they contemplated the future. The nineteenth century had brought great advances, both spiritual and technical. The world had become one, and a new freedom and hope had been gained. There was reason to believe that these advances would continue. Wireless communication was beginning. Strange motor-driven vehicles were appearing in various countries. It had been proved that men could make machines that would carry them in flight. What other miracles might there be in the years just ahead? The press and its communications network now existed to bring tidings of all such things in a new era.

"News, the Manna of a Day" 18

Man's essential need, from the beginning, has been to understand his environment, and to learn to survive within its framework. To do so, he required information. The means and methods for gathering, organizing, and disseminating information useful in meeting that need has been the subject of the preceding pages.

It has been a long story, with its beginnings obscured by the very lack of those media of information now so familiar as to be taken for granted. Not until the art of printing from movable type appeared were the first shadows of ignorance and oppression swept away— printing gave wings to words.

The printing press was a product of man's ingenuity. From it came newssheets, corantos, pamphlets, weekly and daily newspapers, books, and periodicals. The minds of men were stimulated by the ideas and information made available. Out of the creativity resulting there came, among other things, the telegraph and cable, the typewriter and camera, the system of news agencies, the telephone and wireless—all of which advanced the information process.

Through the centuries, kings and generals, statesmen and scholars, churchmen and philosophers, traders and navigators, explorers and scientists, merchants and bankers had occupied positions of power and privilege in the world. They contrived to obtain information necessary for their purposes and their times. Yet even they were dependent upon random sources prior to the age of print. Only within the last 200 years have more than such a privileged few been afforded the opportunity to comprehend their world.

The newspaper press, within that moment of history, became the cutting edge in man's battle against ignorance, isolation, superstition, autocracy, drift, and misunderstanding. It is only stating a fact to say that the printing press, and newspapers in particular, brought a new equality to men, and brought the world into focus. This it had at last accomplished by the first years of the present century. It was the end of a long era in the story of mankind, and the beginning of a new and quite different period.

It is important to recognize, however, that these changes did not occur automatically merely because printing had made possible the dissemination of information. They occurred because men and women made them occur. These were the individual printers, writers, reporters, editors, and publishers who produced the publications and the content of those publications, along with the scientists, inventors, and technicians who gave them the tools with which to work.

These individuals were as important in the history of the world's advance as the greatest statesmen. Their contributions, on balance, may have been more constructive. They formed the *dramatis personae* of the foregoing pages. There were giants among them. There were many bit players and spear-carriers, but few villains.

In the progression from the fifteenth century, printers were at all times important figures. As newspapers prospered and gained freedom to publish current news, the printer yielded center stage to the editor and then to the publisher, as a proprietorial figure. As the newspaper gained importance, however, it did so because a group of reporters entered upon the purposeful and specialized task of seeking and writing news, both locally and in places increasingly remote.

However essential the editors, usually drawn from the ranks of the reporters, and however vital the function of the publisher in the production of the newspaper, the reporter or correspondent at the source of the news was the key personality, as he is today. The quality of his performance—given access to essential sources and freedom to write and publish—must determine the quality of the information presented to readers and to those who undertake to comment upon or interpret events through editorials or other methods.

The reporter tends to be a special breed. Properly speaking, he is just what the term implies—a reporter, and not a participant or advocate. His motivation in becoming a reporter is a very personal thing. It is not a task likely to bring wealth, fame, or even comfort. It is a thing of the mind and spirit. It probably begins with a lively sense of curiosity, an interest in people, things and events, a desire to understand them, and a desire to convey that understanding to others.

A good reporter requires a great breadth of interest and knowledge, and a sense of dedication matching that of a teacher or research scholar. He must have integrity, fairness, and responsibility. He needs patience, stamina, determination, and an element of skepticism, as well as an ability to deal with every sort of person with tact and courtesy. He needs to be able to obtain and sort out facts and produce a well-organized report, often under the pressure of time. Accuracy is a first essential, along with an ability to write a clear and coherent account in a style to capture and hold reader interest. It is not surprising that some are attracted to reporting, particularly in youth, by prospects of adventure and opportunities to observe events first-hand, as well as to see something of the world.

Marco Polo, although not a newsman, surely was moved by those particular impulses and wrote of his observations and experiences in Cathay as a reporter might have done. In later times, there were such other adventurers as Bayard Taylor, Henry Stanley, O'Donovan, Burleigh and Knight, Labouchere and Sala, George Morrison and Ross Colquhoun in a latter-day Cathay, Brinkley and House in Japan, and those men who accompanied polar expeditions.

Where adventure ends and peril begins presents a fine edge. The adventurers faced both, and included reporters who spent years covering wars and revolutions, often in remote parts of the world. Notable among them were Kendall and Gruneisen, Russell and Forbes, Townsend and Coffin, Reid and Villard, Finerty and Davenport, Prior and Villiers, MacGahan and Henty, and Creelman and Palmer. Not a few met death on the battlefield.

There were many of equal courage, sometimes reporting wars, but more concerned with politics, diplomacy, economics, and social problems, or occupying administrative editorial positions, and displaying vision, imagination, and enterprise. They included such men as Franklin and Cobbett, Muddiman and Woodfall, Lloyd and Topliff, Havas, Wolff and Reuter, Bennett and Greeley, Lawson and Stone, Scripps and Pulitzer, and Paz and Mitre. There were such editors as John Delane and C. P. Scott, Moberly Bell, John Edward Taylor, Henry M. Collins, and George Smalley.

Both in the field as reporters, and in the office as editors, there were such men as Crabb Robinson, Edwin L. Godkin, Wallace, Dillon, Chirol, Bourchier, Steed, Engländer, Diehl, Harris, and the five Vizetellys. There were Steevens and James, Nevinson and Mercadier, Bonsal and Chadourne, Walter E. Curtis and Henry R. Chamberlain.

Among those involved in the advance of reporting and the making of newspapers some were more flamboyant than others, but they nevertheless made their contributions. Such would include Richard Harding Davis and Winston Churchill, the younger Bennett, and Hearst and Harmsworth. Women contributing as reporters on the world scene included Flora Louise Shaw, Margaret Fuller Ossoli, Ellen Browning Scripps, and Elizabeth Cochrane (Nellie Bly). There also were such photographers as Fenton, Brady, O'Sullivan, and Hare.

Some of the great figures mentioned here, and others, gave decades of their lives to the business of information. Certain of them were at midpoint in their careers as the twentieth century began, but others had by then completed a quarter-century or more in service. John Merry LeSage and Stoddard Dewey were active for some sixty years. W. H. G. Werndel and Fergus Ferguson of Reuter were reporters in the field for almost fifty years. Engländer, Collins, and Dillon were not far short of that mark. Wallace, Bell, Chirol, Harris, Bellasyse, Steed, Bourchier, Blowitz, Hardman, Saunders, Prior, Villiers, Smalley, Bonsal, Palmer, Seibold, Edwin Arnold, and George Douglas Williams all had careers of from twenty-five to forty years. Nor does that complete the list.

Further, the advance of the press cannot be viewed without tribute to James Watt, father of the industrial revolution. Mention surely must go to Gutenberg himself, and to such contributors to communication and technology as Samuel F. B. Morse, Cyrus Field, John Brett, Wheatstone and Kelvin, Sir John Pender, Alexander Graham Bell, Guglielmo Marconi, Fessenden and DeForest, and to Christopher Sholes, David Napier, Robert Hoe, and Ottmar Mergenthaler. Again, the list is incomplete.

Thomas Hardy once wrote that "War makes rattling good history, but Peace is poor reading." Perhaps that viewpoint explains why much that has been written about the press and its writers has related to war correspondence, while much of substance had been neglected. It is to be hoped that the foregoing pages have put this matter in better perspective. Much of the page-one emphasis in newspapers themselves suggested that war and violence was the most important news of the day. Often it was, but usually it was not. The dramatic and the unusual in the events of the day do "make news," however. It is right that they should be reported, and usually right that they be reported on page one. War is dramatic, and crime, controversy, and catastrophe tend to appear on page one for the same reason. That it does so reflects a realistic editorial appraisal of public interest, and fits the Hardy thesis.

Well-meaning individuals in every community have protested this display of news. Such objections were being heard in the first years of the present century, as they have been heard since. The protests have not been directed at the dramatic and unusual, as such, but at the particular stories published, and upon the manner in which they were written and displayed. The objection was less to stories of war and catastrophes of nature than to stories of crime and controversy. At times, such protests were justified, as for example in the treatment of the Cuban situation between 1895 and 1898 by the *New York Journal* and the *New York World,* and in some of the crime news reports in the *New York Herald* of the 1830s and in the *New York Journal* of the 1890s and later. Taking into account the entire press, however, these were exceptional.

When the press began to function in the fifteenth century, the autocrats of palace and church regarded it as a threat to their established power and privilege, and sought to control it. That "adversary relationship," as it would be described today, has survived to the early twentieth century, and even to the present time, although in greatly modified form.

In the performance of its function, a newspaper reports events as they occur. It examines situations as they exist. It comments editorially upon circumstances with what ever wisdom and judgment it commands. However well it may perform these tasks, not every reader is going to be satisfied. If the reader is satisfied with what he finds in the pages, if what is reported and if what is said accords with his interests or beliefs, he makes no complaint. But this cannot always be.

In 1900, as at present, the news was not always "good." It is natural for readers to prefer pleasant news. But the press must report those unpleasant things that happen or that arise in the relationships between people. To do otherwise, would be to suppress information and to present a distorted picture, perhaps dangerously so. Yet editors find that unthinking readers seem to believe that because the press reports "bad" news, it therefore is responsible for causing such news.

Officials of government, directors of business and industry, members of organizations and institutions whose policies and practices are praised have no complaints about the press. Anything in the least unfavorable, however, produces a different attitude. If their actions or statements prove embarrassing, inexpedient, or inept, they commonly claim "misquotation" or "misunderstanding"; or they claim "misrepresentation" or "malice." If things go wrong they may seek to place the blame on "the media." They find it easy to rationalize such attitudes.

In 1900 many governments, as a heritage from the past, still exercised a control over the press within their countries. Where the press was free, as in the United States in particular, it was able to maintain a "watchdog" function over the interests and welfare of the public, whether with reference to government at all levels, or in other areas. As it still is, even under the best of circumstances, the press was a target of criticism then. This was reasonable enough, since the press as an institution is subject to human error. There was cause for concern, however, lest the more vocal critics of the press, not necessarily without their own special interests, lead enough members of the public to accept a negative view within which a reversal might occur detrimental to the provision of public information. Then, as now, there were persons who failed to grasp the fact that "freedom of the press" was the property of the people, rather than of the press itself, and inseparable from "freedom of speech" and "freedom of worship." There was a failure to realize that there were those, in government and out, ready to seize upon any public indifference or mindless disparagement of the press to hobble it, if they could, even where it was already free.

Having said this, it must be conceded that the press was not without faults in 1900, as the media, collectively, are not without faults at the present time. In 1900, one of the surviving faults was a political partisanship. The introduction of objective news writing after 1860 had helped rid the news columns of the worst such partisanship in some countries, including the United States and Great Britain. But it lingered in other countries, sometimes with the press an actual arm of government, and it lingered virtually everywhere in the form of an editorial policy put forward with considerable bias on the editorial or leader pages. There also was a disposition by many papers to report the news of crime and of some cases before the courts with a strong tendency toward sensationalism, reflected in writing style, placement of the stories on page one, and excesses of typographical or headline display.

Errors of fact and errors in typography also was a fault to which readers then, as now, had reason to object. The first requirement in news reporting is accuracy. Nobody is more disturbed by inaccuracies in print than the reporters and editors with the newspaper in which they appear. Every effort goes to avoid them, to correct them in later editions, and to publish "corrections" when appropriate. A daily newspaper edition, with more than 100,000 words to be processed under pressure of time, is almost certain to have some errors, and only when all human beings are perfect, and all machines as well, is it likely to be otherwise.

Newspapers in 1900, as today, were subject to some objections from readers concerning what was published and what might not have been published. It has never been easy for reporters and editors to draw a precise line, at a precise time, between what should be or must be reported and what need not be reported, while still providing a proper balance of information suited to the particular community in which the newspaper appears. What few members of the reading public realize is that there is always more information available than there is space to accommodate that information. The "news hole," as the term is used, is not limitless. A selection must be made, with decisions as to what is to be used and what omitted. In a free press situation, if something is omitted that a reader seeks it is not omitted for sinister reasons, but because it was crowded out by other news.

Those making a newspaper are aware that the final product is not perfect. They are so caught up in their daily tasks, however, that they have little time on a given day to re-evaluate and change the manner in which they perform those tasks. Nor do they have the power to change established procedures by a mere wave of the hand. They do have their own standards, however, and those standards are as likely as not to be even higher than the standards their critics advance. They are their own critics, and they tend to be defensive when others tell them of their shortcomings. They are professionals, they have their own code of ethics and code of performance. Once the day is over, they are prepared to consider what they might have done differently, and better. Changes may not come the next day, but perhaps by next week or next month new procedures may have been introduced.

It is in this fashion that improvements came in newspaper production prior to 1900, and continue to come. A newspaper reader of today may see little difference in the style of the paper he holds, as contrasted to a copy of earlier date. But if he compared a newspaper of 1850 with one of 1900, or a newspaper of 1900 with one of 1940 or 1970 the differences would be fully apparent.

The press assuredly had not attained perfection in the first years of the twentieth century, nor has it today. But by 1900 it had become so greatly effective as to represent a logical point at which it is proper to sum up the account of man's search for and need for information about his environment and his world. It is, of course, a search that never can end. Great changes and great advances have come since 1900, but that is not a part of this story.

This story, as told here, is one of the emergence of mankind from the darkness of prehistory into the light of the modern-day world. It has been a story of the manner in which information became available to assist man in that journey into the present century, particularly as provided through the press.

"What's past is prologue," Shakespeare wrote in *The Tempest* more than 250 years ago. And the past remains important because it has shaped the present, and has its bearing on the future.

The world is born afresh each day. The newspaper, too, is born afresh each day. The knowledge it brings and the events it reports affect all persons. Another British writer, Matthew Green, a poet following Shakespeare by a century, could say that "to come coffee-house I stray / For news, the manna of a day." By the early twentieth century the "manna of a day" was far more plentiful and far more nourishing. It was indeed a new day and a new century for a new generation in a new era.

Bibliography

Adams, E. D. *Great Britain and the American Civil War.* London, 1925.

Andrews, J. Cutler. *The North Reports the Civil War.* Pittsburgh, 1955.

——. *The South Reports the Civil War.* Princeton, 1970.

Anstruther, Ian. *I Presume: Stanley's Triumph and Disaster.* London, 1956.

Arciniegas, German. "Journalism in Colombia." *Quarterly Journal of Inter-American Relations,* July 1939, pp. 89–95.

Arnold, Matthew. *Friendship's Garland.* London, 1871.

Ashton, T. S. *The Industrial Revolution, 1760–1830.* London, 1948.

Atkins, J. B. *The Life of Sir William Howard Russell.* 2 vols. London, 1911.

Atkins, John Black. "The Work and Future of War Correspondents." *Monthly Review,* September 1901, pp. 81–89.

Austin, Alvin, E. " 'Greatest News Beat' Site Will be Marked." *Editor & Publisher,* 28 March 1953.

Avenel, Henri. *Histoire de la Presse Française Depuis 1789 jusqu'a nos jours.* Paris, 1900.

Babcock, Havilah. "The Press and the Civil War." *Journalism Quarterly,* March 1929, pp. 1–5.

Baehr, Harry W., Jr. *The New York Tribune Since the Civil War.* New York, 1936.

Baker, John Milton, *Henry Crabb Robinson of Bury, Jena, The Times and Russell Square.* London, 1937.

Baker, Ray Stannard. "How the News of the War Is Reported." *McClure's,* September 1898, pp. 491–95.

Barns, Margarita. *The Indian Press.* London, 1940.

Barrett, James Wyman. *Joseph Pulitzer and His World.* New York, 1941.

Barzini, Luigi. *Avventura in Oriente.* Milan, 1959.

Berger, Carl. *Broadsides & Bayonets: The Propaganda War of the American Revolution.* San Raphael, Calif., 1977.

Berger, Meyer. *The Story of The New York Times, 1851–1951.* New York, 1951.

Berryman, John. *Stephen Crane.* New York, 1950.

Blay, John S. *The Civil War: A Pictorial Profile.* New York, 1959.

Bleyer, Willard G. *Main Currents in the History of American Journalism.* Boston, 1927.

Bliven, Bruce, Jr. *The Wonderful Writing Machine.* New York, 1954.

Bloomfield, Leonard. *Language.* New York, 1933.

Blowitz, Henri de. "Journalism as a Profession." *Contemporary Review,* January 1893, pp. 37–43.

———. *Memoirs of M. de Blowitz.* London and New York, 1903.

Blumenfeld, Ralph D. *R. D. B.'s Diary.* London, 1930.

Bodmer, Frederick. *The Loom of Language.* Edited by Lancelot Hogben. New York, 1944.

Bowden, Witt. *The Industrial Revolution.* New York, 1928.

Bowman, W. D. *The Story of "The Times."* New York, 1931.

Boyle, Frederick. *Narrative of an Expelled Correspondent.* London, 1877.

———. *Through Fanteeland to Coomassie: A Diary of the Ashantee Campaigns in Africa.* London, 1874.

Breuil, Henri. *Four Hundred Centuries of Cave Art.* Translated by Mary E. Boyle. London, 1952.

"Britain's Famed Pictorial Weekly Is a Century Old" [Illustrated London News]. *Life,* 16 November 1942, pp. 71-78.

Britton, R. S. *The Chinese Periodical Press, 1800–1912.* Shanghai, 1933.

Brooks, Noah. *Washington in Lincoln's Time.* New York, 1896.

Brown, Charles H. *The Correspondent's War.* New York, 1967.

Brown, Francis. *Raymond of The Times.* New York, 1951.

Brown, Frank James. *The Cable and Wireless Communications of the World.* London, 1927.

Brown, Junius Henry. *Four Years in Secessia.* Detroit, 1866.

Brucker, Herbert. *Freedom of Information.* New York, 1949.

Buchanan, Lemont. *A Pictorial History of the Confederacy.* New York, 1951.

Buck, Sir Edward. *Simla Past and Present.* Calcutta, 1904.

Budge, E. A. W. *Rise and Progress of Assyriology.* London, 1925.

Bullard, F. L. *Famous War Correspondents.* Boston and London, 1913.

Burleigh, Bennet. *Empire of the East, or Japan and Russia at War, 1904–1905.* London, 1905.

———. *Khartoum Campaign.* London, 1898.

Burnham, Lord. *Peterborough Court: The Story of the Daily Telegraph.* London, 1955.

Busoni, Rafaello. *Stanley's Africa.* New York, 1944.

Bussey, H. Findlaten. *Sixty Years of Journalism.* Bristol, 1906.

Caldwell, Louis G. *The American Press and International Communication.* New York, 1945.

Carlson, Oliver. *Brisbane, A Candid Biography.* New York, 1937.

———. *The Man Who Made News: James Gordon Bennett.* New York, 1942.

Carnes, Cecil. *Jimmy Hare, News Photographer.* New York, 1940.

Carter, Samuel. *Cyrus Field: Man of Two Worlds.* New York, 1968.

Carter, Thomas Francis. *The Invention of Printing in China and Its Spread Westward.* 2d ed. rev. by L. Carrington Goodrich. New York, 1955.

Case, Henry J. *Guy Hamilton Scull, Soldier, Writer, Explorer and War Correspondent.* New York, 1922.

Casey, Ralph D., ed. *The Press in Perspective.* Baton Rouge, La., 1963.

Chambers, Julius. *News Hunting on Three Continents.* New York, 1921.

Chappe, Ignace Urbain Jean. *Histoire de la Télégraphie.* Paris, 1824.

Chirol, Valentine. *Fifty Years in a Changing World.* London, 1927.

Christman, Henry M., ed. *The American Journalism of Marx and Engels: A Selection from the New York Daily Tribune.* New York, 1966.

Churchill, Winston. *From London to Ladysmith via Pretoria.* London and New York, 1900.

———. *My Early Life: A Roving Commission.* London, 1930.

———. *The River War, A Historical Account of the Reconquest of the Soudan.* London and New York, 1900.

———. *The Story of the Malakand Field Force.* London, 1898.

Cisneros, Evangelina. *The Story of Evangelina Cisneros, Told by Herself: Her Rescue by Karl Decker.* Illustrated by Frederick Remington. New York, 1898.

Clark, Keith. *International Communications: The American Attitude.* New York, 1931.

Clarke, Arthur C. " 'I'll Put a Girdle Round the Earth in Forty Minutes,' " *American Heritage,* October 1958, p. 40.

———. *Voice Across the Sea.* New York, 1958.

Clarke, Grahame. *Archeology and Society.* 2d rev. ed. London, 1947.

Cochran, Negley D. *E. W. Scripps.* New York, 1933.

Cochrane, Elizabeth [Nellie Bly]. *Nellie Bly's Book: Around the World in Seventy-Two Days.* New York, 1890.

——— *Six Months in Mexico.* New York, 1888.

Codding, George Arthur, Jr. *The International Telecommunications Union: An Experiment in International Cooperation.* Leiden, 1952.

Coe, D. *Marconi, Pioneer of Radio.* New York, 1934.

Coffin, Charles Carleton. *Four Years of Fighting*. Boston, 1898.

Collins, Henry M. *From Pigeon Post to Wireless*. London, 1925.

Colquhoun, Archibald Ross. *China in Transformation*. Rev. ed. New York, 1912.

―――. *Dan to Beersheba: Work and Travel in Four Continents*. London, 1908.

Conférence télégraphique de St. Petersburg, 1875, Documents de la Conférence télégraphique internationale de St. Petersburg. Berne, 1876.

Conyngham, Captain David O. *Sherman's March Through the South, With Sketches and Incidents of the Campaign*. New York, 1865.

Cook, Sir Edward. *Delane of The Times*. New York, 1916.

Cook, Joel. *The Siege of Richmond: A Narrative of the Military Operations of Major General George B. McClellan During the Months of May and June 1862*. Philadelphia, 1862.

Coon, Carleton S. *The History of Man*. New York, 1962.

Coon, Horace. *American Tel. & Tel.* New York, 1939.

Cooper, C. A. *An Editor's Retrospect of Fifty Years of Newspaper Work*. London, 1898.

Cooper, Kent. *Barriers Down*. New York, 1942.

Copeland, Fayette. *Kendall of the Picayune*. Norman, Okla., 1943.

Cortissoz, Royal. *The Life of Whitelaw Reid*. 2 vols. New York, 1921.

―――. *The New York Tribune: Incidents and Personalities in History*. New York, 1923.

Creel, George. "Bold Pathfinder," *Collier's*, 27 February 1932, p. 16.

Creelman, James. *On the Great Highway: The Wanderings and Adventures of a Special Correspondent*. Boston, 1901.

Croker, J. W. *The Croker Papers; The Correspondence and Diaries of the Right Honorable John Wilson Croker, LL.D., F. R. S., Secretary to the Admiralty, from 1809 to 1830*. Edited by Louis J. Jennings. 2d ed. 3 vols. London, 1885.

Crozier, Emmet. *Yankee Reporters, 1861–1865*. New York, 1956.

Current, Richard N. *The Typewriter and the Men Who Made It.* Urbana, Ill., 1954.

Dabney, Thomas Ewing. *One Hundred Great Years: The Story of the Times-Picayune, From Its Founding to 1940.* Baton Rouge, La., 1944.

Dahl, Folke. *A Bibliography of English Corantos and Periodical Newsbooks, 1620–1642.* Stockholm, 1953.

Dana, Charles A. *Recollections of the Civil War.* New York, 1898.

Dasent, A. I. *John Thaddeus Delane, Editor of "The Times": His Life and Correspondence.* 2 vols. London, 1908.

Davidson, Philip. *Propaganda and the American Revolution.* Chapel Hill. N.C., 1941.

Dávila, Carlos G. *The Journalism of Chile.* University of Missouri Bulletin, vol. 29, no. 46, Journalism Series no. 53, edited by Robert S. Mann. Columbia, Mo., 1928.

Davis, Charles Belmont, ed. *Adventures and Letters of Richard Harding Davis.* New York, 1918.

Davis, Elmer. *History of The New York Times, 1851–1921.* New York, 1921.

————. "Must We Mislead the Public?" In *The Press in Perspective.* Edited by Ralph D. Casey. Baton Rouge, La., 1963.

Davis, Oscar King. *Released for Publication.* Boston, 1925.

Davis, Richard Harding. *The Cuban-Porto Rican Campaign.* New York and London, 1899.

————. *With Both Armies in South Africa.* New York, 1900.

————. *A Year from a Correspondent's Notebook.* London and New York, 1898.

Davis, Robert. *Notes of a War Correspondent.* New York, 1910.

Dawson, William Forrest, ed. *A Civil War Artist at the Front: Edwin Forbes' Life Studies of the Great Army.* New York, 1957.

Day, Samuel P. *Down South: Or an Englishman's Experiences at the Seat of the War.* 2 vols. London, 1862.

DeForest, Lee. *Father of Radio: The Autobiography of Lee De-Forest.* Chicago, 1950.

Dennis, Charles H. *Victor Lawson: His Times and His Work.* Chicago, 1935.

Desmond, Robert W. *The Press and World Affairs.* Introduction by Harold J. Laski. New York, 1937.

Dewey, Davis R. "The News of the French Revolution in America." *New England Quarterly,* September 1889, pp. 84–89.

Dicey, Edward. *Six Months in the Federal States.* London and Cambridge, 1863.

Diehl, Charles Sanford. *The Staff Correspondent: How the News of the World Is Collected and Dispatched by a Body of Trained Press Writers.* San Antonio, 1931.

Dillon, Emile J. *Leaves from Life.* London, 1932.

Dinwiddie, William. "Experiences as a War Correspondent." *Harper's Weekly,* 4 June 1904, pp. 862–64.

Doblhofer, Ernest. *Voices in Stone: The Decipherment of Ancients Scripts and Writings.* Translated by Mervyn Savill. New York, 1961.

Documents Relating to the Preparation of the Press Experts Committee. League of Nations: Document C.399.M. 140.1926. Geneva, 1926.

Donald, Robert, ed. *The Imperial Press Conference in Canada, 1920.* London, 1921.

Dorwart, Jeffery M. "James Creelman, the New York World and the Port Arthur Massacre." *Journalism Quarterly,* Winter 1973, pp. 697–701.

Douglass, Paul F., and Bômer, Karl. "The Press as a Factor in International Relations." [The International Combination of News Agencies.] *Annals of the American Academy of Political and Social Science,* July 1932.

Downey, Fairfax. *Richard Harding Davis: His Day.* New York, 1933.

Dugan, James. *The Great Iron Ship.* New York, 1954.

Dunlap, C. E., Jr. *Marconi: The Man and His Wireless.* New York, 1937.

Durant, Will and Ariel. *The Age of Napoleon.* Bk. 1. New York, 1975.

Dyer, Frank Lewis. *Edison, His Life and Inventions*. New York and London, 1929.

Eder, J. M. *History of Photography*. Translated by H. Epstein. New York, 1945.

Eiliassen, Peter. *Ritzaus Bureau, 1866–1916*. Copenhagen, 1916.

Emerson, Edward, Jr. "The Making of a War Correspondent." *Reader*, July 1904.

Emery, Edwin. *The Press and America: An Interpretative History of the Mass Media*. 3d ed. Englewood Cliffs, N.J., 1972.

Escott, T. H. S. *Masters of English Journalism*. London, 1911.

Ewald, William Bragg, Jr. *Rogues, Royalty, and Reporters: The Age of Queen Anne Through Its Newspapers*. Boston, 1956.

Fahie, J. J. *A History of Electric Telegraphy to the Year 1837*. London, 1844.

Farwell, Byron, *The Man Who Presumed*. New York, 1957.

Fay, Bernard. *Notes on the American Press at the End of the Eighteenth Century*. New York, 1927.

Fenn, G. Manville. *George Alfred Henty: The Story of an Active Life*. London, 1907.

Fessenden, H. M. *Fessenden—Builder of Tomorrow*. New York, 1940.

Field, Henry M. *The Story of the Atlantic Telegraph*. New York, 1896.

Fine, Barnett. "When 'Boss' Lord Ruled 'The Sun'." *Editor & Publisher*, 18 February 1922, p. 5.

Finegan, Jack. *Light from the Ancient Past*. Princeton, N.J., 1947.

Finerty, John F. *Warpath and Bivouac*. Chicago, 1890.

"First Phoned Story Published Feb. 13, 1877." *Editor & Publisher*, 14 February 1942.

Fitzler, M. A. H. *Die Entstehung der Sigenannten Fuggerzeitungen in der Wiener Nationalbiblitek*. Baden bie Wien, 1937.

Fogg, William Perry. *"Round the World": Letters from Japan, China, India, and Egypt*. Privately printed. Cleveland, 1872.

Forbes, Archibald. *The Afghan Wars, 1839–42 and 1878–80*. New York, 1892.

———. *Memories and Studies of War and Peace*. New York, 1895.

———. My Experiences of the War Between France and Germany. 2 vols. London, 1871.

———. *Souvenirs of Some Continents*. London, 1885.

———. "War Correspondents and the Authorities." *Nineteenth Century*. January 1880, pp. 185–90.

———. *The War Correspondence of the "Daily News," 1877–1878*. London, 1878.

Ford, Edwin H. and Emery, Edwin, eds. *Highlights in the History of the American Press: A Book of Readings*. Minneapolis, 1954.

Fox Bourne, H. R. F. *English Newspapers*. 2 vols. London, 1887.

Francis, J. C. *Notes by the Way, with a Memoir of Joseph Knight, F.S.A.* London, 1909.

Frédérix, Pierre. *Un Siècle de Chasse aux Nouvelles de l'Agence d'Information Havas a l'Agence France-Presse (1835–1957)*. Preface by André Siegfried. Paris, 1959.

Friedel, Frank. *The Splendid Little War*. Boston, 1958.

"From Journalism to Public Life; When Rt. Hon. L. S. Amery Worked on The Times." *World's Press News*, 15 September 1932, p. 11.

Fulle, Hector. "Getting Into Port Arthur." *Reader*, November-December 1904, pp. 38–47.

Funck-Brentano, Franz. *Les Nouvellistes*. Paris, 1905.

Furlong, Charles Wellington. "Retracing the Epic of 'Darkest Africa'," *New York Times Magazine*, 17 April 1932, p. 8.

Furneau, Rupert. *The Breakfast War*. New York, 1960.

———. *The First War Correspondent; William Howard Russell*. London, 1944.

Furuno, Inosuke, ed. *Tsushinsha shi kankokai*. [History of News Agencies.] Tokyo, 1958.

Gaine, Hugh. *The Journals of Hugh Gaine, Printer*. 2 vols. Edited by Paul Leicester Ford. New York, 1902.

Gardner, Brian. *Mafeking: A Victorian Legend*. London, 1966.

"George Steevens—a prince among descriptive writers." *World Press News*, 17 December 1954.

Gernsheim, Helmut and Alison, eds. *Roger Fenton, Photographer of the Crimean War*. London, 1954.

Gibb, D. E. W. *Lloyd's of London: A Study in Individualism*. New York, 1957.

Giles, Frank. *A Prince of Journalists: The Life and Times of Henri Stefan Opper de Blowitz*. London, 1962.

Gilkes, Lillian. *Cora Crane*. Bloomington, Ind., 1960.

Glyn, Daniel. *The First Civilizations*. New York, 1971.

Gobright. Lawrence A. *Recollections of Men and Things at Washington*. New York, 1869.

Godwin, G. "Century of Communications." *Fortnightly*, June 1937, pp. 732–36.

Gollán, José S. "A Modern Argentine Newspaper." *Bulletin of the Pan American Union*, September 1930.

Gordon, Cyrus H. *The Living Past*. New York, 1951.

Gould, Lewis L., and Greeve, Richard. *Photojournalist: The Career of Jimmy Hare*. Austin, Texas, 1977.

Gramling, Oliver. *AP, The Story of News*. New York, 1940.

Grant, James. *The Newspaper Press: Its Origin, Progress and Present Position*. 3 vols. London, 1871.

Grant, Michael, ed. *The Birth of Western Civilization*. New York, 1964.

Griffin, W. E. *Charles Carleton Coffin*. Boston, 1898.

Grogan, Lady Ellinore. *The Life of J. D. Bourchier*. London, 1926.

Gross, Felix. *Rhodes of Africa*. New York, 1957.

Groth, Otto. *Die Zeitung, ein system der Zeitungskunde*. 33 vols. Mannehim, Berlin and Leipzig, 1928.

Hale, William Harland. *Horace Greeley, Voice of the People*. New York, 1950.

————. "When Karl Marx Worked for Horace Greeley." *American Heritage*, April 1957.

Hales, A. G. *Campaign Pictures of the War in South Africa, 1899–1902*. London, 1900.

————. "The Life of a War Correspondent." *Pall Mall*, February 1901, pp. 204–11.

Hall, Richard. *Stanley, An Adventurer Explored.* Boston, 1975.

Harlow, Alvin, F. *Old Wires and New Waves: The History of the Telegraph, Telephone and Wireless.* New York and London, 1936.

Harlow, Ralph Volney. *Samuel Adams, Promoter of the American Revolution: A Study in Psychology and Politics.* New York, 1932.

Harper, Robert S. *Lincoln and the Press.* New York, 1951.

Harris, Walter Burton. *The Land of an African Sultanate—Travels in Morocco, 1887, 1888, 1889.* London, 1908.

Hartcup, John. *Love Is Revolution: The Story of Camille Desmoulins.* London and New York, 1950.

Hatin, Eugene. *Histoire Politique et Litéraire de la Presse en France.* 8 vols. Paris, 1859–61.

Hawkes, Jacquetta and Woolley, C. Leonard. *Prehistory and the Beginnings of Civilization.* New York, 1962; London, 1963.

Hawkins, Eric and Sturdevant, Robert N. *Hawkins of the Paris Herald.* New York, 1963.

Hearst, William Randolph. *William Randolph Hearst, A Portrait in His Own Words.* Edited by Edmond D. Coblentz. New York, 1952.

Herd, Harold. *The March of Journalism: The Story of the British Press from 1622 to the Present Day.* London, 1952.

Herring, James M., with Gross, Gerald C. *Telecommunications: Economics and Regulations.* New York and London, 1936.

Hibbert, Christopher. *The House of Medici: Its Rise and Fall.* New York, 1975.

Hindle, Wilfred. *The Morning Post, 1772–1937.* London, 1937.

Hird, Frank. *H. M. Stanley, The Authorized Life.* London, 1935.

Hogarth, Paul. *The Artist as Reporter.* New York and London, 1967.

Hohenberg, John. *Foreign Correspondence: The Great Reporters and Their Times.* New York and London, 1964.

Holtman, Robert B., *Napoleonic Propaganda.* Baton Rouge, La., 1950.

Holden, W. Sprague. *Australia Goes to Press.* Detroit, 1961.

Honan, M. B. *The Personal Adventures of "Our Own Correspondent" in Italy.* 2 vols. London, 1852.

Horan, James D. *Mathew Brady, Historian With a Camera.* New York, 1955.

―――. *Timothy O'Sullivan: America's Forgotten Photographer.* New York, 1966.

Hosmer, George Washington. *The Battle of Gettysburg.* New York, 1913.

Hughes, H. M. *News and the Human Interest Story.* Chicago, 1940.

Hudson, Federic. *Journalism in the United States from 1690 to 1872.* New York, 1873.

Hergo, Maria C. "The Argentine Press: Beginnings and Growth." *Journalism Quarterly,* September 1939, pp. 253–58.

Hunt, F. Knight. *The Fourth Estate.* 2 vols. London, 1850.

Hunt, William. *Then and Now: Fifty Years of Newspaper Work.* Hull, 1887.

James, Lionel. *High Pressure.* London, 1929.

―――. *Times of Stress.* London, 1929.

Jebb, Sir Richard C. "Ancient Organs of Public Opinion." In *Essays and Addresses.* Cambridge, 1907.

Jeffrey, William H. *Mitre and Argentina.* New York, 1952.

Jessen, Hans. "Wo Kommt der Aviso Her?" (Amsterdam) *Gazette* 1, 1956.

Johnson, Malcolm. "100th Anniversary of 1st Telegraph Message." *Editor & Publisher,* 20 May 1944, pp. 11, 54.

Jones, Sir Roderick. *A Life in Reuters.* London, 1951.

Judson, Isabella Field, ed. *Cyrus W. Field, His Life and Work.* New York, 1866.

Kanesada, Hanazono. *The Development of Japanese Journalism.* Osaka, 1924.

Kawabé, Kisaburo. *The Press and Politics in Japan.* Chicago, 1921.

Kendall, George Wilkins. *Narrative of the Santa Fe Expedition.* 2 vols. Chicago, 1929.

Kennan, George. "How War News Is Collected." *Outlook,* 11 June 1898, pp. 369–73.

———. *Tent Life in Siberia.* New York and London, 1870.

King, Homer W. *Pulitzer's Prize Editor: A Biography of John A. Cockerill, 1845–1891.* Durham, N.C., 1965.

Kinglake, A. W. *Invasion of Crimea.* 9 vols. 6th ed. London, 1877–88.

Kingsley, Philip. *The Chicago Tribune, Its First Hundred Years.* 3 vols. New York, 1943–45.

Kirk, John W. "The First News Message by Telegraph." *Scribner's Magazine,* May 1892.

Kitchin, F. Harcourt. *Moberly Bell and His Times: An Unofficial Narrative,* London, 1925.

Klarwill, Victor von, ed. *The Fugger News Letters.* Translated by Pauline de Clary. New York, 1922.

———. ed. *The Fugger News Letters: Second Series, 1568–1605.* Translated by L. C. R. Byrne. London, 1926.

Kleinpaul, Johannes. *Fugger News-Letters, 1568–1605.* Leipzig, 1921.

Knight, Oliver. *Following the Indian Wars: The Story of the Newspaper Correspondents Among the Indian Campaigners.* Norman, Okla., 1960.

———. *I Protest, Selected Disquisitions of E. W. Scripps.* Madison, Milwaukee, and London, 1966.

———. "A Revised Check List of Indian War Correspondents, 1866–91." *Journalism Quarterly,* Winter 1961, pp. 81–82.

Knightley, Phillip. *The First Casualty; From the Crimea to Vietnam: The War Correspondent as Hero, Propagandist, and Myth Maker.* New York and London, 1975.

Knowles, L. C. A. *The Industrial and Commercial Revolutions in Great Britain During the Nineteenth Century.* 3d rev. ed. London and New York, 1926.

Knox, Thomas W. *Camp-Fire and Cotton-Field.* New York, 1865.

Kouwenhoven, John A. *Adventures of America, 1857–1900: A Pictorial Record from Harper's Weekly.* New York and London, 1938.

Kreighbaum, Hillier. *Facts in Perspective.* Englewood Cliffs, N.J., 1956.

Kroeber, A. L., ed. *Anthropology Today.* Chicago, 1963.

Labouchere, Henry. *Diary of a Besieged Resident of Paris.* 3d ed. London, 1872.

Land, Myrick. "Two Words That Changed the World." *This Week,* 21 June 1959, pp. 20–23.

Landon, Percival. "War Correspondents and the Censorship." *Nineteenth Century,* 15 September 1932, p. 11.

Lane, Margaret. *Edgar Wallace: The Biography of a Phenomenon.* New York, 1939.

Laney, Al. *Paris Herald; The Incredible Newspaper.* New York, 1947.

Langford, Gerald. *The Richard Harding Davis Years: A Biography of Mother and Son.* New York, 1961.

Laufer, Berthold. *Paper and Printing in Ancient China.* Chicago, 1931.

Lawrence, George Alfred. *Border and Bastille.* London and New York, 1863.

Lazo, Raimundo. "Early Printing in Spanish America." *Bulletin of the Pan American Union,* November 1973, pp. 809–21.

Lee, Alfred McClung. *The Daily Newspaper in America: The Evolution of a Social Instrument.* New York, 1937.

Lin Yu'tang. *A History of the Press and Public Opinion in China.* New York, 1936.

Littell, Blaine. *South of the Moon: On Stanley's Trail Through the Dark Continent.* New York, 1966.

Lowe, Charles. *Tales of a 'Times' Correspondent.* London, 1927.

Löwenthal, Rudolf. "Public Communications in China Before July 1973." *Chinese Political and Social Science Review,* April-June 1938, pp. 42–58.

Lucas, Reginald. *Lord Glenesk and the "Morning Post."* London, 1910.

Lundberg, Ferdinand. *Imperial Hearst: A Social Biography.* New York, 1936.

Lutnick, Solomon. *The American Revolution and the British Press, 1775–1783.* Columbia, Mo., 1967.

Mabie, Carlton. *The American Leonardo: A Life of Samuel F. B. Morse.* New York, 1943.

MacDougall, Curtis D. *Interpretative Reporting.* 3d ed. New York, 1957.

MacGahan, J. A. *Campaigning on the Oxus, and the Fall of Khiva.* 4th ed. London, 1876.

———. *The Turkish Atrocities in Bulgaria.* London, 1876.

———. *Under Northern Lights.* London, 1876.

Mackay, Charles. *Through the Long Day.* London, 1887.

MacKenzie, C. C. *Alexander Graham Bell.* Boston, 1928.

Mackenzie, Fred A. "English War Correspondents in South Africa." *Harper's,* July 1900, pp. 209–11.

———. *The Mystery of The Daily Mail, 1896–1921.* London, 1921.

Maclaurin, W. Rupert. *Invention and Innovation in the Radio Industry.* New York, 1949.

Makower, S. V. *Notes Upon the History of "The Times," 1785–1904.* Edinburgh, 1905.

Mance, Brigadier General Sir Osborne. *International Telecommunications.* London, 1943.

Manning, Olivia. *The Reluctant Rescue.* New York, 1947.

Marble, Annie Russell. *From 'Prentice to Patron: The Life Story of Isaiah Thomas.* New York and London, 1935.

Marcosson, Isaac F. *David Graham Phillips and His Times.* New York, 1912.

Mathews, Joseph J. "The Father of War Correspondence." *Virginia Quarterly Review,* Winter 1945, pp. 111–27.

———. *George W. Smalley: Forty Years as a Foreign Correspondent.* Chapel Hill, N.C., 1973.

———. *Reporting the Wars.* Minneapolis, 1957.

———. "Walter Burton Harris, Times Correspondent in Morocco." *Journalism Quarterly,* September 1940, pp. 227–31.

Matthews, George T., ed. *News and Rumor in Renaissance Europe.* New York, 1959.

McCarthy, Justin and Robinson, Sir John. *The "Daily News" Jubilee.* London, 1896.

McCracken, Harold. *Frederic Remington: Artist of the Old West.* Philadelphia, 1947.

McCutcheon, John T. *Drawn from Memory.* Indianapolis, 1950.

McElroy, John. *This Was Andersonville.* Edited by Roy Meredith. New York, 1957.

McMurtrie, Douglas C. and Farran, Don. *Wings for Words: The Story of Johann Gutenberg and His Invention of Printing.* New York, 1940.

McNaught, Carlton. *Canada Gets the News.* Toronto, 1940.

McRae, Milton A. *Forty Years in Newspaperdom: The Autobiography of a Newspaper Man.* New York, 1924.

Melgund, Viscount. "Newspaper Correspondents in the Field." *Nineteenth Century,* March 1880, pp. 434–42.

Mels, Edgar. "War News—Its Collection and Cost." *Saturday Evening Post,* 2 July 1904, pp. 14–17.

Mengel, Willi. *Ottmar Mergenthaler and the Printing Revolution.* Brooklyn, 1954.

Meredith, Roy. *Mr. Lincoln's Camera Man, Mathew B. Brady.* New York, 1946.

———. *The World of Mathew Brady: Portraits of the Civil War.* New York, 1977.

Meriwether, Walter Scott. "In the Days When the Story Was the Thing." *Editor & Publisher,* 18 February 1922, p. 5.

Millard, Thomas F. "A War Correspondent and His Future." *Scribner's,* February 1905, pp. 242–48.

Miller, Francis Trevelyan, et al., eds. *The Photographic History of the Civil War.* Introduction by Henry Steele Commager. 5 vols. New York, 1957.

Miller, John C. *Sam Adams: Pioneer in Propaganda.* Boston, 1936.

Millis, Walter. *The Martial Spirit.* Boston and London, 1931.

Mills, J. Saxon. *The Press and Communications of Empire.* New York, 1924.

Mitchell, Edward Page. *Memoirs of an Editor.* New York, 1924.

Mitton, Fernand. *La Presse Française: Des Origines a la Révolution.* Paris, 1943.

Moberly Bell, E. H. C. *The Life and Letters of C. F. Moberly Bell.* London, 1927.

Mooradian, Karlen. *The Dawn of Printing.* Journalism Monographs, no. 23. Minneapolis, 1972.

Moore, Frank, comp. *Diary of the American Revolution.* 2 vols. 2d ed. New York, 1967.

Moorhouse, A. G. *Writing and the Alphabet.* London, 1946.

Moran, James. *Printing Presses: Their History and Developoment from the Fifteenth Century to Modern Times.* Berkeley, 1973.

Moreno, G. Galván. *El Periodismo Argentine: Amplia y Documentada Historia Desde sus Origenes Hasta el Presente.* Buenos Aires, 1944.

Morison, Stanley, ed. *The History of the London Times, 1785–1948.* 5 vols. London and New York 1935–1948.

———. *John Bell, 1745–1831.* London, 1930.

Morley, Edith J. *The Life and Times of Henry Crabb Robinson.* London, 1935.

Morris, Joe Alex. *Deadline Every Minute: The Story of the United Press.* Garden City, N.Y., 1957.

Morse, Edward Lind. *Samuel F. B. Morse: His Letters and His Journals.* 2 vols. Boston and New York, 1914.

Mott, Frank Luther. *American Journalism: A History of Newspapers in the United States through 260 years: 1690 to 1950.* New York, 1950.

Mott, Frank Luther and Casey, Ralph D., eds. *Interpretations of Journalism, A Book of Readings.* New York, 1937.

Muddiman, J. G. (J. B. Williams). *The King's Journalist, 1659–1689.* London, 1923.

Nafziger, Ralph O. *International News and the Press.* New York, 1940.

Neilly, J. *Besieged With Baden-Powell.* London, 1900.

Nevins, Allen. *The Evening Post: A Century of Journalism.* New York, 1922.

Nevinson, Henry W. *Changes and Chances.* New York, 1923.

——. *Fire of Life.* London, 1935.

——. *Ladysmith, The Diary of a Siege.* London, 1900.

——. *More Changes More Chances.* New York and London, 1925.

Newhall, Beaumont. *The History of Photography from 1839 to the Present Day.* New York, 1949.

Newman, Henry. *A Roving Commission.* London, 1937.

News Agencies: Their Structure and Operation. UNESCO publication. Paris, 1953.

"The Newspaper Correspondent in the War." *Review of Reviews* [New York], November 1898, pp. 538-41.

Nichols, M. E. *(CP) The Story of the Canadian Press.* Toronto, 1948.

North, S. N. D. *History and Present Condition of the Newspaper and Periodical Press in the United States.* Washington, 1880.

O'Brien, Frank M. *The Story of The Sun.* 2d ed. New York, 1928.

O'Connor, Richard. *The Scandalous Mr. Bennett.* Garden City, N.Y., 1962.

O'Donovan, Edmund. *The Merv Oasis, Travels and Adventures East of the Caspian, during the years 1879, 1880-1881.* 2 vols. London, 1882.

Ogden, Rollo. *The Life and Letters of Edwin Lawrence Godkin.* 2 vols. New York, 1907.

Ogg, Oscar. *The 26 Letters.* 2d ed. New York, 1961.

Older, Mrs. Fremont. *William Randolph Hearst, American.* New York, 1936.

O'Malley, I. B. *Florence Nightingale, 1820-1856.* London, 1931.

Ono, Hideo. *A Tale of Kawara-ban: A History of Mass Communication During the Yedo Period (1590-1868).* Tokyo, 160.

Opie, Iona and Peter. *Oxford Dictionary of Nursery Rhymes.* London, 1951.

O'Shaughnessy, James. "Harden Tells Story of Manila Bay Scoops." *Editor & Publisher,* 18 February 1922, p. 5.

O'Shea, John Augustus. *Leaves from the Life of a Special Correspondent.* 2 vols. London, 1885.

———. *Round-About Recollections.* London, 1892.

Oswald, Clyde. *A History of Printing.* New York, 1928.

Page, Charles A. *Letters of a War Correspondent.* Boston, 1899.

Paine, Albert Bigelow. *Thomas Nast: His Period and His Pictures.* New York, 1904.

Paine, Ralph D. *Roads of Adventure.* Boston, 1922.

Painter, George D. *William Caxton, A Biography.* New York, 1977.

Palmer, Frederick. *Going to War in Greece.* New York, 1897.

———. *With Kuroki in Manchuria.* New York, 1904.

———. *With My Own Eyes: A Personal Story of Battle Years.* Indianapolis, 1933.

Parrington, Vernon. *Main Currents in American Thought.* 3 vols. New York, 1937.

Payne, George Henry. *History of Journalism in the United States.* London and New York, 1920.

Pears, Sir Edwin. *Forty Years in Constantinople.* New York, 1916.

Pearse, E. S. *Four Months Besieged, The Story of Ladysmith.* London, 1900.

Perivier, A. *Napopléon journaliste.* Paris, 1918.

Peterson, Theodore. *Magazines in the Twentieth Century.* Urbana, Ill., 1956.

Phillips, Cabell, ed. *Dateline: Washington; The Story of National Affairs Journalism.* New York, 1949.

Pollard, James E. *The Presidents and the Press.* New York, 1947.

———. *The Presidents and the Press: Truman to Johnson.* Washington, 1964.

Pound, Reginald and Harmsworth, Geoffrey. *Northcliffe.* London and New York, 1960.

Price, Priscilla. *The Life of Henry Morton Stanley.* London, 1930.

Prior, Melton. *Campaigns of a War Correspondent.* Edited by H. L. Bensusan. London, 1912.

Pupin, Michael I. *From Immigrant to Inventor.* New York, 1923.

Ralph, Julian. *At Pretoria: The Capture of the Boer Capitals and the Hoisting of the Flag at Pretoria.* London, 1901.

————. *Making of a Journalist.* New York, 1903.

————. *Toward Pretoria: A Record of the War Between Britain and Boer, to the Relief of Kimberley.* New York, 1900.

————. *War's Brighter Side: The Story of the Friend Newspaper Edited by the Correspondents with Lord Roberts's Forces.* New York, 1901.

Randall, James G. "The Newspaper Problem and Its Bearing Upon Secrecy During the Civil War." *American Historical Review,* January 1918.

Report on the British Press. PEP publication. London, 1938.

Richardson, Albert D. *The Secret Service, the Field, the Dungeon and Escape.* Hartford, Conn., 1965

Richardson, J. Hall. *From the City to Fleet Street.* London, 1927.

Riegel, O. W. *Mobilizing for Chaos.* New Haven, 1934.

"The Rise and Fall of the War Correspondent." *MacMillan's,* August 1904, pp. 301–10.

Rittenhouse, Mignon. *The Amazing Nellie Bly.* New York, 1856.

Robb, Arthur T. [Articles on Confederate news agency.] *Editor & Publisher,* 13, 20, 27 August 1949.

Roberts, Brian. *The Churchills in Africa.* London, 1970.

Robinson, Henry Crabb. *Diary, Reminiscences, and Correspondence of Henry Crabb Robinson, F.S.A., Barrister-at-Law.* Selected and edited by Thomas Sadler, Ph. D. 3 vols. 3d ed. London, 1872.

Robinson, Sir John H. *Fifty Years of Fleet Street.* ·London, 1904.

Rogers, Cornwell B. *The Spirit of Revolution in 1789: A Study of Public Opinion as Revealed in Political Songs and Other Popular Literature at the Beginning of the French Revolution.* Princeton, 1949.

Rosebault, Charles. *When Dana Was The Sun.* New York, 1931.

Rosewater, Victor. *History of Co-operative News-Gathering in the United States.* New York, 1930.

Russell, William Howard. *The British Expedition to the Crimea.* Rev. ed. London, 1858.

———. *My Diary During the Last Great War.* London, 1874.

———. *My Diary North and South.* Edited by Fletcher Pratt. New York, 1954.

———. *The War.* London, 1855.

Russo-Japanese War: A Photographic Descriptive Review from the Reports, and Cables of Collier's War Correspondents of the Great Conflict in the Far East. New York, 1905.

Sala, George Augustus. *The Life and Adventures of George Augustus Sala.* 2 vols. London, 1895.

———. *My Diary of America in the Midst of War.* 2 vols. London, 1865.

Salmon, L. M. *The Newspaper and Authority.* New York, 1923.

———. *The Newspaper and the Historian.* New York, 1925.

Salmon, Ludwig. *Geschichte des Deutschen Zeitungswesens.* 3 vols. Oldenburg and Leipzig, 1906.

Sardella, Pierre. *Nouvelles et Speculations a Venise au Debut de XVIe Siecle.* Paris, 1948.

Sass, Herbert Ravenel. *Outspoken: 150 Years of the News and Courier.* Columbia, S.C., 1953.

de Sauvigny, Guillaume de Bertier. "The American Press and the Fall of Napoleon in 1814." *American Philosophical Society Proceedings* 98, 1954, pp. 337–75.

Schierbrand, Wolf von. "Confessions of a Foreign Newspaper Correspondent." *World's Work,* April 1903, pp. 3355–58.

Schlesinger, Arthur M. *Prelude to Independence: The Newspaper War on Britain, 1764–1776.* New York, 1958.

Schreiner, George Abel. *Cables and Wireless, and Their Role in the Foreign Relations of the United States.* Boston, 1924.

Schwedler, Wilhelm. "Das Nachrichtensystem Weltpresse." *Zeitungswissenschaft,* 1 July 1934.

C. P. Scott, 1846–1932: The Making of The Manchester Guardian. London, 1946.

Scudmore, Frank A. *A Sheaf of Memories.* London, 1925.

Seaver, George. *David Livingstone: His Life and Letters.* New York, 1957.

Seitz, Don C. *Horace Greeley, Founder of the New York Tribune.* Indianapolis, 1926.

———. *The James Gordon Bennetts, Father and Son.* Indianapolis, 1928.

———. *Joseph Pulitzer: His Life and Letters.* New York, 1924.

Seldes, George. *To Tell the Truth and Run.* New York, 1953.

"75th Anniversary of La Prensa." *Bulletin of the Pan American Union.* Washington, D.C., March 1945.

Shaaber, M. A. *Some Forerunners of the Newspaper in England, 1476–1622.* Philadelphia, 1929.

Sharp, Eugene W. "Cracking the Manila Censorship in 1899–1900." *Journalism Quarterly,* December 1943, pp. 280–85.

———. *International News Communications: The Submarine Cable and Wireless as News Carriers.* University of Missouri Bulletin, vol. 28, no. 3, Journalism Series, no. 45. Pamphlet. Columbia, Mo., 1947.

Sheppard, S. T. "The Genesis of a Profession." *United Service Magazine.* March 1907, pp. 569–75.

Siebert, Frederic Seaton. *Freedom of the Press in England, 1476–1776.* Urbana, Ill., 1952.

Simonis, H. *Street of Ink.* London, 1917.

Simpson, J. P. *Pictures from Revolutionary Paris.* Edinburgh and London, 1848.

Smalley, George W. *Anglo-American Memories.* London, 1911.

Smyth, Albert H. *Bayard Taylor.* Boston and New York, 1896.

Smythe, T. C. "War of 1812 Whetted Public Appetite for Straight News." *Editor & Publisher,* 6 February 1965, pp. 47–48.

Snyder, Louis M., and Morris, Richard M., eds. *A Treasury of Great Reporting.* Preface by Herbert Bayard Swope. New York, 1949.

Stallman, E. W. and Hagemann, E. R., eds. *The War Dispatches of Stephen Crane.* New York, 1964.

Stanley, Henry Morton. *The Autobiography of Henry Morton Stanley.* Edited by Dorothy Stanley. New York, 1909.

————. *The Congo and the Founding of Its Free State.* 2 vols. London and New York, 1885.

————. *Coomassie and Magdala: Two British Campaigns.* London and New York, 1874.

————. *The Exploration Diaries of H. M. Stanley.* Edited by Richard Stanley and Alan Neame. New York, 1962.

————. *How I Found Livingstone.* London, 1872.

————. *In Darkest Africa.* 2 vols. London and New York, 1890.

————. *My Early Travels and Adventures in America and Asia.* 2 vols. London and New York, 1895.

————. *Through the Dark Continent.* 2 vols. London and New York, 1878.

————. *Through South Africa.* London and New York, 1898.

Starr, Louis M. *Bohemian Brigade: Civil War Newsmen in Action.* New York, 1954.

Steed, H. Wickham. *The Press.* London, 1938.

————. *Through Thirty Years, 1892–1922, A Personal Narrative.* 2 vols. London, 1924.

Steevens, G. W. *From Capetown to Ladysmith.* New York, 1900.

————. *Things Seen: Impressions of Men, Cities and Books.* Selected and edited by G. S. Street, with a memoir by W. E. Henley. Indianapolis, 1900.

————. *With Kitchener to Khartoum.* New York, 1899.

Steinberg, S. H. *Five Hundred Years of Printing.* London, 1959.

Sterling, Thomas. *Stanley's Way: A Sentimental Journey Through Africa.* New York, 1960.

Stern, Fritz. *Gold and Iron: Bismarck, Bleichroder, and the Building of the German Empire.* New York, 1977.

Stillman, W. J. *The Autobiography of a Journalist.* 2 vols. London, 1901.

Stone, Candace. *Dana and The Sun.* New York, 1938.

Stone, Melville E. *Fifty Years a Journalist.* New York, 1921.

Storey, Graham. *Reuters: The Story of a Century of News-Gathering.* London, 1951.

Stuart, John. *Pictures of the War*. London, 1901.

Suzuki, Hidesaburo. *Early Japanese Newspapers*. Kyoto, 1954.

Swanberg, W. A. *Citizen Hearst: A Biography of William Randolph Hearst*. New York, 1961.

————. *Pulitizer*. New York, 1967.

Symon, J. D. *The Press and Its Story*. London, 1914.

Tarbell, Ida M. *A Reporter for Lincoln*. New York, 1927.

Taylor, Bayard. *The Unpublished Letters of Bayard Taylor in the Hungtington Library*. Edited with introduction by John Richie Schultz. San Marino, Calif., 1937.

————. *A Visit to India, China and Japan in the Year 1853*. New York, 1855.

Tebbel, John. *The Life and Good Times of William Randolph Hearst*. New York, 1952.

Tebbel, John and Jennison, Keith. *The American Indian Wars*. New York, 1960.

Thomas, Ebenezer Smith. *Reminiscences of the Last Sixty-Five Years, Commencing with the Battle of Lexington and Sketches of His Own Life and Times*. 2 vols. Hartford, Conn., 1840.

Thomas, K. E. *The Real Personages of Mother Goose*. Boston, 1930.

Thompson, Robert Luther. *Wiring a Continent: The History of the Telegraph Industry in the United States, 1832–1866*. Princeton, 1947.

Thorold, Algar Labouchere. *Life of Henry Labouchere*. London, 1913.

Thorsen, Svend. *Newspapers in Denmark*. Copenhagen, 1953.

Tibbles, Thomas Henry. *Buckskin and Blanket Days*. New York, 1957.

Tomlinson, John D. *The International Control of Radiocommunications*. Ann Arbor, 1945.

Topliff, Samuel. *Topliff's Travels*. With a Memoir by Ethel Stanwood Bolton. Boston, 1906.

Torres, Teodoro. *Periodismo*. Mexico City, 1937.

Townsend, George Alfred. *Rustics in Rebellion, A Yankee Reporter on the Road to Richmond, 1861–1865.* Chapel Hill, N.C., 1950.

Trevelyan, George Macaulay. *History of England.* London, 1926.

Tribolet, Leslie Bennet. *The International Aspects of Electrical Communications in the Pacific Area.* Baltimore, 1929.

Tudor, William. *The Life of James Otis of Massachusetts, Containing Also, Notices of some Contemporary Characters and Events from the Year 1760 to 1775.* Boston, 1823.

Tyler, Moses Coit. *The Literary History of the American Revolution, 1763–1783.* 2 vols. New York and London, 1897.

Updike, D. B. *Printing Types, Their History.* 3d ed. Cambridge, 1927.

Van Doren, Carl. *Benjamin Franklin.* New York, 1938.

Villard, Henry. *Lincoln on the Eve of '61: A Journalist's Story.* New York, 1941.

———. *Memoirs of Henry Villard.* 2 vols. London and Cambridge, Mass., 1904.

Villiers, Frederic. *Pictures of Many Wars.* London, 1902.

———. *Villiers: His Five Decades of Adventure.* 2 vols. New York and London, 1955.

Vizetelly, E. H. *Reminiscences of a Bashi-Bazouk.* London, 1878.

Vizetelly, Ernest Alfred. *In Seven Lands: Germany, Austria, Hungary, Bohemia, Spain, Portugal, Italy.* New York, 1916.

Waitt, Ernest L. "How the News of the Battle of Lexington Reached England." *New England Magazine,* March 1909, pp. 92–97.

Wang, Y. P. *The Rise of the Native Press in China.* New York, 1924.

Washburn, Stanley. *The Cable Game.* Boston and London, 1913.

Wasserman, Jakob. *H. M. Stanely, Explorer.* Translated from German by Eden and Cedar Paul. London, 1932.

Watson, Elmo Scott. "The Indian Wars and the Press." *Journalism Quarterly,* Winter 1961, pp. 81-82.

———. "Matthew B. Brady, the first man to 'cover' a war with a camera." *Quill,* September 1937, p. 10.

Watson, Thomas A. *Exploring Life.* New York and London, 1926.

Weisberger, Bernard A. *Reporters for the Union.* Boston, 1953.

The WGN (Chicago Tribune). Chicago, 1922.

White, Llewellyn. *The American Radio.* Chicago, 1947.

White, Llewellyn and Leigh, Robert D. *Peoples Speaking to Peoples.* Chicago, 1946.

Wight, John. *Mornings in Bow Street.* Illustrations by George Cruikshank. London, 1875.

Wildes, Harry Emerson. *Social Currents in Japan, With Special Reference to the Press.* Chicago, 1927.

Wilkerson, Marcus W. *Public Opinion and the Spanish-American War.* Baton Rouge, La., 1933.

Wilkie, Franc Bangs. *Pen and Powder.* Boston, 1888.

———. *Thirty-Five Years in American Journalism.* Chicago, 1891.

Wilkinson, Henry Spencer. *Thirty-Five Years, 1874-1909.* London, 1933.

Williams, Francis. *Dangerous Estate: The Anatomy of Newspapers.* London and New York, 1957.

———. *Transmitting World News: A Study of Communications and the Press.* UNESCO publication. Paris, 1953.

Williams, George Forrester. *Bullet and Shell. New York, 1883.*

Williams, Hermann Warner, Jr. The Civil War: The Artists' Record. Boston, 1962.

Williams, T. Harry. "Civil War Papers Spilled Secrets." *Quill,* January-February 1944.

Williams, Valentine. *World of Action.* Boston, 1938.

Wilson, James Harrison. *The Life of Charles A. Dana.* New York, 1907.

Wilson, Quintus C. "The Confederate Press Association: A Pioneer News Agency." *Journalism Quarterly,* June 1949, pp. 160–66.

———. "A Study and Evaluation of Military Censorship in the Civil War." Master's thesis, University of Minnesota, 1945.

Winkler, John K. *William Randolph Hearst: A New Appraisal.* New York, 1955.

Wisan, Joseph E. *The Cuban Crisis as Reflected in the New York Press.* New York, 1934.

Wood, James Playsted. *Magazines in the United States: Their Social and Economic Influence.* New York, 1949.

Woodham-Smith, Cecil. *Florence Nightingale.* New York and London, 1951.

———. *The Reason Why.* New York, 1954.

Woodhead, Henry G. H. *Adventures in Far Eastern Journalism: A Record of Thirty-three years' Experience.* Tokyo, 1935.

Woods, Frederick. *Young Winston's Wars.* New York, 1973.

Woods, N. A. *The Past Campaigns.* 2 vols. London, 1885.

Woolley, C. Leonard. *The Sumerians.* Oxford, 1928.

World Communications: Press, Radio, Television, Film. UNESCO publication. Paris, 1964.

Worsley, Frank and Griffith, Glyn. *The Romance of Lloyd's: From Coffee House to Palace.* London, 1932.

Zobrist, Benedict Karl. "How Victor Lawson's Newspapers Covered the Cuban War of 1898." *Journalism Quarterly,* Summer 1961, pp. 323-31.

Index